CCH BUSINESS OWNER'S TOOLKIT™

TAX GUIDE 2000

A *CCH Business Owner's Toolkit*™ Publication

Susan M. Jacksack, J.D.

CCH INCORPORATED

Chicago

THE CCH BUSINESS OWNER'S TOOLKIT™ TEAM

Susan M. Jacksack is frequently quoted as a small business expert in national publications including *The Wall Street Journal, The New York Times, Money,* and *Worth,* and has made several guest appearances to discuss small business issues on CNBC. She has over 13 years of experience advising and writing for small business owners and consumers on tax, personal finance and other legal topics, and has conducted seminars for new and prospective entrepreneurs on tax issues, business planning, and employment law. Susan is an attorney and a graduate of the University of Illinois, Urbana-Champaign.

Alice Magos has over 35 years of experience running the operations of numerous small businesses. She is the author of the *CCH Business Owner's Toolkit*™ online advice column "Ask Alice." Alice is a popular instructor at small business seminars on accounting, financial planning, and using the Internet; is an accountant and a Certified Financial Planner; and holds degrees from Washington University in St. Louis and Northwestern University.

Joel Handelsman has 20 years of experience writing about business, tax, and financial topics. He has experience with multiple new product and business ventures in the publishing industry, and has held a variety of management positions. Joel is an attorney and holds degrees from Northwestern University and DePaul University.

John L. Duoba has more than 12 years of small business experience in book and magazine publishing, fulfilling various roles in editorial and production management. He has been involved in the publication of scores of titles, with multiple editions and issues raising the total well into the hundreds. John is a professional journalist and holds a degree from Northwestern University's Medill School of Journalism.

Martin Bush has over 15 years of experience providing legal, financial and tax advice to small and large businesses in various industries. He is a frequently quoted small business expert and has appeared on CNBC and National Public Radio. Martin is an attorney and a CPA, and holds degrees from Indiana University and DePaul University.

We would like to acknowledge the significant efforts of the contributors to this book: Bob Barnett, Tom Blazek, Steve Froikin, Catherine Gordon, Tom Lauletta, and Linda Scharf.

Many thanks are also due to Jim Coburn and the software development team: project manager Larry Lee; programmers Alfie Lam, Alan Epperson, Tim Fury, Richard Harrison, Dave Logsdon, John Magby, and Mike Sage; quality controllers Randy Fraley, Jerry Lester and Lue Yarnold; designer Sara Zwern; and web site designer Tony Arguelles.

In addition, we would like to thank Drew Snider for his assistance in the development of this book.

Table of Contents

Part I

Getting Started

Small business owners create the steam – and frequently design the tracks – on which the American economy runs.

Not only are the vast majority of net new jobs in the country created by small businesses, it's entrepreneurs like you who provide most of the innovation in products, services, delivery and marketing methods that continue to transform U.S. culture. The size and unrelenting persistence of our small business sector creates a vast virtual laboratory for testing out new ideas in the local – or national, or global – marketplace.

The entrepreneurial enterprise's small size, and the fact that there is usually only one layer of management, makes it the ideal business form to create and take advantage of newly emerging market niches and technological advances. In fact, it's been said that the best structure for an organization is one in which sales, marketing, operations and administration all sit in the same "business unit": the mind of an entrepreneur.

Being the owner of a small business in America means that you have to wear many hats, and that while you can delegate or outsource many tasks, the ultimate responsibility for all of them remains with you.

One of the most important of these tasks – and some say, one of the most onerous – is to stay on top of your numerous federal income tax obligations.

While many business owners delegate the preparation of tax returns to their accountant or professional preparer, the ultimate responsibility for a missed payment or filing deadline, an improperly claimed deduction, overlooked income, or incomplete records is yours alone.

Whether or not you plan to do your own taxes, you need to create (or at least oversee the creation of) the basic business records that will be used to complete the forms. And you need to know what kind of documentation to save throughout the year, not only to prepare your return, but also in case you're audited and you need to substantiate your responses to the questions on the forms. You can safely assume that a tax auditor won't look kindly on you if your only defense is "I didn't know I had to do that." The old legal saying that "ignorance of the law is no excuse" is perhaps most often applied in tax settings.

While the current U.S. tax code is almost unbelievably complicated – the law, regulations, and explanations run to over 42,000 pages in CCH's best-selling tax publication for professionals – it provides numerous opportunities for tax savings, if you know where to look.

Our goal in this book, and in all *CCH Business Owner's Toolkit*™ products, is to lay out the rules for you as clearly as possible. We know that your immediate concern is to get your taxes filed correctly and on time, so that you get any refund that's due and so you don't get socked with penalties and interest if you're selected for an audit.

We also want to tell you about the many ways you can save taxes by structuring your business operations to take the greatest possible advantage of the existing laws and regulations. While our main focus is on tax issues that impact your business as a sole proprietor,

we'll also discuss taxes that apply to you and your family as individuals.

Tax laws change constantly – in fact, the last two years have seen a major overhaul of the IRS's structure; significant changes in taxpayer's rights; and changes in capital gains, Roth IRAs, the home office deduction, the child tax credit, education tax breaks, and the $500,000 exclusion for gain on sale of a home, to name just a few. It's important to keep up-to-date with all these changes in order to keep your tax bill to the minimum. While we've taken great pains to bring you the latest information and tax forms available up to the date of publication, you can check for any late-breaking developments by going to our Internet site, http://www.toolkit.cch.com.

How To Use This Book

We've designed this book to help you do two things:

(1) to get your tax return filed with as little pain and aggravation (and as large a refund) as possible, and

(2) for the long term, to make you aware of the opportunities for saving tax dollars in your business, and in your personal and family life.

For those of you who are familiar with filing your own returns, this book can be used as a handy reference as you gather your records and work through the forms. Find the topics that apply to you in the Table of Contents or the Index, and go directly to the appropriate section of the book. You'll find the examples, tips, and worksheets scattered throughout the text are a quick way to get a good understanding of the issues.

If you're a new business owner, or haven't tried doing your own taxes before, you may want to read through Part II, *Taxes and Your Business*, from start to finish. It will give you a good, easy-to-understand overview of how the system works. You'll also pick up scores of tax-saving ideas to help you organize your business activities, and to get the greatest possible after-tax return for your effort.

Take advantage of the book's special features to help you work more effectively:

- **Tax Forms:** At the back of the book, you'll find copies of the most commonly used tax forms and tax tables. Copy them, or tear them out and use them directly. You can also download copies of forms through the Internet by going to the IRS web site, http://www.irs.gov, or by calling the IRS at 1-800-TAX-FORM.

- **What's New This Year:** A thumbnail description of the most important changes for small business owners and individuals keeps you up to date.

- **Glossary:** Plain-language definitions of the more commonly used tax terms will help you decipher IRS instructions and other communications.

- **Tax Calendar:** To keep you on track with your due dates and filings, we provide a 1999 calendar of tax-related events.

FREE ONLINE TAX PREPARATION AND FILING

Understanding the tax rules and knowing what to report is half the battle – the other half is gathering all the records, receipts, and other pertinent financial data you've been generating throughout the year, and organizing it so you can actually complete the forms and send them to the IRS.

To that end, we're providing you with the opportunity to use CompleteTax™, an Internet-based tax service, to complete your federal and state tax returns and file them electronically, for free.

Getting started with CompleteTax™ is easy. Just follow these five steps:

1. Go to **http://www.completetax.com/toolkit** and download the special Toolkit™ version of the CompleteTax™ Organizer to your PC.

2. Then you can disconnect from the Internet, and work with the CompleteTax™ Organizer software on your own computer.

3. When you're finished answering all the interview questions, select the "1040" menu option on the CompleteTax™ Organizer to reconnect to the Internet and process your tax return, checking for inaccuracies and omissions.

4. You have the choice of printing and filing the tax return yourself or electronically filing it for speedier processing.

5. If you prefer using the services of a tax professional, you can print the CompleteTax™ Organizer's information for your accountant's use.

As a purchaser of *CCH Business Owner's Toolkit Tax Guide 2000,* you are entitled to use the service to prepare one free federal and resident state tax return. At no additional cost, you can choose to file your federal and resident state return electronically. Note: CompleteTax™ supports electronic filing for 26 states. You can go to the CompleteTax™ "Help" menu for a list of supported states.

Keep your copy of *Tax Guide 2000* handy after you complete the Organizer questions and before you select the "1040" menu option to have your return processed. You'll need some information from the book in order to qualify for a free return. If you need to prepare more than one return, you'll need to provide a credit card number and will be charged $7.50 for each additional tax return. This price includes both the federal and resident state tax returns.

Getting Started with the CompleteTax™ Organizer

The CompleteTax™ Organizer is designed to focus only on the items that are relevant to your business and personal tax situation.

When you download the Organizer and open it for the first time, a Personal Information screen will ask you a number of key questions. Your answers to those questions will determine which of the section tabs will appear on the right.

You may move through the tabs in any sequence. As you open a new section tab, the opening screen for that section will ask you a few basic questions. Your answers will determine which of the topic tabs will appear across the top of the page. To move to each topic, simply click on the tab.

As you answer questions, you'll notice that additional questions may appear, as well as Detail buttons which are used to open up screens that allow you to enter further information. Be sure to answer each "yes" or "no" question to make sure that the correct additional questions appear.

As you enter information, you will notice that a checkmark appears in the topic tab when an item is complete.

When you have finished entering your relevant tax information, you can print the CompleteTax™ Organizer for your records by clicking on the printer icon, or by selecting "File" on the toolbar, and then selecting "Print."

You can submit the Organizer to the CompleteTax™ Internet Service to receive a printed copy of your tax return, and then choose to file your return electronically or to provide the printed Organizer to an accountant or tax preparer who will help you complete your return.

Helpful Functions

- In using the Organizer, whenever you need further information about how to enter a particular item, click on the Help button on the toolbar (marked with a question mark), press F1 to access the Help file, or choose the "Help" menu option.

- Whenever you wish to add additional information about a particular item or transaction, click on the "Tools" button on your screen and select "Notes," or click on the "notes" icon in the icon bar. A blank notepad will appear, and automatically attach to the page you are working on.

- Also in the Tools menu and in the icon bar you'll find a calculator that can be used any time you need to calculate an entry. There is also a calendar to help you track events of the past year.

Importing Data from Personal Finance Software

If you use Quicken or Microsoft Money and have enabled the features that track tax-related items in your software, you can export data from your personal finance software to your CompleteTax™ Organizer. Once the data is in the Organizer, it's easy to review it and make any changes or additions that are necessary.

To import data to the Organizer, you first need to create an export file from the financial software program.

Quicken. For Quicken 6.0 and Quicken 98, 99 or 2000:

1. In Quicken, create a Tax Schedule Report (not a Tax Summary Report).

2. Click the Export button. Quicken displays a dialog box.

3. In the Directories list box, go to your Tax Organizer directory. If you selected the default when you installed the Organizer, this will be c:\taxnbk99.

4. In the File Name field, select a name for the file, but make sure it has a .txf extension. In the Files of Type box, make sure the selected type is Tax export files (*.txf).

5. Click the O.K. button.

In Quicken 2000, when the investment category is used, the data from the investments is combined with the checking account data.

In Quicken 6.0 and Quicken Deluxe 98 or 99, you will have to create a separate capital gains report export file in order to export any data regarding investment sales. To do that, first create a Capital Gains Report in Quicken, then follow steps 2 through 5 above. The CompleteTax™ Organizer will allow you to import one regular tax export file, and one capital gains report, into each Organizer file.

If you have more than one Quicken file containing data that you need for your tax return (for example, you have set up separate Quicken files for business and for personal data), you should import each one into a separate tax organizer file. Be sure to give each

tax organizer file a different name (for example, use "William K. Smith" as the taxpayer's name for one file, and "Bill Smith" in the other file).

Microsoft Money. For users of Microsoft Money 98, 99 or 2000:

1. Create a Tax Software Report.

2. Click the Export button at the bottom right of the screen. Make sure that Tax Exchange Format appears in the Save as Type box.

3. In the File Name field, type a name for the export field, making sure to retain the .txf extension. Include the full path of the directory where you want the file to reside; c:\taxnbk99\export.txf would be an example.

4. Click the O.K. button.

Importing the Data to the Tax Organizer

Once you have created the financial software export files, you're ready to import it into the tax organizer.

Open up the CompleteTax™ Organizer, but do not open a new or existing file. Instead, from the "File" menu, choose "Import TXF file." If you see the name of your export file, click on it, then click the O.K. button.

If you didn't see the name of your export file, you will need to navigate through your directories using the middle "Folders" box until your file appears in the large "File name" box. When you see the name of your file, click on it, then click the O.K. button.

You can now proceed to review the data that has been imported to the Organizer, and add any items that were missed, or correct any figures that don't match your W-2 forms, 1099 or 1098 forms, or other important documents and statements.

What's New This Year

Compared to the major upheavals we've faced in other years, 1999 was fairly calm on the tax front.

Congress spent a lot of time debating possible changes, including a major across-the board tax cut, repeal of the marriage penalty and estate taxes, and targeted tax breaks for lower-middle-class families. The tax cut was vetoed by the President, however, and the parties were ultimately unable to reach a compromise on major changes. As we go to press, the only tax legislation that succeeded in emerging from all the wrangling was an extension of some expiring provisions, partially paid for with a few "loophole closers," otherwise known as tax increases.

As in previous years, there were also a number of inflation-related adjustments to the tax brackets and the various phaseout and deduction amounts, plus some previously scheduled increases in things like the equipment expensing amount.

Here are the highlights of changes in effect for 1999 that you'll want to be aware of:

AMT relief. A waiver of the alternative minimum tax (AMT) rules for those claiming personal tax credits like the child tax credit, the education credits, the adoption credit, the dependent care credit or the credit for the elderly has been extended. Even if the AMT applies, you will get the full benefit of the credits for 1999, as in 1998, under the extension passed by Congress in November. For 2000 and 2001, the temporary AMT relief has been improved so that the personal nonrefundable tax credits may offset both the regular income tax and the tentative minimum tax.

Y2K relief. You may be eligible for a 90-day extension of any tax-related deadline if the IRS determines that you have been affected by a Y2K-related failure, despite your efforts to avoid such problems.

Home office deduction. A newer, more lenient rule for determining whether your home office qualifies for the deduction has finally kicked in for 1999. Beginning this tax season, if the home is the only fixed location where you conduct business management and administrative activities for your business, you will be able to deduct a portion of your insurance; utilities; services; repairs; decorating; casualty losses; and (a) rent or (b) mortgage interest, real estate taxes, and depreciation.

Equipment expensing election. The amount of equipment that can be written off in the same year it was purchased has risen to $19,000 for 1999 (up from $18,500).

Self-employed health insurance. Self-employed people may deduct 60% of health insurance premiums for themselves and their dependents, up from 45% in 1998.

Child tax credit. You can claim a tax credit of $500 for every dependent child under the age of 17, subject to an AGI phaseout range beginning at $75,000 for singles and $110,000 for marrieds filing jointly. This is an increase of $100 per child from last year's $400 credit.

Interest on student loans. You may be able to deduct up to $1,500 of interest on a qualified student loan paid within the first five years of the loan; this represents a $500 increase over last year.

Restriction on installment method. Taxpayers who use the accrual method of accounting may no longer use the installment method of reporting capital gains on the sale of investment or business property.

Estimated tax payment changes. For 2000, if your adjusted gross income (AGI) is higher than $150,000 (or $75,000 for a married person filing separately), you can avoid interest and penalties by paying 108.6% of last year's tax in advance through payroll withholding or estimated tax payments. Previously the safe-harbor amount was 105%.

Personal exemption amount. This amount has increased to $2,750 per person for 1999.

Standard deductions. Standard deduction amounts have increased for 1999, as follows: singles, $4,300; heads of household, $6,350; married filing jointly, $7,200; and married filing separately, $3,600. If you claim an exemption for a dependent who has taxable income, his or her standard deduction will still be the greater of $700, or $250 plus his or her earned income.

Social Security wage base. The maximum amount of wages and net self-employment earnings that are subject to the Social Security portion of the payroll tax has risen to $72,600. For 2000, the limit will be $76,200.

401(k) deferral limits. In 1999, an employee's permitted salary deferral to a 401(k) plan will be $10,000 (no change from 1998).

Earned income credit. The maximum amount of the credit for taxpayers with two children has increased to $3,816; the maximum amount of income you can have and still claim the credit is $10,200 for taxpayers without children, $26,928 for taxpayers with one qualifying child, and $30,580 for taxpayers with two or more qualifying children.

Phaseout of exemptions and deductions. High-income taxpayers begin to lose their personal exemptions when AGI reaches $126,600 for singles, $189,950 for marrieds filing jointly, $158,300 for heads of household, and $94,975 for marrieds filing separately. The phaseout of itemized deductions begins at $63,300 for marrieds filing separately, and $126,600 for all other taxpayers.

Standard mileage rates. For business use of a car, the standard mileage rate is 32.5 cents per mile for the first quarter of 1999, and then drops to 31 cents per mile for the remainder of the year. For charitable use, the rate is 14 cents per mile. For medical expenses, the rate is 10 cents per mile.

Standard meal allowance. For 1999, the SMA is still $30 a day for most areas in the U.S. Some locations in the U.S. are considered high-cost areas

and qualify for higher rates of $34, $38, $42, or $46 per day.

Extension of welfare-to-work credit. Businesses that, in 1998 through December 31, 2001, hire certain persons who had received family assistance can claim a credit for 35% of $10,000 paid to the employee in the first year, and 50% of $10,000 paid in the second year. This credit had previously expired on June 30, 1999 but was retroactively reinstated and extended.

Work opportunity credit. Businesses who hired workers in certain disadvantaged groups can get a credit of up to 40% of their first-year wages for employment of 400 or more hours, and up to 25% for employment of more than 120 but less than 400 hours. This credit had expired on June 30, 1999 but has been extended through December 31, 2001.

Research and experimentation credit. This credit was to expire on June 30, 1999 but was extended through June 30, 2004. However, to hold down the cost, Congress imposed some unusual rules. R&E credits for the period from July 1, 1999 through September 30, 2000 may only be claimed after October 1, 2000. Similarly, credits for the period from October 1, 2000 through September 30, 2001 may only be claimed after October 1, 2001.

Roth IRA conversions. Taxpayers with AGI under $100,000 can convert an ordinary IRA to a Roth IRA if they pay income tax on the entire amount at the time of the conversion. For 1998 only, such taxpayers were allowed to convert to a Roth and pay the tax over the next four years. This grace period has expired, and for 1999 and later years, any conversion tax is due with your tax return for the year of the conversion.

Deductible IRAs when you also are covered by an employer's retirement plan. The amount of adjusted gross income (AGI) you can have and still make deductible contributions to an IRA has increased by $1,000 for this year. The AGI phaseout range is now $31,000 to $41,000 for singles and $51,000 to $61,000 for marrieds filing jointly. When only one spouse is covered by a retirement plan, the other spouse may make deductible contributions, subject to a joint AGI phaseout range of $150,000 to $160,000.

Tax Calendar

FIRST QUARTER

January 10

Employees who work for tips and received $20 or more in tips during December must report them to their employers. Form 4070, *Employee's Report of Tips to Employer*, can be used.

January 18

Make a payment of your estimated tax for the last quarter of 1999 if you did not pay enough income tax through withholding (see page 302). Use Form 1040-ES. You don't have to make this payment if you file your 1999 tax return (Form 1040) and pay any tax due by February 1, 2000.

Farmers and fisherman must pay estimated tax for 1999 using Form 1040-ES. You have until April 17 to file your 1999 income tax return on Form 1040. If you don't pay your estimated tax by this date, you must file your 1999 return and pay any tax due by March 1, 2000 to avoid an estimated tax penalty.

January 31

File your income tax return (Form 1040) for 1999 if you didn't pay your last installment of estimated tax by January 18. This will avoid any penalty for late payment of the last installment.

All employers: Give copies B, C, and 2 of Form W-2 for 1999 to each employee, including household employees.

All businesses: Give annual information statements to recipients of payments you made during 1999, on the appropriate version of Form 1099 or other information return. Payments that are included are:

- compensation for independent contractors
- dividends and other corporate distributions
- interest
- amounts paid in real estate transactions
- rent
- royalties
- amounts paid in broker and barter exchange transactions
- payments to attorneys
- payments of Indian gaming profits to tribal members
- profit-sharing distributions
- retirement plan distributions
- original issue discount
- prizes and awards
- medical and health care payments
- debt cancellation
- cash payments over $10,000

February 10

Employees who work for tips and received $20 or more in tips during January must report them to their employers. Form 4070, *Employee's Report of Tips to Employer*, can be used.

February 28

Businesses must file information returns (Form 1099) with the IRS for certain payments you made during 1999, as described under January 31. Use a separate Form 1096 to summarize and transmit the forms for each type of payment.

If you file Forms 1098, 1099 or W-2G electronically (not by magnetic media), your due date for filing them will be extended to March 31, 2000.

February 29

Employers must file copy A of all W-2 forms and one W-3 transmittal form with the Social Security Administration. If you file electronically, your due date is extended to March 31.

March 1

Farmers and fishermen must file their 1999 income tax return (Form 1040) to avoid an underpayment penalty if they owe estimated tax. However, they have until April 17 to file if they paid their 1999 estimated tax by January 18, 2000.

March 10

Employees who work for tips and received $20 or more in tips during February must report them to their employers. Form 4070, *Employee's Report of Tips to Employer,* can be used.

March 31

If you file Forms 1098, 1099, W-2 or W-2G electronically, this is the due date for filing them with the IRS. The due date for giving the payment recipient a copy of the form is still January 31.

SECOND QUARTER

April 10

Employees who work for tips and received $20 or more in tips during March must report them to their employers. Form 4070, *Employee's Report of Tips to Employer,* can be used.

April 17

File an income tax return for 1999 (Form 1040EZ, 1040A, or 1040) and pay any tax due. If you want an automatic 4-month extension of time to file the return, file Form 4868, *Application for Automatic Extension of Time to File U.S. Individual Income Tax Return.* Then file your tax form by August 15. If you need an additional 2 month extension, file Form 2688, *Application for Additional Extension of Time to File U.S. Individual Income Tax Return,* as soon as possible so the IRS can respond before August 15.

If you paid cash wages of $1,100 or more in 1999 to a household worker, file Schedule H (Form 1040) with your income tax return and report any employment taxes. Report any federal unemployment FUTA tax on Schedule H if you paid total cash wages of $1,000 or more in any calendar quarter of 1998 or 1999 to household employees. Also report any income tax you withheld for your household employees.

Pay the first installment of estimated tax, using Form 1040-ES.

May 10

Employees who work for tips and received $20 or more in tips during April must report them to their employers. Form 4070, *Employee's Report of Tips to Employer,* can be used.

June 12

Employees who work for tips and received $20 or more in tips during May must report them to their employers. Form 4070, *Employee's Report of Tips to Employer,* can be used.

June 15

Make your second installment of quarterly estimated income tax on Form 1040-ES.

If you are a U.S. citizen or resident alien living, working, or on military duty outside the U.S. or Puerto Rico, file Form 1040 and pay any tax, interest, and penalties due.

THIRD QUARTER

July 10

Employees who work for tips and received $20 or more in tips during June must report them to their employers. Form 4070, *Employee's Report of Tips to Employer,* can be used.

August 10

Employees who work for tips and received $20 or more in tips during July must report them to their employers. Form 4070, *Employee's Report of Tips to Employer,* can be used.

August 15

If you have an automatic 4-month extension to file your income tax return for 1999, file Form 1040EZ, 1040A, or 1040 and pay any tax, interest, and penalties due. If you need additional time to file, file Form 2688.

September 11

Employees who work for tips and received $20 or more in tips during August must report them to their employers. Form 4070, *Employee's Report of Tips to Employer,* can be used.

September 15

Third payment of quarterly estimated tax is due, on Form 1040-ES.

FOURTH QUARTER

October 10

Employees who work for tips and received $20 or more in tips during September must report them to their employers. Form 4070, *Employee's Report of Tips to Employer,* can be used.

October 16

File a 1999 income tax return and pay any tax due if you were given an additional 2-month extension.

November 13

Employees who work for tips and received $20 or more in tips during October must report them to their employers. Form 4070, *Employee's Report of Tips to Employer,* can be used.

December 11

Employees who work for tips and received $20 or more in tips during November must report them to their employers. Form 4070, *Employee's Report of Tips to Employer,* can be used.

FISCAL YEAR TAXPAYERS

If you are using a fiscal year as your tax accounting period, Form 1040 is due on the 15th day of the fourth month after the end of your tax year. Estimated tax payment are due on the 15th day of the 4th, 6th, and 9th months of your tax year and on the 15th day of the first month after the end of your tax year.

Chapter 1

The Basics of Tax Planning

Tax planning is a process of looking at various tax options in order to determine *when, whether,* and *how* to conduct business and personal transactions so that taxes are eliminated or reduced.

As an individual taxpayer, and as a business owner, you often will have several different options as to how you want to complete a certain taxable transaction. The courts strongly back your right to choose the course of action that will result in the lowest *legal* tax liability. In other words, *tax avoidance* is entirely proper.

Although tax avoidance planning is legal, *tax evasion* — the reduction of tax through deceit, subterfuge, or concealment — is not. Frequently, what sets tax evasion apart from tax avoidance is the IRS's finding that there was some fraudulent intent on the part of the business owner.

The following are four of the areas most commonly focused on by IRS examiners as pointing to possible fraud:

- a failure to report substantial amounts of income, such as a shareholder's failure to report dividends, or a store-owner's skimming cash from the register without including it in the daily business receipts

- a claim for fictitious or improper deductions on a return, such as a sales representative's substantially overstating travel expenses, or a taxpayer claiming a large deduction for charitable contributions when no verification exists

- accounting irregularities, such as a business's failure to keep adequate records, or a discrepancy between amounts reported on a corporation's return and amounts reported on its financial statements

- improper allocation of income to a related taxpayer who is in a lower tax bracket, such as where a corporation makes distributions to the controlling shareholder's children

A business owner may *not* reduce his or her income taxes by labeling a transaction as something that it's not. So, if payments by a corporation to its stockholders are in fact dividends, calling them "interest" or otherwise attempting to disguise the payments as interest will not entitle the corporation to an interest deduction.

Ultimately, it is the substance, not the form, of a transaction that determines its tax treatment.

How a tax plan works. There are countless tax planning strategies available to a small business owner. Some are aimed at the owner's individual tax situation, some at the business itself. But regardless of how simple or how complex a tax strategy is, it will be based on structuring the transaction to accomplish one or more of these often overlapping goals:

- reducing the amount of taxable income

- reducing your tax rate

- controlling the time when the tax must be paid

- reducing the amount of the tax itself by claiming tax credits

- controlling the effects of the alternative minimum tax

In order to plan effectively, you'll need to estimate your personal and business income for the next few years. This is necessary because many tax planning strategies will save tax dollars at one income level, but will create a larger tax bill at other income levels. You will want to avoid having the "right" tax plan made "wrong" by erroneous income projections. Once you know what your approximate income will be, you can take the next step: estimating your tax bracket.

The effort to come up with crystal-ball estimates may be difficult and by its nature will be inexact. On the other hand, you should already be projecting your sales revenues, income, and cash flow for general business planning purposes. The better your estimates, the better the odds that your tax planning efforts will succeed.

REDUCING TAXABLE INCOME

The primary way to reduce the part of your income that is subject to tax is to take full advantage of all available tax deductions, both business and personal. In order to do this, you must become aware of what is deductible and what isn't, and the special rules that apply to certain types of deductions such as meals and entertainment, automobile expenses, and business travel (see Chapter 6).

In many cases, a business owner can deduct benefits that would otherwise be classified as nondeductible personal expenses. Don't overlook the possibility of purchasing health insurance, investing for your retirement, or providing perks like a company car through your business (see Chapter 6).

But do remember that claiming some kinds of deductions may have a tax impact in later years. An example of this is the recapture of certain depreciation deductions upon the sale of business property (see page 119).

REDUCING YOUR TAX RATE

Although you can't *literally* reduce your federal income tax rate, you can take actions that will have a similar result. These include:

- Choosing the optimum form of business organization (such as sole proprietorship, partnership, or corporation). If your business income is under $75,000 and your business is not a personal service business such as medicine, law, architecture, engineering, accounting, the arts, or consulting, you may be able to save tax dollars by incorporating. Otherwise, the sole proprietorship or pass-through entities (partnerships, LLCs, S corporations) usually offer more tax benefits.

- Structuring a transaction so that some of the money that you receive is classified as capital gains. Long-term capital gains earned by noncorporate taxpayers are taxed at lower rates than ordinary taxable income.

- Shifting income from a high-tax-bracket taxpayer (such as yourself) to a lower-tax-bracket taxpayer (such as your child).

One fairly simple way to do this is by hiring your children. Another possibility is to make one or more of your children a part-owner of your business, so that net profits of the business are shared among a larger group. The tax law limits the usefulness of this strategy for shifting *unearned* income to children under age 14, but some tax-saving opportunities still exist.

When we say "tax bracket," we're referring to the highest federal tax rate that you pay on any of your taxable income. This is the rate that will apply to each additional dollar that you earn, until you earn so much that you graduate to the next bracket. You need to know your current tax bracket in order to make wise tax planning decisions, since many decisions will make sense for those in certain brackets, but not for those in others.

Currently there are five tax brackets for individuals: 15 percent, 28 percent, 31 percent, 36 percent, and 39.6 percent. The dollar amounts at which each bracket begins is different for each filing status (that is, whether you file as single, head of household, married filing jointly, or married filing separately) and are adjusted for inflation each year.

The chart on the bottom of the page shows the income thresholds at which each tax bracket begins for 1999. Note that the dollar amount does not refer to your gross income, but rather, your taxable income — that is, income after you've subtracted any deductions and personal exemptions to which you're entitled.

CONTROLLING THE DUE DATE FOR TAXES

Although your former grade school teachers may not want to hear it, putting something off can sometimes be a good idea.

Putting it another way, "justice delayed" may be "justice denied," but taxes delayed can be taxes minimized!

The idea that we're trying to convey is that it's usually worthwhile to delay the due date for your tax liability, if you can do so legally.

This is true even if you figure that you'll be in the same tax bracket in all relevant years. What you gain is the use of your money for a longer period of time. The advantage may be as little as passbook earnings on the money, or as much as the growth resulting from a needed investment of money or equipment into your business.

Now, you generally don't have the option of actually delaying payment of the income tax you owe. While most taxpayers can get an automatic four-month extension of the time to file their return (e.g., until August 15th), you still have to pay the taxes you owe by April 15th or face penalties and interest payments. It's possible to obtain an extension to pay tax if you can demonstrate to the IRS's satisfaction that you can't pay on time without undue hardship. However, this is not something that you'll want to do unless absolutely necessary, since even with this extension you will owe interest on the unpaid taxes, beginning on the original due date.

What we're really talking about is the fact that it's often possible to delay your taxes indirectly, by taking actions that delay the time when particular income items must be reported on your return.

For small business owners, a common way to do this is to postpone receipt of income until the next year, and accelerate payment of expenses into your current tax year. (This will be much easier to do if you are using the cash method of accounting – see page 41.) This will have the effect of delaying your tax liability to the next quarter, or even the next tax year.

1999 Tax Brackets				
Tax Rate	**Single**	**Married/Joint**	**Married/Separate**	**Head of Household**
15%	$0.50	$0.50	$0.50	$0.50
28%	$25,750	$43,050	$21,525	$34,950
31%	$62,450	$104,050	$52,025	$89,150
36%	$130,250	$158,550	$79,275	$144,400
39.6%	$283,150	$283,150	$141,575	$283,150

Year-End Tax Saving Strategies

- **Delay collections** — Delay year-end billings until late enough in the year that payments won't come in until the following year.

- **Delay dividends** — If you operate your business as a C corporation, arrange for any dividends to be paid after the end of the year.

- **Delay capital gains** — If you are planning to sell assets that have appreciated in value, delay the sale until next year if you can do so without reducing the price significantly.

- **Accelerate payments** — Where possible, prepay deductible business expenses, including rent, interest, taxes, insurance, etc.

- **Accelerate large purchases** — Close the purchase of depreciable personal property or real estate within the current year.

- **Accelerate operating expenses** — If possible, accelerate the purchase of supplies or services, or the making of repairs.

- **Accelerate depreciation** — Elect to expense the cost of new equipment if you are eligible to do so, instead of depreciating the equipment.

Another way to defer the day of reckoning is to plow as much money as you can into qualified, tax-free retirement plans. In most cases, the business will get a tax deduction for the amount contributed, but you won't have to pay income tax on the amounts until you start taking money out of the plan when you retire.

Meanwhile, any income earned on the investments made by the plan will build up, tax-free. As the owner, you have a great deal of control over the way the plan is set up, and there's sure to be a plan that fits into your business goals and retirement objectives.

Postponing Income, Accelerating Deductions

As a general rule of thumb, you should *always* try to minimize your taxes in the present year, even if doing so means you may have to pay slightly more tax in the future.

After all, no one knows what the future holds. The tax laws are constantly changing, and there's a good chance that whatever you think you may owe in the future will be different by the time you get there. Furthermore, economic conditions or personal plans can change, and your business may look entirely different even one year

down the road. In the worst-case scenario, you could die unexpectedly, and in some cases you can avoid tax altogether if you die before paying it.

In broad terms, you can minimize taxes in the current year by postponing the receipt of income so that more of it will be taxed next year, and by accelerating deductions into the current year.

A few more specific ideas for doing this are listed above. (Bear in mind, however, that any strategies aimed at changing the year in which items of income or deduction will be accounted for will be much easier to accomplish if you use the cash method of accounting.)

Using the Accrual Method

Although strategies aimed at changing the year in which income and deductions will be accounted for are usually more difficult to accomplish using the accrual method, this does not mean that they're impossible. You'll need to learn how to navigate through the accrual method accounting rules in a way to reach the tax result that you want:

- If you want to delay taxation of an item of income, make sure that all events fixing the liability for payment are *not* met by year's end.

For instance, if you're selling goods, delay shipment until next year.

- If you want to accelerate a deductible expense into the current year, make sure that all events fixing the liability and amount of payment, and the economic performance, have been completed by year's end. If you are purchasing goods, services, or the use of some property, make sure that you have a valid contract covering all necessary terms, and that the goods, services, or properties are delivered, performed or used by year's end. If you do this, you are "one up" on a business that uses the cash method of accounting: You have received the benefit and deduction for the expense item before you've actually had to pay for it.

Accelerating Income, Postponing Deductions

What if, after looking into your tax situation, you have decided that you should take steps to maximize the amount of income that will be taxed in your present tax year, because you'll probably be in a higher bracket next year? You can accomplish your goal by accelerating income, and postponing expenses into the following year. How do you go about doing this? In most cases, if you simply reverse our suggestions in the box on the previous page, you'll find that you can accomplish your goals. For example, instead of delaying your billings, send out all of your bills early and do everything you can to collect them before year's end.

Again, any strategies aimed at changing the year in which items of income and deduction will be accounted for will be much easier to accomplish if you use the cash method of accounting.

RESTRICTIONS ON TAX PLANNING

The fact that you chose to use one form of transaction rather than another in order to minimize tax will not invalidate a transaction for income tax purposes. The fact that one form is adopted rather than another in order to minimize tax will not necessarily deprive the owner of the tax benefits

sought. However, even if the *form* of a transaction is valid, the IRS will look at the *substance* or true nature of the transaction in order to determine what the tax consequences should be.

Example

Jon Buford, the manager and principal stockholder of Oak Park Micro-Round Bearings, Inc. (a regular, as opposed to an S, corporation), lands a lucrative government contract. Because of this contract, corporate income jumps from $50,000 in 199X, to $500,000 in 199Y. Based on his view that landing the government contract proves that "he's worth a lot more" to the company, Jon raises his corporate salary ten-fold, to $450,000 in 199Y (up from $45,000 for 199X). His corporation takes a compensation-paid deduction of $450,000.

The IRS is likely to see things differently. If $100,000 is reasonable compensation for a manager in Jon's industry, then only that amount will qualify for the compensation deduction, and $350,000 will be treated as a disguised dividend (which does not qualify for the deduction).

Although the IRS says that the substance of a transaction, not its form, determines its tax consequences, a taxpayer who casts a taxable transaction in a particular form may have a difficult time changing his or her mind later, and then trying to convince the IRS that the substance of the transaction differs from its form for tax purposes.

So, the general rule is that the *IRS* may look behind the form of a transaction in order to determine its substance for tax purposes, but *taxpayers* are generally locked into the form of the transaction. The thinking here is that since a taxpayer can freely choose how to set up a transaction, it's only fair to require him or her to live with its tax consequences.

Step Transaction Doctrine

The IRS sometimes uses what is known as the "step transaction" doctrine to argue that the substance of a particular transaction is different from its form. When it relies on this doctrine, the IRS is generally saying that it will not break up a single transaction into two or more steps for income tax purposes.

So, the intermediate steps in an integrated transaction will not be assigned separate tax consequences.

Example

A transfer of property from Able to Baker, followed by Baker's transfer of the same property to Charlie, may, if the transfers are interdependent, be treated for tax purposes as a transfer from Able to Charlie.

Related Taxpayers

The IRS pays close attention to transactions that involve taxpayers who have close business and/or family relationships. In some cases, the tax laws have given the IRS special powers to deal with specific areas where related taxpayers in the past have used their relationships to unfairly cut their taxes.

Examples of this include the denial of interest-paid deductions to businesses that borrow money to purchase life insurance contracts benefiting their officers and employees, and the special accounting rules that apply to interest and expense payments between related parties.

Even beyond those areas in which the IRS has specific powers to deny tax benefits arising from transactions between related taxpayers, you can expect that its agents will closely scrutinize business dealings that you have with family members or other related parties.

Often, the IRS will combine its check of returns for a closely held corporation with a check of returns of the corporation's owners or principal officers, in order to discover any attempts to shift personal expenses to the corporation.

Warning

Among the items that IRS agents are likely to make special checks for are: vacation trips disguised as business trips, purchase of household furnishings or payment of household expenses (such as repairs and mortgage payments) charged off as corporate expenses, and excessive salaries paid to stockholders and relatives.

Chapter 2

Keeping Good Records

Everyone who pays taxes is required to keep accurate, permanent books and records so they can determine the various types of income, expenses, gains, losses, and other items that affect their income tax liability for the year.

BUSINESS-RELATED RECORDS

For business owners, keeping good records takes on special significance, since it's only by keeping a watchful eye on your operations that you can determine whether your business is on the right track.

One of your most important management tools is financial analysis, based on your business records. Here are some of the reasons why you need a good financial recordkeeping system for your business:

Monitoring the success or failure of your business. It's hard to know how your business is doing without a clear financial picture. Am I making money? Are sales increasing? Are expenditures increasing faster than sales? Which expenses are too high based on my level of sales? Do some expenditures appear to be "out of control?"

Providing the information you need to make decisions. Evaluating the financial consequences should be a part of every business decision you make. Without accurate records and financial information, it may be hard for you to know the financial impact of a given course of action. Will it pay to hire another salesperson? How much will another production employee cost? Is this particular product line profitable?

Obtaining bank financing. Before approving a loan, a banker will usually want to see your financial statements: a balance sheet, income statement, and cash flow budget for the most current and prior years, as well as your projected statements showing the impact of the requested loan. A banker may even want to see some of your bookkeeping procedures and documents to verify whether you run your business in a sound, professional manner.

Obtaining other sources of capital. If you need capital and are thinking of taking in an outside investor or a partner, you will need to produce a lot of financial information. Even your suppliers and other creditors may ask to see certain financial records. Such information may be produced by an outside accountant, but it is based on your day-to-day recordkeeping.

Budgeting. All businesses should use a budget for planning purposes. A budget will help keep your business on track by forecasting your cash needs and helping you control expenditures. In addition, if you are seeking bank financing or other sources of capital, a banker or prospective investor will probably want to see your budget as evidence that your business is well planned and stable. You must have solid financial information to prepare a meaningful budget.

Submitting sales taxes. If you collect sales tax from your customers, good records will make it easy for you to compute the tax due and prepare the required reports.

Preparing your income tax return. With good records, preparing an accurate tax return will be easier and you're more likely to be able to do it on time. Poor records may result in your underpaying or overpaying your taxes and/or filing late (and paying penalties). Furthermore, you will have the records necessary to prove your income and deductions, should questions arise or should your return be selected for a tax audit.

Like many small business owners, you may find that it's too expensive to pay an accountant to do routine bookkeeping chores. Someone in your organization must take on the responsibility of keeping an accurate set of financial records. Fortunately, you may find this task easier than you thought, especially if you use your computer.

In most cases, with a little study and help from computer software, you should be able to manage your most basic financial records without the help of an accountant. This includes the daily recording of sales, recording of incoming cash if customers' payments come in after the sale is made, and maintenance of your disbursements. Depending on the size of your business and how it is set up, you may need to maintain other types of records such as accounts receivable and accounts payable ledgers.

Business Bank Accounts

Most small business owners rely primarily on their business checkbook as a recordkeeping device. It's extremely important that you keep a business bank account that is separate from your personal funds. When you make a deposit, you should note the source of the funds – which may be as simple as noting whether the deposit represented business receipts from a certain day or week, an infusion of personal funds, or a loan.

Once you've established your business checking account, you should pay all business expenses (and only business expenses) with a check from that account, or with a credit card. If you must pay an expense with cash, make doubly sure that you save the receipt.

Save Time

If you've graduated from using a manual checkbook to an electronic version, such as that found in Quicken or Microsoft Money, you can easily keep track of your expenses and reconcile your checkbook each month in just minutes. You'll also be able to print out a variety of reports on income and expenses, which is important in case you are ever audited by the IRS. Data from either of these programs can be imported into the CompleteTax™ Tax Organizer and used to make your tax season easier.

The exception to the "don't write checks payable to 'cash' " rule is that when you withdraw earnings from the business for your personal use, you may write a check payable to cash, to yourself, or to your personal bank account.

As your business grows, you may become ready to step up to a small business accounting software package. There are a number of good ones on the market, and we suggest that you poll your friends and associates about the packages they've tried and been happy with. If you work with an accountant, choose a software package that works with his or her system so that data can easily flow back and forth between you.

The IRS does not require you to keep any specific forms of records, so long as your records clearly show your income and expenses for the period. If you use a computerized system, you must be able to obtain printouts of your records that are easily read.

Supporting Documents

From the IRS's point of view, perhaps even more important than your overall business accounting system is your ability to produce the invoices, receipts, and other original documents that prove your items of income and expense.

To show your income, you should have original documents such as cash register tapes, bank deposit slips, receipts, invoices, credit card charge slips, and, if you're an independent contractor, Forms 1099-MISC.

If you carry inventory, you should have canceled checks, cash register tape receipts, credit card sales slips, and invoices.

To show your other business expenses, you should have canceled checks, cash register tapes, account statements, invoices, and credit card slips. Very small expenses paid in cash can be evidenced by a sales receipt.

Ideally, you should have two forms of records for each expense: a document showing you paid the expense, such as a cancelled check or credit card slip, and a document itemizing the expense, such as a sales receipt or invoice from the vendor.

Work Smart

If your financial institution does not provide you with cancelled checks, you can rely on an account statement that shows, for each check, the check number, amount, payee, and date the check amount was posted. Similarly, statements showing electronic funds transfers or credit card statements can also be used. However, these statements should not be your only record of your expenses: you should also have another form of proof for each expense, such as a receipt or an invoice.

SPECIAL DEDUCTION RULES

In many cases, if you don't have records of a particular business expense but it's obvious that you must have incurred it, in an audit situation the IRS will estimate the amount of your expenses and allow you to deduct them. An example would be a retailer who has incomplete records of inventory purchases — the IRS will come up with a reasonable estimate of what the purchases should have been.

However, certain types of expenses, which the IRS has found to be particularly susceptible to cheating, are subject to special documentation rules. The following expenses must generally be proven by

adequate records or other evidence; if you have no records, the deduction will be completely disallowed:

- expenses for travel away from home (including meals and lodging while traveling)

- meals and entertainment expenses

- business gifts

- cars and other means of transportation

- cellular phones, computers, and other property of a kind that is generally used for entertainment or recreation

For all these types of expenses, you must keep receipts for any expense over $75, and for all lodging expenses whatever the amount.

You must also substantiate each individual expense as to: (1) amount, (2) time and place, and (3) business purpose. For entertainment and gift expenses, you must also note the business relationship of the person(s) being entertained or receiving a gift.

These things can be noted on the back of the receipt, or recorded in a formal expense log. For vehicle expenses, you'll also have to keep a mileage log.

Save Money

There is no requirement that you keep a contemporaneous log of your business deductions. However, the closer in time to the expenditure or use that you record the expense (and provide necessary documentary evidence), the more valuable it will be to prove the deduction. Also, if you get into the habit of systematically recording your expenses and all the necessary supporting facts and records, you may discover that you have many more perfectly legitimate deductions than you thought!

Keeping Automobile Records

If you want to deduct expenses for the use of a car for business or employment, for charitable work, or to get to medical appointments, you must keep mileage records of your driving for any of these tax-deductible purposes. In fact, the IRS specifically asks you on your tax return whether you have written evidence of your auto expenses and is likely to deny your deduction if you don't have them.

At a minimum, you should keep a notebook in the car and jot down your odometer reading at the beginning and end of the year. In between, you should jot down your starting and stopping odometer reading for each business trip you take and for any other deductible driving you do, as well as the reason for the trip. Most office supply stores carry notebooks designed for this purpose, in a size that's convenient for glove-box storage.

Save Money

If you have a good memory, you can choose to merely update your mileage records every week or two, but we don't recommend it: It's too easy to forget those short trips to the bank or office supply store. Over the course of the year, those forgotten trips can really add up! It's better to get into the habit of jotting down the facts at the start and end of every trip.

If you commute to a regular place of business, you'll also need to know the distance from your home to your workplace, as well as the number of commuting trips you made during the year, because the IRS specifically asks for this information.

At the end of the year, you'll need to compute the total number of miles you drove during the year and the total number of business miles. Then, you'll divide the number of business miles by the total number of miles driven. The answer you get represents your percentage of business use for the year. Save this number – you'll need it when you compute your deductible vehicle expenses!

Example

Mikio Nagano's initial odometer reading for the year was 23,456, and her ending reading was 33,500. So, her total mileage for the year was 10,044.

During the year, she recorded a total of 34 business trips, with a total mileage of 800 business miles.

So, her business usage of the vehicle was 800/10,044 = .0796, or about 8 percent.

You don't have to keep substantiating records for the business use of any vehicle that, by its very nature, is not likely to be used more than a very minimal amount for personal purposes. This includes various heavy trucks, buses, police and fire vehicles, cranes, forklifts, tractors, and similar vehicles.

For 1999, those using the standard mileage rate can deduct 32.5 cents per mile for every business mile they drove until April 1; as of April 1, 1999, the rate dropped to 31 cents. Those using their car for charitable purposes can deduct 14 cents per mile, and those using their car for deductible medical travel or moving expenses can deduct 10 cents per mile. Parking and tolls may be deducted in addition to these rates, so be sure to ask for a receipt at the toll booth.

Those opting to use the actual cost method for calculating their business-related auto expenses will also have to keep records for all car expenses during the year including gas and oil, cleaning and washing, repairs and maintenance, insurance, interest on a vehicle loan, tires and supplies, parking and garage rental, tolls, motor club membership, personal property taxes, depreciation if you own the vehicle, and lease payments if you lease the vehicle.

Capital Asset Records

For equipment, real estate, and other long-term assets that you use in your business or for investment purposes, you should have records that show when and how you acquired the asset, its purchase price, the cost of any improvements, any Section 179 deduction or tax deductions for depreciation, any deductions taken for casualty losses, when and how you disposed of the asset, the selling price, and any expenses of the sale. You can use the form on page 104 to summarize all this information in one place.

In addition, you should have supporting documents such as purchase and sales contracts or invoices, real estate closing statements, and canceled checks or credit card slips.

These recordkeeping rules generally apply to your personal residence as well. For more details, see page 205.

OTHER PERSONAL RECORDS

In addition to the records described above for automobile use (for charitable, moving, or medical expenses deductions) and for capital assets used as investments, you should retain basic records showing the source of all income you receive, including W-2 forms, 1099 and 1098 forms, and year-end comprehensive statements from financial institutions.

For any deductible item, you should retain documents proving the expense itself (a receipt, bill, or invoice) and proving that you paid it (a canceled check, credit card slip, or bank statement itemizing your checks).

If you are claiming employee business expenses, the recordkeeping rules for each type of expense are the same as those that apply to business owners, as discussed above.

If you receive or pay alimony, you should keep a copy of the separation agreement or divorce decree.

If you are claiming the child care credit, you must keep records of the name, address, and Social Security number or Employer Identification Number of all caregivers.

If you are claiming deductions for charitable contributions, you may need to get a receipt from the organization to which you made the donation, or an appraisal of the item. See page 266 for more details.

If you have gambling winnings, you should be keeping a diary of your winnings and losses that includes the date, type of activity, and location of the establishment, the names of other people who were present, and the amount you won or lost.

HOW LONG MUST YOUR RECORDS BE KEPT?

Your business records and your personal financial records must be retained for as long as they may be relevant for any tax purpose.

Generally, you will need to keep all records that support items on your tax return for at least four years, since the IRS may challenge your return for up to three years after its due date.

Records for capital assets, such as real estate, business equipment, and investments, should be maintained as long as you own the assets, since you will need them in order to determine your taxable gain or loss upon sale of the asset, and you may need them to support depreciation or casualty loss deductions along the way. If you rolled over gain in the asset, as was permitted under the old rollover replacement rule for personal residences, or because you traded some business or investment property in a tax-free exchange, you should keep records of the original asset until you dispose of the asset that took its place.

Also, be sure to keep copies of your income tax return itself. If you have ever made any nondeductible IRA contributions, you must retain the Forms 8606 from each year you made a contribution or received a distribution from any IRAs. But more generally, if your return is ever challenged for something serious such as fraud or not filing a tax return, the IRS can go back in time to examine your returns for as many years as it thinks necessary. The problem is that the IRS computer system might not have accessible copies of your returns from, say, 10 or 15 years ago. Therefore it is very important that you keep copies of your own tax records indefinitely, and preferably forever.

Tax Organizer Tip

Along with your tax returns, we suggest that you keep copies of any worksheets, itemized lists, supplementary records, or even scrap paper you used to organize your tax records. These can be very helpful if you ever need to figure out exactly how you arrived at a particular number on your tax return. The pages that you can print out from CompleteTax™ Organizer can be a useful way to retain all this extra information for your records.

Part II

Taxes and Your Business

If you own a business, your business's tax situation has a tremendous effect on your personal or family tax situation.

At the simplest level, the tax you pay on your business income is unavailable for you to use, so obviously it's in your interest to reduce this tax burden as much as you legally can.

As an entrepreneur, you're likely to face many more volatile income fluctuations than you would as an employee of a large company, and you need to retain absolutely every penny you can to build up a cushion in case things get rough. Saving on taxes is one very important way to reduce your costs and keep more of what you earn.

On the other hand, owning a business also presents numerous opportunities for you to reduce your tax bill by having the business pay for things – for example, family health benefits, a retirement plan, and perhaps even some of the expenses of owning a home, a car, and a computer – that you would otherwise have to

purchase on your own. In addition, if your spouse or other family members work in the business, you may be able to reduce your total tax bill by spreading the income and benefits among more people.

There are limits to how far you can go with these strategies, and numerous rules to follow and records to keep to make sure you stay within the parameters the IRS will permit. But if you become aware of the rules and the techniques that work in your favor, you can save a lot of money.

In Part II, we'll lay out the income tax rules that apply to your business clearly and concisely, to help you file your taxes as quickly and accurately as possible this year, and to tell you about planning strategies you can use to reduce your tax bill in the future.

Warning

As a small business owner, your primary concerns are usually expressed in terms of maximizing your revenue, minimizing your expenses, and ultimately, improving your bottom line. When it comes to taxes, however, the goal is usually the opposite: to defer income or receive it in tax-favored forms such as capital gains or employee benefits, to maximize your expenses by making sure you claim every deduction you're entitled to, and to minimize your taxable net income.

Because of these conflicting goals, which require very different approaches, business owners sometimes fall into the trap of making important business decisions based mainly on the tax consequences.

Don't let the tail wag the dog. Make sure that you consider all the consequences of a transaction or business practice – from a tax, financial, and strategic viewpoint – before finalizing your decision. What sounds good from a tax perspective does not always make sense in terms of your overall business objectives.

Our discussion of the income tax issues faced by your business is organized around seven key subjects.

Chapter 3: Forms of Business Organization provides an overview of how the way in which your business is organized influences your tax situation and the way in which you'll report your income. While this book focuses on the sole proprietorship, we explain how forms such as the partnership, limited liability company (LLC), C corporation, and S corporation operate from a tax perspective.

Chapter 4: Introducing the Schedule C discusses the threshold issues you need to consider, including whether you need to file as a business, how to identify your business, how to select your accounting method and year, and other preliminary matters.

Chapter 5: Business Income discusses the types of income that must be reported on your Schedule C, and for those who carry an inventory, how to compute your cost of goods sold.

Chapter 6: Deductible Business Expenses provides detailed explanations of the most commonly used business deductions, including car and truck expenses, travel expenses, meals and entertainment, employee compensation, health insurance, and retirement plans.

Chapter 7: Capital Assets and Depreciation shows how to handle your costs for real estate, equipment, and other long-term business assets. It also explains what to do when you sell, trade, or dispose of an asset used in your trade or business.

Chapter 8: Business Profit and Self-Employment Tax wraps up our explanation of how to compute your taxable net income, explains how to handle a business loss if you have one, and shows how to compute and pay your self-employment (SECA) tax.

Chapter 9: Business Tax Credits explains the federal tax credits that are available for hiring disadvantaged workers, improving access by the disabled, operating in an Empowerment Zone, and taking certain other actions the government is seeking to promote.

 Tax Organizer Tip

Business-related income and expenses are included in the "Employment" section tab of the CompleteTax™ Organizer. On the first screen of the Employment section, you'll see a list of questions. When you answer "Yes" to the question "Did you have any business income?" a topic tab for "Business Income" will pop up. Click on that tab to get to the main screen for business, which allows you to input your small business information.

As you continue to read through this book, we'll explain unfamiliar terms and tell you how to handle your various items of business income, expense, gain, loss, etc.

Chapter 3

Forms of Business Organization

One of the most important decisions that you made in connection with starting your business was the legal form in which you operate. And, as time passes and your business grows, you may decide to change the form to conform to your changing business goals.

You have a number of choices: a sole proprietorship, a partnership, a corporation (including an S corporation), or a limited liability company (LLC). As you can imagine, there are significant income tax consequences that flow from each of these choices. But as with every business decision you make, don't forget to weigh the tax issues against the non-tax issues.

In this case, you need to think about things like what type of business form will best help you to operate and grow the business, and what form, at your death, will make it easier for you to pass along the business to your heirs as a going concern if you desire.

While this book focuses primarily on tax issues for business owners operating as sole proprietors, it's worthwhile to spend a little time highlighting the differences between that form and the other possibilities. If you own interests in businesses that are organized as corporations, partnerships, or LLCs, we discuss how to report income from these forms of business on your individual tax return at page 171

(salary), page 225 (dividends), and page 237 (partnership, S corporation, and LLC distributions).

SOLE PROPRIETORSHIPS

A sole proprietorship is an unincorporated business with a single owner. It's the most commonly used form for new small businesses, and the easiest form to operate from a tax and recordkeeping perspective. If your business has only one owner, the IRS will presume that it's a sole proprietorship unless you incorporate under state law.

From the IRS's perspective, a sole proprietorship is not a taxable creature in itself. Instead, all of the business's assets and liabilities are treated as belonging directly to the business owner. The annual income and expenses generated by the business are reflected on Schedule C, *Profit or Loss From Business,* or Schedule C-EZ, *Net Profit From Business,* which is part of the business owner's individual tax return (Form 1040).

Beginning on page 33, we'll provide a detailed explanation of the information you need to fill out Schedule C.

For now, just the basics: Your gross revenue from sales and other business income is reported on the top of the Schedule C. Expenses of the business are subtracted from income to arrive at the net profit (or loss) figure at the bottom of the form.

The net profit or loss is carried over from the Schedule C and reported on page 1 of the owner's 1040. This means that there is no separate tax rate schedule that applies to a sole proprietorship — the business owner's individual tax rate will determine the amount of tax paid on the earnings of the business.

The main advantage of a sole proprietorship is simplicity. Because there is only one owner, the accounting rules are much easier to understand and to use. Also, a business owner may transfer money in or out of the business with no tax effects to keep track of.

Example

When you pay yourself as a sole proprietor, you simply withdraw money from your business checking account — you don't have to issue yourself a paycheck and make payroll tax deductions.

Similarly, if you decide to contribute some personal money to the business, you can simply add it to your checking account — you don't have to formally make (and keep track of) your capital contribution as you would with a partnership or a corporation, at least as far as the IRS is concerned.

Sole proprietors are generally required to pay self-employment taxes (see page 135) on all of the business's net profits computed on Schedule C. You must use Schedule SE of the annual income tax return to compute these taxes.

For each quarter, a sole proprietor generally needs to make an estimated tax payment that includes income tax and self-employment tax (see page 306). If you have employees, you may also need to make periodic payments of payroll taxes for them.

When the time comes to sell a business asset or even the business itself, the owner is treated as if he or she sold each individual item that was included in the sale, and gain or loss on each item must be computed separately. Intangible assets such as patents and copyrights are considered assets of the business, and separate gain or loss is computed on them (see page 118).

PARTNERSHIPS

A partnership is an unincorporated business with two or more owners. For businesses with more than one owner, the IRS will presume that your business should be taxed as a partnership unless you have incorporated under state law, or you elect to be taxed as a corporation by filing IRS Form 8832, *Entity Classification Election.*

A partnership is not a taxable entity under federal law — there is no separate partnership income tax, as there is a corporate income tax. Instead, income from the partnership is taxed to the individual partners, at their own individual tax rate.

However, the partnership is required to file a tax return (Form 1065) that reports its income and loss to the IRS, and also reports each partner's share of income and loss on Schedule K-1 of the 1065. For tax purposes, all of the income of the partnership must be reported as distributed to the partners, and they will be taxed on it through their individual returns. This is true whether or not the partners actually received their shares of the income, and even if the partnership agreement requires that the money be retained in the business as partnership capital.

Partnerships are generally the most flexible form of business for tax purposes, since the income and losses distributed to each of the partners can vary (e.g., one partner can receive 40 percent of any profits but 60 percent of any losses), as long as a business purpose other than tax avoidance can be shown for the split.

In the early years of most businesses, the company generates losses rather than profits, and the partnership form allows the partners to use these losses to offset other income they may have from investments or another job. One caveat: The partners may not deduct losses that exceed the amount of their investment in the business. But any losses that can't be deducted as a result of this rule can be deducted in subsequent years if the partner increases his or her investment.

Although the individual partners (not their partnership) are the ones paying the income tax for the business, most of the choices affecting how income is computed must be made by the partnership, rather than by the individual partners on their own returns. These choices include elections of general methods of accounting, methods of depreciation, and accounting for specific items such as organization and business startup expenses and installment sales. Partners are required to treat partnership items in the same way on their individual tax returns as they were treated on the partnership return.

There are a number of nontax factors that may influence your decision as to whether a partnership is the right form of business for you, and we recommend that you seek legal advice in setting up a partnership and writing up the partnership agreement.

LIMITED LIABILITY COMPANIES

The limited liability company (LLC) is a hybrid of a corporation and a limited partnership that is created under state law. For federal tax purposes, an LLC is treated as a partnership and it must file a Form 1065, *U.S. Partnership Return of Income*. (There is an exception to this rule for single-owner LLCs, which are treated identically to sole proprietorships and whose owners must simply file a Schedule C with their Form 1040.)

Under state laws, LLC owners are given the protection from liability that was previously afforded only to corporate stockholders. Although the LLC is a relatively new business form, all of the states have now enacted legislation providing for limited liability companies.

However, while LLCs are treated as partnerships for federal tax purposes, the same is not always true for state tax purposes. Your state department of revenue can tell you the rule in your state.

Comparison with S Corporations

While S corporations (see page 31) also provide limited liability for their owners and favorable pass-through tax treatment, LLCs do provide some special advantages to growing businesses. Like a partnership, an LLC has the ability to make disproportionate distributions to its owners (for example, an LLC member may have a 50 percent ownership interest in the LLC but be entitled to 60 percent of the annual income, if the operating agreement so provides). In

contrast, S corporations must generally make all distributions pro-rata according to the number of shares held by each owner. An LLC can have an unlimited number of investors, but an S corporation is limited to 75 shareholders.

CORPORATIONS

Businesses that are engaged in operations that are considered "risky" or subject to frequent lawsuits are often encouraged by their legal advisors to incorporate. Using a corporate structure can also make it much easier to obtain investment capital and to pass the business down to the owner's children or other successors upon death or retirement.

From a tax perspective, there are two options for corporations under federal income tax law:

- C corporations are what we normally consider "regular" corporations and are subject to the corporate income tax.

- S corporations are corporations that have filed a special election with the IRS. They are not subject to corporate income tax but are treated as similar (but not identical) to partnerships for tax purposes.

There are a number of nontax factors that may influence your decision as to whether a corporation is the right form of business for you, and we recommend that you seek expert legal advice in setting up a corporation and writing up the articles of incorporation.

C Corporations

A C corporation (also known as a regular corporation) is taxed as a separate person or "entity" under the tax law. Income earned by the corporation is normally taxed at the corporate level, using the corporate income tax rates shown in the table on page 30.

After the corporate tax is paid on the business income, any distributions made to stockholders are taxed again at the individuals' rates, as dividends.

Because of these two levels of tax, a regular corporation may be a less desirable form of business than the other types of business entities (sole proprietorships, partnerships, limited liability companies, or S corporations).

This may be true even though regular corporations are taxed at lower tax rates on their first $75,000 in income, when compared to the other business forms.

Comparing Corporations to Other Forms

Because the taxation of income to sole proprietorships and partnerships is determined by the tax bracket that applies to each individual owner, a comparison of tax rates that apply to corporations and to individuals can give you some idea of which form of business would save taxes at a particular income level.

The chart that follows compares the marginal tax rates for tax years beginning in 1999 for corporations, married individuals filing jointly, and for singles. As the table shows, at the lower income levels (non-personal-service businesses with taxable incomes up to $75,000), corporations seem to have the advantage, but this advantage shifts the other way for income between

$75,000 and $283,150. However, the rate comparison is only part of the tax picture to consider: distributions (money taken out) from a partnership are generally taxable only once on the partners' individual returns, while distributions made by a corporation to its shareholders after corporate tax is paid are taxed again as dividends on the shareholders' returns.

Salaries May Offset Tax

In comparing the tax advantages of operating a business as a partnership or sole proprietorship rather than as a corporation, it should be remembered that not all of the corporate profits will be subject to double taxation. The operators of the corporation may withdraw reasonable salaries, which are deductible by the corporation.

These salaries are therefore free from income tax at the corporate level (although the recipients will have to pay individual income tax, and both recipients and the business will have to pay FICA tax, on them). In some cases, the entire net profits of the business may be eaten up by salaries to the owners and other employees, so that no corporate income tax is due.

1999 Tax Rates			
Taxable Income	**C Corporation**	**Married/Joint**	**Single**
0 — 25,750	15%	15%	15%
25,751 — 43,050	15%	15%	28%
43,351 — 50,000	15%	28%	28%
50,001 — 62,450	25%	28%	28%
62,451 — 75,000	25%	28%	31%
75,001 — 100,000	34%	28%	31%
100,001 — 104,050	39%	28%	31%
104,051 — 130,250	39%	31%	31%
130,251 — 158,550	39%	31%	36%
158,551 — 283,150	39%	36%	36%
283,150 — 335,000	39%	39.6%	39.6%
335,001 — 10,000,000	34%	39.6%	39.6%
10,000,001 — 15,000,000	35%	39.6%	39.6%
15,000,001 — 18,333,333	38%	39.6%	39.6%
Over 18,333,333	35%	39.6%	39.6%

Note: Personal service corporations (those whose employees spend at least 95 percent of their time in the field of health, law, engineering, architecture, accounting, actuarial science, performing arts, or consulting) are taxed at a flat rate of 35 percent of net profits.

Warning

If your corporation is profitable but does not pay any dividends for an extended period of time, the IRS is likely to conclude that some of the salaries paid to owners are really disguised dividends. The IRS can disallow some or all of the salary deductions, resulting in a large tax bill plus interest and penalties. If you have a corporation, your best bet is to make sure all salaries are in line with industry standards, and to pay out at least some dividends each year.

S CORPORATIONS

An S corporation is a creature of the federal tax laws. For all other purposes, it's treated as a regular corporation.

This means that to form an S corporation you first have to incorporate under state law.

Then, you must file a special form electing to be taxed under a special provision of the tax law that preserves the corporation's limited liability under state law, but avoids taxation at the corporate level. As a result, the annual income or losses of the S corporation are passed through to shareholders in much the same way that a partnership passes through such items to partners.

One exception is that all S corporation profits, losses, and other items that pass through must be allocated according to each shareholder's proportionate shares of stock. For example, if you own 50% of the stock, you must receive 50% of the losses, profits, credits, etc. This is not the case with a partnership, where one partner can receive different percentages of different tax items if the partnership agreement so specifies.

Because of the restrictive technical requirements for S corporation status, and because the income tax rates on S corporation shareholders are lower than those for C corporations until the taxable income grows to more than $283,151, many business owners choose to operate as S corporations until their businesses "outgrow" this status.

S Corporation Requirements

To obtain S corporation status under the federal income tax law, all of the following requirements must be met:

- The corporation must be a domestic corporation (a corporation organized under the laws of the United States, a state, or territory that is taxed as a corporation under local law).

- *All* shareholders must agree to the election.

- The corporation may not have more than one class of stock (voting and nonvoting shares are not considered to be two separate classes, however).

- The corporation may not have more than 75 shareholders (prior to 1997, the limit was 35)

- The corporation may not have any shareholder that is a nonresident alien or nonhuman entity (such as other corporations or partnerships), unless the shareholder is an estate or trust that is authorized to be an S corporation shareholder under the tax laws, or unless the shareholder is on the list of certain exempt organizations (such as qualified pension, profit-sharing, and stock bonus plans) that are be allowed to be shareholders.

Chapter 4

Introducing the Schedule C

For the rest of Part II, we'll concentrate on issues that apply to businesses organized as sole proprietorships.

If you are the sole owner of a business or operate as an independent contractor, you're going to become very well acquainted with the tax form used by all these businesses: the Schedule C, *Profit or Loss from Business*, or its shorter cousin, the Schedule C-EZ, *Net Profit From Business*.

Although the sole proprietorship is, by definition, a single-owner business, many family businesses are operated in this form even though both spouses consider themselves to be the owners.

If one spouse is the primary business operator, he or she can file as a sole proprietor even if the other spouse fills in as needed or consults on major decisions. If both spouses actively work in the business, you may consider one spouse to be the owner for IRS purposes, and the other may be considered an employee (or possibly even an independent contractor) which will save you the time and trouble of filing partnership tax forms.

You should be aware that under many state marital property laws, both spouses may be considered to be owners of the business assets in case of divorce, regardless of whose name is listed as the owner on the tax forms or the property records.

Work Smart

If both spouses work In the business and you want both to obtain wage credits toward Social Security disability and retirement benefits, you'll generally need to have paychecks issued, and payroll taxes withheld, for the spouse who is not listed as the sole proprietor.

DO YOU NEED TO FILE THIS FORM?

While we suspect that most of you already know the answer to that question, it pays to review the filing requirements just in case your business does not meet them for a particular year.

First of all, the income requirement: If you have $400 or more of business income over and above your expenses, you need to file a Schedule C and a Schedule

SE to pay self-employment tax, even if you would not otherwise have to file a tax return (see page 157).

Although you may know exactly what your business earnings are for normal accounting purposes, if you're close to the $400 threshold or actually had a loss for the year, you'll need to use IRS rules to compute net income for tax purposes in order to know the exact amount. For a complete description of what income you need to include as "business income," see Chapter 5.

Work Smart

Even if your business does have a loss for the year, consider filing a tax return anyway.

That way you can take advantage of the opportunity to carry losses back for two years and/or forward to future years, so you can deduct them in some other year(s) in which you do have a profit.

If your business is just starting out and you have a profit of less than $400, you may want to file a Schedule C to establish your business's existence and show that your business activity was undertaken for a profit motive. In this case, you would not have to file Schedule SE.

If you run more than one business as a sole proprietorship, you'll need to net them together to determine whether you've met the $400 threshold. For example, if one business has a profit of $2,000 and another has a loss of $1,700, your net profit from both businesses is only $300 and you won't need to pay any self-employment tax for the year. We recommend that you do file a Schedule SE anyway, just to demonstrate to the IRS that you computed your taxes correctly.

Do You Have a Profit-Seeking Trade or Business?

In general, in order to file a Schedule C and deduct all your business expenses, you must have been engaged in a "trade or business;" that is, an activity that is carried on for a livelihood or for profit.

A profit motive must be present (though you may in fact have experienced a loss for the year) and some type of economic activity must be conducted.

"Profit" for purposes of these business activity rules means real economic profit, not just tax savings. This profit motive is what separates a business from a hobby, which is an activity engaged in purely for self-satisfaction.

Hobby Loss Rules

What's so bad about hobbies? Well, if you are in business with the objective of making a profit, and it so happens that your deductions exceed your business income for the year, you can claim a loss up to the amount of your total income from all activities. Remaining losses can be carried over into other years.

Your ability to deduct these losses will be limited, however, if the IRS considers your "business" to be a hobby.

Hobby expenses incurred by individuals and even by partnerships and S corporations are generally deductible *only to the extent of the income produced by the hobby*. In other words, you can't use a hobby to generate a tax loss that can be used to shelter your other income. Some expenses, however, that would be deductible on your individual tax return regardless of whether they are incurred in connection with a hobby (such as real estate taxes, mortgage interest, and casualty losses) are deductible even if they exceed your hobby income. These expenses must be used to reduce the amount of the hobby income from which your other hobby expenses can be deducted.

Every bit of your hobby income is reported as "other income" on Line 21 of your Form 1040, *Individual Income Tax Return*. However, expenses associated with the hobby are only deductible if you itemize your deductions. What's more, they are considered "miscellaneous itemized deductions" and you can only deduct the portion of them that, along with any other miscellaneous deductions, exceeds 2 percent of your adjusted gross income.

Although the IRS is not limited in the kind of businesses that it can challenge as being hobbies, businesses that look like traditional hobbies (such as "gentlemen farming" and craft businesses run from the home) may well face a greater chance of IRS scrutiny than other types of businesses.

The absence of income, in itself, does not prevent an activity from being classified as a business activity. You can establish the profit motive of your business under the nine factors used by the IRS, as shown by the chart that follows. A "yes" answer supports a finding of a profit motive, although no one factor settles the matter.

You may also qualify for a presumption that you had a profit motive if your business shows a profit for three of the five years in question.

For a new business, this means that you don't have to show a profit for your first two years. (A narrow exception to this rule applies to horse breeding, training, and racing activities, where profitability must be shown in two out of seven consecutive years.)

If your business qualifies for this presumption, it means that the IRS (not you) has the burden of proving that your business is a hobby. If you don't qualify for the presumption, you may still show that you operated for profit under the nine factors listed below.

The IRS does provide a form (Form 5213, *Election To Postpone Determination as to Whether the Presumption Applies That an Activity Is Engaged in for Profit*, reproduced at the end of the book) on which you can officially elect to have the IRS wait until the first five years are up before examining the profitability of your business. If you use this form, it should be filed within three years of the due date of the return for your first year in business.

However, it's generally not necessary to file the form in order to take advantage of the presumption. If you don't file the form and you are audited by the IRS, you can file the form within 60 days of receiving the IRS notice, as long as your three-year period has not expired.

Nine Factors Used to Show a Profit Motive

1. **How the business is run** — Is the activity carried on in a businesslike manner? Does the owner keep complete, accurate business records and books? Has the owner changed business operations to increase profits?

2. **Expertise** — Does the owner have the necessary expertise to run the business? If not, does he or she seek (and follow) expert advice?

3. **Time and effort** — Does the owner spend the time and effort needed for the business's success? (Spending a lot of time on the activity will not, however, have much value to prove a profit motive if the type of activity has significant personal or recreational aspects.)

4. **Appreciation** — Is it likely that business assets will appreciate in value? (A profit objective can exist where an overall profit would result when the gain from the sale of the asset is added to the other income from the activity, even though a profit is not derived from current operations.)

5. **Success with other activities** — Has the owner engaged in similar (or dissimilar) activities in the past and converted them from unprofitable to profitable enterprises?

6. **History of income or loss** — Were the business losses that were incurred due to the business still being in a startup phase, or because of unforeseen circumstances?

7. **Amount of occasional profit** — Are the amount of occasional profits significant when compared to the size of the owner's investment in the activity, and the amount of losses suffered in other years? (An occasional small profit for an activity generating large losses, or in which the owner has a large investment, will not establish a for-profit objective.)

8. **Financial status of owner** — Is the business activity the only source of the owner's income?

9. **Personal pleasure or recreation** — Is the type of business one that is not usually considered to have elements of personal pleasure or recreation?

Work Smart

How you can go about showing that your activity is operated for profit will depend, in large part, on when you expect it to turn a profit.

Profit possible over short term — *By planning when to receive income and when to purchase items that generate deductions, try to maximize income (and minimize deductions) in at least three years (the "profit" years), and maximize deductions (and minimize income) in the remaining two years (the "loss" years). This may allow you to qualify for the presumption of profit motive discussed above.*

Profit possible only over long term — *If it appears that the business will not be profitable for some years, you won't be able to come within the presumption of profit motive. You'll have to rely on qualifying under the IRS's nine-point inquiry to establish profit motive.*

No possibility of profit — *Face it: What you have here is a hobby. You can try to argue that you qualify under the IRS's nine-point inquiry, but in all likelihood you'll fail. If you want to continue this activity, you may as well either resign yourself to the limitation on hobby losses, or figure out a way to conduct the activity in a way that generates profits.*

More Than One Business?

People who are endowed with an entrepreneurial spirit generally don't limit their efforts to one business activity. It's common for business owners to branch out into sideline activities that may or may not be related to their original activity, and that might be considered a separate business.

For example, a craft supply retailer might also offer classes in various types of arts and crafts. Or, a photography studio might offer photoprocessing of customers' ordinary snapshots, in addition to traditional professional photography. In each case, the question arises: is this a single business, or two businesses that should be reported on two different Schedule Cs?

The tax laws and regulations are not very clear on this issue, probably because the facts and circumstances can vary so much from case to case. Generally speaking, if you have two or more separate business activities, you can't report them both on the same Schedule C. The instructions to Form 5213, *Election*

To Postpone Determination as to Whether the Presumption Applies That an Activity Is Engaged in for Profit, state that in determining whether you are engaged in more than one activity, you must consider all of the following:

- the similarity of the activities

- the business purpose that is (or might be) served by carrying on the activities separately or together in a trade or business or investment setting

- the organizational and economic interrelationship of the activities

These factors are quite vague and subjective, even for the IRS. The general idea, however, is that if you provide similar products or services to similar clients, you have a single business. If you don't, you may have more than one business depending on how close the relationship is between the activities.

Other factors that should be considered include which spouse is the primary operator of the business (for instance, does one spouse run one activity while the other runs a second?) and the locations of the businesses (if you have two different but related businesses that occupy two separate sites, it's more likely that they should be considered two separate businesses).

If you receive income as a "statutory employee," a grouping that includes full-time life insurance agents, agent or commission drivers, commission traveling salespersons, and certain homeworkers, you must report this income on a Schedule C. If you also receive other income as a self-employed person, don't combine the two types of income – you must file a separate Schedule C for each type. See page 48 for more details.

One last factor to keep in mind is that the tax law provides for separate treatment of "passive activities" – basically, income or losses from a passive activity can only be offset by income or losses from other passive activities.

Real estate rentals are most often classified as passive activities which must be reported on Schedule E, *Supplemental Income and Loss*, not Schedule C. So, if your "sole proprietorship" involves some rental or leasing activities, you may need to treat the income and expense from these activities as separate passive activities (see page 214 regarding Schedule E).

Can You Use Form C-EZ?

The IRS does provide a simplified version of Schedule C, known as Schedule C-EZ, *Net Profit From Business*, that can be used by some small business owners, primarily those who work as independent contractors for one or more larger businesses. A copy of Schedule C is reproduced at the end of the book.

Whenever you have an option as to which tax form you can use, it's generally best to use the simplest form that's available to you. There is some evidence that the IRS is less likely to scrutinize tax returns that include the "EZ" versions of the forms.

So, you'll want to use Schedule C-EZ if you're eligible, which means that you:

- operated only one sole proprietorship business during the year

- did not have an inventory at any time during the year

- did not have any employees during the year

- had total business expenses that did not exceed $2,500

- do not deduct expenses for business use of your home

- use the cash method of accounting (see discussion page 41)

- did not have a net loss

- do not have any prior-year unallowed passive activity losses for this business

- are not required to file a Form 4562, *Depreciation and Amortization*, for the year, which means that you did not place any depreciable property into service for the first time this year, and you're not claiming depreciation on any "listed property" such as a car, light truck, motorcycle, cell phone, computer or peripherals, or photographic, audio/video, or communications equipment (for more on depreciation, see page 99).

If you do not meet all of these requirements, you must file Schedule C this year instead of C-EZ.

IDENTIFYING YOUR BUSINESS

Whether you use Schedule C or C-EZ, the top of the form requires you to list your business name (if it's different from your own name), your principal business or profession, your principal business code, and your Employer Identification Number (EIN) if you are required to have one.

Employer I.D. Numbers

Sole proprietors need to have an EIN only if they have one or more employees, if they have a Keogh plan, or if they are required to file excise tax forms such as those for sales tax, alcohol or tobacco.

If you purchase a business for which an EIN is needed, use your own EIN or get a new one – don't use the EIN of the previous owner. If you operate more than one business as a sole proprietor, you should use the same EIN for each one; if you operate businesses in forms other than sole proprietorship, you'll need a separate EIN for each business entity.

To apply for an EIN, you can file a paper Form SS-4, *Application for Employer Identification Number*, with the appropriate IRS Service Center for your state. If you apply by mail, it generally takes about four weeks to receive the number. If you need to file your tax return before you receive the EIN, write "applied for" in the space where the EIN should go.

You can also get an EIN immediately over the phone by calling the number of the Tele-TIN in the chart on the next page; however, you'll still need to fill out a paper SS-4 form and mail or fax it to the Service Center within 24 hours. The IRS representative will give you the correct fax number. The advantage of using this system is that you will receive the EIN immediately and you can use it on your tax forms right away.

Business Codes

Whether you file a Schedule C or C-EZ, you'll need to enter a six-digit business code at the top of the form. We reproduce the complete list of codes on pages 39-40. It's very important that you use the correct business code. If your return is examined by the IRS, the agents may use this code as a screening device to determine whether your income and expenses are unusual for that type of business.

Where to Apply for an EIN	
If your principal business, office or agency, or legal residence in the case of an individual, is located in:	*Call the Tele-TIN number shown or file with the IRS Service Center at:*
Florida, Georgia, South Carolina	Attn: Entity Control, Atlanta, GA 39901 770-455-2360
New Jersey, New York City and counties of Nassau, Rockland, Suffolk, and Westchester	Attn: Entity Control, Holtsville, NY 00501 516-447-4955
New York (all other counties), Connecticut, Maine, Massachusetts, New Hampshire, Rhode Island, Vermont	Attn: Entity Control, Andover, MA 05501 978-474-9717
Illinois, Iowa, Minnesota, Missouri, Wisconsin	Attn: Entity Control, Stop 6800, 2306 E. Bannister Rd., Kansas City, MO 64999 816-926-5999
Delaware, District of Columbia, Maryland, Pennsylvania, Virginia	Attn: Entity Control, Philadelphia, PA 19255 215-516-6999
Indiana, Kentucky, Michigan, Ohio, West Virginia	Attn: Entity Control, Cincinnati, OH 45999 606-292-5467
Kansas, New Mexico, Oklahoma, Texas	Attn: Entity Control, Austin, TX 73301 512-460-7843
Alaska, Arizona, California (counties of Alpine, Amador, Butte, Calaveras, Colusa, Contra Costa, Del Norte, El Dorado, Glenn, Humboldt, Lake, Lassen, Marin, Mendocino, Modoc, Napa, Nevada, Placer, Plumas, Sacramento, San Joaquin, Shasta, Sierra, Siskiyou, Solano, Sonoma, Sutter, Tehama, Trinity, Yolo, and Yuba), Colorado, Idaho, Montana, Nebraska, Nevada, North Dakota, Oregon, South Dakota, Utah, Washington, Wyoming	Attn: Entity Control, Mail Stop 6271, P.O. Box 9941, Ogden, UT 84201 801-620-7645
California (all other counties), Hawaii	Attn: Entity Control, Fresno, CA 93888 209-452-4010
Alabama, Arkansas, Louisiana, Mississippi, North Carolina, Tennessee	Attn: Entity Control, Memphis, TN 37501 901-546-3920
If you have no legal residence, principal place of business, or principal office or agency in any state:	Attn: Entity Control, Philadelphia, PA 19255 215-516-6999

If so, they may decide to dig further into your return (and ask you to produce a lot more records to prove your figures).

In the last several years, the IRS has been making an effort to educate its agents about typical operating procedures in different industries and even in specific types of businesses, so that the agents can more effectively ferret out underreported income and overstated deductions. If you report the wrong business code, the IRS may be judging you by the incorrect standard.

Example

If you operate a retail jewelry business, the IRS has a general idea of the percentage of your revenues that should be eaten up by your cost of goods sold. If you erroneously list your code as "453220" which applies to gift shops, your cost of goods sold may appear to be way out of line and your tax return may be flagged for an audit.

New Principal Business or Professional Activity Codes

These codes for the Principal Business or Professional Activity classify sole proprietorships by the type of activity they are engaged in to facilitate the administration of the Internal Revenue Code. These six-digit codes are based on the new North American Industry Classification System (NAICS) and do not resemble prior year codes.

Select the category that best describes your primary business activity (for example, Real Estate). Then select the activity that best identifies the principal source of your sales or receipts (for example, real estate agent). Now find the six-digit code assigned to this activity and **enter it on line B of Schedule C or C-EZ**

(for example, 531210, the Code for offices of real estate agents and brokers).

Note: *If your principal source of income is from farming activities, you should file **Schedule F** (Form 1040), Profit or Loss From Farming.*

Accommodation, Food Services, & Drinking Places

Accommodation
721310	Rooming & boarding houses
721210	RV (recreational vehicle) parks & recreational camps
721100	Travel accommodation (including hotels, motels, & bed & breakfast inns)

Food Services & Drinking Places
722410	Drinking places (alcoholic beverages)
722110	Full-service restaurants
722210	Limited-service eating places
722300	Special food services (including food service contractors & caterers)

Administrative & Support and Waste Management & Remediation Services

Administrative & Support Services
561430	Business service centers (including private mail centers & copy shops)
561740	Carpet & upholstery cleaning services
561440	Collection agencies
561450	Credit bureaus
561410	Document preparation services
561300	Employment services
561710	Exterminating & pest control services
561210	Facilities support (management) services
561600	Investigation & security services
561720	Janitorial services
561730	Landscaping services
561110	Office administrative services
561420	Telephone call centers (including telephone answering services & telemarketing bureaus)
561500	Travel arrangement & reservation services
561490	Other business support services (including repossession services, court reporting, & stenotype services)
561790	Other services to buildings & dwellings
561900	Other support services (including packaging & labeling services, & convention & trade show organizers)

Waste Management & Remediation Services
562000	Waste management & remediation services

Agriculture, Forestry, Hunting, & Fishing
112900	Animal production (including breeding of cats and dogs)
114110	Fishing
113000	Forestry & logging (including forest nurseries & timber tracts)
114210	Hunting & trapping

Support Activities for Agriculture & Forestry
115210	Support activities for animal production (including farriers)
115110	Support activities for crop production (including cotton ginning, soil preparation, planting, & cultivating)
115310	Support activities for forestry

Arts, Entertainment, & Recreation

Amusement, Gambling, & Recreation Industries
713100	Amusement parks & arcades
713200	Gambling industries
713900	Other amusement & recreation services (including golf courses, skiing facilities, marinas, fitness centers, bowling centers, skating rinks, miniature golf courses)

Museums, Historical Sites, & Similar Institutions
712100	Museums, historical sites, & similar institutions

Performing Arts, Spectator Sports, & Related Industries
711410	Agents & managers for artists, athletes, entertainers, & other public figures
711510	Independent artists, writers, & performers
711100	Performing arts companies
711300	Promoters of performing arts, sports, & similar events
711210	Spectator sports (including professional sports clubs & racetrack operations)

Construction
233110	Land subdivision & land development
233300	Nonresidential building construction
233200	Residential building construction

Heavy Construction
234100	Highway, street, bridge, & tunnel construction
234900	Other heavy construction

Special Trade Contractors
235500	Carpentry & floor contractors
235710	Concrete contractors
235310	Electrical contractors
235400	Masonry, drywall, insulation, & tile contractors
235210	Painting & wall covering contractors
235110	Plumbing, heating, & air-conditioning contractors
235610	Roofing, siding, & sheet metal contractors
235810	Water well drilling contractors
235900	Other special trade contractors

Educational Services
611000	Educational services (including schools, colleges, & universities)

Finance & Insurance

Credit Intermediation & Related Activities
522100	Depository credit intermediation (including commercial banking, savings institutions, & credit unions)
522200	Nondepository credit intermediation (including sales financing & consumer lending)
522300	Activities related to credit intermediation (including loan brokers)

Insurance Agents, Brokers, & Related Activities
524210	Insurance agencies & brokerages
524290	Other insurance related activities

Securities, Commodity Contracts, & Other Financial Investments & Related Activities
523140	Commodity contracts brokers
523130	Commodity contracts dealers
523110	Investment bankers & securities dealers
523210	Securities & commodity exchanges
523120	Securities brokers
523900	Other financial investment activities (including investment advice)

Health Care & Social Assistance

Ambulatory Health Care Services
621610	Home health care services
621510	Medical & diagnostic laboratories
621310	Offices of chiropractors
621210	Offices of dentists
621330	Offices of mental health practitioners (except physicians)
621320	Offices of optometrists
621340	Offices of physical, occupational & speech therapists, & audiologists
621111	Offices of physicians (except mental health specialists)
621112	Offices of physicians, mental health specialists
621391	Offices of podiatrists
621399	Offices of all other miscellaneous health practitioners
621400	Outpatient care centers
621900	Other ambulatory health care services (including ambulance services, blood, & organ banks)

Hospitals
622000	Hospitals

Nursing & Residential Care Facilities
623000	Nursing & residential care facilities

Social Assistance
624410	Child day care services
624200	Community food & housing, & emergency & other relief services
624100	Individual & family services
624310	Vocational rehabilitation services

Information
511000	Publishing industries

Broadcasting & Telecommunications
513000	Broadcasting & telecommunications

Information Services & Data Processing Services
514210	Data processing services
514100	Information services (including news syndicates, libraries, & on-line information services)

Motion Picture & Sound Recording
512100	Motion picture & video industries (except video rental)
512200	Sound recording industries

Manufacturing
315000	Apparel mfg.
312000	Beverage & tobacco product mfg.
334000	Computer & electronic product mfg.
335000	Electrical equipment, appliance, & component mfg.
332000	Fabricated metal product mfg.
337000	Furniture & related product mfg.
333000	Machinery mfg.
339110	Medical equipment & supplies mfg.
322000	Paper mfg.
324100	Petroleum & coal products mfg.
326000	Plastics & rubber products mfg.
331000	Primary metal mfg.
323100	Printing & related support activities
313000	Textile mills
314000	Textile product mills
336000	Transportation equipment mfg.
321000	Wood product mfg.
339900	Other miscellaneous mfg.

Chemical Manufacturing
325100	Basic chemical mfg.
325500	Paint, coating, & adhesive mfg.
325300	Pesticide, fertilizer, & other agricultural chemical mfg.
325410	Pharmaceutical & medicine mfg.
325200	Resin, synthetic rubber, & artificial & synthetic fibers & filaments mfg.
325600	Soap, cleaning compound, & toilet preparation mfg.
325900	Other chemical product & preparation mfg.

Food Manufacturing
311110	Animal food mfg.
311800	Bakeries & tortilla mfg.
311500	Dairy product mfg.
311400	Fruit & vegetable preserving & speciality food mfg.
311200	Grain & oilseed milling
311610	Animal slaughtering & processing
311710	Seafood product preparation & packaging
311300	Sugar & confectionery product mfg.
311900	Other food mfg. (including coffee, tea, flavorings, & seasonings)

New Principal Business or Professional Activity Codes (continued)

Leather & Allied Product Manufacturing
316210 Footwear mfg. (including leather, rubber, & plastics)
316110 Leather & hide tanning & finishing
316990 Other leather & allied product mfg.

Nonmetallic Mineral Product Manufacturing
327300 Cement & concrete product mfg.
327100 Clay product & refractory mfg.
327210 Glass & glass product mfg.
327400 Lime & gypsum product mfg.
327900 Other nonmetallic mineral product mfg.

Mining
212110 Coal mining
212200 Metal ore mining
212300 Nonmetallic mineral mining & quarrying
211110 Oil & gas extraction
213110 Support activities for mining

Other Services

Personal & Laundry Services
812111 Barber shops
812112 Beauty salons
812220 Cemeteries & crematories
812310 Coin-operated laundries & drycleaners
812320 Drycleaning & laundry services (except coin-operated) (including laundry & drycleaning drop off & pickup sites)
812210 Funeral homes & funeral services
812330 Linen & uniform supply
812113 Nail salons
812930 Parking lots & garages
812910 Pet care (except veterinary) services
812920 Photofinishing
812190 Other personal care services (including diet & weight reducing centers)
812990 All other personal services

Repair & Maintenance
811120 Automotive body, paint, interior, & glass repair
811110 Automotive mechanical & electrical repair & maintenance
811190 Other automotive repair & maintenance (including oil change & lubrication shops & car washes)
811310 Commercial & industrial machinery & equipment (except automotive & electronic) repair & maintenance
811210 Electronic & precision equipment repair & maintenance
811430 Footwear & leather goods repair
811410 Home & garden equipment & appliance repair & maintenance
811420 Reupholstery & furniture repair
811490 Other personal & household goods repair & maintenance

Professional, Scientific, & Technical Services
541100 Legal services
541211 Office of certified public accountants
541214 Payroll services
541213 Tax preparation services
541219 Other accounting services

Architectural, Engineering, & Related Services
541310 Architectural services

541350 Building inspection services
541340 Drafting services
541330 Engineering services
541360 Geophysical surveying & mapping services
541320 Landscape architecture services
541370 Surveying & mapping (except geophysical) services
541380 Testing laboratories

Computer Systems Design & Related Services
541510 Computer systems design & related services

Specialized Design Services
541400 Specialized design services (including interior, industrial, graphic, & fashion design)

Other Professional, Scientific, & Technical Services
541800 Advertising & related services
541600 Management, scientific, & technical consulting services
541910 Market research & public opinion polling
541920 Photographic services
541700 Scientific research & development services
541930 Translation & interpretation services
541940 Veterinary services
541990 All other professional, scientific, & technical services

Real Estate & Rental & Leasing

Real Estate
531100 Lessors of real estate (including miniwarehouses & self-storage units)
531210 Offices of real estate agents & brokers
531320 Offices of real estate appraisers
531310 Real estate property managers
531390 Other activities related to real estate

Rental & Leasing Services
532100 Automotive equipment rental & leasing
532400 Commercial & industrial machinery & equipment rental & leasing
532210 Consumer electronics & appliances rental
532220 Formal wear & costume rental
532310 General rental centers
532230 Video tape & disc rental
532290 Other consumer goods rental

Religious, Grantmaking, Civic, Professional, & Similar Organizations
813000 Religious, grantmaking, civic, professional, & similar organizations

Retail Trade

Building Material & Garden Equipment & Supplies Dealers
444130 Hardware stores
444110 Home centers
444200 Lawn & garden equipment & supplies stores
444120 Paint & wallpaper stores
444190 Other building materials dealers

Clothing & Accessories Stores
448130 Children's & infants' clothing stores
448150 Clothing accessories stores
448140 Family clothing stores
448310 Jewelry stores
448320 Luggage & leather goods stores

448110 Men's clothing stores
448210 Shoe stores
448120 Women's clothing stores
448190 Other clothing stores

Electronic & Appliance Stores
443130 Camera & photographic supplies stores
443120 Computer & software stores
443111 Household appliance stores
443112 Radio, television, & other electronics stores

Food & Beverage Stores
445310 Beer, wine, & liquor stores
445220 Fish & seafood markets
445230 Fruit & vegetable markets
445100 Grocery stores (including supermarkets & convenience stores without gas)
445210 Meat markets
445290 Other specialty food stores

Furniture & Home Furnishing Stores
442110 Furniture stores
442200 Home furnishings stores

Gasoline Stations
447100 Gasoline stations (including convenience stores with gas)

General Merchandise Stores
452000 General merchandise stores

Health & Personal Care Stores
446120 Cosmetics, beauty supplies, & perfume stores
446130 Optical goods stores
446110 Pharmacies & drug stores
446190 Other health & personal care stores

Motor Vehicle & Parts Dealers
441300 Automotive parts, accessories, & tire stores
441222 Boat dealers
441221 Motorcycle dealers
441110 New car dealers
441210 Recreational vehicle dealers (including motor home & travel trailer dealers)
441120 Used car dealers
441229 All other motor vehicle dealers

Sporting Goods, Hobby, Book, & Music Stores
451211 Book stores
451120 Hobby, toy, & game stores
451140 Musical instrument & supplies stores
451212 News dealers & newsstands
451220 Prerecorded tape, compact disc, & record stores
451130 Sewing, needlework, & piece goods stores
451110 Sporting goods stores

Miscellaneous Store Retailers
453920 Art dealers
453110 Florists
453220 Gift, novelty, & souvenir stores
453930 Manufactured (mobile) home dealers
453210 Office supplies & stationery stores
453910 Pet & pet supplies stores
453310 Used merchandise stores
453990 All other miscellaneous store retailers (including tobacco, candle, & trophy shops)

Nonstore Retailers
454110 Electronic shopping & mail-order houses
454310 Fuel dealers
454210 Vending machine operators
454390 Other direct selling establishments (including door-to-door retailing, frozen food plan providers, party plan merchandisers, & coffee-break service providers)

Transportation & Warehousing
481000 Air transportation
485510 Charter bus industry
484110 General freight trucking, local
484120 General freight trucking, long-distance
485210 Interurban & rural bus transportation
486000 Pipeline transportation
482110 Rail transportation
487000 Scenic & sightseeing transportation
485410 School & employee bus transportation
484200 Specialized freight trucking (including household moving vans)
485300 Taxi & limousine service
485110 Urban transit systems
483000 Water transportation
485990 Other transit & ground passenger transportation
488000 Support activities for transportation (including motor vehicle towing)

Couriers & Messengers
492000 Couriers & messengers

Warehousing & Storage Facilities
493100 Warehousing & storage (except lessors of miniwarehouses & self-storage units)

Utilities
221000 Utilities

Wholesale Trade

Wholesale Trade, Durable Goods
421600 Electrical goods
421200 Furniture & home furnishing
421700 Hardware, & plumbing & heating equipment & supplies
421940 Jewelry, watch, precious stone, & precious metals
421300 Lumber & other construction materials
421800 Machinery, equipment, & supplies
421500 Metal & mineral (except petroleum)
421100 Motor vehicle & motor vehicle parts & supplies
421400 Professional & commercial equipment & supplies
421930 Recyclable materials
421910 Sporting & recreational goods & supplies
421920 Toy & hobby goods & supplies
421990 Other miscellaneous durable goods

Wholesale Trade, Nondurable Goods
422300 Apparel, piece goods, & notions
422800 Beer, wine, & distilled alcoholic beverage
422920 Books, periodicals, & newspapers
422600 Chemical & allied products
422210 Drugs & druggists' sundries
422500 Farm product raw materials
422910 Farm supplies
422930 Flower, nursery stock, & florists' supplies
422400 Grocery & related products
422950 Paint, varnish, & supplies
422100 Paper & paper products
422700 Petroleum & petroleum products
422940 Tobacco & tobacco products
422990 Other miscellaneous nondurable goods

999999 **Unclassified establishments (unable to classify)**

If you find that your business does not fit neatly into one of the business code categories listed by the IRS, consider whether you might actually be operating more than one business, as discussed on page 36.

If you're still convinced that you're operating only one business, use the code that applies to the majority of your income and expenses. The IRS does provide a code 999999 for business owners that are unable to classify their operations, but we suggest that you use this only as a last resort.

ACCOUNTING METHODS AND TAX YEARS

As a small business owner, you frequently make business decisions that may have important tax implications, whether or not you realize it at the time.

However, there are some tax-related choices that tend to have a more general, long-term effect on how you determine your business income, and possibly even on how you run your business. Often, once made, these choices are more or less permanent — you may not be able to change without the IRS's permission, which may be difficult or time-consuming to get. While some of these decisions may seem rather technical, they can have a significant effect on your tax situation and you should have a basic understanding of the issues at stake.

The most commonly encountered decisions of this nature that you'll face are your choices of an accounting method and a tax year. For those of you who carry an inventory, another important decision relates to your inventory valuation method, discussed on page 52.

Accounting Methods

At the top of the Schedule C or C-EZ the IRS asks you to identify the accounting method you use by checking a box. There are two basic accounting methods available to most small businesses: cash and accrual. If you use a hybrid method (see page 43) or some special method for your industry, you must check the box marked "other" and give the name of the method.

The major difference between cash and accrual is that a cash method taxpayer recognizes income and expenses at the point in time that the money is actually received or paid. In contrast, an accrual method taxpayer generally reports income at the time the sale is made even if the customer does not pay at that time, and reports expenses as they become due rather than by the date that the checks go out.

Most taxpayers use the cash method of accounting for their personal life. It's very simple to use and requires little recordkeeping other than a checkbook register, bank statements and perhaps credit card statements.

You can continue to use the cash method for personal items even if you use the accrual method for your business. And if you have more than one business, you can use different methods for each business as long as you maintain a separate set of accounting books and records for each one.

Cash Method Accounting

The cash method is simple to use because it's usually obvious when you receive money from a customer or other payer, or when you pay an expense with cash, credit card or a check. When money comes in or goes out, it's recorded and recognized for tax purposes.

However, as you would expect, there are a few complicating factors to remember. For one thing, if you are paid in the form of property or services instead of money, or if you pay some of your own debts through some type of barter arrangement, you must recognize these payments at the fair market value of what you give or receive.

You can't delay recognition of income by not taking control of money that you're entitled to receive. Under the cash method, income is recognized when it is actually *or constructively* received. "Constructive receipt" occurs when money is made available to you without restriction, is posted to your account, or is received by your agent.

Example

If a customer pays you with a check on December 30, 1999, you have constructively received the money and must count it as income in 1999, even if you don't cash the check or deposit it into your bank account until sometime in January of 2000.

Similarly, if you receive interest on a money market account, you have constructive receipt of the money when it is credited to your account, not when it is withdrawn.

With most business expenses, the cash method allows you to deduct them in the year that you paid for them. However, some things are not entirely deductible in the year you pay for them; for example, the purchase price of capital assets must be depreciated or amortized over a number of years (see page 99). Generally, if you make advance payments for an expense that apply substantially beyond the end of the current year, the payments must be prorated and deducted proportionately over the period in which the payments apply.

Example

If you purchase a one-year business owner's insurance policy and coverage begins on July 1, 1999, you can only deduct six months' worth of premiums in 1999. The remainder would be deductible in 2000.

Some of the more common items that fall under this rule are amounts paid to obtain a loan, such as prepaid interest, points, and loan origination fees, which must ordinarily be deducted over the course of the loan.

Advance lease payments must be deducted in the year to which they apply, and amounts paid to acquire a lease from another lessee must be deducted evenly over the course of the entire lease.

Accrual Method Accounting

Under the accrual method, you record business income when a sale occurs, whether it be the delivery of a product or the rendering of a service on your part, regardless of when you get paid. You record an expense when you receive goods or services, even though you may not pay for them until later.

To be more precise, under the accrual method you recognize an item of income when all the events that establish your right to receive the income have happened, and when the amount of income you are to receive is known with reasonable accuracy. If you estimate an amount due to you with reasonable accuracy and record it as income, and the amount you eventually receive differs from your estimate, you should make an adjustment to your income in the year you actually receive the payment.

Example

You sold a big-screen television for $800 in December of 1999. You sent out a bill in January of 2000 and the customer paid you later that year. However, when he got the bill, your customer pointed out that your competitor, Store X, was selling the same model for $50 less, so you adjusted your price by $50 to avoid losing the sale.

Under the accrual method, you would recognize $800 of income in 1999, because that is when all events establishing your right to the income took place. You would reduce your 2000 income by $50 to reflect the lower actual payment you received.

The accrual method also says that you recognize an item of expense when you become liable for it, whether or not you pay for it in the same year. Becoming liable means that all events have occurred that establish your obligation, you can determine the dollar amount with reasonable accuracy, and "economic performance" has occurred. Economic performance means that the property or services have been provided or the property has been used.

Work Smart

The accrual method gives you a more accurate picture of your financial situation than the cash method. This is because you record income on the books when it is truly earned, and you record expenses when they are incurred. Income earned in one period is accurately matched against the expenses that correspond to that period, so you get a better picture of your net profits for each period.

Who must use accrual? Any type of business that has an inventory must use the accrual method, at least for sales and for purchases. Inventories are necessary in most marketing, manufacturing, retail, or wholesale businesses, or service businesses in which customers are charged for parts, materials, or components.

There is an exception for artists, authors, and photographers who sell works that they have created by their own efforts. They are not required to assign their qualified creative expenses to the particular works they have created as "cost of goods sold," which generally means they don't need to keep track of inventory costs. "Qualified creative expenses" do not include expenses related to printing, photographic plates, film, videotape, etc., so if you are involved in mass reproduction or publishing of your own creative work, you'll have to use inventory accounting for that part of your business.

Hybrid methods. Since using two different accounting methods can be cumbersome, it's more practical for most businesses that carry inventory to simply use the accrual method for everything.

However, if you wish, you can use a hybrid method that uses accrual to the extent required by law, and uses cash for the remainder of your income and expenses. Consult your accountant for more details on how this would work.

Pros and cons of accrual. Even if your business does not have inventory, if you have a lot of complex transactions during the year you may find the accrual method more desirable, because expenses are deducted in the year in which the income to which they relate is reported. By using the accrual method, your net income tends to be leveled out, avoiding income "peaks" that are subject to higher tax rates.

For some business owners, the accrual method does not necessarily reduce taxes, and may create many unnecessary accounting headaches when compared with the cash method. On the other hand, most accountants feel that the accrual method is the only one that accurately reflects the true financial state of your business.

In selecting the most appropriate accounting method, there's one disadvantage of the accrual method that tax planners like to emphasize — it's considerably more difficult to minimize taxes by shifting items of income and expense from one year to another under the accrual method. The cash-method business owner may be able to collect fees, rents, interest, and other obligations in advance or put off payment until a later year. The cash-method owner can also usually control expenses to some extent by accelerating or deferring payment for items such as advertising, supplies, repairs, interest and taxes.

Controlling income and expenses is not nearly as easy for the accrual-method business owner. He or she can defer some income into the next tax year by shipping and invoicing as little as possible during the closing days of the year, but this may not be worth the cash-flow problem that it may cause. Or the owner can try to accelerate expenses by requesting the delivery and billing of supplies, etc., before the end of the year.

Other Accounting Methods

Certain kinds of businesses can use special accounting methods under the tax law. These include farmers, builders and contractors, and business owners receiving income under long-term contracts. If you're in one of these industries, your accountant can give you more information about your options.

Your Tax Year

Your tax year determines how your taxable income will be computed. All income received or accrued within a single year is reported on that year's tax return, along with all expenses paid or accrued, and the end of the year is the cut-off point for many tax-saving strategies.

In theory, your tax year, which is also known as your accounting period, may be either a calendar year or a fiscal year (a 12-month period that ends on the last day of any month other than December). Whether you knew it or not, you selected your tax year the very first time you filed a tax return as an individual, partnership, corporation, or trust. You must continue to use the same tax year that you used that first time, unless you get IRS permission to change.

Since a sole proprietorship does not exist apart from its owner (at least in the eyes of the IRS), a sole proprietorship must use the same tax year as the owner. The majority of sole proprietors use the calendar year as their tax year, since they must continue to use the same tax year that the owner used in his or her initial individual tax return (and since most of us began filing early in life, we automatically used the calendar year the first time).

Choosing a Fiscal Year

The tax year you use may determine the accuracy with which your business's income is matched with the expenses that generate the income, on your business's financial statements. So, in the case of a business that has seasonal cycles, ideally you would have the accounting period include the entire busy season. The accounting period generally should not begin in the middle of the season.

Example

A ski resort is open only during the months of December through March — the winter resort season. If the books are kept on the basis of a calendar year, the accounting period would split the season, and distortion of income would result.

So, what would appear as a profit as of December 31, the close of the calendar year, may turn out to be a loss, or vice versa, when the entire season from December through March is considered.

Moreover, the use of the calendar year would require the owners to take inventories and make other determinations in the middle of the season when they have the least amount of time available. The use of a fiscal year that included the entire season would allow them to avoid these difficulties.

If the nature of your business is such that the bulk of expenses and receipts for an operating cycle fall in different calendar years, it may be best to select an accounting period that includes both.

Example

Let's say that your business incurs most of its expenses in the fall and gets most of its income in the spring. In any one calendar year, expenses and receipts would have little relation to each other.

Receipts in 1999, for example, would not be offset by corresponding expenses, because these expenses would have been incurred in 1998. The 1999 receipts would be offset by 1999 expenses, although these expenses would relate to 2000 receipts. A fiscal year starting on July 1, August 1, or September 1 would more accurately reflect income for your natural business year.

If you want to switch from a calendar year to a fiscal year (or vice versa), you'll need permission from the IRS, and to get such permission you must demonstrate to the IRS's satisfaction that you have a valid business purpose other than tax avoidance. In most cases, a seasonal business would be able to show a valid business purpose for using a fiscal year. You can request approval by filing IRS Form 1128, *Application to Adopt, Change, or Retain a Tax Year.*

Warning

Except in unusual cases, once you have received permission to change your tax year, the IRS will not allow you to change it again within 10 years.

DID YOU MATERIALLY PARTICIPATE IN THE BUSINESS?

The top section of the Schedule C form asks you to answer yes or no to the question, "Did you materially participate in the operation of this business during 1999?"

Most business owners can safely check the box marked "yes," since owners typically expend much more time and effort on their operations than an employee might. Their participation in the business is not only material, it's absolutely crucial!

The IRS asks this question chiefly to screen out businesses that are really passive, investment activities for their owners instead of actively managed businesses. Passive activities are the classic vehicles for tax shelters, and they are now subject to strict rules regarding deduction of losses (see page 219).

Essentially, the IRS does not want you to try to disguise passive activity losses as regular business losses that are deductible against your ordinary income.

What's more, because passive activity losses can only be deducted against passive activity income, the IRS does not want you to call a profitable business a "passive activity" just so that you can deduct some passive losses against it.

Real estate rentals will always be considered a passive activity that should be reported on Schedule E, not Schedule C, regardless of whether the owner materially participates. An exception exists for real estate professionals who materially participate in the real estate rental activities. See the discussion of rental activities on page 214.

Beyond that important distinction, the IRS has devised a seven-step test for material participation. If you meet any of seven requirements, you have materially participated for the year, and you should check the "yes" box in answer to the question on Schedule C.

If you are married, your spouse's work in the business can be counted towards your own participation hours whether or not you file a joint tax return, and whether or not your spouse is a co-owner of the business.

However, work done primarily as an investor in the business (such as reviewing or analyzing financial statements, or monitoring the finances or operations in a nonmanagerial capacity) does not count toward these tests.

If you do not meet any of these tests, you must check the "no" box, and you may have to complete Form 8582, *Passive Activity Loss Limitations*.

There is an exception for those who own working interests in oil or gas wells – they may check the "yes" box and complete Schedule C whether or not they meet any of the seven tests.

Seven Tests for Material Participation

1. You participated in the activity for more than 500 hours during the tax year.

2. You were substantially the only participant in the activity during the tax year.

3. You participated in the activity for more than 100 hours in the tax year, which was at least as much as any other participant, including employees and independent contractors.

4. The activity involves the conduct of a trade or business, you participated in the activity for more than 100 hours, none of the other six tests apply, and you participated in all such significant participation activities for more than 500 hours during the year.

5. You materially participated in the activity for any five of the preceding 10 tax years.

6. The activity is a personal service activity in which you materially participated for any three prior tax years. A personal service activity is one that involves performing services in the fields of health, law, engineering, architecture, accounting, actuarial science, performing arts, consulting, or any other trade or business in which capital is not a material income producing factor.

7. Based on all the facts and circumstances, you participated in the activity on a regular, continuous basis during the year, and you participated for more than 100 hours. Your participation in management will not count toward this test if anyone else was a paid manager or spent more hours than you in managing the business.

Chapter 5

Business Income

The starting point for computing your income tax is, of course, your gross business income. In this chapter we'll discuss some rules you need to know about what is and isn't reportable business income, and the distinctions between various types of income that must be reported in different places on your tax form.

INCOME REPORTED ON SCHEDULE C

The general rule is that any income you receive that's connected with your business is considered "business income" that should be reported on Schedule C. Income is considered "connected with your business" if it's clear that the payment would not have been made if you did *not* have the business.

The Schedule C provides you with two places to report your income. Line 1 is the place to report the gross income from sales of your product or service to customers. In most cases, this will be the bulk of the income you receive from actually operating your business.

Line 6 is where you report miscellaneous types of income that are not sales revenue. This is where questions arise and the answers can sometimes get complicated, since some types of income that you might consider to be business-related must be reported on other areas of your tax return.

Gross Income from Sales

Income you receive from sales to your customers is reported on Line 1 of Schedule C or C-EZ. You should only report income you received within your tax year, according to your established accounting method (see page 41).

If you work as an independent contractor and you have received one or more 1099-MISC forms from people or businesses you have done work for, the total amount you've received from all such sources is reported on Line 1.

For most people the income has been received in the form of cash, checks, or credit card charges, but if you receive income in the form of goods or services in some type of bartering transaction, you must report the fair market value of whatever you receive.

Example

You own a plumbing business and provide plumbing services for a friend of yours who owns a landscaping business. In return, your friend installs some new shrubs in front of your office. The IRS expects you to report the value of the shrubs and installation as income, although you can deduct any of your costs incurred in providing the plumbing services.

If the shrubs had been installed in front of your home instead of your office, their value would still be reported as business income. However, if you had received the shrubs in exchange for some personal, non-business service such as babysitting, they should be reported as miscellaneous personal income on Line 21 of your Form 1040.

If you receive a negotiable promissory note in payment for a sale and you use the cash method of accounting, the fair market value of the note is reported in gross income at the time you receive it. Accrual method taxpayers would generally recognize the discounted value of the note at the time of economic performance; e.g., when they had provided the services or goods to the customer.

Statutory Employees

Statutory employees occupy a sort of middle ground between independent contractors and regular employees. They can be defined as workers in certain occupations who would not be considered employees under the usual rules, but who have been declared employees under the federal tax laws so that their employers must withhold FICA taxes on their income.

If you are a classified as a statutory employee, you will also report your income on Schedule C, although your employer should give you a W-2 Form that reports this income and shows that payroll taxes were withheld on it.

Because FICA taxes have already been paid by your employer on this income, you don't have to file a Schedule SE and pay Self-Employment Contributions Act (SECA) tax on it. Just be sure to check the box on Line 1 on your Schedule C or C-EZ, so that the IRS doesn't go looking for a Schedule SE that's not there.

If you have both statutory employee income and other income from your own business, do not combine these two types of income on a single Schedule C. You must file two Schedule Cs, and only

the income from your non-statutory-employee business will flow through to your Schedule SE.

People in occupations who may be considered statutory employees are:

- **Full-time life insurance salespersons** who work primarily for one insurance company.

- **Agent and commission drivers** who deliver specified products — individuals who (1) operate their own trucks or the trucks of the persons for whom they perform services, (2) serve customers designated by their principals and customers they solicit on their own initiative, (3) make wholesale or retail sales, and (4) are paid commissions on their sales or earn the difference between what they charge their customers and what they pay their principals for the products or services they sell. Such drivers are statutory employees if they distribute beverages (other than milk), meat, vegetables, fruit, or bakery products, or if they pick up and deliver laundry or dry cleaning.

- **Traveling or city salespersons** (other than agent or commission drivers) who work full time on the principal's behalf and remit orders from customers who are retailers, wholesalers, contractors, or operators of hotels, restaurants, or other businesses whose primary function is the furnishing of food or lodging. The orders must be for items that their customers will resell or will use as supplies in their business operations.

- **Homeworkers** who work on a contract or piecework basis, in their own homes or in the homes of others. For example, persons hired to type up correspondence and to do other word processing jobs on their home computers would be homeworkers.

Statutory employees are entitled to deduct their business expenses on Schedule C, and must pay income taxes on their net income since their employers are not required to withhold income taxes from their pay.

Miscellaneous Business Income

Income other than what you receive from your customers in the ordinary course of business is reported on Line 6 of Schedule C. If you're filing Form C-EZ, you will include this income in your total on Line 1.

Tax Organizer Tip

We suggest that you follow the IRS's lead, and enter any income that will be reported on your Schedule C in the "Business Income" screen found in the "Employment" section tab. On the main "Business Income" screen, you'll see a button marked "Income." When you click on that button you'll go to a screen that permits you to enter your gross receipts or sales, and an itemized list of miscellaneous income amounts.

What kinds of income should be included here? Well, two common types of income that are *not* included are your gains or losses from sales of real or personal business property, which is reported on Form 4797, *Sales of Business Property* (see page 116), and any gains or losses from casualties or thefts, which are reported on Form 4684, *Casualties and Thefts*.

Another type of income that might be considered business income but that must be reported on a different tax form is rental income from real estate, including personal property leased with real estate. This income is reported on Schedule E, *Supplemental Income and Loss*, unless you are a dealer in real estate, a hotel or motel operator, or your business is focused on renting personal property (e.g., formalwear or power tools). See the discussion of Schedule E on page 214.

Investment Income

Income such as interest and dividends from bank accounts, stocks, and bonds are generally *not* considered business income for a sole proprietor, even if you think of them as reserve funds for business downturns. Instead, they are treated as personal items to be reported on Schedule B, *Interest and Ordinary Dividends*, which is part of your Form 1040. Any gains or losses on your investments are reported on Schedule D, *Capital Gains and Losses*.

One exception would be the situation where your business uses an interest-bearing account (for example, a money-market sweep account used in conjunction with your regular checking account). In that case, the interest paid should be reported on Line 6 of Schedule C or Line 1 of the C-EZ.

If you are in the business of lending money or if you

are paid interest on notes receivable that you were given by your customers, you would report that interest income on your Schedule C or C-EZ. Dividends you received on business insurance policies should also be reported there.

Recaptured Depreciation

If you need to report recaptured depreciation because your business use of expensed business equipment or listed property (e.g., cars, computers, cellular phones and other property generally used for recreation) dropped to 50% or less, you would report that recaptured deprecation on Line 6 of Schedule C, after computing the amount on Form 4797. See the discussion of recaptured depreciation on page 119.

Royalties

Royalty income you receive on property you produce as part of your business (for instance, if you're a freelance writer and you receive royalties on a book you wrote) would be considered business income to be reported on Schedule C. But if you receive royalty payments on property you purchased or inherited, the payments should instead be reported on Schedule E, *Supplemental Income and Loss*.

Recovery of Items Previously Deducted

If in 1999 you recovered some item that you deducted in a prior year (such as a state tax refund or, for accrual method taxpayers, a recovery on a previously deducted bad debt), you should recognize the amount as income in 1999. You don't need to go back and amend the previous year's tax return.

However, if the original deduction did not reduce the amount of income tax you owed for that previous year (for instance, if your net income was too low to expose you to taxes), you don't have to include the amount. If this exception applies to you, you should attach a statement to your tax return explaining how you came to your conclusions. This is especially important in the case of tax refunds, since they are reported to the IRS by the taxing body.

Cancelled Debts

The general rule is that if a debt you owe is cancelled or forgiven, you must include the cancelled amount in your gross income. If the debt is connected to your business, it should be reported on Schedule C. The theory behind this is that in most cases you've already received some benefit in exchange for taking on the debt, so in effect, cancelling the debt is equivalent to the lender transferring some type of property to you free of charge.

However, there are a number of exceptions to this rule. One important question to ask is, if you had paid the cancelled amount, would the payment (not just the interest) have been deductible? If so, then the cancelled debt should not be reported as income.

Example

You are a cash-basis business owner and obtained some professional services on credit. Later on, when you were having some cash-flow problems, a portion of the debt was cancelled. You had not already deducted the price of the services, but would have been able to deduct the full price if you had paid it. In this case, you don't have to report the debt cancellation as income.

If you were using the accrual method, you would have recognized and deducted the full professional service expense at the time the services were rendered, so the debt cancellation would have to be treated as income.

Similarly, if you purchase some property for use in your business, and the seller reduces the price after the sale but before you pay for it, cash-method taxpayers don't need to report the reduction as income. Instead, it's simply a price adjustment similar to a discount, and you would record the new lower price as the cost of the property.

Another exception applies to debts that are cancelled in a bankruptcy or because you are insolvent. Generally, such debt forgiveness is not recognized as income to you, perhaps out of recognition that if you can't pay your debts, the government is unlikely to be able to collect any additional taxes from you!

There is also a special exception for forgiveness of qualified real estate business debts, but this gets into rather complicated territory. Consult your tax advisor if, for example, your lender allowed you to refinance some real estate for a lower principal amount, and you think you might qualify for relief under this provision.

Some Non-Income Items

Believe it or not, there are a number of items that the IRS does not require you to report as income or pay tax on:

- contributions to capital; for example, if you deposit personal funds in your business checking account to cover a temporary cash-flow problem

- proceeds from loans

- gifts

- cash discounts for prompt payment of bills (just report the net price after the discount as the amount of the expense; as an alternative, you can credit the amounts to a separate discount account, and include the credit balance in your business income at the end of the year)

- trade discounts you receive from suppliers

- consignments, which are not recognized as sales until the merchandise is actually sold by the person to whom you consigned the goods

- insurance reimbursements, up to the amount of your loss (but if you receive continuation-of-income benefits under a business insurance policy, these amounts must be treated as business income)

- improvements made by tenants to property they rent from you

- like-kind exchanges (see the discussion at page 103)

Damages

If you receive compensation because of a breach of contract or fiduciary duty, patent infringement, or antitrust injury, the amounts must be included in your gross business income. This rule applies to punitive damages as well. You may be entitled to a deduction against this income for legal fees and other expenses you had to pay in order to recover the amounts.

COMPUTING YOUR GROSS PROFIT

As we've discussed above on page 47, the Schedule C has two places to enter your business income. Miscellaneous business income goes on Line 6, while Line 1 is the place to enter your gross receipts from sales.

In most cases, the income reported on Line 1 represents the bulk of your business income. But this is just a starting point. You must make a number of adjustments before arriving at your gross business income.

If, during the year, you booked some income but then accepted some returned merchandise or made an allowance to a customer for unsatisfactory products or services, you must enter the total of these amounts as "Returns and allowances" on Line 2, and subtract them from your gross sales receipts to arrive at your net receipts on Line 3.

"Returns and allowances" can include things like rebates, cash refunds, or merchandise credits. Almost any kind of business can have returns and allowances, including professional service businesses.

If you have no inventory, you can stop here: Your net receipts will be the same as your gross profits, and you can proceed to determine your deductible business expenses (see Chapter 6).

If your business uses inventory, however, you'll need to go through a few more steps to complete the business income portion of your tax return. You need to compute your cost of goods sold, which means determining your change in inventory for the year.

Computing Your Cost of Goods Sold

It's a given that all manufacturers, retailers, and wholesalers must use inventories to accurately track their costs. Other types of businesses, such as those providing professional services or working in the trades, will need to use inventory accounting methods if they bill customers separately for materials and supplies. And under IRS rules all businesses that use inventory must use accrual accounting, at least for purchases and sales of inventory items.

In general terms, the formula used to compute your cost of goods sold is the following:

	Inventory at beginning of year
+	**Purchases or additions during the year**
=	**Goods available for sale**
−	**Inventory at end of year**
=	**Cost of goods sold**

This equation is the basis for Part III on the flipside of the Schedule C. Inventory at the beginning of the year is reported on Line 35, purchases are reported on Line 36 (with a reminder to subtract the cost of items you withdrew for your own personal use), goods available for sale appears on Line 40, inventory at the end of the year is reported on Line 41, and the result is your cost of goods sold on Line 42.

If you are a reseller of goods, these would be the only five items you need. But if you are a manufacturer, things get a little more complicated.

As your additions and purchases during the year, a manufacturer would report the cost of raw materials or parts you purchased for manufacture into a finished product. You would also report the cost of labor on Line 37, including both direct labor costs for production workers, and indirect costs for other employees who perform a general factory function that is necessary for the manufacturing process. On Line 38 you would report the cost of materials and supplies used in the manufacturing process such as hardware, lubricants, abrasives, etc. And on Line 39 you would report the cost of overhead, which includes rent, utilities, insurance, depreciation, taxes, and maintenance for the production facility, as well as the cost of supervisory personnel.

In their accounting records, small manufacturers traditionally use three categories of inventory: raw materials, work in process, and finished goods awaiting sale. As raw materials are purchased, their costs (including delivery charges) are debited to the raw materials account. As materials are taken from storage and used in the manufacturing process, their costs are removed from (credited to) raw materials and added (debited) to the work in process account. The work in process account also collects the costs of direct and indirect labor and factory overhead. When the goods are finished, their costs are transferred (credited) out of work in process and added (debited) to the finished goods inventory. By taking beginning and ending counts of items in each of these three types of inventories, manufacturers can keep a handle on their costs.

Inventory Valuation Methods

Whether you are a retailer or a manufacturer, how do you determine the numbers to plug into the inventory equation?

As a starting point, you need to determine the number of items in your inventory (or each category you use) at the beginning and end of each year. You don't need to physically count your inventory at the end of the year, although that would be the most accurate way to do it. The IRS recognizes that requiring every business to do a complete inventory count on December 31 would be unworkable and would result in poor information, since workers would be rushed and not likely to make an accurate count.

As long as you take regular physical inventory counts at intervals during the year, you may extrapolate your beginning/ending amounts. The inventory at the end of year 1 becomes the beginning inventory for year 2; if there is a discrepancy, you should attach an explanation to your tax return.

But once you know the *number* of each kind of item in your inventory, how do you determine the *value* of the inventory at the beginning and at the end of the year, which will determine the value of inventory

items sold during the year? There are two issues that need to be addressed before you can answer that question:

- Is the original cost, or the current market value, a better way to evaluate your inventory?

- How do you identify the particular inventory items that were sold?

Although there are many possible ways of valuing inventories, the IRS strongly prefers that small business retailers, wholesalers and manufacturers value inventories under either of these methods: (1) cost, or (2) cost or market, whichever is lower.

If you are using the cost method, the value of the inventory would be all the direct and indirect costs of acquiring it. For example, the cost of goods you purchased would be the invoice price, less appropriate discounts, plus transportation or other charges you incur in acquiring the goods. For goods that you produced, the cost would be the cost of labor, materials, and plant overhead used in production. Manufacturers must generally use the uniform capitalization ("unicap") rules to determine exactly which costs are to be included in the formula; if you are subject to these rules, you'll probably need an accountant's help to interpret and apply them. Resellers with average annual gross receipts of $10 million or less for the last three tax years are exempt from the unicap rules.

The second method — the lower of cost or market method — in effect permits you to reduce your gross income to reflect any reduction in the value of inventories. This method is based on the assumption that if the market price falls, the selling price falls correspondingly. If this is so, a business owner will report a lower income, and thus defer until the following year a part of the taxes that would otherwise have to be paid under the cost method. One big drawback to using this method is that you need to compute the value of your inventory both ways in order to determine which is lower.

Case Study — Inventory Valuation

In Year 1, John Newsome purchased merchandise for $50,000 and sold half of the goods for $60,000. On December 31, Year 1, his inventory was $25,000 (under the cost method) and $15,000 (under the lower of cost or market method). In Year 2, he sells the remaining goods for $50,000. If he had used the lower of cost or market method, his income would have been $10,000 less in Year 1 and $10,000 more in Year 2 than if he had used the cost method.

	Cost	Cost or Market
Year 1		
Sales	$60,000	$60,000
Cost of sales (purchases, less ending inventory)	- 25,000	- 35,000
Gross income	$35,000	$25,000
Year 2		
Sales	$50,000	$50,000
Cost of sales (beginning inventory)	- 25,000	- 15,000
Gross income	$25,000	$35,000

In this example, the selling price of the goods in Year 2 is $10,000 less than in Year 1, the same amount by which the market value of the goods sold in Year 1 fell below cost on December 31, Year 1. But suppose that the selling prices do not drop in relation to the market values. Then, the lower of cost or market method may produce a higher total tax over a two-year period than would the cost method because of an imbalance of income and the graduated tax rates. This could happen, for example, if a tax rate increase takes effect in Year 2.

If you are just starting your business and do not use the "Last In, First Out" (LIFO) cost method (see "Identification of Inventory Items," below), you may select either the cost or the lower of cost or market method of accounting.

Save Time

The IRS is less concerned about the nuances of the specific inventory procedures you use, than with your being consistent from year to year so that your inventory method accurately reflects your income.

You must use the same method to value your entire inventory, and you may not change to another method without the IRS's consent.

Identification of Inventory Items

Besides deciding how you will value your inventory — at cost, or at the lower of cost or market — you must also decide how you will identify which items were sold, and which are still in inventory. The most basic way of doing this is called the "specific identification method," which requires you to match each item sold with its cost (or market value).

The specific identification method is easy to understand, but may be totally impractical for your business. It may work well for companies that sell relatively few big-ticket items like cars or pianos. But

if your business has a large, quick-moving inventory of smaller items, you soon would be doing little else than tracking inventory if you had to do it piece by piece.

Example

The "We're Widgets World Wide" ("4W") company, buys and sells thousands of widgets each year. Because 4W depends on several suppliers for widgets, and frequently must outbid other wholesalers for them, the price that 4W must pay usually varies daily. Listed below are just four of the thousands of widgets that came into 4W's inventory in 1999:

- *Widget 2301, bought 1/1/99, $49.00; sold 12/1/99*

- *Widget 3904, bought 6/1/99, $49.50; sold 9/1/99*

- *Widget 5039, bought 6/30/99, $50.45; sold 7/14/99*

- *Widget 7932, bought 7/1/99, $50.20; sold 12/15/99*

Although modern computer-based inventory control systems could allow you to track each widget, the IRS doesn't require this. Instead, you can usually choose one of two identification methods. These systems make broad *assumptions* about which inventory items were sold and which remain in inventory, without reference to the particular inventory items that were actually bought and sold. These two methods are known as the "first-in, first-out" (FIFO) and the "last-in, first out" (LIFO) methods.

The FIFO method assumes that sales are made from the items that have been longest in the inventory. This conforms to the usual business practice of trying to sell the older items first, before they become obsolete, spoiled, or out-of-fashion. This is also the method the IRS prefers.

In contrast, the LIFO method assumes that the most recently purchased items are the ones you sold, and the oldest items are still sitting in your warehouse or on your shelf.

One consequence of using FIFO is that if prices are generally going up over time, your gross income will be matched against the lowest-priced items in your inventory, resulting in higher net profits. In contrast, LIFO would match your gross income against the most expensive items in your inventory, resulting in lower net profits and, consequently, a

lower tax bill. If your business and inventory are constantly growing over time, LIFO will generally be more preferable.

Example

Using the four widgets described in the example above, let's say you know that you sold two of these widgets this year, for a price of $60 each. Under FIFO, you'd be treated as having sold the first two widgets you purchased, so your net income would be $120.00 – ($49.00 + $49.50) = $21.50.

Under LIFO, you'd be treated as having sold the last two widgets you purchased, so your net income would be $120.00 – ($50.45 + $50.20) = $19.35.

The IRS does not favor LIFO, and if you want to use it, you must file IRS Form 970 and follow some very complex tax rules. There is also a "simplified" dollar-value LIFO method available to small businesses (those with average annual gross receipts of $5 million or less for the last three tax years). For more information, see your tax advisor.

Chapter 6

Deductible Business Expenses

Once you know what your gross profit is for the year, it's time to figure out how you can whittle that figure down by subtracting all your deductible business expenses. Digging up every legitimate deduction you have is usually your best bet for reducing your taxable income, and therefore your tax bill, as much as possible in the short run.

In the long run, there may be other ways to save even more tax dollars — such as by shifting income to other tax years and by taking advantage of tax credits — that can take a certain amount of advance planning. But for many small businesses the deduction rules are often the best place to look for tax savings.

Save Money

Getting a tax deduction may be nice, but before you pull out your wallet, make sure that the deductible expense is justified from a business operations perspective. Particularly if you are in the startup phase of your business, the money you have to spend is limited. You don't want to fall into the trap of justifying the purchase of a gold-plated white elephant by saying: "So what if I really don't need it, it's deductible!"

In this chapter we'll explain the basic rules about deductions, so that you'll be able claim all the deductions you've got coming this year and so that, in the future, you can become an expert at spotting deduction opportunities in time to take advantage of them.

To begin with, we'll go through some of the general rules that apply to all business deductions. After that we'll deal with more specific (and fruitful) areas like car expenses, travel and entertainment, and the home office deduction.

Tax Organizer Tip

Most business expenses that will be reported on your Schedule C should be entered into the "Business Income" tab, which is located within the "Employment" section of the CompleteTax™ Organizer.

One notable exception is your home office expenses, which are entered in the "Real Estate" section, under the "Home" tab. Also, contributions to retirement plans on your own behalf are entered in the "Retirement" section of the Organizer.

ORDINARY AND NECESSARY BUSINESS EXPENSES

The first, most basic guideline to remember is that a deduction for an expense paid in connection with your business will be allowed only if the expense is "ordinary and necessary" for the operation of the business.

This doesn't mean that the IRS will attack all sorts of legitimately claimed business deductions, either on the ground that an expense would occur only occasionally (is it ordinary?), or that the expense would be helpful, but not vital to the business (is it necessary?).

In practice the IRS is rather flexible in this regard. It defines "ordinary" as common and accepted in a field of business, and defines "necessary" as helpful and appropriate to your business. "Ordinary" usually refers to expenses that are frequent and ongoing, such as amounts spent on gasoline or business meals, but can also apply to something that you pay only once, such an installation fee for utility service. And an expense does not have to be indispensable to be a necessary expense.

Example

The cost of holiday gifts and cards sent to customers is deductible as a necessary business expense if the items promote healthy customer relations.

However, the cost of a gun purchased for personal protection by an insurance agent, who is sometimes required to make business calls to private homes late in the evening, would not be deductible. While the expense of the handgun might be "ordinary," it is not "necessary" because it is not helpful or appropriate to the business of an insurance agent. It would be considered a nondeductible personal expense.

In addition to being "ordinary and necessary," it has been held that a business expense must also be "reasonable." Whether an expense is reasonable depends upon the facts and circumstances in the particular situation. For example, it has been held that providing a chauffeured luxury car to an employee was not unreasonable given the nature of the employment and the congested area in which the car was driven. Entertainment and meal expenses are not deductible to the extent that they are lavish or extravagant, given the circumstances.

In applying the "ordinary and necessary" and "reasonable" deduction test, the IRS isn't looking to second-guess your business decisions. You can expect that almost any expense that's fairly common for your type of business will pass muster without serious question.

Rather, IRS agents use this test to make sure that the money was actually spent as you claim, and: (1) pertains to the business instead of personal or family needs, (2) is not also being deducted elsewhere on the return (such as in the cost of goods sold computation – see page 51), and (3) is a current, rather than a capital, expense.

Warning

There are a few types of expenses that might be seen as promoting the business, but are specifically made nondeductible. These include items such as lobbying expenses and political contributions, fines and penalties such as parking tickets, and illegal payments such as kickbacks.

For instance, a traveling salesman who receives a speeding ticket must pay it, or risk losing his driver's license and his ability to earn a living. It's arguable that the cost of the ticket is an ordinary and necessary business expense. Nevertheless, the law states that legal fines and penalties are never deductible, so the ticket must be paid out of the salesman's own pocket.

To be deductible, business expenses must be incurred in carrying on an *already existing* trade or business. Costs associated with starting up a business are considered a type of capital expenditure, and are not fully deductible as current expenses (see page 61).

BUSINESS VS. PERSONAL EXPENSES

As a general principal, amounts that you spend for personal or family reasons are not deductible. In many instances this distinction may be difficult to make, especially if yours is a family business or you work out of your home. However, the IRS has been known to come down hard on those who don't keep their personal and business expenses separate, and who attempt to deduct personal living expenses against business income.

Example

A builder was not allowed a business deduction for expenses incurred as a result of his polo playing because he could not show a relationship between those expenses and a true business purpose.

The tax laws contain numerous very specific rules in areas where business expenses are difficult to disentangle from personal expenses. For example, commuting expenses are nondeductible, there are very specific rules on deducting business meals and entertainment, and certain types of property that are commonly used for recreation or amusement are subject to special depreciation rules and more stringent reporting. These rules are discussed in detail in later parts of this chapter.

If an expense is used partly for business and partly for personal purposes, you need to allocate the expense and deduct only the portion that pertains to business usage. The method of allocation depends on the nature of the expense. It can be done on the basis of time, space, usage or some other reasonable method.

Example

If you have an employee who cleans your office and also cleans your house, you can deduct the portion of the employee's wages and payroll taxes that compensate for the hours spent cleaning the office, but not the home. If you drive your car for both business and personal purposes, you must allocate your car expenses on the basis of the mileage driven for business purposes, as opposed to that for personal or commuting purposes.

As a rough rule of thumb, if you're in doubt about whether a particular expense qualifies as a business expense rather than a personal one, ask yourself whether you would still have to pay the expense if you had the same income but didn't work (perhaps all those direct-mail sweepstakes entries finally paid off). If so, there's a good chance that what you have is a personal expense, not a business expense.

To help you decide whether a particular expense is likely to be deductible, we've provided a list of the most common business deductions.

Following that is a list showing common items that usually *won't* be allowed as business deductions. In most cases, a deduction will be denied for these things either because they are nondeductible personal expenses, or because Congress specifically made them nondeductible. Where noted, some of these items may qualify for other tax benefits such as tax credits or recovery through depreciation.

Warning

Just because a particular item does not appear in the second list doesn't mean that it necessarily will be deductible. Any expense may be nondeductible if it does not meet the deduction rules outlined in this chapter. Whether a particular expense meets the deductibility requirements will depend on the facts and circumstances of your particular business.

Some Common Business Deductions

- advertising
- bad debts, for accrual method taxpayers
- bank fees on business accounts
- car and truck expenses
- commissions and fees
- depreciation
- dues for trade and business associations
- employee benefit programs

- meals and entertainment
- office expenses
- pension and profit-sharing plans
- publications
- rent or lease expense
- repairs and maintenance
- supplies and materials
- taxes and licenses

- gifts to customers, suppliers
- insurance (casualty and liability)
- legal and professional services
- travel expenses
- utilities
- wages for employees

Common Nondeductible Expenses

- bar or professional examination fees
- capital expenditures (not fully deductible in the year placed in service, but yearly deductions are allowed to recover cost of item over a specified time period)
- charitable contributions or gifts by a business that's not a C corporation (sole proprietors may deduct contributions on their individual tax returns, rather than on Schedule C).
- clothing, unless it's protective equipment or a uniform that would not be worn during non-working hours
- country or social club dues
- commuting expenses
- estate tax even if largely due to the ownership of a business interest
- expenses, including interest, paid to generate tax-exempt income
- federal income tax
- fines and penalties incurred for violations of law, such as child labor violations, federal income tax penalties, and traffic tickets
- gift tax; inheritance tax
- gifts to employees that are valued at more than $25
- gifts to individuals
- hobby losses
- interest on indebtedness incurred by a business taxpayer to purchase life insurance coverage in excess of $50,000 on the life of any its officers, employees, or other persons having a financial interest in the taxpayer's trade or business
- interest on indebtedness incurred to purchase single premium life insurance contracts, or any life insurance contract under a plan of financing the purchase by withdrawing some or all of the yearly build up in policy cash values
- job hunting expenses (new trade or business)
- life insurance premiums, if the business, or the business owner, is a direct or indirect beneficiary
- lobbying expenses (appearances before legislative bodies and expenses to influence voters)
- partnership organizational expenses, unless amortization election is made
- personal, living or family expenses — however, certain interest, taxes, bad debts, medical expenses, theft or casualty losses, or charitable contributions may be deductible in whole or in part as an itemized deduction on your individual tax return.
- political contributions, including tickets to political dinners
- tax penalty payments
- transfer taxes on business property

NONDEDUCTIBLE CAPITAL EXPENDITURES

One of the principles underlying the rules for tax deductions is that your income for the year should be offset only by those expenses that contributed to earning that income.

Example

If you add floor space to your facility or purchase a new delivery vehicle, you've acquired an asset that will benefit your business for a number of years. If you were allowed to deduct the full cost of such an asset in the year you acquired it, you'd effectively be understating your income during that first year and overstating your income during all the subsequent years that you use the asset in your business.

It may seem as though this shouldn't really be a problem, because everything would come out even in the end. However, what would have happened from the government's perspective is that you would have reduced your taxable income inappropriately in the year of acquisition and deferred the payment of some income taxes, which is not something the IRS usually likes to allow.

So, instead of letting you currently deduct your outlay for items of a more permanent nature (that is, items that will benefit your business beyond the current year), the tax rules provide that such expenditures generally must be capitalized.

What does it mean to "capitalize" an expense? Well, apart from the fact that it means the expense is not fully deductible this year, the act of capitalizing an expense is just an exercise in bookkeeping. The asset becomes a capital asset, against which you can take depreciation deductions each year. Depreciation is discussed at length in Chapter 7.

For now, let's just say that for tax purposes, you'll eventually recover the benefits of a capital expense through (1) annual depreciation deductions for the property and/or (2) a reduced amount of taxable gain or an increased amount of taxable loss when you sell or otherwise dispose of the property.

Although these two results are positive, they are usually not as good as a current deduction for the entire amount of the expense. Unfortunately, you normally won't have a choice as to how to treat a given expense. With certain exceptions, the tax rules specify whether an expense must be capitalized or deducted.

What, Exactly, Is a Capital Expenditure?

One type of capital expenditure occurs when you purchase or otherwise acquire any asset that will benefit your business for more than one year. Expenses that add to the value or useful life of an item of property also are considered capital expenditures.

In contrast, an expense that keeps an asset in an ordinarily efficient operating condition and that does not add to its value or substantially prolong its useful life is generally considered a deductible repair or maintenance expense.

Deciding whether a particular item should be classified as a capital expenditure or as a currently deductible expense is not always easy, particularly if it's debatable whether the expense represents a repair, or an improvement to a capital asset.

However, over time, the IRS and the courts have classified, on a case-by-case basis, some categories of items commonly considered to be capital expenditures. On the next page, we provide a listing of these items as a guide.

Warning

Remember that the same item that was a deductible expense to one taxpayer might be a capital expenditure to another.

That's mainly because the deduct-or-capitalize question does not just involve what was purchased, but also whether its benefits will be expected to last for more than one year. If two taxpayers use an identical item in different ways in their businesses, the item may represent a capital expenditure to one, but a currently deductible expense to the other.

Some Special Rules

In some cases, the tax laws depart from the general deduct-or-capitalize analysis by providing specific rules that govern how you may or must treat certain expenditures. For small business owners, the most commonly applied of these rules are:

- an equipment expensing election that allows you to deduct rather than to capitalize a specified amount of your costs in acquiring new business property (see page 103)

- elections to amortize business startup costs over a 60-month period, including costs associated with organizing a corporation or a partnership (see page 61)

- an election to capitalize rather than deduct taxes and other carrying charges (such as interest) on the property

Common Capital Expenditures

- abstracts of title costs
- appraisal costs paid in obtaining possession of premises
- author's publishing costs
- asbestos removal costs
- basement repair and waterproofing
- boiler patching and welding costs
- burglar alarm installation charges
- business facility improvement costs (for example, waterproofing; replacing a roof; planning, designing, and constructing an addition; remodeling costs)
- cable replacement costs upon sudden failure
- copyright development costs
- credit card membership fees
- drainage costs
- electric wiring costs (new wiring, replacement, and rearrangement)
- electrical system replacement costs
- Federal Communications Commission (FCC) license preparation fees
- fire escapes
- flood protection costs (such as costs of raising floors, or rearranging bins)
- insulation costs
- irrigation system costs
- merger negotiation costs
- office, cost of changing location and equipment
- package design costs
- performance bond premiums
- Security Exchange and Commission (SEC) statement preparation cost
- settlement costs for threatened lawsuit
- well (water) costs
- zoning change costs that increase the value of property beyond the tax year

BUSINESS STARTUP COSTS

Investigating the potential for a new business and getting it started can be an expensive proposition. However, under the general rules for business deductions, you couldn't deduct these expenses because only expenses for an *existing* trade or business can be deducted. By definition, you incur your startup expenses prior to the time that your business is born.

Fortunately, there is a way around this dilemma: If your startup expenditures actually result in an up-and-running business, you can elect to amortize the costs (that is, deduct them in equal installments over a set period of time) over a period of at least 60 months, beginning with the month in which your business opens.

This election enables you to eventually deduct both the cost of investigating the creation of the business and the costs of actually creating it. However, only those costs that would be deductible if they were incurred by an existing trade or business are eligible for the election.

What Costs Qualify?

Investigation expenses that can be deducted over the 60-month period include those relating to business conditions generally, and those relating to a specific business, such as market or product research to determine the feasibility of starting a certain type of business. The costs of checking out the various factors involved in site selection would also be an amortizable investigation expense.

Amortizable costs of creating a business include advertising, wages and salaries, professional and consultant fees, and costs of travel that is necessary before the business actually begins.

What Costs Don't Qualify?

Although they are frequently incurred before a new business goes into operation, the following costs don't qualify for 60-month amortization:

- Startup expenditures for interest, taxes, and research and experimental costs that are otherwise allowed as deductions do not

qualify for amortization. These costs may be deducted when incurred.

- The costs of organizing a partnership or a corporation are not considered startup costs, but they may be eligible for separate amortization.

- The costs attributable to the acquisition of a specific property that is subject to depreciation or cost recovery do not qualify for amortization. Instead, the property should be depreciated under the appropriate rules.

Save Money

It's usually best to claim the 60-month amortization deduction as early as possible if there is any doubt about when the business began operating. If the IRS determines that your business began in a year before the election to amortize startup costs was made, the right to deduct these costs is lost.

What if You Change Your Mind?

If you ultimately decide *not* to go into business, what happens to your costs? The portion of costs you paid to generally investigate the possibilities of going into business at all, or to purchase a non-specific existing business, are considered personal costs and are not deductible. However, the total costs that you paid in your attempt to start or purchase a specific business would be considered a capital expense and you can claim it as a capital loss.

If you purchased any business assets along the way (for instance, some bagel-making machinery), you can claim a loss only if and when you sell or dispose of the property.

Claiming Amortization Expenses

Assuming your business was successfully launched and you want to amortize your startup costs, total up all the costs paid or incurred before your business opened and divide them by 60 months (or longer, if you desire). The result is the monthly deduction amount. Your amortization period will begin with the month in which your business opened.

Example

If you opened on October 31, 1999, you could deduct costs for October, November and December of 1999, which would be equal to 3/60ᵗʰˢ of your total startup costs.

For the first year, your amortization deduction would be shown on Part VI of Form 4562, *Depreciation and Amortization*, and then carried over to your Schedule C as an "other" expense.

You'll need to attach a statement to your tax return itemizing the amortization costs, giving the date each cost was incurred, stating the month your business began operations, and specifying the number of months in your amortization period (not less than 60). The fact that you need to attach this statement precludes you from electronically filing your tax return this year.

In later years, if you are filing Form 4562 for some other reason (generally you must file this form in the first year you put a capital asset into service), you would continue to show your amortization costs on Part VI; if you don't need to file the 4562 in a particular year, simply list your amortization amount as an "other" expense on your Schedule C.

Tax Organizer Tip

When using the CompleteTax™ Organizer, you can treat your total amount of amortizable startup expenditures as a business asset. On the "Business Income" tab, answer "Yes" to the question "Do you have any assets related to this business?" and click on the "details" button to arrive at the "Business Property Depreciation" screen. While you will be amortizing, rather than depreciating, your startup expenses, this entry will serve to jog your memory and remind you to deduct your amortization costs.

SPECIAL DEDUCTION RULES

Having given you a broad overview of the rules for claiming business tax deductions, we're ready to get into the specific rules that apply to the most commonly encountered business deductions:

- expenses for cars, trucks, and other vehicles used in your business

- travel expenses for business trips

- meal and entertainment expenses when you entertain business guests

- business gifts you give to your clients and customers

- the home office deduction, for those with a home-based business

- wages and fringe benefits you provide to your employees

- health insurance for yourself

- retirement plan expenses

Most of these expenses are claimed on Part II of your Schedule C, which asks you to itemize your expenses in 20 categories (some with subcategories). For expenses that don't fit into any of the Part II categories, there is space on the back of the form (Part V) for you to describe and itemize any additional expenses.

Work Smart

If your gut feeling tells you that your dollar amount for any of the IRS expense categories is very large for a business of your type – perhaps large enough to raise an IRS agent's eyebrows – we recommend that you itemize the amounts on the back of the Schedule C. For example, if your travel expenses were unusually large this year, on Line 24a you might write "see itemization in Part V." Then, in Part V, you might break out the expenses into several categories such as "travel – sales calls; travel – conventions; travel – continuing education." This can sometimes save you from receiving an inquisitive letter from the IRS.

For a few categories of expenses, the IRS asks you to first fill out a specific form dealing with the expense, and then to transfer the net amount to your Schedule C. This is true of the home office deduction, and often true of your car expenses and depreciation expenses. There are also a few expenses that may be deducted directly on the front of your Form 1040, such as Keogh or SEP contributions for yourself, and one-half of the self-employment tax.

Also remember that if your business is a type that uses inventory, certain types of costs must be attributed to the inventory and are considered part of your cost of goods sold. As such, these costs will, in effect, be deducted when you sell the inventory to which they are attributed. There is an exception for authors, artists, and photographers who sell works created by their own efforts; these individuals can deduct their expenses without having to use inventory accounting.

See page 51 for more information on costs of goods sold.

TAXES AND VEHICLES

Whether it's down payments, interest payments, gas, tires, or other repairs, operating a car or truck can be expensive. If you're using a vehicle in business, it's important to get any tax breaks that you can for money spent on the vehicle. On the next few pages, we'll examine some of the common tax issues that relate to vehicles.

Obtaining a Business Vehicle

For every business owner, there comes a time when the old set of wheels will no longer suffice. Or, perhaps this was the year you needed a special purpose vehicle such as a delivery truck or van.

At some point, nearly every business owner will have to consider purchasing, leasing, or otherwise obtaining a vehicle. If you've purchased a car this year or are thinking about getting one in the near future, becoming familiar with the following tax issues may help you save money:

- There are several types of excise taxes that may be imposed on the vehicle that you purchase.

- Clean-fuel vehicles such as gas or electric-powered cars are eligible for special tax breaks.

- The expensing election may allow you to deduct up to $3,060 of the cost of a vehicle placed in service in 1999. For more on this, see page 114.

Save Money

Once you've made the decision that you need a vehicle for your business, our first recommendation is that you try to conserve your capital by converting a vehicle you already own to partial or full-time use in your business.

Cars and trucks generally depreciate in value very quickly and are poor investments in and of themselves. If you are the owner of a new business, whatever capital you have should be put into the things that will most directly generate revenue — and that usually won't include a new car.

Excise Taxes on New Cars

You need to be aware of two excise taxes that can hit you when you purchase certain vehicles.

While these taxes apply to all vehicles, not just those used in a business, you may want to keep these rules in mind if you're planning to buy a business vehicle. These taxes may be hidden costs that could influence your decision in terms of choosing a car.

Gas guzzler tax. This tax is imposed on new cars that fail to meet federal fuel economy standards. Although the tax is imposed on the manufacturer, it becomes part of the retail price. Before computing the depreciation deduction for a business car, you must reduce the basis of the car by the amount of any gas guzzler tax you paid. So, you can't recover this tax through depreciation. For more on how depreciation works, see page 99.

Luxury tax. There's also a 6 percent luxury tax (for 1999) on any portion of the sales price of a car that exceeds $36,000. For 2000 and subsequent years, the tax is scheduled to decrease one percentage point each year until it reaches 3 percent in 2002, and the tax will expire after 2002. The dollar threshold above which the tax is imposed is indexed for inflation each year. The tax is collected by car dealers and reported by them to the government.

After-market alterations in the car must be counted as part of the purchase price for purposes of computing the luxury tax, if they occur within six months of the purchase and they exceed $1,000.

If you paid luxury tax on a car you purchased this year, the amount of the tax is not deductible. Instead, you should treat it like a sales tax: Add it to car's tax basis and recover it through depreciation deductions (see page 112).

Save Money

The luxury car tax does not apply to trucks, vans, and sport-utility vehicles that weigh over 6,000 pounds. If you bought a qualifying sports-utility vehicle that cost $50,000 in 1999, this special rule would save you $840 ($50,000 - $36,000 x 6%).

In addition, if you use this type of vehicle for your business, it will also escape the annual depreciation dollar caps (see page 114) and the annual lease income inclusion rules (see page 68).

Special rules for clean-fuel vehicles. If you purchase a conventional automobile and have it retrofitted to convert it to an electric or clean-fuel vehicle, the cost of the additional parts and installation will *not* be subject to the luxury tax. If you purchase a vehicle that was designed to be an electric vehicle, the luxury tax applies only to the portion of the price that exceeds 150 percent of the ordinary luxury tax threshold, or approximately $54,000 for 1999.

More Tax Breaks for New Clean-Fuel Vehicles

There are two other types of tax breaks available to purchasers of alternative-fuel vehicles.

Tax deduction for clean fuel vehicles. To promote the use of vehicles powered by cleaner-burning fuels, a deduction from gross income is permitted for a portion of the cost of these vehicles placed in service before January 1, 2005. Examples of "clean fuels" are natural gas and hydrogen, and fuels that are composed of at least 85 percent methanol, ethanol, alcohol, or ether.

The maximum clean fuel deduction for cars and light trucks is $2,000. For some trucks and vans with a gross weight of more than 10,000 pounds but not more than 26,000 pounds, the maximum deduction is $5,000. For trucks and vans with gross weight of more than 26,000 pounds, the maximum deduction is $50,000. The $50,000 maximum also applies to buses that can seat 20 adult passengers. The deduction should be claimed as an "other expense" on Schedule

C; if the vehicle is used only partly for business, the portion of the deduction that applies to personal use would be included on Line 32 of Form 1040.

Tax credit for electric vehicles. A 10 percent tax credit (based on your purchase price) is allowed for certain electric vehicles placed in service before January 1, 2005. The maximum credit may not exceed $4,000, and will be phased out gradually, beginning with vehicles placed in service after 2001. The allowable credit is claimed on IRS Form 8834, *Qualified Electric Vehicle Credit.*

Using a Vehicle in Your Business

If you use your car, van, or some other type of vehicle exclusively for business purposes, you may generally deduct the full cost of operating the vehicle. But if, like most sole proprietors, you use a vehicle for business on a part-time basis, you will have to allocate your expenses based on your business and personal use.

The business portion of your costs will be deductible on Line 10 of Schedule C; the personal portion will be nondeductible except for any costs of using the vehicle for charitable purposes (see page 265), for medical purposes (see page 262), or for a tax-deductible move (see page 185). Also, if you or your spouse is employed by another business, a portion of the expenses for the car may be deductible as an employee business expense (see page 181).

But what, exactly, is "business use of a car?" Generally, the IRS divides all car usage into three categories: business, commuting, and personal. "Business use" generally means travel between two business destinations, one of which may be your regular place of business. Typical travel expenses that are deductible include expenses for:

- travel from one job to another

- travel from one customer or client to another

- travel from your office or business location in order to perform business tasks, such as to pick up supplies and inventory, to check your business post office box, or to make a bank deposit

In addition, if you have a regular place of business, the

cost of traveling between your home and a temporary work site that is *not* the regular place of business is deductible, regardless of the distance traveled. A temporary work site is a place where you perform services on an irregular or short-term basis. The term "short-term" generally means a matter of days or weeks. Also, if you do *not* have a regular place of business and you travel outside of the metropolitan area in which you work to a temporary work site, you are allowed a deduction for your travel costs. Travel within the metropolitan area would be considered nondeductible commuting.

Commuting expenses. Vehicle expenses incurred in commuting between your home and your main or regular place of business are not deductible expenses. This is true even if you have an advertising display on your car, or you use the commute to listen to business books on tape or to phone your clients.

Save Money

Remember that costs of traveling between your home and a location that is not *your regular place of business are deductible. You can take advantage of this rule by making a business related-stop on the way to work and on the way home, thereby converting your nondeductible commute into deductible business travel!*

Travel from a Home Office

If you work out of your home and your home is your principal place of business (see page 79), you can generally deduct the cost of traveling from your home to any business destination.

Example

If you are a real estate agent and do most of your work at home, you can deduct the expenses that you incur in traveling between your home and the houses you're trying to sell.

Whether your home is your principal place of business is determined under the same standards that apply to home office deductions. Beginning this year (1999), these standards are significantly easier to meet, and a much larger number of people will be able to deduct the costs of driving from their home office to other business-related locations.

Hauling Tools or Equipment

Commuting expenses may be partially deductible if you have to transport heavy or bulky tools, materials, or equipment to and from your workplace.

The catch is that you can only deduct the portion of the cost that is higher than the costs you'd normally face in commuting by that *same* mode of transportation *without* the work equipment. The fact that you would have used a less expensive mode of transportation were it not for the tools is immaterial.

Example

Robert Jensen takes the train from his home to his workplace each workday. His daily round-trip train ticket costs $10.00. Every few months he must bring drafting tools and display charts to his workplace for a presentation. When he transports these tools and materials he uses his car instead of taking the train. Driving to his workplace costs him $20.00 in gas, tolls, and parking fees. However, Jensen cannot deduct the extra $10.00 it costs him when he drives to his workplace, since he would have spent that amount driving regardless of what he was carrying with him.

If, however, Jensen's tools and materials were so bulky that he had to rent a trailer to carry them, he could deduct his costs for renting and parking the trailer.

Keeping Records of Business Use

If, like most business owners, you use your vehicle for both business and personal purposes, you must allocate your vehicle costs for business use separately from those associated with commuting or personal use. Even if you use a particular car or truck *only* for business purposes, you'll need to keep records to prove it unless the vehicle, by its nature, is not likely to be used more than a very minimal amount for personal purposes. Such vehicles would include various heavy trucks, buses, police and fire vehicles, cranes, forklifts, tractors, and similar vehicles. See the discussion of mileage records on page 21.

If you commute to a regular place of business, you'll also need to know the distance from your home to your workplace, as well as the number of commuting trips you made during the year, because the IRS specifically asks for this information.

At the end of the year, you'll need to add up the total

number of miles you drove during the year and the total number of business miles. Then, you'll divide the number of business miles by the total number of miles driven. The answer you get represents your percentage of business use for the year. Save this number – you'll need it when you compute your deductible vehicle expenses!

Example

Joyce King's initial odometer reading for the year was 23,456, and her ending reading was 33,500. So, her total mileage for the year was 10,044.

During the year, she recorded a total of 34 business trips, with a total mileage of 800 business miles.

So, her business usage of the vehicle was 800/10,044 = .0796, or about 8 percent.

How to Compute Your Vehicle Expenses

If you use your vehicle for business driving, there are two methods that can be used to compute your vehicle expense deduction:

- the standard mileage rate, discussed below

- the actual cost method, discussed on page 67

The standard mileage rate is generally easier to use and doesn't require you to keep as many records; however, it's not available to everyone. It will generally be the preferred method if you do relatively little business driving.

The actual cost method may result in a larger deduction, particularly with a relatively expensive car; however, the burden of keeping records for every penny you spend on the car may cause more trouble than the deduction is worth.

Ideally, each year you (or your accountant) should compute your deduction under both methods and compare the results. Then, use the method that gives you the largest deduction in that particular year.

Warning

Remember that whichever method you choose, you may have a taxable gain when you sell or otherwise dispose of a vehicle used in business. See page 116 for more on taxable gains and losses.

The Standard Mileage Rate

If you use the standard mileage rate (SMR) method, you calculate the fixed and operating costs of your vehicle by multiplying the number of business miles traveled during the year by the business standard mileage rate. This rate is set by the IRS and adjusted annually; for 1999, it's 32.5 cents per mile for January through March, and 31 cents for the rest of the year.

While very simple to use, the standard mileage rate is not available to everyone. Specifically, this rate may not be used to compute the deductible expenses for:

- vehicles used for hire, such as taxis

- two or more vehicles used simultaneously, as in fleet-type operations. This does not include situations where you own more than one vehicle (say, a car and a truck) but you don't use them at the same time; in that case, you can still use the SMR.

Save Time

As of 1998, the standard mileage rate can be used for cars that you lease, not just those that you own, provided that you continue to use this method for the entire lease term (or the remainder of the term, for leases that began before 1998).

For all practical purposes, if you want to use the SMR for a car that you own, you must use it in the very first year you place it in service for your business.

If you do that, in later years you can either use the actual cost method or the SMR, depending on which method yields the bigger deduction in any given year.

However, once you use the SMR, you must use the straight-line method of depreciation if you switch to the actual cost method for that car. Ordinarily straight-line gives you a smaller deduction than the quicker MACRS depreciation (see page 100 for a comparison of depreciation methods). The SMR and MACRS are basically incompatible, and if you've ever used MACRS for a car, you can never use the SMR method for that car.

What's included in the SMR? Using the SMR takes the place of deducting almost all the operating and fixed business costs of your vehicle, such as maintenance and repairs, tires, gas, oil, insurance, and license and registration fees.

However, you can still deduct parking fees and tolls that are directly related to business (i.e., not commuting), in addition to the standard mileage rate. For business owners, interest on loans for vehicles and taxes attributable to the operation of these vehicles are also deductible on top of the SMR.

Adjustments for depreciation. When you use the standard mileage rate method, a specific amount is included for depreciation. This means that you can't claim an additional deduction for depreciation when you use the standard mileage rate method.

It also means that if you use the SMR method, when you sell your car and need to determine whether you had any taxable gains, you must adjust the basis of your vehicle for each year the method was used.

You must multiply your business mileage for the year by a specified amount, as shown on the chart that follows, and then reduce your car's basis (and increase your potential taxable gains) by that amount.

Example

If a car was used for 7,000 business miles in 1999, the basis would be reduced by $840 (7,000 x $0.12).

Pre-1990 use of a vehicle in excess of 15,000 miles in one year is disregarded for the purpose of basis adjustment, even if the actual business mileage was higher.

Year method used	Amount of adjustment (cents per mile)
1986	9
1987	10
1988	10.5
1989-91	11
1992-93	11.5
1994-99	12

The Actual Cost Method

When you use the actual cost method of determining your vehicle deduction instead of the SMR, you must keep track of the actual amount of your costs during the year, including all the costs shown on the list below, to calculate your deductible vehicle expenses. The amount of your deduction depends, to a large extent, on how good you are at saving receipts and jotting down your costs throughout the year.

At the end of the year, you'll multiply your total expenses by your percentage of business use of the car. The business use percentage is calculated in the same way as described above, in the discussion of the standard mileage rate method:

business miles/total miles = business use percentage

Actual Cost Car Expenses

The cost of operating a vehicle includes these expenses:

- cleaning, inside and out; waxing
- depreciation, if you own the vehicle
- gas and oil
- insurance
- interest on a vehicle loan

- motor club membership
- parking and garage rental
- personal property taxes
- repairs and maintenance
- tires and supplies

- lease payments, if you lease the vehicle   • tolls

- license fees, if substantially based on the value of the vehicle

The cost of the vehicle itself is not a deductible expense, nor is the cost of a replacement, modification, or extensive repair that prolongs the useful life of the vehicle or increases its value. Instead, these costs are capitalized, which means they are added to your tax basis in the vehicle. These capitalized costs are recovered through depreciation deductions that are taken for a number of years after you place the vehicle in service.

You'll also need to calculate your depreciation amount for the car, as discussed in Chapter 7, *Capital Assets and Depreciation*. This amount is deducted as part of your depreciation expense on Line 13 of your Schedule C, not as part of the car and truck expenses reported on Line 10.

Deducting Vehicle Lease Payments

If you lease a vehicle for your business, you can generally deduct each lease payment as a rental expense. However, when business use of a leased vehicle is less than 100 percent, the rental deduction is scaled down in proportion to the personal use.

Example

If you drive a leased car, and 75 percent of the mileage driven was for business while 25 percent was for personal purposes and commuting, you can deduct only 75 percent of the lease payments.

The percentage of use for business is determined using your mileage records. The amount you deduct for a leased car is reported on Line 20a as rented or leased vehicles, machinery, and equipment; it is not added to the rest of your car and truck expenses on Line 10.

If a vehicle with a fair market value in excess of approximately $15,500 (for 1999) is leased, you must add back an additional amount (i.e., subtract it from your otherwise deductible amount) to offset a portion of the lease payments. This rule was enacted to prevent individuals from using leases to avoid the

luxury car depreciation limits that apply to purchased vehicles. The amounts that must be added back are called "inclusion amounts" and are taken from a price-based table issued annually by the IRS. Tables for 1999, 1998, and 1997 are reproduced on pages 69-71; if you leased your car before 1997, get IRS Publication 463, *Travel, Entertainment, Gift, and Car Expenses*, to find the tables for earlier years.

To use the table, find the value of your car on the first day of your lease term (or on the day you converted your personal car to business use) in the first column, and read across the line to the column that matches the year of your lease to find the dollar value to be included. Then prorate the dollar amount from the table for the number of days of the lease term included in your tax year, and multiply the prorated amount by your percentage of business use for the year (as calculated by using your mileage records).

Example

Let's say that in April of 1998 you leased a new car valued at $20,350 to use in your business. In 1999, your business usage was 75% and you had the car for the entire year. You would use the second table, for cars first leased in 1998, and the column marked "2nd" since this is the second year of your lease. Reading across the line for cars valued between $20,000 and $20,500, the dollar amount is $82. Since you had the car for all of 1999, use 100% of the amount (otherwise you would multiply by a fraction, x/365, where x = the number of days you leased the car). Then multiply $82 by 75%, your percentage of business use, to arrive at an inclusion amount of $61.50. This amount should be subtracted from 75% of your total lease payments to arrive at the amount you can deduct.

Inclusion Amounts for Cars (Other Than Electric Cars) First Leased in 1999

Fair Market Value		Tax Year of Lease[1]				
Over	Not Over	1st	2nd	3rd	4th	5th and Later
$ 17,500	$ 18,000	$ 16	$ 32	$ 48	$ 58	$ 68
18,000	18,500	19	39	59	71	82
18,500	19,000	22	47	69	83	96
19,000	19,500	26	53	80	96	111
19,500	20,000	29	61	90	108	126
20,000	20,500	32	68	101	121	140
20,500	21,000	35	75	111	134	155
21,000	21,500	39	82	122	146	169
21,500	22,000	42	89	132	160	183
22,000	23,000	47	100	148	178	206
23,000	24,000	53	114	169	204	235
24,000	25,000	60	128	190	229	264
25,000	26,000	66	142	212	254	293
26,000	27,000	73	156	233	279	322
27,000	28,000	79	171	253	305	351
28,000	29,000	85	185	275	330	380
29,000	30,000	92	199	296	355	410
30,000	31,000	98	214	316	381	439
31,000	32,000	105	227	338	406	468
32,000	33,000	111	242	359	431	497
33,000	34,000	118	256	380	456	527
34,000	35,000	124	270	402	481	556
35,000	36,000	131	284	423	506	585
36,000	37,000	137	299	443	532	614
37,000	38,000	144	313	464	557	643
38,000	39,000	150	327	486	582	672
39,000	40,000	157	341	507	607	702
40,000	41,000	163	355	528	633	731
41,000	42,000	170	369	549	658	760
42,000	43,000	176	384	570	683	789
43,000	44,000	183	398	591	708	819
44,000	45,000	189	412	612	734	848
45,000	46,000	196	426	633	759	877
46,000	47,000	202	441	654	784	906
47,000	48,000	208	455	675	810	935
48,000	49,000	215	469	696	835	964
49,000	50,000	221	483	718	860	993
50,000	51,000	228	497	739	885	1,023
51,000	52,000	234	512	759	911	1,052
52,000	53,000	241	526	780	936	1,081
53,000	54,000	247	540	802	961	1,110
54,000	55,000	254	554	823	986	1,140
55,000	56,000	260	569	843	1,012	1,169
56,000	57,000	267	582	865	1,037	1,198
57,000	58,000	273	597	886	1,062	1,227
58,000	59,000	280	611	907	1,087	1,256
59,000	60,000	286	625	928	1,113	1,285
60,000	62,000	296	646	960	1,151	1,329
62,000	64,000	309	675	1,002	1,201	1,387
64,000	66,000	322	703	1,044	1,252	1,446
66,000	68,000	335	732	1,086	1,302	1,504
68,000	70,000	348	760	1,128	1,353	1,563
70,000	72,000	361	788	1,171	1,403	1,621
72,000	74,000	374	817	1,212	1,454	1,679
74,000	76,000	387	845	1,255	1,504	1,738
76,000	78,000	399	874	1,297	1,555	1,796
78,000	80,000	412	902	1,339	1,606	1,854
80,000	85,000	435	952	1,413	1,694	1,956
85,000	90,000	467	1,023	1,518	1,821	2,102
90,000	95,000	500	1,094	1,623	1,947	2,248
95,000	100,000 [2]	532	1,165	1,729	2,073	2,394

[1]For the last tax year of the lease, use the dollar amount for the preceding year.
[2]If the fair market value of the car is more than $100,000, see Revenue Procedure 99-14 (1999-5 IRB 56).

Inclusion Amounts for Cars (Other Than Electric Cars) First Leased in 1998

Fair Market Value		Tax Year of Lease[1]				
Over	Not Over	1st	2nd	3rd	4th	5th and Later
$ 15,800	$ 16,100	$ 1	$ 5	$ 8	$ 12	$ 14
16,100	16,400	4	10	16	22	25
16,400	16,700	6	15	25	31	36
16,700	17,000	9	20	33	41	47
17,000	17,500	12	28	43	53	62
17,500	18,000	16	37	56	70	80
18,000	18,500	20	46	70	85	99
18,500	19,000	24	55	83	101	117
19,000	19,500	28	64	96	117	136
19,500	20,000	32	73	110	133	154
20,000	20,500	36	82	123	149	173
20,500	21,000	40	91	136	165	191
21,000	21,500	45	99	150	181	209
21,500	22,000	49	108	163	197	228
22,000	23,000	55	122	183	221	255
23,000	24,000	63	140	210	252	292
24,000	25,000	71	158	236	285	329
25,000	26,000	79	176	263	316	366
26,000	27,000	88	193	290	348	403
27,000	28,000	96	211	317	380	439
28,000	29,000	104	229	343	412	477
29,000	30,000	112	247	370	444	513
30,000	31,000	120	265	396	476	550
31,000	32,000	128	283	423	508	587
32,000	33,000	137	301	449	540	624
33,000	34,000	145	319	476	571	661
34,000	35,000	153	337	502	604	697
35,000	36,000	161	355	529	635	735
36,000	37,000	169	373	556	667	771
37,000	38,000	178	391	582	699	808
38,000	39,000	186	409	608	731	845
39,000	40,000	194	427	635	763	882
40,000	41,000	202	445	662	794	919
41,000	42,000	210	463	688	827	955
42,000	43,000	218	481	715	859	992
43,000	44,000	227	498	742	891	1,028
44,000	45,000	235	516	769	922	1,066
45,000	46,000	243	534	795	955	1,102
46,000	47,000	251	552	822	986	1,140
47,000	48,000	259	570	849	1,018	1,176
48,000	49,000	268	588	875	1,050	1,213
49,000	50,000	276	606	901	1,082	1,250
50,000	51,000	284	624	928	1,114	1,286
51,000	52,000	292	642	955	1,145	1,324
52,000	53,000	300	660	981	1,178	1,360
53,000	54,000	308	678	1,008	1,209	1,398
54,000	55,000	317	695	1,035	1,241	1,434
55,000	56,000	325	713	1,062	1,273	1,471
56,000	57,000	333	732	1,087	1,305	1,508
57,000	58,000	341	750	1,114	1,337	1,544
58,000	59,000	349	768	1,140	1,369	1,582
59,000	60,000	358	785	1,168	1,400	1,619
60,000	62,000	370	812	1,207	1,449	1,674
62,000	64,000	386	848	1,261	1,512	1,747
64,000	66,000	403	884	1,313	1,577	1,821
66,000	68,000	419	920	1,367	1,640	1,894
68,000	70,000	435	956	1,420	1,704	1,968
70,000	72,000	452	991	1,474	1,767	2,042
72,000	74,000	468	1,027	1,527	1,832	2,115
74,000	76,000	484	1,063	1,580	1,896	2,189
76,000	78,000	501	1,099	1,633	1,959	2,263
78,000	80,000	517	1,135	1,686	2,023	2,337
80,000	85,000	546	1,198	1,779	2,134	2,466
85,000	90,000	587	1,287	1,913	2,294	2,649
90,000	95,000	627	1,377	2,046	2,453	2,834
95,000	100,000 [2]	668	1,467	2,178	2,613	3,018

[1] For the last tax year of the lease, use the dollar amount for the preceding year.
[2] If the fair market value of the car is more than $100,000, see Revenue Procedure 98-30 (1998-17 IRB 6).

Inclusion Amounts for Cars First Leased in 1997

Fair Market Value		Tax Year of Lease[1]				
Over	Not Over	1st	2nd	3rd	4th	5th and Later
$ 15,800	$ 16,100	$ 1	$ 5	$ 5	$ 8	$ 10
16,100	16,400	4	10	13	18	21
16,400	16,700	6	15	22	27	32
16,700	17,000	9	20	30	36	44
17,000	17,500	12	28	40	49	58
17,500	18,000	16	37	53	65	77
18,000	18,500	20	46	66	82	95
18,500	19,000	24	55	80	97	114
19,000	19,500	28	64	93	113	132
19,500	20,000	32	73	106	129	151
20,000	20,500	36	82	120	145	169
20,500	21,000	40	91	133	161	187
21,000	21,500	45	99	147	177	205
21,500	22,000	49	108	160	193	224
22,000	23,000	55	122	180	216	252
23,000	24,000	63	140	206	249	288
24,000	25,000	71	158	233	280	326
25,000	26,000	79	176	259	313	362
26,000	27,000	88	193	287	344	399
27,000	28,000	96	211	313	377	435
28,000	29,000	104	229	340	408	473
29,000	30,000	112	247	366	441	509
30,000	31,000	120	265	393	472	546
31,000	32,000	128	283	420	504	583
32,000	33,000	137	301	446	536	620
33,000	34,000	145	319	472	568	657
34,000	35,000	153	337	499	600	693
35,000	36,000	161	355	526	631	731
36,000	37,000	169	373	552	664	767
37,000	38,000	178	391	578	696	804
38,000	39,000	186	409	605	727	841
39,000	40,000	194	427	632	759	878
40,000	41,000	202	445	658	791	915
41,000	42,000	210	463	685	823	951
42,000	43,000	218	481	712	854	989
43,000	44,000	227	498	739	886	1,026
44,000	45,000	235	516	765	919	1,062
45,000	46,000	243	534	792	951	1,098
46,000	47,000	251	552	819	982	1,136
47,000	48,000	259	570	845	1,015	1,172
48,000	49,000	268	588	871	1,047	1,209
49,000	50,000	276	606	898	1,078	1,246
50,000	51,000	284	624	925	1,110	1,282
51,000	52,000	292	642	951	1,142	1,320
52,000	53,000	300	660	978	1,174	1,356
53,000	54,000	308	678	1,004	1,206	1,394
54,000	55,000	317	695	1,032	1,237	1,430
55,000	56,000	325	713	1,058	1,270	1,467
56,000	57,000	333	732	1,084	1,301	1,504
57,000	58,000	341	750	1,110	1,334	1,540
58,000	59,000	349	768	1,137	1,365	1,578
59,000	60,000	358	785	1,164	1,397	1,615
60,000	62,000	370	812	1,204	1,445	1,670
62,000	64,000	386	848	1,257	1,509	1,743
64,000	66,000	403	884	1,310	1,573	1,817
66,000	68,000	419	920	1,363	1,637	1,890
68,000	70,000	435	956	1,417	1,700	1,964
70,000	72,000	452	991	1,470	1,764	2,038
72,000	74,000	468	1,027	1,524	1,827	2,112
74,000	76,000	484	1,063	1,577	1,891	2,186
76,000	78,000	501	1,099	1,630	1,955	2,259
78,000	80,000	517	1,135	1,683	2,019	2,333
80,000	85,000	546	1,198	1,776	2,130	2,462
85,000	90,000	587	1,287	1,909	2,291	2,645
90,000	95,000	627	1,377	2,042	2,450	2,830
95,000	100,000 [2]	668	1,467	2,175	2,609	3,014

[1] For the last tax year of the lease, use the dollar amount for the preceding year.
[2] If the fair market value of the car is more than $100,000, see Revenue Procedure 97-20 (1997-1 CB 647).

Note that as of 1998, you can elect to use the standard mileage rate to compute your auto expenses for a leased car or truck, provided that you use this method for the entire period of the lease. If your lease began before 1998, you would need to use the SMR for the remainder of the lease term.

Claiming Your Business Vehicle Deductions

If you are self-employed, you will deduct your total vehicle expenses on Schedule C or C-EZ of IRS Form 1040.

Part IV of Schedule C or Part III of Schedule C-EZ may be completed if you are claiming the standard mileage rate and you are not required to file IRS Form 4562, *Depreciation and Amortization*, for any other reason.

If you are using the actual cost method and you are entitled to a depreciation deduction, Part V of Form 4562 must be completed, and the appropriate amount must then be transferred to Schedule C. And if you are required to complete Form 4562 for any other reason (i.e., you are claiming some other business depreciation deductions for the year), you must enter your auto expenses on Part V of the Form.

BUSINESS TRAVEL EXPENSES

Travel expenses are one of the most commonly encountered types of business tax deductions. However, this category is also one of the most confusing. When is the cost of a trip deductible as a business expense? How about conventions in other cities? What if you bring your family? It will be easier to plan your business trips, and to combine business with vacation when possible, if you become familiar with the IRS's ground rules.

Basically, to be deductible, your travel must meet two criteria:

- the travel expenses must be incurred in connection with an existing business

- the expenses must be incurred away from home

You can only deduct travel expenses if they are ordinary and necessary expenses that you incur in connection with the pursuit of an existing business. You can't deduct travel expenses to the extent that they are lavish or extravagant — the expenses must be reasonable considering the facts and circumstances. However, the IRS gives you a great deal of latitude here. Your expenses won't be denied simply because you decided to fly first class, or dine in four-star restaurants.

The expenses have to be incurred for an *existing* business — travel expenses you incur in connection with acquiring or starting a new business are not deductible. However, you can add these costs to your startup expenses and amortize them over 60 months – see page 61.

What about travel that has a combined business and personal aspect? Here's where it gets a bit more complicated. The IRS is on the lookout for taxpayers who might try to classify a nondeductible personal trip as a deductible business trip. So, if you travel to a destination and engage in both personal and business activities, you can deduct your traveling expenses to and from the destination only if the trip is *primarily* related to your business.

If the trip is primarily personal in nature you can't deduct any of your airfare, hotel, or other traveling expenses. This is true even if you engage in some business activities while you are there. (You can deduct particular expenses you incur while you're at your destination if they otherwise qualify as business deductions; for example, cabfare to an isolated business appointment.)

The primary purpose of a trip is determined by looking at the facts and circumstances of each case. An important factor is the amount of time you spent on personal activities during the trip as compared to the amount of time spent on activities directly relating to business. Travel expenses outside the U.S. may be further limited if part of your trip is for personal purposes – see the discussion of foreign travel below.

Away From Home

You may only deduct travel expenses incurred when you are "away from home." You are traveling away from home if you meet the following two conditions:

- Your trip is long enough or far away enough that you can't reasonably be expected to complete the round trip without obtaining sleep or rest. This doesn't mean that you need to stay overnight at the destination; for example, it may be that you had an all-day meeting and needed to catch a few hours sleep in a hotel before driving home.

- The travel is away from the general area or vicinity of your tax home.

Generally, your tax home is the entire general area or vicinity (e.g., a city and surrounding suburbs) of your principal place of business.

If you conduct your business in more than one place, you should consider the total time you ordinarily spend working in each place, the degree of your business activity in each place, and the relative amount of your income from each place to determine your "principal" place of business.

If you don't have a regular place of abode and no main place of business, you may be considered an itinerant: your tax home is wherever you work and you can never be "away-from-home." When you are temporarily (a year or less), as opposed to indefinitely, working away from your main place of business, your tax home doesn't change.

Defining Travel Expenses

Generally, deductible travel expenses are the ordinary and necessary expenses that you incur while you're away from home in pursuit of your trade or business. In order to claim travel expenses as deductions, you must keep adequate records and be able to prove the existence, amount, and business purpose of your expenses.

The chart below shows a list of expenses you may be able to deduct as travel expenses, depending on the facts and circumstances.

Meal Costs When Traveling

The cost of dining alone is a deductible expense only if your business trip is overnight or long enough to require that you stop for sleep or rest. (Of course, if you entertain business guests at home or away you may be able to deduct the cost, if you meet the usual deductibility rules for meals and entertainment as discussed on page 75).

In any case, you can deduct only 50 percent of the cost of the meals.

Deductible Travel Expenses

- 50 percent of the cost of meals when traveling (see discussion below)
- air, rail, and bus fares
- baggage charges
- cleaning and laundry expenses
- computer rental fees
- expenses of operating and maintaining a vehicle, including the cost of gas, oil, lubrication, washing, repairs, parts, tires, supplies, parking fees, and tolls
- expenses of operating and maintaining RVs or house trailers
- hotel expenses
- local transportation costs for taxi fares or other transportation between the airport or station and a hotel, from one customer to another, or from one place of business to another, and tips incidental to the foregoing expenses
- public stenographer or clerical fees
- telephone or fax expenses
- tips on eligible expenses
- transportation costs for sample and display materials and sample room costs

---

A special exception to the 50 percent rule for deducting meal costs applies to people who are away from home while working under Department of Transportation regulations. This group of workers includes air transportation employees, interstate truck and bus drivers, railroad employees, and merchant mariners. For these workers, meals will be 55 percent deductible in 1999, 60 percent deductible in 2000 and 2001, 65 percent deductible in 2002 and 2003, 70 percent deductible in 2004 and 2005, 75 percent deductible in 2006 and 2007, and 80 percent deductible in 2008 and thereafter.

Standard Meal Allowance

Assuming that you are traveling away from home for the required length of time, you may elect to deduct half of a Standard Meal Allowance (SMA), rather than half of the actual cost of your meals, laundry, cleaning and tips.

The standard meal allowance for 1999 is $30 a day for most areas in the U.S. Some locations in the U.S. are considered high-cost areas and qualify for higher rates of $34, $38, $42, or $46 per day. These per diem rates are updated periodically to reflect regional inflation and are published at http://www.policyworks.gov on the Internet and in IRS Publication 1542, *Per Diem Rates (for Travel Within the Continental United States)*. Note that these sources also list a per diem rate that includes lodging as well as meals and incidentals, but this combined per diem generally can't be used by self-employed people.

For travel in areas outside the continental U.S., you must use federal per diem rates that are published monthly by the government. The foreign per diem rates can be purchased from the Government Printing Office and are also available on the Internet from the State Department at http://www.state.gov.

Save Time

The advantage to using the standard meal allowance is that you don't have to keep records of actual meal expenses, although you still have to keep records to prove the time, place, and business purpose of your travel.

A disadvantage is that the standard meal allowances are not very generous. Chances are that your actual expenses — and therefore your deductions — would be larger.

Spouses and Dependents

You may be wondering whether you can deduct the cost of bringing your spouse along on a business trip. The answer is generally no.

For the travel expenses of a spouse (or dependent or any other individual for that matter) to be deductible, the spouse (or other person) must also be an employee of the business. In addition, the spouse's travel must be for a bona fide business purpose and the expenses must be otherwise deductible by the spouse.

Conventions, Seminars, Meetings

You can deduct your travel expenses when you attend a convention if you can show that attending the convention benefits your business.

You can satisfy the business relationship test by showing that your business duties and responsibilities tie into the program or agenda of the convention. The agenda doesn't necessarily have to deal specifically with your duties or responsibilities—a tie-in is enough. You must, however, show some kind of income-producing purpose for attending the convention. In any case, you won't be able to deduct any nonbusiness expenses (sightseeing, for example) you incur while attending the convention.

The rules become even stricter when the convention is held outside North America or on a cruise ship. Basically, the IRS doesn't want people deducting their vacations. However, they recognize that at least some of these trips are for bona fide business purposes. Here's what you need to know:

Conventions held outside North America. In order to be able to deduct expenses for attending a convention outside the North American area, the convention must be directly related to your business and it must be as reasonable to hold the convention outside the North American area as in it. You must also satisfy the requirements for deducting business travel expenses outside the U.S.

Conventions held on cruise ships. The following requirements must be met before you can deduct expenses incurred for a convention or seminar held on a cruise ship:

- The convention must be directly related to the active conduct of your business.

- The cruise ship must be a vessel registered in the U.S.

- All of the cruise ship's ports of call must be located in the U.S. (or its possessions).

- You must attach to your income tax return a written statement signed by you that includes the total days of the trip (excluding the days you spent traveling to and from the ship's port), the number of hours each day that you devoted to scheduled business activities, and a program of the scheduled business activities of the meeting.

- You must attach to your income tax return a written statement signed by an officer of the organization or group sponsoring the convention that includes a schedule of the business activities of each day of the convention, and the number of hours you attended the scheduled business activities.

If you meet the requirements, you can deduct up to $2,000 annually of the expense of attending a seminar or convention on a cruise ship.

Foreign Travel

Simply stated, if you travel outside the U.S. purely for business purposes, all your travel expenses of getting to and from your business destination are deductible.

However, if you spend part of your time in a foreign country engaging in personal activities, you may have to allocate your travel expenses in proportion to the number of days you spent on nonbusiness activities during your trip, unless you meet one of the following conditions:

- You were outside the U.S. for a week or less, combining business and personal activities (a week is seven consecutive days, not counting the day you leave the U.S., but counting the day you return to the U.S.).

- You were outside the U.S. for more than a week, but you spent less than 25 percent of the total time you were in a foreign country on personal activities (counting both the day your trip began and the day it ended).

- You can establish that a personal vacation was not a major consideration for the trip.

If you meet one or more of these conditions, you're in luck! Your trip is considered entirely conducted for business and you can deduct all of your business-related travel expenses.

If you don't meet at least one of these conditions and you spent 25 percent or more of your time on personal activities, you'll have to allocate your travel expenses of getting to and from your destination between your business and personal activities to determine your deductible amount. You must allocate your expenses *even if* your trip was primarily for business reasons. Remember, if your trip was primarily for vacation purposes, the entire cost of the trip is a nondeductible personal expense. You would be able to deduct only the expenses that you incurred on the trip that were directly related to your business (if any).

Claiming Your Travel Expenses

Sole proprietors claim their travel expenses, except for any meals or entertainment expenses, on Line 24a of their Schedule C. The full amount of meals and entertainment costs must be reported separately on Line 24b; the tax form asks you to compute 50 percent of this amount on the face of the form to make sure that you're only deducting half of the expenses.

MEAL AND ENTERTAINMENT EXPENSES

As a small business owner, you may often find yourself in the position of having to entertain clients or customers. While this sort of thing is a necessary expense for many small business owners, the costs can really add up. You'll be glad to know that the IRS lets you take a deduction for 50 percent of qualifying entertainment expenses for yourself and your guests.

What requirements must your meal and entertainment expenses meet in order to be deductible? Generally, the answer is that you can deduct ordinary and necessary expenses to entertain a customer or client if:

- Your expenses are of a type that qualifies as meals or entertainment.

- Your expenses bear the necessary relationship to your business activities.

- You keep adequate records and can substantiate the expenses.

Defining Meals and Entertainment

What kind of expenses count as meal and entertainment expenses, for which a 50 percent deduction is allowed? Generally, expenses for any activity considered to provide entertainment, amusement, or recreation fall into this category.

For example, entertaining guests at nightclubs; at social, athletic, and sporting clubs; at theaters; at sporting events; or on hunting, fishing, vacation and similar types of trips is considered deductible entertainment. Meeting personal, living, or family needs of individuals (for example, providing meals, a hotel suite, or a car to business customers or their families) can be an entertainment expense as well.

Entertainment expenses include the cost of meals you provide to customers or clients, whether the meal alone is the entertainment or it's a part of other entertainment (for example, refreshments at a football game). A meal expense includes the cost of food, beverages, taxes, and tips.

You can also deduct 50 percent of business meals or entertainment expenses incurred while:

- entertaining business guests, whether it's at your place of business, a restaurant, or some other location

- attending a business convention, reception, meeting, or luncheon at a club

- traveling away from home on business, whether eating alone or with others on business.

It's important to note that the type of business you run can determine whether an activity is entertainment.

Example

If you're a freelance theater critic who is paid for your reviews, and you attend a theatrical performance in your professional capacity, this is not a 50 percent deductible entertainment expense; instead, it would be a 100 percent deductible business expense. Similarly, if a clothing designer puts on a fashion show to show his designs to a group of store buyers, it would not be considered entertainment. However, if you are an appliance distributor and you put on a fashion show for your retailers and their spouses, the show is considered entertainment and only 50 percent would be deductible.

The cost of entertainment tickets is generally deductible. However, you can only deduct the face value of the ticket *even if* you paid a higher price (for example, if you pay more than face value for a ticket from a scalper, ticket agency, or ticket broker).

You can, however, take the full cost you pay for a ticket into account, even if it's higher than face value, when the ticket is to a sporting event if the event's main purpose is to benefit a qualified charitable organization, the entire net proceeds go to the charity, and volunteers perform substantially all the event's work. Also, the 50 percent limitation on entertainment expenses doesn't apply to any expense covered by a package deal involving a ticket to a charitable sports event.

Entertaining Spouses

Can you deduct the cost of entertainment for your spouse or a customer or client's spouse? You can only deduct these costs if you had a clear business purpose, rather than a personal or social purpose, for providing the entertainment.

Example

You would be able to deduct otherwise permissible entertainment expenses of an out-of-town client's husband when it is impracticable to entertain the client for business purposes without him.

Business-Related Entertainment

Your expenses for meals and entertainment must be closely related to your business in order to be deductible. In the IRS's view, your expenses may qualify if they meet at least one of the following two tests:

- the directly-related test

- the associated-with test

You can't deduct meal and entertainment expenses to the extent that they are lavish or extravagant — the expenses must be reasonable considering the facts and circumstances.

Directly-Related Test

If the entertainment takes place in a clear business setting (for example, you provide a hospitality room at a convention) directly to promote your business, the expense satisfies the directly-related-to test. If you can't meet the clear business setting requirement, the expense must meet *all* of the following requirements:

- You must have more than a vague expectation of deriving some income or other specific business benefit (other than the goodwill of the person entertained) from the meal or entertainment. However, you don't need to show that income or some other business benefit actually resulted from each deducted expenditure.

- During the meal or entertainment, you actively engaged in business discussions.

- The main purpose of the combined business and entertainment was the active conduct of business.

What kind of expenses are generally *not* considered directly related? In situations when entertainment occurs where there are substantial distractions, such as meetings or discussions at night clubs, theaters, or sporting events; meetings or discussions at social gatherings, such as cocktail parties; and situations in which you meet with a group that includes persons other than business associates, for example cocktail lounges, country clubs, golf or athletic clubs, or at vacation resorts. For these types of meal and entertainment expenses, there's a presumption that the directly-related test is not met unless you clearly can show otherwise.

Associated-With Test

Meals and entertainment expenses may be deductible under this test if they meet the following two requirements:

- The expenses are associated with the active conduct of your business.

- The meal or entertainment directly precedes or follows a substantial and bona fide business discussion.

Entertainment that occurs on the same day as the business discussion automatically meets the "directly precedes or follows" requirement.

If the entertainment and the business discussion don't occur on the same day, the facts and circumstances of each case are considered. The relevant facts are the place, date, and duration of the business discussion, whether you and your business associate are from out of town (and the dates of arrival and departure), and the reasons the entertainment didn't take place on the same day as the business discussion.

Whether a business discussion (such as a meeting, negotiation, transaction, etc.) is substantial and bona fide depends on the facts and circumstances of each case. If the IRS challenged you on this, you would have to establish that you actively engaged in the business discussion (not the entertainment) for the purpose of obtaining income or some other type of specific business benefit. However, you *don't* have to show that more time was devoted to business than entertainment.

Claiming Meal and Entertainment Expenses

Your total meals and entertainment expenses would be reported on Line 24b of the Schedule C. This amount should include any meal expenses you incurred while traveling on business.

Line 24c requires you to multiply your total meals by 50 percent and to subtract it from the total, just to be sure that you're only deducting half of these costs. The remaining 50 percent is reported on Line 24d.

BUSINESS GIFT EXPENSES

As a small business owner, you may find yourself giving gifts to clients and customers in the course of your business, particularly around the holidays.

What you may not know is that you can deduct only part of the cost of certain gifts as a business expense.

For purposes of this discussion, a gift is any item that's excluded from gross income of the recipient under the gift tax laws. If an item is excluded from gross income under any other provision, then it's not considered to be a gift. For example, because scholarships are excluded from income under another tax law provision, they are not considered gifts. Similarly, a "gift" to an employee will be treated as taxable compensation for the employee, which is deductible for your business under the normal rules for employees' pay.

Dollar limitation. Basically, the IRS will let your business deduct only $25 or less for business gifts you give to any one person during your tax year.

This means that any number of your employees, co-owners or business partners may give a client business gifts. However, the deduction will be limited to $25 per recipient. Any amount of expense in excess of $25 is disallowed as a deduction.

Example

If you give a client a $50 plant as a gift, you can only take a $25 deduction.

In addition, if you and your spouse both give gifts, you're both going to be treated as one taxpayer, and together you can only deduct gifts of $25 per recipient. This is true even if you have separate businesses, are separately employed, or whether each of you has an independent connection with the gift recipient.

Direct and Indirect Gifts

The $25 limit for business gifts includes both direct and indirect gifts. Figuring out if you gave a direct gift is a pretty straightforward determination. If you gave fruitcakes to each of ABC Corporation's 10 employees, than you made a direct gift to each one of them.

Determining whether you made an indirect gift is trickier because the IRS isn't only going to look at who received the gift, but also at whom you actually intended to benefit by giving this gift.

Example

Let's say you give your client's live-in relative, Aunt Mabel, a single ticket for a basketball game. Now, at the time you gave her the ticket, you probably had a pretty good idea that she would ultimately give the ticket to your client who is an avid basketball fan. So, do you think the IRS will classify this as an indirect gift to your client? You can bet on it.

However, if you have bona fide business dealings with Aunt Mabel (let's say she is your supplier) then the gift is generally not considered an indirect gift. Still, the IRS will look at the gift to see whether your client, Aunt Mabel, (or any family member for that matter), was to have the eventual use or benefit of the gift. If your client is the intended beneficiary it may still be treated as an indirect gift.

Incidental Costs

The $25 limit for business gifts doesn't include incidental costs — for example, packaging, insurance, and mailing costs or the cost of engraving jewelry. Related costs are considered incidental only if they don't add some kind of substantial value to a gift.

Example

Let's say you send someone a fruit basket as a gift. If the basket has a substantial value as compared to the value of the fruit, the cost of the basket is not incidental and it must be included in the $25 limit. On the other hand, the cost of gift wrapping is incidental and doesn't have to be included in the $25 limit.

Exemptions From the Gift Limitations

If you give key chains or pens with your business name on them to customers and clients, are these considered gifts and subject to these rules? In a word, no. The following items are excepted from the $25 limit for business gifts and their cost is deductible without limitation:

- items that cost $4 or less, have your name clearly and permanently imprinted on them, and are one of a number of identical items you widely distribute

- signs, display racks, or other promotional material to be used on the business premises of the recipient

Entertainment Gifts

What happens if you give tickets to a play or sporting event to a customer or client? Is this a gift expense or an entertainment expense? The general rule is that any item that could be considered either a gift or an entertainment expense should be considered an entertainment expense.

However, under certain circumstances, you may have the choice of determining whether an item is either a gift or entertainment expense. For example, if you give a client tickets to go see a play or sporting event, you may treat the tickets as either a gift or an entertainment expense if you don't go with the client to the play or sporting event. If you do go with the client, you *must* treat the cost of the tickets as an entertainment expense – you don't have any choice.

Save Money

If you have the choice of treating an expense as a gift or entertainment, which should you choose? Taking into account the $25 limit for gifts and the 50 percent limitation on entertainment expenses, it's generally advantageous to treat an expense as entertainment when it is over $50. For example, let's say you gave a client ballet tickets that cost $140. If you deduct them as a gift expense, your deduction is limited to $25. If you deduct them as an entertainment expense, your deduction is one-half the cost or $70. Conversely, if you gave a client tickets to a movie premiere that cost $30, you would get a bigger deduction by claiming a gift expense ($25 as opposed to $15 for an entertainment expense).

What about food-related gifts? Should you treat their cost as a meal expense or a gift expense? If you give a customer or client packaged food or beverages that you intend them to use at a later date, treat the cost as a gift expense, not a meal expense.

Claiming Business Gift Expenses

Since Schedule C does not include a separate category for business gift expenses, you would need to list them as an "other" expenses in Part V of the

Schedule C. You don't need to list each gift separately; it's fine to total them up and list them as a single line-item, "gifts."

BUSINESS-RELATED EDUCATION EXPENSES

Self-employed business owners can deduct the cost of seminars; training sessions; and vocational, technical, or academic classes that may or may not lead to a degree, if they are sufficiently related to the business activity. For more information, see the discussion of education expenses for employees on page 182.

THE HOME OFFICE DEDUCTION

If you use a part of your home for business — perhaps to perform paperwork; to store records, inventory, or samples; or even to meet customers — you may be able to claim a tax deduction for some of your expenses of maintaining the home.

Now, you may have heard that the home office deduction is either one of the greatest money-savers available to American small business, or that it is a major red flag that will make you audit bait for the IRS.

Actually, IRS spokespersons have recently stated that the home office deduction is no longer on their radar screen in terms of flagging you for a tax audit. Nevertheless, we recommend that you keep meticulous records of all your expenses. Because the rules for claiming the home office deduction have been significantly liberalized beginning in 1999, the IRS may start paying more attention.

Tax Organizer Tip

As a reminder, your home office expenses should be entered under the tab for "Home" in the "Real Estate" section of the CompleteTax™ Organizer.

Many Deductions, Not Just One

In reality, when we speak of the home office deduction, we're really talking about a series of smaller deductions. These deductions — which may include such items as part of your utility bills, mortgage interest, repairs, and depreciation — are totaled up to get an overall deduction amount which is reported on IRS Form 8829, *Expenses for Business Use of Your Home.* The common denominator among these deductions is that the IRS has devised a single test to determine whether you qualify for all of them.

Some deductions are available even if you don't qualify. A commonly held misconception is that you need to qualify for the home office deduction in order to claim *any* expenses associated with a home or a home-based business. This is simply not true.

For example, home mortgage interest and real estate taxes would be allowed as an itemized deduction on Schedule A of your Form 1040 in any case, even if you can't take a home office deduction. Office supplies, postage, and the cost of bringing a second telephone line into your home for business use may also be deductible. Moreover, you may be able to write off the cost of computers and office furniture you buy to use at home, even if you're not allowed to deduct the cost of the office itself (see Chapter 7 regarding depreciation).

Having said that, we're ready to discuss the details of the home office deduction and to help you calculate your deduction amount.

Qualifying for a Home Office Deduction

The requirements of the home office deduction are fairly strict. Generally, to qualify, your home office must be used exclusively and regularly for business *and* either:

1. be your "principal place of business" *or* be normally used to personally meet with clients or customers

2. be a separate structure that is not attached to your house or residence, in which case it merely has to be used in your trade or business

Exclusive and Regular Business Use

Everyone who wishes to claim the home office deduction must use a portion of the home exclusively and regularly for business.

You don't necessarily have to use the space as an office; it could be a showroom, lab, or storage area. However, you must use it *regularly*, not just occasionally. Ordinarily, "exclusive use" means that the business part of the home may not be used for any personal, family, or investment activities, or for any other business activities that don't meet the home office requirements.

There is an exception to the "exclusive use" requirement if your home is the only fixed location of a retail or wholesale business. In that case, you can deduct expenses that pertain to the use of part of your home for the storage of inventory or product samples.

Example

Patrick Daily's home is the sole, fixed place of his business selling personal computers at retail. He regularly uses half of his basement for inventory storage, although he also uses that part of the basement for personal purposes when his inventory is low.

The expenses allocated to the storage space are deductible even though he does not use that part of the basement exclusively for business.

There is also an exception to this exclusive use requirement for those who operate a child care business in their home. The portion of the home that is used regularly for day care qualifies as a "home office," even if it is also used for personal and family living space. However, day care operators face an additional time restriction: they may only deduct expenses for the actual time the day care center was open (see page 83).

Other Requirements

As we mentioned above, in addition to the exclusive and regular use tests, you must meet *one* of the following requirements:

- The part of the home must be your principal place of business, *or* you must use it as a place to personally meet clients or customers in the normal course of your business (telephone calls don't count).

- If it is a separate structure that is not attached to your house or residence, it merely has to be used in your trade or business.

An important change for 1999. Beginning in 1999, the "principal place of business" definition is significantly easier to meet.

The law has been changed to state that the home office will qualify as the principal place of business if: (a) the office is used by the taxpayer to conduct administrative or management activities of a trade or business, and (b) there is no other fixed location where the taxpayer conducts substantial administrative or management activities of the trade or business.

This means that the fact that you may conduct management activities in a non-fixed location, such as a car or hotel room, will not cause you to lose the deduction. Similarly, the fact that you conduct some management activities in another fixed location of the business will not cause you to lose the deduction, as long as those activities are not "substantial."

Example

Joe Ditto operates his photocopier service and repair business out of his home. His only office is a room in his house used solely for business purposes.

Although Joe never meets with customers in his home office, he spends about 12 hours per week working there, scheduling service calls and writing up orders and other reports. He spends an average of 30 hours per week on service calls at his customers' businesses at various locations in the metropolitan area. Joe keeps the few tools and supplies necessary to his business in the trunk of his car.

As of 1999, Joe's home qualifies for the home office deduction. Even though the essence of his business requires him to service and repair photocopiers at the customers' places of business, and he spends less time in his home office than he does at the customers' offices, his home office is considered his principal place of business because it is the only fixed location from which he conducts administrative and management functions.

The same result would apply to a restaurant owner who serves his customers in a retail setting, but conducts management activities such as ordering food and supplies, scheduling employees' working time, and doing bookkeeping and payroll chores out of his home.

He will qualify for the home office deduction as of 1999, as long as this is the only place he conducts substantial management activies; the fact that some of his employees may condust management activies at the retail location does not matter.

Are You Eligible as an Employee?

If you or your spouse is an employee, including an employee/shareholder of a small corporation, there is another requirement in addition to those discussed above: You must be using your home for the convenience of your employer in order to qualify for the home office deduction. If your employer provides you with office space, you probably can't take the home office deduction because your home would not be considered your principal place of business.

The IRS specifically prohibits you from taking the home office deduction if you rent all or part of your home to your employer and then use the rented portion to work in as an employee.

Computing Your Home Office Deduction Amount

Once you've determined that you qualify for the home office deduction, you can determine the actual dollar amount that you can deduct.

This amount depends on a surprisingly large number of factors. But don't be alarmed – we'll walk you through them.

First, you need to know what you spent for each component of the home office deduction:

- rent if you don't own the home

- mortgage interest and real estate taxes if you do own the home

- depreciation if you own

- insurance, utilities and services, repairs, and decorating, whether you own or rent

- casualty losses whether you own or rent

Of course, for all these expenses, you can only deduct the portion that pertains to your home office, not the full amount that applies to the entire residence. There are two factors to consider in determining the "home office portion":

- space: the size of the area that was used

- time: the portion of the year that the home office was used, if not the entire year

Finally, some business owners will find that their home office deduction is limited by their business income. The tax law states that the home office deduction, plus all your other deductible business expenses, cannot exceed your business income for the year. In other words, the home office deduction cannot be used as a tax shelter to offset other income you (or your spouse) may have.

Business Portion of the Home

An important part of the qualification requirements for a home office is that a portion of your residence be used regularly and exclusively for business purposes, whether it be as an office, a conference room, a lab area, storage room, or some other type of business usage.

But, if you do have an area that you use regularly and exclusively for business, you can deduct a portion of certain expenses relating to your home. For most types of home office expenses, the amount you may deduct depends primarily on the percentage of the space in the residence that is used for business.

There are two common ways to determine this, and you can use whichever method results in the larger deduction.

The first method looks at the number of rooms used for business, divided by the total number of rooms in your house. The second method looks at the square footage of the space used for business, divided by the total square footage of the house.

Example

If you have an eight-room house and use one room as an office, the business use portion will be 1/8 or 12.5 percent of the home. Alternately, if your home office was 168 square feet and your home was a total of 2000 square feet, your business use percentage will be 168/2000 or 8.4 percent.

Most of your home expenses (such as rent or real estate taxes and mortgage interest) must be multiplied by the larger of these two fractions to determine the portion that's deductible as a home office expense.

Day care providers. Home day care operators get a special tax break: They can count all the space they regularly use for their day care business as the "business portion of the home" even though the same space is used for personal or family purposes. For example, they may include the bathroom, the kitchen where day care meals are prepared, and the family bedrooms where naps are taken. However, unlike most home business operators, they must prorate these expenses for the hours in which the day care is offered, as discussed below.

Partial-Year Home Offices

Most people do not start up a new business precisely on January 1. Most likely, you opened your business at some point between January 1 and December 31, and your first year in the home office was not a complete one. Similarly, people who close down their business don't always do it precisely on the last day of their tax year.

As a result, for the first year in which you began using your home office, or the year in which you closed your business, you'll have to prorate your home office expenses based on the percentage of the time your home office was actually used.

Example

If you began using your home office on July 1 of this year and continued to use it through the end of the year, you can use only your expenses for the last half of the year in computing your home office deduction.

Special rules for depreciation. For the first year you begin using your home office, the IRS provides a table showing the fraction of your depreciable basis you can deduct, based on the month in which you started using the office. See Table A-7a on page 129.

For the last year, you'll need to determine the amount of depreciation you'd normally deduct for the year, under the usual rules. Then multiply this amount by a fraction: The numerator will be the number of months that you used the office, and the denominator will be 12. Count the month in which you stopped using the property as half a month. For example, if you stopped using your office in October, the fraction will be 9.5/12.

Day care operators. As mentioned above, home day care operators can count as "business-use space" whatever portion of the home is regularly used for day care purposes, even if the same space is also used for personal living space. However, they must prorate their home office expenses based on their hours of operation.

Example

A home day care operator's expenses for mortgage interest, real estate taxes, depreciation, utilities, and property insurance amounts to $10,000. She estimates that 80% of her home is used regularly for day care activities. The day care center is open 12 hours per day, five days per week, which amounts to 60 hours out of a possible 168.

She must multiply her home office expenses of $10,000 by .80 to arrive at $8,000, which is her business use percentage of these expenses. Then she must multiply this amount by 60/168 to arrive at her allowable deduction of $2,857.

Rent, Interest, and Taxes

For those who rent their home, the major advantage of the home office deduction is that a portion of your rental payments will be deductible. Renters who don't qualify for the home office deduction ordinarily can't deduct any of their rental payments, so working out of your home can result in significant tax savings.

Homeowners. For homeowners, your deduction is not based on the fair rental value of your home. Instead, you may deduct a portion of your real estate taxes and your qualified mortgage interest (but not principal) payments on the home. You can also claim a depreciation deduction to recover some of the home's purchase price.

"Real estate taxes" include the amount of taxes actually paid to the taxing authority on your behalf during the year, which may be different from the amount that your mortgage holder requires you to pay into an escrow account. Real estate taxes do not include amounts paid to any homeowner's association or condominium association. They also don't include

assessments for local benefits like streets, sidewalks, or water and sewer systems – instead, these amounts may be depreciated (see the discussion of home office depreciation, below).

"Qualified mortgage interest" may include interest on a second mortgage or a home equity loan. However, there are dollar limits that apply. Only interest on mortgages up to $1,000,000 used to buy, build, or improve your property, and interest on home equity loans up to $100,000, is considered "qualified." If you think either of these limits might apply to you, consult your tax advisor or get IRS Publication 936, *Home Mortgage Interest Deduction*, for more detailed information on computing your deduction.

For both renters and homeowners, the deductible portion of the rental, tax, or interest payments depends on the percentage of the home's space that is used for business (see page 82 for the rules on computing the business percentage of your home). If you start or stop using the office during the year, the percentage of time that the office is used will also be a factor.

Save Money

Of course, as a homeowner, you can claim all your real estate taxes and qualified mortgage interest as itemized deductions, regardless of whether you use your home for business purposes. Claiming these expenses as part of the home office deduction basically means shifting them to a different tax form (Form 8829).

One major advantage to this shift is that by claiming these amounts as a business deduction, you reduce the net business income on which you must pay self-employment taxes.

For higher income taxpayers, there can be another advantage, because most itemized tax deductions are phased out for those with high levels of income while business expenses, including the home office deduction, are not.

Claiming the home office deduction also means that some of your real estate taxes and mortgage interest will be used to reduce your adjusted gross income (AGI), which in turn can improve your eligibility for numerous tax benefits including IRAs (see page 250), miscellaneous itemized deductions (see page 272), and the deduction for medical expenses that exceed 7.5% of AGI.

Depreciation on a Home Office

If you qualify for the home office deduction and you own your home, you can't directly deduct the price you paid for the home, the principal payments you make on the mortgage, or the fair rental value of the home.

Instead, you can recover the cost of the business percentage of the home through depreciation deductions.

Before you can calculate the dollar amount of your depreciation, however, you will need to know the tax basis of your home. To determine your home's tax basis, you start with the lower of:

- the home's fair market value at the time you begin using the home office, or

- the cost of the home (not including the cost of the land underneath it), plus the value of any permanent improvements you made before using the home office, and minus any casualty losses you deducted before using it.

In most cases you'll be using the second of the two items listed above, but if you suspect that your home has slid down in value since you bought it, you should have an appraisal done when you start using the home office in order to fix the fair market value at that point in time.

The cost of the home generally includes not only the price you paid to the seller, but also various closing costs and settlement fees such as abstract fees, installation of utility services, legal fees, recording fees, surveys, transfer taxes, title insurance, and any amounts you agree to pay on behalf of the seller such as back taxes or interest, sales commissions, or charges for improvements or repairs. Some fees and costs you may not include are insurance premiums, rent for occupancy before closing, and charges connected with getting a loan such as mortgage insurance, credit reports, appraisal fees, loan assumption fees, and points.

You must reasonably allocate the total costs of the property between the land and the buildings on it to compute your tax basis for depreciation. If your sales contract did not explicitly allocate the price, you should allocate the costs on the basis of the fair market values of the land and buildings at the time of purchase. Your realtor or insurance agent may be able to help you make a reasonable estimate of fair market value.

Your tax basis must be multiplied by the business percentage of your home (see page 82), to arrive at the amount you can depreciate.

Once you know the tax basis of the depreciable portion of the home, you multiply it by a percentage determined by the IRS, based on the month and year you bought the home. Table A-7a showing these percentages is included on page 129. Generally speaking, for home offices that you began using for business on or after May 13, 1993, the depreciation period will be 39 years and in every year but the first and the last, the applicable percentage will be .02564. For the first and last years, the fraction will depend on the month in which business use began or ended.

If you began using your home office before May 13, 1993, continue using the depreciation method that you originally started out with.

Capital improvements. If, after you begin using your home for business, you make a significant, permanent improvement to the property (as opposed to a repair) you will need to depreciate this capital expenditure as well. For example, if you put on a new roof or buy a new furnace for your home, you would depreciate the business percentage of the cost of the improvement over 39 years, beginning with the month and year of installation. See page 60 for a list of items that are generally considered capital improvements, not repairs.

Warning

It's important to recognize that when you eventually sell your home, you'll be required to pay tax on the amount of capital gain (if any) that's equal to the amount of depreciation you claimed over the years on your home, including depreciation from a home office. The maximum tax rate on this "recaptured" depreciation is 25%.

Insurance, Utilities, Services, Repairs, and Decorating

If you qualify for the home office deduction, you may claim a portion of certain types of expenses that are associated with your home but are not deductible by the average homeowner. These expenses include insurance, utilities, repairs, security system expenses, maid service, garbage disposal, and decorating expenses.

With all of these expenses, the general rule is that if a given expense pertains only to the home office, the entire expense will be deductible as a "direct" home office expense. If the expense applies to the entire house, it's an "indirect" home office expense and only a proportionate part of it will be deductible. And if the expense applies only to the non-business portion of the house, none of the expense will be deductible. Also, if you did not operate the business for the entire year, you may only deduct expenses that pertain to the portion of the year in which the office was used.

Insurance. You may deduct the business percentage of your homeowner's or renter's insurance as part of the home office deduction.

Do not include the costs of any business insurance you carry or special home office policy riders in this figure. Those costs apply specifically to the business portion of your home, and are fully deductible as ordinary business expenses, not as part the home office deduction. This distinction can become important if your home office deduction is limited by the amount of your business income (see page 86).

Utilities and services. As a general rule, you can deduct the business percentage of your utility payments for heat and electricity, and for services that pertain to the entire house such as trash collection, security services, and maid or cleaning services.

Warning

IRS regulations indicate that lawn service is generally not deductible as part of the home office deduction, even when the home office is used as a meeting place with clients (who presumably view the lawn as they enter the residence).

If you pay for a utility or service that's not used in your business at all, you can't deduct any portion of the expense. For instance, if you buy propane fuel that is used only in your kitchen and your business does not involve cooking, no part of the propane bill is deductible.

If you believe that your business accounts for significantly more (or less) of a particular utility, you should increase (or decrease) your business percentage

of that utility bill accordingly. This is not an exact science, and the IRS will accept a reasonable estimate.

Example

Leona Grossberg is a cosmetics company representative who qualifies for the home office deduction. She has an electric bill of $400 for lighting, cooking, laundry and television. Only the lighting is used for business. She figures that $250 of the bill is for lighting alone. Because she uses 10 percent of the house for business, $25 may be deductible as a business expense.

Telephones. Telephone bills are considered direct business expenses, and are not part of the home office deduction. Therefore, you may be able to deduct a portion of your home or cellular phone bill even if you don't qualify under the home office rules.

In any event, you can't claim any deduction for the basic telephone service on the first telephone line in your home, or on your cellular phone. These are considered to be personal expenses that you would incur even if you did not own a business. However, you *can* deduct any separately stated charges for local or long distance business calls. You can also deduct the cost of bringing a second phone line into your home, if you use the line exclusively for business.

Repairs and decorating expenses. Expenses that exclusively benefit your business (for example, repairing the drywall and repainting a former bedroom that is now your office) are considered "direct" home office expenses and are fully deductible. Expenses that benefit the entire home (for example, patching the roof so it doesn't leak, or recarpeting the entire house) are considered "indirect" home office expenses that are proportionately deductible. And expenses that benefit only the personal portion of the home (for example, installing a whirlpool tub in the master bedroom suite) are not deductible at all.

It's sometimes difficult to distinguish between a repair, which is deductible (fully or partially) in the year it was done, and an improvement, which must be depreciated over the course of property's useful life. The IRS says that an improvement is something that materially adds to the value of your home, considerably prolongs its useful life, or adapts it to new uses. A repair, on the other hand, is something that keeps your home in ordinary efficient operating condition but does not add to the value of your home or prolong its life. If repairs are done as part of extensive remodeling or restoration, the entire job is considered an improvement.

Example

Generally speaking, patching walls and floors, painting, repairing roofs and gutters, fixing a furnace or air conditioner, and mending leaks would be considered repairs. Installing new flooring, roofs and gutters, furnaces, or air conditioners would be considered capital improvements.

Home Office Casualty Losses

If your home office is damaged or destroyed by a burglary or a disaster such as a hurricane, flood, fire, accident, riot, or vandalism, you may be able to deduct some of your losses as part of the home office deduction. For a detailed discussion of casualty loss deductions, see page 267.

If the loss occurs only to the home office, treat it as a "direct" expense that is fully deductible. If it applies to the entire home (such as storm damage to your roof), you can deduct a proportionate part of it as a business expense (based on your business use percentage), and the remainder as a personal expense. If the loss occurred only to the personal part of the home, you may not deduct any of it as a business expense, although you may be able to deduct it as a personal expense.

Business vs. personal loss. The rules for deducting casualty losses are more favorable for business property than for personal property.

For one thing, losses on personal property are subject to two thresholds: a $100 threshold (the first $100 is not deductible at all) and a 10 percent of adjusted gross income (AGI) limit. In other words, after the first $100 is subtracted, you can only deduct the portion of the remaining loss that exceeds 10 percent of your AGI. Neither of these limits applies to casualty losses on business property.

Secondly, business casualty losses are measured using slightly different rules. For both kinds of losses, if the property is only damaged, you must take the *lower* of the decrease in the property's fair market value (FMV) as a result of the loss or the property's adjusted basis before the casualty loss. From this you subtract any insurance reimbursement, to arrive at the amount of loss. If personal property is completely destroyed, use the lower of the property's FMV or adjusted basis before the loss. But if business property is completely destroyed, use the adjusted basis before the loss minus any salvage value; the property's FMV is not considered.

In order to claim a casualty loss on your home office, you must compute the loss both ways. First, compute the amount of loss that you'd be allowed to deduct if the office was *not* used for business, using the $100 and 10 percent-of-AGI thresholds described above.

Then, compute the amount of loss on the home office as a business expense. The easiest way to compute these two amounts is to use IRS Form 4684, *Casualties and Thefts*, as a worksheet. Complete Section A as if the loss were on personal property, and then complete Section B as if the property were business.

While the amount that would be deductible as a personal loss (as shown on Section A) is always deductible as an itemized deduction, the difference between the personal loss and the business loss will only be deductible this year if your business income is sufficient to cover all your business expenses. If not, you can carry over the excess and deduct it next year.

Adjustments to basis. Your deductible casualty losses must be used to reduce your tax basis in the business portion of the home. For the year of the loss and for subsequent years, you will need to use this new basis in calculating your depreciation deductions. For more information, see IRS Publication 946, *How To Depreciate Property*.

Business Income Limitation

With most of your ordinary business expenses, if you have more expenses than you have income, your business can show a net operating loss that may be deductible against any other regular income you have (such as interest, dividends, or income from another job or business). This may even be true if the loss is a "paper loss" resulting from depreciation.

However, it is not true of the home office deduction.

Your home office deduction is limited by the amount of your net business income. If your net income is too low, you won't be able to deduct the entire amount of your home office deduction this year (although you may carry it over and deduct it in a later year when your net business income is higher).

The IRS has developed a rather lengthy computation that must be used in applying this limit, which is incorporated into Form 8829.

Basically, you must start with your gross business income from all sources (sales, interest on bank accounts, etc.), less all of your business expenses that are not part of the home office deduction. This is your tentative profit as shown on Line 29 of your Schedule C, and is the maximum amount you can claim as a home office deduction this year.

Then, subtract the portion of your home office deduction expenses that you could otherwise use as itemized deductions: home mortgage interest, real estate taxes, and casualty losses computed as if the home office was your personal residence. (If the answer is zero or a negative number, you may be better off not claiming the home office deduction, and instead claiming these amounts as regular itemized deductions. This is especially true if you think your tax bracket next year won't be higher than your bracket this year.)

Assuming the answer to the previous step was a positive number, subtract the portion of your home office deduction expenses that would not otherwise be deductible as itemized deductions: insurance, repairs and maintenance services, utilities, and rent if you don't own the home.

Finally, you may subtract the extra business portion of any casualty losses, depreciation on your home, and any carried-over home office expenses from previous years. If the end result is zero or a positive number, you can deduct all your home office expenses. If the end result is a negative number, you may carry over the nondeductible portion to be subtracted on next year's tax return.

Home Office Deduction Forms

As with most other business expenses, the way in which you claim your home office deduction depends on your employment status:

If you are self-employed. Self-employed people must fill out a special form to claim the home office

Case Study

Sylvia Pappas is employed as an outside salesperson, and she meets all the requirements for deducting expenses for a home office. In 1999, her computation of expenses for the business use of her home is as follows:

Gross income from business:	$6,000
less: direct business expenses (business phone, car expenses)	-2,000
Balance:	4,000
less: deductible mortgage interest and taxes	-3,000
Home office deduction limitation	1,000
less: other expenses for business use of home	-2,400
Balance (carried over to the next year)	-1,400

deduction. You must complete Form 8829, *Expenses for Business Use of Your Home,* and then transfer the total to your Schedule C. Unfortunately, Schedule C-EZ, which is a much simpler form, can't be used if you're claiming the home office deduction. The business portion of your home mortgage interest and real estate taxes is claimed on Form 8829 and cannot be claimed again as an itemized deduction on Schedule A of your return.

If you are an employee. Employees are not required to complete Form 8829. Your unreimbursed home office deductions are usually claimed on Form 2106, along with your other unreimbursed employee business expenses.

Then, the total of such expenses is included in your miscellaneous deductions on Schedule A of your individual income tax return. As such, they are subject to the 2 percent floor; in other words, you can deduct only the portion of all miscellaneous expenses that is more than 2 percent of your adjusted gross income.

In some cases, you might be able to avoid filing Form 2106. If your only reason for filing the form would be to claim the home office deduction, and your employer did not reimburse you for any home office expenses, you don't have to file the 2106. Instead, you can claim the deduction directly on the bottom of your Schedule A.

DEDUCTIBLE WAGES FOR EMPLOYEES

If you have employees, you can claim a tax deduction for the salary, wages, commissions, bonuses, and other compensation you pay them. In fact, it's likely that your deductions for employee compensation will be one of your largest deductible expenses.

To be deductible, the compensation must be ordinary and necessary, reasonable in amount, based on services rendered, and actually paid or incurred in the year for which the deduction is claimed (as shown by your payroll records).

The timing of your deduction will depend on whether you use the cash or accrual method of accounting. If you use the cash method, you must deduct your expense for each salary, wage, or benefit payment in the year it's paid to the employee. If you use the accrual method, you must generally deduct the expense when you establish your obligation to make the payment and when the services are performed, even if the actual paycheck is distributed later.

If the compensation is paid in some form other than cash, the deductible amount is generally equal to the fair market value of the property transferred. For example, if you give your employees gold-plated cell phones at Christmas, the cost you paid for the gifts would be deductible.

What is "reasonable" compensation to employees depends on the facts and circumstances at the time the compensation is paid. Ordinarily, the IRS will not challenge the amount of the compensation as unreasonable unless the employee has some control over the employer (e.g., is a large stockholder) or has some personal relationship with the owners.

Warning

This discussion of employees' wages does not include payments to independent contractors. The gross amount you pay an independent contractor is deductible. If, in the course of business, you pay $600 or more to an independent contractor, or you pay $600 or more in rents, services including parts and materials, or attorney fees, you must report the payment on IRS Form 1099-MISC. Give a copy to the contractor by January 31, and send a copy to the IRS by February 28. These rules generally don't apply to payments made to corporations. Form 1099-MISC is a machine-readable form, and you must use the official IRS version (call 1-800-TAX-FORM for a copy) or a pre-approved computer-generated form (software is available in most larger office supply stores).

Awards and Bonuses

You can deduct the cost of any bonuses you pay to your employees, as long as the bonus represents pay for services rather than a gift, and it's reasonable in view of the employee's services and performance.

If you're a cash method taxpayer, you must have paid the bonus before December 31, 1999 in order to deduct it in 1999.

If you're using the accrual method, you can deduct it in 1999 as long as you established the amount and the employee's right to the bonus before the end of the year – you can pay the amount in 2000 if you prefer.

Warning

There is an exception to this rule for related taxpayers: If your bonus-achieving employee is your spouse, child, brother or sister, parent or grandparent, you may only deduct the payment in the year in which the employee reports the payment as income. This means that if the recipient is using the cash method (as most individuals do), you may only deduct the bonus in the year you pay it, after all.

Awards. Employee achievement awards made under a written plan that does not discriminate in favor of highly compensated employees, and which average $400 or less during the year, are deductible as "qualified" plan awards. Other awards are considered "nonqualified" and no more than $400 in nonqualified awards can be deducted for any one employee. No more than $1,600 in total awards, both qualified and nonqualified, can be deducted for any one employee per year.

Loans or Advances

If you make a loan to an employee which you don't expect to be repaid, you can deduct the amount as compensation. If you do expect the loan to be repaid, it would not be deductible unless and until the employee defaults.

If an employee has outstanding loans over $10,000 and you are not charging interest, or you are charging interest at a rate below the applicable federal rate, you may have to report "imputed interest" income at the federal rate, and also report this imputed interest as additional compensation to the employee. You can find out the current applicable federal interest rate by calling the IRS at 1-800-TAX-1040. Consult your tax advisor for more information if you think this rule applies to you.

Vacation Pay and Unpaid Salaries

If you use the cash method, it's simple: You only deduct what you actually paid to your employees during your tax year, whether you're talking about vacation pay or that last December paycheck.

If you're on the accrual method, you may be able to deduct vacation pay or unpaid salaries before the payment is actually made, so long as the employee's right to the payment is fixed and unconditional, and the employee has done the work on which the payment is based. For example, if the employee's pay period ended on December 31 and your paychecks are issued a week later, you could deduct the amount for that last pay period of the year. Accrued vacation pay must be paid within 2½ months to come under this rule.

There is an exception to the rule for employees who are related to you – see the discussion above under "Awards and Bonuses."

Meals and Lodging

If you pay your employees in the form of food or housing, you can deduct your costs of providing these items. You would deduct them as direct costs of your business, not as employees' wages.

Example

If you rent a house for your temporary workers, you can deduct the cost of the rental payments as "rental expenses" on Line 20b of your Schedule C, not as "wages" on Line 26.

Effective in 1998, meals provided to employees for the convenience of the employer are 100% deductible by the employer, but are not taxable to the employees. To be considered "for the convenience of the employer," they must be taken on the business premises.

Tax legislation in 1998 clarified that if an employer provides meals to its employees on the premises, and more than one-half of the employees are receiving the meals "for the convenience of the employer," the meals will not be taxable to any of the employees and the employer can deduct the entire cost of all the meals. The question of exactly what "convenience of the employer" means remains an unsettled question in the law. Generally, if your employees must remain on the premises in order to be available to work if needed, or if the lunch breaks are too short to allow employees to go out to eat, the meals would be considered to be for the employer's convenience.

If the meals do not meet this test, the costs of the meals would be only 50% deductible unless you include the value of the meals in the employee's taxable wages.

Payment of Employees' Expenses

Frequently it happens that employees pay some of your company's expenses out of their own pocket, and then ask you for reimbursement. This is often the case with car, travel, or meal expenses. How do you treat these expenses for tax purposes?

The answer is that reimbursements made under an "accountable plan" are deductible for your business, and are also excluded from the employee's gross income for payroll tax purposes. You would deduct these expenses in the Schedule C categories to which they pertain; for example, reimbursed employee travel expenses would be added to your own travel expenses on Line 24a; reimbursed meals would be reported on Line 24b etc.

However, if the reimbursements are not made under an accountable plan, you must include the reimbursements in the employee's taxable wages on IRS Form W-2. In that case, the employee must generally claim a miscellaneous itemized deduction for the allowable business expenses if he or she wants to get any tax benefits from them. You will be able to deduct the reimbursements as compensation to the employee, on Line 26 of Schedule C, "wages."

The catch is that you are required to withhold income taxes and employment taxes on reimbursements made, or considered made, under a nonaccountable plan because the reimbursements are included in the employee's taxable wages. You'll also have to pay your portion of the payroll taxes on these amounts.

Clearly, reimbursing under an accountable plan is better for both you and your employees, from a dollars-and-cents perspective. So, what is an accountable plan? A reimbursement arrangement that meets the following three requirements is considered an accountable plan:

- The reimbursements must be for your deductible business expenses that are paid or incurred by an employee in the course of performing services for you.

- The employee must be required to substantiate the amount, time, use, and business purpose of the reimbursed expenses to you. In order to do this, the employee should submit an account book, diary, log, statement of expense, trip sheet, or similar record, supporting each of these elements, that is recorded at or near the time of the expenditure. The records should include any supporting documentary evidence, such as receipts. An employee who receives a mileage allowance is considered to have substantiated the amount of the expenses if the employee substantiates the time, place (or use), and business purpose of the travel.

- The employee must be required to return to you any excess of reimbursements over substantiated expenses within a reasonable period of time.

How long is a "reasonable period?" The IRS will generally accept your plan if the employee is required to provide substantiation within 60 days or return unsubstantiated amounts within 120 days after an expense is paid or incurred. Again, you can use a mileage allowance — *even one that exceeds the standard mileage rate of 31 cents per mile* — and if it is reasonably calculated not to exceed the employee's actual or anticipated expenses, it will be treated as meeting this return requirement even if the employee does not have to return the excess of the allowance over the standard mileage rate.

Salaries of Owners

Sole proprietorships may deduct wages paid to employees, but the owner of the business is not considered an employee and the owner's salary or draw is not deductible. All the net profits of the business are taxable income to the owner, and self-employment tax applies to the entire amount (see page 135).

Claiming Deductions for Wages and Benefits

Generally, the value of wages and salaries you pay to your employees is reported on Line 26 of Schedule C. Payments for employee benefit plans are reported separately. Retirement plan contributions are reported on Line 19, and your contributions for all other employee benefit plans are reported on Line 14.

However, if you are a manufacturer, the wages and benefits of production workers, indirect factory workers, and supervisors must be included in your cost of good sold, as discussed on page 51.

Finally, your payments of payroll taxes such as FICA, FUTA, and state unemployment taxes are reported on Schedule C, Line 23, "taxes and licenses."

Warning

You should be aware that if you have employees, you will have some additional tax obligations because of them. You'll need to withhold and/or pay federal, state, and perhaps local income taxes; Social Security and Medicare taxes; federal and state unemployment taxes; and, in some states, disability insurance taxes. All of these payroll taxes must be paid over to the various government agencies, along with employment tax returns; for small employers this is generally done on a quarterly basis. You'll also need to give each employee a W-2 form at the end of the year, detailing their pay and the amounts deducted.

Payroll tax reporting is beyond the scope of this book. For more information, some good references are Hire Manage and Retain Employees for your Small Business, *edited by Joel Handelsman (CCH: 1998), and the IRS's free Publication 15,* Employer's Tax Guide.

EMPLOYEE BENEFIT PLANS

Employee benefits can be considered a special type of fringe benefits – benefits that provide things for employees that, if they purchased them for themselves, would normally be considered personal or family expenses.

You can generally deduct the *cost* of providing benefits such as accident and health plans, group-term life insurance, adoption assistance, dependent care assistance, educational assistance, and welfare benefit funds. These costs would be deductible on the "employee benefits" line (Line 14) of Schedule C.

Note that the issue here is different from the issue of whether the benefit is taxable to the employee for purposes of computing payroll taxes. For payroll tax purposes, some types of benefits are not taxable to the employee for purposes of FICA or income tax withholding, and they are not taxable to you as the employer for FICA or FUTA tax purposes. Common examples of this are health insurance, qualified retirement plan contributions, and group-term life insurance up to $50,000. However, the cost of providing these benefits is deductible by the employer.

Fringe benefits that are not specifically excluded from employees' income under the tax laws must be included in the employee's taxable income, at their value. This is also true when the benefits are of a type that would be excludible if they met all the federal requirements, but for some reason your plan does not meet the requirements. For instance, some types of benefit plans are not permitted to discriminate in favor of highly compensated employees such as the business owners. If the plans do discriminate, the value of the benefits will generally be taxable compensation to the highly compensated employees who receive them. However, the cost of the benefit is still deductible to your business.

Life Insurance

The cost of group-term life insurance coverage up to $50,000 per employee is deductible on the "employee benefits" line of your Schedule C, unless you are directly or indirectly a beneficiary of the policy. Life insurance on yourself as the business owner is not deductible on your Schedule C.

Health Insurance

Group health benefits that you provide to employees and their dependents are generally deductible. However, the cost of your own benefits under the plan are only 60% deductible in 1999.

Unless you operate in Hawaii, there are no federal or state laws that require you to have a health plan. However, if you do have a health plan, your plan must meet certain federal requirements or be subject to punitive excise taxes.

To avoid these excise taxes, your plan must include certain accessibility and portability features, most notably those that impose strict limits on the extent to which preexisting health conditions of employees or their dependents can be used to limit coverage. You must provide COBRA benefits to employees who lose coverage under the plan – that is, you must continue to allow them to purchase coverage at their own expense for up to 18 or 36 months, depending on the reason for the loss of coverage. COBRA coverage is not required, however, if you have fewer than 20 employees.

Work Smart

If you haven't spoken to your insurance representative recently, we suggest you contact him or her to be sure your plan provides the required coverage.

Health Insurance for the Owner

Self-employed individuals can currently deduct only a *portion* of their health insurance premiums. But help is on the way: Full deductibility is being slowly phased in, and by 2003 health insurance premiums will be completely deductible for sole proprietors, partners, LLC members, and S corporation shareholders owning more than 2 percent of the shares.

The deductible portion is determined by the year in which the premium is paid:

Tax Year Beginning In	Percent of Premiums Deductible
1999-2001	60%
2002	70%
2003	100%

Health insurance premiums for yourself and your dependents are deductible on the first page of your Form 1040 (Line 28), rather than on the Schedule C.

As a result, the cost of the premiums serve to reduce your adjusted gross income (AGI), which in turn can increase your ability to take advantage of certain tax breaks like Roth IRAs and tax breaks for education. Since the premiums are not considered an itemized medical deduction, they are not limited by the 7.5 percent of AGI floor, as are most medical deductions.

Save Money

If your spouse is an employee of your business, group insurance premiums for your spouse will be 100 percent deductible as employee benefits. And if you provide health insurance for your employees' spouses and dependents, your own insurance will be deductible as well, since you are the spouse of an employee and qualify for coverage. This may be a good reason to consider hiring your spouse!

Medical Savings Accounts (MSAs)

Under a recently established pilot program, employees of small businesses (50 or fewer employees) and self-employed individuals will be able to set up MSAs to pay health care expenses, provided the accounts are used in connection with high-deductible health insurance.

MSAs are similar to IRAs in the sense that each employee (including yourself) can make tax-free contributions to an account. But instead of withdrawing the funds at retirement as you would with an IRA, you withdraw them to pay for certain types of medical care. In effect, you're being allowed to pay some of your medical costs with pre-tax dollars, which is a lot cheaper than paying for it with post-tax dollars.

Any unused money in the account is allowed to accumulate from year to year, to be used in later years when medical expenses are higher or to be saved until retirement.

At present, MSAs that are exempt from federal income taxes are part of a four-year demonstration project that began in 1997 and ends in 2000, unless Congress decides to renew it. It's limited to the first 750,000 people who sign up and is open only to the self-employed and to businesses with fewer than 50 workers. However, a number of states have MSA laws that permit employers in those states to establish state-tax-exempt MSAs under less restrictive rules.

Here's how MSAs work. A business may offer its employees, or a self-employed person may purchase, a high-deductible health insurance plan (often referred to as a "catastrophic health plan"). For 1999, the deductible must be a minimum of $1,550 for individual coverage and $3,050 for family coverage, and can be as high as $2,300 for an individual and $4,600 for a family (these amounts will be indexed for inflation periodically). The employer and employee may then make tax-free contributions to an MSA. Total annual contributions are limited to 65 percent of the deductible for individuals and 75 percent of the deductible for families.

Contributions. Contributions to the account by an individual are deductible from gross income, and contributions made by an individual's employer are excluded from income (unless they are made through a cafeteria plan). Contributions may be made for a tax year at any time until the due date of the return for that year (not including extensions). Employer contributions must be reported on the employee's W-2. Earnings of the fund are not included in taxable income for the current year.

Withdrawals. Funds may then be withdrawn from the MSA, tax-free, to pay for minor medical expenses — routine checkups, dental exams, eyeglasses, drugs, even minor surgery. Any funds that are left in the MSA at the end of the year remain in the account, and can be used in succeeding years, or saved until retirement. Thus, unlike flexible spending accounts, there is no "use it or lose it" requirement.

If you have few medical expenses over a period of years, the account may grow to a tidy sum. If funds are withdrawn for nonmedical purposes, a 15 percent penalty will be assessed (plus the funds will be taxed as ordinary income). However, after age 65 or if you become disabled, you may use your MSA monies for any purpose, just like an IRA, and pay only the tax on withdrawn funds.

Reporting MSA contributions. The health insurance feature of the MSA would be treated like any other health insurance: Benefits you pay for your employees are reported as employee benefits on Line 14 of the Schedule C, and your own benefits would be included on Line 28 of your Form 1040.

If you make contributions to your employee's MSA accounts (i.e., other than what they voluntarily have deducted from their paychecks), you must do so at a uniform rate or dollar amount. If so, you can deduct the contributions as employee benefits on Line 14 of the Schedule C.

Contributions you make to your own MSA are reported on a special IRS Form 8853, *Medical Savings Accounts and Long-Term Care Insurance Contracts*, and the deductible amount is transferred to Line 25 of your Form 1040.

Long-Term Care Insurance

Long-term health care contracts are relatively new arrangements designed to provide coverage if you become chronically ill or disabled after reaching a specified age, such as 50. Long-term care policies greatly expand the time period over which benefits will be paid out, when compared to standard accident and health policies. Another advantage is that, unlike Medicare coverage, long-term care contracts will cover the cost of custodial care, as well as skilled nursing care. These two advantages often make long-term care contracts a preferred way of pre-funding nursing home care for the elderly.

If certain specified requirements are met, long-term care insurance contracts issued after December 31, 1996 will generally receive the same income tax treatment as accident and health policies.

That means that amounts received under a long-term care insurance contract are nontaxable, although the exclusion is capped at $190 per day on *per diem* contracts (this amount will be adjusted for inflation). It also means that company-paid premiums for long-term care are not taxable for the employee. If you purchase the policy as an individual rather than through your company, the premiums count as deductible medical expenses.

Employer-provided long-term care premiums are deductible by the employer as employee benefits. However, for the business owner, they are treated as health insurance premiums, which means that for 1999, they are only 60 percent deductible.

RETIREMENT PLANS FOR THE SELF-EMPLOYED

Before 1963, sole proprietors and partnerships were allowed have qualified pension and profit-sharing plans for their employees, but the owners of these businesses could not get the tax benefits of the plans. The only way to get the maximum retirement benefits for the owner was to incorporate.

The Self-Employed Individuals Tax Retirement Act of 1962 (also called HR-10 or the Keogh Act) and its later amendments made it possible for owner-employees of unincorporated businesses and other self-employed persons to be covered under qualified retirement plans. Over the years, this tax-favored treatment for retirement plans was extended to individuals not covered by other private qualified retirement plans, and made available through Individual Retirement Accounts (IRA) and Simplified Employee Pension (SEP) plans.

As a self-employed business owner, your major pension options are:

- Keogh plans

- Simplified Employee Pensions (SEPs)

- SIMPLE plans

- Individual Retirement Accounts (IRAs) (discussed on page 250)

Keogh Plans

Generally, a Keogh Plan is a defined benefit or a defined contribution retirement plan set up by a self-employed person or partnership. The plan must meet the same eligibility and coverage requirements, contribution limits, vesting requirements, rules for integration with Social Security, and other plan requirements, as any qualified retirement plan covering corporate employees.

If you have employees, they must be allowed to participate in the Keogh plan. Also, an individual who has another job during the day, but decides to supplement his or her income by turning a weekend avocation into a business, is eligible to open a Keogh plan based on the net earnings derived from the part-time self-employment.

Warning

It's important to remember that to take a deduction for contributions to a Keogh plan on behalf of yourself, you must have some net earnings — you cannot use Keogh plan contributions to create a business loss.

Qualified plans. These plans are those that meet the requirements of the Employee Retirement Income Security Act of 1974 (ERISA) and the federal tax laws, and qualify for four significant tax benefits.

1. The income generated by the plan assets is not subject to income tax, because the income is earned and managed within the framework of a tax-exempt trust.

2. An employer is entitled to a current tax deduction for contributions to the plan.

3. The plan participants (the employees or their beneficiaries) do not have to pay income tax on the amounts contributed on their behalf until the year the funds are distributed to them by the employer.

4. Under the right circumstances, beneficiaries of qualified plan distributions are afforded special tax treatment.

Nonqualified plans. These plans are those not meeting the ERISA guidelines and the requirement of the federal tax laws. They do not get all of the preferential tax treatment of qualified plans, but employers may still deduct contributions to these plans, generally at the time that employees become vested in the benefits. Nonqualified plans are usually designed to provide deferred compensation exclusively for one or more executives.

Requirements for Qualified Plans

To satisfy the general requirements, a qualified plan must be permanent, meaning it cannot have a planned expiration date. Although the employer may reserve the right to change or terminate the plan or to discontinue operations, abandoning the plan for any reason other than business necessity within a few years is evidence that the plan was not a bona fide program from its inception.

The plan must be a definite written program that is communicated to all employees. All plan assets must be held in trust by one or more trustees. The plan must be for the exclusive benefit of the employees and their beneficiaries. Assets can't revert to the employer, except for forfeitures (for example, if an employee leaves before vesting in benefits). Funding can be provided from employer or employee contributions, or both.

Participation/coverage rules. To meet the minimum standards, at least a certain percentage of the non-highly-compensated employees must be covered by the plan and a certain number of those covered employees must actually be in the plan. The plan cannot discriminate in favor of employees who are officers, shareholders, or highly compensated, by making larger contributions on their behalf or providing them with better benefits. The plan may condition eligibility on age and service, but generally cannot postpone participation beyond the date the employee attains the age of 21 and the date on which the employee completes one year of service.

Vesting rules. The process of acquiring a nonforfeitable right to the money being set aside for you is called vesting, and means that you have to stick around in order to earn full benefits. There are two permitted vesting methods: five-year cliff vesting in which the participant becomes fully vested after five years of service (with zero vesting in the first four years) and seven-year gradual vesting in which the participant becomes increasingly vested (usually 20 percent per year) after three years of service. Although the employer can have vesting rules more lenient than these, the rules cannot be more restrictive. An employee must become fully vested no later than the normal retirement age specified in the plan. The plan must also provide rules on how breaks in service affect vesting rights.

When an employee leaves your business, you may "cash out" the employee's pension benefits if the vested portion of the benefits is equal to or less than $5,000. Previously, the dollar threshold was $3,500 rather than $5,000.

Required communications. Each year the employer must furnish a document called a Summary Plan Description, written in plain English understandable to the average plan participant, detailing the amount of pension benefits, requirements for receiving those payments, and any conditions that might prevent someone from receiving them.

Integration with Social Security. Many companies integrate their pension schemes with Social Security. This integration reduces your employer-provided pension benefit by a percentage of the amount of your Social Security benefit. The employer argues that since it must pay over 7 percent in Social Security taxes and also fund the pension program, without integration it is supporting two pension systems.

However, although a certain degree of integration is allowed by law, an employee must be guaranteed at least 50 percent of the pension he or she earned when social security is merged with the pension.

Example

If your employer-provided pension benefit is $2,000 per month and your Social Security benefit is $1,200 per month, the amount you will actually receive from your employer must be at least $1,400 [$2,000-(50% x $1,200) = $1,400]. Your total monthly income may be as low as $2,600 [$1,200 Social Security + $1,400 pension], not the $3,200 you might have anticipated.

Retirement plans (including Keogh plans) are also divisible into the following broad categories: defined benefit plans, defined contribution plans, and hybrid plans.

Defined Benefit Plans

A defined benefit plan is one set up to provide a predetermined retirement benefit to employees or their beneficiaries, either as a certain dollar amount each month, or a percentage of compensation.

Employer contributions to a defined benefit plan are very complex to determine and require the work of an actuary. The assets of the plan are held in a pool, rather than individual accounts for each employee, and as a result, the employees have no voice in investment decisions. Once the plan is established, the employer must continue to fund it, even if the company has no profits in a given year. Since the employer makes a specific promise to pay a certain sum in the future, it is the employer who assumes the risk of fluctuations in the value of the investment pool.

There are three basic types of defined benefit plans:

- **Flat benefit plan** — All participants receive a flat dollar amount as long as a predetermined minimum years requirement has been met.

Example

A plan might pay 20 percent of average compensation for the last five years, or $500 per month, to each retiree with at least 10 years of service.

- **Unit benefit plan** — The benefit is either a percentage of compensation or a fixed dollar amount multiplied by the number of qualifying years of service.

Example

A plan might provide a benefit of 2 percent of the average compensation of the employee's five highest consecutive years, or a $20 monthly retirement benefit, for each year of service.

- **Variable benefit plan** — Benefits are based on allocating units, rather than dollars, to the contributions to the plan. At retirement, the value of the units allocated to the retiring employee would be the proportionate value of all units in the fund.

The maximum annual contribution you can make to a defined benefit plan is one that would be projected to yield a benefit equal to the lesser of $130,000 (in 1999 – this amount may be adjusted for inflation annually), or 100 percent of the participant's average compensation for the three highest consecutive years.

Very few defined benefit plans provide for the benefits to be adjusted each year to reflect the effects of inflation (called the Cost of Living Adjustment, or COLA), so over the years of your retirement, the value or purchasing power of your benefits may shrink considerably.

The Pension Benefit Guarantee Corporation (PBGC). With a defined benefit plan the employer is legally required to make sure there is enough money in the plan to pay the guaranteed benefits. If the company fails to meet its obligation, the federal government steps in. Defined benefit plans are the only type of pension insured by the PBGC. The insurance works similarly to the federal deposit insurance that backs up your bank accounts. If your plan is covered and the sponsoring company goes bust, PBGC will take over benefit payments up to a maximum amount. The insurance protection helps make your pension more secure, but it is not a full guarantee that you will get what you expected.

Defined Contribution Plans

Defined contribution plans, which are less expensive and more flexible than defined benefit plans, are actually a broad range of programs including profit-sharing plans, money-purchase plans, 401(k) plans, and others. Either you alone, or you and your employee, make contributions into the plan, usually based on a percentage of the employee's annual earnings.

Each participant has an individual, separate account. There is no way to determine in advance what the final payout at retirement will be. Each employee's benefits depend on how much was contributed in his or her name and how well the pension fund investments performed. So, the risk of fluctuations in investment return is shifted to the employees.

The government sets a limit on how much can be contributed in your name each year no matter how many different plans you participate in. The total amount that can be contributed in one employee's name is the lesser of $30,000 or 25 percent of the employee's annual earnings. The limits are somewhat lower for the business owner: $30,000 or 20 percent of annual earnings. The contributions are allocated to separate accounts for each participant based on a definite, predetermined formula. Forfeitures can be reallocated to remaining participants.

Profit-sharing plans. Profit-sharing plans are now the most popular type of plan, especially for small businesses. They offer the greatest flexibility in contributions and are simple to administer. Initially developed to encourage hard work and loyalty, the plans encourage companies to set aside money in the employees' names when the company shows a profit. Each year, the employer has the discretion to contribute up to the lesser of $24,000 or 15 percent of compensation for each plan participant. For yourself, you may contribute up to the lesser of $24,000 or 13.0435 percent of your net earnings. The employer may decide *not* to contribute in any given year, if it so desires.

Money-purchase plans. In a money-purchase plan, the employer is obligated to contribute each year even if the company didn't make a profit. The contributions are determined by a specific percentage of each employee's compensation and must be made annually. The employer may contribute up to the lesser of $30,000 or 25 percent of each employee's compensation up to $160,000; for yourself, you may contribute up to $24,000 or 20 percent of your net earnings up to $160,000.

401(k) plans. Many qualified defined contribution plans permit participating employees to make contributions to a plan, so they can save for retirement on a before-tax basis. The employees authorize their employer to reduce their salary and contribute the salary reduction on their behalf to a qualified retirement plan.

In addition to the employees' elective deferrals, an employer can make supplemental contributions on behalf of employees. These employer contributions can be subject to a vesting schedule, but the employees' own contributions must be nonforfeitable.

The employee's elective deferral to all 401(k) plans is limited to $10,000 (in 1999 – this amount is adjusted annually for inflation), and the employer contribution is also subject to separate, complex limitations. Generally, withdrawals from 401(k) plans are not permitted before age 59^1/$_2$ unless the employee retires, dies, becomes disabled, changes jobs, or suffers a financial hardship as defined by Internal Revenue Service regulations. 401(k) plans are often offered in combination with other plans, such as profit-sharing plans.

Save Money

While 401(k) plans are popular with large corporate employers, they are not the most popular plans for small business owners since they severely limit the amount of money a business owner can sock away on his own behalf. If you're going to the trouble and expense of setting up a pension plan, a money-purchase plan would generally offer you more flexibility and the opportunity to defer tax on a much larger nest egg.

Setting up a Keogh plan

To qualify for tax deductions, the Keogh plan must be in writing and must be communicated to the employees. Most Keogh plans follow a standard form (a master or prototype plan) approved by the Internal Revenue Service, and provided by the bank or financial services company that administers the plan. If you prefer, you can set up an individually-designed plan to meet specific needs, but you will usually need the help of a professional in doing so. You can set up a trust or custodial account to invest the funds, or buy a contract from an insurance company.

Reporting Keogh Contributions

Contributions made for employees to a Keogh are reported on Line 19 of Schedule C, "Pension and profit-sharing plans." Contributions made on your own behalf would be reported on Line 29 of your Form 1040.

There are also reporting requirements with regard to the Keogh plan itself. Generally, an annual report on IRS Form 5500 must be filed with the IRS by the last day of the 7th month after the close of the plan year. Single-participant plans can use form 5500-EZ. See the instructions for these forms (available from the IRS by calling 1-800-TAX-FORM, or at their website http://www.irs.gov) or see your professional tax advisor.

Tax Organizer Tip

Contributions you make for employees should be entered as a business expense, in the "Business Income" tab of the "Employment" section. Contributions made on your own behalf should be entered in the "Retirement" section of the CompleteTax™ Organizer.

Simplified Employee Pensions (SEPs)

A simplified employee pension (SEP) is a written arrangement that allows an employer to make contributions toward his or her own and employees' retirement without becoming involved in more complex retirement plans. The contributions are made to special IRAs (SEP-IRA) set up for each individual qualifying employee.

An employer can use IRS Form 5305-SEP to satisfy the written arrangement requirement for a SEP. A SEP can be established at any time during the year, or up to the original due date of the tax return for the year (April 15th for most people). Contributions to the SEP for a given year must be made by the due date of the income tax return, including any extensions, for that tax year.

If you have a SEP plan in place, you don't have to make any contributions to the plan in any given year. But, if you do make contributions for a year, the contributions must be based on a written allocation formula (for example, "2 percent of each employee's pay") and must not discriminate in favor of highly compensated employees.

The SEP rules permit an employer to contribute, and deduct, an annual maximum of 15 percent of the employee's compensation or $30,000, whichever is less, to each participating employee's account. For the business owner, however, the contribution limit is lower. The business owner's maximum contribution is the net earnings of the business, minus the deduction for one-half the self-employment tax, multiplied by a percentage that is somewhat lower than the percentage used to compute the employees' contribution. For example, if your employees were receiving the maximum contribution of 15 percent of pay, you would have to use 13.0435 percent. If your employees receive 10 percent, your percentage would be 9.0909. You can compute your percentage for other rates by taking the employees' rate, expressed as a decimal, and dividing it by that rate plus one.

Example

If the employees' rate was 10.5 percent, you could compute the owner's rate by dividing 0.105 by 1.105 to arrive at .0950, or 9½ percent.

Prior to 1997, an employer could establish a Salary Reduction Arrangement SEP (SARSEP) under which employees could elect to make contributions out of their own pay, up to a certain dollar limit per year, per employee. This choice is called an elective deferral. Although new SARSEPs can no longer be set up, you may continue to make contributions to a SARSEP that was established before 1997. For 1999, the dollar limit for each employee's elective deferrals is $10,000.

SIMPLE Plans

Employers with 100 or fewer employees who received at least $5,000 in compensation during the preceding year can adopt a relatively new type of simplified retirement plan, the Savings Incentive Match Plan for Employees (SIMPLE plan). If you want to establish a SIMPLE, it must be the only retirement plan you have — if you've already established another plan, you'd have to terminate it or convert it to a SIMPLE.

The plan allows employees to make elective contributions of up to $6,000 per year and requires employers to make matching contributions, up to 3 percent of each employee's pay. Alternately, you can decide to make a blanket contribution of 2 percent of each participating employee's pay regardless of whether they make any elective contributions. *These are the only contributions permitted.* You cannot opt to contribute more for older employees, managers, or the business owner.

Assets in the account are not taxed until they are distributed to an employee, and employers may generally deduct contributions to employees' accounts. In addition, the SIMPLE plan is not subject to the nondiscrimination rules or other complex requirements applicable to qualified plans, mainly because the contributions to each employee's account must follow exactly the same formula.

SIMPLE plans may be structured as an IRA or as a 401(k) plan. Contributions to a SIMPLE account are limited to the employee's elective contributions, up to $6,000 per year plus the required matching (nonelective) contributions by the employer, also up to $6,000 per year (these amounts are adjusted for inflation periodically). All contributions to an employee's SIMPLE account must be nonforfeitable. If a SIMPLE plan is adopted, it must be open to every employee who is reasonably expected to receive at least $5,000 in compensation during the current year and received at least $5,000 in compensation from the employer during any two preceding years. Self-employed individuals are also eligible to establish a SIMPLE plan.

Distributions from a SIMPLE account are generally taxed like distributions from an IRA. Participants may roll over distributions from one SIMPLE account to another free of tax. In addition, a participant may roll over a distribution from a SIMPLE account to an IRA without penalty if the individual has participated in the SIMPLE plan for at least two years. However, distributions may not be rolled over tax-free to another type of qualified plan.

Participants who take early withdrawals from a SIMPLE account before age 59 1/2 are generally subject to the 10 percent early withdrawal penalty. However, employees who withdraw contributions during the two-year period beginning on the date that they first began participating in the SIMPLE plan will be assessed a 25 percent penalty tax.

Deducting SIMPLE Contributions

Contributions for employees to a SIMPLE plan would be reported on Line 19 of your Schedule C, as a "pension and profit sharing plan." Contributions for yourself are reported on Line 29 of your Form 1040. There are also reporting requirements associated with setting up and maintaining the plan itself; see IRS Publication 560, *Retirement Plans for Small Business,* for more details.

Chapter 7

Capital Assets and Depreciation

Almost every business must invest in some major equipment, vehicles, machinery, or furniture in order to operate. Some businesses will require assets such as land, a building, patents, or franchise rights. Major assets that will be used in your business for more than a year are known as "capital assets" and are subject to special treatment under the tax laws. Most importantly, you generally can't deduct the entire cost of acquiring such an asset in the year you acquire it.

Why not? Because one of the goals of accounting is to accurately measure a business's gross income, expenses, and net income (earnings) during a given period of time, usually a year. If a business were allowed to reduce one year's gross income by an expense deduction for the total cost of an item that will be used for several years, the result would be an understatement of earnings in the year the asset was purchased, and an overstatement of earnings during the following years.

It follows that, for "capital assets" (assets that have a useful life of more than one year), the cost must be written off (that is, depreciated or amortized) over more than one year.

Theoretically, the cost of an asset should be deducted over the number of years that the asset will be used, according to the actual drop in value that the asset will suffer each year. At the end of each year, you could subtract all depreciation claimed to date from the cost of the asset, to arrive at the asset's "book value," which would be equal to its market value. At the end of the asset's useful life for the business, any undepreciated portion would represent the salvage value for which the asset could be sold or scrapped.

Since the actual drop in value of each business asset would be difficult and time-consuming to compute (if indeed it could be computed at all), accountants use a variety of conventions to approximate and standardize the depreciation process.

For example, the straight-line method assumes that the asset depreciates by an equal percentage of its original value for each year that it's used. In contrast, the declining balance method assumes that the asset depreciates more in the earlier years. The following table compares the depreciation amounts that would be available under these two methods, for an asset that cost $1,000, and is expected to be used for five years and then sold for $100 in scrap.

	Straight-Line Method		Declining-Balance Method	
Year	Annual Depreciation	Year-End Book Value	Annual Depreciation	Year-End Book Value
1	$900 x 20% = $180	$1,000 - $180 = $820	$1,000 x 40% = $400	$1,000 - $400 = $600
2	$900 x 20% = $180	$820 - $180 = $640	$600 x 40% = $240	$600 - $240 = $360
3	$900 x 20% = $180	$640 - $180 = $460	$360 x 40% = $144	$360 - $144 = $216
4	$900 x 20% = $180	$460 - $180 = $280	$216 x 40% = $86.40	$216 - $86.40 = $129.60
5	$900 x 20% = $180	$280 - $180 = $100	$129.60 x 40% = $51.84	$129.60 - $51.84 = $77.76

As you can see, the straight-line method results in the same deduction amount every year, while the declining-balance method results in larger deductions in the first years and much smaller deductions in the last two years. One implication of this system is that if the equipment is expected to be sold for a higher value at some point in the middle of its life, the declining balance method can result in a greater taxable gain that year because the book value of the asset will be relatively lower.

You Must Follow the Rules

Most people realize that if they claim more depreciation than they're entitled to, they may suffer penalties in a tax audit. What you may not know is that if you *don't* claim all the depreciation deductions that you're entitled to, you will still be treated as having claimed them when it comes time to compute your taxable gain or loss upon sale or disposal of the asset.

In some cases, the IRS gives you a choice between two or more different methods, but you must choose one of them — you can't create your own system.

Example

You can't choose to depreciate your computer over three years, when the IRS mandates a five-year period, even though you may know your particular computer will be obsolete and replaced within three years.

If you make a mistake and claim the wrong depreciation amount, you can generally file an amended tax return (Form 1040X) for the year at issue, and correct your deduction. However, if you make the same mistake for two or more consecutive tax years and the mistake is not a simple math error (for example, you realize that you've been using the wrong table), you've effectively chosen an accounting method, and you cannot correct the mistake by filing an amended return. Instead, you must file IRS Form 3115 requesting permission to change accounting methods.

Tax Organizer Tip

On the "Business Income" screen found in the "Employment" section tab in the CompleteTax™ Organizer, the last question on the screen asks whether you have any business assets. By answering "yes" and clicking on the "Details" button, you'll open a screen that allows you to add tax basis and depreciation information for assets used in your trade or business, including your home office.

Which Assets Can Be Depreciated?

In general, property that you own can be depreciated if it meets all of the following requirements:

- It is used in a trade or business (which is the focus of our discussion here), or held for the production of income as investment property.

- It has a finite period of usefulness in your

business that can be estimated with some confidence, and that is longer than one year.

- It wears out, decays, gets used up, becomes obsolete, or loses value from natural causes.

Examples of depreciable assets are cars, computers, office furniture, machines, buildings, and significant additions or improvements to these kinds of property.

See page 59 regarding the distinction between improvements, which must be depreciated, and repairs, which can be fully deducted when made.

Which Assets Are Not Depreciable?

Land is probably the most commonly encountered property that is *not* depreciable. As a rule you can only "recover" the cost of land when you eventually sell it, at which point you'll subtract the cost from the sales price to determine your taxable gain. So, when you purchase a business building and the land on which the building is situated, the cost of the land must be subtracted from the total cost of the property. Only then can you determine the depreciation expense for the building itself.

The costs of clearing, grading, planting, landscaping, or demolishing buildings on land are not depreciable, but are added to the tax basis of the land, so they can reduce your taxable gains on the property when it comes time to sell.

Depreciation is not allowed on personal assets, such as a residence used by you and your family, or an automobile or boat used for pleasure purposes only. If an asset is used partly for personal purposes and partly for business, only the portion of the asset used for business purposes is depreciable.

Other items that are not depreciable are inventory and property you lease or rent from others. However, if you pay for some permanent improvements on property that you lease (for example, you remodel your leased office or store), you can depreciate the cost of the improvements.

Amortizable Assets

Some business assets are not depreciable, but the costs can be recovered through amortization; that is, they can be deducted in a series of equal amounts over a specified period of time. An example of this is the cost of starting your business, which can be deducted over a period of 60 months after the business begins to operate (see page 61).

Intangible assets purchased after August 10, 1993, including agreements not to compete, franchise rights, business licenses, and patents, copyrights, trademarks, trade names, business goodwill, and going concern value that are acquired as part of the acquisition of a substantial portion of a business, must be amortized over the course of 15 years. Most intangible assets acquired before that date cannot be amortized at all; others, such as patents and copyrights, agreements not to compete, designs and patterns, franchises, and customer or subscriber lists, must be depreciated using the straight-line method over their useful life.

Off-the-shelf computer software purchased after August 10, 1993 must be amortized over 36 months from the date of purchase. Customized software purchased after that date must be amortized over a 15-year period. For software purchased before August 11, 1993, if it was purchased as part of a computer, the software should have been treated as part of the computer and depreciated as a single asset; if you purchased the software separately you could depreciate it using the straight-line method over five years (or a shorter period if you could prove that its usefulness was less than five years).

As a general rule, any intangible assets created by your business (rather than purchased from someone else) cannot be depreciated or amortized.

DEPRECIABLE VALUE OF AN ASSET

The starting point to determine how much depreciation you can claim on a business asset is a value for the asset known as its "tax basis." Usually, the tax basis is equal to the asset's purchase price, minus any discounts and plus any sales taxes, delivery charges, installation fees, or other acquisition costs.

Example

If you bought a piece of machinery priced at $1,000, you paid 8 percent in sales tax, and it cost $200 to deliver the item, the tax basis would be $1,280 *and that's the amount that you could write off as depreciation over the life of the asset.*

For real estate, you can also include costs of legal and accounting fees, revenue stamps, recording fees, title abstracts/insurance, surveys, and real estate taxes assumed for the seller. Some special rules apply where you trade in business equipment; see page 103.

If you acquire property by gift, the tax basis for depreciation will be the same as the donor's basis at the time of the gift.

If you convert personal property to business use, the basis will be the *lower* of (a) the fair market value at the time of the conversion, or (b) the cost plus any additions or improvements, and minus any deducted casualty losses, up to the time of the conversion.

Partly Depreciable Assets

Things aren't always so simple. What if, for a single purchase price, you purchase an asset that is only partly depreciable? What you need to do is to allocate the price between the depreciable part and the nondepreciable part.

Example

Raymond Anthony buys some real estate for use in his auto repair business for $100,000. On the lot is a building that was formerly used as a gas station. Considering the size and location of the property, and the size and repair of the building, a fair allocation of the price paid for the property might be $70,000 for the building and $30,000 for the land.

In this example, the $70,000 paid for the building could be recovered through depreciation, while the $30,000 paid for the land could not, because land is not depreciable. But wouldn't it be better to allocate as much as possible to the building (say, $90,000), so Ray's depreciation deductions would be greater and his tax bill would be lower?

Absolutely, but you can expect the IRS to attack your allocation if it doesn't reflect economic reality.

If an IRS auditor raises objections, you may need to bring in a real estate appraisal to support the allocation you use. In some states, real estate tax bills will show a separate assessment for the buildings and the land on a piece of property, which can be useful evidence in an IRS audit. Ideally, the allocation should have been made as part of the sales contract in which you originally acquired the property, and you should be prepared to prove that the allocation was a part of good faith negotiations between yourself and the seller.

If you acquire a number of assets at the same time (for example, you acquire a number of business assets in the course of buying a business), you need to allocate the purchase price among the various assets you purchased. The IRS provides special rules for doing this — consult your tax advisor for more details.

Mixed-Use Property

You also need to make an allocation if you have a single asset that is used partly for business and partly for personal purposes; for example, if you have a home office, or a car that you use sometimes for work and sometimes for family driving.

You will need to allocate the cost of the asset according to the percentage of usage that is strictly for business. For example, if 20 percent of the square footage of your home is used as an office, you may be able to depreciate 20 percent of the cost of the home (see page 84); if 60 percent of the mileage you drive in your car is for business purposes, you may be able to depreciate 60 percent of the cost of the car (see page 113).

For other business assets, the allocation would ordinarily be based on the amount of time you used the asset for business, compared to the amount of time you used it for personal or family purposes.

Example

Although you don't qualify for the home office deduction, you have a computer at home on which you keep a backup copy of your accounting records, and which you use for other business purposes in the evenings. You also use the computer to keep track of your investments, surf the Internet, send and receive social E-mail, etc. Your computer time log (see page 113) shows that you've spent approximately 10 hours per week on the computer for business reasons, and approximately 5 hours per week for other purposes. Therefore, you can depreciate 2/3 of the cost of the computer.

Adjustments to the Basis

If, like most taxpayers, you use the standard depreciation charts to compute your depreciation expense each year, your tax basis for the asset at the time you begin depreciating it will generally remain the same. You will multiply your original basis by a fraction that may change each year. For an example of how this works, see page 110.

In addition to the *original* basis of the asset, you may also need to know your *adjusted* basis if you sell, trade or dispose of the asset, or suffer a casualty loss.

Once you've claimed some depreciation on a piece of business property, the depreciation would be deducted from the cost to arrive at the adjusted basis. It's important that you (or your accountant) keep capital asset records that include the amount of accumulated depreciation you've claimed for each asset over the years, so you can easily compute the adjusted basis when the need arises. You can use the depreciation worksheet on page 104 to keep track of your tax basis over time. These records should be retained as long as you own the asset.

Other events that can require an adjustment to the basis are casualty losses for which you've claimed a tax deduction, or additions or improvements to the property. You'll need to keep a record of these items, too, and save them until you eventually dispose of the property.

When you file your tax return, additions or improvements are treated like separate, depreciable assets that have the same depreciation period as the underlying property. However, when the underlying property is sold, any undepreciated value of the additions or improvements must be added to the asset's tax basis to compute your taxable gains. For more on sales of capital assets, see page 116.

Casualty loss deductions (see page 267) *are* subtracted from your adjusted tax basis in the property as of the year the loss occurred. Once you have a deductible casualty loss, you must use the new, adjusted basis of the property, instead of the original basis, for depreciation purposes. What's more, you can no longer use the tables to compute your depreciation expense. Instead, you'll have to use the actual formulas on which the tables are based. Consult your tax advisor or the IRS's free Publication 946, *How to Depreciate Property*, for details on how this is done.

Effect of Trade-In on Basis

If you trade in some business equipment that was used 100 percent for business for new business equipment of the same asset category, the transaction will not be a taxable event because it will be treated as a "like-kind exchange," as discussed on page 116.

However, the tax basis of the new equipment will be equivalent to the adjusted basis of the old equipment, plus any additional cash you paid for the new equipment. This tax basis represents the maximum amount you can claim as depreciation for the item for tax purposes.

If you trade in a *vehicle* that was used partly for business for another vehicle that will be used in your business, you must use the following computation to determine the tax basis of the replacement vehicle. (For cars acquired before June 19, 1984, consult your tax advisor for the proper method to use.)

The basis for figuring depreciation for the replacement vehicle is:

1. the adjusted basis of the old vehicle, plus

2. any extra amount paid for the replacement vehicle, minus

3. the excess, if any, of the total amount of depreciation that would have been allowable during the years before the trade if 100 percent of the use of the vehicle had been business and investment use, divided by the total amounts actually allowable as depreciation during those years.

To see how this would work, check out the case study that follows.

WRITING OFF ASSETS IN THE FIRST YEAR

As we've been saying, you normally can't take a current business deduction for the entire cost of a capital asset in the year you purchase it, because the asset's usefulness to your business will extend beyond the year of purchase. However, there is an important exception to this rule for small businesses.

Depreciation Worksheet

Description of Property	Date Placed in Service	Cost or Other Basis	Business/ Investment Use %	Section 179 Deduction	Depreciation Prior Years	Basis for Depreciation	Method/ Convention	Recovery Period	Rate or Table %	Depreciation Deduction

Case Study

On August 5, 1995, Sally Fox purchased a car for $9,000. On June 1, 1999, she purchased a new car for $21,500. She was allowed a $2,000 trade-in on the old car and financed the remaining $19,500. Assume depreciation claimed on the old car was $7,200, based on 80 percent business use over those years. Assume further that if the car had been used 100 percent for business reasons, the allowable depreciation would have been $9,000. The basis of the new car for depreciation purposes is computed as follows:

Cost of old car		$9,000
Less: depreciation claimed		– 7,200
Adjusted basis of old car		$1,800
Plus: additional amount paid		+19,500
Total		$21,300
Less:		
Depreciation assuming 100 percent business use	$9,000	
Less: depreciation actually allowable	– 7,200	– 1,800
Adjusted basis of new car		$19,500

A special tax provision allows you the option of claiming a deduction in the first year for the entire cost of qualifying business assets, up to $19,000. If you fully qualify for this deduction, known as the expensing deduction or Section 179 deduction, you can get what amounts to a significant, up-front reduction in the out-of-pocket cost of a needed piece of business equipment.

Example

For 1999, if you are a sole proprietor in the 28 percent tax bracket, the net after-tax cost of buying a $19,000 piece of machinery is reduced to $13,680.

If you want to make use of this election, you must do so on your original tax return for the period, on Form 4562, or on an amended tax return filed before the due date for your original return (including any extensions). If you don't claim it, you cannot change your mind later by filing an amended tax return after the due date.

What Qualifies for the Election?

To qualify for this expensing election, the property that you purchase must be tangible personal property: that is, property other than real estate that can be seen or touched, such as a typewriter, chair, or desk. This includes property that is not a building or a structural component of a building, but is an integral part of manufacturing, production, or extraction, or of furnishing transportation, communications, electricity, gas, water, or sewage disposal services; or a research or storage facility used in connection with any of these processes. It can also be a single-purpose livestock or horticultural structure, or a petroleum products storage facility that is not a building.

An air conditioning or heating unit doesn't qualify, nor does intangible property such as a patent, contract right, stock or bond, etc. To qualify, the property must be something that you actively use in your business, for which a depreciation deduction would be allowed. The property must have been purchased specifically for your business, whether it is new or used — property that you previously owned but recently converted to business use does not qualify. Also, property you acquired by gift or inheritance does not qualify, nor does property you acquired from related persons such as your spouse, child, parent, some other ancestor or descendent, or another business with common ownership.

The property must be used more than 50 percent for business. If you want to expense property that will be used partly for personal or family reasons (e.g., a home computer that you use for business only 75 percent of the time), you can expense only the portion of the property's tax basis that corresponds to its percentage of business use.

Warning

If, in any year after the year you claimed the expensing election, you either sell the property or stop using it more than 50 percent in your business, you may have to recapture or "give back" part of the tax benefits that you previously claimed. The recaptured amount is equal to the difference between the amount you expensed, and the amount you would have been able to depreciate under the normal rules. See page 108 for instructions on how to do this.

So, if you think you'll only be using the equipment for a year or two, it may be better to forego the expensing election and avoid the recapture problem.

Annual Deduction Limit

The maximum amount that can be expensed each year is subject to a ceiling amount of $19,000 in 1999. This dollar amount is scheduled to increase over the next few years:

1999.	$19,000
2000.	$20,000
2001 and 2002	$24,000
2003 and thereafter. . .	$25,000

If the cost of all qualified property placed in service by a business during the year is more than $200,000, the ceiling for that business is reduced by the amount over $200,000. This limit is intended to keep the expensing election targeted toward small businesses.

Example

In 1999, Bobscarts, Inc., a company that manufactures electric golf carts, purchases for $205,000 a machine to be used in its business. Bobscarts would be able to expense $14,000 of the cost of the machine ($19,000 - [$205,000 - $200,000]).

Empowerment zone businesses. If substantially all of the property's use is in a trade or business located in an empowerment zone, the annual deduction limit is $39,000 for 1999. Some special requirements will apply, so consult your tax advisor or IRS Publication 946, *How To Depreciate Property*, if you think this higher limit might apply to you.

Equipment Over the Limit

If you purchased equipment that exceeds the $19,000 limit, you can depreciate the excess amount under the usual rules.

Example

Say that you purchased a full suite of office furniture for $25,000 in 1999, and this was your only capital expense for the year. You could expense $19,000 of the cost in 1999, which would leave a remaining balance of $6,000. You could then depreciate the $6,000 over seven years, yielding a 1999 depreciation deduction of $857.40.

Your total write-off for the furniture in 1999 would be $19,000 + $857.40 = $19,857.40.

If your equipment purchases for the year exceed the expensing dollar limit, you can decide to split your expensing election among the new assets any way you choose.

Save Money

Generally speaking, where you have a choice, it's best to expense those assets with the longest depreciation periods (e.g., seven-year property), so you can claim a quicker write-off for them. If the asset has a shorter depreciation period (e.g., three-year property), expensing it in the first year is not going to make as much of a difference. See page 110 for more on the depreciation periods that apply to various assets.

Special Rules for Cars

For many small business owners, the only time they would even approach the $19,000 limit would be the year they purchase a new car. But as fate would have it, there is a special rule that prevents you from deducting the full $19,000. Generally, for cars, the amount that may be expensed under the special write-off election is limited to $3,060 for vehicles placed in service in 1999 (this amount increases periodically because of inflation). For more details on depreciating your car, see page 112.

Timing Your Purchases

As long as you start using your newly purchased business equipment before the end of the tax year, you get the entire expensing deduction for that year, whether you started using the equipment in January or on December 31st. The amount that can be expensed depends upon the date the qualifying property is placed in service, not when it's purchased or paid for.

Save Money

If, towards the end of your tax year, you're thinking about purchasing equipment that you can expense, you may do well to complete the purchase and start using the property before the end of the year if you can benefit from deducting the property's cost on your current year's tax return.

However, if you expect your taxable income to be much higher in the following year, you may want to hold off on the new equipment until the beginning of the next tax year.

Business Income Limitation

The total cost of property that may be expensed for any tax year cannot be higher than the total amount of taxable income that you get from the active conduct of any trade or business, including any salary or wages from other jobs you (or your spouse) may have.

So, if your business is facing a loss, you might not get the full benefit of the expensing provision. Costs that can't be deducted because of this limit can be carried forward to future years, so the fact that this income limitation rule knocks out a portion of your expensing deduction does not mean that it is permanently lost.

Work Smart

The way in which taxable income is computed under the expensing rules may especially benefit a small business owner who operates the business in either an unincorporated form (a sole proprietorship or partnership) or as an S corporation. This is because in determining the taxable income limit of such taxpayers, all wages and income are included — even those from another job or a separate business activity. Married business owners filing joint returns can also count their spouses' wages and business income.

Sharing the Election

Allocation rules determine how the benefits of the expensing deduction are to be split up between spouses, certain related corporations, partnerships and their partners, and S corporations and their shareholders. These rules are designed to make sure that a purchase of business equipment in a particular year cannot be used by related parties to gain more than the total allowed for expense deductions.

- **Married taxpayers filing separate returns** — For purposes of the expensing amount ceiling, they are treated as one taxpayer. Unless they elect otherwise, 50 percent of the cost of the property is allocated to each spouse.

- **Related corporations** — If you operate your business as a corporation that controls other corporations, the corporations will be limited to one total deduction amount for business property purchased.

- **Partnerships and S corporations** — The deduction limit applies separately to the partnership or S corporation itself and to each partner or S corporation shareholder.

Example

In 1999, Sam Smith and Linda Lane form a partnership to operate a bakery. The partnership buys an oven and a refrigerator for a total cost of $20,000. In addition, Lane also enters into a separate business venture, a flower shop, by herself, for which she buys $3,000 worth of equipment.

Assuming the partnership has taxable income that exceeds $19,000, it can elect to expense up to $19,000 of the cost of the oven and refrigerator. If it does so, *each partner's share of the expensing deduction is $9,500. In addition, Lane can elect to expense the entire $3,000 cost of her equipment, assuming her taxable income derived from the flower shop exceeds $3,000.*

Recapturing the Expensed Amount

Remember that to claim the expensing election for a piece of property, you must use the property more than 50 percent for business purposes. If your business usage drops below 51 percent during some year before the ordinary depreciation period for this property ends (see the chart on page 110), you will have to "give back" or recapture some of the amount you expensed.

To figure the recaptured amount, compare the amount you expensed, and the total amount you would have been entitled to deduct so far under the quickest depreciation method allowed for that type of property (see page 109). If the amount you expensed was greater, the difference between the two amounts must be reported as ordinary income.

The recapture is reported on IRS Form 4797, *Sales of Business Property*, in Part IV at the end of the second page. If the property was listed property, use Column

(b) of Lines 33 through 35. If not, use Column (a). See the case study below for an illustration of how this works.

WHEN DOES DEPRECIATION BEGIN?

Your depreciation or expensing election deductions for a piece of property begin in the tax year in which you place it in service.

That means that just buying a piece of depreciable property is not enough: In order to claim a depreciation deduction for the property in 1999, you must have put it to some productive use in your business before the end of the year.

If you are using the expensing election, the timing doesn't matter much; as long as you began using the property before the end of the year, you get the entire deduction.

But if you have property that's not eligible for the $19,000 expensing election described above (for example, your home office or other business real estate, or the portion of business equipment that exceeds $19,000), the date on which you placed the

---

Case Study

In 1997, John Aboud purchased a new computer to use for in his startup boat chartering business, and expensed 75 percent of the $3,000 cost in the year of purchase. He used the computer 75 percent for business in 1997 and 1998. In July of 1999, John decided to buy a new business computer and retired the old one to his family room, to be used for business purposes only 10 percent of the time. Since John's computer was "listed property" (see page 112), his allowable depreciation must be computed using the straight-line method, over a five-year recovery period. John's recapture amount would be computed as follows:

Section 179 expensing election:	$3,000 x .75 =		**$2,250**
Allowable depreciation:			
1997:	$3,000 x .75 x .10 =	$225	
1998:	$3,000 x .75 x .20 =	$450	
1999:	$3,000 x .10 x .20 =	$ 60	**$ 735**
1999 recapture amount:			**$1,515**

John would report the amounts in bold in Column (b), Lines 33-35, of his IRS Form 4797, *Sales of Business Property*.

---

property in service and the total amount of property placed in service during the year are the two factors that determine how much of a full year's deduction you will get for the first year. If you sell or dispose of the property within the year you got it, you can't claim a depreciation deduction at all.

Mid-Month Convention

Nonresidential real estate, a classification that includes home offices, is treated as being placed in service in the middle of the month in which you actually placed it in service. You will get a deduction for half of that month, plus the rest of the months for the remainder of the year. This principle (known as the mid-month convention) is factored into the depreciation tables used for this type of property (see Table A-7a, page 129).

Half-Year Convention

For most depreciable property other than real estate, no matter what month of the year you begin using the property, you treat it as if you began using it in the middle of the year. So, you will generally get one-half of the first year's depreciation, regardless of when you placed the property in service. Again, this principle (known as the half-year convention) is factored into the depreciation tables used for most depreciable property (see Table A-1, page 126).

Mid-Quarter Convention

However, there's an important exception to the half-year convention described above. Think of it this way: If Uncle Sam were going to give you a half year's tax break for a purchase made *any time in the year*, what would keep you from routinely purchasing all your business assets and starting to use them in the final days of December?

Presumably, that would allow you to get a deduction for a half-year's worth of depreciation, while avoiding any actual cash outlay until late in the year. Good deal? You bet! Unfortunately, the IRS is well aware of this strategy, and has imposed some special rules to prevent you from using it.

These rules, called the mid-quarter convention rules, apply if you place more than 40 percent of your total new property for the year into service in the last quarter. If you do, you will have to use these rules for all assets placed in service during the year. Under the

mid-quarter rules, assets are considered to be placed in service at the midpoint of the quarter in which they were actually placed in service. So, for the first year, depending on which quarter in which you placed the asset in service, you would get the following portions of a full year's depreciation:

First quarter:	87.5%
Second quarter:	62.5%
Third quarter:	37.5%
Fourth quarter:	12.5%

Don't worry about having to use these percentages – they are factored into the depreciation charts used for mid-quarter property, on pages 126-128.

If you want to avoid the mid-quarter rule, you can't be too aggressive about placing a lot of property in service late in the year. However, there may be times when using the mid-quarter convention can work to your advantage. If you place a large, expensive asset in service in the first quarter, you may be able to claim more depreciation by placing slightly more than 40 percent of new assets in service in the last quarter.

Example

If you placed five-year assets with a total value of $10,000 in service at various points during the year, but no more than $4,000 in assets were placed in service in the fourth quarter, you'd ordinarily be able to claim a total of $10,000 x .20 = $2,000 in the first year.

If, however, $5,999 in assets were placed in service in the first quarter and $4,001 in the fourth quarter, your depreciation deduction would be ($5,999 x .35) + ($4,001 x .05), which equals $2,099.65 + $200.05 for a total deduction of $2,300 in the first year.

DEPRECIATION METHODS

The depreciation method that you use for any particular asset is fixed at the time you first place that asset into service. Whatever rules or tables are in effect for that year must be followed as long as you own the property. Since Congress has changed the

Class of Property	Items Included
3-year property	Tractor units, racehorses over two years old, and horses over 12 years old when placed in service.
5-year property	Automobiles, taxis, buses, trucks, computers and peripheral equipment, office machinery (faxes, copiers, calculators etc.), and any property used in research and experimentation. Also includes breeding and dairy cattle.
7-year property	Office furniture and fixtures, and any property that has not been designated as belonging to another class.
10-year property	Vessels, barges, tugs, similar water transportation equipment, single-purpose agricultural or horticultural structures, and trees or vines bearing fruit or nuts.
15-year property	Depreciable improvements to land such as shrubbery, fences, roads, and bridges.
20-year property	Farm buildings that are not agricultural or horticultural structures.
27.5-year property	Residential rental property.
39-year property	Nonresidential real estate, including home offices. (Note: the value of land may not be depreciated.)

depreciation rules many times over the years, you may have to use a number of different depreciation methods if you've owned business property for a long time.

For most business property placed in service after 1986, if you don't claim the equipment expensing deduction for the full cost of the item, the IRS requires you to depreciate the asset using a method called "MACRS," which stands for Modified Accelerated Cost Recovery System. This method categorizes all business assets into classes and specifies the time period over which you can write off assets in each class. The most commonly used items are classified as shown in the chart above. Some assets are not eligible for MACRS depreciation, including intangible assets such as patents, trademarks, and business goodwill. Generally these must be written off in equal amounts over a 15-year period, beginning in the month of acquisition (see page 116). Off-the-shelf computer software must be amortized over 36 months.

Once you know the classification and the tax basis of the asset you need to depreciate (see page 101), you can use a special table provided by the IRS to determine the percentage of the item's tax basis that can be deducted each year. MACRS provides for a slightly larger write-off in the earlier years of the cost recovery period. We include the most commonly used depreciation tables beginning on page 126.

Example

As an example, the following chart shows the depreciation amounts under MACRS for office furniture purchased in 1999 for $10,000, and used 100 percent for business. The amounts in the third column are taken from the MACRS half-year convention table, which is the one most commonly used.

Year	Basis x	Percent =	Deduction
1999	$10,000	14.29%	$1,429
2000	10,000	24.49%	2,449
2001	10,000	17.49%	1,749
2002	10,000	12.49%	1,249
2003	10,000	8.93%	893
2004	10,000	8.92%	892
2005	10,000	8.93%	893
2006	10,000	4.46%	446

Notice that the asset's tax basis does not change over the years – only the percentage used as a multiplier changes each year.

If you do not use the asset 100 percent for business, then each year you must multiply the asset's total tax basis by the business percentage for that year, and then multiply the result by the fraction found in the table.

Example

If, in 2000, you use the office furniture from the previous example only 50% for your business, you would multiple the $10,000 tax basis by .50, and then multiply the result by .2449 to get your final depreciation figure.

Groups of Assets

If you place more than one asset of the same type into service during the year, and the assets are in the same class, with the same recovery period, and use the same depreciation method, you can elect to group the assets into a "general asset account." For example, if you purchase five computers to use in your business in 2000, you can create a general asset account for them.

This basically means that you will treat them as a single asset for depreciation purposes. You can only do this for assets that are used 100% for business in the first year you place them into service.

Warning

Although the general asset account can simplify your recordkeeping, it can also cause problems if you sell one, but not all, of the assets in the group before the end of the recovery period. In that case you might have to recognize the full amount of the sales price as ordinary income (not the sales price minus the tax basis of the item, as in the usual case). You would continue to depreciate the entire group of assets for the remainder of the class life, including the computer you've already sold.

Be sure to check with your tax advisor if you think you want to use a general asset account for large, relatively expensive assets.

Variations on MACRS

The MACRS charts we've provided on pages 126-129 are the most commonly used and generally the most favorable to taxpayers, because they provide for the largest possible deductions in the earliest years. However, you do have the option of using slower depreciation methods.

While normal MACRS uses a 200 percent declining balance method for 3-, 5-, 7- and 10- year property, there is also a 150 percent declining balance method that is available as an option for most business owners, and that *must* be used for all farm property, and for all nonfarm property in the 15- and 20-year property classes. Charts for this method begin on page 129. Most often the 150 percent declining balance method is used for the same recovery periods as normal MACRS, but you do have the option of using the longer ADS recovery periods as described below.

Normal MACRS uses a straight-line method for real estate, which is property in the 27.5- or 39-year class. However, you can also choose to use straight-line depreciation for any other property, if you wish.

Warning

Generally, if you exercise your option to use any of the variations of MACRS you must use it for all assets of the same class that you placed in service during the year. Once you make the election you cannot change it.

Alternative Depreciation System

There is also an alternative MACRS system known as ADS, under which depreciation is deducted over generally longer periods than under regular MACRS, using the straight-line method. The chart beginning on page 133 compares the depreciation periods for various classes of property under the ADS system and MACRS.

The ADS straight-line method must be used in certain situations when normal MACRS is not available; for example, if you've used the Standard Mileage Rate method of deducting vehicle expenses and want to switch to the actual cost method in a later year (see page 66). ADS must also be used if your business use of "listed property" drops to 50 percent or less for a year (see page 113).

For property purchased before 1999, the ADS system *must* be used to compute your alternative minimum tax (AMT) liability, if you're unlucky enough to have to worry about the AMT (see page 301). Taxpayers who have paid or are likely to pay AMT will need to maintain depreciation records under both the alternative system and the regular MACRS. The depreciation tables that must be used for AMT purposes are reproduced beginning on page 130.

Save Time

Things will get a little simpler in the future. For depreciable real estate placed into service in 1999 or later, you will be able to use the same depreciation allowable under MACRS even if you are subject to the AMT, so you no longer have to maintain two sets of records. For non-real estate property purchased in 1999 or later, you may use the MACRS recovery periods for AMT purposes but must use a slower recovery method; namely, either the straight-line or the 150 percent declining balance method, rather than the 200 percent declining balance method.

So, if you think you're likely to be subject to the AMT, you may want to avoid purchasing any new business property at the end of the year. If you can wait until 1999, your depreciation records will be greatly simplified.

You can elect to use the slower ADS depreciation even if you are not required to use it by law; for example, if you want your earnings to appear larger on your income statement, you might opt to use ADS for any new property you purchase because it will result in lower depreciation deductions. However, if you begin depreciating a particular asset using ADS, you must continue using it for the life of the asset — you can never switch back to the ordinary MACRS system. Also, if you elect this method for one item in an asset class, you must use it for all assets of that class that you placed into service that year, unless the asset is real estate.

Pre-1987 Property

If you began operating your business before 1987, you might be using some assets that were put into service before that year. If so, you'll have to continue to use a set of depreciation methods known as "ACRS," which stands for Accelerated Cost Recovery System.

ACRS used shorter recovery periods for most assets

than those currently in use under MACRS. Personal property was classified as 3-year (cars, trucks, racehorses, tractors); 5-year (computers, copiers, equipment, furniture, petroleum storage facilities, single-purpose horticultural and agricultural buildings); or 10-year (theme-park structures, public utility property, manufactured homes and railroad tank cars). The normal ACRS recovery periods for property of these types purchased before 1987 would already have expired, unless a longer period was elected.

Under ACRS, real estate is depreciable over 15 years if placed into service after 1980 but before March 16, 1984; over 18 years if placed into service on or after March 16, 1984 but before May 9, 1985; and over 19 years if placed into service on or after May 9, 1985 through the end of 1986.

To find the depreciation deduction for any of these properties, get a copy of IRS Publication 534, *Depreciating Property Placed in Service Before 1987*, which you can obtain for no charge by calling 1-800-TAX-FORM, or download it from the IRS website at http://www.irs.ustreas.gov.

Even Older Methods

For property placed into service before 1981, you could generally use any reasonable method for depreciating property based on its tax basis, useful life, and salvage value. If you still hold such property and it is not yet fully depreciated, you must continue to use the same method you've established in previous years, or get IRS permission to change your accounting method by filing IRS Form 3115. There is an exception to this rule if you want to change to a straight-line method; in that case, you generally don't need advance permission, although you must attach a statement to your tax return that explains what you're doing. See IRS Publication 534, *Depreciating Property Placed in Service Before 1987*, for more details.

CARS AND OTHER LISTED PROPERTY

Certain types of business property are called "listed property" and are subject to even more depreciation rules and regulations.

Listed property includes:

- cars and other vehicles (but not those over 14,000 pounds, or those that are unlikely to be used for personal purposes because of their design such as construction vehicles, moving vans, tractors etc.)

- cellular phones

- equipment that's normally used for entertainment or recreation such as photographic, audio, communication, and video recording equipment

- computers and peripherals *unless* they are used at a regular business establishment, including an office that qualifies for the home office deduction, and are owned or leased by the business operator

- significant additions or improvements to listed property

Generally, your business use of listed property must exceed 50 percent in order for you to take the special expensing election or to depreciate the property under MACRS. Otherwise, you must use straight-line depreciation under the ADS method, using the appropriate ADS class lives for the items. Depreciation charts for this method are included at page 130, and the class life chart is at page 133.

Warning

Commuting to work is not considered "business use" of the car, even if you do work while driving such as calling customers or dictating letters.

If your employees use your car, you can count as "business use" any mileage they drive for business purposes, plus other mileage if the value of the car's use is treated as compensation to the employees. See page 64 for more on which trips are considered "business use."

If your business use drops below 51 percent in any year after the first year you use the property in your business, but before the property's depreciation period expires, you may have to pay back some of the excess depreciation you claimed.

Specifically, you'll have to treat the difference between the ADS depreciation and the depreciation you actually claimed (including any amount you expensed in the first year) as ordinary income in the first year you no longer use the asset more than 50 percent for business. For an example of how this would work, see the Case Study on page 108.

And, as you might guess, you'll have to keep records showing that your business usage was at least 51 percent of total usage of the property. This means that you should keep a log showing each time the property was used, for how long, and for what purpose.

For cars, your mileage records (see page 21) will generally suffice. For computers, cameras, audio/video equipment etc., you should keep a log noting the date, length of time, and purpose for each use of the item. Personal or family use can simply be designated "personal" but business use should show enough detail to enable you to prove the relationship to your work, if necessary in an audit.

Depreciation Limits for Passenger Cars

While the expensing limit for general business property is $19,000 in 1999, the limit for cars is much lower: $3,060 is the maximum amount of depreciation of any type that can be written off in the first year. This limit does periodically increase to reflect inflation.

The maximum amounts that may be deducted under the MACRS depreciation method (ACRS for cars placed in service before 1987), and/or under the Section 179 expensing election for the first year, are known as the "luxury car limitations," although in reality they apply to cars valued at more than approximately $15,800 in 1999. They are provided by the IRS in the form of a chart, reproduced below.

Note that the maximum annual amounts shown in the chart assume that the vehicle was used 100 percent for business. The amounts must be proportionately reduced if your business use of the vehicle was less than 100 percent.

Year Placed in Service	Depreciation Allowable in—			
	Year 1	Year 2	Year 3	Year 4 and later years
4/3/85 through 1986	3,200	4,800	4,800	4,800
1987 and 1988	2,560	4,100	2,450	1,475
1989 and 1990	2,660	4,200	2,550	1,475
1991	2,660	4,300	2,550	1,575
1992	2,760	4,400	2,650	1,575
1993	2,860	4,600	2,750	1,675
1994	2,960	4,700	2,850	1,675
1995 and 1996	3,060	4,900	2,950	1,775
1997	3,160	5,000	3,050	1,775
1998	3,160	5,000	2,950	1,775
1999	3,060	5,000	2,950	1,775

Example

In 1999, you purchased a new car. Sixty percent of the mileage you drove during the year was for business purposes. So, your maximum depreciation deduction for the first year would be $3,060 x .60 = $1,836.

This table represents the *maximum* depreciation you can claim. For the first year, if you used the car more than 50 percent for business, you may claim a proportionate part of the full amount, regardless of the actual cost of the car.

For later years, you must compute your depreciation on the car using the usual methods, but can't deduct more than the amount shown in the chart. As long as you continue to use the car more than 50 percent for business, you would multiply the business percentage of the car's cost by the percentage shown in the MACRS table for five-year property. The dollar amounts in the chart above, reduced proportionately for any non-business use of the car, acts as a ceiling on the amount of depreciation you can actually claim.

If you use the car 50 percent or less for business, you must use the straight-line ADS method for five-year property for that year, and for every subsequent year.

If you started out depreciating the car under MACRS, but then your business use dropped to 50 percent or less which required you to switch to the straight-line ADS method, you will have to "give back" some of the depreciation you claimed. Specifically, you'll have to report as income the amount (if any) by which the total MACRS depreciation you claimed is greater than the total straight-line depreciation you would have been entitled to claim.

Save Money

If you use a van, truck, or sport-utility vehicle that weighs over 6,000 pounds in your business, it is not subject to the annual depreciation dollar caps or the annual lease income inclusion rules. In addition, the luxury car excise tax does not apply to these types of vehicles.

If you own a relatively lower-priced car (e.g., one that cost less than $15,800 in 1998 or $15,500 in 1999), you can expect to recover the entire basis of the business portion of the car over the six tax years for which the MACRS depreciation deductions are generally claimed.

However, when part of the normal MACRS deduction is disallowed because of the luxury car limitations, you'll recover only a portion of the car's basis during the normal recovery period. In that case, you may continue to depreciate the car for as long as it takes to recover the remaining basis *of the business portion* of the car.

WHEN DOES DEPRECIATION END?

Whatever method you use, you must stop claiming depreciation when the total amount of depreciation you've claimed over the years is equal to your original cost or other basis for the asset, or when you stop using the asset in your business.

Warning

One of the more common mistakes business owners make is to continue depreciating property beyond the end of its recovery period. This is not permitted, except in the case of "luxury cars" where the dollar limits prevented you from claiming the full depreciation amounts within six years after the car's purchase.

If the asset is sold, scrapped, or otherwise disposed of, you can claim a depreciation deduction for the year of disposal, based on the depreciation convention you used. For example, if you were using the usual MACRS method, which includes a half-year convention, you're treated as owning the asset for half of the final year and can claim a half-year's depreciation; if you were using the mid-month or mid-quarter convention, you're treated as owning the asset until mid-way through the month or quarter in which you stopped using it.

CLAIMING YOUR DEPRECIATION DEDUCTIONS

In most cases, your depreciation deductions will be entered on Form 4562, *Depreciation and Amortization*, and then the total amount will be carried over to Line 13 of your Schedule C.

You must file a Form 4562 for the first year you claim depreciation or amortization on any particular piece of property, for any year you claim a Section 179 expensing election (including an amount carried over from a previous year), and for every year you claim depreciation on a car or other vehicle or on any other type of listed property (see page 112). You don't have to file this form if you are simply claiming continued depreciation on property that is not considered listed property, or if you are claiming auto expenses based on the Standard Mileage Rate.

Do not combine depreciation expenses for more than one business or investment activity on the same Form 4562. If you operate more than one business, or if you conduct some other type of activity for which you can deduct depreciation (e.g., you own some rental real estate that will be reported on Schedule E), you'll need to consider each activity's expenses separately in determining whether you need to file a Form 4562 for that business. It's very common to include several 4562s in the same tax return. Just be sure that, at the top of the form, you write the name of the business or activity to which that copy of the form relates, along with its Employer Identification Number if you have one.

If you (and your spouse, if filing jointly) are filing more than one Form 4562, you should use one of the forms as a "master" and complete Part I on that form only. This section of the form computes your Section 179 expensing election and applies the $19,000 limit, and since the limit applies "per taxpayer" rather than "per business activity," you need to total up all your elected amounts in one place.

If you use the worksheet on page 104 to keep track of your depreciable assets, you'll have all the information you need to complete your 4562.

Part V of the form relates to cars and other listed property and should generally be completed first. The total section 179 expensing election claimed for this type of property, if any, is entered on Line 27 and carried over to the front of the form (Line 7). The total amount of regular depreciation on listed property is entered on Line 26 and is carried over to the front of the form (Line 20).

Once you've taken care of Part V, you can go back and complete Part I, which helps you to compute your Section 179 expensing election for any new property placed in service during the year, or any carryover of an elected amount from previous years.

Then, complete Part II for any new property other than cars and listed property placed in service during the year. If you have more than one piece of property in an asset class (for instance, you purchased several pieces of office furniture which are considered seven-year property), your entry for column (c) in Part II will be the total basis for all items in the class, and your entry for column (g) will be the total depreciation deductions for all items in the class.

Part III asks you to total up your depreciation deductions for "old" property — that is, any property not first placed in service in 1999. The total for property placed in service in 1987 or later is entered on Line 17. The total for property place in service before that date is entered on Line 19.

The grand total of your depreciation deductions are calculated on Line 21, and then carried over to the appropriate Schedule C (or other form).

Amortization deductions are treated separately, on Part VI of the Form 4562 (Lines 40-42). Once entered here, they are not added to the rest of your depreciation deductions. Instead, they are carried over as "other expenses" to your Schedule C, and must be listed separately on the back of that form. See page 61 for more on computing your amortization expenses, in the context of business startup expenses.

DISPOSING OF CAPITAL ASSETS

When you sell, scrap, retire, or otherwise remove a capital asset from your business, you'll have to report the change to the IRS and pay tax on any gain from the sale.

The good news is that long-term capital gains are taxed at a lower rate than other income, and if you have a loss on property used in a trade or business, you can deduct it.

Save Money

In some cases, if you trade business property for other business property of the same asset class, you do not need to recognize a taxable gain or loss.

Instead, you'll be treated as making a nontaxable like-kind exchange, in which the tax basis of the old property becomes the tax basis of the new property. The most common situation in which this rule arises is when you trade in an old vehicle for a new one (see page 103).

Consult your tax advisor for more details if you think you may want to arrange another type of like-kind exchange, since there are some very complicated rules to follow.

When you dispose of a capital asset, your gain (or loss) is computed by subtracting your adjusted tax basis for the property from your net proceeds on the sale.

Your proceeds from the sale include the cash you receive in the sale, the fair market value of any property or services you receive, and the value of any of your existing mortgage, loans, and other debts that are assumed by the buyer. From these proceeds you may subtract any costs you had in effecting the sale such as brokers' commissions, advertising expenses, appraisal fees, legal fees, surveys, abstract and recording fees, title insurance, and transfer or stamp taxes.

Your adjusted tax basis is generally your original cost for the property, plus the cost of any improvements or additions, and minus any depreciation you've claimed or casualty losses you've deducted over the years.

If you (or your accountants) have carefully maintained capital asset records for all your assets on forms like the one on page 104, it will be relatively quick and easy for you to compute any taxable gains or losses.

Tax Rate on Capital Gains

If you sell, scrap, retire, or dispose of some business property that you have held for one year or less, gains on it will be taxed at your ordinary income tax rate.

However, if the property was held for more than one year, gains on it will generally be treated as long-term capital gains. While property used in a trade or business is technically not a capital asset in the IRS's view, the tax laws do apply the more favorable capital gains tax rate to this property.

Congress recently acted to reduce the tax rate on long-term capital gains. For property that was sold before May 7, 1997, the maximum tax rate was 28 percent. For property sold on or after that date, the maximum tax rate on long-term capital gains is 20 percent (10 percent for taxpayers in the 15 percent income tax bracket).

For property that was sold after July 28, 1997 but before January 1, 1998, the property had to have been held for 18 months to qualify for the 20 (or 10) percent rate; if the property was held for more than a year but less than 18 months, the old 28 percent maximum would continue to apply. This effectively created a class of "mid-term gains" that caused a great deal of confusion and complication during the 1997 tax season, so Congress acted to eliminate it completely for 1998.

Beginning in 1998 and moving forward, the 20 percent maximum rate applies to property held for more than one year. So, for the moment, we're back to a two-tiered system of short-term gains (property held for one year or less) and long-term gains (property held for more than one year).

More Changes in the Future

Things won't stay that simple for long, however. Beginning in 2001, long-term capital gains property which has been held for more than five years will be taxed at a maximum rate of 18 percent (8 percent for taxpayers in the 15 percent bracket). So, we will once again be faced with three classes of capital gains: short term, long-term, and five-year gains.

The special 18 percent rate will apply only to property first put into service after 2000, except that for taxpayers in the 15 percent tax bracket, the special 8 percent rate applies to property first put into service after 1995.

Taxpayers who already hold assets used in a trade or business on January 1, 2001 may elect to treat the property as having been sold on that date (which involves paying tax on any gains up to that point), if they want to be able to take advantage of the special 18 percent rate for five-year property.

An important exception to the special rate for long-term capital gains is any gain that represents recaptured depreciation as discussed on page 119. Also, sales to close family members or controlled business entities might not be eligible for capital gains treatment, or for deduction of a capital loss, as discussed on page 236.

Calculating Net Capital Gains

Okay, so you understand the basic principle that sales price – cost of selling – adjusted tax basis = taxable gain (or loss). But what happens if you sell more than one capital asset during the year? What if you take a loss on one sale, but a gain on another? How do you determine the amount of your gains or losses, and will they be short- or long-term?

The general principle is that you must net your short-term gains against your short-term losses, to get a total short-term gain or loss. Then, you net your long-term gains against your long-term losses, to get a total long-term gain or loss. Finally, you net your total short-term gain or loss against your total long-term gain or loss.

If the ultimate result is a long-term gain, it will be subject to the maximum capital gains tax rate of 20 percent. If the result is a short-term gain, it will be subject to tax at your regular income tax rate.

If the result is a loss, whether short-term or long-term, up to $3,000 of it will be deductible from your ordinary net income (or up to $1,500 for married people filing separately). If your losses exceed this amount, you can carry them over and deduct them in subsequent years until they are used up.

Allocating Gains of Part-Business Property

For depreciable property that is used for both business and personal purposes, both the tax basis and sale proceeds of the property must be allocated between the two types of usage.

Essentially, the property will be treated as if it were two separate pieces of property. This applies to both real estate (e.g., your home office), and to property like cars, computers, office furniture, and equipment.

As a general rule, the taxable gain or loss on the business portion's disposition will be reported on Form 4797, *Sales of Business Property*.

In contrast, gain or loss on the personal portion will generally be reported on Schedule D of your individual income tax return. Note that any losses on the personal portion of your home or equipment are *not* deductible, although gains on this portion are taxable.

In the case of a home office, a special provision in the law says that up to $250,000 in capital gains (or $500,000 on a joint return) will be excluded upon sale of the home, if the home has been used as a principal place of residence for two out of the last five years before the sale. If you have been using part of your house as a home office for more than three years out of the last five years, you cannot meet the "two out of five years" residence rules for that portion of the home, since you have been using the office as a place of business, not your residence. Therefore, you would need to treat the property as two separate assets, and only the gain on the home would be excludable.

If you have used your home office for no more than three years out of the last five, you do not need to treat the home office as a separate business asset. However, you would still need to recapture any depreciation claimed on the home for periods after May 6, 1997 (see page 120). Except for the recaptured depreciation, the gain on the entire home would be excludible.

Selling a Business

If you sell your sole proprietorship business, each of the assets sold with the business is treated separately.

So, you would need to determine the adjusted basis of each and every asset in the sale (you can lump some of the smaller items together, however, in categories such as office machines, furniture, production equipment, etc.). The problem becomes one of allocation: if you negotiate a total price for the business, you and the buyer must agree as to what portion of the purchase price applies to each individual asset, and to intangible assets such as goodwill. The allocation will determine the amount of capital or ordinary income tax you must pay on the sale.

Allocation of the price can be a big bone of contention. The buyer wants as much money as

Case Study

You've been using a room in your house as a home office for the last four years. Your original basis in the home was $120,000, and you sold it in 1999 for $300,000. Your costs of selling were $21,000. The total area of the home is 2,400 square feet and your office is 120 square feet, or 5 percent of the total.

You must treat the sale as the sale of two pieces of property: your home, which is 95 percent of the total property, and your office, which is 5 percent of the total:

	Home	**Office**
Selling price	$285,000	$15,000
Less: selling expenses	-19,950	-1,050
Amount realized:	265,050	13,950
Cost basis:	114,000	6,000
Less: depreciation	-0	-622
Adjusted basis	114,000	5,378
Gain (amount realized minus adjusted basis)	$151,050	$ 8,572

The sale of the office portion would be reported on Form 4797, *Sales of Business Property*. Because the gain on the "home" portion of the property is less than $250,000, it does not have to be reported; if it had been over that amount (or over $500,000 on a joint return), it would be reported on Schedule D.

possible to be allocated to items that are currently deductible, such as a consulting agreement, or to assets that can be depreciated quickly under IRS rules. This will improve the business's cash flow by reducing its tax bill in the critical first years.

The seller, on the other hand, wants as much money as possible allocated to assets on which the gain is treated as capital gain, rather than to assets on which gain must be treated as ordinary income. The reason is that the tax rate on long-term capital gains is limited to 20 percent (for property held for more than 12 months), while the tax rate on short-term gains or ordinary income can be as high as 39.6 percent. Most small business owners who are successful in selling their companies are in high tax brackets, so the rate differential is very important.

Any gains on property held for one year or less, inventory, or accounts receivable are treated as ordinary income. Amounts paid under noncompete agreements are ordinary income to you and amortizable over 15 years by the buyer, *unless* the IRS successfully argues they are really part of the purchase price. And amounts paid under consulting agreements are ordinary income to you and currently deductible to the buyer.

IRS allocation rules. As you can imagine, the IRS has come up with some rules for making allocations of the purchase price. Generally speaking, they require that each tangible asset be valued at its fair market value (FMV), in the following order: (1) cash; (2) CDs, government securities, readily marketable securities and foreign currency; (3) all other assets except intangible assets, (4) intangible assets such as patents, trademarks, trade names, copyrights, a trained workforce, the value of business records, covenants not to compete, customer relationships, supplier relationships, licenses or permits, and (5) goodwill.

The total FMV of all assets in a class are added up and subtracted from the total purchase price before moving on to the next class. Thus, intangible assets such as goodwill get the "residual value," if there is any. However, remember that FMV is in the mind of the appraiser. You still have some wiggle room in allocating your price among the various assets, provided that your allocation is reasonable and the buyer agrees to it. Your odds are even better if your allocation is supported by a third-party appraisal.

According to IRS rules, the buyer and seller must use the same price allocation, so the allocation will have to be negotiated and put in writing as part of the sales contract. The allocation must be reported to the IRS on Form 8594, *Asset Acquisition Statement Under Section 1060*, which must be attached to the tax returns of both parties for the year in which the sale occurred. The allocation will be binding on both parties unless the IRS determines that it is not appropriate.

Recapture of Depreciation Deductions

If you realize a capital gain on the sale or other disposition of property used in your trade or business, you probably won't get the benefit of the special capital gains tax rate on the entire amount of your gain.

Why not? Because Congress wants to first take back, or "recapture," some of the benefits of the depreciation deductions you've been claiming for all the years you owned the property.

The tax rules for recapture differ, depending on whether the property is real estate or personal property. For business real estate, there is a special, more generous rule for home offices.

Recapture Rules for Personal Property

If you have a capital gain on any depreciable personal property other than real estate, you must report all or part of the gain as ordinary income to reflect the amount of depreciation, and any first-year expensing deductions that were claimed on the asset. The amount that must be reported as ordinary income ("recaptured") is not eligible for the special long-term capital gains rates described above, and is equal to the lesser of:

- the total of depreciation and expensing deductions allowable on the asset, and

- the total gain realized

If the total gain realized is more than the amount that must be recaptured, the excess will be taxed at the long-term capital gain rate, provided that the asset has been held for more than one year. If the total of the depreciation deductions is greater than the gain realized, the entire amount of the gain is reported as ordinary income.

Case Study

On April 30, 1999, Albert Edwards sold a car for $5,000. The original cost of the car in 1994 was $12,000. The car had been driven 75,000 miles, 60,000 of which were attributable to business usage. Edwards used the standard mileage rate to claim car deductions, so his depreciation equals the depreciation component of the SMR for each year, multiplied by the business miles driven that year. Assume the depreciation treated as allowable for those years was $6,300. Edwards sold no other business property during the year. Edwards has a business gain of $700, computed as follows:

	Total	Business (80%)	Personal (20%)
Cost of car	$12,000	$9,600	$2,400
Less: depreciation	-6,300	-6,300	--0--
Adjusted basis of car	5,700	3,300	2,400
Less: sale proceeds	-5,000	- 4,000	-1,000
Gain (loss)	($700)	$700	($1,400)

The full amount of the business gain of $700 is treated as ordinary income because it is less than the amount of depreciation that was taken on the car. Remember, the personal loss is not deductible!

Recapture of Real Estate Depreciation

For sales of real estate used in a trade or business after May 6, 1997, including home offices, the recapture rules apply to real estate as well as personal property. So, if you realize a capital gain on the sale of real estate after that date, you must report all or part of the gain as "recaptured" income to reflect the amount of depreciation you've claimed on the asset. This recaptured amount is taxed at a special maximum rate of 25 percent. The amount that must be recaptured is equal to the lesser of:

- the total depreciation allowable on the asset (except that for home offices, only depreciation for periods after May 6, 1997 counts), and

- the total gain realized

If the total gain realized is more than the amount that must be recaptured, the excess may be reported as a capital gain (for a maximum 20 percent rate) provided that the asset has been held for more than one year.

If the total of the depreciation deductions is greater than the gain realized, the entire amount of the gain is taxed at the 25 percent rate.

Planning for Depreciation Recaptures

If you choose to depreciate a property quickly, the property's adjusted basis will be reduced more quickly than if you had depreciated the property more slowly, and if you sell in the first few years you will have more taxable gain upon sale of the asset.

Moreover, as a general rule, *the faster you depreciate property, the more likely it is that you will have a recapture liability when you sell the property, and the more likely that this liability would be larger than if you have chosen slower depreciation.*

All things being equal, it's probably best to be hit with a recapture in a year in which your business has an operating loss (which can be used to offset the recapture amount), rather than in profit years, when the recapture will increase your taxable income, and possibly even move you into a higher tax bracket.

Warning

Don't let the tail wag the dog. Strategies aimed at the timing or minimization of depreciation recaptures may be worthwhile, but don't fall in the trap of over-focusing on tax issues. First, consider the operational aspects when deciding whether and when you should sell an asset. Tax considerations should run a distant second when making these kinds of decisions.

Foreclosures and Involuntary Conversions

If your property is foreclosed upon, repossessed, or destroyed due to theft, condemnation, or other casualty, you should report the event as a sale of the property.

A foreclosure or repossession is generally treated in the same way as a sale. Your gain or loss for tax purposes is the difference between your adjusted basis in the property, and the amount (if any) you receive. Cancellation of debt is treated as an amount that you received for this purpose.

If your property is lost or destroyed by theft, vandalism, condemnation, or a natural disaster such as a fire, tornado, flood, landslide etc., you may have a taxable gain if you receive some insurance payment, condemnation award, or damages in a lawsuit. If the amount you receive is less than the amount of your loss, you may have a deductible loss provided that the property was used in a trade or business or was investment property.

However, even if there is a taxable gain, you generally can postpone payment of tax on the gain if you reinvest the proceeds in similar property costing at least as much as the amount you received. Your tax basis in the new property would be the same as your tax basis in the old, destroyed property, and you would not be taxed on the cumulative gains until you sell the replacement property. The replacement property would generally have to be purchased within two years of receiving any payments that exceed your tax basis in the old property, or within three years if the property was used in a trade or business, or for investment. A special four-year replacement period applies to homes (and their contents) damaged by Presidentially declared disasters. For a discussion of how to report casualty losses (and gains), see page 267.

Installment Sales

The installment method can be used to defer some tax on capital gains, as long as you receive at least one payment for a piece of property after the year of the sale. It can't be used if the sale results in a loss.

The bad news is that payments for many (or even most) of the assets of your business are not eligible for installment sale treatment. Also, accrual method taxpayers can't use the installment method for sales after the enactment of the 1999 tax law in December.

Assets Eligible for Installment Treatment

Generally, anything on which gains must be treated as ordinary income will not be eligible for installment sale treatment. That includes payments for your inventory, for accounts receivable, and for property that's been used for one year or less. It also includes payments for any personal property or real estate to the extent of any depreciation that must be recaptured, based on deductions you've claimed over the years (see page 119). For all these items, you must pay tax on any gains in the year of the sale, even if you haven't yet received payments for the items.

Looking at it another way, in most cases only gain on assets that have appreciated in value beyond their original purchase price will be eligible for installment sale treatment. In most cases, that means real estate. For older businesses, gain on intangible assets such as goodwill will also be eligible for installment sale treatment, because under the law prior to 1993 goodwill could not be depreciated or amortized (hence, there's no depreciation to be recaptured).

Using the Installment Method

To use the installment method, you must allocate the total purchase price you received among all the assets you've sold in the transaction.

Then, for each asset to which the installment method applies, you must compute your "gross profit percentage." This is basically your gross profit (your selling price minus: the tax basis of the property, selling expenses, and any depreciation recapture) divided by the selling price of the asset. Then, each time you receive a payment from the purchaser, the principal portion of the payment (i.e., everything but the interest) is multiplied by the gross profit percentage to determine the amount that must be reported as taxable gain for the year.

Case Study

Let's say that on January 1, 1999, you sold some commercial real estate. The total price was $600,000, of which $500,000 was allocated to the building and $100,000 was for the land underneath. Selling expenses were $37,500. You originally purchased the property 10 years ago for $300,000 ($250,000 for the building and $50,000 for the land). Over the years you've claimed $61,168 in depreciation using the straight-line method. For simplicity, we'll assume you're a cheapskate and made no capital improvements to the building during the time you owned it.

The buyers made a $200,000 down payment and will pay the rest off at 10 percent interest on a 20-year amortization schedule, except that at five years the unpaid principal will be due in a balloon payment.

First, separate the transaction into two portions: the building, and the land:

	Building	**Land**
Cost basis:	$250,000	$ 50,000
Less: depreciation	-61,168	-0
	188,832	50,000
Plus: expenses of sale	+31,250	+ 6,250
Adjusted basis:	$ 220,082	$56,250

Now let's consider the "building only" portion of the transaction. Your net gains on the sale of the building alone will be the sales price minus the adjusted basis computed above, or $500,000 - $220,082 = $279,918. Since this amount is greater than the $61,168 in depreciation, all of the depreciation you claimed over the years would be "recaptured" and taxed in the year of the sale.

The remainder of your profit on the building, or $218,750 (since $279,918 - $61,168 = $218,750) would be divided by the selling price of $500,000 to arrive at your gross profit percentage for the building: $218,750/$500,000 = .4375, or 43.75 percent.

For the land, no depreciation was deductible, so there is no recapture. Your profit on the land is the price less the adjusted basis, or $100,000 - $56,250 = $43,750. Your gross profit percentage of the land would be $43,750/100,000 = .4375, or 43.75 percent.

For every payment you receive, including the down payment and the balloon, separate the principal from any interest (all interest is taxed as ordinary income).

Of the principal, 1/6 will represent a payment for the land, and 5/6 will represent a payment for the building. Of the payment for the land, 43.75 percent will be taxed as capital gains, and the remainder is a return of your capital, which is not taxed. Of the payment for the building, 43.75 percent of each payment will be taxed as capital gains, and the rest represents either the recaptured depreciation, which was taxed in the year of the sale, or the return of your capital which is not taxed.

Installment sales are reported on IRS Form 6252, *Installment Sale Income*. A separate form should be filed for each asset you sell using this method. You must file this form in the year the sale occurs, and in every later year in which you receive a payment.

If the buyer assumes any of your debt as part of the installment deal, the assumption is treated as a payment to you for purposes of the installment sale rules. If the buyer places some of the purchase price in an escrow account, it's not considered a payment until the funds are released to you, as long as there are some substantial restrictions on your ability to get the money.

If your deal includes an enrapt provision under which you may be entitled to additional payments based on future performance of the business, special rules apply. Please see your tax advisor for details.

REPORTING SALES OF ASSETS

If you sell or dispose of property used in a trade or business, it must be reported on IRS Form 4797, *Sales of Business Property*. This form is divided into several sections, which are used for different types of property.

Part II, "Ordinary Gains and Losses," is used for property held for one year or less, and for property not eligible for the long-term gain rate such as accounts receivable and inventory sold as part of a sale of your business.

Part III, "Gain from Disposition of Property Under Sections 1245, 1250, 1252, 1254, and 1255," is used for reporting the sale of depreciable personal property (known as 1245 property) and depreciable real estate (known as 1250 property). The other forms of property are less commonly used, but a translation is: 1252 property is farmland held more than one year but less than 10 years; 1254 property is oil, gas, or geothermal property place in service before 1987, and 1255 property is property for which you received certain types of government conservation program payments.

Part III is where your depreciation recapture (if any) will be figured. The net result of this section will be carried over to Part II on the front of the form.

Part I is used to report the sale of property not included in Part III, such as land, and gains from installment sales (originally reported on Form 6252 and carried over to Line 4 of Part I) and like-kind exchanges (originally reported on Form 8824).

Finally, Part IV is used to report an event that may not look like a sale, but is treated as a taxable event by the IRS: the recapture of some of your depreciation deductions when your business use of "listed property" drops below 51 percent (see page 112) and the recapture of some of your Section 179 expensing election when your business use drops

below 50 percent for property you've previously expensed.

PURCHASING VS. LEASING

Depreciation generally may be claimed by the *owner* of a capital asset. If you lease your equipment instead of purchasing it, you can't depreciate the equipment. However, you will generally be able to deduct the lease payments you make, at the time that you make them, which can result in a larger tax benefit than you'd get if you bought the equipment outright.

If you lease property that is used for both business and personal purposes, you must prorate the lease payments and deduct only the portion of the lease that corresponds to your business use percentage. See page 102 for more details on how to calculate business usage for various types of property.

Inclusion Amounts for Listed Property

If, instead of purchasing it, you lease your car, computer system, audio/visual equipment, or other listed property as defined on page 112, you may have to include an additional amount known as the "inclusion amount" in your gross income. This extra amount is intended to place you on the same financial footing as someone who has purchased similar equipment and can only deduct the depreciation, which is typically less than your lease payments would be.

If you lease a car, you must calculate an inclusion amount for every year you deduct lease payments; see page 68 for instructions on how this is done.

If you lease some other type of listed property, you only need to calculate an inclusion amount if your business usage of the property drops to 50 percent or less for a year. The inclusion amount is added to your income only for that year.

This could easily happen, for instance, if you have not claimed the home office deduction, but have been leasing a computer predominantly for business at home, and then you find that your family is using the computer more than you!

Inclusion Amount Worksheet for Leased Listed Property Used 50% or Less for Business

1. Fair market value of the asset _____

2. Business/investment use for the first year that business use is 50% or less _____

3. Multiply line 1 by line 2 _____

4. Rate from Table A-19 (below) _____

5. Multiply line 3 by line 4 _____

6. Fair market value of the asset _____

7. Average business/investment use for all years property was leased before the first year that investment use fell to 50% or less _____

8. Multiply line 6 by line 7 _____

9. Rate from Table A-20 (below) _____

10. Multiply line 8 by line 9 _____

11. Add lines 5 and line 10. This is your inclusion amount _____

RATES TO FIGURE INCLUSION AMOUNTS
FOR
LEASED LISTED PROPERTY

Table A-19. **Amount A Percentages**

Recovery Period of Property Under ADS	First Tax Year During Lease in Which Business Use is 50% or Less											
	1	2	3	4	5	6	7	8	9	10	11	12 & Later
Less than 7 years	2.1%	−7.2%	−19.8%	−20.1%	−12.4%	−12.4%	−12.4%	−12.4%	−12.4%	−12.4%	−12.4%	−12.4%
7 to 10 years	3.9%	−3.8%	−17.7%	−25.1%	−27.8%	−27.2%	−27.1%	−27.6%	−23.7%	−14.7%	−14.7%	−14.7%
More than 10 years	6.6%	−1.6%	−16.9%	−25.6%	−29.9%	−31.1%	−32.8%	−35.1%	−33.3%	−26.7%	−19.7%	−12.2%

Table A-20. **Amount B Percentages**

Recovery Period of Property Under ADS	First Tax Year During Lease in Which Business Use is 50% or Less											
	1	2	3	4	5	6	7	8	9	10	11	12 & Later
Less than 7 years	0.0%	10.0%	22.0%	21.2%	12.7%	12.7%	12.7%	12.7%	12.7%	12.7%	12.7%	12.7%
7 to 10 years	0.0%	9.3%	23.8%	31.3%	33.8%	32.7%	31.6%	30.5%	25.0%	15.0%	15.0%	15.0%
More than 10 years	0.0%	10.1%	26.3%	35.4%	39.6%	40.2%	40.8%	41.4%	37.5%	29.2%	20.8%	12.5%

To calculate your inclusion amount for items other than cars, you need to know the fair market value of the item on the first day of the lease term. Alternately, if the capitalized cost of the item is specified in the lease, you must treat that amount as the "fair market value."

Then, you can use the worksheet above to determine your inclusion amount. The final result from the worksheet must be included as "other income" on Line 6 of your Schedule C.

As we've said, inclusion amounts for listed property other than cars are included in gross income only in the first year that business use drops to 50 percent or less.

There is an exception to this rule if the lease term began within the last nine months of your tax year and extends into the next year, and you did not use the property more than 50 percent for business in the first year of the lease. In that case, you would calculate your average business use percentage for the first and second calendar years (Worksheet Line 2) and the percentage amount for the first year (Worksheet Line 4). The inclusion amount would be added to your income for the second year, not the first.

True Leases vs. Financial Leases

In certain situations, the IRS may deny your deduction of lease payments if it audits your return and concludes that your lease is not in reality a true lease, but a financial lease, which can be treated as an installment or conditional sale. To understand why the IRS would even care whether you characterize your acquisition as a lease or a purchase, consider the following example:

Example

Jiffy Company is interested in a piece of equipment that sells for $25,000. However, instead of purchasing the equipment, Jiffy negotiates to lease the equipment for three years at an annual rent of $8,500. The lease grants Jiffy the option to purchase the equipment at the end of the lease for $2,400. The fair rental value of the equipment is only $3,000. Why would Jiffy and the leasing company do this?

From Jiffy's perspective, leasing the equipment allows it to effectively recover the equipment's cost over three years via its deductions of the rental payments. If it had purchased the equipment, it likely would have recovered the cost over five years via depreciation deductions. And the IRS really frowns upon the improper acceleration of deductions.

From the lessor's perspective, leasing the equipment allows it to spread its recognition of income over the three-year lease period. The improper deferral of income is another thing the IRS dislikes. Furthermore, the lessor would be able to claim depreciation deductions with respect to the equipment while it is being leased and thereby reduce its current income even more.

If the IRS does recharacterize your lease as a sale, your rental payments will not be deductible. Instead, you'll be entitled to depreciation deductions as the owner of the property for tax purposes. Moreover, a portion of your rental payments, which the IRS effectively recharacterizes as being installment payments on a purchase price, will likely be considered interest that you can currently deduct.

The leasing transaction in the example above is one that the IRS would likely recharacterize. What types of factors attract the IRS's attention? Here are some examples:

- A portion of your rental payments establishes equity in the leased property.

- You acquire title to the property after paying a specified amount of rent.

- Your rental payments are made over a relatively short period of time and are inordinately large in comparison to the amount required to purchase the property.

- Your rental payments substantially exceed the fair rental value of the property.

- You can acquire the property under a purchase option for a price that is nominal in relation to the property's value at the time you can exercise the option or that is nominal in comparison to your total payments under the lease.

- A portion of your rental payments is specifically designated as being interest or is readily recognizable as being the equivalent of interest.

If any of these factors describe an equipment lease you're preparing to enter, you should proceed with caution to avoid interest and penalties if the IRS recharacterizes the transaction. If you have any doubt as to how the IRS may view the lease, have your accountant or lawyer review the agreement.

Table A-1. **3-, 5-, 7-, 10-, 15-, and 20-Year Property**
            Half-Year Convention

Year	Depreciation rate for recovery period					
	3-year	5-year	7-year	10-year	15-year	20-year
1	33.33%	20.00%	14.29%	10.00%	5.00%	3.750%
2	44.45	32.00	24.49	18.00	9.50	7.219
3	14.81	19.20	17.49	14.40	8.55	6.677
4	7.41	11.52	12.49	11.52	7.70	6.177
5		11.52	8.93	9.22	6.93	5.713
6		5.76	8.92	7.37	6.23	5.285
7			8.93	6.55	5.90	4.888
8			4.46	6.55	5.90	4.522
9				6.56	5.91	4.462
10				6.55	5.90	4.461
11				3.28	5.91	4.462
12					5.90	4.461
13					5.91	4.462
14					5.90	4.461
15					5.91	4.462
16					2.95	4.461
17						4.462
18						4.461
19						4.462
20						4.461
21						2.231

Table A-2. **3-, 5-, 7-, 10-, 15-, and 20-Year Property**
            Mid-Quarter Convention
            Placed in Service in First Quarter

Year	Depreciation rate for recovery period					
	3-year	5-year	7-year	10-year	15-year	20-year
1	58.33%	35.00%	25.00%	17.50%	8.75%	6.563%
2	27.78	26.00	21.43	16.50	9.13	7.000
3	12.35	15.60	15.31	13.20	8.21	6.482
4	1.54	11.01	10.93	10.56	7.39	5.996
5		11.01	8.75	8.45	6.65	5.546
6		1.38	8.74	6.76	5.99	5.130
7			8.75	6.55	5.90	4.746
8			1.09	6.55	5.91	4.459
9				6.56	5.90	4.459
10				6.55	5.91	4.459
11				0.82	5.90	4.459
12					5.91	4.460
13					5.90	4.459
14					5.91	4.460
15					5.90	4.459
16					0.74	4.460
17						4.459
18						4.460
19						4.459
20						4.460
21						0.557

Table A-3.　3-, 5-, 7-, 10-, 15-, and 20-Year Property
　　　　　Mid-Quarter Convention
　　　　　Placed in Service in Second Quarter

Year	Depreciation rate for recovery period					
	3-year	5-year	7-year	10-year	15-year	20-year
1	41.67%	25.00%	17.85%	12.50%	6.25%	4.688%
2	38.89	30.00	23.47	17.50	9.38	7.148
3	14.14	18.00	16.76	14.00	8.44	6.612
4	5.30	11.37	11.97	11.20	7.59	6.116
5		11.37	8.87	8.96	6.83	5.658
6		4.26	8.87	7.17	6.15	5.233
7			8.87	6.55	5.91	4.841
8			3.33	6.55	5.90	4.478
9				6.56	5.91	4.463
10				6.55	5.90	4.463
11				2.46	5.91	4.463
12					5.90	4.463
13					5.91	4.463
14					5.90	4.463
15					5.91	4.462
16					2.21	4.463
17						4.462
18						4.463
19						4.462
20						4.463
21						1.673

Table A-4.　3-, 5-, 7-, 10-, 15-, and 20-Year Property
　　　　　Mid-Quarter Convention
　　　　　Placed in Service in Third Quarter

Year	Depreciation rate for recovery period					
	3-year	5-year	7-year	10-year	15-year	20-year
1	25.00%	15.00%	10.71%	7.50%	3.75%	2.813%
2	50.00	34.00	25.51	18.50	9.63	7.289
3	16.67	20.40	18.22	14.80	8.66	6.742
4	8.33	12.24	13.02	11.84	7.80	6.237
5		11.30	9.30	9.47	7.02	5.769
6		7.06	8.85	7.58	6.31	5.336
7			8.86	6.55	5.90	4.936
8			5.53	6.55	5.90	4.566
9				6.56	5.91	4.460
10				6.55	5.90	4.460
11				4.10	5.91	4.460
12					5.90	4.460
13					5.91	4.461
14					5.90	4.460
15					5.91	4.461
16					3.69	4.460
17						4.461
18						4.460
19						4.461
20						4.460
21						2.788

Table A-5. **3-, 5-, 7-, 10-, 15-, and 20-Year Property**
Mid-Quarter Convention
Placed in Service in Fourth Quarter

Year	Depreciation rate for recovery period					
	3-year	5-year	7-year	10-year	15-year	20-year
1	8.33%	5.00%	3.57%	2.50%	1.25%	0.938%
2	61.11	38.00	27.55	19.50	9.88	7.430
3	20.37	22.80	19.68	15.60	8.89	6.872
4	10.19	13.68	14.06	12.48	8.00	6.357
5		10.94	10.04	9.98	7.20	5.880
6		9.58	8.73	7.99	6.48	5.439
7			8.73	6.55	5.90	5.031
8			7.64	6.55	5.90	4.654
9				6.56	5.90	4.458
10				6.55	5.91	4.458
11				5.74	5.90	4.458
12					5.91	4.458
13					5.90	4.458
14					5.91	4.458
15					5.90	4.458
16					5.17	4.458
17						4.458
18						4.459
19						4.458
20						4.459
21						3.901

Table A-6. **Residential Rental Property**
Mid-Month Convention
Straight Line—27.5 Years

Year	Month property placed in service											
	1	2	3	4	5	6	7	8	9	10	11	12
1	3.485%	3.182%	2.879%	2.576%	2.273%	1.970%	1.667%	1.364%	1.061%	0.758%	0.455%	0.152%
2–9	3.636	3.636	3.636	3.636	3.636	3.636	3.636	3.636	3.636	3.636	3.636	3.636
10	3.637	3.637	3.637	3.637	3.637	3.637	3.636	3.636	3.636	3.636	3.636	3.636
11	3.636	3.636	3.636	3.636	3.636	3.636	3.637	3.637	3.637	3.637	3.637	3.637
12	3.637	3.637	3.637	3.637	3.637	3.637	3.636	3.636	3.636	3.636	3.636	3.636
13	3.636	3.636	3.636	3.636	3.636	3.636	3.637	3.637	3.637	3.637	3.637	3.637
14	3.637	3.637	3.637	3.637	3.637	3.637	3.636	3.636	3.636	3.636	3.636	3.636
15	3.636	3.636	3.636	3.636	3.636	3.636	3.637	3.637	3.637	3.637	3.637	3.637
16	3.637	3.637	3.637	3.637	3.637	3.637	3.636	3.636	3.636	3.636	3.636	3.636
17	3.636	3.636	3.636	3.636	3.636	3.636	3.637	3.637	3.637	3.637	3.637	3.637
18	3.637	3.637	3.637	3.637	3.637	3.637	3.636	3.636	3.636	3.636	3.636	3.636
19	3.636	3.636	3.636	3.636	3.636	3.636	3.637	3.637	3.637	3.637	3.637	3.637
20	3.637	3.637	3.637	3.637	3.637	3.637	3.636	3.636	3.636	3.636	3.636	3.636
21	3.636	3.636	3.636	3.636	3.636	3.636	3.637	3.637	3.637	3.637	3.637	3.637
22	3.637	3.637	3.637	3.637	3.637	3.637	3.636	3.636	3.636	3.636	3.636	3.636
23	3.636	3.636	3.636	3.636	3.636	3.636	3.637	3.637	3.637	3.637	3.637	3.637
24	3.637	3.637	3.637	3.637	3.637	3.637	3.636	3.636	3.636	3.636	3.636	3.636
25	3.636	3.636	3.636	3.636	3.636	3.636	3.637	3.637	3.637	3.637	3.637	3.637
26	3.637	3.637	3.637	3.637	3.637	3.637	3.636	3.636	3.636	3.636	3.636	3.636
27	3.636	3.636	3.636	3.636	3.636	3.636	3.637	3.637	3.637	3.637	3.637	3.637
28	1.97	2.273	2.576	2.879	3.182	3.485	3.636	3.636	3.636	3.636	3.636	3.636
29							0.152	0.455	0.758	1.061	1.364	1.667

Table A-7. **Nonresidential Real Property**
Mid-Month Convention
Straight Line—31.5 Years

Year	Month property placed in service											
	1	2	3	4	5	6	7	8	9	10	11	12
1	3.042%	2.778%	2.513%	2.249%	1.984%	1.720%	1.455%	1.190%	0.926%	0.661%	0.397%	0.132%
2-7	3.175	3.175	3.175	3.175	3.175	3.175	3.175	3.175	3.175	3.175	3.175	3.175
8	3.175	3.174	3.175	3.174	3.175	3.174	3.175	3.175	3.175	3.175	3.175	3.175
9	3.174	3.175	3.174	3.175	3.174	3.175	3.174	3.175	3.174	3.175	3.174	3.175
10	3.175	3.174	3.175	3.174	3.175	3.174	3.175	3.174	3.175	3.174	3.175	3.174
11	3.174	3.175	3.174	3.175	3.174	3.175	3.174	3.175	3.174	3.175	3.174	3.175
12	3.175	3.174	3.175	3.174	3.175	3.174	3.175	3.174	3.175	3.174	3.175	3.174
13	3.174	3.175	3.174	3.175	3.174	3.175	3.174	3.175	3.174	3.175	3.174	3.175
14	3.175	3.174	3.175	3.174	3.175	3.174	3.175	3.174	3.175	3.174	3.175	3.174
15	3.174	3.175	3.174	3.175	3.174	3.175	3.174	3.175	3.174	3.175	3.174	3.175
16	3.175	3.174	3.175	3.174	3.175	3.174	3.175	3.174	3.175	3.174	3.175	3.174
17	3.174	3.175	3.174	3.175	3.174	3.175	3.174	3.175	3.174	3.175	3.174	3.175
18	3.175	3.174	3.175	3.174	3.175	3.174	3.175	3.174	3.175	3.174	3.175	3.174
19	3.174	3.175	3.174	3.175	3.174	3.175	3.174	3.175	3.174	3.175	3.174	3.175
20	3.175	3.174	3.175	3.174	3.175	3.174	3.175	3.174	3.175	3.174	3.175	3.174
21	3.174	3.175	3.174	3.175	3.174	3.175	3.174	3.175	3.174	3.175	3.174	3.175
22	3.175	3.174	3.175	3.174	3.175	3.174	3.175	3.174	3.175	3.174	3.175	3.174
23	3.174	3.175	3.174	3.175	3.174	3.175	3.174	3.175	3.174	3.175	3.174	3.175
24	3.175	3.174	3.175	3.174	3.175	3.174	3.175	3.174	3.175	3.174	3.175	3.174
25	3.174	3.175	3.174	3.175	3.174	3.175	3.174	3.175	3.174	3.175	3.174	3.175
26	3.175	3.174	3.175	3.174	3.175	3.174	3.175	3.174	3.175	3.174	3.175	3.174
27	3.174	3.175	3.174	3.175	3.174	3.175	3.174	3.175	3.174	3.175	3.174	3.175
28	3.175	3.174	3.175	3.174	3.175	3.174	3.175	3.174	3.175	3.174	3.175	3.174
29	3.174	3.175	3.174	3.175	3.174	3.175	3.174	3.175	3.174	3.175	3.174	3.175
30	3.175	3.174	3.175	3.174	3.175	3.174	3.175	3.174	3.175	3.174	3.175	3.174
31	3.174	3.175	3.174	3.175	3.174	3.175	3.174	3.175	3.174	3.175	3.174	3.175
32	1.720	1.984	2.249	2.513	2.778	3.042	3.175	3.174	3.175	3.174	3.175	3.174
33							0.132	0.397	0.661	0.926	1.190	1.455

Table A-7a. **Nonresidential Real Property**
Mid-Month Convention
Straight Line—39 Years

Year	Month property placed in service											
	1	2	3	4	5	6	7	8	9	10	11	12
1	2.461%	2.247%	2.033%	1.819%	1.605%	1.391%	1.177%	0.963%	0.749%	0.535%	0.321%	0.107%
2-39	2.564	2.564	2.564	2.564	2.564	2.564	2.564	2.564	2.564	2.564	2.564	2.564
40	0.107	0.321	0.535	0.749	0.963	1.177	1.391	1.605	1.819	2.033	2.247	2.461

Table A-13. **Straight Line**
Mid-Month Convention

Year	Month property placed in service											
	1	2	3	4	5	6	7	8	9	10	11	12
1	2.396%	2.188%	1.979%	1.771%	1.563%	1.354%	1.146%	0.938%	0.729%	0.521%	0.313%	0.104%
2-40	2.500	2.500	2.500	2.500	2.500	2.500	2.500	2.500	2.500	2.500	2.500	2.500
41	0.104	0.312	0.521	0.729	0.937	1.146	1.354	1.562	1.771	1.979	2.187	2.396

Table A-8. **Straight Line Method**
Half-Year Convention

Year	Recovery periods in years							
	4	5	6	9	10	15	18	20
1	12.5%	10.0%	8.33%	5.56%	5.0%	3.33%	2.78%	2.5%
2	25.0	20.0	16.67	11.11	10.0	6.67	5.56	5.0
3	25.0	20.0	16.67	11.11	10.0	6.67	5.56	5.0
4	25.0	20.0	16.67	11.11	10.0	6.67	5.55	5.0
5	12.5	20.0	16.66	11.11	10.0	6.67	5.56	5.0
6		10.0	16.67	11.11	10.0	6.67	5.55	5.0
7			8.33	11.11	10.0	6.67	5.56	5.0
8				11.11	10.0	6.66	5.55	5.0
9				11.11	10.0	6.67	5.56	5.0
10				5.56	10.0	6.66	5.55	5.0
11					5.0	6.67	5.56	5.0
12						6.66	5.55	5.0
13						6.67	5.56	5.0
14						6.66	5.55	5.0
15						6.67	5.56	5.0
16						3.33	5.55	5.0
17							5.56	5.0
18							5.55	5.0
19							2.78	5.0
20								5.0
21								2.5

Table A-9. **Straight Line Method**
Mid-Quarter Convention
Placed in Service in First Quarter

Year	Recovery periods in years							
	4	5	6	9	10	15	18	20
1	21.88%	17.5%	14.58%	9.72%	8.75%	5.83%	4.86%	4.375%
2	25.00	20.0	16.67	11.11	10.00	6.67	5.56	5.000
3	25.00	20.0	16.67	11.11	10.00	6.67	5.56	5.000
4	25.00	20.0	16.67	11.11	10.00	6.67	5.56	5.000
5	3.12	20.0	16.66	11.11	10.00	6.67	5.55	5.000
6		2.5	16.67	11.11	10.00	6.67	5.56	5.000
7			2.08	11.11	10.00	6.67	5.55	5.000
8				11.12	10.00	6.66	5.56	5.000
9				11.11	10.00	6.67	5.55	5.000
10				1.39	10.00	6.66	5.56	5.000
11					1.25	6.67	5.55	5.000
12						6.66	5.56	5.000
13						6.67	5.55	5.000
14						6.66	5.56	5.000
15						6.67	5.55	5.000
16						0.83	5.56	5.000
17							5.55	5.000
18							5.56	5.000
19							0.69	5.000
20								5.000
21								0.625

Table A-10. **Straight Line Method**
Mid-Quarter Convention
Placed in Service in Second Quarter

Year	Recovery periods in years							
	4	5	6	9	10	15	18	20
1	15.63%	12.5%	10.42%	6.94%	6.25%	4.17%	3.47%	3.125%
2	25.00	20.0	16.67	11.11	10.00	6.67	5.56	5.000
3	25.00	20.0	16.67	11.11	10.00	6.67	5.56	5.000
4	25.00	20.0	16.66	11.11	10.00	6.67	5.56	5.000
5	9.37	20.0	16.67	11.11	10.00	6.67	5.55	5.000
6		7.5	16.66	11.11	10.00	6.67	5.56	5.000
7			6.25	11.11	10.00	6.66	5.55	5.000
8				11.12	10.00	6.67	5.56	5.000
9				11.11	10.00	6.66	5.55	5.000
10				4.17	10.00	6.67	5.56	5.000
11					3.75	6.66	5.55	5.000
12						6.67	5.56	5.000
13						6.66	5.55	5.000
14						6.67	5.56	5.000
15						6.66	5.55	5.000
16						2.50	5.56	5.000
17							5.55	5.000
18							5.56	5.000
19							2.08	5.000
20								5.000
21								1.875

Table A-11. **Straight Line Method**
Mid-Quarter Convention
Placed in Service in Third Quarter

Year	Recovery periods in years							
	4	5	6	9	10	15	18	20
1	9.38%	7.5%	6.25%	4.17%	3.75%	2.50%	2.08%	1.875%
2	25.00	20.0	16.67	11.11	10.00	6.67	5.56	5.000
3	25.00	20.0	16.67	11.11	10.00	6.67	5.56	5.000
4	25.00	20.0	16.66	11.11	10.00	6.67	5.56	5.000
5	15.62	20.0	16.67	11.11	10.00	6.67	5.55	5.000
6		12.5	16.66	11.11	10.00	6.67	5.56	5.000
7			10.42	11.11	10.00	6.66	5.55	5.000
8				11.11	10.00	6.67	5.56	5.000
9				11.11	10.00	6.66	5.55	5.000
10				6.95	10.00	6.67	5.56	5.000
11					6.25	6.66	5.55	5.000
12						6.67	5.56	5.000
13						6.66	5.55	5.000
14						6.67	5.56	5.000
15						6.66	5.55	5.000
16						4.17	5.56	5.000
17							5.55	5.000
18							5.56	5.000
19							3.47	5.000
20								5.000
21								3.125

Table A-12. **Straight Line Method**
Mid-Quarter Convention
Placed in Service in Fourth Quarter

Year	Recovery periods in years							
	4	5	6	9	10	15	18	20
1	3.13%	2.5%	2.08%	1.39%	1.25%	0.83%	0.69%	0.625%
2	25.00	20.0	16.67	11.11	10.00	6.67	5.56	5.000
3	25.00	20.0	16.67	11.11	10.00	6.67	5.56	5.000
4	25.00	20.0	16.67	11.11	10.00	6.67	5.56	5.000
5	21.87	20.0	16.66	11.11	10.00	6.67	5.55	5.000
6		17.5	16.67	11.11	10.00	6.67	5.56	5.000
7			14.58	11.11	10.00	6.67	5.56	5.000
8				11.11	10.00	6.66	5.56	5.000
9				11.11	10.00	6.67	5.55	5.000
10				9.73	10.00	6.66	5.56	5.000
11					8.75	6.67	5.55	5.000
12						6.66	5.56	5.000
13						6.67	5.55	5.000
14						6.66	5.56	5.000
15						6.67	5.55	5.000
16						5.83	5.56	5.000
17							5.55	5.000
18							5.56	5.000
19							4.86	5.000
20								5.000
21								4.375

Table A-14. **150% Declining Balance Method**
Half-Year Convention

Year	Recovery periods in years						
	3	5	7	10	15	20	25
1	25.0%	15.00%	10.71%	7.50%	5.00%	3.750%	3.000%
2	37.5	25.50	19.13	13.88	9.50	7.219	5.820
3	25.0	17.85	15.03	11.79	8.55	6.677	5.471
4	12.5	16.66	12.25	10.02	7.70	6.177	5.143
5		16.66	12.25	8.74	6.93	5.713	4.834
6		8.33	12.25	8.74	6.23	5.285	4.544
7			12.25	8.74	5.90	4.888	4.271
8			6.13	8.74	5.90	4.522	4.015
9				8.74	5.91	4.462	3.774
10				8.74	5.90	4.461	3.584
11				4.37	5.91	4.462	3.583
12					5.90	4.461	3.584
13					5.91	4.462	3.583
14					5.90	4.461	3.584
15					5.91	4.462	3.583
16					2.95	4.461	3.584
17						4.462	3.583
18						4.461	3.584
19						4.462	3.583
20						4.461	3.584
21						2.231	3.583
22							3.584
23							3.583
24							3.584
25							3.583
26							1.792

Table A-15. **150% Declining Balance Method**
Mid-Quarter Convention
Property Placed in Service in First Quarter

Year	Recovery periods in years						
	3	5	7	10	15	20	25
1	43.75%	26.25%	18.75%	13.13%	8.75%	6.563%	5.250%
2	28.13	22.13	17.41	13.03	9.13	7.008	5.685
3	25.00	16.52	13.68	11.08	8.21	6.482	5.344
4	3.12	16.52	12.16	9.41	7.39	5.996	5.023
5		16.52	12.16	8.71	6.65	5.546	4.722
6		2.06	12.16	8.71	5.99	5.130	4.439
7			12.16	8.71	5.90	4.746	4.172
8			1.52	8.71	5.91	4.459	3.922
9				8.71	5.90	4.459	3.687
10				8.71	5.91	4.459	3.582
11				1.09	5.90	4.459	3.582
12					5.91	4.460	3.582
13					5.90	4.459	3.582
14					5.91	4.460	3.582
15					5.90	4.459	3.582
16					0.74	4.460	3.582
17						4.459	3.582
18						4.460	3.582
19						4.459	3.581
20						4.460	3.582
21						0.557	3.581
22							3.582
23							3.581
24							3.582
25							3.581
26							0.448

Table A-16. **150% Declining Balance Method**
Mid-Quarter Convention
Property Placed in Service in Second Quarter

Year	Recovery periods in years						
	3	5	7	10	15	20	25
1	31.25%	18.75%	13.39%	9.38%	6.25%	4.688%	3.750%
2	34.38	24.38	18.56	13.59	9.38	7.148	5.775
3	25.00	17.06	14.58	11.55	8.44	6.612	5.429
4	9.37	16.76	12.22	9.82	7.59	6.116	5.103
5		16.76	12.22	8.73	6.83	5.658	4.797
6		6.29	12.22	8.73	6.15	5.233	4.509
7			12.23	8.73	5.91	4.841	4.238
8			4.58	8.73	5.90	4.478	3.984
9				8.73	5.91	4.463	3.745
10				8.73	5.90	4.463	3.583
11				3.28	5.91	4.463	3.583
12					5.90	4.463	3.583
13					5.91	4.463	3.583
14					5.90	4.463	3.583
15					5.91	4.462	3.583
16					2.21	4.463	3.583
17						4.462	3.583
18						4.463	3.583
19						4.462	3.583
20						4.463	3.583
21						1.673	3.583
22							3.583
23							3.583
24							3.582
25							3.583
26							1.343

Table A-17. **150% Declining Balance Method**
Mid-Quarter Convention
Property Placed in Service in Third Quarter

Year	Recovery periods in years						
	3	5	7	10	15	20	25
1	18.75%	11.25%	8.04%	5.63%	3.75%	2.813%	2.250%
2	40.63	26.63	19.71	14.16	9.63	7.289	5.865
3	25.00	18.64	15.48	12.03	8.66	6.742	5.513
4	15.62	16.56	12.27	10.23	7.80	6.237	5.182
5		16.57	12.28	8.75	7.02	5.769	4.871
6		10.35	12.27	8.75	6.31	5.336	4.579
7			12.28	8.75	5.90	4.936	4.304
8			7.67	8.74	5.90	4.566	4.046
9				8.75	5.91	4.460	3.803
10				8.74	5.90	4.460	3.584
11				5.47	5.91	4.460	3.584
12					5.90	4.460	3.584
13					5.91	4.461	3.584
14					5.90	4.460	3.584
15					5.91	4.461	3.584
16					3.69	4.460	3.584
17						4.461	3.584
18						4.460	3.584
19						4.461	3.584
20						4.460	3.584
21						2.788	3.585
22							3.584
23							3.585
24							3.584
25							3.585
26							2.240

Table A-18. **150% Declining Balance Method**
Mid-Quarter Convention
Property Placed in Service in Fourth Quarter

Year	Recovery periods in years						
	3	5	7	10	15	20	25
1	6.25%	3.75%	2.88%	1.88%	1.25%	0.938%	0.750%
2	46.88	28.88	22.41	14.72	9.88	7.430	5.955
3	25.00	20.21	17.24	12.51	8.89	6.872	5.598
4	21.87	16.40	13.26	10.63	8.00	6.357	5.262
5		16.41	13.10	9.04	7.20	5.880	4.946
6		14.35	13.10	8.72	6.48	5.439	4.649
7			13.10	8.72	5.90	5.031	4.370
8			4.91	8.72	5.90	4.654	4.108
9				8.72	5.90	4.458	3.862
10				8.71	5.91	4.458	3.630
11				7.63	5.90	4.458	3.582
12					5.91	4.458	3.582
13					5.90	4.458	3.582
14					5.91	4.458	3.582
15					5.90	4.458	3.582
16					5.17	4.458	3.583
17						4.458	3.582
18						4.459	3.583
19						4.458	3.582
20						4.459	3.583
21						3.901	3.582
22							3.583
23							3.582
24							3.583
25							3.582
26							3.135

Table B-1. **Table of Class Lives and Recovery Periods**

Asset class	Description of assets included	Recovery Periods (in years)		
		Class Life (in years)	GDS (MACRS)	ADS
SPECIFIC DEPRECIABLE ASSETS USED IN ALL BUSINESS ACTIVITIES, EXCEPT AS NOTED:				
00.11	**Office Furniture, Fixtures, and Equipment:** Includes furniture and fixtures that are not a structural component of a building. Includes such assets as desks, files, safes, and communications equipment. Does not include communications equipment that is included in other classes.	10	7	10
00.12	**Information Systems:** Includes computers and their peripheral equipment used in administering normal business transactions and the maintenance of business records, their retrieval and analysis. Information systems are defined as: 1) Computers: A computer is a programmable electronically activated device capable of accepting information, applying prescribed processes to the information, and supplying the results of these processes with or without human intervention. It usually consists of a central processing unit containing extensive storage, logic, arithmetic, and control capabilities. Excluded from this category are adding machines, electronic desk calculators, etc., and other equipment described in class 00.13. 2) Peripheral equipment consists of the auxiliary machines which are designed to be placed under control of the central processing unit. Nonlimiting examples are: Card readers, card punches, magnetic tape feeds, high speed printers, optical character readers, tape cassettes, mass storage units, paper tape equipment, keypunches, data entry devices, teleprinters, terminals, tape drives, disc drives, disc files, disc packs, visual image projector tubes, card sorters, plotters, and collators. Peripheral equipment may be used on-line or off-line. Does not incude equipment that is an integral part of other capital equipment that is included in other classes of economic activity, i.e., computers used primarily for process or production control, switching, channeling, and automating distributive trades and services such as point of sale (POS) computer systems. Also, does not include equipment of a kind used primarily for amusement or entertainment of the user.	6	5	5
00.13	**Data Handling Equipment; except Computers:** Includes only typewriters, calculators, adding and accounting machines, copiers, and duplicating equipment.	6	5	6
00.21	**Airplanes (airframes and engines), except those used in commercial or contract carrying of passengers or freight, and all helicopters (airframes and engines)**	6	5	6
00.22	**Automobiles, Taxis**	3	5	5
00.23	**Buses**	9	5	9
00.241	**Light General Purpose Trucks:** Includes trucks for use over the road (actual weight less than 13,000 pounds)	4	5	5
00.242	**Heavy General Purpose Trucks:** Includes heavy general purpose trucks, concrete ready mix-trucks, and ore trucks, for use over the road (actual unloaded weight 13,000 pounds or more)	6	5	6
00.25	**Railroad Cars and Locomotives, except those owned by railroad transportation companies**	15	7	15
00.26	**Tractor Units for Use Over-The-Road**	4	3	4
00.27	**Trailers and Trailer-Mounted Containers**	6	5	6
00.28	**Vessels, Barges, Tugs, and Similar Water Transportation Equipment, except those used in marine construction**	18	10	18
00.3	**Land Improvements:** Includes improvements directly to or added to land, whether such improvements are section 1245 property or section 1250 property, provided such improvements are depreciable. Examples of such assets might include sidewalks, roads, canals, waterways, drainage facilities, sewers (not including municipal sewers in Class 51), wharves and docks, bridges, fences, landscaping shrubbery, or radio and television transmitting towers. Does not include land improvements that are explicitly included in any other class, and buildings and structural components as defined in section 1.48-1(e) of the regulations. Excludes public utility initial clearing and grading land improvements as specified in Rev. Rul. 72-403, 1972-2 C.B. 102.	20	15	20

Table B-2. **Table of Class Lives and Recovery Periods**

Asset class	Description of assets included	Class Life (in years)	GDS (MACRS)	ADS
		Recovery Periods (in years)		
	DEPRECIABLE ASSETS USED IN THE FOLLOWING ACTIVITIES:			
01.1	**Agriculture:** Includes machinery and equipment, grain bins, and fences but no other land improvements, that are used in the production of crops or plants, vines, and trees; livestock; the operation of farm dairies, nurseries, greenhouses, sod farms, mushroom cellars, cranberry bogs, apiaries, and fur farms; the performance of agriculture, animal husbandry, and horticultural services.	10	7	10
01.11	**Cotton Ginning Assets**	12	7	12
01.21	**Cattle, Breeding or Dairy**	7	5	7
01.221	**Any breeding or work horse that is 12 years old or less at the time it is placed in service****	10	7	10
01.222	**Any breeding or work horse that is more than 12 years old at the time it is placed in service****	10	3	10
01.223	**Any race horse that is more than 2 years old at the time it is placed in service****	*	3	12
01.224	**Any horse that is more than 12 years old at the time it is placed in service and that is neither a race horse nor a horse described in class 01.222****	*	3	12
01.225	**Any horse not described in classes 01.221, 01.222, 01.223, or 01.224**	*	7	12
01.23	**Hogs, Breeding**	3	3	3
01.24	**Sheep and Goats, Breeding**	5	5	5
01.3	**Farm buildings except structures included in Class 01.4**	25	20	25
01.4	**Single purpose agricultural or horticultural structures (within the meaning of section 168(l)(13) of the Code)**	15	10***	15
10.0	**Mining:** Includes assets used in the mining and quarrying of metallic and nonmetallic minerals (including sand, gravel, stone, and clay) and the milling, beneficiation and other primary preparation of such materials.	10	7	10
13.0	**Offshore Drilling:** Includes assets used in offshore drilling for oil and gas such as floating, self-propelled and other drilling vessels, barges, platforms, and drilling equipment and support vessels such as tenders, barges, towboats and crewboats. Excludes oil and gas production assets.	7.5	5	7.5
13.1	**Drilling of Oil and Gas Wells:** Includes assets used in the drilling of onshore oil and gas wells and the provision of geophysical and other exploration services; and the provision of such oil and gas field services as chemical treatment, plugging and abandoning of wells and cementing or perforating well casings. Does not include assets used in the performance of any of these activities and services by integrated petroleum and natural gas producers for their own account.	6	5	6
15.0	**Construction:** Includes assets used in construction by general building, special trade, heavy and marine construction contractors, operative and investment builders, real estate subdividers and developers, and others except railroads.	6	5	6
57.0	**Distributive Trades and Services:** Includes assets used in wholesale and retail trade, and personal and professional services. Includes section 1245 assets used in marketing petroleum and petroleum products.	9	5	9****
57.1	**Distributive Trades and Services—Billboard, Service Station Buildings and Petroleum Marketing Land Improvements:** Includes section 1250 assets, including service station buildings and depreciable land improvements, whether section 1245 property or section 1250 property, used in the marketing of petroleum and petroleum products, but not including any of these facilities related to petroleum and natural gas trunk pipelines. Includes car wash buildings and related land improvements. Includes billboards, whether such assets are section 1245 property or section 1250 property. Excludes all other land improvements, buildings and structural components as defined in section 1.48-1(e) of the regulations. See *Gas station convenience stores* in chapter 3.	20	15	20
79.0	**Recreation:** Includes assets used in the provision of entertainment services on payment of a fee or admission charge, as in the operation of bowling alleys, billiard and pool establishments, theaters, concert halls, and miniature golf courses. Does not include amusement and theme parks and assets which consist primarily of specialized land improvements or structures, such as golf courses, sports stadia, race tracks, ski slopes, and buildings which house the assets used in entertainment services.	10	7	10
	Certain Property for Which Recovery Periods Assigned A. Personal Property With No Class Life Section 1245 Real Property With No Class Life		7 7	12 40

* Property described in asset classes 01.223, 01.224, and 01.225 are assigned recovery periods but have no class lives.

** A horse is more than 2 (or 12) years old after the day that is 24 (or 144) months after its actual birthdate.

*** 7 if property was placed in service before 1989.

**** Any high technology medical equipment as defined in section 168(i)(2)(C) which is described in asset guideline class 57.0 is assigned a 5-year recovery period for the alternate MACRS method.

Chapter 8

Business Profit and Self-Employment Tax

Once you have added up all your gross business income, and you've dug up all your deductible business expenses for the year, you can calculate your net business income by subtracting your expenses from your income. Hopefully, you still have some income left over after expenses are deducted, and this amount is your profit for tax purposes.

This calculation is made on the bottom of the front page of your Schedule C or on Line 3 of your C-EZ. If you have more than one Schedule C, the results from each one are computed separately.

The results from any and all Schedule Cs you have are totaled up and carried over to your individual income tax return (Form 1040, Line 12), where they will become part of your adjusted gross income (AGI). If you are filing jointly with your spouse, the net income from any Schedule Cs filed by your spouse is also included.

Owning a business is full of surprises, both good and bad. In some years you may find that your expenses exceed your gross business income, which means that you have a loss for the year. This can be deducted

against any other income you or your spouse may have, or carried over to other years in which you have more income, provided you meet certain requirements, as discussed on page 139 below.

Your net business income is important for another reason: it is the amount on which you must pay self-employment taxes. So, your net business profit or loss is also carried over to Line 2 of Schedule SE, which is used to compute your self-employment (SECA) tax.

SELF-EMPLOYMENT TAX

Brand-new business owners are sometimes surprised to find out that in addition to their federal income taxes, they must also pay a significant percentage of their income as SECA taxes.

The Self-Employment Contributions Act (SECA) tax is basically the business owner's version of the FICA tax that employees pay. Like FICA, it is made up of your "contributions" to both the Social Security and Medicare programs. However, the tax rate for the self-employed under SECA is twice the rate that employees must pay on their paychecks as FICA tax, to reflect the fact that employees pay one-half of the FICA tax and employers pay the other half.

What Income Counts?

For starters, you don't have to worry about paying the SECA tax at all if your total business income, from all Schedule Cs combined, is less than $400. But if your total income is $400 or more, you must file a Schedule SE and pay SECA tax on your entire profits, including the first $400.

If you are filing jointly and your spouse also files one or more Schedule Cs, each spouse must count his or her own income separately.

Example

You own two small businesses and file two schedule Cs. Business A had net income of $80,000 and Business B had a net loss of $5,000. Your spouse also operated a business as a sole proprietor, and had net income of $20,000. On Line 12 of your Form 1040, you would report all Schedule C income earned by both you and your spouse: $80,000 + $20,000 - $5,000 = $95,000.

However, for SECA tax purposes, your total net business income would be $80,000 - $5,000 = $75,000. Your spouse's total net income for SECA purposes would be $20,000. You must each file one Schedule SE and attach both of them to your joint Form 1040.

Since it's the net income from your *business* that is the basis of SECA tax, certain types of income are not included: interest and dividends, sales of business property or other assets, and rental income from real estate or personal property. There's an exception to this rule if generating that income is your core business; for instance, if you are a real estate developer in the business of renting or selling property, you operate a bank, or you are in the rent-to-own business. Do not count any income from your hobbies, as defined on page 34.

Farmers

Farmers who file Schedule F with their Form 1040 must include as self-employment income their net income from farming, as shown on Line 36 of their Schedule F.

Partners

Partners, also, must include their distributions from the partnership as well as any guaranteed payments they receive for their services as net self-employment income. These amounts should be shown on the Schedule K-1 information return that you receive from the partnership at the end of the year. For all general partners, this is true whether you are an active or inactive member of the partnership. For limited partners, you need only to include any guaranteed payments, such as salary or professional fees received during the year.

There is an exception to this rule if the partnership is an investment club, and the club limits its activities to investing in CDs and securities, and collecting income on the investments.

If you are a retired partner, you do not need to include your retirement income received from the partnership in net earnings from self-employment if all of the following are true:

- You are receiving periodic payments for life.

- Your share of the partnership capital has been fully repaid. The partnership owes you nothing but the retirement payments.

- You performed no services for the partnership this year.

Corporate Payments

If you are an S corporation shareholder, unlike a partner, your distributions from the organization generally do not count as self-employment income and are not subject to SECA tax. However, if you are a shareholder and also an officer of the company who performs substantial services, you are considered an employee. Some reasonable amount of compensation for your services must be considered salary or wages, on which regular payroll taxes, including Social Security, Medicare, and income tax withholding, must be paid.

Corporate directors of either C or S corporations who receive fees are not considered employees. Instead, their fees are considered self-employment income. However, if you are a corporate officer or other employee, your income is subject to regular payroll taxes (including FICA) and you aren't considered self-employed for purposes of SECA tax.

Religious Exemptions

There are some special exemptions from self-employment income that may apply if you are a member of certain religions, or you work for a religious group.

If you are a member of a religious order who has taken a vow of poverty, you are exempt from self-employment tax as long as you are working for the church or a church agency. But if you are working for yourself, you must pay SECA tax.

If you have not taken a vow of poverty, but you are a minister, member of a religious order, or a Christian Science practitioner, you can get an exemption from SECA tax if you file IRS Form 4361, *Application for Exemption from Self-Employment Tax for Use by Ministers, Members of Religious Orders, and Christian Science Practitioners.* To get a copy, call the IRS at 1-800-TAX-FORM.

If you are a member of a recognized sect that has been in existence since December 31, 1950 and that is opposed to insurance, you may be exempt from Social Security and Medicare tax (and thus, SECA tax) if you are conscientiously opposed to pension plans or life, disability, or medical insurance and you waive all Social Security benefits. To get the exemption, you must file IRS Form 4029, *Application for Exemption from Social Security and Medicare Taxes and Waiver of Benefits,* which you can obtain by calling 1-800-TAX-FORM.

If none of the above apply to you and you are an employee of a church or church-controlled organization that has itself elected exemption from Social Security and Medicare taxes, you will have to pay SECA tax if you are paid $108.28 or more in a year by the church or organization.

Aliens

Aliens who are residents of the United States are generally subject to the same rules as U.S. citizens, including SECA tax rules. Residents of the Virgin Islands, Puerto Rico, Guam, or American Samoa are also subject to SECA tax. Self-employment activities of U.S. citizens in these regions plus the Northern Mariana Islands are subject to SECA tax.

Nonresident aliens will be subject to SECA tax on income earned in the U.S. unless they are citizens of a country that has a social security agreement or treaty in effect with the U.S. If an agreement is in effect, the terms of the agreement will dictate the rules. Currently there are agreements with Austria, Belgium, Canada, Finland, France, Germany, Greece, Ireland, Italy, Japan, Korea, Luxembourg, the Netherlands, Norway, Portugal, Spain, Sweden, Switzerland, and the United Kingdom. For more information, contact a country's social security agency, or the U.S. Social Security Administration, Office of International Policy, P.O. Box 17741, Baltimore, MD 21235.

Other Miscellaneous Income

If you are the executor or administrator of a deceased person's estate, your fees are exempt from SECA tax and are simply reported as miscellaneous income on Line 21 of your Form 1040. An exception to this rule applies if you are a professional fiduciary, or the estate includes an active trade or business that you participate in and your fees are related to operating the business, or your administrative duties are so extensive over a long period of time that they should be considered a trade or business. In any of these cases, you'd need to file a Schedule C to report the income and, in turn, a Schedule SE to report self-employment income.

Since statutory employees already have FICA tax withheld from their payments, they do not have to pay SECA tax. See page 48 for more on statutory employees.

Fees received as a notary public are not subject to SECA tax.

The $72,600 Ceiling

In computing your SECA tax, the Medicare portion of the tax is imposed on 2.9% of all your net business income, with no upper limit.

The Social Security portion of the tax is 12.4%, but it only applies to the first $72,600 you earn in 1999. This dollar amount increases every year to reflect increases in the average American wage. In 2000, the wage ceiling will be $76,200.

For purpose of determining whether you meet the $72,600 ceiling, only your own earnings – and not those of your spouse – are counted.

If you have earnings from a regular job, or perhaps more than one job, your employer will automatically be withholding FICA tax on your wages. Your wages, salary, bonus, tips, etc. earned on the job will count towards the $72,600 amount, and at most your SECA tax will apply to the difference.

Overpayments of FICA tax

If you had more than one job during the year, and the total of all your income from those jobs added up to more than $72,600, it's likely that too much Social Security tax has been withheld from your paychecks.

Take a look at the amount in Box 4 on all of your W-2 Forms. If you add them up and the sum is more than $4,501.20, you've paid too much tax. The overpayment (what you've paid, minus $4,501.20) can be claimed as a subtraction from your tax bill on Line 62 of Form 1040. You cannot use Form 1040EZ or Form 1040A to claim this overpayment.

Computing Your SECA Tax

Your SECA tax is computed by filling out either the long or the short version of Schedule SE.

Most people can use the short version of the form. Those who cannot include those whose total wages, tips, salary and earnings from self-employment were more than $72,600 in 1999; religious workers who owe self-employment taxes (see discussion above); or farmers or low-income people using one of the optional methods discussed below (which generally require you to pay higher SECA taxes).

Unless you are using one of the optional methods, to compute your SECA tax you will transfer your net self-employment income to Lines 1 and 2 of the short SE form or the long SE.

Then, you will multiply your total net self-employment income by 92.35% to get your taxable net earnings from self-employment. This fraction has the effect of giving you a deduction from your income for one-half of the SECA taxes you'd otherwise have to pay, to reflect the fact that employees don't have to pay FICA tax on the portion of FICA that their employers pay them.

Then, multiply the result by 15.3% to arrive at your SECA tax, unless your combined wages, tips, salary, bonus and your net earnings from self-employment are greater than $72,600. If they are, you will be using the long form of Schedule SE, which will allow you to make sure you're paying Social Security only on the first $72,600 you make.

Finally, you will enter the amount of your SECA tax on Line 5 of the short SE or Line 12 of the long SE, and then transfer it to Line 50 of your Form 1040 and add it to the income tax you owe.

Don't forget the very last step, which is to give yourself an income tax deduction for one-half of your SECA tax (computed on Line 6 of the short SE and Line 13 of the long one). This amount is transferred to Line 27 of your Form 1040. It has the effect of allowing you to avoid paying income tax on one-half of your SECA tax amount, just as employees do not have to pay income tax on the amount of FICA tax that their employers pay for them.

Optional Methods

As we mentioned above, there are two optional methods of computing your SECA tax.

To understand why these optional methods exist, you have to realize that Social Security disability and retirement benefits are conditioned on your having worked a certain amount during your lifetime; generally you need to have worked for at least 40 calendar quarters (or 10 years) in which you were covered by Social Security and earned a minimum amount. For 1999, you must earn $740 to get a quarter of coverage; if you earn $2,960 or more you will be credited with four quarters.

When the Social Security system was enacted, people who were relatively close to retirement, or who had been out of the workforce or had worked for many years at very low-paying jobs, were in danger of not qualifying for retirement benefits. This is less of a problem today, when most workers earn many more quarters than the minimum needed to qualify; however, there are still a few people who might be in danger of falling outside the Social Security system if they did not have a special way to qualify. In particular, some farmers whose income fluctuates a great deal from year to year and who often suffer an annual financial loss may need some help in gaining more quarters of coverage.

Hence, the optional methods of computing net earnings from self-employment, which operate by allowing you to pay SECA tax as if your net earnings were higher than they actually were.

Can I Use the Optional Methods?

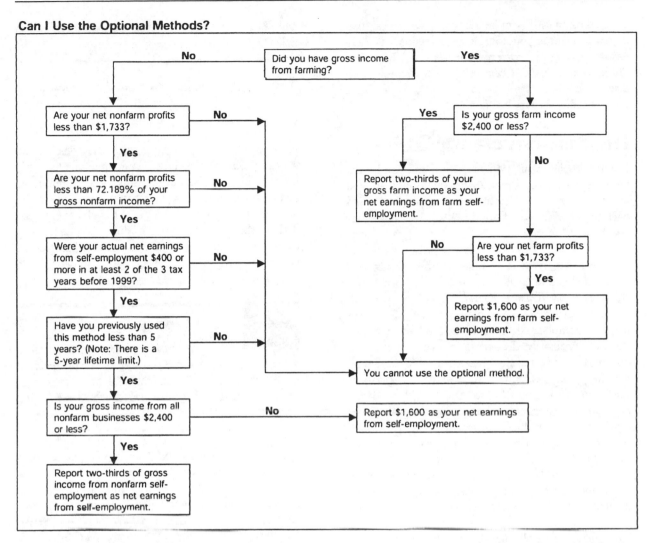

There is a special optional method for farmers, and a slightly less lenient method for low-income non-farmers. Either of these methods can also help you if you are entitled to the Earned Income Credit (EIC) and increasing your net self-employment income will help you to obtain a higher EIC amount.

The flow chart above will tell you whether or not you qualify to use one of these methods. If you are eligible, Part II of the long version of Schedule SE will walk you through the computations.

NET OPERATING LOSSES

If you're like most small business owners, you won't see a profit in your first year of operation. And as your business grows, you may face one or more years in which your business's expenses exceed its income.

In other words, the business may have a loss for the year.

Although it may be small comfort, if you have a loss, you'll normally be able to deduct it from your total income from other business ventures or from any salary, wages, or other earnings. If the business loss exceeds your total income for the year, any unused portion of the loss, which is known in the tax laws as a net operating loss (NOL), can be used to offset income and reduce taxes in another year.

The net operating loss deduction is an exception to the general income tax rule that your taxable income is determined on the basis of your current year's events. This deduction allows you to offset one year's losses against another year's income. A net loss from the operation of a trade or business, casualty losses, and losses resulting from employee business expenses are included in this computation, but losses from a trade or business are the most common occurrence.

Calculating an NOL can be tricky and we suggest that, if you have one, you consult a professional to help ensure you do it correctly, or get the IRS's free Publication 536, *Net Operating Losses*. The following discussion is intended to give you a basic understanding of how NOLs work

Do You Have an NOL?

If you complete your 1999 tax return and you have a negative number on Line 37 of your Form 1040, you may have an NOL that may potentially be carried over to other years. If so, 1999 will be called your "NOL year."

The next step is to determine whether or not you have a deductible NOL. Schedule A of Form 1045, *Application for Tentative Refund*, should be used to compute the amount of your NOL. This can become complicated, because a number of things that are ordinarily deductible on your tax return cannot be deducted for purposes of determining whether you actually have an NOL: personal exemptions for yourself, spouse, and dependents; net capital losses, which are subject to different carryover rules; nonbusiness losses; NOL deductions from other years; and nonbusiness deductions such as alimony, medical deductions, charitable deductions, real estate tax on your residence, deductible IRA contributions, or the standard deduction if you don't itemize.

Net operating losses may be carried back for two years (or for three years, in the case of a casualty loss) before the year of the loss (called the NOL year). The loss is used to offset the taxable income of those previous years, for the earliest year first. Any unused portion of the loss may be carried forward for up to 20 years after the NOL year. If the entire loss isn't used up within the permitted period, no further net operating loss carryover is permitted.

To "carry a loss back," you may file a Form 1045 within one year of the end of the NOL year, or you can file an amended tax return for the year in question within three years of the NOL year.

Example

If your NOL year was 1999 and you filed your tax return on April 15, 2000, you can file Form 1045 any time on or after April 15 of 2000 but before January 1, 2001, to claim a refund for 1997. Or, you

can file a 1040X for 1997 any time before April 15 of 2003.

Whichever form you use to claim the carryback, you must use Schedule A of Form 1045 to compute the amount of the NOL.

A taxpayer can elect to forgo the carryback period, instead choosing to deduct the net operating loss only over the next 20 years in the future. If so, you must attach a statement to your tax return for the NOL year, or to an amended return for that year filed within six months of its due date excluding extensions. The statement must assert that you are electing to forgo the carryback period under Section 172(b)(3) of the Internal Revenue Code.

Save Money

Because carrying back a net operating loss to a prior tax year can result in a quick tax refund, it will usually be unwise to pass up the carryback period, unless you're quite sure that your business will be in a higher tax bracket in the future.

When you carry back an NOL, you must refigure your tax for the carryback year by recomputing your adjusted gross income (AGI) for that year. Then you must recompute any items that were limited by your AGI amount, such as the special allowance for passive activities, taxable Social Security benefits, IRA deductions, and excludable savings bond interest.

Next, refigure your taxable income if needed to reflect the change in your itemized deductions for medical expenses, casualty losses, miscellaneous itemized deductions, and the overall limit on itemized deductions and phaseout of personal exemptions for higher-income taxpayers. You will also have to refigure your AMT, if it applied to you. However, do not refigure your self-employment tax for the carryback year.

If you don't use up your entire NOL in the first carryback year, you may have a carryover, and you'll need to use Schedule B of Form 1045 to compute the amount.

If you carry forward an NOL, things are a little simpler. You would list your NOL figure as a negative amount on the "other income" line of Form 1040, and attach a statement showing how you computed the NOL.

Chapter 9

Business Tax Credits

Besides taking care to claim every single tax deduction that you qualify for, you can minimize your income tax bill by claiming any and all the business tax credits available to you.

When they're available, tax credits are generally a better deal than tax deductions would be, because credits are subtracted directly from your tax bill. On the other hand, deductions are subtracted from the *income* on which your tax bill is based.

So, a dollar's worth of tax credit reduces your tax bill by a whole dollar, but a dollar's worth of deductions lowers your tax bill by only 36 cents if you're in the 36-percent bracket, by 28 cents if you're in the 28-percent bracket, etc. If you have a choice between claiming a credit or a deduction for a certain expense, you're generally better off claiming the credit.

As wonderful as tax credits can be, with the IRS (as you've probably figured out by now) there's almost always a catch. In this case, the catch is that business tax credits are only available for certain very specific situations. Many of them apply only to certain industries (like restaurants and bars, or energy producers). And credits come with a set of very complicated rules, which you (or, more likely, your tax pro) must follow in order to claim them.

Before the 1986 tax simplification, federal income tax credits were available for many of the investments a small business might typically make. Now, however, most credits are very narrowly targeted to encourage you to take certain actions that lawmakers have deemed desirable; generally, to benefit disadvantaged or low-income individuals or the environment. There are also a few credits designed to prevent double taxation, and a few designed to encourage certain investments that are considered socially beneficial.

The forms and procedures used to calculate and claim business tax credits are quite complicated. In fact, we recommend that you leave the technical details to your tax adviser. However, we do provide an outline of the basic rules, including the dollar limits, carryback and carryforward rules, and recapture rules, so you can decide whether to pursue arranging your business affairs to take advantage of a credit.

CREDITS FOR CERTAIN TAXES

You might not believe it, but sometimes the IRS does have a heart. It occasionally gives certain people a break for taxes that might be considered unfair.

There are four business tax credits that give a "rebate" for certain kinds of taxes.

Credit for FICA Tax on Tips

Under current law, employees who get $20 or more in tips in a single month must report their tips to their employers. If you have tipped employees, you have to pay Social Security and Medicare (FICA) taxes to the tune of 7.65 percent on tips that are reported to you, even though you don't have any control over the amounts. The purpose of the rule is to make sure that tipped employees are adequately covered by Social Security pension, disability, and survivors' benefits. However, the rule was believed to place a particularly heavy burden on the restaurant industry.

So, if your business is one that provides food or beverages for customers to consume on or off the premises, and if your waiters, waitresses, or delivery personnel are customarily tipped by your patrons, you're entitled to a tax credit for any FICA taxes you pay on the tips.

The upshot of all this? Your workers receive Social Security credits towards their future benefits on account of the tips, but you don't have to pay for these benefits. Note that there's an exception to the general credit rule: If you pay your employees below the minimum wage, with the expectation that tips will bring them up to the minimum, you can't claim the credit for FICA on the portion of the tips that is used to bring them up to the minimum wage.

No double-dipping is allowed. If you are eligible for and decide to claim this credit, you can't deduct the FICA taxes on which the credit is claimed as a business expense. However, because tax credits are generally worth more than deductions, this is not usually a problem.

The FICA tax credit is claimed on Form 8846, *Credit for Employer Social Security and Medicare Taxes Paid on Certain Employee Tips*, and is part of the general business credit.

The total of all your general business credits can't reduce your current year's tax bill below the larger of (a) your tentative minimum tax or (b) 25 percent of the part of your regular tax bill that exceeds $25,000.

Gasoline Tax Credit

You can claim a credit for any federal excise taxes you pay on gasoline and special fuels (like undyed diesel, heating oil, liquefied petroleum gas, and compressed natural gas), when you use the fuel for certain purposes: for farming; for nonhighway purposes of your trade or business; for intercity, local, or school buses; or for export or foreign trade. You can't claim this credit for any personal (nonbusiness) use, so forget about claiming it for your snowmobile or pleasure boat! The credit is claimed on Form 4136, *Credit for Federal Tax Paid on Fuels*. It is *refundable*, meaning that the IRS will pay it to you even if you have no tax liability for the year.

Foreign Tax Credit

You can claim a credit for foreign income taxes, or taxes imposed by possessions of the U.S., that you paid or accrued during the tax year. For example, you might have become liable for foreign taxes on profits from overseas operations or investments. You can elect to deduct these taxes instead of taking the credit, if you prefer, although claiming the credit will generally save you more money. The credit is claimed on Form 1116, *Foreign Tax Credit*.

Prior Years' AMT Credit

If you paid alternative minimum tax (see page 301) in a prior year, you may be eligible for a credit for a portion of it against your regular tax liability for the current year, and for subsequent years as well. The credit is claimed on Form 8801, *Credit for Prior Year Minimum Tax—Individuals, Estates, and Trusts*.

Save Time

If you have paid AMT in prior years and think you might be eligible for this credit, see your tax adviser. The AMT rules are a morass of confusion, and interpretation of them is best left to professionals.

CREDITS BENEFITING DISADVANTAGED GROUPS

The tax laws have historically been used to encourage certain activities that the government deems desirable, but that people might not otherwise undertake on their own because the economic rewards are perceived as insufficient. This group of tax credits is a good example of that type of policy.

Welfare-to-Work Credit

A tax credit is provided to employers who hire qualified long-term family assistance (AFDC or its successor program) recipients. The credit is equal to 35 percent of up to $10,000 of wages in the first year and up to 50 percent of up to $10,000 in the second year of employment, for a two-year maximum credit of $8,500 per employee. The credit is available for employees hired between January 1, 1998 and January 1, 2002, and is claimed on Form 8861, *Welfare-to-Work Credit.*

Work Smart

Note that if you claim the welfare-to-work credit for an employee, you can't also claim the work opportunity credit for that employee. The welfare-to-work credit is more generous, so it will usually be more beneficial to claim it, rather than the work opportunity credit, where the employee would qualify for both.

Work Opportunity Credit

This credit was designed to provide an incentive to hire persons from certain disadvantaged groups that have a particularly high unemployment rate (including urban youths, government assistance recipients, ex-convicts, disadvantaged Vietnam vets, and vocational rehabilitation referrals). It was created in 1996 to replace the expired targeted jobs credit. The credit is claimed on Form 5884, *Work Opportunity Credit.*

The work opportunity tax credit is available for a limited time — it applies to the wages of employees who began work after October 1, 1996, and before January 1, 2002.

For employees who began work before October 1, 1997, the credit is for 35 percent of up to $6,000 of each worker's first-year wages, for a maximum credit of $2,100. For summer youth employees, the maximum credit is 35 percent of up to $3,000 of wages paid during a 90-day period, for a maximum credit of $1,050.

For workers who began work after October 1, 1997 and up to January 1, 2002, the credit percentage has been increased to 40 percent for employment of 400 or more hours, and dropped to 25 percent for employment of at least 120 but less than 400 hours. The 35 percent credit for summer youth employees is unchanged.

The credit applies to the wages of the following groups:

- families receiving cash welfare benefits for at least nine months

- veterans who are members of families receiving assistance or food stamps

- high-risk youth aged 18 through 24 on their hiring date who live in an empowerment zone or enterprise community

- vocational rehabilitation referrals certified to have a physical or mental disability

- qualified summer youth employees aged 16 or 17 on the hiring date who live in an empowerment zone or enterprise community and perform services during a 90-day period between May 1 and September 15 who have not previously worked for the employer

- ex-felons hired not more than one year after the later of their conviction or release from prison, who are members of low-income families

- individuals aged 18 to 24 who are in families that have been receiving food stamps for six months

- Supplemental Security Income (SSI) recipients

Most of these individuals, other than the summer youth employees, must be employed for at least 180 days or 400 hours to qualify; as of October 1, 1997, this requirement was reduced to 120 hours and days are no longer counted.

Disabled Access Credit

Under the Americans with Disabilities Act of 1990 (ADA), businesses that are open to the public ("public accommodations," in legal language) must help or accommodate persons with disabilities seeking to use their services. They must also remove physical barriers to the disabled, if removal is "readily achievable."

Example

The regulations say that moving tables in a restaurant is "readily achievable," but widening a doorway is not.

What's more, any renovations or new construction must include provisions for access by the disabled, in accordance with certain very technical specifications.

Small businesses that are faced with making changes to obey the ADA have been given a "carrot," in the form of a tax credit, to encourage them to comply with the law. For any year, you may claim a credit for 50 percent of your eligible access expenditures that exceed $250 but don't exceed $10,250. So, you can't claim more than $5,000 in any one year.

The "eligible access expenditures" include not only expenses for removal of physical barriers (in renovations, but not new construction), but also expenses for deaf interpreters; readers for the blind; equipment or devices to make services available to the deaf, blind, or other disabled persons; or similar expenses.

Save Money

If you anticipate that your disabled accommodation expenses will exceed $10,250, try to spread them over more than one year in order to take maximum advantage of the tax credit.

This tax credit is available only to small businesses— that is, those having: (1) gross receipts of $1 million or less, or (2) having no more than 30 full-time employees.

The disabled access credit is claimed on Form 8826, *Disabled Access Credit*, and is part of the general business credit discussed on page 148.

Empowerment Zone Employment Credit

If your business is located in a federal "empowerment zone," and you hire workers who also live and work within the zone, you can get a tax credit for 20 percent of the first $15,000 of wages paid to each of your workers. The workers can be full-time or part-time, so long as substantially all of their work is done within the zone and as part of your trade or business. You can't count wages paid to employees who worked for less than 90 days (unless the worker became disabled or was fired for misconduct); employees who are closely related to you; employees who own 5 percent or more of the business; or employees at golf courses, country clubs, massage parlors, hot tub facilities, suntan facilities, racetrack or gambling facilities, or liquor stores.

Where are these zones? They are certain designated parts of Atlanta, Baltimore, Chicago, Detroit, New York, and Philadelphia; portions of Clinton, Jackson, and Wayne Counties in Kentucky; portions of Bolivar, Sunflower, Leflore, Washington, Humphreys, and Holmes Counties in Mississippi; and portions of Starr, Cameron, Hidalgo, and Willacy Counties in Texas. If you live in one of these cities or areas, contact your city or county government to find out the exact boundaries of the empowerment zones.

Beginning in 1998, portions of Washington, D.C. have been designated as an Enterprise Zone that is eligible for the Empowerment Zone wage credit. This law is scheduled to expire on December 31, 2002.

Also, under tax legislation passed in 1997, up to 20 more empowerment zones may be designated for use beginning in 2000. Five of these will be in rural areas, and 15 will be in urban areas.

The empowerment zone employment tax credit is claimed on Form 8844, *Empowerment Zone Employment Credit*.

Indian Employment Credit

If your business is located on an Indian reservation, and you have employees who live on or near the reservation, you may be eligible for a special tax credit. You can claim a credit for 20 percent of your wages or health insurance costs for the year (up to $20,000 per employee) that exceed the total of comparable costs you had in 1993. However, the employee must be an enrolled member, or the spouse of an enrolled member, of an Indian tribe.

The credit is claimed on Form 8845, *Indian Employment Credit*.

Community Development Corporation Credit

The government wants to encourage you to make gifts or long-term loans to certain organizations that provide employment and business opportunities to low-income individuals. So, you can claim a tax credit for 5 percent of the amount you contribute, for each of 10 tax years beginning with the year you make the contribution. Eventually, you'll get tax credits for 50 percent of the contribution.

If the contribution is a gift, you can also take a charitable contribution deduction for the full amount, in the year you make it. If the contribution is a loan, the loan term must be at least 10 years. The CDC must be one of 20 organizations selected by the Secretary of HUD.

The CDC contribution credit is claimed on Form 8847, *Credit for Contributions to Selected Community Development Corporations.*

Low-Income Housing Credit

A tax credit is available for low-income housing that's constructed, rehabilitated, or acquired after 1986. The credit amounts to 70 percent of the qualified basis of non-federally subsidized units, or 30 percent of the qualified basis of units financed with tax-exempt bonds or other federal subsidies, but it must be claimed over a period of 10 years. The property must continue to meet the "low-income" requirements for at least 15 years. If you purchase qualified property on which the credit is being claimed, before the 10-year period is up, you may be able to "step into the shoes" of the seller and claim the remainder of the credit.

The credit is claimed on Form 8586, *Low-Income Housing Credit.*

Warning

If you're interested in investing in low-income housing to take advantage of the tax credit, you will definitely need the assistance of an attorney who is well-versed in this very complicated subject.

CREDITS BENEFITING THE ENVIRONMENT

Currently, the largest group of tax credits are those designed to encourage energy conservation or other actions to help the environment. However, most of these credits are very narrowly targeted, so the number of people eligible for them is actually quite small.

Credit for Qualified Electric Vehicles

If you purchase a new electric vehicle, you can receive a tax credit for 10 percent of the purchase price (up to $4,000). Any part of the cost that you elect to expense in the first year under Section 179 is not eligible for the credit, and the credit amount reduces the tax basis of the vehicle. The credit is claimed on Form 8834, *Qualified Electric Vehicle Credit.*

Energy Credit

An energy credit is allowed for 10 percent of the cost of the following types of property placed in service during the year: (1) equipment that uses solar energy to generate electricity, heat or cool a structure, provide hot water, or provide solar process heat; or (2) equipment used to produce, distribute, or use geothermal energy stored in rocks, water, or steam. The property must be depreciable (i.e., tangible personal property used in your business).

The energy credit is part of the investment tax credit, and can be recaptured (paid back to the IRS) if the qualifying property is sold or disposed of before the end of its recovery period. It is claimed on Form 3468, *Investment Credit.*

Reforestation Credit

For those in timber production, the 10 percent reforestation credit applies to up to $10,000 of the expenses you incur each year to forest or reforest your property. The property must be held for growing trees for sale or use in the commercial production of timber products. The reforestation credit is part of the investment tax credit and is claimed on Form 3468, *Investment Credit.*

Alternative Fuels Credit

A producer of "alternative fuels" can claim a tax credit for the domestic production and sale of such fuels to unrelated persons. The fuels eligible for the credit include oil and gas produced from nonconventional sources like shale and tar sands, geopressured brine, Devonian shale, coal seams, biomass, certain types of processed wood, etc.

For the most part, the production facilities or wells must have been placed in service or drilled before 1993; the placed-in-service date for gas produced from biomass and synthetic fuel produced from coal has been extended through June 30, 1998. The credit must be reduced by any energy investment credit allowed for the property used to produce the alternative fuel.

There's no IRS form for this credit — if you want to claim it, you (or your tax pro) must attach a page showing how you computed it to your Form 1040, *U.S. Individual Income Tax Return*.

Alcohol Fuels Credit

Producers of alcohol fuels or mixtures such as gasohol or ethanol can receive a tax credit for any sales or use of such fuels. The alcohol fuels credit is part of the general business credit. It's claimed on Form 6478, *Credit for Alcohol Used as Fuel*.

Enhanced Oil Recovery Credit

If you begin or significantly expand a domestic oil recovery project that uses certain tertiary recovery methods — such as the injection of liquids, gasses, or other matter — to increase crude oil production, you can take a credit for 15 percent of your qualified enhanced oil recovery costs for the tax year. The enhanced oil recovery credit is part of the general business credit. It's claimed on Form 8830, *Enhanced Oil Recovery Credit*.

Renewable Resources Electricity Production Credit

This credit is based on electricity that was produced from wind or closed-loop biomass (organic material grown exclusively for electricity production) and sold to third parties, from facilities placed in service after 1992 and before July 1, 2002, or wind energy facilities placed in service after 1993 and before July 1, 2002. The credit will apply to electricity produced by poultry waste facilities placed in service in 2000 and 2001.

The credit for calendar year 1999 is 1.7 cents per kilowatt-hour of such electricity sold. The credit is claimed on Form 8835, *Renewable Electricity Production Credit*.

CREDITS FOR CERTAIN INVESTMENTS

A small number of tax credits remain for investments that are not necessarily targeted towards the disadvantaged or the environment. In some cases, investments that take advantage of one of these credits can become, in effect, a tax shelter for cash-rich small businesses. Consult your tax adviser for more details.

R&E Credit

The research and experimentation (R&E) credit encourages businesses to increase the amounts they spend on scientific research. The credit expires on June 30, 2004. However, credits for the period from July 1, 1999 to September 30, 2001 can only be claimed after October 1, 2000. To claim a credit for this period, you may use an amended return, an application for expedited refund, an adjustment of estimated tax, or other similar means. Consult your tax advisor for details.

The credit generally equals 20 percent of the amount by which your research expenses for the year are higher than your "base amount," which is a figure based on the percentage of gross receipts you spent on research for 1984 through 1988. New companies' base amounts are set by a formula in the law.

To qualify for the credit, the research must be done for an existing business, and must be technological in nature (not research in the social sciences, arts, or humanities). It must relate to a new or improved function, performance, reliability, or quality. Qualified expenses includes in-house research, and 65 percent of the cost of research done by a person other than an employee of the taxpayer.

The R&E credit is claimed on Form 6765, *Credit for Increasing Research Activities*.

Orphan Drug Credit

The orphan drug credit is designed to encourage development of drugs for diseases and conditions that are so rare that drug development would otherwise be economically unfeasible.

The credit is equal to 50 percent of the qualified clinical testing expenses for the year. The orphan drug credit operates in much the same fashion as the R & D credit, except that there is no requirement that expenses exceed those for a base period. Where the same expenses would qualify for both the orphan drug credit and the R & D credit, you must choose between them — the same expenses can't be claimed as a credit twice. The orphan drug credit is claimed on Form 8820, *Orphan Drug Credit.*

Rehabilitation Credit

This tax credit is designed to encourage the rehabilitation of older real estate or certified historic buildings. It allows you to take a tax credit for the expenses you have for renovating, restoring, or rehabilitating (but not enlarging or adding new construction to) certain structures. The percentage of expenses you can take as a credit is 10 percent for buildings originally placed in service before 1936, and 20 percent for buildings listed in the National Register of Historic Places. If a project involves both rehabilitation and enlargement, only the costs of rehabilitation are eligible for the credit.

If you claim this credit, you must reduce the depreciable tax basis of the property by the amount of the credit.

The rehabilitation credit is part of the investment tax credit, and can be recaptured (paid back to the IRS) if the qualifying property is sold or disposed of within five years of the time it's placed in service. The credit is claimed on Form 3468, *Investment Credit.*

CLAIMING FEDERAL INCOME TAX CREDITS

Once you've decided that one or more of the available tax credits apply to you, how do you go about claiming it? The short answer is, you don't — you leave it up to your tax pro, because the rules for most credits are too complicated for the average small business owner to handle.

However, we're including the basic concepts here, so that you can ask intelligent questions of your accountant or lawyer, and see that he or she is earning the fees that you pay.

There are a number of steps you must take in the process of computing and claiming your tax credits:

First, compute your regular tax liability. You need to know what your income is for the year, subtract all your allowable deductions, and compute your tax liability on that basis (as if you had no credits). If you're a sole proprietor, part of the process will be completing Schedule C, *Profit or Loss From Business,* so you can determine your net income for your business.

Second, compute your alternative minimum tax (AMT) liability, if any. Generally, credits cannot be claimed to the extent that they would reduce your tax bill below your tentative minimum tax. See page 301 for a discussion of how AMT works.

Third, compute your nonrefundable credits and subtract them in the prescribed order. The order is important because each credit is limited to the amount of the tax minus the credits previously taken. Claim credits in the following order:

1. personal nonrefundable credits, such as the credit for child and dependent care, the credit for the elderly and disabled, the adoption credit, the child credit, and the credit for interest on certain home mortgages

2. the foreign tax credit

3. the alternative fuels credit

4. the credit for qualified electric vehicles

5. the general business credit, which is made up of the following parts: the investment credit, the work opportunity credit, the welfare-to-work credit, the alcohol fuels credit, the research credit, the low-income housing credit, the enhanced oil recovery credit, the disabled access credit, the renewable energy production credit, the empowerment zone employment credit (which is part of the general business credit but is not claimed on Form 3800), the Indian employment credit,

the employer FICA credit on tips, the orphan drug credit, and the community development corporations credit. The investment credit, in turn, is made up of the rehabilitation credit, the energy credit, and the reforestation credit.

Fourth, compute any carryback or carryover amounts, as discussed below.

Finally, compute and subtract your refundable credits from your remaining tax liability, if any. Refundable credits include the earned income credit, credit for any income taxes withheld on your paycheck, and the credit for gasoline and special fuels taxes. If subtracting these credits leaves you with a tax liability below zero, the IRS will send you a check for the difference.

Dollar Limits on Credits

In most cases, the limit on the credits you can claim for the year is computed as follows: take your regular tax liability, subtract your tentative minimum tax liability, and the result is the dollar limit on credits you can claim for the year. The credits are subtracted in a prescribed order, and some, including the general business credit, have additional limits that must be observed.

Tax Forms To Use

Most of the credits must be computed on their own special IRS forms. In addition, if you are claiming more than one of the components of the general business credits, if you have a carryback or carryover, or a credit from a passive activity, you will also need Form 3800, *General Business Credit*, to compute any limitations on the combined credit components.

The General Business Tax Credit

In order to provide some uniform rules about dollar limitations, carrybacks and carryforwards, and other technical details, many of the federal income tax credits available to businesses that were discussed above are lumped together and treated as components of the "general business credit."

The order in which the components are claimed is important. If you plan to claim more than one of these credits for the year, you must claim them in the prescribed order, using Form 3800, *General Business*

Credit — that way, if you exceed your credit dollar limit for the year, the credits further down the list will be the ones that are carried back or carried over to other years.

Dollar Limits on General Business Credits

Your total general business credit for the year can't exceed your net income tax, minus the greater of (1) your tentative minimum tax, or (2) 25 percent of your net regular tax liability that is more than $25,000 ($12,500 for marrieds filing separately). Your net income tax is your net regular tax liability plus your alternative minimum tax.

Carrybacks and Carryforwards

If the dollar limitations on the general business credit prevent you from claiming all of it in the year that it was earned (the "credit year"), for credits arising in 1998 and later, you can carry unused amounts back for one year, and forward for 20 years. The foreign tax credit may be carried back to the past two years and forward for five years, if it is necessary to use it up. To claim a carryback, you must generally file an amended return (Form 1040X, *Amended U.S. Individual Income Tax Return*) for the tax year to which you're carrying the credit. You can also apply for a quick refund of taxes for a prior year by filing Form 1045, *Application for Tentative Refund*.

The Investment Tax Credit

The investment tax credit is a credit against your federal income tax. Currently, it's made up of three components: the rehabilitation credit, the energy credit, and the reforestation credit. The investment tax credit is itself one of the components of the general business credit and is subject to the limitations, carryback and carryforward rules, etc. that apply to all the other components of that "umbrella" credit. The investment credit is claimed on Form 3468, *Investment Credit*.

Basis Adjustment

When you claim an investment tax credit for a business asset, you must generally reduce the depreciable tax basis of the property. The basis reduction would be equal to 100 percent of the rehabilitation credit you claimed, and 50 percent of the reforestation and energy credits.

Part **III**

Personal Tax Issues

The first half of this book dealt with the many questions and issues that can arise on the business portion of your tax return. In many cases, keeping your business taxes low is the best way to keep your overall tax bill as low as possible.

However, even if your business occupies the majority of your time and efforts, and presents the most thorny issues at tax time, don't neglect the personal and family side of your tax return.

For a sole proprietor, the income tax forms you need to file for your business (Schedules C and SE of Form 1040, and perhaps other forms depending on your business activity) are only one part of your individual income tax return that you must file.

Personal and family tax issues must be sorted out and addressed in the course of preparing your return. Depending on the age, size, income level and activities of your family, the personal side of your tax return may be as complicated as the business side.

What's more, there are numerous opportunities to save money on taxes on the personal side. Buying or refinancing a home, contributing to a regular or Roth IRA, investing in higher education, or riding the Wall Street rollercoaster all present you with potential tax

breaks. If you become familiar with the rules and keep up with the annual changes, you will be able to take advantage of all the breaks available to you.

Our discussion of non-business tax issues is organized into the following topical areas:

Chapter 10: Filing Status and Exemptions explores the basic questions of who must file a tax return, who qualifies as a dependent, and what are your options as to filing jointly or separately if married, or as single or head of household if not married.

Chapter 11: Employment Income and Related Deductions discusses the tax treatment of income reported to employees on W-2 forms, as well as income received by farmers, and various types of miscellaneous income such as unemployment benefits, disability benefits, and gambling winnings. This chapter also discusses tax breaks that may be claimed by employees and the self-employed, including moving expenses, the tax credit for child and dependent care, and miscellaneous deductions for employee business expenses.

Chapter 12: Real Estate covers the tax benefits of owning a home, such as the itemized deductions for home mortgage interest and real estate taxes. It also addresses the issues that must be faced by investors in real estate, or those who rent out their home or a vacation home for some part of the year. Finally, this chapter discusses recordkeeping for homeowners and the tax consequences of selling a home or other real estate.

Chapter 13: Investments discusses the tax treatment of interest and dividend income; capital gains on investment sales; and income from other entities such as estates and trusts, partnerships, LLCs and S corporations, and REMICS. Also discussed are itemized deductions related to investments, and special rules for handling the investment income of a minor child.

Chapter 14: Retirement explains how to report periodic payments from pension and annuity plans, as well as lump-sum distributions and Social Security benefits. It also covers all the rules related to IRAs – both Roth and traditional – whether you are making contributions or taking distributions.

Chapter 15: Standard and Itemized Deductions covers the standard deduction as well as itemized deductions not discussed elsewhere in the book: medical and dental expenses, state and local taxes, interest, charitable contributions, casualty and theft losses, and

miscellaneous itemized deductions. It also explains the limit on itemized deductions that applies to high-income taxpayers.

Chapter 16: Tax Credits and Miscellaneous Issues for Families deals with some of the latest new tax breaks for individuals: the $500-per-child tax credit, tax benefits for adoption, and tax breaks for education. It also covers the credit for the elderly and the disabled, and the earned income credit for low-income families. The tax aspects of alimony and child support are also discussed.

Chapter 17: Calculating Your Tax explains how to pull everything together and calculate the amount of federal income tax you owe, so you can determine the amount of your refund (or the amount you'll have to send in to the government). It also discusses two other types of taxes you may have to pay: payroll taxes on household employees, and the alternative minimum tax.

Chapter 18: Dealing with the IRS covers the mechanical issues of when and where to file your tax return, how to get an extension, and how to figure your quarterly estimated tax bill, and offers some tips on dealing with IRS audits.

Chapter 10

Filing Status and Exemptions

The federal income tax laws impose five different tax rates on individual taxpayers – that is, taxpayers that are not corporations. Since 1993, the rates have been set at 15 percent, 28 percent, 31 percent, 36 percent and 39.6 percent.

Each succeeding rate applies to a tier of your income. The first portion of your taxable income is taxed at 15 percent, the next portion is taxed at 28 percent, a third portion may be taxed at 31 percent, any income above that is taxed at 36 percent and, for very high earners, all income above a certain level is taxed at 39.6 percent.

Although the five rates are the same for everyone, the dollar levels at which the different tax rates kick in depend on your "filing status" — that is, whether you file your tax return as a single individual, as a head of household, or as married filing jointly or separately. For almost any given income level, the IRS tax tables provide four different amounts of tax that will apply, depending on filing status.

Your filing status is the first item you need to complete on your tax return, after your name, address, and Social Security number. This is appropriate, because your filing status is the starting point for determining whether you need to file a tax return at all, and, if you must file a return, the tax rates that will apply to your income.

Your status also has a wide-ranging effect in determining how numerous other tax rules will apply to you including the standard deduction, IRA contribution limits, credits for children or for education expenses, taxation of Social Security benefits, credits for the elderly or disabled, the adoption credit, the earned income credit and the phaseouts of exemptions and deductions for high-income taxpayers.

Once you've determined your filing status, you need to know how many personal exemptions you can claim, since the law allows you to exempt $2,750 of your income from tax for each member of your family in 1999.

The rules are fairly straightforward for most people. You can claim one exemption for yourself, one for your spouse if married and filing jointly, and one for each minor child living with you. But what about your older children, parents, extended family members you support, or children from a previous marriage? The surprisingly complex rules are explained on page 161.

Tax Organizer Tip

When inputting information into the CompleteTax™ Organizer, show your filing status on the "Taxpayer" tab in the "Personal" section. If you indicate that your filing status is married, a tab section will appear for your spouse's information. If you answer "yes" to the question, "Do you have any dependents?" a tab will appear for your dependents' information.

CHOOSING YOUR FILING STATUS

To claim your filing status on IRS Form 1040A or Form 1040, you simply check the box in front of the status that applies to you. If you choose "married filing separate returns," you'll need to enter the name of your spouse on Line 3, and also include your spouse's Social Security number at the top of the form directly below your own. This is required so that the IRS can match up your two forms in case of an audit. If you choose "head of household" status, you must enter on Line 4 the name of your qualifying person if it is a child who's not your dependent (see page 161).

Taxpayers who are able to file Form 1040EZ can only use "single" or "married filing jointly." If they are married, they must write both spouses' names and Social Security numbers on the return, which automatically places them in the "joint filers" category; otherwise they will be considered single.

While actually claiming your filing status on your tax return couldn't be simpler, knowing which status to claim is not always so easy. The primary factor in determining your status is whether you are married or not. If you are married, you and your spouse must decide whether to file jointly or separately (see page 153). In some cases, recently widowed persons can be treated as married, and some married people who are not living with their spouses can be treated as single.

Generally, if you are not currently married, you can be classified as a "head of household" if you meet the requirements for supporting at least one other person,

or as "single" if you don't. Head of households face a significantly lower tax rate than singles for the same level of income, but must file IRS Form 1040A or 1040 to claim this status.

Are You Married?

The rule for determining marital status is a simple one. If you are married on the last day of the tax year (December 31, for most people), you are considered to be married for the whole year. Conversely, if you are divorced during the year and don't remarry before December 31, you will be considered unmarried for the entire year.

Save Money

If you are planning a winter wedding and your income level is much higher or lower than that of your future spouse, marriage can actually lower your tax bill, and a December wedding would be preferable to a January wedding. If you are married by December 31, you'll be treated as if you were married for the whole preceding year.

However, if you and your intended have relatively similar income levels, marriage is more likely to increase your tax bill. In that case, waiting until January to get married will allow you one extra year of more favorable single status.

In a divorce situation, the parties are considered to be married until a final decree of divorce or legal separation is issued. The validity of the divorce is determined under the law of the state of domicile (legal residence). Taxpayers who live apart and have obtained an interim decree of divorce or separation, but have not yet been granted a final decree, are treated as married for tax purposes.

What about common-law marriages? Generally speaking, if your state recognizes such marriages and you meet all the state law requirements, the IRS will recognize your marriage as well.

Spouses Living Apart

A special rule allows a married person who is living apart (but not necessarily legally separated) from the spouse, and who is caring for a dependent child, to be treated as single and eligible to use the head of household filing status. In the absence of this rule, these individuals would probably have to file as "married filing separately," a much less advantageous status.

In order to take advantage of this special rule, all of the following conditions must be met:

- You must file a separate tax return.

- You must pay more than half of the cost of maintaining your household for the year.

- Your spouse must not have been a member of your household during the last six months of the tax year.

- Your household must, for more than six months of the year, have been the principal home of at least one of your dependent children. See page 161 for the definition of "dependent." "Child" includes your legally adopted children and foster children; however, if the child is a foster child, he or she must reside in your household for the entire year.

Recently Widowed Persons

An exception to the "December 31 rule" for determining whether a person is considered to be married applies to those whose spouses have died in the past year.

Generally, you can file a joint return with your spouse for the year in which your spouse dies, and you'll be treated as married for the entire year. You can also claim the whole personal exemption for the deceased spouse. However, in order to file jointly, you must have the consent of the personal representative (executor or administrator) of the deceased spouse's estate, if you are not the representative.

This rule does not hold if you remarry within the year. In that case, you can file jointly with your new spouse, but not with the old one. The return of the deceased spouse would have to be filed as "married filing separately" for the final year.

Qualifying widows or widowers. Some surviving spouses can continue to use the "married filing jointly" tax rates for up to two years *after* the year in which their spouse died. To take advantage of this option, all of the following must be true:

- You have not remarried.

- Your home was the principal residence of a dependent child or stepchild for the entire year, and you must have provided more than half of the cost of maintaining the home.

- You must have been eligible to file a joint return with your deceased spouse in the year he or she died.

Surviving spouses who meet these tests and are able to continue using the joint return rates are called "qualifying widows or widowers" and must check off the box for that filing status on Line 5 of Form 1040. They must also write the year in which their spouse died in the blank provided for that purpose on Line 5, so that the IRS can be sure they aren't using this status for more than two years after the year the death occurred.

As a result, they have the advantage of continuing to use the joint return tax amounts in the tax table, although they may not claim a personal exemption for the deceased spouse for any year after the year in which the spouse died.

Most Married People File Jointly

If you're married, you and your spouse must decide whether to file jointly or separately.

In the vast majority of cases, filing jointly will result in a lower total family tax bill. The tax rates for joint filers have the effect of "leveling out" the income, exemptions, and deductions of each spouse, so that each spouse is essentially treated as having half of the total net income. For slightly more than half of married couples, this results in a "marriage bonus," so that the couple pays less in tax than they would if they each made the same income and were single. This is usually the case where one spouse's earnings are much higher than the other's.

For couples where each spouse makes roughly the same income, however, there is often a "marriage penalty" in which the second wage earner's income pushes the couple into a higher tax bracket than either spouse would face if they were single. This situation can sometimes, but unfortunately not often, be helped if the couple files separately rather than jointly.

However, the IRS does not smile on couples who file separately, perhaps because it has to incur the extra charges of processing two tax returns rather than only one.

In order to strongly encourage married couples to file jointly, Congress has provided that for people who are treated as "married," certain tax benefits are available *only* if a joint return is filed, as shown in the chart that follows (but note that certain legally separated couples or spouses living apart from each other are not treated as "married" for this purpose – see page 152). When you consider the effects of not being able to claim any of these benefits, it's usually clear that filing separately would result in a larger tax bill.

Joint Returns May Be Prohibited

In a few limited situations, married taxpayers have no choice and must file separately:

- if the spouses have different tax years, and this difference is not due to the death of either spouse (if filing separately is not beneficial, either spouse may be able to obtain IRS consent to change to a "matching" tax year by filing Form 1128, *Application to Adopt, Change, or Retain a Tax Year*, after consent is obtained, you can file jointly)

- if either spouse is, at any time during the year, a nonresident alien and the couple chooses not to treat the nonresident alien spouse as a U.S. resident subject to tax on worldwide income (see page 156 for more on this situation)

- if a spouse has died during the year, and the personal representative of the estate elects to file a separate return

---

Tax Breaks Not Available to Married People Filing Separately

- the dependent care credit (see page 189)

- the earned income credit (see page 290)

- the HOPE scholarship credit (see page 286)

- the lifetime learning credit (see page 287)

- the deduction for interest on education loans (see page 288)

- the adoption credit (see page 282)

- the exclusion for interest income on Series EE U.S. Savings Bonds used for higher education expenses (see page 224)

- the $2,000 deduction for IRA contributions for a nonworking or low-income spouse (see page 250)

In addition, married couples who lived together at any time during the year must file jointly in order to claim any of the following:

- the more lenient phaseout rules (i.e., phaseout between $150,000 and $160,000 in AGI) for the IRA deduction when a spouse is covered by an employer's pension plan (see page 252)

- the credit for the elderly or the disabled (see page 284)

- the $25,000 rental loss allowance under the passive loss rules (see page 219)

Beyond these listed items, you should be aware that if a couple files separately and one spouse itemizes his or her deductions, the other spouse must follow suit - the standard deduction may not be used. Also, if either spouse is receiving Social Security benefits, the amount of benefits on which income tax must be paid is higher for spouses filing separately.

When Is a Separate Return Better?

If spouses file separately, each must report only his or her own income, exemptions, and deductions on his or her tax return. However, in community property states, the general rule is that each spouse must report one-half of the combined community income.

To be absolutely certain whether joint or separate returns are better, you should compute your tax liability both ways and compare the results. It's especially important to run the numbers where one or both spouses may be liable for the alternative minimum tax (see page 301).

Itemized Deductions

If both spouses have similar income levels but one spouse has a much higher amount in deductible expenses, it may be advantageous to file separately.

For example, medical expenses are deductible only to the extent that they exceed 7.5 percent of the taxpayer's adjusted gross income (AGI). If one spouse had the majority of the family medical expenses, the 7.5 percent threshold may be easy to overcome if only that spouse's income is counted. A similar situation exists for miscellaneous itemized deductions, including employee business expenses (2 percent of AGI threshold) and nonbusiness casualty losses (10 percent of AGI threshold).

However, keep in mind that if one spouses itemizes deductions, the other will have to itemize as well, even if the second spouse winds up with few or no allowable deductions. If you're a high-income earner, it may also be important to consider how separate filing alters the impact of the limitation on itemized deductions faced by high-income taxpayers (see page 273).

Dependents

If you have dependents and file separately, you must divide their exemptions between yourself and your spouse, but no single exemption can be split.

Save Money

If you have numerous dependents and one spouse claims them all, you might come out ahead, particularly if the other spouse's income is so high that his or her personal exemptions would be phased out. Just make sure that the spouse who claims the exemptions can meet all the tests for claiming each dependent as described on page 161; generally this would require that the spouse claiming the exemptions earned enough money to provide more than one-half of the dependents' support.

Limiting Your Liability for the Return

It's important to note that if you file a joint tax return with your spouse, both of you are legally responsible for the accuracy of information shown on the tax return, as well as for the entire amount of tax that is owed.

Spouses who are separated often file separate returns simply because they do not have access to complete financial information about the other party.

In other situations, where one spouse actually suspects that the other spouse is not being completely truthful, he or she should consider filing a separate return to avoid possible civil or criminal penalties.

It is possible, but difficult, to obtain "innocent spouse relief" and avoid having to pay taxes, interest and penalties on amounts that were actually owed by the other spouse. You must establish that you did not know, and had no reason to know, that your joint return failed to report some income or claimed some erroneous deductions, credits, or other tax breaks. If so, you can be relieved of liability for tax on that item.

To obtain innocent spouse relief, you have to apply for it using IRS Form 8857, *Request for Innocent Spouse Relief*, which can be obtained by calling 1-800-TAX-FORM. You must file this form within two years after the IRS begins collection activities.

Work Smart

One recent change in the law permits a taxpayer who is divorced, legally separated or living apart from a spouse for at least one year to limit his/her liability in instances where a former spouse may have made erroneous statements on a previous joint tax return.

To make the election, the ex-spouse must file IRS Form 8857, and establish the unpaid taxes that should be allocated to the other spouse. The election can't be made if the IRS demonstrates that the spouse seeking the election had actual knowledge of the matter relating to the unpaid taxes when the return was signed. This is a more lenient standard than the innocent spouse relief rule, but it is available only to spouses who have split up.

The divorced husband or wife has two years after the IRS begins collection activities to make this election of separate liability, which will excuse the innocent spouse from paying any additional taxes owed or interest and penalties on the item(s) in question.

Nonresident Alien Spouses

If a U.S. citizen or resident alien is married to a nonresident alien, a joint return may not be filed unless both spouses file an election with the IRS to treat the nonresident alien as a resident alien.

While it may appear that a nonresident alien who has no income from U.S. sources need not be concerned with filing status, since he or she is not subject to taxation by the U.S. government, the filing of a joint return may at least reduce his or her spouse's U.S. tax bill on income subject to U.S. taxation. If the nonresident alien has U.S. source income, an election for a joint return may be doubly beneficial, since he or she may be taxed on the U.S. income anyway.

Contrast Between Tax Treatments

Nonresident aliens who are not treated as resident aliens generally are taxed only on their income from U.S. sources. Investment income from U.S. sources is taxed at a flat 30 percent rate. Regular U.S. income tax rates for a married person filing separately are imposed on income from a job in the U.S. This income may be offset by deductions.

In contrast, when a nonresident alien is treated as a resident alien, he or she is subject to U.S. taxation on worldwide income (i.e., income from foreign sources as well as U.S. sources). However, as with any other U.S. citizen or resident alien, the alien is eligible for a foreign tax credit or an itemized deduction for taxes paid to a foreign government on income earned in those countries. The alien may also exclude up to $74,000 of foreign earned income from U.S. taxation (in 1999 and may be eligible to exclude or deduct some of the cost of foreign housing.

How to Make the Election

You can make the election to treat a nonresident alien spouse as a resident alien by attaching a statement to that effect, signed by both you and your spouse, to the joint return for the first tax year of the election. The election is effective for all later tax years unless it is revoked by the spouses or the IRS, one spouse dies, or the spouses are legally separated. It will also be suspended as of any year in which neither spouse is a U.S. citizen or a resident alien.

Are You a Head of Household?

Next to the joint return rates, the best tax rate schedule applies to single taxpayers who qualify for head of household (HOH) status.

However, some complicated rules determine whether you are eligible to file as an HOH. Whether you are divorced or have never been married is not important; what is important is that you maintain a home for one or more of your children or dependent relatives.

More specifically, for the year in question you must be maintaining your own principal place of residence, and you must have as a member of your household, for more than half of the tax year, one or more of the following "qualifying persons":

- Your child (including your legally adopted child), your child's descendent, your stepchild, or a foster child who's lived with you all year. This person need not be your dependent, unless he or she is married on the last day of the tax year. If the person is married on that date, you must be eligible to treat him or her as a dependent; that is, the person must have had less than $2,750 in gross income for 1999 unless he or she is under age 19 or is a student under age 24; the person must have received more than one-half of his or her financial support from you; and the person must not file a joint return.

- Any other *relative* for whom you can claim a dependency exemption (see page 161). "Relative" includes:

    — parent or grandparent

    — brother or sister

— half-brother or half-sister

— stepbrother or stepsister

— stepparent

— parent-in-law

— brother- or sister-in-law

— son- or daughter-in-law

— aunt, uncle, niece or nephew by blood

If you are not married, and you can't qualify as a head-of-household, you are treated as single for federal income tax purposes.

Maintaining a Household

In order to be considered to be "maintaining a household," you must provide more than one-half the cost of keeping up a home. Costs of maintaining a household include rent or mortgage interest, real estate taxes, insurance on the home, repairs, utilities, and food eaten in the home. They do not include the costs of clothing, education, medical treatment, vacations, transportation, life insurance, or the value of services.

Save Money

The test described above for "maintaining a household" is less demanding than the test for supporting a dependent, discussed on page 164. As a result, you may be entitled to file as an HOH even though you can't claim any dependency exemptions.

One common situation where this rule comes into play is where a couple is divorced, and the lower-paid spouse retains custody of the children. The couple may agree to give the dependency exemptions to the noncustodial parent (because that parent can gain more tax benefits from the exemptions), but the custodial parent would still retain the tax benefits of filing as an HOH.

Residing in the Same Household

You must live in the same household as your "qualifying person" *unless* the person is your father or mother. In that case, you can be an HOH if you pay for at least half the cost of maintaining your father or mother's main home for the entire year, even if your parent(s) lives apart from you in a house or apartment, or in a nursing home or other care facility for the elderly.

If the "qualifying person" is anyone other than your mother or father, the person must live in your household for more than half of your tax year. However, temporary absences for vacations, illnesses, military service, or time spent in college are permissible for either you or the qualifying person, provided that you reasonably anticipate that the absentee will return and you continue to maintain a household during the absence.

Also, if the qualifying person is born or dies during the tax year so that he or she is alive for less than six months in the year, you can still file as an HOH if the qualifying person lived with you for the whole period in which he or she was alive during the year.

WHO MUST FILE A RETURN?

If you're reading this book, you probably don't have any doubt about whether you need to file a tax return. Most small business owners need to file, because anyone with net self-employment income of $400 or more must file a tax return to report and pay their self-employment tax.

However, you may have questions about whether your child, parent, or some other person for whom you're responsible needs to file a return.

The basic rule is that if you are a citizen or resident of the United States, or a resident of Puerto Rico, you must file a tax return if you have gross income at or above a certain dollar amount. The dollar amount depends on your filing status, and on your age if you are 65 or older at the end of the year. The same rules apply to U.S. citizens living outside the United States.

If you are a nonresident alien, different rules may apply which are not covered in this book. See IRS Publication 519, *U.S. Tax Guide for Aliens*.

Filing Thresholds for 1999

If your gross income meets or exceeds the following levels and you are under age 65, you must file a tax return:

Single	$ 7,050
Head of Household	$ 9,100
Married Filing Jointly	$12,700
Married Filing Separately	$ 2,750
Qualifying Widow or Widower	$ 9,950

If you are 65 or older on or before January 1, 2000, you can add $1,050 to the amounts shown above for single or head of household, or $850 to the amount for married filing separately. On a joint return, if both spouses are 65 or older you can add $1,700 to the amount shown, so the threshold would be $14,400.

Filing for Dependents

Children or other people who can be claimed as dependents on someone else's tax return (see discussion below) generally must file a tax return if they have more than $700 of unearned income (interest, dividends, capital gains), or earned income over $4,300, or their total income was more than the larger of $700 or their earned income plus $250.

If the dependent is age 65 or over or blind, he or she generally must file a return if gross income was more than $1,750 for singles or $1,550 for marrieds. If the dependent was *both* 65 or over *and* blind, you can add to these amounts an extra $1,050 for singles or $850 for marrieds.

When tallying up a dependent's income, "unearned income" includes interest, dividends, capital gains, unemployment compensation, taxable Social Security benefits, pensions, annuities, and trust distributions. "Earned income" includes wages, salaries, tips, and net income from a business; it also includes taxable scholarship and fellowship grants.

If the child or other dependent is too young or otherwise incapable of filing a tax return, his or her parent, guardian, or other legally responsible person must file the tax return for the dependent. In that case the responsible adult filing the return would sign the return for the dependent, and add their own name; for example, "John Jones, Jr., by John Jones, parent of minor child."

If the child is under age 14 and his or her only income is interest and dividends, the parent has the option to include the child's income on the parent's return by filing IRS Form 8814, *Parent's Election to Report Child's Interest and Dividends*, along with the parent's return.

Save Money

Combining the child's income with that of the parents would save the child from having to file his or her own tax return; however, it frequently results in a slightly larger tax bill since the child's income will increase the parents' AGI and possibly reduce the deductible portion of the parents' itemized medical expenses, miscellaneous deductions, casualty losses, and IRA deductions. There are many other tax breaks that are phased out at higher levels of AGI and that can potentially be lost or reduced if a child's income is combined with the parents' income, so in most cases the family will be better off if the child files a separate return.

Others Who Must File a Tax Return

Even if you don't have sufficient income to meet the filing thresholds for your filing status, you must file a tax return in order to get an IRS refund for any overpaid estimated taxes or amounts withheld from your paycheck.

You must also file a tax return if any of the following apply to you:

- You received an advance earned income credit from your employer (this would be shown in Box 9 of your W-2 Form).

- You had net earnings from self-employment of at least $400, as shown on Schedule C or C-EZ.

- You had wages of at least $108.28 from a church or church organization that is exempt from Social Security (see page 137).

- You owe any special taxes, such as: uncollected FICA tax on tips, uncollected FICA tax on group-term life insurance over $50,000, alternative minimum tax (AMT – see page 301), tax on a pension plan or IRA, tax on a medical savings account (MSA), recapture tax on a home purchased with a federally subsidized mortgage, recapture of the qualified electric vehicle credit, or recapture of investment credit or low-income housing credit (see page 145).

Which Tax Form Should You Use?

For business owners, the answer to this is cut and dried: If you file a Schedule C or C-EZ, or if you must report a taxable sale of business property, you must file the "long form" (Form 1040) for your federal income tax.

Since some of you may have dependents who must file tax returns, or may be overseeing tax preparation for other people who do not own a business, we'll go over the rules for the shorter income tax forms as well. The general idea is that you should always use the simplest tax form that applies to you.

If you cannot use the 1040EZ or the 1040A under the rules discussed below, you must use the regular 1040 form.

Rules for Form 1040EZ

The simplest, one-page tax form has become more and more complicated in recent years, and as a result it can be used by more and more taxpayers.

You can use the 1040EZ if all of the following are true:

- Your filing status is single, or married filing jointly.

- You (and your spouse, if filing jointly) were both under 65 and not blind.

- You are not claiming any dependents (but you may use this form if you are claimed as a dependent on someone else's tax form)

- Your taxable income is less than $50,000.

- Your income is only from wages, salaries, tips, unemployment compensation, Alaska Permanent Fund dividends, taxable scholarship and fellowship grants, and taxable interest of $400 or less.

- You're not claiming a student loan interest deduction or an education credit

- You did not receive any advance earned income credit payments.

- If you were a nonresident alien at any time in 1999, your filing status is married filing jointly.

- You do not owe any household employment taxes on wages you paid to a household employee (see page 302).

Rules for Form 1040A

Form 1040A is the "medium form." It's not quite as long as Form 1040, but can be used if you don't qualify for the 1040EZ and meet all of the following requirements:

- Your taxable income is less than $50,000.

- Your only income is from wages, salaries, tips, IRA distributions, pensions and annuities, taxable Social Security or railroad retirement benefits, taxable scholarships or fellowships, interest, dividends (including Alaska Permanent Fund dividends) and unemployment compensation.

- Your only adjustments to income are the deduction for contributions to an IRA or the student loan interest deduction; you don't have an adjustment for a medical savings account, moving expenses, penalty on early withdrawal of savings, or alimony.

- You are claiming the standard deduction rather than itemized deductions.

- Your only taxes are the income tax as shown in the Tax Table, the alternative minimum tax, and/or the advance earned income credit (EIC).

- Your only tax credits are the child tax credit, the credit for child and dependent care expenses, the credit for the elderly and the disabled, the EIC, and/or the adoption credit.

Rules for Using Form 1040

You must file your income taxes using Form 1040 if *any* of the following are true.

1. You had $400 or more in self-employment income.

2. Your taxable income is $50,000 or more.

3. You choose to itemize your deductions.

4. You received capital gain distributions (e.g., from a mutual fund) or nontaxable dividends.

5. You had taxable gain from the sale of your home or other property, barter income, alimony income, taxable refunds of state or local income taxes, or self-employment income (including farm income).

6. You sold or exchanged capital assets or business property.

7. You had any of the following adjustments to gross income: payments to a medical savings account; moving expenses; payments for self-employed health insurance; one-half of the self-employment tax; payments to a Keogh, SEP or SIMPLE retirement plan; penalty for early withdrawal of savings; alimony paid; certain required repayments of supplemental unemployment benefits; jury duty pay turned over to your employer; qualified performing artists' expenses; or other allowable adjustments to income.

8. Your Form W-2 shows uncollected FICA tax on tips or group-term life insurance over $50,000 in Box 13.

9. You received $20 or more in tips in any one month and did not report all of them to your employer.

10. You received or paid accrued interest on securities transferred between interest payment dates.

11. You receive a distribution from a foreign trust, or you had a bank, securities, or other financial account in a foreign country at any time during the year.

12. You have to recapture an investment tax credit, a low-income housing credit, a qualified electric vehicle credit, or an Indian employment credit you claimed in a previous year.

13. You have to recapture tax on the disposition of a home purchased with a federally subsidized mortgage.

14. You have to pay tax on excess golden parachute payments.

15. You claim any of the following tax credits: mortgage interest credit, foreign tax credit, any general business credit (see page 148), credit for prior years' AMT, credit for fuel from a nonconventional source, credit for federal tax on fuels, qualified electric vehicle credit, or the regulated investment company credit

16. You file any of the following forms: Form 2555, *Foreign Earned Income;* Form 2555-EZ, *Foreign Earned Income Exclusion;* Form 4563, *Exclusion of Income for Bona Fide Residents of American Samoa;* Form 4970, *Tax on Accumulation Distribution of Trusts;* Form 4972, *Tax on Lump-Sum Distributions;* Form 5329, *Additional Taxes Attributable to Qualified Retirement Plans (Including IRAs), Annuities, Modified Endowment Contracts, and MSAs;* Form 8271, *Investor Reporting of Tax Shelter Registration Number;* Form 8814, *Parents' Election to Report Child's Interest and Dividends;* Form 8853, *Medical Savings Accounts and Long-Term Care Insurance Contracts.*

EXEMPTIONS AND THE DEPENDENCY TEST

In computing how much of your income is actually subject to federal income tax, you're automatically entitled to subtract two amounts: a personal exemption and a standard deduction. The sum of these amounts is not taxed, period. Of course, you can choose to itemize your deductions rather than claiming the standard deduction, if itemizing would result in a lower tax bill. Deductions are discussed in Chapter 15; the remainder of this chapter explains personal exemptions and how to determine whether a particular person is your dependent or not.

The rule is that one (and only one) personal exemption is available for every individual – adult or child. The amount of the exemption is $2,750 for 1999 and is indexed for inflation every year.

So, on a joint return, you could automatically claim one exemption for yourself and one for your spouse, for a total of $5,500. You can claim an exemption for your spouse even if he or she died during the year, provided you have not remarried. However, if you obtain a final decree of divorce, you can't claim your spouse's exemption.

If you are married filing separately, you can claim your spouse's exemption on your own return only if your spouse had absolutely no gross income for the year and was not the dependent of any other individual.

Besides the personal and spousal exemptions, you should also claim an exemption for each of your dependents. The catch is that if you can claim a dependency exemption for an individual, that person may not claim a personal exemption on his or her tax return.

Warning

There is nothing optional about this rule. If you are eligible to claim, say, an exemption for your child who is away at college, you cannot choose to let the child claim his or her own exemption even if you want to. This is true even if you are going to lose some or all of your personal exemptions because your income is too high (see page 167).

One possible way around this rule is to make a hefty gift to the child in one year, and then refrain from paying more than half of the child's support in later years. The child could use the gift money to support himself or herself and could then claim the personal exemption on his or her own return.

Claiming Your Dependents' Exemptions

To claim an exemption for a dependent, you must use IRS Form 1040A or the long Form 1040. You must write each dependent's first and last name and Social Security number on Line 6C of either form, and also write in the dependent's closest relationship to you (or your spouse, if filing jointly).

Then, you must total up your dependents in three categories: children who live with you, children who don't live with you because of divorce or separation, and other dependents. The total number of exemptions (including one for yourself and, if applicable, your spouse) is entered on Line 6d of either form.

Social Security Number Required

You must list a Social Security number on your tax return for each dependent, even if the dependent was born late in 1999. Otherwise, your dependency deduction may be denied.

If you don't have a number for one of your dependents and don't expect to get it before April 15th, file an extension request on IRS Form 4868, *Application for Automatic Extension of Time to File U.S. Individual Income Tax Return,* so that you have an extra four months in which to obtain a number. In the meantime, you or your dependent should get a number from the Social Security Administration by filing Form SS-5, *Application for a Social Security Card,* as soon as possible. Contact your local SSA office for more information.

If you are adopting a child who has been placed with you by an authorized agency, you may be able to claim an exemption for the child. If you don't know the child's Social Security number you can get an adoption taxpayer identification number from the IRS by filing Form W-7A, *Application for Taxpayer Identification Number for Pending U.S. Adoptions.* You can call the IRS at 1-800-TAX-FORM to get a copy of this form.

Similarly, if your dependent is a resident or nonresident alien, you will need to get a special identification number from the IRS by filing Form W-7, *Application for IRS Individual Taxpayer Identification Number.*

Tests for Dependency

Deciding whether a given household member is your dependent is usually obvious. In most cases, the person is a minor child living with one or both parents, and there is no doubt that the child is being supported by his or her parent(s).

However, in cases where a child who has substantial income is a member of the household, where an extended family lives under one roof, or where a family supports someone who is living elsewhere, there may be questions as to whether a certain individual qualifies for a dependency exemption. The IRS has come up with a five-part test to determine whether a person is really your dependent.

Briefly, if the individual meets all of the following tests, he or she is your dependent and is not permitted to claim an individual exemption on his or her own tax return:

- the member-of-household or relationship test

- the citizenship test

- the joint return test

- the gross income test

- the support test

Each of these tests is described in more detail below. If your child meets all five of the tests, you can claim a full exemption for the child even if he or she was born on the last day of the year.

If your child or other dependent died during the year but would otherwise have met all five tests, you can still claim the exemption for the dependent.

The Member-of-Household or Relationship Test

Basically this test is met if the individual is closely related to you *or* was a member of your household for the entire year.

Relationship Test

A person automatically meets this test if he or she is one of the following:

- your child, grandchild, or great-grandchild (legally adopted children are treated as children; before legal adoption, a child is treated as your child if he or she was placed with you by an authorized agency and is a member of your household)

- your stepchild (but not a step-grandchild)

- your brother, sister, stepbrother, stepsister, half-brother, or half-sister

- your parent, grandparent, or other direct ancestor (but not a foster parent)

- your stepfather or stepmother (but not a step-grandparent)

- your aunt, uncle, niece, or nephew by blood; that is, the brother or sister of your father or mother, or the child of your brother or sister

- your father-in-law, mother-in-law, son-in-law, daughter-in-law, brother-in-law, or sister-in-law

The person must bear the listed relationship to you or, on a joint return, to your spouse. You don't need to show that the person is related to the particular spouse who actually provided the financial support unless you are married filing separately.

Example

Peter Lake is the primary support for the uncle of his wife, Vera, although the uncle lives in his own apartment. If the Lakes file a joint return, they may claim the uncle as a dependent. However, if they file separately, neither spouse can claim the exemption because Peter does not bear the required relationship to the uncle or live with him for the whole year, and Vera does not provide more than one-half of the uncle's support.

You may have noticed that your spouse is not on the list of close relationships, above. That's because the spousal exemption is not treated as a dependency exemption, and the five tests do not apply to your spouse. On a joint return, you can automatically claim the exemption for your spouse, simply because you're married. If you file separately, you can claim the exemption for your spouse only if the spouse had no gross income at all and was not the dependent of any other taxpayer. However, in that situation you'd ordinarily have a much lower tax bill if you filed jointly.

Member of Household Test

If the individual is not a close relative under the IRS's definition, he or she can still meet the first test by living with you for the entire year as a member of your household.

Temporary absences from the home will not cause you to fail this test, whether it's you or the dependent who's absent. Temporary absences may be due to illness, education, business, vacation, military service, or temporary placement in a nursing home. If a person died or was born during the year, but was a member of the household for the entire time he or she was alive during the year, the test was met.

Foster children (or adults) can be treated as dependents if they live with you for the entire year, *unless* you receive payments as a foster parent from a state government, a political subdivision, or a tax-exempt child-placement agency. If you receive any such payments, you can't claim a dependency exemption for the child.

Save Money

If you receive some payments as a foster parent, you can claim a charitable deduction for the excess expenses, if your actual expenses for the child are higher than the amount of payments you receive.

Exception for employees. Your maid, babysitter, *au pair*, or any other employee is not considered your dependent even if the employee lived in your household for the entire year.

Citizenship Test

This test for dependency status is met if the person is a U.S. citizen or resident alien, or is a resident of Canada or Mexico for at least part of the calendar year in which your tax year begins.

Children are usually considered to be citizens or residents of their parents' country. In most cases, children born of an American parent are considered to be U.S. citizens for dependency purposes, even if the other parent is a nonresident alien and the child does not live in the U.S., Mexico, or Canada.

Foreign exchange students placed in American homes for a temporary period are not considered U.S. residents, so they don't qualify for a dependency exemption.

Joint Return Test

This test refers to the tax return (if any) filed by the dependent, not your own tax return. In most cases, you can't claim a dependency exemption for any married person who files a joint return with his or her spouse.

There is an exception to this rule if both of the following are true:

- Neither the dependent nor his or her spouse is required to file a tax return, but they file one merely to get a refund.

- Neither the dependent nor his or her spouse would owe any tax if they filed separately rather than jointly.

Gross Income Test

This is another either/or test. The dependent must either (a) be your child who is age 18 or younger, or age 23 or younger and a student, *or* (b) have gross income that is less than the amount of the dependency exemption for the year, which means less than $2,750 for 1999.

Some Definitions

The definition of "child" includes a stepchild, legally adopted child, or a child placed with you by an authorized agency for legal adoption. A foster child who was a member of your household for the entire year is also considered your child.

The child must meet the age requirement for the entire year. If the child was not a student, you don't meet the test for the year in which the child turns 19, even if the child was 18 for most of the year. For that year, the child must have income that is lower than the exemption amount or you'd lose the exemption.

The definition of "student" means a full-time student for some portion of at least five months in the calendar year. Therefore, you can usually count your child as a dependent for the year in which he or she graduates from school.

The school can be an elementary school; middle school; junior or senior high school; a college or university; or a technical, trade, or mechanical school. However, it can't be a correspondence school, night school, or an on-the-job training course (certain on-farm training courses are permitted, though). People who work in co-op programs that are part of the school's prescribed course of study are considered full-time students. Also, students who attend some classes at night as part of a full-time program are considered full-time students.

Income Under $2,750

If the person is not your minor child or your child who is a full-time student under age 24, the amount of income he or she received in 1999 must have been under $2,750.

You must count all the taxable income the person received during the year, whether in the form of money, property, or services. "Income" includes all unemployment compensation and the taxable portion of any pension income, but does not include gifts, support from you, or tax-exempt Social Security payments.

Also not included are scholarship funds used for tuition, fees, books, or equipment needed for school, or income received by a totally and permanently disabled person for working in a sheltered workshop.

Support Test

The final part of the dependency test requires that you provide more than half of the person's total support during the calendar year.

Save Time

In practice, most parents of minor children are assumed to provide at least half of the support. They don't need to do the formal calculations described below unless the dependent received a significant amount of income during the year and spent it on "support items" as described below.

Technically speaking, to apply the support test you must first calculate the total amount spent for the individual's support during the year, and then calculate how much of that support was provided by you (or your spouse, if filing jointly). If you provided more than half, the individual meets this test to be your dependent.

Total Support for the Year

The first step is to determine how much was actually spent on the individual's support during the year.

"Total support" includes amounts spent to provide food, clothing, lodging, education, medical and dental care, health insurance, recreation, transportation, and similar necessities. Other items can be included, depending on the situation. For example, if you pay someone to provide child care or disabled dependent care, you can include the payments as support even if you claim a tax credit for them.

Items not included as support are federal, state and local taxes; life insurance premiums; funeral expenses; savings and investments; and scholarships received by your child if the child is a full-time student.

Each item you provided is valued at its actual cost. In the case of lodging, the cost is determined as a portion of the fair rental value of the home provided to the dependent. The fair rental value usually includes utilities and furnishings.

Where the precise cost of the support items provided to the dependent can't be determined (e.g., the value of groceries consumed by the person is unknown), you must compute the cost of the item for the entire household in the year, and assign a proportionate share to each member of the household.

Where Did the Support Come From?

Once you know the total value of support received by the individual, you must compute how much of it was provided by yourself (and your spouse, if filing jointly) and then compare the amounts. If you provided one-half or more of the total support, the individual is your dependent under this test.

In some cases, the individual may be receiving income from outside sources such as Social Security, a welfare program, an educational institution, or other individuals. None of this income is treated as support provided by you.

If you are an employer of the individual (for example, if you hire your child to perform office work), the wages you pay are not treated as support provided by you. Also, if the individual takes out a loan and uses the proceeds for educational or other expenses, the loan proceeds count toward total support but not toward support provided by you.

However, the fact that the individual is receiving outside income does not automatically mean that it is being used to support that individual. Amounts that the person saves or invests, or spends on non-support items like life insurance, are not treated as support. This is true even if you encourage the person to save his or own money (and perhaps to open an IRA) and you make up for the amount saved by providing a comparable amount of support.

You can use the worksheet provided on the next page to see whether a particular dependent qualifies under the support test.

Case Study

Troy Smith owns a home in which he lives with his wife, two children, and his mother, Blanche. Blanche is a U.S. citizen and receives annual pension benefits of $3,000, of which $1,800 is taxable gross income. She spends her entire pension on clothing, recreation, and other support items.

Troy's total food expenses for the household were $5,000. He also paid his mother's medical expenses, amounting to $4,000. The fair rental value of the room furnished to Blanche, based on the cost of comparable rooming facilities, was $2,400 per year.

Blanche's total support is computed as follows:

Fair rental value of lodging:	$ 2,400
Direct expenses paid by Blanche:	3,000
Medical expenses paid by Troy:	4,000
Blanche's share of food expenses:	1,000
Total support:	$10,400

Because Troy furnished support worth $7,400, he paid more than one-half of Blanche's support and can claim her as a dependent.

If we change the facts slightly to provide Blanche with nontaxable Social Security benefits of $8,000 in addition to her $3,000 pension, she would remain Troy's dependent as long as she spent less than Troy did ($7,400) on her own support. The remainder of her pension and benefits could be saved or invested, perhaps with the idea that upon her death the savings would go to Troy's children.

Worksheet for Determining Support

Income of the Person You Supported	
1) Did the person you supported receive any income, such as wages, interest, dividends, pensions, rents, social security, or welfare? (If yes, complete lines 2, 3, 4, and 5. If no, go to line 6.)	☐ Yes ☐ No
2) Total income received	$
3) Amount of income used for support	$
4) Amount of income used for other purposes	$
5) Amount of income saved	$
(The total of lines 3, 4, and 5 should equal line 2)	
Expenses for Entire Household (where the person you supported lived)	
6) Lodging (Complete item a or b)	
a) Rent paid	$
b) If not rented, show fair rental value of home. If the person you supported owned the home, include this amount in line 20.	$
7) Food	$
8) Utilities (heat, light, water, etc. not included in line 6a or 6b)	$
9) Repairs (not included in line 6a or 6b)	$
10) Other. Do not include expenses of maintaining home, such as mortgage interest, real estate taxes, and insurance.	$
11) Total household expenses (Add lines 6 through 10)	$
12) Total number of persons who lived in household	
Expenses for the Person You Supported	
13) Each person's part of household expenses (line 11 divided by line 12)	$
14) Clothing	$
15) Education	$
16) Medical, dental	$
17) Travel, recreation	$
18) Other (specify)	$
19) Total cost of support for the year (Add lines 13 through 18)	$
Did You Provide More Than Half?	
20) Amount the person provided for own support (line 3, plus line 6b if the person you supported owned the home)	$
21) Amount others provided for the person's support. Include amounts provided by state, local, and other welfare societies or agencies. Do not include any amounts included on line 2.	$
22) Amount you provided for the person's support (line 19 minus lines 20 and 21)	$
23) 50% of line 19	$

Is line 22 more than line 23?

Yes. You meet the support test for the person. If the other exemption tests are met, you may claim an exemption for the person.

No. You do not meet the support test for the person. You cannot claim an exemption for the person unless you can do so under a multiple support agreement.

Support Test for Children of Divorced or Separated Parents

Special rules apply for determining who can claim the dependency exemption for a child in cases where the parents are divorced, legally separated, or have lived apart for the last six months of the calendar year, and are not filing a joint tax return.

For these rules to apply, the support provided by the parents is combined, and the sum must be greater than one-half of the child's total support. The parent who has custody of the child for the greater part of the year is generally treated as the parent who has provided more than one-half of the child's support.

The question of who has custody of the child is normally determined under the divorce decree, separation agreement, or custody agreement. If there is no such agreement, physical custody of the child is the controlling factor.

The parent who does not have custody of the child for the greater portion of the year can take the dependency exemption if either:

- The custodial parent waives the exemption by signing IRS Form 8332, *Release of Claim to Exemption for Child of Divorced or Separated Parents*, or a similar statement.

- A decree or agreement signed before 1985 provides that the noncustodial parent gets the exemption, and that parent provided at least $600 for the child's support during the year.

Multiple Support Agreements

A situation that frequently arises, particularly with elderly persons, is that a number of people are contributing to an individual's support but no one is paying more than one-half of the support.

The IRS has devised a special rule to cover situations where two or more individuals would have been eligible to claim the dependency exemption if not for the support test, and together these individuals provide more than half of the support.

They can agree among themselves that one of them who provides more than 10 percent of the support will get the exemption. Each of the others must sign an IRS Form 2120, *Multiple Support Declaration*, or

another written statement agreeing not to claim the exemption for that year. These forms or statements must be filed along with the income tax return of the person who's claiming the exemption.

In making the decision as to who will get the most tax savings from the exemption, it's important to consider the marginal tax rates of the eligible contributors as well as the effect of the phaseout of personal exemptions discussed below.

Example

Amy, Betty, Carl, and Donald together provide 80% of the total support for their mother, Evelyn in the following amounts:

Amy	35%
Betty	20%
Carl	20%
Donald	5%
	80%

Evelyn receives nontaxable Social Security benefits to cover the remaining 20% of her expenses.

Because Amy, Betty, and Carl all provide more than 10% of Evelyn's support, they may choose which one of them should get the exemption, provided that the other two sign statements to that effect. Donald does not need to sign a statement since his contributions were not greater than 10%.

PHASEOUT OF EXEMPTIONS FOR HIGH-INCOME FAMILIES

Taxpayers in the higher brackets will find that, even if they are entitled to one or more exemptions for dependents, they may not get the full benefit of the exemptions on their tax return. In fact, your dependency exemptions may be phased out entirely if your income is high enough.

The threshold amounts of adjusted gross income (AGI) at which you must begin to reduce your personal exemptions are adjusted each year for inflation. The amounts shown in the chart below apply for 1999.

Filing Status	Phaseout Begins At:	Phaseout Complete Above:
Married filing separately	$ 94,975	$156,225
Single	126,600	249,100
Head of household	158,300	280,800
Married filing jointly	189,950	312,450

If your income exceeds the amount at which the phaseout begins for your filing status, you have to determine the amount of the excess income, and divide it by $2,500 ($1,250 if married filing separately). Take this result and round it up to the nearest whole number. Then multiply this whole number by two percent. Your answer is the percentage by which you must reduce your otherwise allowable exemptions.

Reverse Planning for Exemptions

While those in lower income brackets will want to arrange their affairs to allow as many people as possible to qualify as dependents, it can sometimes pay to "reverse plan" for those in higher income brackets. If you stand to partially or completely lose your exemptions, but you have dependents that have significant taxable income of their own from wages or investments, you might consider allowing some of your dependents to "lose" their dependent status in the future so they will be able to claim their own personal exemptions.

An added benefit of this strategy stems from the fact that individuals who may be claimed as dependents on your tax return are allowed a lower standard deduction on their own tax return. As long as they are considered dependents, they may claim only the greater of $700 or the amount of their earned income as a standard deduction. If dependent status is lost, they will be eligible for the full $4,400 standard deduction for singles in 2000.

In the case of a child who is age 14 or older, you might also consider transferring some additional income-producing assets to the child to ensure that the child will be able to use the full amount of the exemption and the higher standard deduction.

Case Study

Lincoln and Shabona Park are married and have one child, Grant. The Parks file a joint return and have a joint adjusted gross income of $220,500. They claim three exemptions. The reduction of the Parks' exemptions for 1999 will be calculated as follows:

Adjusted gross income	$220,500
Less: threshold for joint filers	- 189,950
Amount exceeding threshold	$ 30,550

The $30,550 figure is divided by $2,500 to reach the result of 12.22. Rounding up 12.22 to the nearest whole number gives us 13. 13 x 2% = 26%, which is the percentage of their exemptions that the Parks will lose.

Because the Parks would have an unreduced exemption amount of 3 x $2,750 = $8,250 for 1999, and 28% x $8,250 = $2,145, the Parks may claim exemptions of only $6,105 ($8,250 - $2,145).

Example

Mary and Carl Black file jointly, have one child, and have a taxable AGI of $240,000 for 1999. Their daughter, Carrie, is a college student who earns $5,000 in summer employment and also has $5,000 in investment income. It may be beneficial to have Carrie pay more than one-half of her own support so that she may claim a personal exemption on her tax return.

FILING RETURNS FOR THE DECEASED

If your spouse or another family member passes away during the year, a tax return may have to be filed for him or her.

The rule is that if the deceased person met any of the filing thresholds for the year so that he or she would have been required to file a tax return if alive, then a final return for the year of death must be filed.

Example

A tax return must be filed for a single person over age 65 if he or she had already received taxable income over $8,100 for the year, or more than $400 in self-employment income.

What income is included, in determining whether the thresholds are met and in filing the tax return itself? On the final income tax return, you report only income that the decedent received (for cash-basis taxpayers) or accrued (for accrual basis taxpayers) up to the date of death. Any income received or accrued after that date is ordinarily reportable on the estate's income tax return. If the account is transferred immediately to another beneficiary (such as to the joint owner on a bank account), the beneficiary must report any income earned after the date of death.

If the decedent receives any year-end 1099 forms from banks, savings and loans, brokerages, mutual fund companies, or other financial institutions reporting interest or dividends earned both before and after death, the institutions must be contacted so they can correct their records and issue corrected 1099 forms. Special care should be taken to make sure that the new 1099 forms correctly allocate the amounts between the final individual return and the estate or beneficiary's income tax return.

If the decedent had a capital loss in the period before death, it can be netted against capital gains as discussed on page 235. Any remaining loss up to $3,000 can be deducted on the final return; if the loss exceeded $3,000, the remainder cannot be deducted by the estate or carried over to any succeeding tax years.

Due Dates and Filing Requirements

The due date for the final tax return is the same due date the deceased person would have faced if alive, which is generally April 15th of the year after the year of death, although extensions may be available under the usual rules.

The person responsible for filing the final return is the individual's executor, administrator, or personal representative, if one has been appointed.

An "executor" is the person named in the deceased's will to gather the deceased assets, pay debts and taxes, and distribute any remaining assets according to the directions in the will. An "administrator" has similar duties but is appointed by the probate court if no executor was named, or the named executor is unable to serve. The term "personal representative" is used to refer to both executors and administrators. Often, but not always, a surviving spouse is chosen as the personal representative.

If no personal representative has been formally appointed by the time the tax return is due, the surviving spouse (if there is one) is responsible for filing the last tax return. If there is no surviving spouse, the person who is in charge of the deceased's property must file the final return, and would write the words "Deceased," the decedent's name, and the date of death across the top margin of the tax return.

Filing Status on the Final Return

If the decedent was married at the time of death and the surviving spouse does not remarry before the end of the year, the decedent's final return can be in the form of a joint return with the surviving spouse. The income reported is that of the decedent for the portion of the year he or she was alive, and that of the spouse for the entire calendar year. A full personal exemption can be claimed for the decedent even if his or her income was less than the minimum filing amount.

Filling a joint return usually results in significantly lower overall taxes, but this election must be agreed to by both the surviving spouse and the personal representative (if there is one who is not the surviving spouse). Otherwise, both the survivor and the decedent will have to file as "married filing separately."

If a personal representative was not appointed before the date the tax return is due, but is later appointed, he or she can file an amended return to change the deceased's filing status. If the status will be changed from "separate" to "joint," the surviving spouse must agree to the change. If the status will be changed from "joint" to "separate," the personal representative must file a separate return for the deceased within one year from the due date of the return; in that case, the original joint return would become the separate return of the surviving spouse.

The personal representative or other person filing the final return must sign it, and state his or her capacity; e.g., "Sharon Smith, executor for the estate of Sally Ann Smith." If the final return is a joint return with the surviving spouse, the spouse must also sign it.

Claiming the Decedent's Refund

The surviving spouse can claim a refund on a final joint return, and no special forms are necessary.

However, if the deceased's return is filed separately, the person filing the return must generally attach IRS Form 1310, *Statement of Person Claiming Refund Due a Deceased Taxpayer*, with the return. A court-appointed personal representative can avoid filing this form if he or she attaches a copy of the court certificate showing the appointment.

Chapter 11

Employment Income and Related Deductions

Many business owners have working spouses who are pulling down a salary, and who will need to report income and associated deductions from a W-2 on their joint return.

What's more, many business owners themselves start out as moonlighters while holding down a day job for a larger company. Even after a small business is established, it's not uncommon (or a bad idea) for the owner to have another job on the side, to provide supplemental income when business is slow.

If any of these scenarios apply to you, you'll need to be aware of the rules for reporting income from a job on your tax return.

Some of you may also have farm income that must be reported on Schedule F, or other types of miscellaneous income. In this chapter we'll provide you with a list of various types of income that are or are not taxable, and tell you how to handle the taxable ones on your income tax return.

The second part of this chapter will discuss employee business expenses, such as expenses for cars, travel, entertainment, and job-related education. We'll also cover the rules for two types of tax breaks that can apply to both those who are self-employed, and those who are employed by others: deductible job-related moving expenses, and child or dependent care credits, for those who can claim them.

Tax Organizer Tip

Most of the income and deduction items we'll be discussing in this chapter should be entered in the "Employment" section of the CompleteTax™ Organizer. Some types of miscellaneous income (such as gambling income and any unemployment benefits) are entered in the "Miscellaneous" section.

EMPLOYMENT INCOME

For the most part, employees have it very easy when it comes to reporting their taxable earnings.

They simply look at the W-2 forms they've received from their employers, take the number in Box 1 of the W-2, and report it on Line 1 of Form 1040EZ, or Line 7 of Form 1040A or Form 1040.

If they had more than one job during the year, or they are filing jointly with a spouse, they must add up all the numbers in Box 1 from all the W-2s that they (and their spouse) received, and report the total on Line 7.

There are numerous types of employee benefits that are exempt from federal income tax. For example, health and accident insurance, qualified retirement plan contributions, certain types of education assistance, reimbursements for business expenses, qualified transportation benefits, and group-term life insurance up to $50,000 can all be excluded if certain conditions are met. However, it will be up to your employer to determine whether or not you've received nontaxable benefits, to determine the appropriate value of the benefits, and to adjust your taxable earnings amount accordingly so that only the taxable amount is reported in Box 1.

Your employer must give you a W-2 Form by February 1st of 2000 to report all taxable salary, tips, wages and other compensation earned in 1999. A copy of each W-2 you (or your spouse, if filing jointly) receive must be attached to your tax form.

If the employer makes a mistake in these calculations, you must inform the employer and ask for a corrected Form W-2. Employers send a copy of all W-2s directly to the government, and if your reported income does not match what the employer has reported, you may get a letter from the IRS asking for more tax money, plus interest, and penalties.

If you don't receive a W-2 at all, you should contact the employer to find out why not, and ask that one be sent to you. If this doesn't work and by February 15th you still haven't received a W-2, call the IRS at 1-800-TAX-1040 to ask them to help you fill out a copy of Form 4852, *Substitute for Form W-2*.

Employees' Fringe Benefits

Certain types of fringe benefits that you may receive from your employer have been singled out for special treatment by the IRS.

If you received these benefits during the year, your employer must determine the amount that it expects to be deductible on your tax return, and does not

include that amount in your taxable wages as reported in Box 1 of your W-2 Form. However, you will have to report the amount separately, somewhere else on your tax return.

The benefits to which this applies are:

- **Dependent care benefits:** If your employer reports these in Box 10 of your W-2, you must file IRS Form 2441, *Child and Dependent Care Expenses*, to determine whether you can exclude the full amount from your taxable income. See page 196.

- **Adoption benefits:** If your employer reports these in Box 13, code T, you must file IRS Form 8839, *Qualified Adoption Expenses*, to determine whether you can exclude the full amount from your taxable income. See page 282.

- **Employer's contributions to a Medical Savings Account (MSA):** If your employer reports these in Box 13, code R, you must file IRS Form 8853, *Medical Savings Accounts and Long-Term Care Insurance Contracts*, to determine whether you can exclude the full amount from your taxable income.

- **Advance Earned Income Credit payments:** If your employer reports these in Box 9, you must report them on Line 54 of your Form 1040, or Line 33 of Form 1040A. You will also have to complete Schedule EIC.

If any of these benefits apply to you, you will have to complete the applicable form to determine whether some of the benefit amount might have to be added back in to your taxable income on Line 7 of Form 1040 or 1040A.

There are a number of other items that may have to be included in your total on Line 7, which are discussed in more detail below.

Excess Salary Deferrals

If the amount shown in Box 13 of your W-2 exceeded $10,000 and the "deferred compensation" box in Line 15 was checked, you must include the amount above $10,000 in Line 7. (If your plan was a tax-sheltered annuity plan or an eligible plan of a state or local government or non-profit organization, a higher limit may apply. Contact your employer if you have questions about your plan, or see IRS Publication 575 for details.)

Corrective Distributions

If too much of your salary was withheld or contributed to a retirement plan (other than an IRA) and your employer corrected the amounts, the corrections should have been reported to you on Form 1099-R, and you must include the amounts that were repaid to you on Line 7.

Disability Pensions

If you received a disability pension reported on Form 1099-R and you have not reached the minimum retirement age set by your employer, report the amount on Line 7. Otherwise, pensions are reported on Lines 16a and 16b of Form 1040, or Lines 11a and 11b of Form 1040A.

Back Pay Awards

If you received a settlement or a judgment for back pay, it should be reported to you on a W-2 Form and included in the total on Line 7. The taxable amount can include damages, unpaid life insurance premiums, or unpaid health insurance.

Severance Pay

Severance pay is taxable compensation and should be reported on Line 7. Also include any amounts you receive to compensate for cancellation of an employment contract.

Tips

If you or your spouse received tips from customers in 1999, any tips that exceeded $20 in a single month should have been reported to your employer over the course of the year. These tips should be reported to you in Box 1 of your W-2 Form.

If, in addition to your reported tips, your employer allocated tips to you (as shown in Box 8 of your W-2) you generally must add these amounts to your Line 7 salary and wages. Allocation is done for employees of larger restaurants, bars, or similar businesses when an employee's reported tips did not equal at least 8 percent of the employer's gross sales that were attributable to you. When you add your allocated tips to your Line 7 wages, remember that FICA tax has not been paid on these tips. Therefore, you will also

have to File IRS Form 4137, *Social Security and Medicare Tax on Unreported Tip Income*, to compute and pay the FICA tax, and you will have to file IRS Form 1040 (not 1040A or 1040EZ).

You do not have to add your allocated tips in Box 8 to your reported tips in Box 1 (and pay the extra FICA tax on Form 4137) if you kept a daily record of tips in 1999. In that case, you can use your actual amount of tips, as shown in your tip diary or records.

Work Smart

Technically, all employees who receive tips are supposed to keep a daily tip record – otherwise, how can they accurately report their tips to their employers each month? In actuality, the IRS recognizes that this recordkeeping duty is not always carried out. This is the reason that larger employers have to make a tip allocation.

As an employee, you can save yourself from having to pay unexpectedly large amounts of taxes on April 15th if you carefully keep track of your tips during the year. All it takes is a notebook showing your name, the employer's name, and, for each workday, the date, amount of cash tips, amount of credit card tips, and amount of any non-cash tips. If you split your tips with other workers you must also write down the names of the other employees and the amounts you paid to them.

Clergy and Religious

Clergy members must include in their income offerings and fees they receive for performing religious ceremonies such as weddings, baptisms, funerals, etc. But if the offering is made to the religious organization, it is not taxable to you. If you're a clergy member or retired clergy (but not a teacher or administrator of a church school or college), you do not pay tax on the rental value of a home or a housing allowance that's paid as part of your salary, and designated a housing allowance by the church or organization that employs you. If you own the home, you may deduct real estate taxes and mortgage interest (see page 199) even if you pay these expenses with your housing allowance.

Members of religious orders who have taken a vow of poverty and who turn their wages or salary over to the order are not taxed on these earnings, provided that they perform the services as duties required by the order, for the church or another agency of the church or an associated institution. If they work outside the church, they must pay tax on the income.

MISCELLANEOUS FORMS OF INCOME

The general rule is that, if you are a U.S. citizen, you must report all income from any source and any country – your total worldwide income – unless it is explicitly exempt under U.S. law. This includes income received in the form of money, property, or services. The following pages explain how to report some commonly encountered forms of income.

Alaska Permanent Fund Dividend Income

If you receive this type of income, you should receive a statement from the State of Alaska showing the total amount. Report it on Line 21 of Form 1040, on Line 12 of the 1040A, or Line 3 of the 1040EZ.

Alimony

For the treatment of alimony paid, as well as alimony received, see page 280.

Cancelled Debts

If you had a debt that was cancelled by the person to whom you owe money, the debt may be treated as taxable income. It will not be taxable if the cancellation was intended as a gift, or as a bequest. It will also not be taxable if the debt was cancelled in a bankruptcy case or when you are insolvent.

Certain student loans that are cancelled because the student worked for a certain period of time in a certain profession (such as teaching) are not treated as income. To qualify, the loan generally must have been made by an educational institution, a tax-exempt organization, or a government agency or instrumentality.

See also the discussion of cancelled business debts on page 49.

Corporate Director Fees

Report these on Line 7 of Form 1040 or 1040A, or Line 1 of Form 1040EZ. Generally, you should receive a W-2 Form showing these payments in Box 1.

Court Awards, Damages, and Legal Settlements

These amounts are either taxable or nontaxable, depending on the nature of the injury that they are designed to compensate you for.

Compensatory damages for personal physical injury or physical sickness are not taxable. However, the following types of damages would be taxable as ordinary income:

- Interest on any type of award

- Compensation for lost wages or lost profits

- Punitive damages

- Amounts received to settle pension rights, if you did not contribute to the plan

- Compensation for patent or copyright infringement

- Compensation for breach of contract

- Compensation for interference with business operations

- Back pay and damages for emotional distress in a Civil Rights Act claim.

Credit Card Insurance Payments

If you receive payments under an insurance plan that makes your credit card payments if you cannot pay because of unemployment, illness, or injury, you must report as "other income" on Line 21 of Form 1040 the amount of benefits you receive during the year that exceeds the amount of premiums you paid during the year.

Disability Pay

If you receive payments because of disability under a plan paid for by your employer, the benefits will be taxable; if you paid for the plan yourself, they are not taxable. "Paying for the plan yourself" includes paying through payroll deductions that were made from your after-tax income. If you paid for the plan through pre-tax payroll contributions, as in a cafeteria-plan arrangement, the benefits you receive are taxable.

Certain types of military and government disability pensions are not taxable. VA disability payments are not taxable, including awards made retroactively after retirement for length of service, and the equivalent of VA benefits that would have been paid if you receive a lump-sum disability severance award. Disability payments for combat-related injuries, or injuries sustained in a terrorist attack while serving as a U.S. government official, are tax-exempt. Also persons who were eligible to receive a disability payment before September 25, 1975 may generally exclude their disability payments.

If the benefits are taxable, they are reported on Line 7 of Form 1040 or 1040A until you reach minimum retirement age. Beginning on the day after you reach minimum retirement age under your employer's plan, the benefits are treated as pension benefits and reported on Lines 16a and 16b of Form 1040, or on Lines 11a and 11b of Form 1040A.

Dividends

See the discussion in Chapter 13.

Election Official Fees

If you are paid for performing services as an election officer or worker, you should receive a W-2 Form reporting this income. Include it in the total reported on Line 7 of Form 1040 or Form 1040A, or on Line 1 of Form 1040EZ.

Estate and Trust Income

See the discussion of investment income in Chapter 13.

Executors and Trustees

If you are not in the business of being a professional fiduciary, fees you receive in these capacities are treated as "other income" to be reported on Line 21 of Form 1040. If being a fiduciary is part of your trade or business, or your duties are so extensive as to constitute a trade or business for a substantial period of time, you will have to report the fees you receive on Schedule C or C-EZ. See Chapter 13.

Gains and Losses

See the discussion of investment gains and losses in Chapter 13.

Gambling Winnings

If you have winnings from a lottery, raffle, or some other gambling activity, it must be reported on Line 21 of Form 1040. If any taxes were withheld from your winnings, you should receive a Form W-2G that shows the total paid to you in Box 1, and the amount of income taxes withheld in Box 2. Be sure to include the amount in Box 2 in the amount of taxes paid on Line 57 of your 1040.

Hobby Income

Income you receive from an activity that is not considered a for-profit business (see page 34) is reported as "other income" on Line 21 of Form 1040. Expenses you incurred in generating this income are deductible as miscellaneous itemized deductions on Schedule A.

Illegal Income

Bribes, kickbacks, push money, stolen or embezzled funds, and other illegal income must be reported on Line 21 of Form 1040, or on Schedule C or C-EZ. While obviously this is rarely done, failure to report opens the door to imposition of tax fines and penalties, as well as criminal penalties, on illegal activities.

Interest

See the discussion in Chapter 13.

Jury Duty Pay

All jury duty pay you receive must be reported as "other income" on Line 21 of Form 1040. If the pay is turned over to your employer, you should treat the amount you repay to your employer as an adjustment to income on Line 32. Write "Jury Pay" and the amount that was repaid on the dotted line next to Line 32.

Pension Benefits

For a discussion of the treatment of retirement and Social Security payments, see Chapter 14.

Prizes and Awards

If you win a prize in a contest, drawing, or raffle, you must report it on Line 21 of Form 1040. If the prize takes the form of a car, merchandise, a gift certificate, or free services, the fair market value of the item is the value that you must report.

There is a very narrow exception for prizes in recognition of past accomplishments (such as a Nobel, Pulitzer, literary prize, citizen-of-the-year award, etc.). You don't have to include the award as income if you were selected without any action on your part to enter the contest, you don't have to perform future services, and you transfer the award directly to a tax-exempt charitable organization or government unit.

Refunds or Recoveries of Previously Deducted Items

If you recover or receive back an amount that you had already deducted on a prior year's return, you generally must report the recovered amount as income in the year you receive it. This rule saves you the trouble of having to file an amended tax return for the prior year.

State or local income tax refunds are the most commonly encountered items of this type. Therefore, they have been assigned their own line (Line 10) on Form 1040. If you itemized your deductions in the year to which the refund applies, you must report the refund as income on Line 10. If you did not itemize, you don't have to report the refund since you didn't gain any tax benefit from it. Federal tax refunds are not reported because you cannot claim an itemized deduction for your federal taxes.

This rule – the rule that you must report the refund or recovery only if you got some tax benefit from it in a previous year – applies generally to all types of refunds and recoveries, except that recoveries other than state and local tax refunds, credits and offsets are reported on Line 21 of Form 1040.

You only have to report recoveries of items to the extent that they helped your itemized deductions to exceed the standard deduction for the year in question.

Example

In 1998, your filing status was single, which would have qualified you for a standard deduction of $4,250. Instead, you claimed itemized deductions of $5,000.

In 1999, you received a $1,000 refund of state income tax. Since your itemized deductions minus your standard deduction was only $750, you must report $750 of the recovery as income for 1999. The remaining $250 of the recovery is not taxable.

If your deduction for the item was less than the amount you recovered, you only have to report a taxable recovery for the amount that you had actually deducted.

Example

In 1998, your employee business expenses were $1,000, but since your adjusted gross income was $40,000, you faced the 2 percent of adjusted gross income limitation on miscellaneous deductions (including employee business expenses). So, you had to subtract $40,000 x .02 = $800 from the expense amount, to arrive at an allowable deduction of $200.

In early 1999 your employer reimbursed you for $300 of your business expenses. Your taxable recovery is limited to the amount you deducted, or $200.

Taxpayers who itemized their deductions for the year to which the recovery applies, but had their deductions limited because they were high-income taxpayers (see page 272), must go through some special calculations to determine how much of the recovery they must report. Basically, this involves determining how much of a deduction they would have been able to claim for the item if it were reported accurately, as compared to the amount they actually were able to claim for the item, taking the limitation into account.

Example

In 1998, $9,000 in state income taxes were withheld from your paycheck, but you could only *deduct $3,600 of these taxes because your itemized deductions were reduced by 3% of the amount by which your income exceeded $124,500. In 1999, you received a state tax refund of $2,000. If you had correctly reported your state taxes for 1998 as $7,000, your itemized deduction for taxes would have been $1,800. Therefore, the difference between what you actually claimed, and what you should have claimed, is your reportable recovery amount ($3,600 - $1,800 = $1,800).*

Rents and Royalties

See the discussion in Chapter 13.

Scholarships

Scholarship or fellowship grants are excludable from income if you are a degree candidate, and the amounts received are for tuition, fees, books, supplies, or equipment required for courses. Room and board do not qualify. If you receive payments for services, they must be included in your taxable income even if such services are required of all candidates for the degree.

Veterans' Administration payments are not taxable. Qualified tuition reduction for undergraduates, or tuition waivers or reductions for graduate students engaged in teaching or research activities, are not taxable.

If you received taxable money under a grant, you must report it on Line 7 of your 1040 form, whether or not it was reported on a W-2 form.

Social Security Benefits

See the discussion in Chapter 14.

State Tuition Programs

Distributions from a qualified state tuition program are tax-free up to the amount that was contributed to the program; amounts over the contributions are taxable.

Unemployment Compensation

All unemployment compensation you may receive is taxable. If you received any during the year, you should receive a Form 1099-G showing the amount that was paid to you. Report it on Line 19 of Form 1040, Line 12 of Form 1040A, or Line 3 of Form 1040EZ.

If you receive supplemental unemployment benefits from a fund that was created by your employer, these benefits are taxable for income tax purposes and are reported on Line 7 of Form 1040 or 1040A.

If you received payments from a union, they are reported on Line 21 (the "Other Income" line) of Form 1040. And if you received payments from a private unemployment fund to which you contributed, only the portion that exceeds your total contributions are taxable, and reported on Line 21.

Nontaxable Income

The following items are generally not reported as taxable income.

- Accelerated death benefits under a life insurance contract that are paid to a terminally or chronically ill person by the insurance company or a viatical settlement company

- Accident and health insurance benefits

- Black lung benefits

- Cash rebates (for example, you receive $500 after purchasing a new car)

- Casualty insurance and other reimbursements for theft or casualty loss (see page 267)

- Child support payments

- Damages for physical injury or sickness

- Energy conservation subsidies provided by public utilities for purchase or installation of energy-saving devices in dwellings

- Federal Employees' Compensation Act payments

- Foster-care payments, unless you are paid for care of more than five people age 19 or older, or you receive difficulty-of-care payments for more than five people age 19 or older, or more than 10 people under 19

- Gifts, bequests, and inheritances

- Government cost-of-living allowances for civilian employees stationed outside the continental U.S. or in Alaska

- Life or accident insurance proceeds, unless the policy was turned over to you for a price. However, if you cash in a policy, you must include in taxable income any amount that exceeds the total premiums you paid less any rebates, refunds, dividends, or unrepaid loans.

- Living expenses paid by insurance, because of a casualty loss to your home, to the extent the payments compensate for extra expenses you would not have had if the casualty had not occurred

- Long-term care insurance benefits from qualified plans, up to $190 per day or $69,350 per year (in 1999).

- Medical savings account withdrawals, if used to pay for qualified medical expenses for you, yourself, or your dependents (withdrawals to pay for health insurance premiums are qualified expenses only if you are unemployed, buying COBRA continuation coverage, or buying long-term care coverage)

- Mileage allowance for transporting schoolchildren, if you are not in the business of transporting them

- Military allowances

- Supplemental Security Income (SSI) payments

- Veterans' benefits

- Welfare benefits, including disaster relief grants, mortgage assistance programs, and payments to reduce cost of winter energy

- Workers' compensation

FARM INCOME

Farmers must report their income from farming in a variety of different ways.

If you are in the trade or business of farming, you must complete and file Schedule F, *Profit or Loss from Farming,* along with your IRS Form 1040. This form is very similar to Schedule C and most of your expense deductions, tax credits, and gains and losses are computed using the same rules discussed in Part II for small business owners. For example, for the treatment of car or truck expenses, see page 63 relating to small business car or truck expenses. For the treatment of sales of assets, see page 116 relating to sales of business assets.

Note that sales of livestock held for breeding, dairy, draft, or sport purposes are treated as sales of business assets reported on Form 4797, *Sales of Business Property*, while sales of livestock raised or purchased for resale are reported on Schedule F.

Schedule F, Line E, asks whether you "materially participated" in the farming business. The standard for "material participation" for this question relates to the passive activity rules and is basically the same as the standard for materially participating in a small business; see page 44 for more details.

As a farmer, you can be treated as materially participating under two additional situations: (1) if you are a retired or disabled farmer, and you materially participated for five of the eight years preceding your retirement or disability, or (2) if you are a surviving spouse of a farmer, you actively manage the farm, and the property used for farming meets the special use valuation of a farm property under the estate tax rules.

Net farm income as computed on Schedule F is carried over to Line 18 of Form 1040, and self-employment tax is computed on the Schedule F net income using Schedule SE. See the discussion of self-employment taxes on page 135.

Beginning in 1998, a special rule permits farmers to average their income over three years. This will allow you to pay less in taxes in an unusually good year. If you elect to average farm income, you must complete Schedule J and file it with your Form 1040. You'll figure the current year's tax by following these steps:

1. Subtract the elected part of your current year's taxable farm income (elected farm income) from your total taxable income.

2. Figure the tax on the amount in Step 1 using the current year's tax tables or tax rate schedules.

3. For each of the previous three years, make the following computation:

(a) Add one-third of the current year's elected farm income to your taxable income for that year.

(b) Figure the tax on the amount in (a) using the tax tables or rate schedules for that year.

(c) Subtract that year's actual tax from the tax in (b).

4. Add the amounts in step 3(c) to the amount in Step 2. The result is the tax for the current year.

Rent Based on Crop or Livestock Sharing

If you are involved in a crop or livestock sharing arrangement with a tenant who does most of the work of operating the farm and you don't meet the special active participation test described below, you should report your income and expenses on Form 4835, *Farm Rental Income and Expenses*, instead of Schedule F. In that case, your net income from Form 4835 is carried over to Schedule E, *Supplemental Income and Loss*. It is treated like rental income and will not be subject to self-employment tax.

In order to use this form (and avoid self-employment tax on the income), you must *not* have materially participated in the activity. You *did* materially participate if you meet one of the following four tests:

1) You do any three of the following four things: pay or stand good for at least half the direct costs of producing the crop; furnish at least half the tools, equipment, and livestock used in producing the crop; consult with your tenant; inspect production activities periodically.

2) You regularly and frequently make, or take an important part in making, important management decisions.

3) You work 100 hours or more spread over five weeks or more in activities connected with crop production.

4) You do things which, considered in their total effect, show that you are materially and significantly involved in the production of the farm commodities.

Rent Based on Flat Charge

Finally, if you rent cropland, farm buildings, etc. for a flat charge (rather than a percentage of the value of the yield produced by the tenant), report the activity directly on Schedule E, *Supplemental Income and Loss*. Again, net income from this type of activity will not be subject to self-employment tax.

More Farming Information

Farmers are subject to some special, generally more lenient accounting rules and some very specific rules about income recognition. We recommend that you get a copy of the IRS's free Publication 225, *Farmer's Tax Guide*, for help in completing Schedule F or Form 4835. For more on Schedule E, see Chapter 12.

EMPLOYEE BUSINESS EXPENSES

If you've read Part II of this book, you know that business owners must report their sales and other income on Schedule C, and then are entitled to deduct all their legitimate business expenses before arriving at the net income that will be subject to tax.

If you are an employee, your income from your job is reported to you on a W-2 form, and the expectation is that your employer is providing you with the location, materials, tools and equipment, and other things you need to do your work. However, it's not always the case that employers pay for *all* of an employee's business expenses.

So, the IRS does give employees the opportunity to claim some tax deductions if you spend money on your job; e.g., on business meals and entertainment, local transportation, gifts, travel, education, supplies, tools, uniforms and other customary business expenses, so long as the expenses are considered reasonable and meet certain requirements.

The way in which your business expenses are written off for tax purposes depends on whether your employer reimburses you for your expenses and, if so, what type of reimbursement plan the employer uses.

Generally speaking, you'll get the full benefit of all your allowable deductions if they are reimbursed by your employer under what is known as an "accountable plan." This is a plan under which you have to report and document your expenses for your employer, and you have to return any expense allowance amounts over and above the expenses you have proven. Your employer then subtracts the reimbursements from your taxable income when filling out your annual W-2 form, so you pay no tax on the amount of the reimbursements.

Unreimbursed Expenses

If you have expenses that are not reimbursed by your employer, or if your employer does not use an accountable plan, you'll generally have to claim the nonreimbursed expenses on Form 2106, *Employee Business Expenses*. In some cases you may be able to use Form 2106-EZ, *Unreimbursed Employee Business Expenses*. Then the total amount of your expenses from either of these forms is transferred to Line 20 of Form 1040 Schedule A, *Itemized Deductions*.

Warning

We might as well warn you upfront that Schedule A requires that your employee business expenses be classified as "miscellaneous deductions" that must be reduced by 2 percent of your adjusted gross income (AGI) before they can be deducted. In other words, you'll automatically lose the benefit of some of your expenses, up to the amount of 2 percent of AGI.

And, if you can't itemize your deductions because all of your deductible expenses don't add up to more than the standard deduction for your filing status (see page 257), you will lose the tax benefits of your employee business expenses entirely.

Therefore, it becomes very important to keep track of your expenses so that your allowable deductions will be as large as possible. Sometimes a few extra dollars of expenses will make the difference when you're deciding whether it's worthwhile to itemize in a particular year.

This is the basic story, but as you might guess, there are a few wrinkles to be aware of. On the next few pages, we'll first go over the most common types of employee business expenses, and then explain exactly how to claim them on your tax return.

What Expenses are Deductible for Employees?

For the most part, employees can deduct all "ordinary and necessary" business expenses, using the same definition that is used by a business owner. An "ordinary" expense is one that is common and accepted in your line of work. A "necessary" expense is one that is appropriate or helpful for the work you do, even if it's not absolutely indispensable to your business.

For employees, expenses may be considered "unnecessary" if you could have been reimbursed for them, but you neglected to ask the employer for reimbursement.

As a general principle, amounts that you spend for personal or family reasons are not deductible. While it's sometimes difficult to tell the difference, the IRS has specific rules in a number of areas (such as car expenses, travel, meals and entertainment, and education) to help you determine what portion of an expense is truly business-related. If you pay for property or have some other expense for both business and personal purposes, you must allocate the expense between the two types of usage. The allocation must be made on a reasonable and consistent basis, depending on the nature of the expense.

Example

If a car is used partly for business and partly for personal purposes, the allocation is based on the number of miles driven during the year for business, compared to the miles driven for personal use. If you use a room in your home as a home office, the allocation is based on the number of square feet in the office as compared with the square footage of the home.

See page 57 for more information on how to make this type of allocation.

Certain expenses, while they may be ordinary and necessary, must be treated as capital expenditures.

Generally speaking, the cost of equipment or business real estate that will be used for more than one year must be treated as a capital expenditure and depreciated. Employees may claim a depreciation deduction for equipment they need in their job (such as a cellular phone or a laptop computer) and would use a separate Form 4562, *Depreciation and Amortization*, to compute the proper amount. The result from Form 4562 would be carried over to Line 4 of the Form 2106 or 2106-EZ. For a detailed explanation of capital assets, depreciation, and how to treat the sale of a business asset, see Chapter 7.

Finally, certain types of expenses are not deductible even if they meet the "ordinary and necessary" tests, and are not personal or capital expenses. This category includes illegal payments (e.g., bribes or kickbacks) and payments of fines or penalties (such as parking or traffic tickets).

Cars, Meals and Entertainment, Travel, Home Offices, and Gifts

The very most commonly deducted employee business expense is undoubtedly the cost of a car. The IRS has a large number of very specific rules about deductible costs of operating a vehicle. The rules for employees are basically the same as the rules for self-employed people, as described beginning on page 63.

One departure from the ordinary rules that employees should be aware of is that an employee using the actual expense method cannot deduct any part of the interest payments on a car loan (while a self-employed person can).

In order to claim the deduction for car expenses, you'll have to keep records that satisfy the IRS. The best way to be sure you'll get to claim all your deductions is to keep a written record of your business mileage whenever you drive, and also keep a record of all car expenses as you pay them. It's a good idea to save all your receipts for expenses as well. See the discussion of recordkeeping in Chapter 2.

If your employer pays you a mileage allowance, you can simplify your recordkeeping a bit. Generally, if the mileage allowance is no higher than the government's standard mileage rate (32.5 cents per mile for January through March of 1999, and 31 cents thereafter) you will only be required to prove to the employer the time, number of miles, and business purpose of your car trips, and this will be enough to satisfy the IRS. If, however, your employer pays you more than the standard mileage rate (SMR), the SMR amount will be shown in Box 13 of your W-2 Form with Code L, and the excess will be reported as taxable income to you in Box 1 of the W-2 Form.

For employees, car expenses can be reported on Form 2106-EZ if you own your car and use the standard mileage rate for 1999, and if you are not required to file Form 2106 for any other reason. Otherwise, you must use Form 2106 to report car expenses.

Meals, entertainment, travel, gifts, and home offices. Most other types of employee business expenses follow the same rules that apply to small business owners. For the rules regarding meals and entertainment, see page 75. For rules on deductible travel expenses, see page 72. For rules on business gifts, see page 77. And for rules on home offices, see page 79. Note that for an employee to claim a home office expense, he or she must be using the office for the convenience of the employer (not just his or her own convenience), in addition to meeting all the other requirements for the home office deduction.

Employees' Education Expenses

Educational expenses for employees can yield tax benefits under two different law provisions, each of which has its own detailed requirements.

In addition, as of last year there are several new types of tax credits that apply to educational benefits for all individuals, not just employees. For a discussion of the Hope Scholarship Credit and the Lifetime Learning Credit, see page 286; for a discussion of the exclusion of education loan interest, see page 289.

In this section, we'll concentrate on two types of educational benefits: employer-provided educational assistance, and qualifying work-related education.

Employer-provided assistance. Up to $5,250 per year can be provided to an employee as reimbursement for educational expenses as part of an employee benefit plan. Tuition, fees, books, supplies, and tools are considered reimbursable "educational expenses." The tax law does not require the education to be related to the job, or part of a degree program, although some employers may impose these requirements under their particular plan. However, the courses may not be for graduate-level or professional education (such as medicine, law, or a master's or Ph.D. degree). Furthermore, this tax break is scheduled to expire as of January 1, 2001 and courses beginning after that date will not be covered.

Work Smart

Note that the benefits must be provided under a written plan that does not discriminate in favor of officers, shareholders, or highly compensated employees, and no more than five percent of the benefits provided during a year can be paid to the business owner's family. Therefore, small business owners can't use this type of plan to finance their own or their family's education.

If you receive benefits under this type of plan, they are completely tax-free, and they will not be reported

as income on your W-2 form. You don't have to take any further action to claim your exemption.

Work-related education. If you don't receive employer-provided assistance under the type of plan described above, or if the assistance you receive is more than $5,250 per year or is for graduate-level education, there is another law provision under which you may receive a tax break for education.

Under the qualifying, work-related education rules, education of any type (whether or not it leads to a degree, and whether it is technical, vocational, undergraduate, graduate, or professional) will be deductible if it meets either of these requirements:

1. The education must be required by your employer or the law to keep your present salary, status, or job (and serve a business purpose of your employer).

2. The education must maintain or improve skills needed in your present work, including refresher courses, seminars, and academic courses.

However, even if the education meets these requirements, it is not qualifying education if either:

1. It is needed to meet the minimum educational requirement of your present trade or business as in effect when you first got the job.

2. It is part of a program of study that can qualify you for a new trade or business, even if you have no plans to enter that trade or business. Bar review or CPA review courses or exams don't qualify.

The education must relate to your present work, not just to work you may enter in the future or work that you held in the past. However, if you stop work for a year or less (for example, to go to school full-time) and then resume your work, this temporary absence will not render the education nonqualifying.

If all of these rules are met, you can deduct your educational expenses. Furthermore, if the employer reimburses you for these expenses, it can be treated as a nontaxable working-condition fringe, and the reimbursements should not be reported as taxable income on your W-2 form. Nondiscrimination rules do not apply to this type of working-condition fringe benefit, so small business owners can take advantage of this deduction as well.

Types of expenses that qualify. Under the qualifying work-related education expense rules, you can deduct a much broader range of expenses: the costs of tuition, fees, books, supplies, transportation and travel costs, and other expenses such as the cost of research, typing and copying when writing a paper as part of an educational program.

Generally, you can deduct the standard mileage rate of 32.5 cents per mile for the first quarter of 1999 and 31 cents thereafter, for the mileage you drive one way from work to school; alternately, you can deduct the cost of bus, subway, train, cab, or even airfare to get to school. If you are regularly employed and go to school on a temporary basis (generally, irregularly or for a matter of days or weeks), you can also deduct the cost of going from school to home. However, if you go from home directly to school you can deduct the round-trip costs only if you are going from home to school on a temporary basis.

If you drive, you can choose to use the actual cost method to compute your vehicle costs (see page 67); however, this generally involves a great deal of recordkeeping for very little payback. Regardless of whether you use the standard mileage rate or the actual cost method, you can always deduct the cost of parking and tolls.

If you must travel and stay overnight to get to school or to a particular seminar, training course, trade or business association meeting, etc., you can deduct the cost of travel, lodging, and 50 percent of the cost of meals for yourself under the usual rules related to travel (see page 72). However, you cannot deduct the cost of travel that is in itself a form of education – there must be some type of specific class, seminar, convention, etc., involved.

Claiming work-related education expenses. For employees, if you are deducting transportation, travel, or meals in connection with qualified education, these should be added to your other expenses of the same type and deducted on IRS Form 2106 or 2106-EZ.

Example

You traveled 10 miles from work to school and 12 miles from school back home, and made this trip once a week for a six-week period. Since this was a "temporary" situation you can deduct the cost of driving 22 miles, for each of the six classes, or a total of 132 miles. This mileage would be added to any other business mileage you drove during the year and

reported on Line 13 of Form 2106, or Line 8A on Form 2106-EZ.

Other education costs of employees (the costs of tuition, fees, books, supplies, etc.) would normally be reported on Line 4 of either Form 2106 or 2106-EZ.

If you are self-employed, education costs would be reported on Schedule C, with most costs being reported on Line 27 as "other expenses" but the costs for your car or truck, meals, and travel being added to Lines 10, 24b, and 24a respectively. If you file Schedule C-EZ, deduct these expenses on Line 2.

More Employee Business Expenses

Along with the expenses we've already mentioned, you can deduct almost any other ordinary and necessary business expense you have as an employee. Some of the more common ones are discussed below.

Computers. You can claim a first-year expensing election for a home computer (see page 103) if you use it more than 50 percent for business; otherwise, or for later years, you may depreciate the business percentage of the cost. See Chapter 7 for the rules related to long-term business assets.

Dues. You can deduct membership fees and dues to professional societies, the chamber of commerce, boards of trade, business leagues, civic or public service organizations, real estate boards, or trade associations if membership helps you in your job; however, you can't deduct any portion of the dues that is used for lobbying or political activities. Your organization should tell you the percentage of your dues, if any, that are used for this purpose. Dues to airline clubs, social clubs, or country clubs are not deductible.

Office furniture used at home. Even if you can't claim the home office deduction, you can expense or depreciate the cost of a desk, chair, file cabinets, lighting, etc. you use when you work at home, provided you meet the usual requirements (see Chapter 7).

Subscriptions. You can deduct the cost of professional, trade, or business publications and newspapers.

Telephones. The installation and monthly charges for the first telephone line you bring into your home is not deductible. But if you have a second line for business, or you can determine the cost of specific long-distance or local charges for business calls, you can deduct those amounts even if you don't qualify for the home office deduction.

Work clothes and uniforms. These are deductible only if you must wear certain items as a condition of your employment and they are not suitable for normal wear; for example, firefighters, delivery people, waiters, health care workers, and others required to wear specific uniforms may claim the deduction, but not those who are merely required to conform to a dress code, or to dress in a certain style or color. If your clothing qualifies, so does the cost of upkeep and cleaning. You can also deduct the cost of protective clothing or items like hard-hats, safety glasses, work gloves, steel-toed boots, etc.

Other deductions. Here are a few more potentially deductible items that are often overlooked:

- Breakage fees

- Business cards

- Business liability or malpractice insurance, for wrongful acts committed on the job

- Damages for breach of employment contract that you pay to your former employer

- Legal fees (for example, to negotiate an employment contract)

- Medical exams required by the employer

- Occupational taxes and license fees

- Office supplies and postage; for example, items you use at home

- Passport fee for a business trip

- Tools and other supplies used in your work

- Union dues

Claiming Employee Business Expenses

If you receive an advance to pay for your employee business expenses, or reimbursements for expenses you have already incurred, the way you report your expense depends on how your employer reimburses you.

The key distinction to be made is whether the employer's plan is "accountable" or "nonaccountable." Your employer should be able to tell you which type it is using.

Accountable plans. If the plan is accountable, and you are reimbursed for the exact amount of the expense, you are among the lucky ones. Your reimbursements are simply excluded from your income – that is, they are not reported as income on your W-2 form, and you don't have to pay income tax, Social Security tax, or Medicare tax on them. You don't have to file a Form 2106 to claim your expenses as deductions, because they are already subtracted from your pay.

Under accountable plans, you report your expenses to the employer, and provide it with all the receipts, credit card slips, and other documentation you would normally need for the IRS. This takes the place of retaining all these records in case the IRS asks for them.

Nonaccountable plans. However, if the plan is not considered accountable, or if your employer does not reimburse you for all of your allowable expenses, you'll have to claim the deductions on your tax return.

Your employer will include any reimbursements it makes in your taxable income (in Box 1 on your W-2), and will withhold income tax, Social Security tax, and Medicare tax on them. Any reimbursements that are *not* reported in Box 1 must be subtracted from your deductible expenses on Form 2106, *Employee Business Expenses.*

If you are not reimbursed for your employee business expenses (other than taxable amounts included in Box 1), you can generally report your expenses on Form 2106-EZ, *Unreimbursed Employee Business Expenses,* provided that if you are claiming vehicle expenses, you are using the standard mileage rate (SMR) to compute your expenses.

If you use the actual expense method of claiming car expenses, or if you were reimbursed for expenses, you will have to use the longer Form 2106, *Employee Business Expenses.*

Save Time

If you are not claiming any car, parking and tolls, local transportation charges, travel, or meals and entertainment expenses, and you didn't receive any reimbursements that weren't reported as taxable income, you don't have to use either version of the 2106. Instead, you can simply claim these expenses as miscellaneous deductions on Line 20 of Schedule A.

However, you may want to file a Form 2106 anyway, particularly if you are claiming a large amount of expenses, just to provide the IRS with some additional information and, hopefully, prevent them from writing you a letter that questions your deduction.

Some special rules. Qualified performing artists, and disabled employees with impairment-related work expenses, are subject to some special, more lenient ways to claim their employee business expenses.

A qualified performing artist can deduct employee business expenses as an adjustment to gross income (on Line 32 of Form 1040). As a result, such artists don't need to itemize expenses to get the benefits of their deductions. They would still need to complete Form 2106 to compute their expenses, and then write the total amount and "QPA" on the dotted line next to Line 32 on the 1040.

Qualified performing artists are those who perform services for at least two employers during the tax year, receive at least $200 from two different employers, have related performing-arts business expenses over 10 percent of their gross income, and have adjusted gross income of not more than $16,000 before deducting those expenses. If married, the artist must file jointly unless living apart from the spouse at all times during the tax year, and joint adjusted gross income may not be more than $16,000 before deducting the expenses.

Employees with physical or mental disabilities, who have impairment-related work expenses, can deduct those expenses without regard to the usual 2 percent of adjusted gross income threshold for miscellaneous deductions. They would complete Form 2106 or 2106-EZ, and enter impairment-related expenses directly onto Line 27 of Schedule A, *Itemized Deductions.*

DEDUCTIBLE MOVING EXPENSES

Moving to a new location to take a new job or start a new business is something that doesn't happen every year. However, if you did move last year, your moving costs may have eaten up a significant portion of your income.

The tax laws permit some limited tax breaks for job-related moves, if you meet all the requirements. If your employer pays for some or all of the costs, you won't be taxed on the reimbursements. And if you pay for the costs yourself, you can deduct them "above the line"; that is, you don't have to itemize your deductions in order to get the benefit of your moving expenses. Moreover, your moving expense deduction will serve to reduce your Adjusted Gross Income, which may help you qualify for other tax breaks that are phased out at higher AGI levels.

Which Moves Qualify?

Before you can start to add up the amounts you spent on your move, you have to determine whether your move met the IRS's requirements for a deductible move.

There are three parts to the test that you must meet:

1. Was the move closely related to the start of work?

2. Did the move meet the distance test?

3. Did your work in the new location meet the time test?

Closely Related to Start of Work

For any moving expenses to be deductible, your move must have been closely related to the start of work in your new location, in both time and in space.

Being closely related in time means that the expenses occurred within one year before, or one year after, you go to work or start a business in the new location.

You may qualify for an exemption from this rule if you have a good reason for incurring the expense of moving outside the one-year period.

Example

You were transferred to a new job on the West Coast and began working there, but the rest of your family did not move from the Midwest until 18 months later so that your son could finish high school. The costs of moving your family would be deductible even though they were incurred more than one year after your new job began.

Being closely related in place generally means that the distance from the new job to the new home is not more than the distance from the new job to the old home.

Again, there may be an exception to this rule if you can show that either your employer requires you to live at the new home as a condition of employment, or you will actually spend less time or money commuting to the new job from your new home.

For purposes of measuring distances, the "new job" is considered to be located at your principal place of work, which is the place where you spend most of your working time. If there is no one location where you spend most of your time, consider your principal place of work to be the main office, station, check-in point, or place where you receive instructions. If you have more than one job, you'll have to decide which is your main job, based on the time spent at each job, the amount of work you do at each place, and the amount of money you earn at each place.

Also, your "home" for these purposes means your main home, not a summer home, second home, or a home kept up by other family members.

Distance Test

There is another test related to distance that must be met if you want to deduct moving expenses.

The distance between your old home and your new job must be at least 50 miles farther than the distance from the old home to the old job. In other words, your new job would have increased your commuting distance by at least 50 miles, if you hadn't moved.

Example

Sally travels 60 miles one way to get to work. She takes a new job that would require her to travel 65 miles and, since she feels the extra time makes her commute just too long, she bites the bullet and buys a new home only two miles from the new job. Sally cannot deduct her moving expenses, because the new job would only have increased her commute by five miles.

For those who are seeking their first full-time job or have been out of the workforce for a significant period of time, the new place of work must be at least 50 miles from your old home.

Time Test

The third and final test for a deductible move is that, if you're an employee, in the first year after you start work in the new location you must work full time for at least 39 weeks.

If you are self-employed (as a sole proprietor or partner), you must work full time for at least 39 weeks in the first year, and you must also work full time for at least 78 weeks in the first two years.

The weeks need not be consecutive, and they don't have to be with the same employer or in the same business activity if you are self-employed. "Full-time work" means whatever is considered full time in your occupation and region. Also, vacation time or time off because of illness, strikes, layoffs, natural disasters, or similar causes counts as time worked. If you are using the self-employed rule, you can count time spent as an employee as well as time working for your own company towards the 78-week requirement.

This rule can be waived only if your work is cut short due to death or disability, or if you obtained full-time work but you were transferred by the employer or were laid off for a reason other than misconduct.

If you are filing a joint return, the move is deductible if either spouse meets the 39-week test, or the 78-week test if self-employed. However, time worked by one spouse can't be added to time worked by the other spouse.

Example

K.C. Jones decides to move from Boston to Dallas because he believes there are better job prospects there. He moves himself and his family to Dallas at his personal expense, where he finds a job with an oil company. After working full-time for 30 weeks, his job ends. He then moves to Santa Fe and gets a job there, which he holds for more than 39 weeks.

Meanwhile his wife, Tracy, found a job in Dallas at the same time as her husband and worked there for nine weeks after he left for Santa Fe. Since Tracy met the 39-week requirement for work in Dallas, the entire family's move from Boston to Dallas is deductible if the couple files a joint return. Since K.C. met the 39-week requirement in Santa Fe, the family's moving expenses from Dallas to Santa Fe will also be deductible.

Obviously, the one-year period after you begin work in a new location might not coincide with your tax year, which is a calendar year for most individuals. The IRS very graciously allows you to deduct your moving expenses on this year's tax return even if you have not yet met the 39-week or 78-week requirements, as long as you reasonably expect to meet them within the allotted time.

If it later turns out that you can't meet the test, and you don't qualify for any of the exceptions, you have a choice: either amend your tax return for the year you claimed the moving expenses using IRS Form 1040X, or add back the expenses as miscellaneous income to your tax return for the year in which you fail the test.

Example

You moved in December of 1999 to transfer to a new location and take a different job with your employer of 20 years, and because it seemed likely that your job would continue indefinitely, you deducted your moving expenses on your 1999 tax return.

However, in May of 2000, your employer offers you a buy-out for early retirement, and you decide to accept the offer and retire to the beach. Because you did not work for 39 weeks at the new location, your moving expenses were rendered nondeductible. You could file an amended return for 1999 to rescind the deduction; however, since your income (and your tax rate) is lower in 2000 due to your retirement, you decide instead to report the moving expenses as miscellaneous income (on Line 21 of your Form 1040) in 2000.

Some Special Rules

There are special, more lenient rules on moves for the military, and for those who move back to the U.S. to retire or because their spouse has died.

First, the rules for members of the U.S. Armed Forces: You can deduct moving expenses and do not have to meet the time or distance tests described above if you are moving because of a permanent change of station. If a member of the armed services is imprisoned, deserts, or dies, a permanent change of station for the spouse or dependents includes a move to the place of enlistment; the member's, spouse's or dependent's home of record; or a nearer point in the United States. Finally, if the military moves a member and his or her family to or from separate locations, the moves are treated as a single move to the new main job location and all moves will be deductible.

Retirees whose former main job location and main home were outside the U.S. can deduct their moving expenses to the U.S. or one of its possessions without having to meet the time test described above, provided they are permanently retiring.

Spouses or dependents of people who die overseas can deduct expenses for a move that begins within six months of the death. The deceased person must have had a main job location outside the U.S., and the survivor(s) must have been living there also.

Which Moving Expenses are Deductible?

In general, there are only two categories of expenses that can be deducted as moving expenses:

1. the cost of moving household goods and personal effects, including temporary storage costs

2. the cost of a one-way trip for all household members to the new home, including lodging expenses (but not meals)

"Household members" includes all who reside in both the old and the new location, but does not include domestic help or tenants unless they're your dependents (see the rules for dependents, page 161).

The trip must be taken by conventional, reasonable means considering the circumstances of the move; if you make side trips along the way, the side trips are not deductible expenses.

If you travel by train, air, bus, etc., the cost will generally be the cost of the tickets, plus taxis or other ground transportation if applicable. If you travel by car, you have the choice of deducting 10 cents per mile (in 1999), or your actual expenses for gasoline, oil, repairs, etc. In either case, you can also deduct parking fees and tolls. It's not necessary that all family members travel together or by the same method.

The cost of the trip includes the cost of lodging along the way, including lodging in the vicinity of your old home within one day of the time you could no longer stay in the old home because your furniture was moved, and expenses for the day you arrive in the new location.

The cost of moving household goods and personal effects includes the possessions of all members of the household as defined above, including pets and cars. It includes costs of packing, crating, and insuring them. It also includes the cost of storing them for up to 30 consecutive days between the time they are removed from your old home, and are delivered to your new home. If goods are being moved from another location besides your old residence, you can't deduct more than the cost of moving them from your old residence.

Example

John Grey is moving from Chicago to Los Angeles. John also wants to move furniture and other personal effects stored at his parents' home in New York. He can deduct the cost of moving goods from both Chicago and New York, but for the New York items, he can only deduct an amount equivalent to what it would have cost to move them from Chicago.

A Special Rule for Foreign Moves

For a move by a U.S. citizen or resident alien to a new place of work outside the U.S. or its possessions, the moving expense deduction also includes the reasonable expenses of moving household goods and personal effects to and from storage, and the cost of storing such items for part or all of the period during which the taxpayer worked at the new, foreign location as his or her principal place of work.

However, if the individual also qualifies for the foreign earned income exclusion (see page 156), unreimbursed moving expenses may be disallowed to the extent that they are allocated to or chargeable against the excluded earned income.

Nondeductible Moving Expenses

The following are now considered nondeductible expenses, although you may remember that some of them were deductible as moving expenses under prior law. If your employer reimburses you for any of these expenses, the reimbursements are taxable (and your employer should add them to your taxable income, as shown in Box 1 of your W-2 Form).

- any part of the purchase price of your new home

- car license plates, stickers, or other registration

- drivers' licenses

- expenses of breaking or getting a lease

- expenses of buying or selling a home

- home improvements to help sell your home

- loss on the sale of your home

- losses from disposing of club memberships

- meal expenses

- mortgage prepayment penalties

- pre-move househunting trips

- real estate taxes

- refitting carpets and draperies

- security deposits

- storage charges other than those incurred in a 30-day period between when your goods were moved, and when they arrived at the new home

- temporary living expenses

Claiming Moving Expenses

Moving expenses are reported on IRS Form 3903, *Moving Expenses,* which is one of the simpler and more self-explanatory tax forms that you will run across. Moves to a location outside the U.S. are reported on Form 3903-F, *Foreign Moving Expenses.* If you move to more than one location during the year, you'll need to fill out two forms.

Either of these forms will ask you to add up your total moving expenses in the two categories of deductible expenses described above. Then, you will subtract any reimbursements you receive from your employer that were not included in Box 1 of your W-2 form along with your other taxable wages. The amount of these reimbursements, if any, should have been shown in Box 13 of your W-2 form and marked with Code P.

If your employer's payments were higher than your deductible expenses, you must report the excess as income from wages, salaries, or tips on Line 7 of your 1040 Form.

If your expenses were higher than any reimbursements you received, the difference will be your deductible moving expenses, which are carried over to Line 26 of your 1040 Form. You cannot claim moving expenses on either Form 1040EZ or 1040A.

Timing the Deduction

If you, like most people, are a cash-method taxpayer, you can deduct your moving expenses either when you owe them, or when you pay them. If you moved near the end of the year, you may be able to deduct some expenses in two different calendar years.

If you are reimbursed for moving expenses by your employer, you may be able to deduct the expenses in the year you receive reimbursement, even if that's not the same year that you paid the expenses. You can do this if either of the following is true:

1. You actually paid the expenses in the year preceding the reimbursement.

2. You actually paid the expenses in the year after you received the reimbursement, and you paid them on or before the due date of the tax return for the reimbursement year.

THE CREDIT FOR CHILD AND DEPENDENT CARE

Congress and the IRS both recognize that in many situations you have to spend money to make money. This is especially true of working parents, many of whom would find it impossible to look for a job, let alone actually work at it, without paying someone to look after their children. Those who are responsible for looking after an aged parent or a disabled relative often find themselves in the same position.

To lighten some of the extra burden that falls upon working parents and those caring for disabled dependents, Congress has provided three basic types of tax benefits for employees or the self-employed:

- the credit for child or dependent care

- the exclusion for employer-provided care

- the earned income credit (EIC)

This section will focus on the first two of these tax benefits. The EIC is discussed on page 290.

There is also a $500-per-child credit for 1999, up from $400 in 1998, but it is available to all parents and does not depend on whether or not one or both parents work outside the home. For a discussion of this credit, see page 281.

You Must Choose Your Benefit

To some extent, the child and dependent care credit, and the exclusion for employer-provided dependent care assistance, are mutually exclusive. If you use one, you might be totally or partially precluded from using the other.

Thus, if your employer offers any assistance for dependent care, you'll have to decide which strategy saves you more money: taking advantage of your employer's assistance program or claiming the tax credit. In certain limited circumstances you might be able to combine methods.

Save Money

The decision as to which tax break is best for you depends on factors including the kind of assistance your employer offers, your marginal tax bracket (see page 15 if you don't know your bracket), whether you have one qualified dependent or more, and the amount of qualified expenses you had this year.

As a rule of thumb, if you have an adjusted gross income of more than approximately $25,000, you'll save more money by taking full advantage of any assistance offered

by your employer, even if that means giving up the tax credit.

In other situations, the answer is not so simple and you may have to figure out your tax bill both ways before you can tell which strategy is best for you.

How the Tax Credit Works

If your employer does not offer any type of dependent care assistance, this tax credit may be your only chance to recover some tax benefits for your child or other dependent care expenses. It's available in varying degrees to anyone who has children under the age of 13, who supports a disabled relative, or who has a disabled spouse.

If your employer does provide dependent care assistance, the tax credit may still be a better deal, particularly if you are in the 15 percent marginal tax bracket. If you meet all the qualifications described on the following pages, you can reduce your tax bill by up to $720 if you have one qualifying dependent, or by up to $1,440 if you have two or more.

If your employer provides only a small amount of dependent care assistance (under $2,400 for one child or under $4,800 for more than one), but you have expenses that exceed what your employer paid, you may be able to take advantage of your employer's plan and claim the tax credit for your excess expenses. See page 196.

How Much Is the Credit Worth?

Basically, the credit works like this: you get a tax credit of between 20 and 30 percent of your qualifying child care expenses, but you can only count expenses of up to $2,400 for one dependent, or up to $4,800 for two or more dependents.

Whether you can claim 20 percent, 30 percent, or somewhere in between depends on your adjusted gross income (that is, your net taxable income before subtracting your exemptions or deductions).

The following table shows the applicable percentages. Note that, unlike many dollar benchmarks in the tax laws, these figures are *not* adjusted for inflation each year. For those with AGIs above $28,000, the maximum credit will be $480 for one child, or $960 for two children.

Adjusted Gross Income		Percentage of Expenses	Maximum Credits	
Over	_But Not Over_		_One Person_	_More Than One_
$0	$10,000	30%	$720	$1,440
$10,000	$12,000	29%	$696	$1,392
$12,000	$14,000	28%	$672	$1,344
$14,000	$16,000	27%	$648	$1,296
$16,000	$18,000	26%	$624	$1,248
$18,000	$20,000	25%	$600	$1,200
$20,000	$22,000	24%	$576	$1,152
$22,000	$24,000	23%	$552	$1,104
$24,000	$26,000	22%	$528	$1,056
$26,000	$28,000	21%	$504	$1,008
$28,000	no limit	20%	$480	$ 960

Eligibility for the Credit

As you might expect, there a number of requirements you must meet before you can claim any portion of the tax credit. The requirements are summed up in the checklist that follows, and described in more detail below.

Eligibility Requirements To Claim the Child or Dependent Care Credit

- You must have incurred expenses for the care of at least one qualifying person.

- The expenses must have been incurred to allow you to work or to look for work.

- You (and your spouse, if married) must keep up a home in which you live with the qualifying person (exceptions exist for divorced or separated parents).

- You (and your spouse, if married) must have earned some income during the year, unless you or your spouse were disabled or a full-time student.

- The care provider must be someone that you can't claim as a dependent.

- You must identify the care provider by name and Social Security number (or employer I.D. number).

- If married, you must file a joint return unless you meet the "abandoned spouse" exception.

- To claim the expenses you must file IRS Form 2441, _Child and Dependent Care Expenses,_ along with your Form 1040, or file Schedule 2 along with your Form 1040A. You can't claim the expenses by filing Form 1040EZ.

Qualifying Person

There are three basic categories of people who may be qualifying persons for purposes of this credit:

- Any child under the age of 13 for whom you can claim a dependency exemption. For more details about dependency exemptions, see page 161.

- Any dependent, regardless of age, who is disabled. For purposes of this rule only, "dependent" means any disabled dependent who received more than half of his or her total support from you, even if the dependent received more than $2,750 in gross income for the year.

- Your disabled spouse, regardless of age, amount of support, or place of abode.

"Disabled" means having a physical or mental condition that makes the person incapable of dressing, feeding, or cleaning himself or herself. Also, if a person requires constant attention to prevent injury to self or others, the person is considered disabled.

If a person meets the requirements for only part of the year, you can count only the expenses you had during the period he or she was qualified.

Example

Lois and Kent Clark enrolled their dependent son, Jimmy, in an after-school program because neither of them arrives home from work before 5:30 in the evening. Jimmy turned 13 on March 15, 1999. When figuring their 1999 tax credit for child care, Lois and Kent can count the cost of the program only through March 14.

Child of separated or divorced parents. Ordinarily, the custodial parent, or the parent who has actual custody of the child for more than half of the year, is the parent who can claim the child as a "qualifying person." This is true even if the other parent is entitled to the child's dependency exemption under the divorce decree. This rule applies if you are legally divorced or separated, or if you've lived apart from your spouse for all of the last six months of the year.

Social Security number required. You will need to report the Social Security number of your qualifying persons (up to two) on Form 2441 or on Schedule 2 of Form 1040A.

Keeping Up a Home

In order to meet this test, you (and your spouse, if married) must pay at least half of the expenses of maintaining your household for the year, and the qualifying individual must live there with you.

The costs of maintaining a household include:

- Rent
- Mortgage interest
- Property taxes
- Utility charges
- Home repairs
- Food eaten at home
- Homeowner's or renter's insurance

Costs of maintaining a household do not include:

- Clothing
- Vacations, recreation
- Education
- Life insurance
- Transportation
- Mortgage principal
- Medical treatments
- Permanent improvements or replacement of property

Living in the home. Individuals are considered to be living in the home if it continues to be their main home, even if they are temporarily away because of illness, school, business, vacations, military service or a custody agreement. So, either you or your qualifying person can be temporarily absent without failing this requirement.

Earned Income Test

Another requirement for claiming the tax credit is that you (and your spouse, if you're married) must have some earned income during the year. You can only claim child care expenses up to the amount of the lower of your income or your spouse's earned income.

"Earned income" includes your net earnings from self-employment, wages, salaries, tips, other employee compensation, strike benefits, and any disability pay that is taxable as wages.

It does not include pensions, annuities, Social Security benefits, worker's compensation, interest, dividends, unemployment compensation, or scholarship or fellowship grants (except amounts paid for teaching, research, or other services).

Exception for disabled spouses or student-spouses. So long as one spouse is working, the other spouse may be a nonworking disabled person or a full-time student without losing the credit.

If this situation applies to you, the nonworking spouse will be treated as having earned $200 a month for one qualifying person, or $400 for more than one qualifying person, for every month in which the spouse was physically or mentally incapable of self-care or was a full-time student at an elementary school; junior or senior high school; college university; or technical, trade, or professional school. This does not include night school or correspondence school. Therefore, if the nonworking spouse was a student or disabled for the entire year, you will be able to claim the maximum amount of expenses.

"Full-time student" means a person maintaining a schedule that is considered full-time by the institution attended, but the schedule must extend over some part of at least five months of the year.

This $200- or $400-per-month rule applies to only one spouse per month. If both you and your spouse are unemployed because each is either disabled or a full-time student (or for any other reason), you cannot claim dependent care expenses for the month because of the work-related expenses test discussed below.

Work-Related Expenses

The tax credit for child and dependent care expenses was intended only to help those who incur these expenses in order to enable them to earn income. So, you can only claim expenses that are work-related; that is, they must be necessary to allow you to work or to look for work.

Example

You can't claim expenses for a babysitter while you run errands or do volunteer work.

If you are married, the expenses must be required to allow both you and your spouse to work or to look for work, unless one of you meets the criteria above for being disabled or a full-time student.

"Work" includes any gainful full-time or part-time work, self-employment, and even work performed in your own home, but does not include volunteer work.

If you are actively looking for work, you can claim expenses for the period of your job search, but only up to the amount of your actual earned income for the year (or your spouse's income, if lower).

Kinds of Expenses To Count

A wide variety of child or dependent care expenses are counted. The care can be provided in your own home, another's home, or at a daycare center. However, if the care is provided outside your home, the qualifying person must be either your dependent under age 13, or any other qualifying person who regularly spends at least eight hours each day in your household. In other words, boarding school does not qualify.

If you use a dependent care center (that is, a place that provides care for more than six persons and charges a fee), the center must comply with all applicable state and local regulations.

Expenses of caring for the qualifying person do not include amounts spent for food, clothing, and entertainment unless the costs can't be separated out of the other costs you pay for the individual's care.

Education. You can count the total cost of sending your child to school if the child is not yet in first grade, and the amount you pay for schooling is incidental to the cost of care.

If your child is in the first grade or higher, or the cost of care can be separated from the cost of school, you can only count the cost of care.

Examples

Carla Webb sends her three-year-old child to a nursery school that provides lunch and educational activities as a part of its preschool program. She can count the total cost of the school in figuring her credit.

However, Wilbur Mudd sends his five-year-old child to kindergarten in the morning. In the afternoon, the child *attends an after-school daycare program in the same school. Mudd's total tuition cost is $3,000, of which $1,800 is for the after-school program. Only the after-school program qualifies in figuring Mudd's credit.*

Camp. You can deduct the full cost of sending your child to day camp, provided the money was spent to ensure the child's well-being during your absence from the home while at work. However, the cost of sending your child to overnight camp is not deductible at all.

Household services. If you pay someone to perform household services, you can count the fees or wages as long as the services are at least partly for the well-being and protection of a qualifying person.

In this context, household services are the ordinary and usual services done in and around your home that are necessary to run your home. They can include the services of a nanny, babysitter, nurse's aid, housekeeper, maid, or cook, but not a driver, bartender, or gardener.

If one individual performs some services that don't qualify (e.g., your cook doubles as a driver), you can't count the part of the payment that applies to the non-household services. However, you don't have to allocate the payments if only a small part applied to nonqualified purposes.

Example

Basil Holmes pays a housekeeper to care for his children, aged nine and 15, so that he can work. The housekeeper spends most of the time doing normal household work, but also spends 30 minutes each day driving the children to and from school.

Holmes can treat the entire expense of the housekeeper as work-related, because the time spend driving is minimal. He doesn't need to apportion the housekeeper's wages between the two children, because the household services are at least partly for the care of the nine-year-old, who is a qualifying person. However, he can only count the first $2,400 that he pays the housekeeper for the year, because he has only one qualifying person (the 15-year-old is too old to qualify).

Meals and lodging that you provide to a household worker count as child or dependent care expenses.

If the person performing services in your home is your employee, you may have to pay federal and state employment taxes (Social Security, Medicare, and unemployment taxes – see page 302). If the services qualify for the dependent care credit, any taxes you pay on the services are also qualified expenses.

Prepaid or postpaid expenses. If you prepaid for some 2000 child care expenses in 1999, you can claim them only in the year that the dependent care is actually received. In that case, you'll fill out your Form 2441 (for Form 1040) or Schedule 2 (for Form 1040A) for 2000 as if the prepaid expenses were paid in the same year that the care was received.

However, if you received some care in 1999 but won't pay for it until 2000, you can claim the care only in the year you paid for it. You will have to file Forms 2441 and 1040 (not Form 1040A and Schedule 2) in order to get any credit for this care.

Dependent care assistance provided by your employer. Any child or dependent care expenses that were paid for or reimbursed by your employer can't be counted for purposes of the tax credit for dependent care.

Moreover, if you received any such assistance from your employer, you will have to subtract the amount of assistance from your applicable credit expense limit (the limit is $2,400 for one qualifying person and $4,800 for more than one). If the answer is a positive number, that answer is the maximum amount of expenses you can claim when computing your tax credit for dependent care. For more on employer-provided assistance, see page 196.

Payments to Dependents or Household Members

Payments that you make to a person for whom you or your spouse can claim a dependency exemption, or to your child who is under the age of 19 at the end of the year even if not your dependent, can't be counted for purposes of the dependent care credit.

You can count work-related expenses that you pay to persons who live in your home, even if they are related to you, as long as they are not your dependents. This includes payments to live-in babysitters or housekeepers.

Identification of Care Provider

You must provide the IRS with the name, address, and Social Security number (for individuals) or the Employer Identification Number (for organizations) of the person or organization that provided the care. The information must be included on Part I of Form 2441 or Schedule 2.

I.D. numbers are not required if the care provider is a tax-exempt organization, such as a church or nonprofit school. In that case, simply write "tax-exempt" in the space provided for an I.D. number.

If the care provider refuses to give you all the information you need, you should report whatever information you have on the tax form you use to claim the credit. On the bottom of the second page of the form, you should write a note saying that you asked the care provider for the information but he or she didn't give it to you.

Joint Return

If you're married at the end of the tax year, you must file a joint return in order to claim this credit. The only exception to the joint return rule is that you can be considered unmarried if you are legally separated, or if all of the following are true:

- You file a separate return.

- Your home is the home of a qualifying person for more than half the year.

- You pay more than half the cost of keeping up your home for the year.

- Your spouse does not live in your home for the last six months of the year.

If all of these apply to you, you can claim the credit on your separate tax return.

Medical Expense Deductions

Some expenses, like the costs of at-home nursing care for a disabled dependent, would ordinarily be deductible as medical expenses; if they enable the taxpayer to be gainfully employed, they can also qualify as employment-related dependent care.

However, you can't use the same expenses for both the medical deduction and the dependent care credit. You'll have to decide which tax benefit will help you more.

Generally speaking, if you have a choice, it's better to maximize your child or dependent care credit up to the applicable dollar limitations ($2,400 for one qualifying person, or $4,800 for two or more). If your expenses exceed this limitation, any excess that qualifies as a medical deduction should be treated as such.

Remember that only medical expenses that exceed 7.5 percent of your adjusted gross income are deductible, and high-income taxpayers may lose some of their deductions above 7.5 percent (see page 273). If you do have sufficient medical expenses to exceed the 7.5 percent threshold, and your tax bracket is 28 percent or higher, you may be better off claiming the expenses as a medical deduction.

Example

During 1999, John and Mary Davis paid $10,000 of work-related expenses for the care of their physically handicapped daughter. The work-related expenses were for services performed in the Davis home and qualified as medical expenses. The Davises adjusted gross income for 1999 was $60,000.

If they take the maximum of $2,400 of these expenses into account for purposes of the dependent care credit, they can claim a 20% credit of $480, and treat the balance, or $7,600, as medical expenses. Because the Davises had no other medical expenses, they can deduct $3,100 ($7,600 minus 7.5% of $60,000, or $4,500) as a medical expense. Since they are in the 28% bracket, the $3,100 deduction saves them $868 in taxes. Total tax savings: $480 + $868 = $1,348.

However, if they claim the full $10,000 as a medical expense, subtracting the 7.5% of AGI amount ($4,500) leaves a deduction of $5,500. In the 28% bracket, this deduction would save $1,540 in taxes. The Davises are better off forgoing the child and dependent care credit, and instead claiming the full medical expense deduction for their daughter's expenses.

Claiming the Credit

To claim the credit for child and dependent care expenses, you need to fill out Parts I and II of IRS

Form 2441, *Child and Dependent Care Expenses,* if you're filing IRS Form 1040. If you are filing the 1040A, you may use Schedule 2, Parts I and II.

Either of these forms requires you to provide identification information for both the care provider(s) and the qualifying children or disabled persons. The forms help you to compute your credit by comparing your allowable expenses with your wages and other earnings (and those of your spouse, if married). Your credit amount as shown on Line 9 of the 2441 is carried to Line 41 of your Form 1040, where it will be directly subtracted from the taxes you owe. If you use Schedule 2, the credit amount as shown on Line 9 is carried to Line 26 of Form 1040A.

If you are using Form 2441 to claim a credit for expenses you incurred in 1998 but did not pay until 1999, you can increase the amount of credit you can claim, but you will have to attach a statement to your tax return explaining how you computed the credit, as well as the name, I.D. number, and address of the care provider for the 1997 expenses. Get IRS Publication 503, *Child and Dependent Care Expenses,* for more details. You can obtain any IRS Publication for free by calling 1-800-TAX-FORM; most popular publications are also posted on the IRS website at www.irs.gov.

DEPENDENT CARE PROVIDED BY YOUR EMPLOYER

In order to retain valued employees and improve the corporate image, and at the same time gain tax benefits for themselves, many companies offer some type of financial help to employees who must pay for child or dependent care in order to work.

These benefits can take a number of forms. In some cases, the employer has set up on-site daycare centers, to which employees can send their young children. In other cases, employers subsidize the costs of child care by reimbursing employees for certain expenses.

However, the majority of companies that provide dependent care assistance do so by allowing employees to contribute part of their pretax wages to individual accounts under a "Flexible Spending Arrangement." The money is then used to reimburse the employee for child or dependent care expenses.

All these types of assistance can be provided to the employee as tax-free fringe benefits, provided certain rules are met.

Employers may also offer a number of other dependent-related services, such as referrals to area day care centers, seminars or informational meetings, or employee assistance programs that provide counseling for personal problems that affect an employee's work. In most cases, these benefits are considered tax-free fringe benefits for employees because they fall into the category of *"de minimis"* benefits. Their value is relatively small and difficult to measure, so the IRS essentially ignores them when it comes to imposing taxes.

Dependent Care as a Fringe Benefit

Your employer can provide you with a substantial amount of dependent care assistance as a nontaxable fringe benefit. However, it must meet certain criteria.

From the employee's standpoint, the most important requirement is probably the fact that the amount of tax-free assistance is limited to $5,000 a year per family, or to the total amount of the lower-paid spouse's salary, whichever is lower. If one spouse is totally disabled or a student, that spouse is treated as earning $200 per month for one dependent, or $400 per month for two.

Unlike the child and dependent care credit, employer-provided dependent care can be claimed by a married couple filing separately. In that case the maximum dollar limit is $2,500 per spouse. Only the spouse whose employer provides assistance can claim the exclusion; if both spouses' employers provide assistance, they can each claim $2,500.

Warning

To qualify for tax benefits, the dependent care assistance must be offered by the employer under a written plan that does not discriminate in favor of the most highly paid workers. The tax laws say that no more than 25 percent of the amounts paid by the employer for dependent care assistance during the year may be provided for shareholders or owners (or their spouses or dependents), who own more than 5 percent of the stock or of the capital or profits interest in the employer on any day in the year. This means that dependent care programs generally can't be used by very small, family-owned businesses.

Rules for tax credit apply. The kinds of dependents and expenses that may be covered by an employer's dependent care plan are the same as those that would qualify for the tax credit for child and dependent care. So, the rules relating to keeping up a home for at least one qualifying individual, the earned income test, the work-related expenses test, and the other rules discussed on pages 191-195 all apply to the employer-provided assistance.

Salary Reduction Arrangements

Employers can give you tax-free dependent care assistance in a number of ways. Dependent care assistance is usually delivered by means of a Flexible Spending Arrangement, or FSA plan. Under such plans, employees request that an annual amount of up to $5,000 be withheld in equal installments from their paychecks and set aside in a special account by the employer. The employees benefit because the salary reductions are made before any federal income, Social Security, or Medicare taxes are paid – in effect, the employee is able to pay for child care with pretax dollars.

Save Money

Where both spouses work for employers that provide FSAs, and one spouse has a salary that is higher than the Social Security ceiling ($72,600 for 1999), the other spouse should be the one to sign up for the FSA to maximize family tax savings. This is because FSA amounts are not taxed for income, Social Security, and Medicare taxes. Your "discount" for using the FSA will be greater if you would otherwise have been subject to Social Security taxes on the amount.

During the year, each employee using an FSA submits bills for daycare, babysitting, and other qualified expenses to the plan, and is reimbursed up to the amount set aside in his or her individual account. Requests for reimbursement are monitored to make sure that the expenses are work-related, apply to a qualified individual, and meet the other requirements.

One drawback to the arrangement is that you must decide how much you want to contribute to your FSA once a year, usually in November or December for the coming year. Once requested, the amount may not be changed during the calendar year unless you experience a "major life event" such as a birth, death, marriage, or divorce.

If you don't have enough qualifying expenses during the year to use up your FSA contributions, you forfeit the remainder of your account back to your employer.

Comparison with the Tax Credit

Child care expenses for which you're paid or reimbursed under an employer's plan cannot be used again in determining whether you're eligible for the tax credit for child and dependent care, discussed beginning on page 189. Obviously, if your employer doesn't offer any assistance, the tax credit is your only choice.

One difference between the two types of tax breaks is especially important for those with only one child or qualifying individual. Under the tax credit, you are only allowed to count the first $2,400 you spend for care of that individual. However, under the employer assistance plan, you may count up to $5,000, whether it's spent on one person or several.

The second factor to consider is your tax bracket. If you're in the 28% bracket, your federal tax "discount" for using the employer's plan will probably equal 35.65% of your allowable expenses (28% federal income tax + 7.65% FICA tax), unless your salary is over the Social Security ceiling. Even if it is, you'll still have a 29.45% discount (28% income tax + 1.45% Medicare tax). However, families with taxable income higher than $28,000 who use the tax credit will get a credit of only 20% of their allowable expenses.

A third factor to consider is the alternative minimum tax or AMT. Ordinarily, if you are subject to the AMT, your tax credit may be limited or potentially extinguished. This won't happen in 1999, since a special law provision prevents individual credits such as the child and dependent care credit from triggering the AMT for this year only.

However, employer-paid dependent care assistance is subtracted from your adjusted gross income before the AMT is calculated, so it will not be affected by the AMT calculation (and in fact can help you to avoid the AMT by keeping your AGI lower).

Reduced Retirement Benefits

One more factor to consider when deciding whether to take advantage of your employer's plan or to go for the tax credit is the Social Security angle.

Because you don't pay social security tax on the amounts that are withheld from your paycheck to fund your dependent care reimbursement account, these amounts aren't counted as part of your salary when you eventually retire and collect Social Security benefits. So, you might qualify for a slightly lower benefit at retirement because of the dependent care benefits you're getting now.

In most cases, this benefit reduction would be slight, particularly if you have a long working career but receive dependent care benefits for only a few of those years. Moreover, it's generally better to save tax dollars now, rather than to pay more tax now in the hope of getting a larger retirement benefit 20 or 40 years down the road. It's quite likely that the rules for computing Social Security benefits will have changed by then, anyway.

Claiming Employer-Provided Assistance

If your employer provided you with any dependent care assistance in 1999, it should have been reported in Box 10 of your W-2 Form. If more than $5,000 was provided, the extra amount is taxable and should have been included in Box 1 of the W-2.

To report this amount, you need to complete Parts I and III of Form 2441, *Child and Dependent Care Expenses*, if you are filing Form 1040. If you are filing Form 1040A, you can use Schedule 2 of that form and, again, complete Parts I and III.

Note that either of these forms will ask you whether you forfeited any benefits this year; that is, whether you had more deducted from your paycheck than you were able to claim reimbursement for. If you have a forfeiture, you don't have to pay taxes on this amount. However, if the amount you had withheld from your paycheck was more than your total wages (or those of your spouse, if married, which is the more likely scenario) you can only deduct the dependent care assistance up to the amount of the wages earned. Anything above that amount would be taxable and must be included in your taxable income amount on Line 7 of your Form 1040 or 1040A.

Chapter 12

Real Estate

For many people, a home is not only a shelter for their family, but also the only real tax shelter available.

The opportunity to reduce your income taxes by deducting your mortgage interest payments, the points you may have paid when taking out your loan, and your real estate taxes is one of the most important reasons for owning a home.

In order to claim these tax breaks, you'll need to itemize your deductions. It's important to note that if you're itemizing in order to claim home mortgage and real estate taxes, you'll also be able to claim any itemized deductions for state and local income taxes, charitable contributions, casualty losses, employee business expenses and other miscellaneous deductions that exceed 2 percent of your adjusted gross income (AGI), and medical expenses that exceed 7.5 percent of your AGI. These deductions can save you many tax dollars – and most people who don't own a home can't take advantage of them.

On the next few pages we'll outline the major rules you need to know in order to maximize your home-related tax deductions. This chapter will also discuss how to handle the purchase or sale of your principal residence. Generally the first $250,000 in gains on the sale of your home will be tax-free (and the first

$500,000 will be tax-free, if you are married filing jointly), provided that you meet certain requirements. Losses on sales of your personal residence are generally not deductible, unless you used part of the property for business purposes or rented it out.

Finally, for those of you who own investment real estate, we'll discuss the rules related to reporting rental income and deductions, and handling the purchase or sale of rental property, including second homes.

Tax Organizer Tip

The deductible expenses and income discussed in this chapter would all be entered in the "Real Estate" section of the CompleteTax™ Organizer.

THE HOME MORTGAGE INTEREST DEDUCTION

In most cases, you can deduct all of the interest you pay on any loan that is secured by your home, whether the loan is called a mortgage, a second (or third, fourth, fifth, etc.) mortgage, a home equity loan, a line of credit, or a home improvement loan. Your lender will mail you an end-of-year statement that breaks down your house payment into components, and tells you exactly how much interest you paid. You can't deduct the portion of the payment that goes towards repaying the principal amount of the loan.

A loan "secured by your home" means that, under the loan agreement, the lender has the right to take the house ("foreclose") if you don't make the payments. This generally means that if you or your spouse take a loan from a 401(k) plan at work to make a down payment on a house, you can't deduct interest on the 401(k) loan because it is not secured by a mortgage on the house.

Generally, as long as the loan is secured by the home, if doesn't matter what you actually spend the money on. For example, you can take out a home equity loan and use the money to buy a car, take a vacation, consolidate credit card debts, or anything else you choose. However, the dollar limits discussed below can differ, depending on how the loan proceeds are spent.

Limits on Deductibility

Beginning in the late 1980s, Congress placed certain limits on the types and amounts of loans that qualify for the mortgage interest deduction.

If you took out a mortgage on or before October 13, 1987, all of the interest is fully deductible, regardless of the amount of the loan. This is called "grandfathered debt."

If you had such a mortgage and you refinanced it after that date, the new mortgage is treated as grandfathered debt to the extent of the principal balance remaining on the pre-October 13, 1987 loan. Any mortgage amount over that limit may be eligible for treatment under category (A) or (B) discussed below.

If you had established a home equity line-of-credit as of October 13, 1987 and you borrowed amounts against it after that date, then those amounts are treated under category (A) or (B), below, depending on how the proceeds were used. Amounts borrowed before that date are fully deductible grandfathered debt.

Post-1987 Loans

Loans that were taken out after October 13, 1987, will qualify for the mortgage interest deduction if they meet the criteria in either (A) or (B):

(A) Interest paid on mortgages used to buy, build, or substantially improve your first or second home is deductible, to the extent that the total of all these mortgages, plus any grandfathered debt, does not exceed either the lower of:

1. the total cost to buy or build the home, plus the cost of any improvements

2. $1 million (for married taxpayers filing separately, this second limit is $500,000 each)

(B) Interest paid on mortgages used for any other purpose is deductible only to the extent that such mortgages totaled $100,000 or less throughout the year. (The limit is $50,000 each for married taxpayers filing separately.) You can't deduct the interest, however, if you used the money to generate tax-exempt interest (e.g., if you bought tax-free municipal bonds).

Another limit to be aware of is that if the total amount of all loans secured by a home is more than the fair market value (FMV) of the home, you can't deduct interest on the portion of debt that exceeds the FMV. In recent years, some lenders in some areas of the country have been willing to extend loans that exceed 100 percent of the home's value; the interest on the excess portion of the debt is not deductible.

If you are married filing separately, who gets to deduct the interest? Generally, the deduction should be split according to who is liable for the debt, which in turn generally reflects the ownership in the home. However, a spouse filing separately generally cannot deduct any more interest than he or she actually paid. If you own the home jointly and the interest was paid from joint funds or equally by both of you, each spouse should deduct half the interest payments. In other situations, the answer can get more complicated, and your tax adviser may have to check state law (or you can avoid the problem by simply choosing to file jointly).

To sum up: the maximum total amount of non-grandfathered debt that will qualify for the mortgage interest deduction is $1,100,000 per individual or couple.

Mixed-Use Mortgages

If you took out a mortgage after October 13, 1987 and use the money both to buy, build, or substantially improve the home and for other purposes, then it is considered a mixed-use mortgage. The loan amount must be divided between categories (A) and (B) above, to determine whether the deductibility limits have been reached.

Example

Alice Gamos took out a $100,000 mortgage to buy her home in 1986. In March of 1994, when the home had a fair market value of $220,000 and she owed $95,000 on the mortgage, she took out a second mortgage of $80,000. She used $60,000 of the loan proceeds for home improvements and the remaining $20,000 for other personal purposes.

All of the interest is deductible. The interest on the first mortgage is deductible simply because it was taken out before October 13, 1987.

Of the second mortgage, the $60,000 used to improve the home falls into category (A), above. The $60,000 must be added to the balance on the existing loan to be sure that the $1 million limit is not exceeded; in this case, $60,000 + $95,000 = $155,000, well short of $1 million. The remaining $20,000 is subject to the limits on home equity loans in category (B); because it is less than $100,000, it is fully deductible.

Which Homes Qualify?

You can deduct mortgage interest on both your main home and one other qualified residence each year, but all the mortgages on both homes must be combined for purposes of the dollar limits discussed above.

If more than one person owns the home (for instance, you purchased a vacation home jointly with your brother), each of you can deduct your proportionate part of the interest.

A "home" for tax purposes can be a house, condominium, cooperative, mobile home, motor home, timeshare condominium, or boat. At a minimum, the "home" must contain sleeping space, a toilet, and cooking facilities.

If the home is a condominium, you can deduct interest paid on a mortgage you take out to purchase your individual unit. If there is a blanket mortgage over the entire property, you can deduct interest on the portion of the blanket mortgage that applies to your unit. Similarly, if you own a co-op, you can deduct interest paid on a mortgage to purchase shares in the building that pertain to your individual unit; you can also deduct interest paid or incurred by the corporation on loans taken out to acquire, construct, alter, rehabilitate, or maintain the co-op buildings or land.

Your main home is generally the place where you spend the most time.

Save Money

If you have a second home that you don't rent out to others, it can be treated as your "other qualified residence," even if you don't set foot in it all year. If you have several vacation homes, you can claim the interest deduction for a different home each tax year.

If you rent out your vacation home to others for any part of the year, it is a qualified residence only if you use if for personal purposes for more than 14 days or more than 10 percent of the rental days in the tax year, whichever is longer. If you don't use it long enough, it is considered "rental property" and a different set of rules apply. These rules are covered beginning on page 214.

Timeshares

In the case of a timeshare arrangement, you count your use and rental of the home only during the time you have a right to use it.

Example

If you have the right to use a timeshare condo for one week each year, you could claim the mortgage interest deduction for a loan on the condo if you either use the week or leave the condo vacant for the week. If you rented it for even one day during the week, you'd lose the deduction for the year since it would be impossible for you to meet the greater-of-14-days-or-10-percent rule.

Home Being Built

You can treat a home that is under construction as a qualified home for a period of up to 24 months, but only if it becomes your qualified main or secondary home at the time it is ready for occupancy. The 24-month period can start any time on or after the day construction actually begins.

Save Money

If you delay making a mortgage payment and, consequently, have to pay an extra "late fee" to the lender, the late fee is deductible as home mortgage interest, as long as it was not for a specific service performed by the lender.

Prepaying Your Mortgage Interest

If you, like most individuals, are a cash-method taxpayer, you ordinarily deduct interest in the year that you pay it. However, if you prepay your mortgage interest, you can't fully deduct the prepaid amount in the year you pay it. Instead, you must deduct the interest in the year to which it applies (but see the exception for "points," below).

An apparent exception to this rule applies if you make your first payment of the next tax year during the last month of the preceding year (for example, you make your January 1st mortgage payment sometime in December). Mortgage interest is due after the month to which it applies; therefore, your January 1st payment is for interest you owe for the month of December and can be deducted in the earlier year.

Work Smart

Be aware that if you use this strategy to reduce your taxes, the mortgage interest statement you receive from your lender may not reflect that last pre-January 1st payment. If not, you should deduct the correct amount on your tax return and attach a short statement explaining why the lender's statement is incorrect.

Interest Paid at Settlement

At the settlement or closing on a new home loan, it's common for the buyer to be charged a small amount of "prepaid interest." This generally represents mortgage interest on your loan amount from the day of settlement to the end of the current month, so it's less than an ordinary monthly mortgage payment.

Such prepaid interest is deductible home mortgage interest, and since it applies to the portion of the month immediately following the closing date, for calendar year taxpayers it would be deductible for the same tax year in which the closing date falls.

You cannot count as "interest" the fees your lender charges you to make the loan, such as an application fee, appraisal fee, credit check fees, fees for private mortgage insurance (PMI), etc. These amounts are not deductible, nor are they added to the cost of your home for purposes of calculating gains or losses when you sell.

Points

As mentioned above, as a general rule you can't deduct prepaid interest ahead of the year to which it relates. The most common form of prepaid interest is "points."

A point is a charge paid by the borrower to the lender upon taking out the loan. One point equals one percent of the amount borrowed; thus, on a $100,000 loan, three points equals $3,000, but on a $250,000 loan, three points equals $7,500.

Under the general rule, you could deduct points as mortgage interest but you'd have to spread your deduction for points out over the entire life of the loan, even though you actually paid the amount if the first year.

Fortunately, there is an exception that allows many borrowers to deduct their points in the year paid.

Points on Home Mortgage or Improvement Loans

You may deduct points in the year you pay them if all of the following are true:

1. The loan is used to buy or improve your principal home, and the loan is secured by the home. Thus, second mortgages or home equity loans qualify if the proceeds are used for home improvement – but not otherwise.

2. The payment of points is an established business practice in your area.

3. The points paid don't exceed the number of points generally charged in the area. If lenders in

your area generally charge three points and you pay four, you can deduct the first three in the first year. The fourth point must be deducted over the entire term of the loan.

4. The points aren't paid in place of amounts that are usually separate charges, such as appraisal, inspection, title, or attorney fees

5. The points are computed as a percentage of the principal amount of the mortgage.

6. If the loan is used to buy your main home, you must have provided funds at the time of closing that are at least equal to the points charged, outside of the money obtained from the lender. For this purposes, the funds you provided don't have to be applied specifically as payment of points; they can be applied to your down payment, earnest money, or other funds actually paid over at closing.

The deduction for points applies only to buyers, and not to sellers, of homes. If the seller pays some points to enable the buyer to get a loan, the buyer may deduct the points. The seller treats the amount paid as a selling cost that helps to reduce his or her taxable profits on the sale.

Second Homes

The rules above apply only to your main home. If you pay points on a loan secured by a second home, those points can only be deducted over the entire term of the loan.

Refinancing

Points paid in refinancing a mortgage on your main home are generally not deductible in the year paid. They must be prorated and deducted over the entire loan period.

However, if the proceeds of your refinancing are used both to pay off the old mortgage and to pay for home improvements, the portion of the points that pertain to the home improvements can be deducted in the first year. The remaining portion must be prorated over the loan's entire term.

Mortgage Paid Off Early

If your mortgage is paid off early (perhaps because you sell the home, refinance to get a lower interest

rate, or make enough extra principal payments to retire the loan), at that time you can deduct any portion of points on the old loan that have not yet been deducted.

Example

Sharon Flint refinanced her mortgage in 1995 to get a lower interest rate. At that time, she paid $3,000 in points that were required to be spread over the 15-year term of her new loan. Through 1998, she had deducted $800 of the points. In 1999, Sharon paid off her mortgage in full. She can then deduct the remaining $2,200 of points in 1999.

Mortgage Credit Certificates (MCCs)

If you reside in one of the few states or localities that have chosen to issue MCCs and you obtain a certificate, then you can claim a tax credit (rather than a deduction) based on the amount of interest you paid. Generally, credits are more valuable than deductions because they reduce your taxes dollar-for-dollar, while deductions reduce your taxes by only a percentage of the amount in question (i.e., if you're in the 28 percent tax bracket, a deduction reduces your taxes by 28 percent of the dollar amount of your mortgage interest).

Even within the localities that issue MCCs, these certificates are generally available only to first-time homebuyers whose income is below the median income for the area where they live. If you are eligible for the credit, it must be claimed on IRS Form 8396 *Mortgage Interest Credit*, which must be filed with your Form 1040.

Claiming the Home Mortgage Interest Deduction

If you paid mortgage interest to a financial institution, by January 31st you should receive a Form 1098 reporting the amount of interest and points you paid during the previous year.

The amount shown in Box 1 of the 1098 is the amount of interest you paid, and the amount shown in Box 2 is the amount of points paid. These amounts are added together (and if you have a mortgage on a second home, add the amounts on the 1098 from that mortgage also), and entered on Line 10 of Schedule A *Itemized Deductions.*

If the amounts shown on Form 1098 don't agree with what you actually paid (for example, the bank did not add in the interest from that extra payment you made at the end of December), enter the correct amount but attach a short statement to the return explaining the discrepancy.

If you paid interest that was not reported on a 1098, it should be entered on Line 11 of the Schedule A. In most cases this will be interest you paid to an individual, such as a seller who took back a mortgage, or your rich Uncle Harry who lent you the money for part of the down payment. You'll need to enter the person's name, Social Security number, and address on the dotted lines next to Line 11.

On Line 12, report any points that were not reported on Form 1098 (for example, if you paid off a loan you had already refinanced at least once).

Lines 10, 11, and 12 are added up, together with any amount on Line 13 for investment interest (see page 240), and the total is entered on Line 14 of the Schedule A. Certain high-income taxpayers may have all of their itemized deductions limited – see page 273 for more details.

THE DEDUCTION FOR REAL ESTATE TAXES

Next to the home mortgage interest deduction, the most important tax break for homeowners is probably the deduction for state and local taxes, including real estate taxes.

Your real estate taxes are fully deductible, whether they are imposed by the state, county, city, township, or some other local government body.

You can deduct taxes on all your real estate – your deduction is not limited to only two principal residences, as it is with the home mortgage interest deduction. Real estate taxes you paid on all real estate you own for personal or family purposes is deductible on Line 6 of Schedule A, *Itemized Deductions.*

However, if you own commercial or residential rental real estate, the taxes would be deducted on your Schedule E, *Supplemental Income and Loss* (see page 216) or on Form 4835 for farms (see page 179), not Schedule A. See also page 213 for information about real estate that is rented out some of the time, and used for personal purposes at other times.

Deductible "taxes" do not include charges for services performed, such as a unit fee for water consumed or a periodic fee for trash removed. Taxes also don't include assessments for local benefits that tend to increase the value of your property, such as for the construction of streets, sidewalks, or sewers. Any such charges must be added to the tax basis of your property – they'll eventually reduce the amount of taxable profit on your property when you sell.

However, there is a distinction to be made between *improvements* and *repairs.* Assessments for repairs, such as repair of a broken sidewalk, or for maintenance, such as mowing, are deductible if the charges are broken out separately on your tax bill.

The general rule is that the person who owns the real estate and, therefore, owes the taxes is the person who can deduct them, provided that he or she actually paid the amounts. Co-owners should divide the tax bill and the deduction according to the percentage of their ownership interest. If you pay taxes for someone else (for example, your aged parent) on property that they own, you cannot deduct them.

However, if you are divorced and your separation agreement or divorce decree requires you to pay real estate taxes on property owned jointly by you and your ex-spouse, the amount you pay on the ex-spouse's portion may be deductible as alimony (see page 280).

Condos and Co-Ops

You can't deduct homeowners' association assessments, including condominium association assessments, if they are for maintaining common areas and/or for the recreation, health, safety, and welfare of residents.

However, condo owners can deduct real estate taxes assessed against the unit. In some jurisdictions, the unit owner receives a single assessment covering both the unit and the percentage interest that the owner has in the common elements of the condo building or community. In other jurisdictions, the unit owner receives an assessment against his or her unit, and the condominium association receives an assessment covering all the common elements. The association collects a share of its tax bill from each unit owner. Each owner can deduct the share of this bill that he or she pays.

Co-op owners. Under a cooperative housing arrangement, the owner in a co-op building does not own title to the building or to any real estate. Rather, he or she owns shares of stock in a corporation; the corporation, in turn, owns title to the land and building. The shareholder receives a proprietary lease entitling him or her to occupy a unit within the building. Nevertheless, the tenant-shareholder can deduct amounts paid to the co-op corporation, to the extent that they represent his or her proportionate share of real estate taxes paid or incurred by the corporation.

When Taxes Are Deductible

You can deduct real estate taxes that are imposed on you and that you paid either at the settlement or closing of a sale, or to a taxing authority during the year.

If your monthly house payment includes an amount placed in the care of the lender ("escrow") to be saved up and used to pay real estate taxes when due, you can deduct only the amount that the lender actually pays to the taxing body even though this may be more or less than the amount you have contributed to escrow during the year. You cannot deduct the portion of your escrow payment that goes to pay homeowner's insurance, unless you have a qualifying home office (see page 79 for complete details on the home office deduction).

Taxes Paid at Settlement

At the closing, it's customary for the seller and the buyer to allocate the real estate taxes for the current year between themselves. If taxes for the year have already been paid, the buyer may have to pay a portion of that amount to the seller; on the other hand, if the taxes for the year are not yet due, the seller will generally give the buyer a credit for the portion that the seller is estimated to owe. Occasionally, one party will agree to pay all taxes for the year.

For federal tax purposes, the actual arrangements made between the buyer and the seller don't matter.

Instead, taxes for the year of sale must be divided between the parties on the basis of the number of days each party owned the property during the year. The seller can deduct the taxes up to the date of sale; the buyer can deduct taxes beginning with the date of sale through the rest of the year.

Generally, the seller can claim this deduction in the year of sale; the buyer may claim the deduction only when the tax bill is actually paid – which sometimes means the following year.

Example

Gus Pappageorge's property tax year is the same as the calendar year, but the property taxes are not due until the following October 31 (e.g., 1999 taxes are payable by October 31, 2000).

On March 2, 1999, Gus sells his home to Joel Page. The 1999 real estate taxes on the home are $4,500. Gus is treated as having paid $740 of the tax (he owned the home for 60 days out of 365; $4,500 x 60/365 = $739.73). He can deduct this amount in 1999.

Joel is treated as having paid the remainder of the tax or $3,760. He must deduct this amount in 2000 because the taxes will not be paid until then.

Buying a Home

If you bought a home in 1999, you've undoubtedly been busy with a glut of activities including shopping for a house and a mortgage, negotiating the purchase price, moving, and setting up your household in a new location.

You can add to this list of duties one fairly simple, but important task: collecting and retaining the records that show the basis of your home.

Why Track Your Basis?

While some brokers and advisers will tell you that keeping track of your basis is now unnecessary, since the first $250,000 in gain on sale of your home won't be taxed (see page 210) and probably won't even need to be computed, you're on much safer ground if you retain these records.

Knowing the basis of your home is important for several reasons besides computing your gain when you eventually sell the home.

For example, if you suffer a casualty loss to the home, your deductible losses may be limited by the amount of your tax basis in the home. If you don't have accurate records of that, you may lose some of your tax benefits at a time when you need them most.

If you ever decide to rent out some or all of your home (for example, if you decide to move when the housing market is very slow and you need to find a tenant to cover your mortgage payments with some income for an extended period of time), you'll need to know your tax basis in order to determine your depreciation deductions. Similarly, if you ever decide to use part of your home for business (see page 79), depreciation is usually computed on the business portion of the home's tax basis.

If you purchased your first home many, many years ago and since then you've moved several times, deferring gain each time by purchasing a more expensive home under the old rollover replacement rule, you may have deferred tens or hundreds of thousands of dollars already, and the basis of your current home may be very low. If so, you may hit the $250,000 in capital gains mark very quickly.

Finally, if it turns out that you stay in your home for a long time, you should realize that the $250,000 exclusion of taxable gain on the sale of the home is not indexed for inflation. The value of the exclusion is bound to be eroded as time passes.

Example

If we look at the exclusion in today's dollars, at a modest 3 percent inflation rate, the value of $250,000 in ten years will be only $186,023. In 20 years it will be worth $138,418, and in 30 years it will be worth only $102,996 in 1999 dollars.

Long-time homeowners may well find that they end up paying some capital gains tax on their home, but they may pay more than necessary if they haven't kept track of their basis over the years.

And all of this assumes that Congress won't change the law to either increase or, more likely, decrease the amount of the exclusion or change the rules for claiming it!

Computing Your Initial Basis

The starting point for your home's tax basis is the sales price and the charges you paid upon purchasing or building the home (if you did not purchase the home but acquired it by gift, inheritance, transfer in a divorce, etc., see the discussion on page 208). The key document that you'll need for tax purposes is the HUD statement or other settlement document that shows all the settlement costs paid by yourself and the seller.

Of course, for legal purposes, you'll also want to keep the signed sales contract that shows the legal description of the property, the sales price, and the terms of your sale in a safe place like your safe deposit box at the bank. But the settlement statement will generally provide the information you need for tax purposes.

Work Smart

You should keep these documents for at least as long as you own the home, but preferably for the rest of your life since it may turn out that your executor or heirs need this information.

To compute your basis for a home that you purchased, start with the sales price you paid, which is generally composed of your down payment (including any earnest money) plus the principal amount of any mortgage or other debt you took out or assumed.

If you built the home, the starting point would be your basis in the land the home is built on, plus the costs of building the house including labor and materials, contractor's fee, architect fee, building permit charges, and legal fees directly connected with building the home. If you worked on the home yourself, you can count the value of materials and supplies you used, but not the value of your labor.

Settlement or Closing Costs

In addition to the direct costs of the house, you can add to your basis certain costs that you paid at the settlement or closing.

First of all, remember that prepaid interest or points are deductible in the year of the purchase, under the rules outlined above. Real estate taxes for the day of the purchase and afterwards are also deductible by you, whether you paid them or the seller actually paid them. Real estate taxes up to and including the day before the sale are deductible by the seller. If either party actually paid taxes for any period when they did not own the home, the amount of taxes they paid is not deductible, but is added to their tax basis in the property.

Other settlement costs that are can be added to your basis are listed below, along with some costs that may not be added to your basis. The general rule of thumb is that you can deduct most fees directly associated with acquiring the home, as opposed to costs associated with living in it, but you can deduct only those fees that you would have had if you had paid cash for the home. In other words, costs specifically incurred to take out a mortgage are not deductible.

Items Added to Purchaser's Tax Basis

The following items are commonly paid at settlement and can be added to your tax basis:

- attorney's fees

- abstract fees

- charges for installing utility services

- transfer and stamp taxes

- surveys

- owner's title insurance

- unreimbursed amounts that the seller owes but that you pay for back taxes or interest, recording fees for the deed or the mortgage, charges for improvements or repairs done before the sale, and selling commissions

Items Not Added to Purchaser's Tax Basis

The following items are *not* added to your basis and are not deductible:

- fire or liability insurance premiums

- charges for using utilities

- rent for occupying the home before closing

- any other fees or charges connected with occupying the home

- charges connected with getting or refinancing a mortgage loan, such as: FHA mortgage insurance premiums or VA funding fees, private mortgage insurance (PMI) premiums, loan assumption fees, cost of a credit report, cost of a preapproval or prequalification letter, fee for an appraisal required by the lender, and application fees, document fees, and any other miscellaneous fees imposed by the lender

Home Acquired by Gift, Inheritance or Other Transfer

If you received the home (or the part you did not already own) as part of a settlement in a divorce, you generally have no gain or loss at the time of the transfer. Thereafter you will essentially "stand in the shoes" of your former spouse and take whatever basis he or she had in the property, as to the part you received in the settlement. If the home was originally purchased by you and your former spouse together, the basis of the home will generally be figured based on its cost, as discussed above.

If you received your home by bequest or inheritance, your initial basis is the fair market value of the home on the date of the former owner's death, or the alternate valuation date if the estate is using that date for estate tax purposes. If an estate tax return was filed, use the amount shown for the home on the tax return. If the estate was too small to require the filing of an estate tax return, you may need to get an appraisal showing the home's value as of the date of death. Special rules apply where in community property states, where the death of one spouse causes the home to pass to the other spouse. Consult your attorney or tax professional for more details.

If you received the home as a gift, your initial tax basis will generally be the same as that of the person who gave it to you. You can add to this basis the part of any federal gift tax paid by the donor that is attributable to the increase in the home's value. See IRS Publication 551, *Basis of Assets*, or your tax adviser for more details.

Home That Was Purchased Under Rollover Replacement Rule

Under the tax laws that were in effect before May 7, 1997, you could avoid capital gains tax on the sale of your home if, within two years before or after the sale, you purchased and lived in another main home that cost more than the sales price of the old home.

If you took advantage of this rule in previous years, the gain on the sale of your earlier homes was deferred, not wiped out. The amount of gain you would otherwise have recognized (and paid tax on)

was deducted from the cost of your replacement home, so the basis of your current home is likely to be somewhat lower than your cost.

If this is your story, you'll need to look back into your tax records for the IRS Form 2119, *Sale of Your Home*, that was filed in the year you sold your most recent earlier home. That form (which became obsolete for sales after 1997) required you to compute the adjusted basis of the replacement home, which is what you must use as the initial basis.

Adjustments to Your Home's Basis

Over the years that you own your home, your initial tax basis may need to be adjusted to reflect several kinds of events.

The most common reason for an addition to your basis is that you made a permanent improvement, such as a room addition, kitchen remodeling, installation of air conditioning or heating, new sidewalks or landscaping, etc. "Improvements" are generally defined as things that add to the value of the home, prolong its useful life, or adapt it to new uses. In contrast, "repairs" are things that keep your home in good working condition and maintain, but do not add to, its value. However, if jobs that would normally be considered repairs are done as part of a larger improvement project, all of the expenses can be treated as an improvement and added to your basis.

As you complete and pay for improvements, you should retain receipts and cancelled checks for the payments you make. You may find it helpful to use a form like the one that follows to keep track of your improvements over the years.

Save Money

Although the list of improvements included in the form concentrates on big-ticket items, remember that an improvement need not be large in order to be deductible. For example, drapery rods, window shades, bathroom towel racks, updated lighting fixtures, and even new handles on your kitchen cabinets can all be considered "improvements." If you keep careful track of these items over the years, they can really add up.

Capital Improvements Worksheet (keep for your records)

These are improvements made to your home that add to its value, prolong its useful life, or adapt it to new uses. Examples are listed below.

Caution: *Do not include improvements that are no longer part of your main home. For example, if you put wall-to-wall carpeting in your home and later replaced it with new wall-to-wall carpeting, do not include the cost of the first carpeting as a capital improvement.*

(a) Type of Improvement	(b) Year	(c) Amount	(a) Type of Improvement	(b) Year	(c) Amount
Additions			**Heating & Air Conditioning**		
Bedroom			Heating system		
Bathroom			Central air conditioning		
Deck			Furnace		
Garage			Duct work		
Porch			Central humidifier		
Patio			Filtration system		
Storage shed			Other		
Fireplace					
Other			**Electrical**		
			Light fixtures		
Lawn & Grounds			Wiring upgrades		
Landscaping			Other		
Driveway					
Walkway			**Plumbing**		
Fence			Water heater		
Retaining wall			Soft water system		
Sprinkler system			Filtration system		
Swimming pool			Other		
Exterior lighting					
Other			**Insulation**		
			Attic		
Communications			Walls		
Satellite dish			Floors		
Intercom			Pipes and duct work		
Security system			Other		
Other					
			Interior Improvements		
Miscellaneous			Built-in appliances		
Storm windows and doors			Kitchen modernization		
Roof			Bathroom modernization		
Central vacuum			Flooring		
Other			Wall-to-wall carpeting		
			Other		

Total capital improvements. Add the amounts in column (c). Enter the total here and on line 8 of the **Adjusted Basis of Home Sold Worksheet** on page 4. . . . . $ _____

Besides additions or improvements, you may need to record an increase in your home's tax basis if you pay a special assessment to your taxing body for a local improvement such as a sidewalk, paving an alley, etc. You should also increase your basis by the amounts you spend to restore damage to your home caused by a casualty, vandalism, etc.

Decreases to your basis will need to be made for the following amounts:

- casualty losses, whether they are covered and reimbursed by insurance, or not covered by insurance and deductible (see page 267)

- payments you receive for granting an easement or right-of-way

- depreciation, if you used your home for business or rental purposes (see page 217)

- residential energy credit claimed for the cost of energy-related improvements that you added to the basis of your home (the credit was available from 1977 through 1987)

- energy conservation subsidy that was excluded from your gross income because it was received from a public utility after 1992 to buy or install any energy conservation measure

- adoption credit you claimed for improvements that you added to the basis of your home, and nontaxable adoption assistance received from your employer that you used for improvements that you added to the basis of your home (see page 283)

- the First-Time Homebuyer Credit for the District of Columbia. For property purchased before January 1, 2002, a first-time homebuyer of a principal residence in the District of Columbia is entitled to a tax credit of up to $5,000 of the amount of the purchase price of the residence. The amount of the credit is phased out for individual taxpayers with modified adjusted gross income (AGI) between $70,000 and $90,000 ($110,000 and $130,000 for joint filers). If you qualify for the credit, you must complete IRS Form 8859, *District of Columbia First-Time Homebuyer Credit*, and attach it to your tax return for the year of the sale.

SELLING YOUR HOME

Because of changes to the tax laws that went into effect in May of 1997, most homeowners will be exempt from paying tax on gains from the sale of their main home.

More specifically, every two years you can exclude up to $250,000 in gains when you sell your home, provided that you have both owned and used your home as a principal residence for at least two of the five years immediately preceding the sale.

Married couples can exclude up to $500,000 in gains if they file a joint return, provided that both spouses meet the two-year use test, at least one spouse can meet the two-year ownership test, and neither spouse has excluded gain from the sale of another home in the last two years (counting sales since May 6, 1997).

As a reminder, losses on the sale of your personal residence are not deductible. There is an exception to this rule if part of your home was rented out or used for a home office (see page 79), or your home was converted to a rental property before you sold it. In any case, only losses on the business portion of the home would be deductible. See page 116 for more on sales of rental or commercial real estate.

Two Years of Ownership and Use

To take advantage of the exclusion, you must have *owned* and *used the home as a principal residence* for at least two of the five preceding years. The two years for each test need not have occurred at the same time.

Example

In 1992, Sharon Rose was living in a rented apartment. The apartment was converted into a condominium, and in 1995 Sharon purchased her apartment. In 1997, Sharon became ill and on April 14 of that year, she moved to her daughter's home. She never moved back to the condo and on July 10, 1999, she sold it.

Sharon can exclude up to $250,000 in gain on the sale of her condo because she met both tests, at different times. Her five year-period began on July 10, 1994 and ended on July 10, 1999. Within that period she lived in the condo from July 10, 1994 until April 14, 1997, which is more than two years. Also within that period she owned the home from sometime in 1995 until July 10, 1999, which is also more than two years.

In tallying up the time periods, you can count short periods of absence for vacation, seasonal absences, or any other temporary absence (generally, anything under one year) as time that you spent using the home.

Also, there are some grandfathering provisions in the law, which say that if you previously owned a home and rolled over the capital gains from that home into your current home under the old rollover-replacement rule, you can count the time you owned and/or lived in that previous home towards your two-year period. To take advantage of this exception, you can't have sold another home within two years of your sale, or since May 7, 1997 (whichever period is shorter). This is true even if your previous home was condemned or destroyed.

Finally, if you can't meet the two-year rules because you became physically or mentally incapable of self-care, you qualify for the exemption if you owned and lived in the home for at least one year.

Reduced Exclusion

You might qualify for a partial exclusion even if you don't meet the two-year rules, if the reason that you can't meet them is because you suffered a "change in place of employment, health, or unforeseen circumstances." Exactly what type of "change" is serious enough to warrant this tax break has not yet been defined in the regulations or any official pronouncements by the IRS. If you think this exception might apply to you, for the time being, we advise you to think about what a "reasonable" person would think was justification for moving. For example, taking a job in another city; moving to a warmer, drier part of the country due to severe asthma; or selling your home because of a drop in income would probably warrant a partial exclusion.

You can compute a partial exclusion by using the worksheet below.

If You Are Married

If you and your spouse file a joint return for the year, you can exclude up to $250,000 in gain if either spouse meets the ownership and use test, and up to $500,000 if both spouses meet the use test and at least one spouse meets the ownership test.

If each spouse sells a different home, each spouse can deduct up to $250,000 in gain provided that each meets the ownership and use test with regard to their own home.

Work Smart

This rule can come into play if, for example, an older couple gets married and each spouse brings a home into the marriage. If they want to sell the old homes and purchase a new one together, they can sell either home before or after the marriage without losing the full exclusion; furthermore, it's not necessary to buy a home that costs more than either (or both) of the homes to qualify for a tax break, as under prior law.

Reduced Exclusion for Gain on Sale of a Principal Residence

Complete Column B only if you are married and filing a joint return.

	You	Your Spouse
(1) Maximum amount	$250,000	$250,000
(2a) Number of days you used the property as a main home during the 5-year period ending on the date of sale		
(2b) Number of days you owned the property during the 5-year period (if one spouse owned it longer than the other, enter the longer period in both columns)		
(2c) Enter the smaller of Line 2a or 2b.		
(3) Are you or your spouse excluding gain from the sale of another home after May 6, 1997? If no, skip Line 3 and enter the number of days from Line 2c on Line 4. If yes, if the other home was sold before this one, enter the number of days between the date of sale of the other home and the date of the sale of this home. Otherwise, skip Line 3 and enter the number of days from Line 2c on Line 4.		
(4) Enter the smaller of Line 2c or Line 3.		
(5) Divide the amount on Line 4 by 730 days.		
(6) Multiply the amount on Line 1 by the decimal on Line 5.		
(7) Add the amounts in columns a and b of Line 6. This is your reduced maximum exclusion.		

If one spouse dies before a sale is accomplished, the other spouse can use the decedent's time of ownership and use in order to qualify for the exemption.

Divorce

If a home is transferred from one spouse to the other as part of a divorce settlement, the recipient is treated as having owned the home during any time the donor owned it.

Also, in cases where the home is not sold for a while after the divorce (for example, the couple agrees to maintain joint ownership, so one spouse can live there with the children until they finish high school), you are considered to have used the property as your main home during any period when you owned it, and your spouse or former spouse is allowed to use it under a divorce or separation instrument.

Calculating Gains on Sale

To determine the amount of your gains, and whether the $250,000 or $500,000 exemption is large enough to save you from paying any tax on the sale of your home, compute your gains as shown in this example:

Example

Kelly Vargas, a single person, sold her main home on September 15, 1999. She had owned and lived in it as her main home for seven years. She computed her gain as follows:

Selling price of home	*$195,000*
Minus: selling expenses	*- 15,000*
Amount realized on sale	*$180,000*
Minus: adjusted basis of home	*- 50,000*
Gain on sale	*$130,000*

Since Kelly's gain is less than $250,000, she will not be taxed on the sale.

Selling expenses that Kelly can subtract from the selling price of her home include the broker's commission, title insurance or abstract fees, legal fees, recording fees, advertising, escrow fees, geological surveys, and interest reimbursed on money borrowed for an option to purchase.

Reporting Gains on Sales

Historically, the IRS had required all homeowners to complete and file IRS Form 2119, *Sale of Your Home*, in the year that they sell a home. Form 2119 is no longer required for 1998 and thereafter. Those who owe some tax on the sale of a principal residence will report the sale as short-term or long-term gain on Schedule D, *Capital Gains and Losses*. If you owned the home for up to one year, any non-exempt gain would be considered short-term gain taxable at ordinary rates, and if you owned the home for more than one year, it would be taxed at the long-term rate, which is a maximum of 20 percent, or 10 percent for taxpayers in the 15 percent bracket.

Home Offices

If you have used part of your home as a home office (see page 79), you haven't been using that part of your home as a principal residence at the same time.

Therefore, if you've used your home office for more than three of the past five years, you will have to divide up your property into two pieces: the "principal residence" part, on which up to $250,000 gain may be excluded, and the "business" part, which is treated as a taxable sale of business real estate, as discussed in Chapter 7.

You'll have to compute the gain on each portion of the house separately. Assuming the home was owned for at least one year, the maximum tax rate on the business portion will be the long-term capital gains rate of 20 percent. However, the amount of gains up to the amount of any depreciation ever claimed on the home will be taxed at a rate of 25 percent.

If you have *not* used your home office for more than three of the last five years, you can exclude most of your gains on the sale of the home. However, you'll still have to pay a 25 percent tax on gains up to the amount of any depreciation claimed for periods after May 6, 1997.

Separating your property into the "home" portion and the "business" portion is generally necessary whenever you use some of the property for commercial or rental activities, and some for living space. Another situation where this frequently arises is illustrated in the case study for part-rental property.

Case Study

Tom Stonehouse, a 72-year-old taxpayer, owns a four-unit apartment building that he had purchased five years ago. He occupies one unit as his personal residence and rents out three units. Desiring to move to a warmer climate, Tom decides to sell the building and move in with his nephew. Tom's records show the following:

Cost of building	$80,000
Capital improvements	+ 8,000
	$88,000
Less: Depreciation on rental units	- 10,100
Adjusted basis	$77,900

Tom sells the building for $220,000 and incurs selling expenses of $10,000. Since only one-fourth of the building was used as his personal residence, Tom would compute his gain as follows:

	Apartment Residence (1/4)	Rental Building (3/4)
(1) Selling price	$55,000	$165,000
(2) Selling expenses	-2,500	-7,500
(3) Amount realized (adjusted sales price)	$52,500	$157,500
(4) Basis (including improvements)	$22,000	$ 66,000
(5) Depreciation		-10,100
(6) Adjusted basis	$22,000	$ 55,900
(7) Realized gain [(3) minus (6)]	$30,500	$101,600
(8) Gain subject to exclusion	$30,500	
(9) Gain subject to tax		$101,600

Of the gains subject to tax on line (9), $10,100 would be taxed at a 25 percent rate since it represents deprecation that must be recaptured, and the remainder would be taxed at a maximum rate of 20 percent.

VACATION HOME RENTALS

A second home in the country, a condo in the city, or a houseboat on the lake can all be a pleasant place to spend your vacation. They can also be made to partially pay for their own costs, if you can rent them out to others for at least a few days or weeks each year.

The IRS basically uses a two-week *de minimus* rule. If you rent out a vacation home for two weeks or less during the year, you don't have to report any rental income you receive, but you can't deduct any rental expenses you have (except for the normal home mortgage interest and real estate tax deductions you'd have anyway). Essentially the IRS will ignore this small amount of rental activity.

If you have property that is rented out for more than 14 days during the year, and you or your family, or any co-owner or his or her family, use it for personal purposes for *even one day* of the year, you have to divide all the expenses of the property into two buckets: "personal" and "rental."

The rental expenses will generally be deductible on Schedule E, *Supplemental Income and Loss,* and the personal expenses will not be deductible except for mortgage interest, real estate taxes, and casualty losses that you could ordinarily claim on Schedule A.

On Schedule E you can deduct the entire amount of expenses that apply only to renting, such as advertising, commissions, credit checks, etc. For all expenses that apply to the entire home, such as mortgage interest, real estate taxes, insurance, utilities, and repairs and maintenance on the furnace, roof, electric system, etc., you must generally divide the expenses on the basis of days spent for personal use, compared to days that the property was rented at a fair market rate; the total need not add up to 365 days.

When counting days of "personal use," you must include any days that you donated the use of your property to a charitable organization (for example, if you allowed a charity to auction off a week in your lakefront house). Also count as "personal" any days that you traded with someone else for the use of a different property, or any days for which you charged less than fair market rent. However, don't count as "personal" the days you stayed in the home because you were having repairs or maintenance done, even if your family stayed with you.

Example

You have a cabin in the mountains that you generally rent out during a three-month ski season; this year, the rental agent was only able to rent the property for 60 days out of the 90 days it was available. You donated a week of this unrented period to a local charity. Also, you spent a week at the cabin cleaning and making repairs before the rental period began.

You would count as "personal use" the 7 days you donated to charity, and you would count as "rental use"

the 60 days you actually rented the property. Therefore, 7/67 of your expenses would be treated as "personal" and deductible, if at all, on Schedule A. 60/67 of your expenses would be treated as "rental" and deductible on Schedule E, subject to the limits discussed below. The 7 days spent cleaning and making repairs do not count as either personal or rental use.

Dwelling unit used as a home. An even more severe restriction applies if you (or your family, or any co-owners or their families) use the property for personal purposes for more than the greater of 14 days, or 10 percent of the days it is rented out to others.

In that case, not only do you have to apportion your expenses between the "rental" and the "personal" portion, but also if your rental expenses exceed your rental income for this mixed-use property, you can only deduct your expenses up to the amount of your income. Any remaining expenses can be carried over and deducted in the next year, however.

You don't have to apply this additional limit if you converted rental property to a personal residence during the year.

You also don't have to apply it if you converted a personal residence to a rental during the year and you rented or tried to rent it out for at least 12 months, or if you would have rented it for at least 12 months except that you sold or exchanged the property before the 12 months were up.

You can use the following worksheet to compute the additional limit on rental deductions for a mixed-use property.

RENTAL REAL ESTATE INCOME AND EXPENSES

If you rented out residential or commercial real estate during the year, you will normally report your income and expenses from this activity on Part I of Schedule E, *Supplemental Income and Loss.*

Worksheet for Figuring the Limit on Rental Deductions for a Dwelling Unit Used as a Home

Use this worksheet only if you answer "yes" to all of the following questions.
- Did you use the dwelling unit as a home this year?
- Did you rent the dwelling unit 15 days or more this year?
- Are the total of your rental expenses and depreciation more than your rental income?

1. Enter rents received . . . . _____

2a. Enter the rental portion of deductible home mortgage interest (see instructions) . . . . _____
  b. Enter the rental portion of real estate taxes . . . . _____
  c. Enter the rental portion of deductible casualty and theft losses (see instructions) . . . . _____
  d. Enter direct rental expenses (see instructions) . . . . _____
  e. **Fully deductible rental expenses.** Add lines 2a–2d . . . . _____

3. Subtract line 2e from line 1. If zero or less, enter zero . . . . _____

4a. Enter the rental portion of expenses directly related to operating or maintaining the dwelling unit (such as repairs, insurance, and utilities) . . . . _____
  b. Enter the rental portion of excess mortgage interest (see instructions) . . . . _____
  c. Add lines 4a and 4b . . . . _____
  d. **Allowable operating expenses.** Enter the smaller of line 3 or line 4c . . . . _____

5. Subtract line 4d from line 3. If zero or less, enter zero . . . . _____

6a. Enter the rental portion of excess casualty and theft losses (see instructions) . . . . _____
  b. Enter the rental portion of depreciation of the dwelling unit . . . . _____
  c. Add lines 6a and 6b . . . . _____
  d. **Allowable excess casualty and theft losses and depreciation.** Enter the smaller of line 5 or line 6c . . . . _____

7a. **Operating expenses to be carried over to next year.** Subtract line 4d from line 4c . . . . . _____
  b. **Excess casualty and theft losses and depreciation to be carried over to next year.** Subtract line 6d from line 6c . . . . _____

Enter the amounts on **lines 2e, 4d, and 6d** on the appropriate lines of Schedule E (Form 1040), Part I.

Worksheet Instructions

Follow these instructions for the worksheet above. If you were unable to deduct all your expenses last year, because of the rental income limit, add these unused amounts to your expenses for this year.

Line 2a. Figure the mortgage interest on the dwelling unit that you could deduct on Schedule A (Form 1040) if you had not rented the unit. **Do not** include interest on a loan that did not benefit the dwelling unit. For example, **do not** include interest on a home equity loan used to buy, build, or improve the dwelling unit, or to refinance such a loan. Enter the rental portion of this interest on line 2a of the worksheet.

Line 2c. Figure the casualty and theft losses related to the dwelling unit that you could deduct on Schedule A (Form 1040) if you had not rented the dwelling unit. To do this, complete Section A of Form 4684, treating the losses as personal losses. On line 17 of Form 4684, enter 10% of your adjusted gross

income figured **without** your rental income and expenses from the dwelling unit. Enter the rental portion of the result from line 18 of Form 4684 on line 2c of this worksheet.

Note. Do **not** file this Form 4684 or use it to figure your personal losses on Schedule A. Instead, figure the personal portion on a separate Form 4684.

Line 2d. Enter the total of your rental expenses that are directly related only to the rental activity. These include interest on loans used for rental activities other than to buy, build, or improve the dwelling unit. Also include rental agency fees, advertising, office supplies, and depreciation on office equipment used in your rental activity.

Line 4b. On line 2a, you entered the rental portion of the mortgage interest you could deduct on Schedule A if you had not rented out the dwelling unit. Enter on line 4b of this worksheet the rental portion of the mortgage interest you could not deduct on Schedule A because it is **more than** the limit on home

mortgage interest. **Do not** include interest on a loan that did not benefit the dwelling unit (as explained in the line 2a instructions).

Line 6a. To find the rental portion of excess casualty and theft losses, use the Form 4684 you prepared for line 2c of this worksheet.

A. Enter the amount from line 10 of Form 4684 . . . . . _____

B. Enter the rental portion of **A** . _____

C. Enter the amount from line 2c of this worksheet . . . . _____

D. Subtract **C** from **B**. Enter the result here and on line 6a of this worksheet . . . . . . _____

Allocating the limited deduction. If you cannot deduct all of the amount on line 4c or 6c this year, you can allocate the allowable deduction in any way you wish among the expenses included on line 4c or 6c. Enter the amount you allocate to each expense on the appropriate line of Schedule E, Part I.

Schedule E has space for up to three different real estate or royalty properties. Line 1 asks you to identify the type of property (such as "apartment building," "store," etc.) and the street address. You should also show your percentage of ownership in the property, if you (and your spouse, if filing jointly) own less than 100 percent. If you own, say, half of the property with another owner, you would report half of the income and half of the expenses on your tax return, regardless of which of you actually received the check for the income or paid the expenses out of pocket.

For each property, you are asked to answer "yes" or "no" to the question of whether you or your family

used it for more than the greater of 14 days or 10 percent of the total days rented. See the discussion on page 213 explaining how to make the count.

Income and expenses for each property are reported separately in columns A, B, and C, and the totals from all properties combined are entered in the "totals" column. If you have more than three properties, use as many copies of Schedule E as you need. Just be sure to fill out the "totals" column on only one of the copies, which will become the "master."

Schedule E is not used to report farm rental income if the rent is paid in the form of a percentage of the crops or livestock produced on the farm. In that case, you must use Form 4835, *Farm Rental Income and Expenses*, instead (see page 179). But if the farm rent is paid in terms of a flat fee, use Schedule E.

Also, if you provide a large number of services to tenants in a residential property, you may have to treat your activity as being more akin to running a hotel (reported on Schedule C) than investing in real estate. The IRS says that providing maid service to tenants can transform your activity into a business, not a Schedule E rental. However, providing occasional cleaning or concierge services would probably not be sufficient to change the nature of your activity.

Rental Real Estate Income

Rent you recognize during the year for each property under your accounting method is entered in the appropriate column, on Line 3. For most taxpayers, this means all rent received during the calendar year, whether it's received directly or indirectly (for example, if your tenant makes repairs for you in exchange for a rent credit, or pays some tax, utility, or repair bills you owe under the terms of the lease).

If you receive a security deposit, it doesn't count as rent unless and until you determine that you're entitled to keep some of the deposit because your tenant violated the lease or damaged your property in some way. Also, if your tenant buys out the remainder of the lease term with a cash payment, the payment counts as rent. However, if you receive some rent in advance of when it's due, you must count it as income regardless of your accounting method.

If you are leasing the property with an option to buy, the payments you receive are considered rent. If and when the tenant exercises the option to buy, payments received after the date of the sale would be considered part of the selling price.

Rental Property Expenses

Expenses paid on your rental property are reported on Lines 5 through 18 on Part I of Schedule E. The rules for most of these expenses are the same as those discussed in Chapter 6 for small businesses, or in the first part of Chapter 12 for real estate taxes and mortgage interest.

The major categories of expenses that you can deduct are listed on the front of Schedule E. On the next page we discuss a few of the more important types of deductible expenses, and a few types of expenses that are often forgotten.

Interest Expenses

There is no upper dollar limit on the amount of mortgage interest you can deduct on rental property, as there is with home mortgage interest.

Furthermore, you can deduct almost any type of interest you pay when you borrow money to further your rental activity, such as interest on a revolving charge account or even credit card late fees.

Example

You purchase new kitchen appliances for a home that you rent out to others, and charge the amounts on your department store credit card. You can deduct the interest charges until you pay off the appliances.

The loan need not be secured by the property, but you must be liable for repayment, and the proceeds of the loan must be used for the rental activities. If you don't use the money immediately to pay for a particular expense (such as to buy or improve the property) you must keep records showing where the loan money went.

Save Time

Ideally, you should keep a separate bank account for each major type of activity you have. Don't commingle funds from your small business with funds from your rental activities. Having separate checking accounts, and separate deposit and check records, will also help you to limit the scope of an IRS audit if one of your activities (but not the others) draws the focussed attention of the IRS.

Unlike other types of investment interest, interest on loans pertaining to rental real estate activities in which you actively participate (see page 219) is not limited by the amount of income you receive from the activity.

However, you can't deduct prepaid interest, and there is no exception for points paid to obtain a mortgage on a rental property as there is with home mortgage loans. Consequently, points you pay to obtain a mortgage for commercial or residential property must be spread over the life of the loan, and deducted in equal amounts over the entire period.

Fees and charges you pay to obtain a mortgage on rental real estate, such as application fees, appraisals, abstract fees, recording fees, cannot be deducted as interest but can be amortized (deducted evenly) over the life of the mortgage.

Repairs vs. Improvements

The discussion that begins on page 59 regarding how to distinguish between repairs, which can be deducted in the year they are paid for, and improvements, which must be depreciated over a time period that matches the class life of the asset, applies to rental real estate as well.

Depreciation

Generally speaking, all assets that will be used for more than one year (and are not trivial in cost, such as paper clips or extension cords) are treated as capital assets.

For property used in your rental activity, you *cannot* make the election to expense up to $19,000 in new equipment in the year you purchase it, under Section 179 of the tax law.

Instead, you'll have to depreciate your rental property, any capital improvements you make to it, and any tools or equipment you need to carry out this activity, such as power mowers or tools, vacuum cleaners, and even your computer, cellular phone, and answering machine.

Aside from the lack of availability of the Section 179 expensing election, all the rules for depreciation discussed in Chapter 6 apply equally to rental real estate. If the real estate is used for residential purposes, such as an apartment building, rental house, mobile home, houseboat, etc., the buildings and any capital improvements on it must be depreciated over 27.5 years. If the property is used for other commercial purposes, it must be depreciated over 39 years. Land itself is never depreciable; only the buildings and improvements on the land can be written off.

If you purchased property for personal use and then changed it to rental use, your depreciable basis will generally be the lesser of its adjusted basis, or its fair market value at the time of the conversion.

Depreciation is claimed on Form 4562, *Depreciation and Amortization*. Don't mix depreciation on rental property with any depreciation claimed on business assets; instead, file a separate Form 4562 for each activity you engage in.

Other Rental Expenses

The chart that follows shows some of the types of expenses you may be able to deduct.

Save Money

Unfortunately, you cannot deduct the cost of your own labor if, for example, you paint a rental apartment or install a lock yourself instead of hiring a painter or a locksmith. However, if you hire a non-owner (such as your child or, possibly, your spouse), you can deduct the payments.

Other Rental Deductions

The following is a list of other frequently overlooked rental deductions.

- 50% of meals and entertainment expenses while traveling, or when entertaining business guests

- cleaning supplies

- credit check fees for tenants

- finance charges on a credit card used for business

- janitorial or cleaning service

- legal fees related to drawing up leases, resolving disputes with tenants or repair contractors, tax advice, etc; however, legal fees incurred in connection with buying or selling the property are added to the property's tax basis

- landscaping maintenance

- local licenses, taxes, inspection fees etc.

- car and truck expenses or local transportation expenses, to inspect the property, collect rents, interview prospective tenants, or to call on contractors, suppliers, vendors, your insurance agent etc; if you claim these expenses, be sure to report them on Form 4562, *Depreciation and Amortization*

- miscellaneous repairs and maintenance

- rental fees for power tools, painting equipment, etc.

- safe deposit box rental, if you keep your deed, mortgage, or insurance policy there

- stamps, if you pay bills by mail

- stationery

- tax return preparation, if you pay someone to complete your Schedule E, associated depreciation tax forms, etc.

- telephone calls, although you can't deduct any part of the first telephone line into your residence

Gains and Losses from Rental Activities

Like any business-related activity, to calculate your taxable profits from rental activities, you subtract your deductible expenses from your gross income, and if the answer is a positive number, you have a taxable profit or gain. This will be initially reported on Line 22 of Schedule E.

In the case of real estate rental activities, it frequently happens that the answer isn't positive, it's negative, and you have a loss for the year. In some cases it's only a "paper loss" because you deducted depreciation expenses that don't represent out-of-pocket expenses, but in other cases it is a real loss. Investors in real estate are frequently willing to accept small losses in the short term, if they believe that their property will appreciate sufficiently over the years to result in a big gain over the long term.

However, the IRS is ever vigilant against the possibility that you are merely trying to create a tax shelter for other types of income. Therefore, there are some special rules that may prevent you from deducting some (or all) of your real estate losses.

At-Risk Limitations

Line 22 says that if the result is a loss, you may have to fill out IRS Form 6198, *At-Risk Limitations*. The at-risk limitations apply to relatively few small-business owners, and they don't apply to losses from holding real estate placed in service before 1987 (except mineral property).

In a nutshell, if they apply, the at-risk rules limit your deductible losses to the amount that you have at risk and could actually lose from the activity.

A taxpayer is "at risk" to the extent of cash and the adjusted basis of property contributed to the business activity, as well as to the extent of loans on which he or she is personally liable or has provided collateral. Having insurance will not render you "not at risk" nor cause you to have to fill out this form. A real estate lessor is "not at risk" to the extent that he or she is protected by non-recourse financing not secured by real estate, guarantees by others, stop-loss agreements or similar arrangements.

If any of these items apply to you and you are not at risk for some amounts in your rental activities, you may have to complete Form 6198. You can obtain a copy of this form and its instructions from the IRS by calling 1-800-TAX-FORM, or by downloading it from the IRS website at www.irs.ustreas.gov.

Passive Activity Losses

Line 23 of Schedule E cautions you that for some people, real estate losses are limited regardless of the at-risk rules.

In contrast to the at-risk limitations, the passive activity loss rules apply to a larger group of taxpayers. They generally prevent taxpayers with adjusted gross income (AGI) above $100,000 from deducting some or all losses from real estate rentals, other than the rental of your home that was also used for personal purposes.

There is an exception to these rules for real estate professionals, defined as those who spend more than 750 hours per year and more than half their working time in developing, managing, and/or selling real estate.

If you're not a real estate professional, here's the basic rule: Taxpayers with modified AGI of $100,000 or less can deduct up to $25,000 in net losses from rental real estate activities in which they "actively participate." If you are married, you must file a joint return to take advantage of this deduction unless you lived apart from your spouse for the entire year; in that case, you can deduct up to $12,500 in losses on a separate tax return.

"Active participation" means that you have significant participation in making management decisions or arranging for others to provide services. These management decisions might include approving new tenants, deciding on rental rates and terms, and approving capital or repair expenditures. However, you're not considered to have "actively participated" if you own less than 10 percent of the property.

"Modified AGI" means your AGI as shown on Form 1040, Line 33, without taking into account any passive activity losses, taxable Social Security benefits, deductible IRA contributions, the deduction for one-half the self-employment tax, and the exclusion for amounts received under an employer's adoption assistance program. Also, if you filed Form 8815, *Exclusion of Interest from Qualified U.S. Savings Bonds*, you must add back the savings bond interest excluded on Line 14 of that form.

If your modified AGI is more than $100,000, if you don't materially participate, if you have more than $25,000 in real estate losses, or if you are carrying over any losses that were not allowed in previous years, your losses may be limited. Generally, the rule is that you can deduct passive losses to the extent that you have passive income from other activities, and all rental real estate activities are treated as passive. For information on which trade or business activities are treated as passive, see page 44.

If you have more passive losses from real estate than you have passive income, your deduction of $25,000 will shrink as your AGI rises. You'll lose $1 of the deduction for every $2 that your AGI rises above $100,000; if your modified AGI is $150,000 or more, you can't deduct any excess passive losses this year.

If your losses are limited under any of these rules, you must complete Form 8582, *Passive Activity Loss Limitations*. The allowed loss, if any, shown on the bottom of Form 8582 is transferred to Line 23 of Schedule E.

Losses that cannot be deducted in the current year are carried over to later years until they can be offset by passive income, until you can use the special $25,000 deduction, or until you sell your entire interest in the property to an unrelated third party.

SALE OF RENTAL REAL ESTATE

If you sell or dispose of any rental real estate during the year, the sale will be reported on Form 4797, *Sales of Business Property*. For detailed information, see the discussion of disposing of capital assets beginning on page 116.

Chapter 13

Investments

For a large number of taxpayers, reporting interest and dividends on investments is very simple. Just collect all the 1099-INT and 1099-DIV forms you've received at the beginning of 1999, enter the amounts in Schedule B of Form 1040 or Schedule 1 of Form 1040A, add up the totals, transfer them to the front page of your main tax form, and you're done.

However, if you bought or sold any investments during the year, or if you had any of the many types of investments that followed special rules including mutual funds, tax-free municipal bonds or bond funds, U.S. Savings Bonds, OID interest, nominee interest, amortizable bond premiums, accrued interest, foreign investments, or income from partnerships, S corporations, trusts, or estates, your situation will be a little more complicated.

You may also have some investment-related deductions for interest, investment advice, financial publications or software, or custodial fees. We'll help you deal with those as well.

If you have a child with investment income, you may have the option to report that income on your own return, or to file a separate tax return for the child. This issue is discussed beginning on page 238.

Tax Organizer Tip

Most investment-related data should be entered in the "Investment" section of the CompleteTax™ Organizer. However, information about royalty income and expenses, and investment real estate, should be entered in the "Real Estate" section.

INTEREST INCOME

Interest from bank accounts or accounts at other financial institutions, certificates of deposits, and bonds should be reported to you by the payer on Form 1099-INT. These forms should be sent out by the end of January.

Save Time

If you receive an incorrect 1099 form, you should contact the financial institution involved and ask them to issue a corrected one. Copies of all 1099s are sent to the IRS and are matched with your tax return. Mix-ups are especially prone to occur if your bank completed a merger this year and, for example, your bank accounts were reported to the IRS under a different bank's name than the one you used on your tax return, or if you had multiple accounts at a single bank and they were not all reported on the same 1099.

As a general rule, if you are required to file Schedule B or Schedule 1, every total shown in Box 1 of every 1099 that you receive should appear on your tax form somewhere, so that the IRS knows you are reporting it. If your institution reported multiple accounts on the same form, you should report them the same way. If they sent you separate 1099 forms for different accounts, report them separately.

If you received $400 or less in interest from all sources and none of the special situations described below apply to you, you don't have to file a separate schedule reporting interest, although you can if you wish.

If you do receive more than $400 in taxable interest, you must complete Parts I and III of Schedule B (for Form 1040) or Part I of Schedule 1 (for 1040A).

Save Money

If any federal income tax was withheld on your interest income, it will be reported in Box 4 of Form 1099-INT. Be sure to include this as "federal income tax withheld" on Line 57 on the back of your 1040, or Line 35 on the 1040A. You can generally avoid backup withholding (which is done at the 31 percent rate) if you provide your financial institution with an accurate Social Security number for the owner of the account.

What Is "Interest"?

Generally, the payer of the amount you receive will distinguish between interest and dividends, and will send you the appropriate form reporting the correct dollar amount you received during the year.

Some items that you might consider to be "interest" are treated as dividends by the IRS (for example, income from money market funds) and some things you might think of as "dividends" are treated as interest (for example, dividends from tax-free municipal bond funds).

Other items that are commonly called "dividends" but that are treated as interest and reported in Part I of Schedule B are income from accounts in cooperative banks, credit unions, domestic building and loan associations, domestic savings and loans, federal savings and loans, and mutual savings banks.

U.S. Government Obligations

Interest on all government bonds is taxable for federal income tax purposes, but it is tax-free for state and local income tax purposes.

Generally, interest on treasury notes and bills is paid either at maturity (for instruments with a maturity of one year or less) or at six-month intervals. You must report it in the year you receive it.

There is a special rule for Series E or EE U.S. Savings Bonds. While interest on these bonds accrue each year, if you're a cash-basis taxpayer, you don't have to pay tax on the interest until you cash in the bond, and most people choose to go this route. However, you do have the option of reporting and paying tax on this interest each year, if you want to avoid a big tax bill in the final year or if you think you'll be in a higher tax bracket at that time.

If you've been accruing interest on savings bonds without reporting it, you can switch to the annual reporting method without seeking IRS permission, but you'll have to switch for all bonds you own, and you'll have to report and pay tax on all interest owed on all bonds to date. You can also switch back to the "postpone recognition of interest" method later, but you'll have to write to the IRS for permission in that case.

Save Money

If your minor child was given U.S. Savings Bonds at birth or soon thereafter, and you haven't been reporting annual interest, you might think about switching to the "annual reporting" method in the year your child turns 14. For that year and all later years, the child's interest income will no longer be taxed at the parent's (usually higher) tax rate. Since savings bonds generally mature in 30 years, your child will probably be in a lower tax bracket at age 14 than he or she will be at age 30 or 31 when the bond is cashed, and under the annual reporting method, a minimum of about half the interest will be taxed at the lower age-14 rate.

Also, see page 224 for information about the special tax break for savings bonds redeemed to pay for higher education expenses.

Tax-Exempt Interest

While you don't have to pay ordinary income tax on it, the IRS wants to know how much tax-exempt interest you are receiving, and in some cases it can be used to limit your qualification for certain other tax breaks. Therefore, tax-exempt interest from state and local municipal bonds, including mutual funds that invest in these bonds, must be listed on the dotted lines provided for detailed information under Line 1 on the Schedule B, but it is not included in the "Amount" column on the right side of the page.

Tax-exempt interest is not required to be reported to you on Form 1099-INT or Form 1099-DIV, but your financial institution will generally send you a notice or year-end statement that includes the annual amount.

Work Smart

To clearly differentiate your tax-exempt interest, some tax practitioners recommend splitting the "dotted line" area into two columns labeled "tax-exempt" and "taxable," to make it very clear how much of which types of interest you've received. Or, you may want to add a separate page to your return that clearly details these amounts.

The total amount of tax-exempt interest you receive during the year must also be carried over to the front of your tax return, on Line 8b of both Form 1040 and 1040A.

Penalty on Early Withdrawal of Savings

If you paid a penalty for the early withdrawal of funds from a time savings account or certificate of deposit, you can deduct it, even if it exceeds the interest income you earned on the account during the year.

You must first report the gross amount of interest that would have been paid or credited to your account during the year without the penalty, on Line 1 of Schedule B. Then, you deduct the penalty amount on Line 30 of Form 1040 (you can't claim this deduction on Form 1040A or –EZ).

You don't have to compute the amount of the deduction, because it will be shown in Box 2 of your Form 1099-INT.

Special Situations

If any of the following items apply to you, you'll have to complete Part I of Schedule B or Schedule 1, even if you received $400 or less in total interest: you received interest from a seller financed mortgage, nominee interest, accrued interest, original issue discount (OID), or amortizable bond premiums; or you are claiming the exclusion for Series EE U.S. Savings Bonds used for higher education expenses.

Seller-Financed Mortgages

If you are holding a mortgage on property that the buyer is using as a personal residence, you must list the amount of interest received from the buyer as your first interest item on the lines provided for details under Line 1 of Schedule 1 or B. Also include the buyer's name, Social Security number and address. If you don't, you can get socked with a $50 fine.

Nominee Interest

If two or more people are listed as owners on a bank account or another type of investment account, the associated 1099-INT form will generally be sent to the person whose Social Security number is listed first on the account. The bank will report to the IRS that all income on the account was paid to that person. However, tax on the income should actually be split among all owners of the account, according to their proportionate ownership interest (which is determined under state law, but generally reflects the proportions that each person originally contributed to the account).

If you received a 1099-INT form that includes interest that is actually owed to someone else (for example, another joint owner of the account who is not your spouse), you can avoid tax on the full amount if you give the actual owner an 1099-INT form by the end of January, and file a copy of this form with the IRS along with IRS Form 1096, *Annual Summary and Transmittal of U.S. Information Returns*, by the end of February.

In that case, you would report on Line 1 of Schedule B the full amount shown on the 1099-INT you received; after you list all your taxable interest items, subtract the amount of interest you reported to the other owners and label it "nominee distribution." Then show the result (total interest minus nominee distribution) on Line 2.

Original Issue Discount on Bonds

Original issue discount (OID) is a feature of bonds that are purchased for less than their face value. The discount, or the difference between the amount you paid for the bond and its "face value" (face value is the amount you get at maturity) is generally taxed as it is earned each year, even though you won't actually receive it until the bond matures. A zero-coupon bond is an example of a bond with OID. You don't have to report OID from U.S. Savings Bonds, or from bonds with a maturity of one year or less.

Generally, if you are deemed to receive OID you'll receive an information return (Form 1099-OID) from the issuer of the bond, or from the brokerage or other institution holding your bonds.

Save Money

Remember that your tax basis in the bond is increased by the amount of OID you report over all the years that you own it, thus reducing the amount of capital gains tax that will be due when you sell the bond.

Income from a bank certificate of deposit, or a similar type of instrument at another institution, that has a maturity longer than one year can also be considered a form of OID, but it's generally reported to you on Form 1099-INT.

Accrued Interest

If you purchased a bond between interest dates and paid some accrued interest to the seller, this interest is taxable to the seller. If you find that it has been reported to you on a 1099-INT Form, you should, as your last item reported in the Line 1 area of Schedule B, take a subtotal of all reported interest, and then subtract the amount of accrued interest that was paid and is rightfully taxable to others. Be sure to label the amount you subtract "accrued interest." The remainder of the interest will be reported on Line 2.

Amortizable Bond Premiums

If you paid a premium to buy a bond (that is, you paid more than the bond's face value, most likely because the bond's stated interest rate is higher than the current interest rate at the time you bought it), you can make the election to deduct a portion of the premium each year while you hold the bond.

If you make this election, you must make it for every bond you own and for every bond you purchase in the future, until you revoke the election. You'll probably need the assistance of your accountant or financial advisor in determining the amount of amortization to deduct. If the bond was acquired after 1987, you can deduct this amount from the rest of your interest income on Line 1 of Schedule B. Take a subtotal of your interest income, subtract the amortizable bond premium (label it "ABP") and report the remaining interest on Line 2.

If the bond is a tax-exempt issue, you *must* amortize any premium you paid in your own records, but you can't deduct the amortization. Instead, it will reduce your tax basis in the bond and will potentially increase your capital gains when you sell the bond.

Savings Bonds Used for Higher Education

If you redeemed Series E or EE U.S. Savings Bonds in 1999 to pay higher education expenses you had this year, you may be able to avoid paying tax on the bond interest.

The operative word here is "may." There are a lot of restrictions and requirements on this tax break, and many people find that it doesn't actually help them.

The first requirement is that the bonds must have been issued in 1990 or later, to a person who was at least 24 years old before the bond's issue date.

Save Time

The "24 or older at the time the bond was issued" rule eliminates all those bonds your children may have received when they were born or at birthdays, graduations, or other milestone events. In effect, it usually means that the parents must be the owners of bonds used to pay for their children's education.

Also, to qualify for the tax break, your income (not your child's, even if he or she is the one in college) must be below certain limits. For singles or heads of households, in 1999 the tax break begins to be phased out at $53,100 of AGI and is completely phased out at $68,100. For marrieds filing jointly, the phaseout begins at $79,650 and is complete at $109,650. Marrieds filing separately can't claim the exclusion at all.

If you can meet these requirements, a bond that was issued in your name or your spouse's name qualifies if you paid higher education expenses for yourself, your spouse, or your dependent children. Qualified education expenses include only tuition and fees – not room and board. However, as of 1998 you can include any contribution you make to a qualified state prepaid tuition program as an educational expense.

The qualified educational expenses must be reduced by any nontaxable scholarships, veterans' education assistance, benefits under a qualified state tuition program, or nontaxable employer-paid education benefits. Also, you cannot use the same expenses to qualify for the savings bond exclusion and either the Hope credit or the Lifetime Learning credit (see page 287).

Then, compare your qualified education expenses with the total amount of proceeds from any savings bonds you redeemed – "proceeds" includes principal as well as interest. If the total proceeds are less than your total qualified expenses, you can exclude all the interest on the bonds.

If the total proceeds were more than the total expenses, you can only exclude some of the interest. To find out how much, divide your qualified expenses by the total bond proceeds to get a percentage, and multiply that percentage by the interest you received on the bonds. That's the amount of interest you can exclude, unless you're subject to the AGI limits.

If your AGI is within the phaseout range, take your AGI, subtract the bottom rung of the phaseout range (see above), and divide the result by $15,000 if single, or $30,000 if married. The resulting percentage is multiplied by your excludible interest (as calculated in the preceding paragraph), and the result is the amount of the exclusion you lose because your AGI was too high.

The exemption must be computed on IRS Form 8815, *Exclusion of Interest From Series EE U.S. Savings Bonds Issued After 1989*, which must be attached to your Form 1040 or 1040A.

Work Smart

If you claim this exclusion, make sure that you retain records such as tuition bills, cancelled checks, or credit card statements showing the amount of your qualified higher education expenses. You'll also need to keep a record of the bonds you redeemed including the serial number, issue date, face value, and redemption proceeds. You can use optional IRS Form 8818 to keep this record (call 1-800-TAX-FORM or go to the IRS's website at www.irs.gov to get a copy).

DIVIDENDS

If you received dividends from a corporation in which you owned stock, they will generally be reported to you on a copy of IRS Form 1099-DIV. The ordinary dividends you received are shown in Box 1 on the form. However, you must report all dividends you receive even if you don't receive the 1099-DIV, for example, if you took some distributions from your small C corporation business that should be treated as dividends, not salary.

You'll also receive a Form 1099-DIV from mutual funds or real estate investment trusts (REITs) that pay dividends during the year. If the total amount of all ordinary dividends you received for 1999 from all sources is $400 or less, you don't have to itemize your dividends on Schedule B of Form 1040 or Schedule 1 of Form 1040A. If they totaled more than $400, you must complete Part II of the Schedule B or Schedule 1.

An exception to the $400 dollar rule applies if you received some dividends as a nominee (that is, some dividends were reported as income to you on a 1099-DIV form, but they really belonged to another taxpayer who is not your spouse, perhaps because you were joint owners of the account). In that case, you must complete Part II even if total dividends were less than $400; show your total dividends received, and then subtract the amounts you reported to the nominees on another 1099-DIV. The net result will be the total taxable dividends.

If you did receive dividends as a nominee, you'll have to send a 1099-DIV to the actual owner(s) of the dividends by February 1, plus a copy to the IRS along with Form 1096 by March 1. If you need to file these forms, you must use official forms printed with special, machine-readable ink – you can't use paper forms that you downloaded from the Internet and printed from your home computer.

Call the IRS at 1-800-TAX-FORM and ask them to send you copies of the official forms.

What are "Dividends"?

Some items that you might think of as interest are treated by the IRS as dividends, and vice versa. For example, distributions by money market mutual funds are considered "dividends," but ordinary distributions by tax-free municipal bond mutual funds are treated as "interest." See the discussion on page 222.

As of 1998, "ordinary dividends" you received from mutual funds reported in Box 1 of the 1099-DIV *do not* include the amount of any long-term capital gains distributions (i.e., net gains from sales of securities by the fund, which are passed through to the shareholders). Instead, these capital gains distributions are reported to you in Box 2, and you report them directly on Schedule D, *Capital Gains and Losses*, Line 13. This allows you to more easily compute your tax at the special, lower long-term capital gains rate on Schedule D.

You must report and pay tax on the gross amount of all the ordinary dividends you were entitled to receive, even if you never actually received them because you reinvested them through a common-stock dividend reinvestment plan (DRIP) or a mutual fund reinvestment plan. If you paid any commissions or fees for reinvesting, you may be able to deduct them as investment expenses– see page 241.

Save Money

If you do reinvest dividends, make sure that you keep track of them by saving the annual statements on which they are reported. If you keep good records, when you sell the investment, you'll be able to add the reinvested amounts to your basis in the investment, and pay less in capital gains tax. If you lose your records, in some cases the issuer of the stock or mutual fund will be able to tell you what your reinvestments were, but they might not be able to locate records that go back as far as you need.

If you sold stock after a dividend was declared, but before it was paid, you are still treated as having received the dividend, and you must pay tax on it.

Nontaxable Distributions

Some of the amounts reported to you on Form 1099-DIV will not be taxable, because they are really a return of your original investment, or a return of capital. If you received this type of distribution, it will generally be reported in Box 3. Once you have received all capital you paid in to the investment, any further amounts will be taxable income.

While return of capital amounts will not appear on your tax return, you should keep a record of them, since they must be used to reduce your basis in the stock when you sell.

Stock dividends and distributions. If a corporation of which you're a shareholder pays dividends in the form of shares of stock, or spins off a subsidiary and gives all shareholders of record some shares in the newly created company, the distribution is not taxable until you sell the shares at some point down the road.

An exception to this rule applies if you receive stock or stock options or rights when you or any other shareholder had the choice between receiving such rights or cash, or when different shareholders receive different types of stock or stock options. In that case, the stock or options would be taxable at their fair market value. For more information on this subject, see the IRS's free Publication 550, *Investment Income and Expenses*.

Liquidating distributions. If the corporation is being liquidated, you may receive payments shown in Boxes 8 or 9 of Form 1099-DIV. These are nontaxable distributions to the extent that they repay your basis in the investment. If you receive more than your basis, the excess will be considered capital gains. If you ultimately receive less than your basis, you may have a deductible capital loss. See the discussion of gains and losses beginning on page 227.

Dividends on an insurance policy. Occasionally, certain forms of insurance companies send "dividends" to their policy holders, generally in years when the company has taken in more premium payments than it needs for operating expenses, reserves, and benefit payouts. These dividends are treated as a rebate of premiums you paid and are not taxable as dividends on Schedule B.

FOREIGN INVESTMENT ACCOUNTS AND TRUSTS

While we're on the subject of Schedule B, if you were required to complete Part I or II of Schedule B because you had more than $400 in interest payments or ordinary dividend distributions in 1999, you must also complete Part III. Also, every taxpayer who had a foreign account or was a beneficiary, grantor, or transferor to a foreign trust must complete Part III.

Part III asks you to answer "yes" or "no" to two questions. The first question is, did you, at any time during the tax year, have an interest in or signature or other authority over a bank account, securities account, or other financial account? However, do not check the "yes" box if the combined value of the accounts was $10,000 or less during the year; if the accounts were with a U.S. military banking facility; or if you are an officer or employee of a commercial bank supervised by a U.S. agency, or of a domestic corporation listed on a national exchange or with assets of more than $1 million or with at least 500 shareholders, and you had no personal interest in the account.

Otherwise, check the "yes" box if you own more than half of the stock in a company that owns one or more foreign bank accounts, or you directly own or have an interest in such an account. This does not include foreign securities held in a U.S. securities account.

If you checked the "yes" box, you must write the name of the country or countries on Line 7b, and also file Form TD F 90-22.1, *Report of Foreign Bank and Financial Accounts*, with the Treasury Department by June 30, 2000. This is not a tax form, so don't attach it to your tax return. You can still get a copy of this form by calling 1-800-TAX-FORM, or you can download it from the IRS's website at www.irs.gov.

The second question is, did you receive a distribution from, or were you the grantor of or transferor to, a foreign trust? You may have to file IRS Form 3520, *Annual Return to Report Transactions with Foreign Trusts and Receipt of Certain Foreign Gifts*. This form can get complicated, so we suggest that you check with your tax advisor if you think it may apply to you.

Foreign Tax Credit

If you paid taxes to a foreign country, either directly or through a conduit such as a mutual fund, you may be entitled to a tax credit. Generally you have the option of claiming foreign taxes as an itemized deduction on Schedule A, or claiming the foreign tax credit on Form 1116, *Foreign Tax Credit*.

Save Time

Claiming the credit will nearly always save you more money, but this form is relatively lengthy and complicated to fill out, so it might not be worthwhile unless you've paid large amounts in foreign taxes. For more information, get IRS Publication 514, Foreign Tax Credit for Individuals.

STOCK, BOND, AND OTHER CAPITAL ASSET SALES

If you sold any stocks, bonds, options, or other securities; a home or other real estate; art, antiques, rugs, jewelry, precious metals, other collectibles, or property used in a trade or business or used to generate income; or if you had any capital gains distributions from mutual funds or REITs; you will have to complete and file Schedule D, *Capital Gains and Losses*, and file it with your Form 1040. You won't be able to use either the 1040A or the 1040EZ form.

Some of these items are first reported on another tax form, and then the results computed on that form are transferred to the appropriate line of Schedule D.

Example

Sales of property used in a trade or business, including business real estate, must first be reported on IRS Form 4797. See Chapter 7 for a discussion of the rules that apply to these kinds of assets. Form 8824 is used to report like-kind exchanges (see page 103), and Form 6252 is used to report installment sales (see page 121). All of these forms will separate your long-term gains and losses from your short-term gains and losses, and they will generally require you to transfer the amounts to Part I (short-term) and Part II (long-term) of the Schedule D. Short-term gain or loss from Form 4797, however, is transferred directly to Line 14 of Form 1040.

For special rules related to the sale of your home, see page 210.

Capital Gains Tax Rate

The advantage of capital gains, as opposed to ordinary income, is that the basic maximum tax rate on capital gains for property held for more than one year is 20 percent, and the maximum is only 10 percent for taxpayers who'd otherwise be in the 15 percent bracket. In contrast, ordinary income can be taxed at 28, 31, 36, or 39.6 percent.

Work Smart

You may recall that in 1997, depending on when the sale occurred, there was a special category of "mid-term gains" that were taxed at 28 percent if the property was held for more than one year but no more than 18 months, while property held for more than 18 months was considered "long-term" and gains on it were taxed at 20 percent.

Beginning in 1998, thankfully, all gains held for more than one year are taxed at the long-term rate, and we no longer have to compute any mid-term gains.

There are some situations where other rates will apply to gains on certain types of property. The long-term capital gains rate on business or investment real estate (called "section 1250 property" on the tax forms) will be 25 percent up to the amount of depreciation on the property while you owned it. Also, the long-term capital gains rate on collectibles such as art, rugs, jewelry, precious metals or gemstones, stamps or coins, fine wines, or antiques is 28 percent.

For small business owners, capital gains has another advantage worth mentioning. Unlike the money you earn in your business, capital gains are not subject to the 15.3 percent self-employment tax. However, if a major activity of your business is buying or selling property that would be capital gains property in the hands of the average taxpayer – for example, you're a dealer in coins or stamps, or you're a real estate developer – you will have to treat your gains on sales as ordinary business income, reported on Schedule C rather than Schedule D. In that case, you would be subject to self-employment tax on these gains.

Computing Capital Gains

Generally, the proceeds of any stock, bond, or other securities you sold during 1999 will be reported to you on IRS Form 1099-B by the brokerage or financial institution that carried out the sale for you. The form will state the proceeds from the sale in Box 2 (except for certain futures contracts, reported in Boxes 6 – 9).

The institution may choose to report the gross proceeds, or the net proceeds (gross proceeds minus any commissions, option premiums, state or local transfer taxes, brokers' fees, etc.), in Box 2. Next to the amount reported, the appropriate box for the method used should be checked. If the broker reported net proceeds, you can simply enter the amount shown for each item in column (d) of Part I or II, Schedule D; otherwise, you'll have to check the broker's statements or other notices or documents you've received to determine the amount of commissions and other transaction costs you can deduct.

In the most general terms, your net proceeds, minus your tax basis for the item, will be the amount of capital gains you must report.

For each item you sold, you'll be asked to give a short description of the item (such as "100 shares of IBM common stock"), the date purchased, the date sold, the sales price, the cost or other basis, and the gain or loss you realized. If you run out of space on Schedule D, you can use Schedule D-1, *Continuation Sheet for Schedule D*, or you can create your own continuation sheet by repeating all the column headings on another piece of paper.

Which Asset Sales Are Reported?

Sales of inventory or other items held as stock-in-trade in your business are not considered capital assets. Sales of this type of property are reported on Schedule C or C-EZ (see page 47). Similarly, sales of accounts receivable or notes you received in the ordinary course of business are reported on Schedule C, as are any sales of copyrighted literary or musical compositions or artwork you created.

If you have a gain on property held for personal use such as a home, car, furnishings, clothing, etc. it will be taxable on Schedule D (but see page 210 regarding the exemption for gains on personal residences); if you have a loss, you can't deduct it. If you do have a loss on non-real estate property held for personal use, you don't have to report the sale at all.

Virtually any property that you hold as an investment will generate a taxable gain, or a deductible loss, that should be reported on Schedule D, or on one of the more specialized forms that feed into Schedule D:

- Form 4797, for sales of property used in a trade or business (see Chapter 7)

- Form 4684, for involuntary conversions due to casualties or theft (see page 267)

- Form 8824, if you made one or more like-kind exchanges (see page 103)

- Form 6781, if you had gains or losses from Section 1256 contracts and straddles (these are generally regulated futures contracts, foreign currency contracts, and certain options contracts, or hedging positions; for more information, see IRS Publication 550, *Investment Income and Expenses*)

- Form 6252, if you received payments for the asset over more than one year (but installment sale treatment is not permitted for stocks, bonds, and other securities sold by cash-basis taxpayers); see page 121

What Counts as a "Sale"?

Generally, if you receive money or other property in exchange for your asset, a sale has occurred and Uncle Sam will want a cut.

A redemption of stock, or a redemption or retirement of a bond, is considered a sale, and should be reported even if you have no gains or losses on the transaction (for instance, if you held a bond until maturity and received an amount exactly equal to your tax basis).

You can have a taxable gain caused by a casualty loss, although this can generally be avoided by purchasing replacement property for the items that were damaged or destroyed – see page 267 for more details.

Also, if stock, stock options or rights, or bonds that you owned became worthless, you may have a deductible loss. The "sale" is treated as occurring on the last day of the year in which the item became worthless, which means that your holding period (for determining whether the loss was short- or long-term) ends on December 31. If this applies to you, on the line where you report the sale, write "worthless" in Columns (c) and (d) of Part I or II, Schedule D, which is the space provided for the date and amount of the sale).

Save Money

If you learned this year that securities you own became worthless in some earlier year, you can file an amended tax return on Form 1040X for the year in which the investment became worthless, and deduct the loss. You must claim the deduction within seven years of the due date of your return for loss year, or within two years of the date you paid taxes for that year, whichever is later.

Bad debts. Occasionally, a taxpayer may be able to take a deduction for a bad debt not related to their trade or business. However, in order to deduct a nonbusiness bad debt, you must already have some basis in the debt – that is, you must have loaned out your cash, or you must already have included some expected money in your income. If you're a cash-basis taxpayer, you can't deduct a bad debt if someone merely reneges on a promise to pay you some income such as wages, rent, fees, interest, or dividends, unless you had already included the amount in taxable income (although you might be able to deduct the expense you had in earning this income). You should also have some documentation that the debt exists, such as a signed promissory note or loan agreement.

If you do have a deductible bad debt, you would record it as a short-term capital loss on Line 1, Part I of Schedule D. Enter the name of the debtor, and write "statement attached." Be sure to attach a statement to your tax return that shows the name of the debtor, and any business or family relationship you have with him or her; a description of the debt, the date it became due, and the amount; the efforts you made to collect it; and why you decided it was completely worthless (e.g., the debtor went bankrupt or legal action to collect would probably not result in any payment).

You can only deduct a nonbusiness bad debt in the year it became totally worthless; however, if you discover that a debt had become worthless in an earlier year, you can file an amended tax return within seven years of the due date for that year's taxes. Use Form 1040X.

Nontaxable transactions. There are a few types of transactions that are not considered taxable events. For one thing, if you redeem shares of a money market mutual fund, it's not a taxable event because the value of each share is fixed at $1. Your redemption price for each share will be exactly the same as your tax basis in each share, so no gain or loss is recognized.

Any transfer of property from one spouse to another, either while married, or incident to a divorce or separation agreement, is not taxable. Generally, the spouse receiving the property must continue using the same tax basis as the property had in the hands of the donor spouse (which means that the recipient will eventually get stuck with the capital gains tax bill when the property is sold).

Exchanging one life insurance policy for another or for an endowment or annuity contract, exchanging an endowment contract for an annuity contract or for another endowment contract that provides for regular payments beginning no later than the date on the original contract, or exchanging one annuity contract for another is not a taxable event, as long as the insured person or annuitant is the same under both the old contract and the new one.

Certain types of stock trades are not taxable events:

- exchanges of stock for other stock in the same corporation, as long as the exchange is common stock for common, or preferred stock for preferred, whether the trade is between two stockholders or between the corporation itself and a stockholder

- exchanges of stock for other stock in the same or a different corporation that occur because of a merger, acquisition, recapitalization, or some other form of reorganization, provided certain rules are followed

- conversion of a convertible bond into stock shares, or convertible preferred into common shares, according to the terms of the security

- transfers of property to a corporation in exchange for stock in the corporation, if you (or your group of investors) own at least 80 percent of the corporation after the transfer (for small businesses, this generally means that incorporating your business is not a taxable event)

Aside from these listed exceptions, you can't treat a trade of one type of stock, bond, note, beneficial interest, or partnership interest for another as a nontaxable like-kind exchange.

However, if you exchange other types of business or investment property (such as a store for an apartment building, a car for a truck, etc.), you may be able to avoid tax on the exchange if certain rules are met. In most cases we'd advise you to see a professional tax advisor to make sure that your transaction qualifies under the "like-kind exchange" rules and that you retain proper records, including the tax basis of the new property you receive, for the transaction.

What Is the Basis?

The starting point for determining the tax basis of an asset you purchased is its cost, plus any commissions or other transaction fees you pay on the sale.

If you didn't purchase the asset, determining the basis can be more complicated.

If you received property from your spouse, you'll take the same basis that your spouse had before the transfer.

If you received property in a nontaxable exchange, your basis will generally be the same as that of the asset(s) you gave up, plus any cash you added into the bargain.

If you received property as a bequest or inheritance, your basis will be the fair market value of the property on the date of death, or on the alternative valuation date if the decedent's executor chooses to use that date for estate tax purposes. Special valuation rules may apply to a farm or a closely-held business, but generally, the value shown on the estate tax return is the value that you must use. If there was no estate tax return, you may need to have the property appraised.

Save Time

For securities traded on a national exchange, you won't need an appraisal, and values are usually readily available for any date you need — consult your attorney or accountant for information.

If you received property in exchange for services, the fair market value of the property was taxable to you at the time you received it, and that FMV is the property's basis. If your right to receive the property was restricted or not fully vested, your basis will generally be the FMV at the time you no longer have a substantial risk of forfeiting it, unless you elected to pay tax on the property at an earlier point in time. For more information, see IRS Publication 525, *Taxable and Nontaxable Income.*

If you received property as a gift, your basis will generally be the same basis that the donor had at the time the gift was made. There is an exception to this rule if the fair market value of the property was lower than the donor's basis at the time the gift was made, and if you sell the property at a loss. In that case, you must use the FMV at the time of the gift.

Example

The rule described above can sometimes lead to a strange result.

Let's say your uncle made you a gift of some investment property having an adjusted basis of $10,000 at the time of the gift. The FMV at the time of the gift was $9,000. You later sell the property for $9,500. Your basis for figuring gain would be the donor's basis, or $10,000, but considering your sales price of $9,500, you would not have a gain. However, your basis for figuring loss would be the FMV or $9,000, but considering your sales price of $9,500 you would not have a loss.

In this case, you don't have a taxable gain or a loss. When reporting the sale on Schedule D, list the item's basis as being the same amount as the sales proceeds.

Adjustments to Basis

Stocks, bonds, and collectibles are not subject to depreciation deductions, unlike real estate investments and assets used in your trade or business. However, you may need to make some other types of adjustments to the tax basis of this kind of asset while you hold it.

If you deducted the amortization of bond premiums (see page 224), the deductions will reduce your basis in the bond. Conversely, if you were required to report original issue discount (OID) as income (see page 224) you should increase the basis of the bond to reflect the amounts you included as income.

If you received corporate dividends in the form of stock, the additional shares (or fractions of shares) were not taxable when you received them, but as a result of the distribution, you will have to recompute your basis in the shares you own. A similar computation is necessary if stock that you own splits.

Basically, to compute the new basis of your shares, you take your existing basis in the investment, and divide it among the shares you now own as a result of the distribution or split.

Example

Flo Plummer originally bought 100 shares for a net $50 per share after commissions, so her original basis for the investment is $5,000. After several years the shares split 3-for-2, and she now has 150 shares. Her total basis has remained the same — $5,000 — but since it is now spread over more shares, her basis in each share is $33.33.

Reinvested shares. If you participate in a dividend reinvestment plan of a corporation or a mutual fund, don't forget to add the amount of all your reinvested dividends over the years to the basis of your investment. Otherwise, you'll be taxed twice on the dividends: once when you receive them as income, and once when you sell them as capital gains.

What Is the Holding Period?

As we've mentioned above, long-term gains (on property held more than one year) are taxed at a special lower rate, generally at no more than 20 percent; gains on property held for one year or less is taxed at your ordinary income tax rate, which may be as high as 39.6 percent. Short-term gains are reported in Part I of Schedule D, and long-term gains are reported in Part II.

Save Money

When counting the days that you held the property, the holding period begins on the day after you bought the property, or the day after the trade date for stocks and other securities sold in an established market. This can be a trap for the unwary — try to avoid selling investments exactly one year after you bought them, or you'll end up with short-term, not long-term, gain.

If you acquired property in a nontaxable trade, your holding period for the property will begin on the day following the date you acquired the original property that you gave up in the trade.

If you received property by gift and your basis is determined by your donor's basis (see page 230), your holding period begins when the donor acquired the property. If you must use the FMV at the time of the gift as your basis, your holding period begins when you received the gift.

If you received the property by bequest or inheritance, your holding period is always considered "long term" and you will get the benefit of the lower tax rate on capital gains even if you sell the property the day after you receive it.

Warning

If you are selling inherited property within one year of receiving it, report it as a sale of long-term property in Part II of Schedule D, and write "INHERITED" in Column (b) instead of the date you received the property. Otherwise, the IRS may question your long-term treatment.

If you sell stock that you acquired as part of a spin-off or stock dividend, your holding period begins on the same date as the original investment.

Multiple Stock Purchases on Different Days

If you've made more than one purchase of shares of the same company's stock or the same mutual fund, perhaps because you were participating in a dividend reinvestment plan, or because you were dollar-cost averaging by making regular periodic investments over an extended period of time, determining the basis and the holding period of the shares sold can be more complicated.

If you sold the entire investment and you stopped reinvesting dividends more than a year before the sale, it's fairly simple. The entire gain will be considered long-term, to be reported in Part II of Schedule D. Just total up the costs of all the purchases you made over the years (less any transaction costs) and that will be your tax basis, to be entered in Column (e). In Column (b), write "various" instead of all the dates you actually purchased shares.

If you continued to reinvest income or make purchases up to the date of sale, you can follow the same procedure described above, except that any dividends reinvested or purchases made within the

last year will be reported in Part I of Schedule D for short-term gains. Total up these dividends or purchases and use that amount as the cost basis for the short-term portion of the gains. Then multiply the number of shares (including fractional shares) purchased with those dividends by the price per share on the date of sale, and use that amount as the sales proceeds (Column (d)) to arrive at your short-term gains.

If you sold only part of your investment, and you purchased shares at various times during the year(s), you may have a choice as to which shares you can treat as the ones you sold. If, before the sale, you inform your broker or financial institution as to which specific shares you want to sell, you can treat those specifically identified shares as the ones that were sold. This gives you the opportunity to plan (some would say manipulate) the timing and amount of your gains.

Example

If, at various times over the course of several years, you purchased 100 shares of AT&T at $35, 200 shares at $42, and 100 shares at $55, and you now want to sell 200 shares, you can tell your broker to sell the most recently purchased shares. In that case, your tax basis would be 100 x $42 plus 100 x $55 = $9,700. However, if the most recent purchase was less than one year ago, you would probably prefer to tell the broker to sell the 200 shares purchased at $42, to take advantage of the lower tax rate.

If you don't specifically identify the shares of stock that you sold, the IRS requires you to assume that the shares you sold were the first ones you purchased. Since over time, stock prices tend to rise, this first-in, first-out (FIFO) method tends to result in higher gains reporting. It's not surprising that the IRS prefers it. On the upside, it will usually result in your reporting long-term gains if at all possible, rather than short-term gains.

If you own shares in a mutual fund and want to sell some, but not all, of them, it will be very difficult, if not impossible, to ask the fund in advance to sell specific shares. You can use FIFO to determine your basis and holding period for the shares you sell.

However, you can also use something called "average cost basis," which is an average of the prices you paid for all shares you own at the time of the sale. Many mutual fund companies will automatically calculate average cost at the time of the sale, and if they do, this is an easy way to report your sale. If it's not automatically calculated, however, it can be very difficult to compute.

Once you choose a method for selecting the shares you sold in a partial sale (e.g., FIFO, specific identification, or average cost), you must stick with it for that particular investment. For more information, see IRS Publication 564, *Mutual Fund Distributions.*

Capital Gains Distributions

If you own shares in a mutual fund or real estate investment trust (REIT) that pays out capital gains to shareholders every year or so, these amounts are also reported on Schedule D. The mutual fund company will report the long-term gains on sales of securities during the year, and report them in Box 2a of Form 1099-DIV. Any short-term gains are included in the amount of ordinary dividends, and they are simply taxed as dividends.

So, total up your capital gain distributions and report them all on Line 13 of Schedule D. If your only reason for filing Schedule D would be to report capital gains from Box 2a of one or more 1099-DIVs, you can instead report the gains on Line 13 of Form 1040. However, in that case you must figure your tax using the worksheet on page 32 of the 1040 Instructions to get the benefit of the special 20% tax rate on capital gains.

Undistributed Capital Gains

Some mutual funds and REITs keep their long-term gains and pay tax on them, rather than distributing them to shareholders. If you've invested in one of these, you'll receive an IRS Form 2439, *Notice to Shareholder of Undistributed Long-Term Capital Gains.* Attach Copy B to your Form 1040.

Your undistributed capital gains will appear in Box 1a of the Form 2439, and it will be reported on Line 11 of Schedule D. You can claim a tax credit for the amount of tax paid by the fund or REIT on Line 63 of your Form 1040. Just check Box "a" indicating that the payment was shown on Form 2439.

Save Money

You should also keep a copy of Form 2439 in your records, so that when you sell the investment, *you can increase its tax basis by the difference between the gain you reported over the years, and the tax credit you claimed. If you do, it will reduce the amount of capital gains you report for the sale.*

Special Situations

There are several types of transactions or situations that call into play a number of more technical rules. In some cases, the special rules will operate to disallow the tax break for capital gains. If any of the situations discussed below (sales to related parties, wash sales, short sales, commodity sales, straddles, or gains on qualified small business stock) apply to you, you may need the assistance of a tax professional to sort out the facts and make sure that you pay the least possible amount of tax.

Sales to Related Parties

If you sell capital assets to a close family member, or to a business entity that you own or control, you might not get all the benefits of the capital gains tax rates, and you might not be able to deduct all of your losses.

Gain on sale of depreciable property. If you sell property to a corporation or partnership of which you directly or indirectly have more than 50 percent of the control, and the property is depreciable in the hands of the party who receives it, the gain will be taxed at ordinary rates, rather than the special lower capital gains tax rate.

Losses on sales or trades of property. If you sell or trade property at a loss, other than in the complete liquidation of a corporation, you can't deduct the loss if the transaction is directly or indirectly between you and the following types of related parties:

- members of your family, including your spouse, siblings or half-siblings, ancestors, or descendants

- a partnership or corporation in which you control more than 50 percent of the interests

- a tax-exempt or charitable organization controlled by you or a member of your family

Losses on sales between certain closely related trusts or business entities controlled by the same owners are also disallowed. If you sell multiple pieces of property, and some are at a gain while others are at a loss, the gains will generally be taxable while the losses cannot be used to offset the gains. What's more, when the related person or entity sells the item, he or she (or it) won't be allowed to deduct, as a capital loss, the amount of losses that were disallowed to the original seller.

Like-kind exchanges. If you trade business or investment property to a related party, ordinarily no gain or loss is recognized (under the usual rules – see page 103). However, if the related party sells the property he or she received within two years, both parties will be taxable on any gains they deferred through the exchange. This two-year rule does not apply if the sale occurred because of the death of either related person, an involuntary conversion (due to casualty loss, condemnation, etc.), or if the parties can establish that the main purpose of the exchange and later sale were not mainly designed to avoid taxes.

Wash Sales

If you sold any stock, bonds, or stock options at a loss and then purchased substantially identical securities within 30 days before or after the sale, the loss on the sale will not be deductible. Essentially, it will be ignored because your sale was a "wash." However, you can add the disallowed loss to the basis of your new investment, so that you are not in a worse position than you were before the sale. Moreover, you can add your holding period for the old stock to that of the new stock, for purposes of determining the holding period when you eventually sell the new investment.

Short Sales, Commodity Sales, and Straddles

A short sale occurs when you sell property that you don't actually have, or don't wish to part with at the present time. The sale occurs in two steps. First you make the sale, and then at some later date, you close the sale by either buying the promised property and delivering it to the buyer, or giving up some property you already own.

Generally, a short sale is taxable at the time the property is delivered (the second step, above). The amount of time you actually held the property delivered to the buyer determines whether it's a long-term or short-term gain or loss.

A straddle is any set of offsetting positions on personal property (generally, stock or other securities). For example, a straddle can consist of a call option and a put option written at the same time on the same number of shares. Generally, you can deduct a loss on one position only to the extent that it exceeds unrecognized gains you have in offsetting positions.

The wash sale rules take on special significance in the context of short sales. Moreover, numerous other technical rules apply to short sales, straddles, and to sales of options and commodities. If you are involved in any of these types of investments, we suggest you talk to your tax advisor or get the IRS's free Publication 550, *Investment Income and Expenses,* for more information.

Qualified Small-Business Stock

A special tax break is designed to help qualifying small businesses raise capital by allowing long-term noncorporate investors in original issue stock to cut the tax on their profit. If a five-year holding period is met, qualifying investors can exclude 50 percent of their gains. The nonexcluded portion is taxed at the maximum rate of 28 percent, for an effective tax rate of 14 percent. However, one-half of the excluded gain is a preference item for AMT purposes (see page 301).

In order to qualify for this special break, taxpayers must jump through a large number of hoops.

Qualifying for the Small-Business Stock Exclusion

The 50 percent capital gains exclusion applies only to gain on eligible stock (1) originally issued by a qualifying corporation after August 10, 1993, and (2) held for more than five years. The highlights of this break follow:

- The stock must be acquired in an exchange for money or other property (other than stock), or as compensation for services provided to the corporation (other than acting as the stock's underwriter).

- The small business must be a regular C corporation; it must have $50 million or less in aggregate capital as of the date of stock issuance; and at least 80 percent by value of corporate assets must be used in the active conduct of one or more trades or businesses.

- The corporation cannot be involved in the performance of personal services (such as health or law) or in the finance, banking, leasing, real estate, farming, mineral extraction, or hospitality industries. A number of other types of businesses, such as mutual funds and REITs, are also disqualified.

- The exclusion for each eligible corporation applies only to the extent that the gain does not exceed the greater of (1) 10 times the taxpayer's adjusted basis in the stock disposed of during the tax year (post-issuance additions to basis are disregarded), or (2) $10 million ($5 million for marrieds filing separately), reduced by gain excluded in earlier years from sales of stock in the corporation.

- Although a post-issuance purchaser of otherwise qualified stock doesn't get the exclusion, the tax break is preserved for those who receive such stock as a gift or due to the death of the original purchaser. The transferor's holding period also carries over to the transferee. Similar rules apply to qualified stock distributed by a partnership to its partners.

- Individuals can roll over, tax-free, gain realized on the sale or exchange of qualified small business stock provided that the proceeds are used to purchase other qualified small business stock within 60 days of the sale.

Netting Short-Term and Long-Term Gains and Losses

We're into the final stretch of the Schedule D, the part where you actually compute your gains and losses.

In Part I of Schedule D, you'll net your short-term gains and losses from sales of investment assets, as well as any from bad debts, casualty losses, installment sales, and like-kind exchanges, and also from partnerships, S corporations, or estates and trusts as reported on Schedule K-1 (see page 237). You'll also net any carryovers of short-term losses from previous years. By "netting" we mean that your total short-term losses are subtracted from your total short-term gains, and the result will be a net gain or loss.

Then, in Part II of Schedule D, you go through the same process with your long-term gains and losses. In Part II you are required to report separately (in Column (g)) any long-term gains or losses from art, jewelry, antiques, precious metals, etc., which are termed "collectibles," and up to 50 percent of the eligible gain on qualified small business stock (see page 234), which are taxed at a 28 percent rate. The result will be a net long-term gain or loss.

Then, you net your short-term gain or loss against your long-term gain or loss.

Gains. If the result is a gain, it must be reported on Line 13 of the 1040 Form. Then, go on to complete the rest of your 1040 Form. After you complete the rest of your income, adjustments, and deductions, and you're ready to figure out the actual amount of tax you owe, you must come back to Part IV of the Schedule D to compute your taxes using the special lower rates for various types of capital gains.

Part IV of Schedule D looks much more daunting that it actually is. You must follow the directions for each line, to the letter, but if you do that you'll effectively separate out any gains on collectibles and eligible small business stock, or on unrecaptured real estate depreciation, and tax them at 28 percent and 25 percent, respectively. The computations will also help you find out whether you're in the 15 percent bracket and, if so, tax your long-term capital gains at only 10 percent. If you're in a higher tax bracket, Part IV will apply the 20 percent rate and give you the exact amount of tax you owe.

A note on Line 25, which asks for your unrecaptured section 1250 gain, if any: This refers to depreciation you claimed on business or investment real estate over the years. If you invested in any REITs or mutual funds that invest directly in real estate, the amounts you need will be shown in Box 2c of Form 1099-DIV.

If you sold any business or commercial real estate last year, you'll need to see the directions for Schedule D in order to complete this item. If you didn't receive a copy with your IRS tax package and instructions, you can get a copy by calling 1-800-TAX-FORM.

Losses. If you subtract your losses from your gains and the net result is a loss, you can claim a capital loss on your tax return. Transfer the loss amount to Line 13 of your Form 1040, and enclose it in parentheses to indicate that it should be subtracted from your other income items.

If your capital loss for 1999 is more than $3,000 (more than $1,500 for marrieds filing separately), you may not be able to deduct the entire loss. In most cases any amount above $3,000 will have to be carried over to later years, and deducted at the rate of $3,000 per year until the entire loss is used up. When you carry over a loss, it retains its character as short-term or long-term. The worksheet included below will help you to calculate your carryover amounts.

Save Money

When you complete the worksheet, be sure to keep a copy in your records so that you remember to deduct the carryover loss next year, and so that you have proof of the amounts in case you are audited.

Capital Loss Carryover Worksheet—Line 18
(keep for your records)

Use this worksheet to figure your capital loss carryovers from 1999 to 2000 if Schedule D, line 18, is a loss and **(a)** that loss is a smaller loss than the loss on Schedule D, line 17, **or (b)** Form 1040, line 37, is a loss. Otherwise, you do not have any carryovers.

1. Enter the amount from Form 1040, line 37. If a loss, enclose the amount in parentheses . . . .   1. _____

2. Enter the loss from Schedule D, line 18, as a positive amount . . . .   2. _____

3. Combine lines 1 and 2. If zero or less, enter -0- . . .   3. _____

4. Enter the **smaller** of line 2 or line 3 . . . .   4. _____

   Note: *If line 7 of Schedule D is a loss, go to line 5; otherwise, enter -0- on line 5 and go to line 9.*

5. Enter the loss from Schedule D, line 7, as a positive amount . . . .   5. _____

6. Enter any gain from Schedule D, line 16   **6.** _____

7. Add lines 4 and 6 . . . .   7. _____

8. **Short-term capital loss carryover to 2000.** Subtract line 7 from line 5. If zero or less, enter -0-. . . . . . .   8. _____

   Note: *If line 16 of Schedule D is a loss, go to line 9; otherwise, skip lines 9 through 13.*

9. Enter the loss from Schedule D, line 16, as a positive amount . . . .   9. _____

10. Enter any gain from Schedule D, line 7   **10.** _____

11. Subtract line 5 from line 4. If zero or less, enter -0- . . . .   **11.** _____

12. Add lines 10 and 11 . . . .   12. _____

13. **Long-term capital loss carryover to 2000.** Subtract line 12 from line 9. If zero or less, enter -0- . . . . . .   13. _____

INCOME FROM ESTATES AND TRUSTS

If you were a beneficiary of an estate or trust in 1999, the estate or trust will have to file its own income tax return on Form 1041. Then, each beneficiary's share of income, deductions, credits and other tax items is reported to him or her on a Schedule K-1. One copy of each K-1 is filed with the estate or trust's income tax return, and each beneficiary receives a copy of his or her own K-1.

If you receive a K-1 from an estate or trust, don't file it with your tax return. Instead, each item that is separately stated on the K-1 is transferred to the appropriate section of your own Form 1040. For example, Line 1 on the K-1, "Interest income," should be transferred to Line 1, Part I, of your own Schedule B.

For the average trust, most items on the K-1 consist of interest, dividends, and capital gains and will be transferred to your Schedules B and/or D. However, if the trust operates a business or some rental real estate, income from these activities will be reported on Part III of your Schedule E, *Supplemental Income and Loss.*

The K-1 form contains line-by-line instructions as to exactly where on your tax form each item must be reported. If you disagree with the treatment or amount of any item, you'll need to take it up with the trustee or other fiduciary who prepared the K-1s, and ask them to change their treatment on the copy filed with the IRS. If you can't reach an agreement, you can file IRS Form 8082, *Notice of Inconsistent Treatment or Administrative Adjustment Request,* to explain the discrepancy.

Note that the amounts reported to you on the K-1 may be different from the amounts you actually received. If the trust instrument requires that the beneficiaries be paid all current income, each beneficiary will be taxed on his or her own share, whether or not he or she has actually received it (for example, if there is a time lag and the fiduciary did not pay the income over until the tax returns were filed).

INCOME FROM PARTNERSHIPS, LLCS, AND S CORPORATIONS

A partnership is not a taxable business entity, but while it generally pays no tax on its income, it must file a tax return with the government on Form 1065, U.S. Partnership Return of Income. As part of the Form 1065, it will include a Schedule K-1 for each partner showing his or her share of all partnership tax items. The partner then must report these items on the appropriate line of his or her tax return, generally in Part II of Schedule E

Limited liability companies (LLCs) with multiple owners are treated as if they were partnerships under federal tax law, so they will also file for 1065 and give each LLC member a copy of his or her Schedule K-1.

Warning

While the partnership will report your share of any partnership losses on your K-1, you might not be able to deduct them all. Your deductions are generally limited to your tax basis: the amount you have invested in the partnership, plus your share of any partnership liabilities, net income or gains, and minus previous distributions to you. The partnership isn't responsible for keeping track of your tax basis as time passes; you are. However, the K-1s you receive over the years will generally provide a good foundation for your records.

S corporations may have to pay some tax in certain circumstances. For the most part, however, they follow the partnership pattern of passing through most items of income, deductions, credits, etc. to the shareholders through a K-1 form. The shareholders report these items on their own Form 1040, generally in Part II of Schedule E.

Passive activities. If you own a partnership, LLC or S corporation interest that is classified as a passive activity (see page 44) and you have losses for the year, you will have to complete Form 8582, *Passive Activity Loss Limitations,* to compute your allowable passive losses. Generally passive losses are allowed only to the extent that you have passive income for the year. Any amounts that are disallowed are generally deductible in full in the year you dispose of the activity. For more information, see IRS Publication 925, *Passive Activity and At-Risk Rules,* which can be obtained for free by calling 1-800-TAX-FORM or by accessing the IRS website at www.irs.gov.

ROYALTY INCOME

"Royalties" can generally be described as payments you receive for the use of your property, that are based in some way on the number of units sold.

The two types of royalties most commonly encountered are royalties for the use of copyrights, trademarks, and patents, and royalties from the extraction of oil, gas, or minerals from your property. However, other types of royalties are possible, such as those paid for the use of a name, the sale of products using certain proprietary processes, etc. In any case, income and deductions related to your royalties are generally reported on Schedule E, *Supplemental Income and Loss.*

However, if you are in business as a self-employed artist, author, photographer or inventor, and the royalties relate to a self-created copyright, trademark, or patent, you would report the payments as part of your business income on Schedule C.

Similarly, if you hold an operating oil, gas, or mineral interest in land, you would report your gross income and expenses on Schedule C or C-EZ. Numerous special rules apply to the ownership and taxation of mineral property, and they're beyond the scope of this book. If you own any investments of this nature, we recommend that you consult a qualified tax professional for details.

INCOME FROM REMICS

A real estate mortgage investment conduit (REMIC) is basically an entity formed to hold a number of mortgages secured by property, and to pay out the income to investors.

If you hold a "regular" interest in a REMIC, your investment income is treated as interest, and it will be reported to you on Form 1099-INT and Form 1099-

OID. You'll have to report any OID, or market discount that applies, under the rules for bonds discussed on page 224. The issuer should send you a notice with enough information to allow you to calculate the amounts to include in income. A "regular" interest is one that unconditionally entitles the holder to a specific principal amount. Any interest payments must be based on a specified interest rate (or formula for a variable rate) or a specified percentage of the interest on the mortgages.

Any interest in a REMIC that is not a "regular" interest is a "residual" one. If you own a residual interest, you should receive a Schedule Q from the issuer at the end of the year. Information from the Schedule Q is transferred to Part IV of your Schedule E, *Supplemental Income and Loss,* according to the instructions on Schedule Q. Don't file the Schedule Q itself with your tax return.

INVESTMENT INCOME OF YOUR MINOR CHILD

If a child that you can claim as a dependent had total income of more than the larger of (a) $700 or (b) up to $4,300 of earned income plus $250 in unearned income from interest, dividends, or investments, he or she must report this income on a tax return of some sort.

If the child had income of $7,000 or more, he or she *must* file an individual tax return on Form 1040-EZ, 1040A or 1040, regardless of age.

However, if the child was under 14 at all times during 1999 (that is, the child did not turn 14 until January 1, 2000 or later), and the child's income was less than $7,000, you may be able to elect to report the child's income on your own tax return. Alternately, if an under-14-year-old reports income on his or her own individual tax return, he or she may have to attach Form 8615 and pay the "kiddie tax" as discussed on page 239.

Reporting Your Child's Income on Your Tax Return

If all of your child's income was in the form of interest, dividends, and capital gain distributions (e.g., from mutual funds), and the amount is more than $700 but less than $7,000, you can elect to report the income on your own return rather than filing a separate return for the child.

The IRS allows you to treat your child's income as your own, ostensibly to save you time. For a child under 14, all unearned income above $1,400 must be taxed at the parent's rate, and including the income on your return forces you to calculate this amount.

However, the time you could actually save is minimal at best. If you decide to go this route, you must also complete a Form 8814, *Parents' Election to Report Child's Interest and Dividends*, for each child and attach it to your tax return.

Save Money

Even more important than the time element is the fact that you're likely to pay more tax if you report your child's income on your own return.

This is primarily because you will have to include your child's income in arriving at your own adjusted gross income (AGI), and having a higher AGI can cause you to lose or reduce numerous tax breaks including deductible contributions to an IRA; itemized deductions for medical expenses, casualty and theft losses, and miscellaneous deductions; your credit for child and dependent care; the per-child tax credit; the Hope scholarship credit; the lifetime learning credit; the deduction for interest on education loans; etc. Moreover, you could also increase the amount of personal exemptions and itemized deductions you'd lose under the phaseout for higher income taxpayers (see page 273).

Furthermore, the additional tax you owe on April 15th because of your child's income can cause you to pay penalties, if you don't increase your withholding or make estimated tax payments to cover it.

If you do decide to report your child's income on your own tax return, and you are married filing separately, the parent with higher income must report all of the children's income on his or her own return. Similarly, if the parents live together but are not married, the higher-income parent must report.

If the parents are divorced or legally separated, the parent with custody for the greater part of the year should include the child's income. If the custodial parent has remarried and is filing separately with a stepparent, the stepparent should include the child's income if the stepparent's income is higher than the custodial parent's.

You cannot report the child's income on your own return if any tax was withheld from the child's income, or if he or she made estimated tax payments during the year. In that case, the child would have to file his or her own return.

If you report the child's income, you can't claim any deductions for the child, such as a higher standard deduction if the child was blind, the deduction for a penalty on early withdrawal of savings, or any itemized deductions such as investment expenses or charitable contributions.

Save Money

If your child had any capital gain distributions from mutual funds, make sure that you include these on your Schedule D, rather than reporting them with the rest of the child's income on Line 6 of your Form 8814. Otherwise, your child won't get the benefit of the special 20 percent maximum tax rate on capital gains.

Reporting a Child's Income on Another Return

If your child is required to file a tax return, we recommend that you have him or her file a separate return on Forms 1040-EZ, 1040A, or 1040.

If the child is under 14 at all times during the year and investment income of more than $1,400, he or she will have to complete Form 8615 and attach it to the individual return. In that case, Form 1040-EZ can't be used.

The purpose of the Form 8615 is to impose the "kiddie tax" – that is, to make sure that a child's unearned income is taxed at the parents' top marginal tax rate, for all children under 14. Therefore, you will have to complete your own tax return before the child's can be finished, since you will need to enter the amount of your AGI and the amount of your income tax on the Form 8615. If the parents are filing separately, use the return of the parent with higher income.

If you have more than one child with investment income over $1,400, you'll have to complete the tax returns for all the children as part of the same process, since you need figures from all of the other children's Forms 8615 in order to complete each child's return.

If you or any of your children had capital gains income, these returns can become very complicated. The IRS provides examples, worksheets and instructions for computing the correct amount of tax in its free Publication 929, *Tax Rules for Children and Dependents*. You may find it easier to report your children's income on your own return as described above than to follow the IRS's instructions, however.

Warning

If your child can't file a tax return by himself or herself (as is usually the case), a parent or guardian must complete it and pay the tax. If the child cannot sign the return, the parent should sign the child's name, and then write, "By (parent's signature), parent (guardian) for minor child." If you sign the return in this way, you can deal with the IRS in all matters on behalf of the child. If you don't sign the return, you may have to file Form 2848, Power of Attorney and Declaration of Representative, if you need to deal with the IRS beyond merely filing the return.

INVESTMENT-RELATED EXPENSES

If you have investment-related income, it's likely that you'll have at least a few investment-related expenses as well. Unfortunately, many taxpayers aren't able to deduct these expenses because most of them are classified as miscellaneous itemized deductions, which are only deductible to the extent that they exceed 2 percent of your adjusted gross income.

However, if you have interest expenses related to your investments, it may be a different story. Read on to see how to deduct your interest and other expenses related to investments.

Investment Interest Deduction

The tax laws make a big distinction between interest on loans you take out for personal purposes, and loans you take out for your business, or to produce income through investments.

Interest on loans used for personal purposes is not deductible unless it's qualified home mortgage interest or, in some cases, interest on student loans.

However, you can deduct interest on loans taken out to purchase business assets or inventory, for working capital, or for some other business-related reason. Interest on business-related loans would be deductible on your Schedule C (see page 49).

If you take out a mortgage or other loans related to your ownership of investment real estate, the interest would be deductible on Schedule E (see page 216).

You may also be able to deduct interest on margin loans from your broker, or other loans you took out in order to purchase investments. These loans are the focus of our discussion in this section.

Where Did the Money Go?

It doesn't matter what, if anything, you use for collateral in order to get the loan. What the IRS is looking at is *how you spent the money*. If you spent the money on property that produces dividends, interest, annuities, royalties, or gains or losses, and it is not a trade or business or a passive activity, it will be considered "investment interest." However, you can't deduct interest on loans taken out to purchase tax-exempt investments, such as municipal bonds; on loans taken out to purchase single-premium life insurance, annuity, or endowment contracts; or on loans to purchase certain types of straddles.

Since the IRS is interested in where the money went, you need to be sure that you have a paper trail, including deposit slips, cancelled checks, or account statements (and preferably all three) so that you can prove you actually spent the money on investment property. If you took out a loan and deposited the proceeds in your bank account (for example, while you investigated a number of investment opportunities), any interest you pay is considered "investment interest" unless and until you spend the money on personal items.

We mentioned that interest related to passive activities is not considered "investment" interest. This may seem strange, considering that most people think of passive activities as precisely that – investments, rather than actively conducted businesses. However, the IRS draws another distinction between (a) passive activities, losses (and deductions) for which can only be offset by income from other passive activities, and (b) portfolio or investment assets. For that reason, you may deduct passive activity interest from passive activity income, and investment interest from investment income – the lines may never cross. For more on the definition of what is or isn't a passive activity, see page 44.

Limits on Deductible Interest

The general rule is that you may deduct interest on investment-related loans, up to the amount of your investment income for the year. If you paid more interest than the income you received, you can carry over the disallowed portion of the income to later years, when you can offset it by other investment income.

Your allowable deduction for investment interest is calculated on IRS Form 4952, *Investment Interest Expense Deduction.* You must complete this form and attach it to your return unless all of the following are true:

- Your only investment income was from interest or dividends; that is, you had no annuity or royalty income, no rental income from nondepreciable property, no equity-financed lending activities, and no interests in partnerships or LLCs licensing intangible property. In counting investment income, you must include investment income reported to you by any partnerships or S corporations on a K-1, by an estate or trust, or your child's investment income that you elected to report on your own return.

- You have no other deductible expenses connected with the production of interest or dividends.

- Your investment interest is less than or equal to your total investment income.

- You have no carryover interest deductions from previous years.

If even one of the previous statements is not true, you must complete Form 4952. Luckily, this form is relatively simple. It will ask you to add up your investment income, subtract any deductible investment expenses, and then subtract interest payments up to the remaining investment income.

In adding up your investment income, we mentioned above that you can include investment income of a child, if you opted to report that child's income on your own return. There's another option to consider, which is that you can, if you want, include some or all of your capital gains for the year, including any capital gains distributions from mutual funds. However, if you do, your deductions will offset those gains and you will lose the benefit of the special, lower 20 percent tax rate on capital gains.

Save Money

If you're expecting to have significantly more investment income in later years, you may be better off not including the capital gains so that you get the benefit of the lower 20 percent rate this year. Instead, carry over the interest deduction to next year, so it offsets more of your ordinary income at higher tax rates.

In subtracting your deductible investment expenses on this form, you only need to subtract the expenses you will actually be able to deduct; that is, expenses that exceed 2 percent of your adjusted gross income (AGI). If your itemized deductions are limited because your AGI is very high (see page 273), include only investment expenses that are left, after the limit is applied.

The total amount of allowable investment income is transferred from Form 4952 to Line 13 of Schedule A, *Itemized Deductions.*

Investment Expenses

You can deduct, as a miscellaneous itemized deduction, investment expenses you incurred to produce, manage, or collect income, dividends, gains, losses, etc. that are taxable to you.

The catch is that, like all miscellaneous deductions, the portion that is equal to 2 percent of your AGI will not be deductible. For most taxpayers, it means that these expenses are "lost." Still, it pays to look over your records and see how much you can dig up. You may surprise yourself.

What do investment expenses include? Things like subscriptions to investment on-line services; publications or newsletters; ongoing accounting or attorney fees related to the investment; investment advice; money management fees; dividend or automatic reinvestment plan fees; clerical help; the indemnity bond premium you'd pay to replace lost or missing securities; safe deposit box rent; custody fees for sponsored investment plans; trustee fees for revocable trusts; investment expenses passed through to you from an S corporation, partnership, or REMIC; and even office rent.

Some items are not deductible, but must be added to the tax basis of the investment, to reduce your capital gains when you sell: broker's commissions, state or local transfer taxes, and any fees to set up the investment.

Some items are not deductible at all: transportation to stockholder meetings, expenses of attending investment-related seminars and conventions, and expenses related to tax-exempt investments. If you have some expenses (for example, financial advisory fees) that relate to both taxable and tax-exempt income, you have to prorate the expenses and deduct only the part pertaining to taxable expenses.

Claiming Your Deduction

Your investment expenses are among the miscellaneous deductions that must be listed on Line 22 of Schedule A, *Itemized Deductions*. If you don't have room to list the categories of expenses you paid on the dotted lines following Line 22, you can attach additional sheets of paper to your return.

Chapter 14

Retirement

Because of the ups, downs, and other unpredictable changes that are part of life in a small business, sole proprietors need to plan carefully for their needs in retirement. Having a good retirement plan allows you to build up a solid investment fund outside your business and gain significant tax benefits along the way – and as an added benefit, qualified retirement plans offer some protection from creditors should some unexpected event threaten your business and personal assets.

While we've already discussed how to deduct your contributions to a business-related retirement plan in Chapter 6, you or your spouse may be receiving payments from retirement plans from former employers, or you may have purchased a commercial annuity that provides you with income. This chapter will explain the treatment of both periodic or annuity-type pension payments, and lump-sum distributions.

If you're receiving Social Security benefits, you'll need to be able to calculate the portion (if any) that is taxable. We'll provide a simple worksheet that explains how.

And finally, this chapter discusses individual retirement accounts, a type of plan that's gotten a lot of attention lately because of the addition of Roth

IRAs to the menu in 1998, and the enhanced availability of regular deductible IRAs under recent law changes.

 Tax Organizer Tip

Both distributions from retirement plans including IRAs and annuities, and contributions to such plans, should be entered in the "Retirement" section of the CompleteTax™ Organizer.

DISTRIBUTIONS FROM A PENSION PLAN OR ANNUITY

First, a few definitions and explanations. Distributions from retirement and annuity plans can be made in several ways, depending on the terms of the plan. The typical types of distribution choices are:

- **Annuities.** Usually paid under a contract, this alternative makes regular distributions, generally in equal monthly amounts based on the life expectancy of the beneficiary.

- **Installments.** This alternative can offer a variety of payout periods and equal or unequal payments.

- **Lump sum.** This form of payout distributes the entire vested balance in one payment. It can be made in cash, in securities, or both.

Common types of annuities are:

- **Fixed period.** Distributions are made at regular intervals and have a predetermined amount and period of duration.

- **Single life.** Distributions are made at regular intervals, but payouts end at the beneficiary's date of death.

- **Joint and survivor.** The first annuitant receives a predetermined amount at regular intervals for life. After his or her death, the survivor receives a predetermined amount at regular intervals for life, which can be the same as, or different from, the original amount

- **Variable.** Distributions may fluctuate as a function of profits or economic indices, but the payout period is either fixed in duration or set only for the recipient's life. Employer-provided plans generally do not permit variable distributions, but some annuities purchased through insurance companies may.

Annuities and Pension Plan Installment Payments

Generally, amounts distributed by a qualified retirement plan or annuity are taxable to the recipient as ordinary income in the year they are received. The big exception to this rule is that if the taxpayer made any nondeductible or after-tax contributions to the plan, a portion of each payment will be tax-free, to reflect the amount of his or her contributions.

If you received pension or annuity payments during the year, you should receive an information return, Form 1099-R, from the plan sponsor. This form shows the gross amount of the payments in Box 1, the taxable amount in Box 2a, and the amount of federal income tax withheld (if any) in Box 4. If any tax was withheld, you'll have to attach a copy of the 1099-R to your tax return.

The taxable amount in Box 2a is generally the amount of income you must report on Line 16b of your 1040 or Line 11b of the 1040A, although in some cases you will need to modify these amounts. If your pension was fully taxable, leave Line 16a or 11a blank; these lines are used only if some portion of the payment represents a return of your original after-tax investment in the plan.

The plan sponsor, insurance company, or other payer will withhold federal income tax from your pension or annuity payments unless you specify in writing that you choose not to have tax withheld. If you don't want tax to be withheld on these payments (or if you need to change the withholding amount), notify the payer. You will generally be asked to fill out a form (IRS Form W-4P, or a substitute) showing your correct address and Social Security number. If there is no withholding on your pension, you may need to make quarterly estimated federal tax payments — see page 306.

Partially Nontaxable Payments

Some employment-based retirement plans are "noncontributory" — the employer pays for the entire plan on behalf of the employees. Others, such as 401(k) plans, permit employees to make voluntary, pre-tax contributions from their paychecks. Payments from either of these types of plans are fully taxable when the employee eventually receives the benefits.

However, if you, as an employee, made some *nondeductible, after-tax* contributions to the pension over the years, or if you purchased a commercial annuity with after-tax funds, you can recover the amount of your contributions tax-free over the period you are to receive the payments. A portion of each payment you receive will be nontaxable. Generally, the amount of the after-tax contributions that you received during the year will be shown in Box 5 of the 1099-R, but if your pension began before 1993, the payer is not required to compute this amount.

How is the nontaxable portion of the payment computed? It depends on the date the pension or annuity payments began. Congress has changed the rules several times over the years, so there are a number of different methods that are being used for 1999.

If the payments began after November 18, 1996, and they are from a qualified retirement plan payable over your life, or your life and that of your beneficiary, you are required to use the "Simplified Method." You can use the worksheet below to figure your taxable annuity amount. After you have recovered your entire cost in the plan, the entire benefit will be fully taxable.

If the payments began after July 1, 1986 but before November 19, 1996, you may use the Simplified Method if the payments are from a qualified plan; you also have the option of using the General Rule Method. You may be able to switch from one method to the other within three years of your first pension year, by filing an amended return on Form 1040X using your new method for the first pension year and for each subsequent year.

If you received the payments from something other than a qualified retirement plan, such as a commercially purchased annuity or a nonqualified plan, you must use the General Rule Method. This

method computes your investment in the contract as a percentage of your expected return, based on your life expectancy under IRS tables. With the General Rule method, as with the Simplified Method, you can exclude the portion of the payments that represent your investment in the plan up to the point where you have recovered your entire cost for the plan; after that point, the entire payment is taxable. For detailed information on how the General Rule works, and worksheets and actuarial tables you can use to compute your taxable benefit amount, get IRS Publication 939, *General Rule for Pensions and Annuities.*

If the payments began before 1987, you can continue to take your monthly exclusion for as long as you receive the payments, even if you ultimately receive more tax-free benefits than the total amount of your contribution.

Simplified Method Worksheet (Keep for Your Records)

1. Total pension or annuity payments received this year. Also, add this amount to the total for Form 1040, line 16a, or Form 1040A, line 11a . . . . $ _____

2. Your cost in the plan (contract) at annuity starting date . . . . _____

3. Age at annuity starting date: If **after** Nov. 18, 1996, enter:

55 and under	360
56–60	310
61–65	260
66–70	210
71 and over	160

   . . . . _____

4. Divide line 2 by line 3 (See *Caution* if you received payments in prior years.) . . . . . _____

   Caution: If your annuity starting date is **before Nov. 19, 1996** (and you received payments in prior years), skip lines 3 and 4. You do not need to recompute the tax-free monthly amount. Enter your monthly exclusion computed in prior years on line 4.

5. Multiply line 4 by the number of months for which this year's payments were made . . _____

6. Any amounts previously recovered tax free in years after 1986 . . . . _____

7. Subtract line 6 from line 2 . . . . _____

8. Enter the lesser of line 5 or line 7 . . . . _____

9. **Taxable pension for year.** Subtract line 8 from line 1. Enter the result, but not less than zero. Also add this amount to the total for Form 1040, line 16b, or Form 1040A, line 11b $ _____

   Note: If your Form 1099-R shows a larger taxable amount, use the amount on line 9 instead.

10. Add lines 6 and 8 . . . . _____

11. Balance of cost to be recovered. Subtract line 10 from line 2 . . . . $ _____

If the annuity started in 1999 and is based on the life of more than one person, the recovery period must be determined by combining the ages of the annuitants, and using the following table:

Combined Age of Annuitants	Number of Payments
Not more than 110	410
More than 110, up to 120	360
More than 120, up to 130	310
More than 130, up to 140	260
More than 140	210

Death benefit income exclusion. If you are the beneficiary of an employee who died before August 21, 1996, you may be eligible to exclude up to $5,000 of the benefits you receive. This exclusion does *not* apply if the employee had already been receiving a joint and survivor annuity at the time of death and you are the survivor.

If it does apply in your situation, the $5,000 is treated as an additional contribution by the worker, so you can add $5,000 to the amount shown on Line 2 of the worksheet on the preceding page. In that case, the amount of the pension shown as taxable on the 1099-R form you get from the pension sponsor will be too high. Be sure to use the correct amount, regardless of what the 1099-R form says.

Lump-Sum Distributions

If you received a lump-sum distribution from a qualified retirement plan, or from an annuity or endowment policy you bought from an insurance company, you may have several choices to make that can have a major effect on the tax on your benefits.

First of all, you won't be taxed on any portion of the payment that represents your cost of the plan — that is, any premiums you paid or after-tax contributions you made.

Generally, you have the option of receiving your payment in cash, or rolling it over into an IRA or another qualified plan (such as a new employer's

401(k) plan, or one established by your own business). The amount that represents your investment in the contract is not eligible for a rollover, however. The plan sponsor will report only the taxable amount in Box 2a of Form 1099-R, and that is the amount you can roll over to an IRA.

If you don't roll the payment into an IRA but receive it in cash, the taxable portion of it will be taxed as ordinary income in the year it is received, unless you are one of the few people who still qualify for any of the special tax treatments described below (capital gains treatment, or 5- or 10- year averaging). What's more, you may have to pay an extra 10 percent penalty if the distribution was made "prematurely." In any case, 20 percent of your payment will be withheld for income taxes.

If you roll the amount over into an IRA, you can generally avoid current taxation on the lump-sum, and the amount invested in the IRA will build up tax-free. However, you will be taxed at ordinary rates on all withdrawals as you take money out of the IRA, unless you elect to convert the IRA to a Roth IRA (see page 253).

Rollovers to an IRA

You can avoid current tax on some or all of your lump-sum distribution by rolling it over into an IRA account.

Work Smart

If you go this route, you'll also have the option of rolling the payment into your own small business's plan or another employer's plan at some

point down the road, provided you keep the payment in a new IRA account (sometimes called a "conduit IRA") that's separate from any other IRAs you may have established.

You'll need to make the rollover within 60 days of receiving the lump sum, and you cannot revoke this decision once you make it.

If you make a direct, trustee-to-trustee rollover from your retirement plan to the IRA sponsor, there will be no income tax withholding on your lump-sum payment.

However, if you accept the lump sum in cash with the intention of rolling it over within 60 days, the retirement plan sponsor must withhold 20 percent of the payment for income taxes. In order to avoid all taxes on your lump sum, you will need to roll over 100 percent of the amount, which means that you will have to find some other source (perhaps even a loan) to temporarily replace the 20 percent that was sent to the IRS. Then, when you get your tax refund for the year, you can replenish the other source or repay the loan.

If you do roll over a lump sum you received in 1999, you will receive a 1099-R Form from the plan sponsor that shows the amount paid to you in Box 1. Report the total amount on Line 16a of Form 1040, or 11a of Form 1040A. Report any amount that was *not* rolled over on Line 16b or Line 11b (if you rolled over the entire amount, enter a zero on Line 16b or 11b). You will also need to write the word "rollover" in the margin of your tax return, next to Line 16 or 11.

If you don't roll over the entire amount and you are under age 59½, you may have to pay a 10 percent "premature distribution" tax on the amounts you took in cash – see the discussion on page 249 below.

Lump Sums Taxed as Ordinary Income

Generally, if you receive a lump sum from a retirement plan, any portion that is not rolled over into an IRA will be taxed as ordinary income. This can have the effect of pushing you into a much higher tax bracket than you'd usually face.

There is an exception for lump sums (or portions of them) that are taken in the form of the employer's securities. For example, if your qualified plan invested in your employer's stock and so permits, you may take the stock itself with you, rather than the cash value of the stock, when you retire or separate from employment. The value of the stock will not be taxed until you sell it some years down the road, when it will be treated as a capital gain.

You do have the option to include in your gross income, for the year you receive the stock distribution, the net unrealized appreciation (NUA) in the stock up to the date of withdrawal from the plan. If you want to take advantage of this option, the NUA must be reported on IRS Form 4972, *Tax on Lump-Sum Distributions*, and will generally be taxed at the long-term capital gains rate of 20 percent.

Special Lump-Sum Options

If you were older than 59½ before you received a lump sum from a qualified employee retirement plan, you may have some other options that can reduce your tax bill. You may qualify for capital gains treatment for a portion of the payment, and you may be able to use the 5- or 10-year averaging method to calculate the tax on any portion that doesn't qualify for capital gains treatment. To use any of these special treatments, you must complete IRS Form 4972, *Tax on Lump-Sum Distributions*, and attach it to your tax return.

To be eligible to use any of the special tax treatments, you must have received the entire balance from all plans of your employer in which you participate, in the same tax year, and you can use any of these treatments only once in your lifetime. You must be receiving the lump-sum due to separation from employment or death of an employee, or be older than age 59½, and you must have participated in the employer's plan for the last five years. A distribution made after a self-employed plan participant becomes totally and permanently disabled also qualifies for special treatment.

If you are receiving a lump sum as a survivor of an employee-participant, the employee must have turned 59½ before he or she died. Generally, you (or the employee, if you are receiving the payment as a survivor) must have been born before 1936 to qualify for the special treatments, except that persons born in 1937 or later may qualify for 5-year averaging if they received the payment after turning 59½. Five-year averaging will no longer be available after 1999, however.

If you want to use any of these special treatments, you must use 5- or 10-year averaging, and/or capital gains treatment, for the entire payment. You can *not* roll over *any* of the lump sum to an IRA. It's an all-or-nothing choice.

Save Money

As a very general rule of thumb, if you qualify for 5- or 10- year averaging and you think you will need to use the money before the end of the 5- or 10-year period, you may come out ahead by choosing one of these special tax options. If you won't need the money for the next 10 years, a rollover to an IRA may serve you better. However, to fine-tune your decision, we suggest that you consult a financial planning professional or accountant who can crunch the numbers for you, based on the amount of your lump sum and your particular situation.

Capital Gains Treatment

If you were born before 1936 and you participated in the plan before 1974, the portion of the distribution that resulted from participation before 1974 may qualify for capital gains treatment – that is, you can choose to have it taxed at a flat rate of 20 percent. If any of your payment pertains to pre-1974 participation, the plan sponsor will provide you with the amount in Box 3 of your Form 1099-R.

5- or 10-Year Averaging

The portion of the payment that doesn't qualify for capital gains treatment (or the entire payment, if you so choose) can be taxed as if you received it over the course of 5 years using current tax rates, or, if you were born before 1936, over the course of 10 years using (higher) 1986 rates. You pay this tax only once, in the year you receive the payment, but the averaging treatment usually has the effect of taxing your payment in a lower tax bracket than you'd otherwise face.

If you choose the 5-year option, you'll basically figure your tax on 20 percent of the amount using the normal 1999 tax rates for a single person as shown in the following table, and then multiply this figure by five to arrive at your tax on the lump sum.

1999 Five-Year Averaging Rate Table

Amount Subject to Averaging:		The Tax Is	Of The Amount Over
Over	But Not Over		
$ 0	$25,750	15%	0
25,750	62,450	$3,862.50 + 28%	$25,750
62,450	130,250	14,138.50 + 31%	62,450
130,250	283,150	35,156.50 + 36%	130,250
283,150	. . . . . .	90,200.50 + 39.6%	283,150

If you choose the 10-year option, you'll basically figure your tax on 10 percent of the amount using a special chart based on the 1986 tax rates for a single person, as shown below. Then multiply this amount by 10 to find your total tax on the lump sum.

10-Year Averaging Rate Table

Amount Subject to Averaging:		The Tax Is	Of the Amount Over
Over	But Not Over		
$ 0	$1,190	11%	0
1,190	2,270	$ 130.90 + 12%	1,190
2,270	4,530	260.50 + 14%	2,270
4,530	6,690	576.90 + 15%	4,530
6,690	9,170	900.90 + 16%	6,690
9,170	11,440	1,297.70 + 18%	9,170
11,440	13,710	1,706.30 + 20%	11,440
13,710	17,160	2,160.30 + 23%	13,710
17,160	22,880	2,953.80 + 26%	17,160
22,880	28,600	4,441.00 + 30%	22,880
28,600	34,320	6,157.00 + 34%	28,600
34,320	42,300	8,101.80 + 38%	34,320
42,300	57,190	11,134.20 + 42%	42,300
57,190	85,790	17,388.00 + 48%	57,190
85,790	. . . . . .	31,116.00 + 50%	85,790

If you think you want to use any of the special tax methods, Part III of Form 4972 will walk you through the computations, and help you choose the method that will result in the lowest total tax bill.

Ten Percent Penalty

If you receive a lump-sum distribution under conditions that the IRS considers "premature," you may be subject to a 10 percent excise tax penalty, in addition to the ordinary income tax on the amount. You can generally avoid this tax by rolling over the entire amount into an IRA and leaving it there; just remember that nearly identical penalties apply for premature distributions from IRAs.

As a general rule, a 10 percent penalty applies for taking a lump-sum distribution before age 59½. A higher penalty (25 percent) applies for taking a distribution from a SIMPLE plan within the first two years of participation. Your 1099-R should show a distribution code of "S" in Box 7 if this 25 percent rate applies.

The 10 percent penalty does not apply to qualified plans or IRAs if the distributions are:

- made to a beneficiary or the estate of the plan participant on or after the participant's death

- made because you are totally and permanently disabled

- made as part of a series of substantially equal periodic payments, at least annually, over your life (or life expectancy) or the joint lives (or expectancies) of you and your beneficiary; if from a qualified employee plan, benefits must start after separation from service

Work Smart

If you want to take advantage of this last exception, talk to your financial planner about setting up a series of equal payments. There are a number of ways to calculate the payments that are acceptable to the IRS, and your choice among them should depend on things like the size of your lump sum and whether you need more or less cash from the plan each year. However, once you set up a method, you must stick with it. If you deviate from your chosen method before the end of five years or your attainment of age 59 ½ (whichever takes longer), for any reason other than death or disability, you'll generally have to pay a recapture tax, plus interest, on all distributions received thus far.

For more on premature distributions from IRAs and some special exceptions that can apply, see page 255.

The 10 percent penalty does not apply to qualified plans if the distributions are:

- made to you after you separated from service if the separation occurred during or after the calendar year in which you reached age 55

- not more than your deductible medical expenses (those over 7½ percent of your AGI), whether or not you itemized deductions in 1999

- paid to alternate payees (such as a divorced spouse) under a qualified domestic relations order (QDRO)

- made to you if, as of March 1, 1986, you were separated from service and began receiving benefits from the plan under a written election that provides a specific schedule of benefit payments

- made to correct excess deferrals, excess contributions, or excess aggregate contributions

The 10 percent penalty does not apply to payments from deferred annuity contracts *not* purchased by qualified employer plans (i.e., deferred annuities you purchased from a commercial provider) if the payments are:

- allocable to investment in a deferred annuity contract before August 14, 1982

- from an annuity contract under a qualified personal injury settlement

- made under an immediate annuity contract

- made under a deferred annuity contract purchased by your employer at the termination of a qualified retirement plan or qualified annuity that is held by your employer until you separate from service

Reporting the Excise Tax

If you owe only the extra 10 percent tax on premature distributions, and distribution code 1 is shown in Box 7 of your 1099-R, you can simply enter 10 percent of your taxable distribution on Line 53 of Form 1040. Write "no" on the dotted line next to Line 53 to show that you don't have to file Form 5329.

Otherwise, you must complete IRS Form 5329, *Additional Taxes Attributable to IRAs, Other Qualified Retirement Plans Annuities, Modified Endowment Contracts, and MSAs* and attach it to your tax return. This form is also required if you meet an exception to the tax, but your 1099-R form does not show distribution code 2, 3, or 4 in Box 7, or the code is incorrect.

TAXATION OF SOCIAL SECURITY BENEFITS

Depending on your total annual income, a portion of your Social Security benefits, or those of your spouse if filing jointly, may be subject to income tax.

If the total of your taxable pensions, wages, interest, dividends, and other taxable income, plus any tax-exempt interest income, plus half of your Social Security benefits are more than a base amount, some of your benefits will be taxable. The base amount is $0 for marrieds filing separately who lived with their spouses at any time during the year; $25,000 for singles, heads of households, and marrieds filing separately who didn't live with their spouses; and $32,000 for those who are married filing jointly. These dollar amounts are not indexed for inflation.

The amount of your Social Security benefits that you must include in taxable income depends on the total of your income plus half of your benefits. The higher the total, the more benefits that must be included in taxable income. You may have to pay income tax on anywhere from 50 percent to 85 percent of your Social Security benefits.

You can use the chart that follows to compute the amount of your Social Security benefits that are subject to tax.

INDIVIDUAL RETIREMENT ACCOUNTS (IRAs)

Individual Retirement Accounts (IRAs) function as personal, tax-qualified retirement savings plans. Anyone who works, whether as an employee or self-employed, can set aside up to $2,000 per year in an IRA, and the earnings on these investments grow, tax-deferred, until the eventual date of distribution. Moreover, certain individuals are permitted to deduct all or part of their contributions to the IRA. Beginning in 1998, you may be able to set up a "Roth IRA," contributions to which are not deductible, but from which withdrawals at retirement won't be taxed.

IRAs are set up as trusts or custodial accounts for the exclusive benefit or an individual and his or her beneficiaries. You can set up an IRA simply by choosing a bank, mutual fund, brokerage house or other financial institution to act as trustee or custodian. The institution will give you the necessary forms to complete. A lesser-known alternative is to purchase an individual retirement annuity contract from a life insurance company. An individual cannot be his own trustee.

Contributing to Your IRA

The most that you can contribute to your retirement IRA in any year is the smaller of $2,000, or an amount equal to your compensation includible in income for the year.

The same limit applies if you have more than one IRA, or more than one type of IRA. The contribution must be from "compensation," which means wages, salaries, commissions, net self-employment income, and other sources of earned income. It does not include deferred compensation, retirement payments, or portfolio income such as interest or dividends. When both a husband and wife have compensation, the limit applies separately to each, so that as much as $4,000 can be contributed.

If one spouse does not work or has very little income, a married couple filing jointly may still contribute up to $2,000 for each spouse's account, as long as the couple's joint earned income exceeds their joint IRA contributions. Separate accounts must be used for each spouse.

An IRA can be established, and/or a contribution made, after year-end. It must be made no later than the due date for filing the income tax return for that year, not including extensions. This generally means that you have until April 15th of the following year to make the contribution, and to deduct it on your tax return if you qualify for the deduction.

You don't have to contribute the full $2,000 every year. You may skip a year or even several years. You

Figuring Your Taxable Benefits

Before you start: Is your filing status *Married filing separately?*
    No. Go to question 1.
    Yes. Did you live apart from your spouse all year?
        No. Go to question 1.
        Yes. Do the following if you file:
            Form 1040: Enter "D" to the left of line 20a, then go to question 1.
            Form 1040A: Enter "D" to the right of the word "benefits" on line 13a, then go to question 1.

1. Enter the total amount from box 5 of ALL your Forms SSA–1099 and RRB-1099 . . . .   **1.** _____
   Note: *If line 1 is zero or less, stop here; none of your benefits are taxable.*
   Otherwise, go on to line 2.
2. Enter one-half of line 1 . . . .   **2.** _____
3. Enter the total of the amounts from:
   Form 1040: Lines 7, 8a, 8b, 9-14, 15b, 16b, 17-19, and 21.
   Form 1040A: Lines 7, 8a, 8b, 9, 10b, 11b, and 12 . . . .   **3.** _____
4. *Form 1040A filers:* Enter the total of any exclusions for qualified U.S. savings bond interest (Form 8815, line 14) or for adoption benefits (Form 8839, line 22)
   Form 1040 filers: Enter the total of any exclusions/adjustments for:
   • Qualified U.S. savings bond interest (Form 8815, line 14)
   • Adoption benefits (Form 8839, line 22)
   • Foreign earned income or housing (Form 2555, lines 43 and 48, or Form 2555-EZ, line 18), and
   • Certain income of bona fide residents of American Samoa (Form 4563, line 15) or Puerto Rico   **4.** _____
5. Add lines 2, 3, and 4 . . . .   **5.** _____
6. *Form 1040A filers:* Enter the amount from Form 1040A, line 15. *Form 1040 filers:* Enter the amount from Form 1040, line 32, minus any amount on Form 1040, line 24 . . . .   **6.** _____
7. Subtract line 6 from line 5 . . . .   **7.** _____
8. Enter $25,000 ($32,000 if married filing jointly; $0 if married filing separately and you lived with your spouse at any time during 1998) . . . .   **8.** _____
9. Subtract line 8 from line 7. If zero or less, enter -0- . . . .   **9.** _____
   Note: *If line 9 is zero or less, stop here; none of your benefits are taxable. (Do not enter any amounts on Form 1040, line 20a or 20b, or on Form 1040A, line 13a or line 13b. But if you are married filing separately and you lived apart from your spouse for all of 1998, enter -0- on Form 1040, line 20b, or on Form 1040A, line 13b.) Otherwise, go on to line 10.*
10. Enter $9,000 ($12,000 if married filing jointly; $0 if married filing separately and you lived with your spouse at any time during 1998) . . . .   **10.** _____
11. Subtract line 10 from line 9. If zero or less, enter -0- . . . .   **11.** _____
12. Enter the **smaller** of line 9 or line 10 . . . .   **12.** _____
13. Enter one-half of line 12 . . . .   **13.** _____
14. Enter the **smaller** of line 2 or line 13 . . . .   **14.** _____
15. Multiply line 11 by 85% (.85). If line 11 is zero, enter -0- . . . .   **15.** _____
16. Add lines 14 and 15 . . . .   **16.** _____
17. Multiply line 1 by 85% (.85) . . . .   **17.** _____
18. **Taxable benefits.** Enter the **smaller** of line 16 or line 17 . . . .   **18.** _____

   • Enter the amount from line 1 above on Form 1040, line 20a, or on Form 1040A, line 13a.
   • Enter the amount from line 18 above on Form 1040, line 20b, or on Form 1040A, line 13b.
   Note: *If you received a lump-sum payment in this year that was for an earlier year, also complete Worksheet 2 or 3 and Worksheet 4 to see whether you can report a lower taxable benefit.*

may resume making contributions in a later year, but you cannot "catch up" for years no contribution was made.

If you contribute more than the allowable amount, a 6 percent excise tax penalty will be assessed. This penalty is due for the year of the excess contribution and for each year thereafter until corrected. However, you can generally avoid this tax by removing any excess contributions by the end of the tax year for which they were made.

1999 Maximum IRA Deduction if Covered by a Retirement Plan		
If you file a single return and AGI is no higher than:	If you file a joint return and AGI is no higher than:	Maximum deduction is lesser of 100% of compensation or
$31,000	$51,000	$2,000
$32,000	$52,000	$1,800
$33,000	$53,000	$1,600
$34,000	$54,000	$1,400
$35,000	$55,000	$1,200
$36,000	$56,000	$1,000
$37,000	$57,000	$ 800
$38,000	$58,000	$ 600
$39,000	$59,000	$ 400
$40,000	$60,000	$ 200
$41,000	$61,000	$ 0

No contributions may be made to an inherited IRA, in a form other than cash, or during or after the year in which the individual reaches age 70½. For Roth IRAs, however, there is no upper age limit on when contributions can be made.

Deductible IRA Contributions

Everyone is eligible to establish and maintain an IRA, but whether your contributions into the IRA this year will be deductible depends on your (or, if married, you and your spouse's) income level and whether or not you are covered by another pension plan at work.

If neither you nor your spouse is covered under another retirement plan, you may both take full advantage of the tax deduction for the amount contributed, regardless of your income level.

If the individual making the contribution is covered under another retirement plan, the amount of the contribution eligible for deduction is determined by the filing status and adjusted gross income (AGI) of the couple, as shown on Line 33 of their Form 1040. Note that the test here is AGI – not earned income.

That means that interest, dividends, capital gains, etc. are included in the total; what's more, AGI for this purpose is computed without considering the exclusion of Series EE bond interest shown on Form 8815, or the exclusion of employer-paid adoption expenses shown on Form 8839.

The table above shows the limits that apply for 1999. Under the Taxpayer Relief Act of 1997, these dollar amounts will increase in the future. For both single and joint returns, the phaseout will increase by $1,000 per year in 2000 through 2002, by $6,000 in 2003, and then by $5,000 per year for the next three years. Ultimately, in 2007 the phaseout range for joint returns will be $80,000 to $100,000, and the range for singles will be $50,000 to $60,000.

AGI limits when only one spouse is covered. Beginning in 1998, if the individual making the contribution is not covered by another retirement plan at work, but his or her spouse is covered by such a plan, the non-covered individual may make deductible contributions to an IRA. The AGI phaseout range for such contributions is $150,000 to $160,000, as shown on the following chart.

Maximum Contribution When One Spouse is Covered by a Retirement Plan	
If you file a joint return and AGI is no higher than:	Maximum deduction is lesser of 100% of compensation or
$150,000	$2,000
$151,000	$1,800
$152,000	$1,600
$153,000	$1,400
$154,000	$1,200
$155,000	$1,000
$156,000	$ 800
$157,000	$ 600
$158,000	$ 400
$159,000	$ 200
$160,000	$ 0

If your contribution to an IRA is deductible, you don't need to file any special form to claim it, nor do you need to itemize deductions on Schedule A.

Simply write the amount of your contribution (and your spouse's contribution, if married filing jointly) on Line 23 of Form 1040, or Line 15 of Form 1040A.

Roth IRAs

As of 1998, some taxpayers can set up an IRA that is backloaded, meaning that the contributions are not deductible, but the withdrawals from the account, including all the buildup in value over the years, are tax-free as long as certain conditions are met; namely, that the withdrawals are made five years or more after the account was opened, and after you attain age 59 1/2 or have become disabled.

Joint filers with income under $150,000 can make full contributions of $2,000 apiece to Roth IRAs; for those with income between $150,000 and $160,000, the contribution amount is phased down, until it is phased out completely at $160,000. For singles, the phase-out range is between $95,000 and $110,000, and for marrieds filing separately, the range is between $0 and $10,000.

Since contributions to Roth IRAs are not deductible, they are not reported on Form 1040 or 1040A.

You may be able to convert a "regular" IRA to a Roth IRA, if your adjusted gross income is under $100,000 (single or joint) The catch is that you must pay current income tax on the entire converted amount. If the conversion took place in 1998, the IRS allowed you to spread the tax over four years. The converted amount must remain in the account for five years; if it is withdrawn prematurely a 10 percent penalty will apply and any tax due on the conversion that has not already been paid (for instance, if it was to have been spread forward for four years) will become due in the year of the withdrawal.

If you make a conversion from a traditional IRA to a Roth, you must report the conversion on IRS Form 8606, *Nondeductible IRAs*. If you converted in 1998 and elected to spread the amount over four years, report this year's taxable amount on Form 1040, line 15b.

Nondeductible IRA Contributions

To the extent that you can't meet the requirements for deductible IRAs or Roth IRAs, you may still make a *nondeductible* contribution to an IRA.

However, your total annual contributions to any type of retirement IRA may not exceed $2,000.

Just be sure that whatever you do, you don't mix deductible and nondeductible contributions in the same account. The earnings on nondeductible contributions will still accumulate on a tax-deferred basis, and when you make withdrawals from your account, you'll be able to receive your original contributions (but not the additional buildup in value over the years) tax-free.

To report nondeductible contributions, you must file Form 8606, *Nondeductible IRAs,* with your tax return.

Warning

If you do decide to make nondeductible IRA contributions, you should be aware that when you make withdrawals from the account after retirement, every withdrawal will be treated as if it included both taxable and nontaxable amounts. The computations of what percentage of each payment is nontaxable can become quite complicated, and you may need the assistance of an accountant or tax advisor to figure them out.

IRA Transfers and Rollovers

The shifting of funds from one IRA trustee/custodian directly to another trustee/custodian is called a transfer. It is not considered a rollover because nothing was paid over to you. You can have as many transfers as you like each year; transfers are tax-free, and there are no waiting periods between transfers. They don't have to be reported on your tax return.

A rollover, in contrast, is a tax-free distribution to you of assets from one IRA or retirement plan that you then contribute to a different IRA or retirement plan. Under certain circumstances, you may either roll over assets withdrawn from one IRA into another, or roll over a distribution from a qualified retirement plan into an IRA. If the distribution from a qualified plan is made directly to you, the payer must withhold 20 percent of it for taxes. You can avoid the withholding by having the payer transfer the funds directly to the trustee/custodian of your IRA.

To avoid tax, a rollover must be made within 60 days of receipt of the distribution. You cannot deduct the rollover contribution, but you must report it on your tax return, as follows: Enter the total amount of the distribution on Line 15a of Form 1040 or Line 10a of Form 1040A; then enter the taxable amount, if any (i.e., any amount that was not rolled over) on Line 15b or Line 10b. If you are rolling over a distribution from an employer's plan to an IRA, the distribution and the taxable portion (if any) are reported on Lines 16a and 16b of Form 1040, or Lines 11a and 11b of Form 1040A.

Rollovers not completed within 60 days can have horrible tax consequences. First of all, they are treated as taxable distributions. On top of the regular income tax on the entire amount, you may also have to pay a 10 percent excise tax penalty if the distribution was considered "premature" (see page 255). If you place the amount into another IRA account, you must treat it as a brand-new IRA contribution for the tax year in which it is made, and another 15 percent excise tax penalty will apply to any portion of the amount that exceeds $2,000. These defective rollovers must be reported on Form 5329, *Additional Taxes Attributable to IRAs, Qualified Retirement Plans, Annuities, Modified Endowment Contracts, and MSAs.*

A rollover from one IRA to another enables you to change your investment strategy and enhance your rate of return. It can also be used to obtain a short "bridge loan" from yourself, since you'll have the use of the funds for any purpose you want, for up to 60 days. This type of rollover may be made only once a year, but the once-a-year rule applies separately to each IRA you own. If property other than cash is received, that same property must be rolled over. Except for an IRA received by a surviving spouse, an inherited IRA cannot be rolled over into, or receive a rollover from, another IRA.

Withdrawals/Distributions from an IRA

In general, all withdrawals from a regular, deductible IRA account are fully taxable and reported on Line 15b of Form 1040, or Line 10b of Line 1040A. However, if you made any nondeductible contributions to IRAs over the years, a portion of your withdrawal will be treated as a withdrawal of the nontaxable cost basis of your IRAs, and no tax or penalties will apply to this portion.

Premature Withdrawals

Speaking of penalties, there are a number of rules limiting the withdrawal and use of your IRA assets. Violation of the rules generally results in taxation of the withdrawn amount as ordinary income *plus* a penalty equal to 10 percent of the withdrawal. The rules apply equally to SEP-IRAs and IRAs established under SIMPLE plans, except that the penalty for a withdrawal from a SIMPLE plan within the first two years of participation is 25 percent. Also, there are more lenient rules for Roth IRAs, discussed below.

Generally, you violate the rules if you withdraw assets from your regular IRA before you reach the age of 59 1/2. However, there are a number of exceptions to these rules for cases that might be considered hardship withdrawals. If you can use any of these exceptions, you won't have to pay the penalty, but you will still be taxed at ordinary rates on the amount of the withdrawal. Also, you must complete IRS Form 5329, *Additional Taxes Attributable to IRAs, Other Qualified Retirement Plans (Including IRAs), Annuities, Modified Endowment Contracts, and MSAs,* and give the reason that the distribution is escaping from the penalty.

First, if you become disabled before you reach age 59½, you don't have to pay the additional 10 percent tax if you can furnish proof of your disability, as determined by your physician.

Second, you can receive distributions from your IRA that are a series of substantially equal distributions over your life (or life expectancy) or the lives of you and your beneficiary (or your joint life expectancies). You must use an IRS-approved calculation method, you must take at least one distribution annually, and you must continue the payment method until you reach age 59½ or for five years, whichever is longer. If you want to take advantage of this exception, consult your tax advisor or get IRS Publication 590, *Individual Retirement Arrangements,* for further information.

Third, there is an exception that allows you to take penalty-free distributions from an IRA if the amounts are used to pay medical expenses in excess of 7.5 percent of adjusted gross income, or if the distributions are used to pay health insurance premiums for yourself, your spouse, or dependents if you lost your job, you received unemployment compensation for 12 consecutive weeks, you made the withdrawals during the year you were unemployed or the following year, and you made the withdrawals no later than 60 days after you were reemployed. Self-employed persons can use this exception if they would have met all the requirements except for the fact that they could not receive unemployment benefits because they had been self-employed.

Fourth, as of 1998, you can take a penalty-free withdrawal of up to $10,000 from any type of IRA to purchase a first home for yourself, your spouse, your child or spouse's child, your grandchild or spouse's grandchild, your parent or other ancestor, or your spouse's parent or other ancestor. A "first home" actually means the person's first home within the last two years.

Fifth, 1998 was the first year that you can take a penalty-free withdrawal from an IRA that is not a Roth IRA to pay certain higher education expenses for yourself, your spouse, your children, or your grandchildren. Qualified higher-education expenses include tuition, fees, books, supplies, or equipment; if the individual is at least a half-time student, room and board are also qualified expenses.

Finally, if you make a contribution to an IRA (perhaps mistakenly), you take no deduction for it, and you withdraw your contribution before the due date (including extensions) of your income tax return for that year, the withdrawal is not a taxable distribution. However, any interest or income on the amounts (which must also be withdrawn) are treated as taxable income in the year the contribution was made. The income must be reported on Form 5329.

Withdrawals from a Roth IRA

Generally, to avoid tax and penalties, after you first establish a Roth IRA account you cannot take any withdrawals within five years. Furthermore, a withdrawal after five years must be made under one of the following four conditions: you have attained age 59½, you became disabled, the distribution was to pay qualified first-time homebuyer expenses, or the withdrawal was made to a beneficiary after your death. If you follow these rules, there will be no tax on your Roth IRA withdrawals.

However, if you do violate the rules when you take early withdrawals from a Roth IRA, the withdrawals are treated as first coming from any income on the account, and there is no tax or penalty on the amount to the extent that the withdrawals don't exceed the income. There is an exception to this rule if the Roth account was established by rolling over a regular IRA account – in that case, the amount rolled over must remain in the Roth account for five years, or you will face tax and the 10 percent penalty.

Taxable withdrawals from a Roth IRA are reported on IRS Form 8606, *Nondeductible IRAs*.

Withdrawals from Partially Nontaxable IRAs

If you've ever made nondeductible contributions to any of your IRAs, then whenever you take a distribution from a non-Roth IRA, part of the distribution will be treated as coming from the nontaxable part. You must compute the taxable and nontaxable portions of the withdrawals by completing IRS Form 8606, *Nondeductible IRAs*, and attaching it to your tax return. This can be a complicated process, so make sure that you follow the instructions to the form very closely.

Mandatory Withdrawals

You must begin taking distributions from an IRA no later than April 1st of the year following the year in which you reach age 70½, or the year in which you retire, whichever is later. For any year after your 70½ year, you must take the minimum distribution by December 31st of that year. There's an exception to this rule for Roth IRAs, which carry no mandatory distribution requirements.

The amount of your mandatory distributions must be calculated under one of several formulas in the tax laws; if you take less than the required distribution, you may have to pay a 50 percent excise tax on the amount not withdrawn as required. You can always take more than the required amount (assuming you're over age 59½) but the extra withdrawals don't count towards your minimums for future years.

Generally, you compute your minimum distribution for 1999 by taking your total balance in all IRA accounts as of December 31st of 1998, plus your contributions made for 1999. Divide this balance by one of the following life expectancies: your remaining life expectancy, or the remaining joint life expectancy of yourself and your oldest beneficiary. Life expectancy tables can be found in IRS Publication 590, *Individual Retirement Arrangements (IRAs)*. In the first year you take a minimum distribution, you must decide whether, for each subsequent year, you're going to simply subtract one year from the life expectancy you used last year, or recompute your remaining expectancy based on the tables. Once you pick a method, you must stick with it unless the terms of your IRA account (i.e., the rules set up by the financial institution) provide otherwise.

The minimum distribution rules refer to the dollar amounts you must withdraw. You must calculate the minimum withdrawals *separately* for each account that you have (mainly because the IRS lets you have different beneficiaries on different accounts). You can actually make all the withdrawals from a single account, or spread the required withdrawals across all of your accounts in any manner you choose.

Warning

Computing minimum IRA distributions can be a rather daunting task, especially if you've established numerous IRAs over the years. Many financial institutions are willing to help you compute the minimums if you consolidate your accounts with them. Otherwise, you might consider hiring a financial planner or accountant to help you set up a withdrawal schedule, since the 50 percent penalty for making a mistake in this area is quite severe.

Special rules, too numerous to relate here, apply if your beneficiary is not your spouse and is more than 10 years younger than you, if you change beneficiaries, if your beneficiary dies or if you receive an inherited IRA account. For more detailed information, see IRS Publication 590, *Individual Retirement Arrangements (IRAs)*.

Chapter 15

Standard and Itemized Deductions

Throughout this book, we've discussed a wide range of deductible expenses, in the context of the type of income to which they pertain

For example, Part II of this book dealt extensively with tax deductions relating to your small business. Chapter 11 covered deductible employee business expenses and moving expenses, and Chapter 12 covered deductions related to rental real estate, and to the home mortgage interest and real estate tax deductions for your home. Chapter 13 discussed deductions related to investment income.

In this chapter, we're going to wrap up our discussion of tax deductions, by first exploring the choice between using the standard deduction and itemizing your deductions on Schedule A of Form 1040.

Second, we'll discuss in more detail the few types of itemized deductions that we haven't covered elsewhere: the deductions for medical expenses, charitable contributions, casualty deductions, taxes other than real estate, and other miscellaneous deductions.

Finally, we'll explain how those of you in the higher income ranges may be required to cut back your itemized deductions, and suggest some ways to minimize the damage for those of you who are affected by the phaseout.

THE STANDARD DEDUCTION

Almost any taxpayer who does not wish to itemize deductions in any particular year can choose to use the standard deduction. For 1999, the standard deduction amounts for most individuals will be:

Single	$4,300
Head of Household	$6,350
Married Filing Jointly	$7,200
Married Filing Separately	$3,600

Those who can be claimed as a dependent on someone else's return must generally use a standard deduction of the greater of $700, or the dependent's earned income plus $250. However, the dependent's standard deduction may not be greater than the normal deduction for someone with the same filing status; for example, a single dependent with a lot of earned income can't claim a standard deduction higher than $4,300.

Those who are 65 years old or older at the end of the year, or who are blind, or who file jointly with a spouse who has one or both of these attributes, get a somewhat higher standard deduction. For those who are single or heads of households, being over 65 or blind merits an extra $1,050 added to the normal deduction amount; being both over 65 and blind merits an extra $2,100. For those who are married, each of these conditions for either spouse merits an extra $850 whether you file separately or jointly.

Example

Sarah and Jay Jackson are both over age 65 at the end of 1999, and Sarah is blind. They are filing a joint tax return. Their standard deduction for 1999 is computed as follows: $7,200 + $850 + $850 + $850 = $9,750.

Anna Thompson is Sarah's elderly mother, whom Sarah and Jay claim as a dependent. Anna has no earned income. Her standard deduction is $700 + $1,050 = $1,750.

Who Can't Use the Standard Deduction?

There are a very few people who aren't eligible to use the standard deduction. Most importantly, if you are married and filing separately from your spouse, and one of you itemizes deductions, the other must itemize as well or use a standard deduction of zero. This is the IRS's way of making sure you don't abuse the situation by having one spouse claim all the itemized deductions for the couple, while the other spouse claims a full standard deduction.

Others who can't use the standard deduction are nonresident aliens, or those who were both nonresident and resident aliens during the year, unless they are married to U.S. citizens or residents and elect to be taxed as residents for the year; and those who are filing a tax return for a short tax year because they are changing to a fiscal year.

Claiming the Standard Deduction

To claim the standard deduction, enter the appropriate amount on Line 36 of your Form 1040, Line 21 of Form 1040A, or Line 5 of Form 1040EZ.

If you (or your spouse, if filing jointly) are over age 65 and/or blind, you must use Form 1040A or 1040, and you'll also have to check boxes showing your status on Line 35 (Form 1040) or Line 20a (Form 1040A).

ITEMIZED DEDUCTIONS

If your deductible personal and family expenses, as defined by the IRS, add up to more than the standard deduction for your filing status, *and* you have the records to prove them, you should itemize your deductions instead of claming the standard deduction. To do that, you'll have to file Form 1040, and complete Schedule A and attach it to your tax return.

Save Time

As a general rule, most taxpayers who own their own homes will come out ahead by itemizing; those who don't are unlikely to be able to itemize unless they have extraordinary amounts of medical expenses, charitable gifts, or casualty losses during the year.

Schedule A divides your itemized deductions into six major categories: medical and dental expenses, state and local taxes, interest, gifts to charity, casualty and theft losses, and miscellaneous deductions. We'll discuss each of these categories on the next few pages.

Tax Organizer Tip

When using the CompleteTax™ Organizer to pull together your personal tax-related information, most of the items that are discussed in this chapter should be entered in the "Deductions" section of the organizer.

The major exception to this rule is deductible interest, which should be reported according to the type of loan for which it was paid: home mortgage or investment real estate interest should be reported in the "Real Estate" section; other investment interest should be reported in the "Investment" section; business-related interest should be reported in the "Business Income" tab of the "Employment" section; and qualified student-loan interest should be reported in the "Other Expenses" tab of the "Miscellaneous" section.

MEDICAL AND DENTAL EXPENSES

You can deduct the amount of medical and dental expenses you had during the year that were not reimbursed by insurance. You can also deduct the amount of health insurance premiums you paid out of pocket – that is, not including amounts paid by your employer, or paid with pre-tax dollars through withholding from your paycheck.

However, your medical and dental expense deduction is extremely limited in that only the portion that exceeds 7.5 percent of your adjusted gross income (as shown on Line 33 of your Form 1040) is deductible. For that reason, generally only those with severe chronic or catastrophic medical problems or those who must pay for their own health insurance will benefit from this deduction.

Save Money

For self-employed people in 1999, 60% of health insurance premiums for themselves, their spouse, and dependents are deductible directly on the front of Form 1040 (Line 28), rather than on Schedule A. You're eligible to claim this deduction for any months that you were not covered or eligible to be covered under an employer's plan for yourself or your spouse.

The good news is that this 60% of health insurance is not subject to the 7.5% of AGI limitation; you can deduct it on the front of your Form 1040 whether or not you itemize. The 60% limit is scheduled to rise to 70% in 2002, and will go up to 100% in 2003.

The remaining amount of your premiums (40% for 1999) can be deducted as a regular itemized medical deduction on Schedule A.

Tax Organizer Tip

We suggest that you include the 60% of health insurance that's deductible directly on Form 1040 in the "Business Income" tab of the "Employment" section of the CompleteTax™ Organizer. If you click on the "General Information" button on the "Business Income" screen, you'll see a box where the amount of insurance can be reported. The other 40% of your health insurance should be included in the "Medical Expenses" screen of the "Deductions" section.

Whose Medical Expenses Are Deductible?

You can deduct your own medical expenses, those of your spouse, and those of anyone you can claim as a dependent (see page 161 for rules on dependency status). For a married couple filing jointly, this makes it simple – you can add up both spouses' expenses, those of all your children, and those of any other dependents you are supporting in the hopes of reaching the 7.5 percent AGI limit.

However, if you're married filing separately, this means that you can deduct only those expenses that you actually pay for yourself or your spouse, and those that you actually pay for anyone claimed as a dependent on your separate return. Once again, you can see why filing separately is often unattractive for most married couples.

For divorced or separated parents, the IRS is slightly more lenient. As long as either parent can claim the child as a dependent, both parents can deduct any medical expenses they personally paid for the child.

If you are adopting a child, you can deduct expenses that you paid for the child before the adoption was finalized, so long as the child qualified as your dependent at the time the expenses were incurred or paid. If you pay back an adoption agency or anyone else (such as a birth mother) for medical expenses after the adoption goes through, you can deduct the expenses, except for those incurred before the adoption negotiations began. See also the discussion of the adoption tax credit on page 282.

Deductible Medical and Dental Expenses

- abortions, if legal

- acupuncture treatments

- alcoholism treatments, both inpatient treatments (including meals and lodging), and transportation costs to attend Alcoholics Anonymous meetings if you attend under medical advice

- ambulance payments

- artificial limbs

- birth control pills, injections, devices

- Braille books and magazines, to the extent that they cost more than an ordinary book or magazine

- capital expenses for equipment installed in your home, to the extent that they don't increase the value of your home, provided that the main purpose is medical care for yourself, your spouse or a dependent, or to accommodate the residence to such a person's disabled condition. The following are not treated as increasing the value of your home: adding entrance or exit ramps; widening doorways or hallways; installing railings, support bars, or other modifications to bathrooms; lowering or modifying kitchen cabinets or equipment; moving or modifying electrical outlets or fixtures; installing lifts other than elevators; modifying stairways; installing handrails or grab bars; modifying hardware; or grading ground or making other modifications outside doorways. However, elevators and air conditioning systems generally do increase the value of your home to some extent, and would not be fully deductible. Any operation and upkeep expenses (such as electric bills) for such capital improvements would be deductible, even if the original improvement was only partly deductible.

- car modifications to accommodate a disability, and the amount by which a specially modified car costs more than an ordinary car, but not operating expenses for the car

- chiropractors

- Christian Science practitioners

- contact lenses, including the cost of equipment and supplies to clean and maintain them

- crutches, walkers, canes, etc.

- dental treatment including x-rays, fillings, braces, extractions

- dentures, bridges, and implants

- drug addiction treatments at an inpatient facility, including room and board

- drugs if medically prescribed, and insulin, but not over-the-counter drugs

- eyeglasses and eye exams

- guide dogs or other animals to help the blind, hearing impaired, or people with other physical disabilities; including food, vet. bills, and other care expenses

- HMO premiums, deductibles, and copayments

- hearing aids

- home care, to the extent the services are of a type generally performed by a nurse; most personal or household services don't qualify unless they qualify as long-term care (see below)

- hospital services, including room and board for inpatients

- insurance premiums for policies that cover hospitalization, surgical fees, X-rays, prescription drugs, replacement of lost contact lenses, and HMOs, PPOs, etc. Long-term care policies are also deductible within limits (see below). Insurance premiums are not deductible if they are exempt from tax because they are paid under an employer-sponsored plan. However, you can deduct any deductibles, copayments, and noncovered charges under your insurance plan.

- laboratory tests and fees

- lead-based paint removal to prevent a child who has or has had lead poisoning from eating the paint (You can deduct the cost of removing or covering the paint with wallboard or paneling, but not the cost of repainting.)

- legal fees that are necessary to gain access to mental health treatment or other medical treatment, but not for the management of a guardianship estate or financial affairs

- lifetime care — advance payments for care under an agreement with a retirement home, or for treatment of dependents with disabilities

- lodging, up to $50 per night per person, while away from home to obtain medical care from a doctor or licensed medical facility, provided there's no element of vacation or lavish accommodations (You can deduct lodging for the person receiving the care and a companion.)

- long-term care contracts, if they are guaranteed renewable; have no cash surrender value; provide that refunds other than in case of death or policy cancellation may be used only to reduce premiums or increase benefits; and cover medical, therapeutic, maintenance, and personal care required by a chronically ill person under a plan of care prescribed by a licensed health care practitioner. A chronically ill person must be unable to perform at least two activities of daily living without substantial assistance, or require substantial supervision to prevent injury due to cognitive impairment. Payments from such contracts are not taxed, up to $190 per day (for 1999 – this amount may be increased for inflation). Any unreimbursed expenses are deductible. Also, premiums for such insurance are deductible up to the following annual amounts: age 40 or less -- $210; age 41 to 50 -- $400; age 51 to 60 -- $800; age 61 to 70 -- $2,120; and age 71 and above -- $2,660.

- medical information plans that keep your medical history available

- medical savings account contributions are deductible on Form 8853, *Medical Savings Accounts and Long-Term Care Insurance Contracts,* and not as an itemized medical deduction, see page 92 (Any amounts reimbursed by your medical savings account cannot be claimed as an itemized deduction.)

- medical services of physicians, surgeons, specialists, or other medical practitioners such as osteopaths and podiatrists

- Medicare Part B premiums deducted from Social Security checks, and Part A premiums for those who are not eligible for Social Security but voluntarily enroll in Medicare (Medicare payroll taxes are not deductible.)

- mentally retarded home costs, or those for similar disabilities

- nursing home costs, if the main reason for being there is to get medical care

- nursing services connected with caring for the patient's condition, as well as bathing and grooming, but not household help unless the expenses qualify as long-term care expenses (If the nursing services qualify, you can also deduct the cost of food and lodging for the nurse, as well as payroll taxes.)

- organ, bone marrow, etc. donation expenses, whether or not the donation is successfully completed

- oxygen and oxygen equipment

- psychiatric care, psychoanalysis, and psychologist counseling, but not marriage counseling

- schools, education, and tutoring costs for the blind, disabled, and learning disabled, including room and board

- sterilization

- surgery that is legal and not purely cosmetic, even if it is elective

- telephone equipment for the hearing-impaired

- television modifications or special equipment for the hearing impaired

- therapy treatments, such as physical, occupational, or speech therapy

- transportation to obtain medical care, for a parent who must go with a child who needs care, or for a nurse traveling with a patient. Transportation expenses for cars can be computed as the actual cost of gas and oil, or at the rate of 10 cents per mile (in 1999); to this amount you can add parking fees and tolls. You can also deduct bus or cab fare, train or plane tickets, etc.

- wigs purchased for cancer patients to improve mental health, if on the advice of a physician

- wheelchairs

- x-rays, MRIs, etc.

Expenses That Are Not Deductible Medical Expenses

- babysitting or child care to enable you to obtain medical treatment

- cosmetic surgery including hair transplants, electrolysis, and liposuction, unless necessary to correct a congenital abnormality, an injury, or a disfiguring disease

- dancing lessons, swimming lessons, etc., even if they are recommended by a doctor

- diaper service, unless necessary to relieve the effects of a particular disease

- funeral expenses

- health club dues or treatments, unless related to a specific medical condition (not just general health and well-being)

- illegal operations, treatments, and drugs

- insurance premiums for life, disability, or accident insurance; policies that pay a stated amount each week if you are hospitalized; or the portion of your car insurance that covers medical expenses

- maternity clothes

- meals, unless part of inpatient care

- over-the-counter drugs

- stop-smoking programs

- trips to enhance general health even if taken on advice of a doctor

- vitamins, herbs, etc. to enhance general health

- weight loss programs

STATE AND LOCAL TAXES

Generally, you don't have to pay federal tax on the amount of state and local taxes you pay. There are a few exceptions to this rule (most notably, sales tax) and a rather strict definition of what, exactly, is a "tax" instead of a license, but generally the principle holds true.

We've already discussed real estate taxes, which are deducted on Schedule C for business property, on Schedule E for rent producing property, and on Line 6 of Schedule A for personal residence property (see page 204).

Income Taxes

The other big-ticket item among deductible taxes are state and local income taxes, in areas that have them. You can deduct all state and local income taxes that have been withheld from your paycheck during 1999 as shown on Form W-2, from your pension on Form 1099-R, from investment income on Forms 1099-INT or 1099-DIV, or from other payments on Form 1099-MISC.

Deduct tax payments in the year that you make them. If it later turns out that you get a refund, don't subtract the refund from your otherwise deductible taxes – include it as income on Line 10 of Form 1040, but only if you itemized deductions in the year to which the refund pertained.

On the other hand, if your withheld state and local income taxes were not enough to cover your tax bill for last year and you had to send in a check along with your tax return last April 15, don't forget to include the amount as taxes paid in 1999.

State Disability Fund Taxes

If you, as an employee, had amounts withheld from your paycheck to pay taxes to one of the following state benefit funds, you can deduct the amounts: California, New Jersey, New York Nonoccupational Disability Benefit Fund, Rhode Island Temporary Disability Fund, or Washington State Supplemental Worker's Compensation Fund.

Foreign Income Taxes

Generally, you have the choice between deducting foreign taxes on Schedule A, or claiming a tax credit for them on Form 1116. Usually, the credit will do you the most good. See the discussion on page 227.

Personal Property Taxes

In some states, taxes are imposed on the value of certain non-real-estate property that you own such as cars, trucks, or investments. You can deduct such taxes on Line 7 of Schedule A, but only to the extent that they are based on the value of the item.

Example

Your state charges an annual motor vehicle registration tax based on 1% of the car's value plus 50 cents per hundred pounds. You paid $167 based on the car's value ($15,000) and its weight. You *can deduct only the $150 that reflects 1% of the car's value.*

Other Taxes

Several types of taxes might be deductible on other parts of your tax return:

- Any taxes paid as part of your business operations are deductible on Schedule C.

- Self-employment tax you paid on your own net earnings is deductible up to 50 percent of the amount paid, on Line 27 of Form 1040 (see page 135).

- Payroll taxes on nannies, babysitters, etc. may be deductible as part of the dependent care credit (see page 302).

- If you received income in respect of a decedent, you can deduct the portion of the decedent' federal estate tax that applied to this income, as a miscellaneous deduction not subject to the 2 percent of AGI floor (Line 27 of Schedule A). The decedent's executor should tell you the relevant amounts, if they apply to you.

You can't deduct penalties, fines, or license fees paid for personal purposes such as driver's licenses, dog tags, marriage licenses, etc.

INTEREST

Two major categories of interest payments are deductible on Schedule A: qualified home mortgage interest, which is discussed on page 199, and investment interest, which is discussed on page 240.

Some other types of interest are deductible in other places on your tax return. Business-related interest payments are deducted on Schedule C (see Chapter 6), interest on rent-producing property is deductible on Schedule E (see page 216), and, as of 1998, qualified student loan interest is deductible on Line 24 of your Form 1040 (see page 288).

GIFTS TO CHARITIES

Making a gift of cash or property can be a good way to save some money on your tax bill, as well as to do some good for a cause you believe in.

You can generally deduct contributions to, or for the use of, qualified charities that you made during 1999, and in some cases you can deduct your out-of-pocket expenses incurred while donating your time to the charity. For small business owners, gifts made by your business should be deducted on Schedule A, not Schedule C.

Qualifying Organizations

Not all organizations that solicit your funds qualify as charities, to which gifts are deductible. Generally, only the groups listed below can qualify:

1. corporations, trusts, funds, foundations, or community chests organized and operated for charitable, religious, scientific, literary, or educational purposes or for the prevention of cruelty to children or animals, or that foster national or international sports competitions. This includes churches, synagogues, temples, mosques and other religious institutions; nonprofit schools and hospitals; groups like Salvation Army, Red Cross, Goodwill Industries, Girl Scouts; medical research organizations; and nonprofit museums and cultural institutions

2. veterans' organizations

3. domestic fraternal societies, orders, and associations operating under the lodge system, only if used for charitable purposes

4. certain nonprofit cemetery companies or corporations, unless used for care of a particular lot or crypt

5. the United States, a state, a possession, or any political subdivision of a state, possession, or an Indian tribal government

In most cases the charity must be a U.S. organization, but if you have Canadian income you may be able to deduct contributions to Canadian charities, and if you have income from sources in Mexico you may be able to deduct contributions to Mexican charities.

Gifts that Don't Qualify for the Charitable Deduction

- gifts to civic leagues, social and sports clubs, labor unions, and Chambers of Commerce

- gifts to groups run for personal profit

- gifts to groups whose purpose is to lobby for law changes

- gifts to homeowner's associations

- direct donations to needy individuals or families

- gifts to political groups or candidates for public office

- cost of raffle, bingo, or lottery tickets

- dues, fees, or bills paid to fraternal organizations, country clubs, or similar groups

- tuition

If you're in doubt about whether a particular organization qualifies for tax-deductible contributions, ask them directly, or check IRS Publication 78, which lists most qualified organizations. You can also call the IRS at 1-800-TAX-1040 to find out.

Which Contributions Are Deductible?

You can deduct outright gifts of money or property that you make to a qualified charity, or that you place in a trust for the use of the charity.

However, if you receive some benefit from the gift, you can only deduct the portion of the gift that exceeds the value of the benefit you receive.

Example

Jim and Shirley Jackson paid $1,000 for a table at a dinner to benefit a children's aid organization. They and eight friends attended the dinner, which would have ordinarily cost $30 per person. The Jacksons can deduct $1,000 less the $300 value of the dinners, or $700.

If you purchase items at a charitable sale or auction, you can only deduct the portion of the price you paid that exceeds the value of the item.

You can generally deduct the entire membership fee or dues you pay to a qualified organization, provided that you receive only nominal benefits in exchange, such as discounts on goods and services, free parking, and free or discounted admission to the group's events, or if you receive only token items such as mugs, T-shirts, calendars, etc.

If you make a payment over $75 that is partially in exchange for some goods or services, the organization must give you a written statement that tells you the amount you can deduct.

Donated Services

Although you can't deduct the value of your time, you can deduct the out-of-pocket expenses you incur in donating your time and efforts to a charity. The expenses must be unreimbursed, and directly connected with the services.

If you use your car in the service of the charity, you can deduct your actual cost of gas and oil, or you can deduct 14 cents per mile. However, you'll have to keep written records of the mileage you drive, the name of the charity and the purpose for which you drove, and the records should be made at or near the time you actually did the driving.

You can deduct travel expenses, including meals and lodging, if you travel away from home to perform services for a charity, or if you are a chosen representative of a qualified organization at a convention. However, you can't deduct travel expenses if you attend a convention only as a member, rather than a chosen representative. In any case, you can't deduct the costs of bringing your spouse or dependents along, and you can't deduct costs of sightseeing, parties, etc.

Foster parents can deduct any expenses for caring for their foster children that exceed the nontaxable payments they received (if any). If you host a foreign exchange student under an agreement with a qualified organization, you can deduct up to $50 for each month or half-month that the student lives with you.

Contribution Valuation and Recordkeeping

If you give cash or checks, the value of the gift is easy to determine. If the value is less than $250, you must keep a cancelled check or credit card slip, a receipt, or some other reliable written record or evidence.

If the cash gift was $250 or more, your own records won't be enough. You must get a written acknowledgement of the gift from the organization which states the amount of the gift, and the amount of goods or services you received in return (if any). For gifts made in 1999, you must get this acknowledgment before you file your tax return for 1999, or (if later) the due date of the return, including extension.

If you made more than one small donation (under $250) to the same group, but the total for the year was more than $250, don't worry about getting a statement from the organization. Each gift is counted separately, unless you wrote two checks on the same day to the same organization.

If you made gifts through payroll deductions (such as to the United Way), you don't need an acknowledgement letter unless any single deduction exceeded $250. In that case, save a copy of your pay stub and also a pledge card stating that the organization does not provide goods or services in exchange for payroll contributions.

Noncash Gifts

If you donate property to a charity, the value of the donation is sometimes difficult to determine. Generally the value of the gift is the fair market value of the property at the time of the donation, but there are some exceptions to this rule.

If you're donating used clothing, furniture, household goods, toys, books, etc., the value of the gift is the same as you would pay in a thrift or consignment shop. You should keep an itemized list of the goods you donate and, if possible, get the charity's representative to stamp or sign it; at a minimum, they should give you a receipt for the goods you donate showing the name of the charity and date.

Similarly, if you're donating a car, boat, etc., you should determine the current fair market value, and get a receipt describing the item from the charity.

If you donate items from your inventory (for example, you're a restaurant owner and you donate the food for a charitable event) you can deduct the cost of the items to you, not their value.

If you donate property that has increased in value, the amount that you can deduct depends on whether, if you had sold the property, you would have realized ordinary gains or capital gains. For ordinary gains property (most property you held for a year or less, works of art you created, or inventory) you can deduct only the lower of fair market value at the time of the gift, or your basis in the property (which is generally your cost).

However, if the property would have resulted in capital gains if you had sold it, you can use the fair market value at the time of the gift. This includes stocks and bonds held for more than one year, real estate, and depreciable business property held for more than one year.

Documenting noncash gifts. For noncash contributions under $250, you need to get a receipt from the charity showing its name, the date, and a reasonably detailed description of the property. You also need to keep records showing the property's fair market value, and its cost if it has appreciated in value.

For noncash contributions of $250 to $500, you must get a written acknowledgement of your contribution from the charity, stating how much (if anything) you received in return for your gift.

If you made total noncash gifts over $500 for the year, you must complete and attach to your tax return IRS Form 8283, *Noncash Charitable Contributions*. If any single gift or group of similar gifts was valued at over

$5,000, you must also get an appraisal of the item from a qualified appraiser. The cost of the appraisal itself is not a charitable contribution, but can be deducted as a miscellaneous deduction on Line 22 of Schedule A.

CASUALTY AND THEFT LOSSES

If you've suffered the results of a theft, accident, fire, flood, or some other casualty during the year, you may be able to deduct some of your unreimbursed losses.

Save Money

In particular, it's important to know that if you're in an area that was declared a federal disaster area by the President, the tax deduction for your casualty losses can be claimed retroactively, by treating them as if they occurred in the previous year and filing an amended tax return for that year. This allows you to receive a quick tax refund – money that you can use right away.

Casualty losses are treated somewhat differently depending on whether the loss occurred to property used in your trade or business, property used to generate investment income, or property used for personal or family purposes. However, regardless of the type of property, the loss must first be reported on IRS Form 4684, *Casualties and Thefts*. For that reason we're going to discuss all types of casualties, both business and personal, on the next few pages.

What Is a Casualty?

A casualty is a sudden, unexpected, or unusual loss or damage to some property you own. Examples of events that typically cause casualty losses are earthquakes, hurricanes, tornadoes, floods, storms, volcanic eruptions, shipwrecks, cave-ins, sonic booms, fires, car accidents, airplane crashes, riots, vandalism, burglaries, larcenies, or embezzlement. Examples of events that are not considered deductible casualties are progressive deterioration caused by age, wind and weather, wood rot, termites or other insect infestation, or drought.

Work Smart

There are situations where insect infestation can be considered a casualty for tax purposes, if the destruction was very sudden and severe. Also, drought can be considered a casualty if the property was used for a trade or business or in some other transaction entered into for profit, such as an investment in farmland.

Simply misplacing or losing property does not qualify as a tax-deductible casualty, even though your insurance company may consider it a reimbursable loss. However, if you lose property in conjunction with another accident, it may qualify. For instance, if you were involved in a car accident that scattered your property into the surrounding area and some of your jewelry was never found, you can deduct the loss of the jewelry.

Work Smart

Losses of business inventory can be treated as either a casualty loss, or as part of your cost of goods sold.

Treating this kind of loss as part of your cost of goods sold will generally mean that you'll have less net income from your business, which, depending on your income level, may save you some Self-Employment Contributions Act (SECA) tax.

Measuring the Loss

First of all, only losses to your property are deductible. You can't deduct the loss of earnings if your business is damaged in a fire, nor can you deduct the loss of time you spent cleaning up after the fire (although you could deduct the cost of hiring a clean-up crew for your business, but not for a fire in your home). For personal losses, you can't deduct the extra living expenses you may have such as renting a car after your personal automobile was damaged in an accident.

How do you measure the amount of damage to your property? The IRS uses a rather conservative yardstick. You must use either the property's adjusted tax basis immediately before the loss, or the property's decline in fair market value due to the casualty, *whichever is lower*. IRS Form 4684 requires you to compare these two figures and will only allow you to deduct the smaller amount. This means that if your property has increased in value since you purchased it, you're out of luck, and you can only deduct the property's cost. However, if your property has decreased in value, your loss is limited to the lower current value.

Your adjusted tax basis for property generally is equal to the costs of acquiring it, plus the cost of any improvements, less any depreciation deductions or previous casualty losses. See Chapter 7 for more details on calculating your tax basis.

Example

You purchased a table at an auction for $100. Later you discovered that the table was actually an antique and its fair market value was $1,000. If the table was destroyed in a fire, your loss would be limited to the $100 you paid for it.

If the property was totally destroyed in a casualty, rather than just damaged, the value of the loss depends on what the property was used for. If it was used for personal purposes, the rule stated above still holds. But if it was used in a business or to produce income, you simply use the property's adjusted tax basis after the loss, minus any salvage value – the fair market value does not come into play at all.

If a single casualty or theft involves more than one piece of property, you must calculate the value of the loss separately for each item. There's an exception to this rule if the loss was to your home or other personal-use real estate. In that case, you can treat the entire property as a single item (including all buildings, improvements, trees and landscaping). But generally, each item will be listed in a separate column on the appropriate section of your IRS Form 4684.

Proving the Loss

In order to claim a deduction for your casualty loss, you must be prepared to prove it. Specifically, if your tax return is audited, you should be prepared to show all of the following:

- that you owned the property

- the amount of your basis in the property

- the pre-disaster value of the asset

- the reduction in value caused by the disaster

- the lack or insufficiency of reimbursement to cover the costs

To claim the deduction, generally, you must be the owner of the property. Therefore you can't claim a loss for the destruction of property owned by, say, your dependent parent. If more than one person owns the property, the loss must be allocated among the owners in proportion to their ownership interests. However, if the risk of loss was shifted to you by a contract, you can claim a deduction even if you didn't own the property.

Example

If the rental agreement for your office space says that you must pay for any damages to the building resulting from a casualty, then you are entitled to claim a loss deduction for the damages.

Proving the basis of business property is generally not a problem, since you should have adequate records of the property's original cost or other basis, plus any additions or subtractions to the basis, for tax and accounting purposes.

For personal property, proving the basis may be more difficult. For larger items such as your home, you should have retained the sales contract or closing documents in your safe-deposit box, but for furniture, cars, clothing, household items etc., it's quite impractical to save every sales slip. Perhaps luckily, since these items typically depreciate in value over time, their loss would generally be measured by the fair market value at the time of the casualty, not their cost basis to you.

Appraisals and Other Evidence

A professional appraisal is often the best evidence you can obtain of the value of property before and after a casualty. Ideally, the appraiser would be someone who was at least passingly familiar with your property before and after the theft, who has adequate knowledge of sales of comparable property in the area, who is familiar with conditions in the area, and who uses conventionally accepted appraisal methods.

Save Money

The cost of obtaining an appraisal is not itself part of your casualty loss, but it can be deducted as a miscellaneous itemized deduction (see page 272).

While professional appraisals are nice to have, they are not always required, especially for inexpensive items. An insurance adjuster's appraisal may do just as well. If you sell the property after the casualty, the sales price will be evidence of its fair market value (FMV).

For cars, you can often rely on "blue books" or similar sources that provide retail values for cars by age, make, model, condition, mileage, etc.

For property that has been damaged, you can use the cost of cleaning it up or repairing it to bring it back to its condition before the casualty as a measure of the difference in fair market value before and after the casualty, so long as the repairs do not actually increase the property's value above its pre-casualty value. Finally, if you have photographs (before and/or after), videotapes, an insurance inventory, any receipts or other documentation, they may all be useful in establishing the property's value.

Work Smart

You may find the IRS's free Publication 584, Nonbusiness Disaster, Casualty, and Theft Loss Workbook, helpful if your home and personal belongings have been largely destroyed by a disaster. It goes through the house room by room and prompts your memory with lists of items commonly found in a typical home, which can also be useful in filing your insurance claim. You can get a copy by calling 1-800-TAX-FORM.

Loss Reimbursements

If your property loss was covered by insurance, you must submit a timely claim for reimbursement with the insurance company in order to deduct any casualty losses for property damage. The exception to this rule is that if your policy requires you to pay a deductible amount, this amount counts as a loss even if you don't file a claim.

Once you've determined the amount of your loss, you must subtract the value of the insurance reimbursements you received, to arrive at your deductible casualty loss. If the reimbursements are greater than your losses as calculated under IRS rules, you may actually have a gain as a result of the casualty.

Example

If you are reimbursed on the basis of your home's appreciated value, but for tax purposes you can only claim the original cost of the home as a loss, you may experience a gain upon receiving the insurance money. You can generally avoid paying tax on the gain if you purchase qualified replacement property within two years – see page 270 below.

Insurance payments are the most common form of reimbursement for casualty losses, but you will also have to count any condemnation awards, disaster relief grants, or cancellation of disaster relief loans. However, if you receive money to help you recover from a disaster that is not specifically earmarked for repair or replacement of damaged property, it is not considered a reimbursement for tax loss purposes.

If your insurance company pays you for living expenses because you have to move out of your damaged home, these payments are not subtracted from your casualty loss. However, you may have to declare some of the payments as taxable income, if they exceed the actual amount of the extra expenses you had.

Example

You had a fire in your apartment and had to move out for a month and stay in a hotel. Your rent is normally $500 per month, but the hotel cost $1,200. Your insurance company paid $1,000 for living expenses.

You don't have to subtract any of the payment from your allowable casualty loss. The amount by which your hotel bill exceeds your rent ($1,200 - $500 = $700) is tax-free. However the remaining $300 would have to be declared as extra income on Line 21 of Form 1040, unless you can show that your food, transportation, and other costs were $300 higher for the month because of the damage to your home.

If, at the time your tax return is due, you haven't yet received the final word from your insurance company on what your reimbursement will be, you must take a stab at an approximation, and subtract that amount. If it later turns out that you receive less than you expected, you can deduct the difference as a casualty loss on the tax return for the later year in which the insurance claim is finalized.

If it turns out that you receive more than you expected, you will have to include the excess amount in income in the year you receive it. However, if any part of your original deduction did not reduce your tax bill, you don't have to include that part of the reimbursement in your income.

Example

In December of 1999, you suffered a personal loss of $5,000 and expected to receive $3,000 from your insurance company. However, due to the application of the $100-plus-10 percent rule (discussed below), you were unable to deduct any of your loss in 1999. If, in 2000, you actually receive $5,000 from the insurance company, you don't have to declare any of it as income.

Calculating the Tax Deduction

For losses of trade or business property, or property used to produce rentals or royalties, once you've calculated the amount of your loss and subtracted the amount of your reimbursement, the remainder is your deductible loss (or gain).

For losses of income-producing property that is not described above (for example, investments such as stocks, bonds, gold, silver, and works of art), your casualty losses are added to your itemized miscellaneous deductions. All of these deductions are added together, 2 percent of your adjusted gross income is subtracted, and the remainder is your deductible amount.

Limits on Personal Losses

For thefts or casualties of personal or family property, your deductible loss is much more strictly limited. After calculating the amount of your loss and subtracting any reimbursements, you must subtract $100 for each casualty, theft, or accident you suffered during the year, regardless of the number of items that were damaged or destroyed during the event.

If you are married filing jointly, a single $100 reduction applies for each event, but if you are filing separately, each spouse who claims a loss must subtract $100, for a total of $200 per event for jointly owned property. If only one spouse owned the property at issue and you are filing separately, that spouse is the only one who can claim a deduction (and must apply the $100 reduction).

After the first $100 is subtracted, you're not in the clear yet. You must again reduce your deductible loss by a full 10 percent of your adjusted gross income as shown on Line 33 of your Form 1040. As a result, small personal casualty losses are unlikely to bring you any tax benefits.

Mixed-use property. If you suffered damage to your home, part of which you were using as a home office, or to your car, which you sometimes used for business, you have mixed-use property and your loss must be proportionately divided between the two types of usage. You will actually treat the event as if it were two separate losses. The $100 and 10 percent of AGI reduction applies only to the personal portion of the loss. For more on casualty losses to home offices, see page 86.

Casualty Gains

If you receive insurance reimbursement that is more than your adjusted basis in the destroyed or damaged property, you may actually have a gain as a result of the casualty or theft. However, the fact that a gain exists does not necessarily mean that it will be taxable right away. You will probably be able to defer the gain to a later year (or perhaps indefinitely) if you purchase qualified replacement property.

First, in calculating your gain, remember that you can subtract from your reimbursement any expenses you incurred in obtaining the reimbursement, such as the expenses of hiring an independent insurance adjuster.

Then, if you spend the same amount as the remainder of the insurance money you received, either repairing or restoring the property, or in purchasing replacement property, you can postpone tax on the gain. However, you must make the replacement within two years of the end of the tax year in which you have the gain. If the loss was to your main home, and the area was declared a federal disaster area, you have more time: up to four years after the end of your tax year in which you have the gain.

The replacement property must be similar or related in use to the property that was destroyed. For instance, if your car was destroyed, you can replace it with another car, but not with a piano. If your home was destroyed, you can replace it with another main residence such as a home or a condo, but not with a store building. If the property was investment real estate, then other investment real estate will qualify as a replacement, but not a second home. However, if the property was business or income-producing property located in a federally declared disaster area, any business-use property will qualify.

You cannot postpone a casualty gain of more than $100,000 by purchasing replacement property from a related party, such as a corporation you control.

However, you can replace property and defer gain by purchasing a controlling interest in a corporation that owns similar property, as long as you own at least 80 percent of the stock.

If you purchase replacement property, you will have to reduce the tax basis of the new property to reflect the casualty gain you postponed.

Example

Emily Gates' home of several years was destroyed by fire. Her basis in her home was $60,000. Her insurance company reimbursed her in the amount of $100,000. So, Emily had $40,000 of realized gain on the involuntary conversion of the property ($100,000 - $60,000 = $40,000).

Emily spent the entire $100,000 insurance proceeds building a new home and thereby qualified for deferral of tax on all her gain. Her basis in the replacement home is $60,000, the cost of her new home reduced by the amount of her unrecognized gain ($100,000 - $40,000 = $60,000).

If Emily had spent only $90,000 of the $100,000 of insurance money to build a new home, she would have to recognize taxable gain with respect to the $10,000 that was not reinvested. Her basis in the new home would still be $60,000 (her $90,000 cost reduced by the $30,000 of gain that was not recognized).

Reporting a Loss or Gain on Your Tax Return

If you have a loss to personal-use property, you must fill out Section A of Form 4684. Each item is reported in a separate column on this form (if a large number of items were lost or damaged, you can use reasonable categories such as "clothing," "jewelry," "furniture," etc. Separate copies of Form 4684 must be used if you suffered more than one casualty during the year; transfer the amounts from Line 12 of all the forms you used to Line 13 on one of the forms and

use that as the "master" for the remainder of the questions. Ultimately, you will transfer the loss amount to Schedule A as an itemized casualty loss deduction.

If you have a taxable gain as a result of a casualty to personal-use property, use Section A of Form 4684, and transfer the gain amount to Schedule D, *Capital Gains and Losses.* The gain will be treated as short-term or long-term, depending on whether you held the property for one year or less, or for more than one year. If you elect to defer gain by purchasing qualified replacement property, you won't have to transfer the gain to Schedule D, but you must attach a statement to your tax return explaining the date and details of the casualty or theft, the amount of insurance, how you figured the gain, and that you are choosing to postpone gain by purchasing replacement property.

If you've already done the replacing, include information about the property, the postponed gain, the basis adjustment that reflects the postponed gain, and any remaining (unpostponed gain) you are reporting on Schedule D. If you make the replacement in a later year, attach a statement including this information about the replacement property to the tax return for that later year. If you expected to replace property but then didn't, or replaced at less than the full amount, you'll have to go back and amend your tax return for the year you claimed the loss.

Business or Income Property

If you had a loss to income-producing property, complete Section B of Form 4684, and transfer the loss to Schedule A as a miscellaneous itemized deduction.

If you had a gain to income-producing property, or if you had a gain or loss to trade or business property or rental or royalty property, complete Section B of Form 4684 and then transfer the gain or loss to Form 4797, *Sales of Business Property.* Again, you can elect to postpone tax on the gains by purchasing replacement property and attaching a statement to that effect to your tax return, as described above under "Reporting a Loss or Gain on Your Tax Return."

Timing the Deduction

Casualty losses must generally be deducted in the tax year in which the loss event occurred. However, if you suffered a loss in a presidentially declared federal disaster area, you may deduct your loss in the preceding year. To do this, you must file an amended tax return for the preceding year, and figure the loss and the change in taxes exactly as if the loss actually occurred in that preceding year. If you did not itemize your deductions in that preceding year, you can go back and add any other itemized deductions (such as mortgage interest, taxes, charitable contributions, etc.) that you would have been able to deduct in that year. You generally must make this choice by the due date (not including extensions) for the tax return of the year that the loss actually occurred.

Save Money

If your losses were very large, and exceed your income for the year, you may have a net operating loss (NOL) for the year. You can use an NOL to lower your taxes for a previous year, allowing you to get a tax refund for the earlier year. You don't have to be in business to claim an NOL due to a casualty or theft loss, but the rules for claiming NOLs are fairly complex, and we recommend that you consult your tax advisor for advice on the mechanics of amending your prior year's return to claim this deduction.

MISCELLANEOUS ITEMIZED DEDUCTIONS

We've already discussed two categories of miscellaneous itemized deductions: Chapter 11 covered deductible employee business expenses, and Chapter 13 discussed deductions related to investment income. For people who have them, these are usually the biggest-ticket items under the "miscellaneous" umbrella. Line 20 is used to report employee business expenses transferred from Form 2106 or 2106-EZ, and Line 22 is used to report investment expenses. We've also discussed hobby expenses in Chapter 4 – hobby expenses are deductible on Line 22 as well. However, there are a number of other things that count as miscellaneous itemized deductions.

Job Search Expenses

Expenses that you pay in looking for another job in your present occupation can be deducted, even if you don't find a new job. However, you can't deduct the expenses of looking for your first job or a job after you've been out of the workforce for an extended period of time. You also can't deduct expenses of seeking the first job in a new occupation.

If your job search qualifies, you can deduct costs for things like writing, printing, and distributing a resume; using an employment agency, outplacement agency or career counselor; and for traveling to interviews or to a different city to look for work. If you use the standard mileage rate to deduct car expenses, use the business rate of 32½ cents per mile for January through March of 1999, and 31 cents thereafter

Tax Preparation Expenses

You can deduct, as a miscellaneous expense, amounts that you pay to determine the amount of any tax due, to pay the tax, or to claim a refund or contest the amount of tax due. This applies to federal income tax, as well as any other type of tax that you pay.

So, you can deduct the cost of purchasing books like this one, of copying your tax returns, and even postage costs for obtaining a return receipt when you mail your tax forms. If you pay a fee to file your tax return electronically, you can deduct that cost. If you get professional help in preparing your return or in obtaining appraisals needed to determine the amount of tax due, you can deduct those fees.

Investment-Related Deductions

You can deduct, as a miscellaneous itemized deduction, investment expenses you incurred to produce, manage, or collect income, dividends, gains, losses, etc. that are taxable to you. These expenses are discussed in more detail at the end of Chapter 13.

The Two Percent Limit

All of the miscellaneous expenses we've discussed so far are subject to the 2 percent of adjusted gross income (AGI) limit. That is, you must total up all your allowable expenses, and subtract 2 percent of your AGI as shown on Line 33 of your Form 1040. If anything remains, that is the amount you can deduct as an itemized deduction on Line 26 of Schedule A.

Items Not Subject to the Limit

There are a few types of miscellaneous deductions that are not subject to the 2 percent limit. If you have any of these, they are totaled up and reported on Line 27 of your Schedule A. They are:

- amortizable premiums on taxable bonds (see page 224)

- federal estate tax that was paid on income in respect of a decedent (see page 169)

- gambling losses, up to the amount of gambling winnings (the full amount of winnings are reported as income on Line 21 of Form 1040)

- impairment-related work expenses of persons with disabilities

- repayments you had to make of income you reported in earlier years, if more than $3,000

- unrecovered investment in a pension

THE LIMIT ON ITEMIZED DEDUCTIONS

Unfortunately, at higher levels of income, your hard-won and carefully documented itemized deductions will be phased out, and you won't be able to deduct them in the current year – or ever.

As we noted on page 167, this is true of personal exemptions as well. However, while personal exemptions can be phased out completely if your income is high enough, the situation with itemized deductions is a little better – they won't be reduced by more than 80 percent.

Save Money

Regardless of whether your itemized deductions are phased out, you always have the option of using the standard deduction for your filing status, which remains the same no matter how high your income rises.

Income Levels that Trigger the Phaseout

The adjusted gross income (AGI) levels at which the phaseout of itemized deductions begins are adjusted annually for inflation. For 1999, they are:

- $126,600 for singles, heads of households, and married people filing jointly

- $63,300 for marrieds filing separately

If your AGI as shown on Line 33 of your tax return is higher than the applicable threshold, you have to subtract the threshold amount from your income. The remaining amount of AGI is multiplied by 3 percent. The answer you get is subtracted from the total amount of affected deductions, and you can only deduct the remainder. However, in no event will your deductions be reduced by more than 80 percent of their value.

Deductions Subject to the Phaseout

Not all deductions are affected by the phaseout, but most of the larger ones are:

- home mortgage interest

- taxes

- charitable contributions

- miscellaneous itemized deductions that are subject to the 2 percent limit, including employee business expenses

---

- federal estate tax in respect of a decedent

- impairment-related work expenses

- amortizable bond premiums on bonds acquired before 10/23/86

- unrecovered investment in a pension

- repayments of income previously taxed

Deductions Not Subject to the Phaseout

- medical and dental expenses

- gambling losses

- investment interest expenses

- nonbusiness casualty and theft losses

Note that whatever limits are applicable to the particular type of deduction (for example, the $100,000 limit on home equity loans, or the two percent limit for miscellaneous deductions) are applied first, before computing the amount of the phaseout.

Case Study

Boris and Natasha are married taxpayers who file jointly. In 1999 they had adjusted gross income (AGI) of $339,450 and itemized deductions of $23,700. Their only allowable deductions were for home mortgage interest, real estate taxes, and charitable contributions.

Boris and Natasha can deduct only $17,251, computed as follows:

AGI	$339,450
Less: threshold amount	-126,600
Excess over threshold:	$212,850
Multiplier	x .03
Reduction required	$ 6,386
Unreduced deductions	$ 23,700
Less: reduction required	- 6,386
Deductions that may be claimed:	$17,314

Minimizing the Effect of the Phaseout

If your family income is high enough to be affected by the phaseout of itemized deductions, your marginal tax rate may actually be several percentage points higher than the rates shown on page 15. The negative effects of the phaseout can sometimes be reduced by careful tax planning.

Reduce Taxable Income

The most basic strategy, of course, would be to reduce your adjusted gross income below the threshold for your filing status. Business owners can do this more easily than other taxpayers, because their ability to plow earnings back into the business is virtually unlimited.

Some other simple ways of doing this include maximizing your contributions to any retirement plans available to you, or to a nondeductible IRA or Roth IRA. While these IRA contributions won't lower your AGI for the current year, they will lower your taxable income in the future because earnings on the accounts are tax-free.

Another simple strategy is to receive investment income in a nontaxable form, by investing in tax-free municipal bonds. You might also decide to invest more heavily in non-dividend paying growth stocks, to avoid receiving currently taxable dividends.

You may also want to consult a financial planner or tax expert who can suggest more specific ways to trim your current income, including various family income-splitting tactics, charitable remainder trusts, etc.

Reverse Planning for Deductions

If it looks as if you're going to lose some percentage of your deductions anyway, you might want to reduce some of your deductible expenses. In particular, consider paying down your home mortgage or refinancing it at a cheaper rate, since the interest deduction is less valuable to you.

If, like many business owners, your income fluctuates from year to year, you might be able to pay for more deductible expenses in years when you have lower income and the deductions are less likely to be reduced.

Example

Charitable gifts should be made in January of a low-income year, rather than in December of a high-income year.

Chapter 16

Tax Credits and Miscellaneous Issues for Families

So far, we've discussed most of the tax issues that affect you in your capacity as a business owner, an employee, an investor, a homeowner, or a retiree.

In this chapter, we're going to tie up the loose ends by discussing a number of tax issues that pertain primarily to your family situation. First, we'll discuss the treatment of alimony, which is deductible by the person who pays it and is taxable to the person who receives it.

Next, we're going to cover a number of special tax breaks based on your family situation, including the new $500-per-child tax credit, the adoption expense exemption and credit that were added in 1997, and the credit for the elderly and the disabled.

We'll also discuss the new tax breaks for education, including the Hope Scholarship credit, the Lifetime Learning credit, education IRAs, and the exclusion of interest on certain student loans. We'll conclude with

a discussion of the earned income credit for lower-income families and individuals.

Tax Organizer Tip

Information regarding any alimony, adoption expenses, or education expenses that qualify for the Hope Scholarship or Lifetime Learning credits can be entered in the CompleteTax™ Organizer, in the "Miscellaneous" section.

Because the child tax credit and the earned income credit can be somewhat complicated to compute, we suggest you enter the information for these credits directly on the worksheets provided in this book. Information on the credit for the elderly and disabled, if it applies to you, can be entered directly on the relevant tax form.

ALIMONY

There are basically three ways in which money or property can change hands between divorced or divorcing spouses: child support, alimony, and division of property.

Two of these methods (child support payments and division of property) are generally non-events in terms of your taxes. Child support payments don't affect your taxes at all, unless you fall behind and have your tax refund confiscated to pay child support in arrears (more about that on page 299). And property transfers from one spouse to another either during a marriage, or transfers within one year after the divorce or pursuant to a divorce or separation agreement, are not taxable events for either party.

However, alimony is a different story. Although alimony (also known as spousal support) is generally out of fashion with most divorce courts, it is still afforded favorable treatment by the IRS.

Alimony is normally deductible by the person who pays it, and is taxable income to the recipient.

Because the purpose of alimony is to provide support from a higher-income person to a lower-income ex-spouse, the person paying alimony will very frequently be in a higher tax bracket than the person receiving it. Thus, a tax savings occurs that, in effect, causes Uncle Sam to pay part of the alimony.

Example

John is required by the divorce decree to pay Mary $1,000 a month in alimony. John is in the 28% bracket, so he gains a $280-per-month tax deduction, and his actual out-of-pocket cost for alimony is $720 per month. If Mary is in the 15% bracket, she must pay $150 in tax on the $1,000 alimony payment, and she keeps $850. The $130 difference between what John paid out-of-pocket and what Mary got to keep is "paid" by Uncle Sam.

Because alimony is treated so favorably, the IRS has devised a set of rules that are designed to keep people from treating as alimony those payments that are really a property settlement or child support.

Definition of Alimony

In order to be treated as deductible alimony, payments made from you to your spouse (or ex-spouse) must meet all of the following requirements:

- The payments must be in cash, check, or money order.

- The payments must be received by or on behalf of your spouse under a divorce or separation document (including a final decree, a temporary court order, or a written separation agreement between the two of you). Payments you make to third parties on behalf of your spouse, such as for your spouse's medical expenses, housing costs, taxes, tuition, etc., can qualify.

- You and your spouse must not opt out of alimony treatment by stating in the divorce decree that the payments aren't to be considered alimony for federal income tax purposes.

- If you and your spouse have received a final decree of divorce or decree of separate maintenance, you may not be living in the same household when the payment is made. If the payment was made under temporary orders and the decree is not yet final, it is okay to be living in the same home.

- The payer's obligation to make payments must end when the recipient dies, and there must be no liability to make any payment in cash or property as a substitute after the death.

- You and your spouse may not file a joint tax return with each other for the year.

- If any portion of the payment is considered by the IRS to be child support, that portion can't be treated as alimony.

Distinguishing Alimony from Child Support

The IRS will treat a payment as child support to the extent that it could in the future be reduced or ended when some event happens relating to your child, such as the child's death, marriage, graduation from high school or college, getting a job, reaching a specified age or income level, etc.

Even if the divorce decree is drafted to avoid mentioning any child-related events, the payment will be presumed to be child support if it will be reduced or ended within six months before or after your child reaches age 18 or 21, or, if you have more than one child, if the payments are to be reduced on two or more occasions, and each occasion takes place not more than one year before or after a different child reaches a certain age. The "certain age" must be between 18 and 24, and must be the same for each child.

Example

Michael is to pay Lisa Marie, his former wife, $2,000 per month in alimony. However, the payments are to be reduced to $1,500 per month on January 1, 2005, and to $1,000 per month on January 1, 2008. When the first reduction is scheduled to occur, the couple's first child, Michael Jr., will be 20 years, 5 months, and one day old. The second reduction will occur when their second child, Priscilla, is 22 years, 3 months, and 9 days old.

Because each reduction will occur within 1 year of a child's attainment of the age of 21 years and 4 months, and the total reductions are equal to $1,000, $1,000 of each "alimony" payment is considered to be nondeductible child support for tax purposes.

The rules discussed above apply to alimony in most states. However, in community property states, there are some differences in the way alimony is treated if paid before the divorce is final (e.g., under a temporary order). If you live in Arizona, California, Idaho, Louisiana, Nevada, New Mexico, Texas, Washington, or Wisconsin, you'll want to check with your lawyer or tax advisor about the tax treatment of temporary alimony you pay or receive.

Recapture of Frontloaded Alimony

To prevent a property settlement from being disguised as alimony, a provision in the federal tax law requires that when large sums of alimony (over $15,000) are paid in the first or second year following the divorce, but significantly less is paid in the third year, a portion of the alimony deducted by the payer in the first two years is recaptured by being added back to the payer's taxable income in the third year. This has the effect of "recapturing" the lost tax for the IRS.

If this recapture rule applies, the spouse who received the alimony (and had initially been required to include it in income) is entitled to a corresponding deduction in the third year.

The rule does not apply to alimony paid under temporary support orders (i.e., before the final decree is issued) nor does it apply when the reason for the drop-off in alimony in the third year was that the recipient died or remarried, or that less alimony was paid because the amount of alimony was based on a fixed portion of the payer's income from a business, property, or other compensation.

If the recapture rule applies to you, you can use the following worksheet to determine the amount to be recaptured.

Worksheet for Recapture of Alimony

Note: Do not enter less than zero on any line.

1. Alimony paid in **2nd year** . . . . _____
2. Alimony paid in **3rd year** . . . .
3. Floor $15,000

4. Add lines 2 and 3 . . . . _____
5. Subtract line 4 from line 1 . . . . _____
6. Alimony paid in **1st year** . . . .
7. Adjusted alimony paid in **2nd year** (line 1 less line 5) . . . . _____
8. Alimony paid in **3rd year** . . . . _____
9. Add lines 7 and 8 . . . . _____
10. Divide line 9 by 2 . . . . _____
11. Floor $15,000

12. Add lines 10 and 11 . . . . _____
13. Subtract line 12 from line 6 . . . .
14. **Recaptured alimony.** Add lines 5 and 13 . . . . * _____

Reporting Alimony Payments

Reporting alimony is simple – you don't need to file an extra tax form to do it. However, you must use the long income tax form (Form 1040) instead of Form 1040EZ or 1040A.

If you received alimony, write the amount on Line 11 of Form 1040. If you paid alimony, write the amount on Line 31a, and also write the recipient's Social Security number on Line 31b. If you paid alimony to more than one person, write one person's number on Line 31b, and attach a statement to your return showing an itemization of how much you paid to each person, and listing each recipient's SSN.

THE CHILD TAX CREDIT

Beginning in 1998, Congress instituted a new $400-per-child tax credit for every dependent child who is 16 or under at the end of the year, and who is a U.S. citizen or resident alien. This credit has increased to $500 in 1999 and later years.

A qualifying child is one who meets the dependency tests (see page 161), and is your natural or adopted child, grandchild or great-grandchild, stepchild, or a foster child. "Adopted child" includes a child placed with you for adoption even if the adoption has not been finalized. A foster child must have lived with you the entire year to qualify unless the child was born or died during the year.

Like most of the tax credits and other breaks that have been enacted lately, there is an income limitation on the people who can claim this credit. The phaseout of the credit begins at modified adjusted gross income (AGI) of $110,000 for joint filers, $75,000 for singles and heads of household, and $55,000 for marrieds filing separately. You will lose $50 of your total child credit for each $1,000 (or fraction of $1,000) of your modified AGI that exceeds the applicable threshold. For this purpose, modified AGI includes the amount shown on Line 33 of Form 1040 or Line 18 of Form 1040A, plus any foreign earned income exclusion, foreign housing exclusion, and income from U.S. possessions, if any.

Example

Stephen Cooper and his wife Sally have three children, which would qualify them for a child tax credit of $1,500 in 1999. Their modified AGI is $119,500, which exceeds the threshold of $110,000 by $9,500. Therefore, they will lose $50 x 10 = $500 of their credit, leaving a remaining credit of $1,000.

Claiming the Credit

After you determine whether and how many of your dependents qualify for the credit, you must remember to check the box next to the names of the qualifying children on the front of your tax form (the boxes are in Column 4 of Line 6c on Form 1040 or 1040A).

The child tax credit is subtracted from your tax bill after several of the other credits; namely, the credit for child and dependent care expenses, the credit for the elderly and the disabled, and the new education credits described below. You will need to compute the amounts of any of those credits that apply to you before you can determine the amount of tax that's left over, and therefore is available to be reduced by your child tax credit. The tax credit is not refundable, so that if your tax bill, after the credits mentioned above,

is less than your child tax credit, you'll lose some or all of your child credit.

There is an exception to this rule if you have three or more children. In that case, you may be able to claim the "additional child tax credit" which might be refundable, to the extent that it, plus any earned income credit you can claim, does not exceed the amount of Social Security taxes you paid.

You'll need to use the worksheets that follow to determine the actual amount of your child tax credit or additional child credit. If you had three or more children and your tax bill is too low to allow you to claim all of your child credit, you must complete and file IRS Form 8812, *Additional Child Tax Credit,* in order to be able to claim the extra refundable amount.

Child Tax Credit Worksheet—Line 43

▶ Keep for your records.

1. $500.00 × _____ . Multiply and enter the result .... 1. ____

   Enter number of qualifying children

2. Are you filing **Form 2555, 2555-EZ, or 4563,** or are you excluding income from Puerto Rico?
   - ☐ **No.** Enter the amount from Form 1040, line 34.
   - ☐ **Yes.** Enter your **modified adjusted gross income** } ... 2. ____

3. Enter the amount shown below for your filing status:
   - Married filing jointly, enter $110,000
   - Single, head of household, or qualifying widow(er), enter $75,000 } ... 3. ____
   - Married filing separately, enter $55,000

4. Is line 2 more than line 3?
   - ☐ **No.** Skip lines 4 and 5, enter -0- on line 6, and go to line 7.
   - ☐ **Yes.** Subtract line 3 from line 2 .... 4. ____

5. Divide line 4 by $1,000. If the result is not a whole number, round it up to the next higher whole number (for example, round 0.01 to 1) .... 5. ____

6. Multiply $50 by the number on line 5. .... 6. ____

7. Subtract line 6 from line 1. If zero or less, **stop here;** you **cannot** take this credit .. 7. ____

8. Enter the amount from Form 1040, line 40 .... 8. ____

9. Is line 1 above more than $1,000?
   - ☐ **No.** Add the amounts from Form 1040, lines 41, 42, and 44. Enter the total.
   - ☐ **Yes.** Enter the amount from the worksheet on the next page } ... 9. ____

10. Subtract line 9 above from line 8 .... 10. ____

11. **Child tax credit.** Enter the **smaller** of line 7 or line 10 here and on Form 1040, line 43 11. ____

*If line 1 above is more than $1,000, you may be able to take the **Additional Child Tax Credit.***

Line 9 of Child Tax Credit Worksheet (keep for your records)

Use this worksheet **only** if you checked "Yes" on line 9 of the worksheet

1. Add the amounts from Form 1040, lines 41, 42, and 44. Enter the total . . . . **1.** _____

2. Are you claiming any of the following credits: the adoption credit (**Form 8839**), the mortgage interest credit (**Form 8396**), or the District of Columbia first-time homebuyer credit (**Form 8859**)?

   ☐ **No.**   **Stop here**; enter the amount from line 1 above on line 9 of the worksheet.

   ☐ **Yes.** Enter the amount from line 7 of the worksheet .   **2.** _____

         Next, complete Form 1040, lines 52, 59a, 59b, and 62 if they apply to you. Then, go to line 3 below.

3. Enter the total social security and Medicare taxes withheld from your pay (and your spouse's if filing a joint return). These taxes should be shown in boxes 4 and 6 of your W-2 form(s). If you worked for a railroad, see below . . . . **3.** _____

4. Enter the total of the amounts from Form 1040, line 27 and line 52, plus any uncollected social security and Medicare or RRTA tax on tips or group-term life insurance. This tax should be shown in box 13 of your W-2 form(s) with codes **A** and **B** or **M** and **N**.   **4.** _____

5. Add lines 3 and 4 . . . .   **5.** _____

6. Add the amounts from Form 1040, lines 59a and 62. Enter the total . . . . . .   **6.** _____

7. Subtract line 6 from line 5. If zero, **stop here**; enter the amount from line 1 above on line 9 of the worksheet . . . . **7.** _____

8. Subtract line 7 from line 2. If line 7 is more than line 2, enter -0-. This is your child tax credit for purposes of figuring the credits listed on line 2   **8.** _____

    Next, complete the applicable credit form(s) listed on line 2. Use the amount from line 8 above in place of the amount from Form 1040, line 43. Then, go to line 9 below.

9. Enter the total of any adoption credit from Form 8839, line 14, mortgage interest credit from Form 8396, line 11, and District of Columbia first-time homebuyer credit from Form 8859, line 11 . .   **9.** _____

10. Add lines 1 and 9. Enter the total here and on line 9 of the worksheet . . . .   **10.** _____

Railroad Employees. Include the following taxes in the total on line 3 above.

- Tier 1 tax withheld from your pay. This tax should be shown in box 14 of your W-2 form(s) and identified as "Tier 1 tax."
- If you were an employee representative, 50% of the total Tier 1 tax and Tier 1 Medicare tax you paid for 1999.

Work Smart

The child tax credit, education tax credit, and the tax credit for adoption were not originally designed to count against the alternative minimum tax (AMT). As a result, with the addition of these credits some taxpayers who would normally never need to look at the AMT tax forms would actually have had to pay AMT this year because their regular tax bill was being reduced significantly by the credits.

The good news is that Congress has granted some relief. These credits will be allowed against the AMT taxes and eligible families won't lose their credits for 1998 through 2001.

The bad news is that the relief expires in 2002. Unless Congress extends the law, many families who claim these credits will have to calculate and perhaps even pay AMT after 2001. For more on the AMT, see page 301.

TAX BENEFITS FOR ADOPTION

As of 1997, two new tax breaks for adoptive parents became available: an exclusion of up to $5,000 paid under an employee benefit plan that pays for adoption expenses, and a tax credit for up to $5,000 for expenses that were not reimbursed by your employer. For either of these tax breaks, the amount is increased to $6,000 for adoptions of children who are U.S. citizens or residents, and are determined to be "special needs children" by a state.

However, both tax breaks begin to be phased out for those with adjusted gross income (AGI) over $75,000. If your income is $115,000 or more, you can't claim any tax benefits for adoptions.

Qualifying Expenses

For both of these tax breaks, adoption expenses are defined in the same way. They include:

- adoption fees

- court costs

- legal fees

- traveling expenses (including meals and lodging)

- other expenses directly related to the legal adoption of an eligible child

The child must be under 18 years old, or physically or mentally incapable of self-care. You can't deduct expenses for adoptions that violate state law, that involve surrogate parent arrangements, that involve adopting your spouse's child, or that are allowed as a credit or deduction under any other federal income tax rule (for example, medical expenses that can be claimed as itemized deductions are not adoption expenses).

If eligible, you can take advantage of both the employer-provided benefits and the adoption tax credit, but you can't use the same expenses to qualify for two different tax breaks.

Example

In 1999 the adoption of your son was finalized, and you had paid a total of $7,000 in qualified expenses for the adoption. Your employer reimbursed you for $5,000 of your expenses. Therefore, you can claim a tax credit for the other $2,000 in qualified expenses in 1999.

Special Needs Children

To be considered a special needs child, a state must determine that the child cannot or should not live with his or her parents, and that unless financial assistance is provided, it's unlikely that the child will be adopted because of factors such as the child's ethnic or minority background, the child's age, the fact that the child is a member of a sibling group, or the child's medical condition or mental or physical handicap.

Dollar Limits on the Exclusion and Credit

The dollar limits for both the exclusion and the credit apply "per adoption effort." Therefore, if your adoption spans two or more years, you can only claim total credits of $5,000 (or $6,000 for a special needs child) over all the years that you paid expenses. You could also claim an additional $5,000 (or $6,000) in excluded employee benefits, if your employer provides an adoption assistance plan.

If the child is a U.S. citizen or resident, you can claim the tax benefits whether or not your adoption effort is successful. However, if you attempt to adopt one child and the adoption falls through, upon which you attempt to adopt another child, the entire chain of events counts as one "adoption effort." If you adopt two (or more) children, each child's adoption would count as a separate adoption effort even if you adopt the children at the same time (for example, if you adopt a sibling group).

Phaseout of Benefits at Higher Income Levels

To determine whether your income is high enough to cause you to lose some of the adoption benefits, add up your adjusted gross income as shown on Line 33 of Form 1040, or Line 18 of Form 1040A. You must add to this amount the amount of any tax-free adoption benefits you received from your employer, and also any foreign earned income exclusion, foreign housing exclusion or deduction, or excluded income from U.S. possessions.

If your AGI, as modified above, is $75,000 or less, you qualify for the entire dollar amount of the credit and/or exclusion. If your AGI is $115,000 or more, you won't qualify at all. If your AGI is in between these amounts, your credit and exclusion will both be reduced in proportion to how high your income is in relation to the $40,000 phaseout range. By working through IRS Form 8839, *Qualified Adoption Expenses*, you'll compute the limitation if one applies.

Example

If your modified AGI is $85,000, the amount that exceeds $75,000 is $10,000. Since $10,000 is ¼ of the phaseout range, you will lose ¼ of *the adoption credit and also ¼ of the exclusion, so the maximum benefit you could claim for either the exclusion or credit for a non-special-needs child would be $3,750. If you were eligible for both the credit and exclusion, you could claim a maximum of $7,500 in total benefits.*

Claiming the Exclusion or Credit

If you are married, you must file a joint return with your spouse to claim either the credit or the exclusion, unless (1) you are legally separated, or (2) you have lived apart from your spouse for the last six months of the year and your home is the child's home for more than half the year, and you paid more than half the cost of keeping up your home for the year.

Both the exclusion of employer-paid adoption benefits and the tax credit for adoption must be claimed on IRS Form 8839, which must be attached to either Form 1040 or 1040A.

The exclusion is claimed on Part III of the form. Note that any employer-paid benefits are excluded from income taxation, but are still taxable for purposes of Social Security and Medicare tax. The total amount of adoption benefits you received should be shown in Box 13 of your W-2 Form. If your employer excluded more benefits than you are entitled to (for example, because your spouse is employed, thus raising your AGI above $75,000), you may have to add some of the amount in Box 13 to your taxable wages shown in Box 1.

You should generally claim the exclusion in the year your employer pays you for the expenses, but for foreign adoptions, you must claim the exclusion in the later of the year the adoption becomes final or the year of the payment. Unsuccessful foreign adoptions don't qualify for the exclusion.

The tax credit is claimed on Part II of the form. For adoptions of children that are U.S. citizens or residents, you may claim expenses in the year after they are paid or the year the adoption is final, whichever is earlier. If you pay expenses in a year after the year the adoption is final, claim the credit for those expenses in the year you pay them. Again, if the child is a foreign child, you must claim the expenses in the later of the year the adoption becomes final, or the

year you paid them. Unsuccessful foreign adoptions do not qualify for the credit.

Carryovers of Unused Credits

The adoption tax credit is subtracted from your income tax bill, after the subtraction of any credit for child and dependent care expenses, any credit for the elderly or disabled, any mortgage interest credit, and the education credits. If your tax bill is not all that large to begin with, you may find that you're not able to take full advantage of all the credits you're entitled to.

If that is the case, any unused portion of your adoption tax credit for 1999 can be carried over to the next year to be subtracted from your 2000 tax bill. If there are still unused portions of the credit, you can carry it forward for up to four more years.

Child's Identification Number

If your adoptive child can not obtain a Social Security number, or an ITIN for a resident or nonresident alien, you must obtain an adoption taxpayer identification number by completing IRS Form W-7A, which you can obtain by calling 1-800-TAX-FORM.

CREDIT FOR THE ELDERLY AND DISABLED

A tax credit is available to certain low-income individuals if they are at least age 65 or older before the close of the tax year, and to individuals under age 65 if they are retired with a permanent and total disability, and have taxable disability income from a public or private employer.

If you're married at the end of the tax year, you and your spouse must file a joint return to claim this credit, unless you did not live with your spouse at any time during the tax year. In that case, you can file either jointly or separately.

You must be a U.S. citizen or resident to claim this credit, unless you're married to a U.S. citizen or resident, and you both elect to be treated as U.S. residents (and taxed on your worldwide income).

Income Limits for the Credit

Because of the way the credit is structured, your credit will be phased out completely under the following circumstances:

- For singles, your credit will be zero if you have an adjusted gross income (AGI) for the year of $17,500 or more, or if you receive $5,000 or more in nontaxable Social Security, railroad retirement, or veteran's benefits or pension, annuity, or disability benefits that are excluded from your gross income.

- If you are married and file a joint return, and either you or your spouse (but not both) qualify for the credit, your credit will be zero if your joint return adjusted gross income is $20,000 or more, or if you or your spouse receive $5,000 or more in nontaxable Social Security, railroad retirement, or veterans' benefits or pension, annuity, or disability benefits that are excluded from gross income.

- For marrieds filing jointly, if both you and your spouse qualify for the credit, your credit will be zero if your joint return adjusted gross income is $25,000 or more, or if you or your spouse receive $7,500 or more in nontaxable Social Security, railroad retirement, or veterans' benefits or pension, annuity, or disability benefits that are excluded from gross income.

- If you are married and file a separate return, you will not be entitled to any credit unless you are living apart from your spouse for the entire tax year. Even if you qualify, your credit will be zero if you have an adjusted gross income of $12,500 or more, or receive $3,750 or more in nontaxable Social Security, railroad retirement, or veterans' benefits or pension, annuity, or disability benefit that are excluded from your gross income.

Clearly, before you can determine your credit amount, you'll have to determine how much (if any) of your Social Security benefits are taxable, as discussed on page 250.

Computing Your Credit

If you qualify and have income below the limits described above, your starting point for computing the credit is an amount that is determined by your filing status: $5,000 if you are single or married filing jointly with one spouse qualifying for the credit, $7,500 if you are filing jointly and both spouses qualify for the credit, or $3,750 if you are married filing separately.

Then, reduce this amount dollar-for-dollar for pension, annuity, or disability benefits that are excluded from your gross income and also for nontaxable Social Security, railroad retirement, or veteran's benefits payable under a VA program. If you file a joint return, you must combine all benefits paid to both you and your spouse.

Your initial credit amount is further reduced by one-half the amount by which your AGI exceeds one of the following amounts: $7,500 for singles, $10,000 if married filing jointly, or $5,000 if married filing separately.

Finally, multiply the amount that remains after all these subtractions by 15 percent to arrive at your credit amount.

Example

Assume that you are age 66 and single, have an adjusted gross income (AGI) of $8,500 for 1999, and receive $4,000 of nontaxable Social Security benefits for the year. You would determine your credit for the elderly as follows:

Initial amount	*$5,000*
Less: social security benefits	*-4,000*
Reduced initial amount	*1,000*
Less: one-half of AGI above $7,500	*-500*
	500

Credit: $500 x 15% = $75

Special Rules for Disabled People Under Age 65

If you are permanently and totally disabled and are under age 65, special rules apply to determine your credit. Your initial amount may not exceed your taxable disability income for the tax year. Thus, your initial amount is the lesser of your applicable initial amount based on your filing status, as described above, or your disability income for the year.

You are considered to be permanently and totally disabled if you are unable to engage in any substantial gainful activity by reason of any medically determinable physical or mental impairment that can be expected to last for not less than 12 months, or to result in death.

You must furnish proof of your disability to the IRS. Generally this means you must attach a physician's statement, certifying the disability, to your tax return, using the statement on page 4 of the instructions for either Schedule R (for Form 1040) or Schedule 3 (for Form 1040A). You don't have to attach a statement if you filed one in an earlier year and the doctor signed line B on the statement.

TAX BREAKS FOR EDUCATION

Beginning in 1998, a new group of tax benefits has become available to those who are pursuing higher education for themselves, their spouse, or their dependents.

In this section we'll describe the similarities and differences between the Hope Scholarship credit, the Lifetime Learning credit, education IRAs, and the deduction for interest on qualified student loans. In most cases you have to choose among these benefits, since the same student is not permitted to use two different education tax breaks in the same year.

Save Money

For each student, in a given year you can only take advantage of one of the following: Hope Scholarship credit, Lifetime Learning credit, or withdrawal from an education IRA.

For those who qualify, the Hope Scholarship credit will generally save you the most tax money. If you don't qualify, the Lifetime Learning Credit is generally the next-best tax break. Since education IRAs only became available in 1998, they are unlikely to help current students; however they can be a useful way to start an education fund for a new baby or young child. For those who have recently graduated, the student-loan interest deduction provides a measure of relief.

The Hope Scholarship Credit

If you, your spouse, or a dependent for whom you claim an exemption was enrolled at least half-time in the first or second year of college in 1999, you may benefit from the Hope Scholarship credit.

The credit is for the first $1,000 of qualified expenses incurred by the student, and 50 percent of the next $1,000, so that the full credit of $1,500 applies if the student has at least $2,000 in expenses.

The Hope credit is available for each student in your family who meets the qualifications:

- he or she is enrolled in the first or second year of postsecondary education

- is enrolled in a program that leads to a degree, certificate, or other recognized academic credential

- is taking at least one-half of the normal full-time load of classes, for at least one academic period beginning during the calendar year

- has not been convicted of a drug-related felony

The only expenses that count toward the credit are tuition and fees required for attendance. Generally, the expenses can be deducted in the year the class begins, if the expenses were paid during that year. However, if you prepay expenses during one year, for a course that begins in the first three months of the following year, you can count those expenses toward the credit in the year they was paid.

Eligible institutions are any accredited public, nonprofit, or for-profit postsecondary institution eligible to participate in federal student aid programs.

Income-Related Phaseout

Unfortunately, the Hope Scholarship credit (as well as the Lifetime Learning credit) is phased out for those at higher income levels.

Warning

Although either the student or the parent (but not both) can claim a Hope Scholarship or Lifetime Learning credit, you can't avoid the high-income phaseouts for either of these credits by having the student claim the credit, unless the student is not claimed as a dependent on the parent's tax return.

The phaseout occurs in the income range of $40,000 to $50,000 for singles and the range of $80,000 to $100,000 for marrieds filing a joint return. To determine whether your credit will be affected by the phaseout, you must consider your modified adjusted gross income; that is, your AGI as shown on Line 33 of Form 1040 (or Line 18 on Form 1040A), plus any foreign earned income exclusion, plus amounts derived from sources in American possessions if you are a resident of the possession (Guam, American Samoa, the Northern Mariana Islands, or Puerto Rico).

The phaseout is computed by reducing the amount of your credit by a fraction. The fraction is found by taking the amount of your modified AGI that exceeds $40,000 (or $80,000 if filing jointly) and dividing it by $10,000 (or by $20,000 if filing jointly).

Example

Steve and Kit are married filing jointly, and have twin sons who are both freshmen in college in 1999. For each of the boys, tuition costs exceed $2,000. Steve and Kit would normally have a Hope credit of $1,500 for each son, or $3,000 in total.

However, their AGI is $85,000 so they must reduce

their credit as follows: their AGI exceeds $80,000 by $5,000, and they divide $5,000 by $20,000 to get a fraction of ¼. Therefore, ¼ of their credit will not be allowed, and they can claim a Hope credit of only $2,250 for 1999.

Claiming the Credit

To claim the Hope Scholarship credit (or the Lifetime Learning credit described below) you must complete IRS Form 8863, *Education Credits*, and attach it to your Form 1040 or 1040A. These credits are subtracted from your tax bill after the credit for child and dependent care expenses, the credit for the elderly and the disabled, and the child tax credit – and if all these credits reduce your tax bill to zero, you will lose any unclaimed amount of the education credits, because they may not be carried over into a subsequent year.

Lifetime Learning Credit

For those who have two years of college under their belt and can't qualify for the Hope credit, the Lifetime Learning credit provides a smaller tax benefit for an unlimited number of years in which you took one or more postsecondary educational courses. The courses can apply towards an undergraduate, graduate, or professional degree, certificate program, or other academic credential. You can claim the credit for yourself, your spouse if filing jointly, and any dependents for whom you claim an exemption on your tax return.

This credit is worth 20 percent of the first $5,000 in higher education expenses *per family*. Therefore, the maximum amount of credit you can claim is $1,000. If one or more students in the family are eligible for the Hope credit, other family members may use the full $5,000 of the Lifetime Learning credit. However, a single student cannot use both credits; he or she must choose between them.

The Lifetime Learning credit applies to tuition and fees (as with the Hope credit) and the same higher-income phaseout methods apply. To claim the credit, you must use Form 8863, *Education Credits*, and attach it to your tax return. Don't forget that if the education was job- or business-related, you might be able to deduct it instead of claiming the credit. See page 182.

Education IRAs

A third type of tax break for educational expenses that first became available in 1998 is the education IRA. "IRA" is something of a misnomer because this type of account is not designed to survive into the beneficiary's retirement. However, the account works similarly to a Roth IRA in that contributions are not deductible, but interest and dividends that build up within the account are tax-free, and amounts withdrawn from the account under proper circumstances will not be taxed.

Education IRAs are set up on a per-child basis, with a bank or other financial institution approved by the IRS. Each child must have one or more separate accounts, and the child, a parent, grandparent or friend may contribute up to $500 to the account each year. More than one person can contribute on behalf of the same child, but the total contributions for that child cannot exceed $500. No contributions can be after the child turns 18, and no contributions can be made in the same year that a contribution is made to a qualified state tuition program on behalf of the child.

Income Restrictions

The person who contributes to the account must have a modified adjusted gross income (AGI), as computed for the Hope Scholarship and Lifetime Learning credits, of less than $110,000 or less than $160,000 if the contributor files a joint return.

As you might expect, there is a phaseout range for contributions of from $95,000 to $110,000 for singles and from $150,000 to $160,000 for joint filers. If you fall within the range, your contribution is limited as follows: Take the amount by which your modified AGI exceeds the lower limit of the phaseout range that applies to you, and divide it by $15,000 (or by $10,000 in the case of a joint return). The result will be a decimal number that should be multiplied by $500 to determine the amount of the contribution you can't make.

Work Smart

If your income is high enough to fall within the phaseout range, you can avoid losing any of the contribution by having someone with lower income, such as a grandparent or family friend, make a contribution for the child.

Distributions from Education IRAs

If a distribution is taken from an education IRA, the amount will not be taxed to the extent that it does not exceed the beneficiary's qualified higher education expenses. For this purpose, qualified expenses include tuition, fees, books, supplies and equipment, and if the child is at least a half-time student, up to $2,500 each year for room and board. Virtually any accredited postsecondary educational institution will qualify.

If the distribution does exceed the child's educational expenses, the excess portion of the distribution will be taxable to the child to the extent that it represents the tax-free earnings on the account (the original contributions will be recovered tax-free). In addition, a 10 percent additional tax will apply to the taxable portion of the distribution, unless the distribution was made because of the beneficiary's death, disability, or because the beneficiary received a scholarship or some other nontaxable education benefit (such as employer-paid benefits). If the beneficiary dies, the balance must be distributed to his or her estate within 30 days.

Education IRAs can be rolled over to a different trustee, so long as the rollover occurs within 60 days of the withdrawal from the original account. Once a rollover is made, you must wait at least 12 months before making another one.

The balance remaining in an education IRA must be distributed within 30 days after a beneficiary reaches age 30. To avoid tax on the distribution at age 30 (or indeed at any time) the beneficiary on the Education IRA account can be changed, with no tax consequences, if the new beneficiary is the child's child or descendent, stepchildren or descendent, sibling or their descendent, parent or grandparent, stepparent, or the spouse of any of these family members.

Student Loan Interest

If you paid interest on a student loan in 1999, you may be eligible to deduct some or all of the interest you paid, whether the loan was for your own education, your spouse's, or that of a child or anyone else who was your dependent at the time the education was undertaken.

However, only interest paid in the first 60 months that interest payments are required is deductible, and for 1999, the maximum deduction is $1,500. The deductible amounts are scheduled to rise to $2,000 for 2000, and $2,500 for 2001 and later years. If you refinance the loan you can still claim the deduction, but refinancing does not extend the original 60-month period.

The deduction is phased out for those with modified adjusted gross income between $40,000 and $55,000 if you are single, or between $60,000 and $75,000 if filing a joint return. You can't claim this deduction at all if you are married filing separately, or if you can be claimed as a dependent on someone else's return.

For purposes of this deduction, "modified adjusted gross income" is computed by taking the AGI amount from Line 33 of Form 1040, and adding back any foreign earned income exclusion, foreign housing exclusion or deduction, and the exclusion of income for residents of American possessions.

To figure the limit, take the portion of your modified AGI that exceeds $40,000 (or $60,000 if you are married filing jointly) and divide it by $15,000. The resulting decimal should be multiplied by your interest deduction to determine the amount that you will lose due to your high level of income.

Which Loans Qualify?

Beyond the dollar amount of the interest ($1,000) and the AGI restrictions, this tax break also places some limits on the types of loan, the expenses that the loan had to be used for, and the type of education the student was pursuing.

The loan must have been taken out to pay qualified higher education expenses, which include the costs of tuition, fees, room and board, books, equipment, and other necessary expenses such as transportation. However, you must reduce these costs by any employer-provided educational benefits received by the student, any nontaxable distributions from an education IRA, any savings bond interest that was nontaxable because it was used for education expenses, any nontaxable scholarships or veteran's education benefits, or any other nontaxable payments other than gifts, bequests or inheritances.

Qualified educational institutions for this purpose include virtually any accredited postsecondary institution, including those conducting internship or residency programs in hospitals or health care facilities. However, to be eligible the student must have been enrolled in a degree, certificate or similar program, and must have been carrying at least one-half the normal full-time load.

Claiming the Deduction

You don't need to fill out any special forms to claim the student loan interest deduction, and you don't need to itemize your deductions to take advantage of it. The deductible amount is simply written on Line 24 of Form 1040, or Line 16 of Form 1040A, and subtracted from your income.

The Earned Income Credit

A special tax credit, known as the earned income credit or EIC, is available to lower-income taxpayers who have at least some earnings from personal services during the year. For 1999, the credit is available to most workers between the ages of 25 and 64 with an adjusted gross income (AGI) of less than $10,200. Workers with one qualifying child may get the credit if their AGI is less than $26,928, or less than $30,580 if they have more than one qualifying child.

However, if you have investment income of $2,350 or more, you won't qualify for the credit. Investment income includes taxable and nontaxable interest and dividends, capital gains, net income from rental of personal property, net royalty income, and net income from passive activities shown on Schedule E, including real estate rentals (see IRS Publication 596, *Earned Income Credit*, if you are on the borderline and need to know exactly which lines on Schedule E to look at in determining your passive income).

All of these ceiling amounts are adjusted for inflation each year.

 Work Smart

The extraordinary thing about the EIC is that if your credit is higher than the tax you'd

otherwise owe, you will get the difference as a "refund" from the IRS. This extra payment from the federal government is intended to reward lower-income persons for working.

Are You Eligible for the Credit?

In order to be eligible for the EIC in 1999, you must earn at least $1 during the year at a job or self-employment, and meet the income requirements discussed above.

If you are claiming the higher credit based on having one or two children, each child must meet certain requirements. The child may be your natural child, grandchild, stepchild, foster child, or adopted child.

The child must be under the age of 19, and must live with you for more than half your tax year. However, if the child is a student he or she may be up to 23 years old. If the child is permanently and totally disabled, age doesn't matter. If the child is a foster child, he or she must live with you for all of your tax year. A child who is married does not qualify you for the EIC, unless you can claim a dependency exemption for the child. Also, if a child qualifies you for the EIC, that child cannot claim the EIC himself or herself.

If you have a foster child, you should note that beginning in 2000, a foster child won't qualify for the EIC unless he or she lived with you for the entire year, was cared for like your own child, and either (a) was your relative or (b) was placed in your home by a state or nonprofit agency.

If you're married, you must file a joint tax return with your spouse to claim the EIC. Both spouses' income counts in determining the amount of the credit. There's an exception for persons who are treated as unmarried because their spouses have not been a member of the household during the last six months of the tax year; these people can still claim the EIC when they file their tax returns as single or as a head of household.

If two or more taxpayers seek to claim the same child in their bid for the EIC (e.g., a parent and grandparent living in the same household with a child) only the person with the highest AGI may claim the credit. If the child spends exactly half the year in each of two households, nobody can claim an EIC based on that child.

How the Credit Is Computed

The basic EIC is computed in two stages. First, you start with a certain percentage of your earned income up to a certain amount. This is the maximum basic EIC. For 1999, the maximum is $347 if you have no children, $2,312 with one qualifying child, and $3,816 if you have two.

Then, you subtract a percentage of the portion of your AGI that exceeds a specified level. For this part of the computation, you must count all your taxable income, whatever the source – not just earned income. What's more, you must also add in any nontaxable interest you received, any capital losses, any nontaxable retirement plan payments unless they were rolled over into an IRA, and 75 percent of any losses you had in your business or farm. You must also include certain nontaxable earned income, such as 401(k) contributions, nontaxable dependent care and adoption benefits, and the value of food and lodging provided for the convenience of the employer.

The EIC amount is phased down as your income gets higher, and at a certain point it's phased out completely. To find the actual amount of your EIC, you must complete the EIC worksheets reproduced below. The EIC tables referred to in the worksheet are those at the end of this chapter.

Also, if you are claiming a higher EIC amount because you have one or more qualifying children, you must also complete Schedule EIC and attach it to your tax return. The credit amount will be transferred to Line 59a on Form 1040, or Line 37a of Form 1040A.

Line 5 of EIC Worksheet
(keep for your records)

If filing a joint return and your spouse was also self-employed or reported income and expenses on Schedule C or C-EZ as a statutory employee, combine your spouse's amounts with yours to figure the amounts to enter below.

---

1. **If you are filing Schedule SE:**
   a. Enter the amount from Schedule SE, Section A, line 3, or Section B, line 3, whichever applies. . . . . **1a.** _____
   b. Enter the amount, if any, from Schedule SE, Section B, line 4b . . . . . . **1b.** _____
   c. Add lines 1a and 1b . . . . . . **1c.** _____
   d. Enter the amount from Form 1040, line 27 . . . . **1d.** _____
   e. Subtract line 1d from line 1c . . . . **1e.** _____

2. **If you are NOT required to file Schedule SE** (for example, because your net earnings from self-employment were less than $400), complete lines 2a through 2c. But **do not** include on these lines any statutory employee income or any amount exempt from self-employment tax as the result of the filing and approval of **Form 4029** or **Form 4361.**
   a. Enter any net farm profit or (loss) from Schedule F, line 36, and farm partnerships, Schedule K-1 (Form 1065), line 15a . . . . **2a.** _____
   b. Enter any net profit or (loss) from Schedule C, line 31, Schedule C-EZ, line 3, Schedule K-1 (Form 1065), line 15a (other than farming), and Schedule K-1 (Form 1065-B), box 9 . . . . **2b.** _____
   c. Add lines 2a and 2b. Enter the total even if a loss . . **2c.** _____

3. **If you are filing Schedule C or C-EZ as a statutory employee,** enter the amount from line 1 of that Schedule C or C-EZ . . . . **3.** _____

4. Add lines 1e, 2c, and 3. Enter the total here and on line 5 of the worksheet on page 38 even if a loss. If the result is a loss, enter it in parentheses and read the **Caution** below . . . . **4.** _____

   Caution: *If line 5 of the Earned Income Credit Worksheet is a loss, subtract it from the total of lines 3 and 4 of that worksheet and enter the result on line 6 of that worksheet. If the result is zero or less, you **cannot** take the earned income credit.*

Earned Income Credit Worksheet—Line 59a
(keep for your records)

Caution: *Be sure to include all your income on lines 1, 2, 4, 5, and 8 below. An incorrect amount may increase your tax or reduce your refund.*

1. Enter the amount from Form 1040, line 7 . . . . . **1.** _____

2. If you received a taxable scholarship or fellowship grant that was not reported on a W-2 form, enter that amount here . . . . **2.** _____

3. Subtract line 2 from line 1 . . . . **3.** _____

4. Enter any **nontaxable earned income** (see the next page). Types of nontaxable earned income include contributions to a 401(k) plan, and military housing and subsistence. These should be shown in box 13 of your W-2 form . **4.** _____

5. If you were self-employed **or** used Schedule C or C-EZ as a statutory employee, enter the amount from the worksheet on the next page . . . . **5.** _____

6. Add lines 3, 4, and 5 . . . . **6.** _____

7. Look up the amount on **line 6** above in the **EIC Table** on pages **40–42** to find your credit. Enter the credit here . . **7.** _____

   If line 7 is zero, **stop.** You **cannot** take the credit. Enter "No" directly to the right of Form 1040, line 59a.

8. Enter your **modified AGI** (see this page) . . . . . . **8.** _____

9. **Is line 8 less than—**
   - $5,670 if you do not have a qualifying child?
   - $12,460 if you have at least one qualifying child?

   ☐ **Yes.** Go to line 10 now.

   ☐ **No.** Look up the amount on **line 8** above in the **EIC Table** on pages **40–42** to find your credit. Enter the credit here . . . . **9.** _____

10. **Earned income credit.**
    - If you checked "Yes" on line 9, enter the amount from line 7.
    - If you checked "No" on line 9, enter the **smaller** of line 7 or line 9 . . . . **10.** _____

Next: Take the amount from line 10 above and enter it on Form 1040, line 59a.

AND

If you had any nontaxable earned income (see line 4 above), enter the amount and type of that income in the spaces provided on line 59b.

AND

Complete **Schedule EIC** and attach it to your return ONLY if you have a qualifying child.

Note: *If you owe the alternative minimum tax (Form 1040, line 51), subtract it from the amount on line 10 above. Then, enter the result (if more than zero) on Form 1040, line 59a. Also, replace the amount on line 10 above with the amount entered on Form 1040, line 59a.*

1999 Earned Income Credit (EIC) Table

 This is **not** a tax table.

1. To find your credit, read down the "At least – But less than" columns and find the line that includes the amount you were told to look up from your EIC Worksheet.

2. Then, read across to the column that includes the number of qualifying children you have. Enter the credit from that column on your EIC Worksheet.

Example. If you have one qualifying child and the amount you are looking up from your EIC Worksheet is $4,875, you would enter $1,658.

If the amount you are looking up from the worksheet is—		And you have—		
At least	But less than	No children	One child	Two children
		Your credit is—		
4,800	4,850	347	1,641	1,930
4,850	4,900	347	1,658	1,950
4,900	4,950	347	1,675	1,970
4,950	5,000	347	1,692	1,990

If the amount you are looking up from the worksheet is—		And you have—		
At least	But less than	No children	One child	Two children
		Your credit is—		
$1	$50	$2	$9	$10
50	100	6	26	30
100	150	10	43	50
150	200	13	60	70
200	250	17	77	90
250	300	21	94	110
300	350	25	111	130
350	400	29	128	150
400	450	33	145	170
450	500	36	162	190
500	550	40	179	210
550	600	44	196	230
600	650	48	213	250
650	700	52	230	270
700	750	55	247	290
750	800	59	264	310
800	850	63	281	330
850	900	67	298	350
900	950	71	315	370
950	1,000	75	332	390
1,000	1,050	78	349	410
1,050	1,100	82	366	430
1,100	1,150	86	383	450
1,150	1,200	90	400	470
1,200	1,250	94	417	490
1,250	1,300	98	434	510
1,300	1,350	101	451	530
1,350	1,400	105	468	550
1,400	1,450	109	485	570
1,450	1,500	113	502	590
1,500	1,550	117	519	610
1,550	1,600	120	536	630
1,600	1,650	124	553	650
1,650	1,700	128	570	670
1,700	1,750	132	587	690
1,750	1,800	136	604	710
1,800	1,850	140	621	730
1,850	1,900	143	638	750
1,900	1,950	147	655	770
1,950	2,000	151	672	790
2,000	2,050	155	689	810
2,050	2,100	159	706	830
2,100	2,150	163	723	850
2,150	2,200	166	740	870
2,200	2,250	170	757	890
2,250	2,300	174	774	910
2,300	2,350	178	791	930
2,350	2,400	182	808	950
2,400	2,450	186	825	970
2,450	2,500	189	842	990
2,500	2,550	193	859	1,010
2,550	2,600	197	876	1,030
2,600	2,650	201	893	1,050
2,650	2,700	205	910	1,070
2,700	2,750	208	927	1,090
2,750	2,800	212	944	1,110
2,800	2,850	216	961	1,130
2,850	2,900	220	978	1,150
2,900	2,950	224	995	1,170
2,950	3,000	228	1,012	1,190
3,000	3,050	231	1,029	1,210
3,050	3,100	235	1,046	1,230
3,100	3,150	239	1,063	1,250
3,150	3,200	243	1,080	1,270
3,200	3,250	247	1,097	1,290
3,250	3,300	251	1,114	1,310
3,300	3,350	254	1,131	1,330
3,350	3,400	258	1,148	1,350
3,400	3,450	262	1,165	1,370
3,450	3,500	266	1,182	1,390
3,500	3,550	270	1,199	1,410
3,550	3,600	273	1,216	1,430
3,600	3,650	277	1,233	1,450
3,650	3,700	281	1,250	1,470
3,700	3,750	285	1,267	1,490
3,750	3,800	289	1,284	1,510
3,800	3,850	293	1,301	1,530
3,850	3,900	296	1,318	1,550
3,900	3,950	300	1,335	1,570
3,950	4,000	304	1,352	1,590
4,000	4,050	308	1,369	1,610
4,050	4,100	312	1,386	1,630
4,100	4,150	316	1,403	1,650
4,150	4,200	319	1,420	1,670
4,200	4,250	323	1,437	1,690
4,250	4,300	327	1,454	1,710
4,300	4,350	331	1,471	1,730
4,350	4,400	335	1,488	1,750
4,400	4,450	339	1,505	1,770
4,450	4,500	342	1,522	1,790
4,500	4,550	347	1,539	1,810
4,550	4,600	347	1,556	1,830
4,600	4,650	347	1,573	1,850
4,650	4,700	347	1,590	1,870
4,700	4,750	347	1,607	1,890
4,750	4,800	347	1,624	1,910
4,800	4,850	347	1,641	1,930
4,850	4,900	347	1,658	1,950
4,900	4,950	347	1,675	1,970
4,950	5,000	347	1,692	1,990
5,000	5,050	347	1,709	2,010
5,050	5,100	347	1,726	2,030
5,100	5,150	347	1,743	2,050
5,150	5,200	347	1,760	2,070
5,200	5,250	347	1,777	2,090
5,250	5,300	347	1,794	2,110
5,300	5,350	347	1,811	2,130
5,350	5,400	347	1,828	2,150
5,400	5,450	347	1,845	2,170
5,450	5,500	347	1,862	2,190
5,500	5,550	347	1,879	2,210
5,550	5,600	347	1,896	2,230
5,600	5,650	347	1,913	2,250
5,650	5,700	347	1,930	2,270
5,700	5,750	342	1,947	2,290
5,750	5,800	339	1,964	2,310
5,800	5,850	335	1,981	2,330
5,850	5,900	331	1,998	2,350
5,900	5,950	327	2,015	2,370
5,950	6,000	323	2,032	2,390
6,000	6,050	319	2,049	2,410
6,050	6,100	316	2,066	2,430
6,100	6,150	312	2,083	2,450
6,150	6,200	308	2,100	2,470
6,200	6,250	304	2,117	2,490
6,250	6,300	300	2,134	2,510
6,300	6,350	296	2,151	2,530
6,350	6,400	293	2,168	2,550
6,400	6,450	289	2,185	2,570
6,450	6,500	285	2,202	2,590
6,500	6,550	281	2,219	2,610
6,550	6,600	277	2,236	2,630
6,600	6,650	273	2,253	2,650
6,650	6,700	270	2,270	2,670
6,700	6,750	266	2,287	2,690
6,750	6,800	262	2,304	2,710
6,800	6,850	258	2,312	2,730
6,850	6,900	254	2,312	2,750
6,900	6,950	251	2,312	2,770
6,950	7,000	247	2,312	2,790
7,000	7,050	243	2,312	2,810
7,050	7,100	239	2,312	2,830
7,100	7,150	235	2,312	2,850
7,150	7,200	231	2,312	2,870
7,200	7,250	228	2,312	2,890
7,250	7,300	224	2,312	2,910
7,300	7,350	220	2,312	2,930
7,350	7,400	216	2,312	2,950
7,400	7,450	212	2,312	2,970
7,450	7,500	208	2,312	2,990
7,500	7,550	205	2,312	3,010
7,550	7,600	201	2,312	3,030
7,600	7,650	197	2,312	3,050
7,650	7,700	193	2,312	3,070
7,700	7,750	189	2,312	3,090
7,750	7,800	186	2,312	3,110
7,800	7,850	182	2,312	3,130
7,850	7,900	178	2,312	3,150
7,900	7,950	174	2,312	3,170
7,950	8,000	170	2,312	3,190
8,000	8,050	166	2,312	3,210
8,050	8,100	163	2,312	3,230
8,100	8,150	159	2,312	3,250
8,150	8,200	155	2,312	3,270
8,200	8,250	151	2,312	3,290
8,250	8,300	147	2,312	3,310
8,300	8,350	143	2,312	3,330
8,350	8,400	140	2,312	3,350
8,400	8,450	136	2,312	3,370
8,450	8,500	132	2,312	3,390
8,500	8,550	128	2,312	3,410
8,550	8,600	124	2,312	3,430
8,600	8,650	120	2,312	3,450
8,650	8,700	117	2,312	3,470
8,700	8,750	113	2,312	3,490
8,750	8,800	109	2,312	3,510

(Continued)

1999 Earned Income Credit (EIC) Table Continued   (Caution: This is *not* a tax table.)

If the amount you are looking up from the worksheet is—		And you have—			If the amount you are looking up from the worksheet is—		And you have—			If the amount you are looking up from the worksheet is—		And you have—			If the amount you are looking up from the worksheet is—		And you have—		
At least	But less than	No children	One child	Two children	At least	But less than	No children	One child	Two children	At least	But less than	No children	One child	Two children	At least	But less than	No children	One child	Two children
		Your credit is—					Your credit is—					Your credit is—					Your credit is—		
8,800	8,850	105	2,312	3,530	13,850	13,900	0	2,086	3,518	16,650	16,700	0	1,638	2,928	19,450	19,500	0	1,191	2,339
8,850	8,900	101	2,312	3,550	13,900	13,950	0	2,078	3,507	16,700	16,750	0	1,630	2,918	19,500	19,550	0	1,183	2,328
8,900	8,950	98	2,312	3,570	13,950	14,000	0	2,070	3,497	16,750	16,800	0	1,622	2,907	19,550	19,600	0	1,175	2,318
8,950	9,000	94	2,312	3,590	14,000	14,050	0	2,062	3,486	16,800	16,850	0	1,614	2,897	19,600	19,650	0	1,167	2,307
9,000	9,050	90	2,312	3,610	14,050	14,100	0	2,054	3,476	16,850	16,900	0	1,606	2,886	19,650	19,700	0	1,159	2,297
9,050	9,100	86	2,312	3,630	14,100	14,150	0	2,046	3,465	16,900	16,950	0	1,598	2,876	19,700	19,750	0	1,151	2,286
9,100	9,150	82	2,312	3,650	14,150	14,200	0	2,038	3,455	16,950	17,000	0	1,591	2,865	19,750	19,800	0	1,143	2,275
9,150	9,200	78	2,312	3,670	14,200	14,250	0	2,030	3,444	17,000	17,050	0	1,583	2,855	19,800	19,850	0	1,135	2,265
9,200	9,250	75	2,312	3,690	14,250	14,300	0	2,022	3,434	17,050	17,100	0	1,575	2,844	19,850	19,900	0	1,127	2,254
9,250	9,300	71	2,312	3,710	14,300	14,350	0	2,014	3,423	17,100	17,150	0	1,567	2,834	19,900	19,950	0	1,119	2,244
9,300	9,350	67	2,312	3,730	14,350	14,400	0	2,006	3,413	17,150	17,200	0	1,559	2,823	19,950	20,000	0	1,111	2,233
9,350	9,400	63	2,312	3,750	14,400	14,450	0	1,998	3,402	17,200	17,250	0	1,551	2,812	20,000	20,050	0	1,103	2,223
9,400	9,450	59	2,312	3,770	14,450	14,500	0	1,990	3,392	17,250	17,300	0	1,543	2,802	20,050	20,100	0	1,095	2,212
9,450	9,500	55	2,312	3,790	14,500	14,550	0	1,982	3,381	17,300	17,350	0	1,535	2,791	20,100	20,150	0	1,087	2,202
9,500	9,550	52	2,312	3,816	14,550	14,600	0	1,974	3,371	17,350	17,400	0	1,527	2,781	20,150	20,200	0	1,079	2,191
9,550	9,600	48	2,312	3,816	14,600	14,650	0	1,966	3,360	17,400	17,450	0	1,519	2,770	20,200	20,250	0	1,071	2,181
9,600	9,650	44	2,312	3,816	14,650	14,700	0	1,958	3,350	17,450	17,500	0	1,511	2,760	20,250	20,300	0	1,063	2,170
9,650	9,700	40	2,312	3,816	14,700	14,750	0	1,950	3,339	17,500	17,550	0	1,503	2,749	20,300	20,350	0	1,055	2,160
9,700	9,750	36	2,312	3,816	14,750	14,800	0	1,942	3,328	17,550	17,600	0	1,495	2,739	20,350	20,400	0	1,047	2,149
9,750	9,800	33	2,312	3,816	14,800	14,850	0	1,934	3,318	17,600	17,650	0	1,487	2,728	20,400	20,450	0	1,039	2,139
9,800	9,850	29	2,312	3,816	14,850	14,900	0	1,926	3,307	17,650	17,700	0	1,479	2,718	20,450	20,500	0	1,031	2,128
9,850	9,900	25	2,312	3,816	14,900	14,950	0	1,918	3,297	17,700	17,750	0	1,471	2,707	20,500	20,550	0	1,023	2,118
9,900	9,950	21	2,312	3,816	14,950	15,000	0	1,910	3,286	17,750	17,800	0	1,463	2,697	20,550	20,600	0	1,015	2,107
9,950	10,000	17	2,312	3,816	15,000	15,050	0	1,902	3,276	17,800	17,850	0	1,455	2,686	20,600	20,650	0	1,007	2,096
10,000	10,050	13	2,312	3,816	15,050	15,100	0	1,894	3,265	17,850	17,900	0	1,447	2,676	20,650	20,700	0	999	2,086
10,050	10,100	10	2,312	3,816	15,100	15,150	0	1,886	3,255	17,900	17,950	0	1,439	2,665	20,700	20,750	0	991	2,075
10,100	10,150	6	2,312	3,816	15,150	15,200	0	1,878	3,244	17,950	18,000	0	1,431	2,655	20,750	20,800	0	983	2,065
10,150	10,200	2	2,312	3,816	15,200	15,250	0	1,870	3,234	18,000	18,050	0	1,423	2,644	20,800	20,850	0	975	2,054
10,200	12,500	0	2,312	3,816	15,250	15,300	0	1,862	3,223	18,050	18,100	0	1,415	2,633	20,850	20,900	0	967	2,044
12,500	12,550	0	2,302	3,802	15,300	15,350	0	1,854	3,213	18,100	18,150	0	1,407	2,623	20,900	20,950	0	959	2,033
12,550	12,600	0	2,294	3,792	15,350	15,400	0	1,846	3,202	18,150	18,200	0	1,399	2,612	20,950	21,000	0	951	2,023
12,600	12,650	0	2,286	3,781	15,400	15,450	0	1,838	3,192	18,200	18,250	0	1,391	2,602	21,000	21,050	0	943	2,012
12,650	12,700	0	2,278	3,771	15,450	15,500	0	1,830	3,181	18,250	18,300	0	1,383	2,591	21,050	21,100	0	935	2,002
12,700	12,750	0	2,270	3,760	15,500	15,550	0	1,822	3,171	18,300	18,350	0	1,375	2,581	21,100	21,150	0	927	1,991
12,750	12,800	0	2,262	3,750	15,550	15,600	0	1,814	3,160	18,350	18,400	0	1,367	2,570	21,150	21,200	0	919	1,981
12,800	12,850	0	2,254	3,739	15,600	15,650	0	1,806	3,149	18,400	18,450	0	1,359	2,560	21,200	21,250	0	911	1,970
12,850	12,900	0	2,246	3,729	15,650	15,700	0	1,798	3,139	18,450	18,500	0	1,351	2,549	21,250	21,300	0	903	1,960
12,900	12,950	0	2,238	3,718	15,700	15,750	0	1,790	3,128	18,500	18,550	0	1,343	2,539	21,300	21,350	0	895	1,949
12,950	13,000	0	2,230	3,708	15,750	15,800	0	1,782	3,118	18,550	18,600	0	1,335	2,528	21,350	21,400	0	887	1,939
13,000	13,050	0	2,222	3,697	15,800	15,850	0	1,774	3,107	18,600	18,650	0	1,327	2,518	21,400	21,450	0	879	1,928
13,050	13,100	0	2,214	3,686	15,850	15,900	0	1,766	3,097	18,650	18,700	0	1,319	2,507	21,450	21,500	0	871	1,917
13,100	13,150	0	2,206	3,676	15,900	15,950	0	1,758	3,086	18,700	18,750	0	1,311	2,497	21,500	21,550	0	863	1,907
13,150	13,200	0	2,198	3,665	15,950	16,000	0	1,750	3,076	18,750	18,800	0	1,303	2,486	21,550	21,600	0	855	1,896
13,200	13,250	0	2,190	3,655	16,000	16,050	0	1,742	3,065	18,800	18,850	0	1,295	2,476	21,600	21,650	0	847	1,886
13,250	13,300	0	2,182	3,644	16,050	16,100	0	1,734	3,055	18,850	18,900	0	1,287	2,465	21,650	21,700	0	839	1,875
13,300	13,350	0	2,174	3,634	16,100	16,150	0	1,726	3,044	18,900	18,950	0	1,279	2,454	21,700	21,750	0	831	1,865
13,350	13,400	0	2,166	3,623	16,150	16,200	0	1,718	3,034	18,950	19,000	0	1,271	2,444	21,750	21,800	0	823	1,854
13,400	13,450	0	2,158	3,613	16,200	16,250	0	1,710	3,023	19,000	19,050	0	1,263	2,433	21,800	21,850	0	815	1,844
13,450	13,500	0	2,150	3,602	16,250	16,300	0	1,702	3,013	19,050	19,100	0	1,255	2,423	21,850	21,900	0	807	1,833
13,500	13,550	0	2,142	3,592	16,300	16,350	0	1,694	3,002	19,100	19,150	0	1,247	2,412	21,900	21,950	0	799	1,823
13,550	13,600	0	2,134	3,581	16,350	16,400	0	1,686	2,992	19,150	19,200	0	1,239	2,402	21,950	22,000	0	792	1,812
13,600	13,650	0	2,126	3,571	16,400	16,450	0	1,678	2,981	19,200	19,250	0	1,231	2,391	22,000	22,050	0	784	1,802
13,650	13,700	0	2,118	3,560	16,450	16,500	0	1,670	2,970	19,250	19,300	0	1,223	2,381	22,050	22,100	0	776	1,791
13,700	13,750	0	2,110	3,550	16,500	16,550	0	1,662	2,960	19,300	19,350	0	1,215	2,370	22,100	22,150	0	768	1,781
13,750	13,800	0	2,102	3,539	16,550	16,600	0	1,654	2,949	19,350	19,400	0	1,207	2,360	22,150	22,200	0	760	1,770
13,800	13,850	0	2,094	3,529	16,600	16,650	0	1,646	2,939	19,400	19,450	0	1,199	2,349	22,200	22,250	0	752	1,759

(Continued)

1999 Earned Income Credit (EIC) Table Continued   (Caution: *This is **not** a tax table.*)

If the amount you are looking up from the worksheet is— At least	But less than	No children	One child	Two children
22,250	22,300	0	744	1,749
22,300	22,350	0	736	1,738
22,350	22,400	0	728	1,728
22,400	22,450	0	720	1,717
22,450	22,500	0	712	1,707
22,500	22,550	0	704	1,696
22,550	22,600	0	696	1,686
22,600	22,650	0	688	1,675
22,650	22,700	0	680	1,665
22,700	22,750	0	672	1,654
22,750	22,800	0	664	1,644
22,800	22,850	0	656	1,633
22,850	22,900	0	648	1,623
22,900	22,950	0	640	1,612
22,950	23,000	0	632	1,602
23,000	23,050	0	624	1,591
23,050	23,100	0	616	1,580
23,100	23,150	0	608	1,570
23,150	23,200	0	600	1,559
23,200	23,250	0	592	1,549
23,250	23,300	0	584	1,538
23,300	23,350	0	576	1,528
23,350	23,400	0	568	1,517
23,400	23,450	0	560	1,507
23,450	23,500	0	552	1,496
23,500	23,550	0	544	1,486
23,550	23,600	0	536	1,475
23,600	23,650	0	528	1,465
23,650	23,700	0	520	1,454
23,700	23,750	0	512	1,444
23,750	23,800	0	504	1,433
23,800	23,850	0	496	1,423
23,850	23,900	0	488	1,412
23,900	23,950	0	480	1,401
23,950	24,000	0	472	1,391
24,000	24,050	0	464	1,380
24,050	24,100	0	456	1,370
24,100	24,150	0	448	1,359
24,150	24,200	0	440	1,349
24,200	24,250	0	432	1,338
24,250	24,300	0	424	1,328
24,300	24,350	0	416	1,317
24,350	24,400	0	408	1,307
24,400	24,450	0	400	1,296
24,450	24,500	0	392	1,286
24,500	24,550	0	384	1,275
24,550	24,600	0	376	1,265
24,600	24,650	0	368	1,254
24,650	24,700	0	360	1,244
24,700	24,750	0	352	1,233
24,750	24,800	0	344	1,222
24,800	24,850	0	336	1,212
24,850	24,900	0	328	1,201
24,900	24,950	0	320	1,191
24,950	25,000	0	312	1,180
25,000	25,050	0	304	1,170
25,050	25,100	0	296	1,159
25,100	25,150	0	288	1,149
25,150	25,200	0	280	1,138
25,200	25,250	0	272	1,128
25,250	25,300	0	264	1,117
25,300	25,350	0	256	1,107
25,350	25,400	0	248	1,096
25,400	25,450	0	240	1,086
25,450	25,500	0	232	1,075
25,500	25,550	0	224	1,065
25,550	25,600	0	216	1,054
25,600	25,650	0	208	1,043
25,650	25,700	0	200	1,033
25,700	25,750	0	192	1,022
25,750	25,800	0	184	1,012
25,800	25,850	0	176	1,001
25,850	25,900	0	168	991
25,900	25,950	0	160	980
25,950	26,000	0	152	970
26,000	26,050	0	144	959
26,050	26,100	0	136	949
26,100	26,150	0	128	938
26,150	26,200	0	120	928
26,200	26,250	0	112	917
26,250	26,300	0	104	907
26,300	26,350	0	96	896
26,350	26,400	0	88	886
26,400	26,450	0	80	875
26,450	26,500	0	72	864
26,500	26,550	0	64	854
26,550	26,600	0	56	843
26,600	26,650	0	48	833
26,650	26,700	0	40	822
26,700	26,750	0	32	812
26,750	26,800	0	24	801
26,800	26,850	0	16	791
26,850	26,900	0	8	780
26,900	26,950	0	*	770
26,950	27,000	0	0	759
27,000	27,050	0	0	749
27,050	27,100	0	0	738
27,100	27,150	0	0	728
27,150	27,200	0	0	717
27,200	27,250	0	0	706
27,250	27,300	0	0	696
27,300	27,350	0	0	685
27,350	27,400	0	0	675
27,400	27,450	0	0	664
27,450	27,500	0	0	654
27,500	27,550	0	0	643
27,550	27,600	0	0	633
27,600	27,650	0	0	622
27,650	27,700	0	0	612
27,700	27,750	0	0	601
27,750	27,800	0	0	591
27,800	27,850	0	0	580
27,850	27,900	0	0	570
27,900	27,950	0	0	560
27,950	28,000	0	0	549
28,000	28,050	0	0	538
28,050	28,100	0	0	527
28,100	28,150	0	0	517
28,150	28,200	0	0	506
28,200	28,250	0	0	496
28,250	28,300	0	0	485
28,300	28,350	0	0	475
28,350	28,400	0	0	464
28,400	28,450	0	0	454
28,450	28,500	0	0	443
28,500	28,550	0	0	433
28,550	28,600	0	0	422
28,600	28,650	0	0	412
28,650	28,700	0	0	401
28,700	28,750	0	0	391
28,750	28,800	0	0	380
28,800	28,850	0	0	370
28,850	28,900	0	0	359
28,900	28,950	0	0	348
28,950	29,000	0	0	338
29,000	29,050	0	0	327
29,050	29,100	0	0	317
29,100	29,150	0	0	306
29,150	29,200	0	0	296
29,200	29,250	0	0	285
29,250	29,300	0	0	275
29,300	29,350	0	0	264
29,350	29,400	0	0	254
29,400	29,450	0	0	243
29,450	29,500	0	0	233
29,500	29,550	0	0	222
29,550	29,600	0	0	212
29,600	29,650	0	0	201
29,650	29,700	0	0	191
29,700	29,750	0	0	180
29,750	29,800	0	0	169
29,800	29,850	0	0	159
29,850	29,900	0	0	148
29,900	29,950	0	0	138
29,950	30,000	0	0	127
30,000	30,050	0	0	117
30,050	30,100	0	0	106
30,100	30,150	0	0	96
30,150	30,200	0	0	85
30,200	30,250	0	0	75
30,250	30,300	0	0	64
30,300	30,350	0	0	54
30,350	30,400	0	0	43
30,400	30,450	0	0	33
30,450	30,500	0	0	22
30,500	30,550	0	0	12
30,550	30,580	0	0	3
30,580 or more		0	0	0

*If the amount you are looking up from the worksheet is at least $26,900 but less than $26,928, your credit is $2. Otherwise, you cannot take the credit.

Chapter 17

Calculating Your Tax

Now that you know how to report your income, deductions, exemptions, and the special tax breaks and credits you might be entitled to in your business or personal life, it's time to pull the whole thing together and calculate the amount of tax you owe.

In this chapter we'll explain how to compute your income taxes, and we'll also discuss a couple of other types of tax you may have to report and pay on your tax return: the alternative minimum tax (AMT), and payroll taxes on household employees.

COMPUTING AND PAYING INCOME TAX

To review what we've covered so far, the basic formula for federal income taxes is:

total income – adjustments = adjusted gross income

AGI – deductions and exemptions = taxable income

Taxes are then calculated based on the amount of your taxable income. From this initial tax bill, your allowable credits are subtracted, and any additional taxes (like AMT, self-employment taxes, and payroll taxes on household help) are added, to arrive at the amount of taxes you actually owe for the year.

Many people can calculate their taxes using the tax tables provided at the end of this book. Simply take the taxable income amount from Line 39 of Form 1040, Line 24 of Form 1040A, or Line 6 of Form 1040EZ, go to the tax tables and find the line in the bold-faced column that includes your income amount, and read across to the right to find the column that pertains to your filing status. The amount shown at the intersection between the income line and the filing status column will be your tax.

If your taxable income is $100,000 or more, you can't use the tables. Instead, you must use the tax rate schedules that follow the end of the tables.

Some taxpayers must use other forms to calculate their initial tax bills. If you have a net capital gain shown on Schedule D, you must calculate your tax by following the directions for each line on the back of Schedule D, to take advantage of the lower 20 percent rate on long-term capital gains. If you have farm income and choose to use income averaging, calculate your tax using Schedule J, *Farm Income Averaging*. If you are filing a return for a child under age 14 who had more than $1,400 in investment income, you must compute the child's tax using Form 8615, *Tax for Children Under Age 14 Who Have Investment Income of More than $1,400*.

After you've determined your tax amount using one of the methods described above, add to it any tax amount shown on Form 8814, *Parents' Election to Report Child's Interest and Dividends*, or on Form 4972, *Tax on Lump-Sum Distributions*. Write the total amount of your tax on Line 40 of Form 1040, Line 25 of Form 1040A, or Line 10 of Form 1040EZ.

Claiming Your Credits

From your initial tax bill, you will subtract any of the nonrefundable tax credits that apply to you in 1999:

1. the credit for child and dependent care expenses (see page 189)

2. the credit for the elderly or the disabled (see page 284)

3. the child tax credit (see page 280)

4. the education credits (see page 286)

5. the adoption credit (see page 282)

6. the foreign tax credit (see page 227)

7. the mortgage interest credit, claimed on Form 8396 (see page 203)

8. the District of Columbia first-time homebuyer credit, claimed on Form 8859

9. the credit for prior year's minimum tax, claimed on Form 8801 (see page 301)

10. the credit for a qualified electric vehicle, claimed on Form 8834 (see page 145)

11. the general business credit (see page 148)

12. the empowerment zone employment credit (see page 144)

Note that none of these credits can be claimed on Form 1040EZ, and only the first five can be claimed on Form 1040A. The full list of credits may be claimed on Form 1040.

Add Your Other Taxes

Now that you've calculated your income tax bill, you must add in any other taxes that you owe:

- the self-employment tax, as shown on Schedule SE (see page 135)

- the AMT, as shown on Form 6251 (see page 301)

- any Social Security and Medicare tax on tip income not reported to your employer, as shown on Form 4137

- additional tax on improper distributions or excess contributions to IRAs, other retirement plans, or medical savings accounts, as shown on Form 5329 (see pages 251, 249, and 92, respectively)

- advance earned income credit payments you received, as shown on your W-2 (although this is not, strictly speaking, a tax, it's treated as one for purposes of the computation)

- employment taxes on household help, as shown on Schedule H (see page 302)

- any recapture of the investment tax credit on Form 4255, low-income housing credit on Form 8611, qualified electric vehicle credit on Form 8611, or Indian employment credit on Form 8845

- any recapture of federal mortgage subsidies on Form 8828, the 10 percent tax on retirement benefits that exceed plan formulas for business owners, and the tax on accumulation distributions of trusts on Form 4970

Note that none of these are reported on Form 1040EZ, and only the advance earned income credit may be reported on Form 1040A. If you owe any of the other listed taxes, you must file Form 1040.

Subtract Your Payments

After you've determined the dollar amount of all the tax that you owe, you must subtract the amounts of the payments you've made during the year. This includes both tax that was withheld on a paycheck, as shown in Box 2 of any W-2 forms you (or your spouse, if filing jointly) received, and any estimated tax payments you made during the year.

Save Money

Don't forget to add in any income tax withheld from pension checks or investment income such as interest and dividends, as shown on your 1099 forms.

Refundable tax credits are treated as if they were payments that you made. Therefore, if you had an earned income credit (EIC) amount for 1999, or if you claimed the additional child credit (see page 281), it will be added to your other tax payments. In effect, the credit will increase the refund you get (or at least reduce your tax bill).

If you are filing after April 15th because you requested an extension on Form 4868 (see page 305), include any amount you sent in with that form on Line 61 of Form 1040. If you overpaid your Social Security tax (see page 138), report the overpaid amount on Line 62. And if you have any credit on Form 2439, *Notice to Shareholder of Undistributed Long-Term Capital Gains,* or Form 4136, *Credit for Federal Tax Paid on Fuels,* include those amounts on Line 63 since they are treated as tax payments.

Refunds and Payments

Your total tax payments are subtracted from your total tax owed, to see whether you are due a refund, or must pay more when you file your tax return.

If you're due a refund, you have a couple of choices. You can ask the IRS to electronically deposit the amount in your bank account, by using the space provided to write down your bank routing number (the first nine-digit number that appears on the last line of your check) and your bank account number (the number that immediately follows the routing number).

If you prefer, you can have some or all of your refund applied to your 2000 estimated tax, by writing the amount you want to apply on Line 67 of Form 1040, or on Line 42 of Form 1040A.

Save Time

For those who will owe estimated tax for 2000 and are filing by April 15th, applying your refund to 2000 can be a good solution because your first estimated payment is also due on April 15th. Simply rolling the amount due you for 1999 into the account for 2000 saves you the time and trouble of writing an additional check to the IRS.

If you don't elect to receive an electronic deposit or to have your refund applied to your 2000 taxes, you will receive a paper check from the government, generally within six weeks.

Offset of Refunds for Debts

If you owe certain types of debts, the IRS will keep your refund and apply it to the amount you owe. This applies to those who owe back child support, a previous year's taxes, or a federal nontax debt such as a student loan. If an offset occurs, you will get a notice from a federal agency known as Financial Management Service. FMS will provide information to you about the amount, date, and nature of the offset. If the debt is back child support, the notice will indicate the state to which the offset amount was paid, and give you a contact in the state that would handle concerns or questions regarding the delinquent debt that resulted in the tax refund offset.

If you file jointly and it is your spouse who owes the debt, the IRS may keep the entire refund. However, you can get your portion of the refund by filing IRS Form 8379, *Injured Spouse Claim and Allocation.*

Paying Your Taxes

If your tax return shows that your prepaid taxes are less than the taxes you actually owe, you'll have to send some money in with your tax forms. If you owe more than $1,000 and more than 10 percent of the tax shown on your return, you may also owe a penalty (see page 309 for a discussion of the tax penalties). You can, if you wish, send in the amount you owe without the penalties – the IRS will compute the penalties and interest you owe and send you a bill later.

We generally recommend that you let the IRS compute your penalty, since the computation is extremely complicated and time consuming.

However, the standard IRS computation assumes that you received your income evenly over the year. If in fact you received most of your income in one or two quarters, you will have to file IRS Form 2210 in order to show that.

Make your check payable to the United States Treasury, and be sure to write the year and the tax form (e.g., "1999 Form 1040"), your Social Security number, and your name and address on the check.

Work Smart

If you are filing jointly, write the name and Social Security number of the spouse whose name appears first on the front of your tax form. Otherwise the IRS might not apply the payment to the correct account.

If you send in a check, you must also complete Form 1040-V, *Payment Voucher*, and include it with your tax return. The IRS requests that you don't staple the check to your return, but simply enclose it in your envelope.

Signing Your Return

You must sign your tax return before the IRS will accept it – if you don't, the document will probably be returned to you so you can sign it. Make sure that both spouses sign the return if you're filing jointly.

If you are filing a return for a minor child, sign the child's name, and add "By (your signature), parent (or guardian) for minor child." The parent who signs the child's return will be authorized to deal with the IRS if any questions arise about the return.

Assembling and Mailing Your Tax Return

Each form that you need to attach to your Form 1040 or 1040A has an "attachment sequence number" printed in its upper right-hand corner. When assembling your tax return, place the forms in order of their sequence, with Form 1040 (or 1040A) on top. If you have any supporting statements or schedules, attach them all at the end, in the same order as the forms or schedules they refer to.

Be sure to write your name and Social Security number on the top of each tax form, just in case they are separated. And staple a copy of any W-2 forms you received to the front of the return.

Where to Send Your Tax Return	
If your legal residence is located in:	File with the IRS Service Center at:
Florida, Georgia, South Carolina	Atlanta, GA 39901-0002
New Jersey, New York City and counties of Nassau, Rockland, Suffolk, and Westchester	Holtsville, NY 00501-0002
New York (all other counties), Connecticut, Maine, Massachusetts, New Hampshire, Rhode Island, Vermont	Andover, MA 05501-0002
Illinois, Iowa, Minnesota, Missouri, Wisconsin	Kansas City, MO 64999-0002
Delaware, District of Columbia, Maryland, Pennsylvania, Virginia	Philadelphia, PA 19255-0002
Indiana, Kentucky, Michigan, Ohio, West Virginia	Cincinnati, OH 45999-0002
Kansas, New Mexico, Oklahoma, Texas	Austin, TX 73301-0002
Alaska, Arizona, California (counties of Alpine, Amador, Butte, Calaveras, Colusa, Contra Costa, Del Norte, El Dorado, Glenn, Humboldt, Lake, Lassen, Marin, Mendocino, Modoc, Napa, Nevada, Placer, Plumas, Sacramento, San Joaquin, Shasta, Sierra, Siskiyou, Solano, Sonoma, Sutter, Tehama, Trinity, Yolo, and Yuba), Colorado, Idaho, Montana, Nebraska, Nevada, North Dakota, Oregon, South Dakota, Utah, Washington, Wyoming	Ogden, UT 84201-0002
California (all other counties), Hawaii	Fresno, CA 93888-0002
Alabama, Arkansas, Louisiana, Mississippi, North Carolina, Tennessee	Memphis, TN 37501-0002
American Samoa, Puerto Rico, or nonpermanent residents of Guam or the Virgin Islands	Philadelphia, PA 19255-0002
Guam permanent residents	Dept. of Revenue and Taxation, Government of Guam, P.O. Box 23607, GMF, GU 96921
Virgin Islands permanent residents	V.I. Bureau of Internal Revenue, 9601 Estate Thomas, Charlotte Amalie, St. Thomas, VI 00802
Foreign countries, and all APO and FPO addresses:	Philadelphia, PA 19255-0207

Work Smart

Whenever you send a tax form or, for that matter, any other correspondence to the IRS, we recommend that you use certified or registered mail so that you get a return receipt. If you ever need proof that you mailed your documents on time, and that the IRS received them, you'll have it.

If you're filing close to the deadline, you can also use next-day or second-day service from Airborne Express, DHL Worldwide Express, Federal Express, or United Parcel Service. Any of these services can tell you how to get written proof of the mailing date.

THE AMT

Because some taxpayers — particularly wealthy taxpayers — have been so successful in their efforts to legally minimize their tax bills, Congress came up with another way to tax them: the alternative minimum tax (AMT). The AMT provides a formula for computing tax that ignores certain preferential tax treatments and deductions that taxpayers would otherwise be entitled to claim.

So, many taxpayers are required to compute their income tax liability twice: once under the regular method and once again under the AMT method. An individual will be subject to the AMT if his or her AMT liability is more than the regular tax liability for the year.

What types of things can trigger the AMT? The most common items that can cause you to become subject to the AMT are listed below. These items must be added back to your taxable income in order to compute your AMT:

- all personal exemptions

- the standard deduction, if you claimed it

- itemized deductions for state and local income taxes, and real estate taxes

- itemized deductions for home equity loan interest (this does not include interest on a loan to buy, build, or improve your home)

- itemized deductions for miscellaneous deductions

- itemized deductions for any portion of medical expenses that exceed 7.5 percent of AGI but not 10 percent of AGI

- deductions you claimed for accelerated depreciation that exceed what you could have claimed under straight-line depreciation

- differences between gain or loss on the sale of property for AMT purposes and for regular tax purposes; these differences most commonly occur as a result of the different depreciation methods required under AMT, as described above

- addition of certain income from incentive stock options

- changes in income from installment sales, since the installment sale method generally can't be used for AMT purposes

- changes in certain passive activity loss deductions

- deductions relating to oil and gas investments, or drilling or mining operations

- interest on certain private activity bonds that would otherwise be tax-exempt

If you have large amounts of any items on this list, and your adjusted gross income exceeds the exemption amounts discussed below, you (or your accountant) should compute your AMT liability on IRS Form 6251, *Alternative Minimum Tax — Individuals*, to determine whether you must actually pay any AMT. We've reproduced this form at the end of the book for reference, to allow you to decide whether you need to complete it or not. If you do need to complete it, you can get a free copy of the form's instructions by calling 1-800-TAX-FORM, or by downloading them from the Internet at www.irs.ustreas.gov/prod/forms_pubs/forms.html.

Children under age 14 who have investment income of more than $5,000 should also complete Form 6251 to see whether they owe any AMT.

It's also important to know that while most tax credits are not allowed for AMT purposes, for 1998 through

2001, the new tax credits for individuals will not cause you to have to pay AMT. These credits include the child or dependent care credit, the $500-per-child credit and the Hope scholarship credit that are available after 1997, the lifetime-learning tuition tax credit that began in July of 1998, the D.C. homebuyer's credit, and the credit for interest on certain home mortgages. For 1999 and later years, you will probably need to calculate your AMT liability if you claim any of these credits.

AMT Rates and Exemptions

The AMT method does provide each taxpayer with a flat dollar amount that is completely exempt from tax. The dollar amount of your exemption depends on your filing status. The exemption amounts are:

- $45,000 if married filing jointly

- $33,750 if single or head of household

- $22,500 if married filing separately

These amounts are not indexed for inflation and have been in place since 1992.

If your taxable income for AMT purposes (called AMTI) exceeds the exemption amount, you will be subject to a 26 percent AMT rate on the first $175,000 of AMTI that exceeds the exemption amount, and a 28 percent rate on any AMTI above this $175,000 amount.

The AMT exemption amounts are phased out for taxpayers having AMTI exceeding the specified income levels. Under these rules, the exemption available to married couples filing jointly is eliminated entirely if AMTI exceeds $330,000. The amount where the exemption is reduced to zero is $247,500 for single individuals and heads of households, and $165,000 for married taxpayers filing separately.

Work Smart

There's no doubt about it — the AMT can play havoc with your tax planning. If your AMT liability and your regular tax liability tend to be approximately equal from year to year, your best bet is to maintain this stability. If your deductions are not so evenly spaced and you tend to have great fluctuations in income from year to year, you may be able to shift some AMT-triggering

items from an AMT year to a non-AMT year, so as to reduce your liability in a non-AMT year almost to the point at which you would become subject to the AMT. Your tax professional can tell you whether this might be possible in your individual situation.

Credit for Prior Year's Minimum Tax

If you paid AMT last year, or you had a minimum tax credit carryforward from last year, you may be able to claim a tax credit on Form 8801, *Credit for Prior Year Minimum Tax*. You can get a copy of this form by calling 1-800-TAX-FORM or downloading it from the Internet at www.irs.ustreas.gov/prod/forms_pubs/forms.html.

PAYROLL TAXES ON HOUSEHOLD EMPLOYEES

If you are a working parent or, for that matter, anyone who sets out to hire a maid, babysitter, caregiver for an elderly relative, or some other kind of domestic help, it may come as a surprise to discover that you'll be required to pay significant amounts in employment taxes.

Warning

For various reasons, the person you hire may not want you to withhold taxes, preferring to be paid "under the table" in cash. However, the tax laws provide penalties, sometimes substantial ones, for noncompliance. If you went for several years without paying Social Security and Medicare taxes, for example, the back taxes, interest, and penalties you'd owe could add up to hundreds or even thousands of dollars. Employers who have paid their domestic workers in cash, without paying payroll taxes, have been surprised to find that if a former employee files for unemployment benefits, the state will report them to the IRS, triggering an audit that goes back many years.

Are You an Employer?

You don't have to pay taxes on payments that you make to independent contractors, because they are treated as business owners themselves, and they're responsible for paying their own self-employment taxes. If you get domestic workers through an agency, the agency is generally considered the employer. But if you use independent workers and your arrangement gives you the right to control not only the type of work that must be done, but how it must be done (such as what specific tasks must be done by a maid, what cleaning products should be used, etc.), you will be considered an employer.

Generally, you must pay employment taxes if you paid any one employee cash wages of $1,100 or more in 1999 (unless the worker was a student under age 18 at any time during the year). You must also pay if you paid total cash wages of $1,000 or more in any calendar quarter to any number of household employees. However, if you hire your spouse or your child under age 21, you don't need to pay any payroll taxes. If you hire your parent, you don't pay federal unemployment tax, and you don't need to pay Social Security or Medicare tax unless your parent cares for a child who lives with you and is under 18 or disabled, and you are divorced and not remarried, you are widowed, or you're married to a person whose physical or mental condition prevents him or her from caring for the child.

Payroll Tax Rates and Forms

If you are required to pay employment taxes on domestic help, you can pay them along with your regular income tax on Form 1040. However, you will need to complete Schedule H, *Household Employment Taxes*, and attach it to your tax return. Call 1-800-TAX-FORM to get a copy of this form and its instructions, which will walk you through the procedures for completing the form. Also ask for a

copy of IRS Publication 926, *Household Employer's Tax Guide*, which explains more about the responsibilities of employers, including the need to file annual W-2 forms for each employee.

If you are required to pay payroll taxes on your employee's paycheck, the FICA tax rate that you'll pay is 7.65 percent of the employee's paycheck, and you should withhold an equal amount (7.65 percent of pay) from the amount you give your employee. FICA taxes include Social Security and Medicare. You may choose to pay your employee's portion of the tax, if you wish. You will also have to pay federal unemployment taxes, generally at a 0.8 percent rate (be sure to check with your state department of labor for the rules on state unemployment tax, since you will generally have to pay that tax as well).

You don't have to withhold income tax from your household employee's paycheck unless you want to. However, you may have to make advance payments of the employee's earned income credit, if the employee asks you to. See IRS Publication 926 for more details.

As mentioned above, you can report all the employment taxes you owe for domestic workers during 1999 on your 1999 tax return. However, you may have to pay an estimated tax penalty if your total tax bill, including taxes on household workers, is over $1,000 more than the tax you prepaid throughout the year through estimated tax payments or payroll withholding.

To avoid this penalty, it's generally necessary to estimate the household taxes you'll be liable for during the year, and use your estimate to increase the withholding amount on any paychecks you receive, or add the amount to your quarterly estimated tax payments during the year (see page 306).

Chapter 18

Dealing with the IRS

As a small business owner, it's important for you to be aware of what your tax payment obligations are and when they are due.

There's no sinking feeling like the one you have when you thought you had a cash surplus on your books, and then suddenly you have to make a payment to the IRS that depletes your entire balance. Worse yet is the scenario where the funds have been spent elsewhere because you didn't realize a tax payment was due. With a good awareness of your filing and payment obligations, you won't find yourself in this situation or subject to penalties for late filing or payments.

So, this chapter includes information on:

- due dates for regular returns and payments

- estimated tax payment information

- penalties for underpayments or late returns

Finally, we'll end with a discussion of other situations in which you may need to deal with the IRS. We'll give you a list of common errors that trigger IRS letters, and we'll provide some advice on what to expect if you are audited.

DUE DATES FOR TAX RETURNS

For calendar year taxpayers, the due date for filing and payment of tax due on individual income tax returns is April 15.

Work Smart

As a general rule, if a due date that is set by law falls on a Saturday, Sunday, or federal legal holiday, it is delayed until the next day that isn't a Saturday, Sunday, or legal holiday. However, a statewide legal holiday delays a due date only if the IRS office where you are required to file your returns is located in that state.

If you want an automatic four-month extension to file your return, you can file Form 4868, *Application For Automatic Extension of Time To File U.S. Individual Income Tax Return*, by April 15. Your actual return would then be due on August 15.

Warning

It's important to realize that the automatic extension only applies to the filing of your return, not to the payment of any tax that may be due. You must pay any tax that you estimate will be due for 1999 by April 15 of 2000, or you may be subject to interest and penalties on overdue taxes, as discussed below.

If you can't get everything filed by August 15 and you decide that you want an additional two-month extension to file your returns, you must file Form 2688, *Application for Additional Extension of Time to File U.S. Individual Income Tax Return,* by August 15. This additional two-month extension is not automatic — you must give the IRS a reason as to why you need the additional time to file. Examples of good reasons would be if your records are unavailable, if you are waiting for information from a third party, or if you have been ill or out of the country.

Work Smart

If you know you are going to need more time than the four-month automatic extension, it's wise to apply for the additional two-month extension as soon as possible. Because the second extension is not automatic, the sooner you know whether the IRS has granted it, the better!

If the IRS grants you this two-month extension, your return must be filed by October 15. Remember, the two-month extension applies only to the filing of your return, not to the payment of any tax you may owe.

Fiscal Year Taxpayers

If you are a sole proprietor who uses a fiscal year rather than a calendar year, you must file your individual income tax return (including all the applicable schedules) no later than the 15th day of the fourth month after the end of your tax year.

You are entitled to the same automatic four-month extension to file your return that a calendar year taxpayer is entitled to, but you must file for the extension on Form 4868 by the due date for filing the return. The due date for the filing of your return is then the 15th day of the fourth month after the original due date of your return. You may apply for an additional two-month extension (which will be granted at the IRS's discretion). You should file the

extension request on Form 2688 by the 15th day of the fourth month of your automatic extension.

If the second extension is granted, your return will be due on the 15th day of the second month after your automatic four-month extension was granted.

ESTIMATED TAX PAYMENTS

If you are a small business owner, chances are good that you will have to make estimated tax payments.

Estimated tax payments are used to pay tax on income that is not subject to withholding. This, of course, includes income from self-employment (estimated tax payments cover both income tax and self-employment tax). Even if you receive a salary from a job you hold in addition to running your own business, you may still have to make estimated tax payments if the amount of tax being withheld from your salary is insufficient.

Who Must Make Estimated Tax Payments?

You're probably asking yourself, "do I have to make estimated tax payments for 2000?" By answering "yes" or "no" to these three questions, you'll have your answer:

1. Do you expect to owe $1,000 or more for 2000, after subtracting any income tax withholding and credits from your total tax? If the answer is no, you are not required to pay estimated tax. If the answer is yes, go on to the next question.

2. Do you expect your income tax withholding and credits to be at least 90 percent of the tax you'll owe for 2000? If the answer is yes, you are not required to pay estimated tax. If the answer is no, go on to the next question.

3. Do you expect your income tax withholding and credits to be at least 100 percent of the tax shown on your 1999 return? (If your 1999 adjusted gross income was more than $150,000, or more than $75,000 for marrieds filing separately, substitute 108.6 percent in the preceding sentence). If the answer is yes,

you are not required to pay estimated tax. If the answer is no, you must make estimated tax payments.

Save Money

The IRS treats tax payments that are made through payroll withholding as being made evenly through the year, regardless of when the withholding is actually done. If you or your spouse is receiving a paycheck, you can avoid the need to make estimated tax payments and retain the use of more money throughout the year, if you arrange to have extra tax withheld from your paycheck during the last month of the year.

You can do this by filing a revised Form W-4 with your employer (or your spouse's employer) during December of 2000. To avoid penalties, the extra withholding must be a dollar amount that brings your total tax withholding for the year at least up to the lesser of (a) 100 percent of the amount you expect to owe minus $1,000, (b) 90 percent of the amount you expect to owe, or (c) 100 percent of the amount you owed last year (105 percent for high-income taxpayers).

Calculating Your Estimated Tax Payments

If you are required to make estimated tax payments, how much do you have to pay?

Your total tax payments during the year (that is, before January 15th of the next year) must add up to the lower of these two amounts: (1) 90 percent of the tax you owe for the current year, or (2) 100 percent of the tax you owed for last year. (If your 1999 adjusted gross income was more than $150,000, or more than $75,000 for marrieds filing separately, substitute 105 percent in the preceding sentence.) "Tax you owe for the year" includes federal income tax and any self-employment (SECA) tax due on your business income.

"Total tax payments" includes any tax withholding on any paychecks, investment income, pensions, or any other income you receive (or that your spouse receives, if filing jointly). If the difference between any withholding during the year and the amount computed in the paragraph above is $1,000 or more, it must be made up with estimated tax payments.

The best way to do this is to look at each major item on each tax form and schedule that you filed this year, and make a guess as to whether it will change for next year. If you think there will be a change, estimate what the change will be (for instance if your real estate tax bill on your office will rise by 10%, that will reduce the amount of net income from your business on Schedule C, and increase the amount of itemized real estate taxes deductible on Schedule A). Then, determine how the cumulative changes will affect your tax bill to arrive at a ballpark estimated bill. From this expected tax bill, subtract any withholding that will be done, and the amount remaining, minus $1,000, is what you need to pay in estimated taxes. Many business owners go through this exercise at least twice a year: around April 15th, and then again sometime in the third quarter of the year.

The IRS provides a worksheet on which you can make this calculation, as part of the instructions to Form 1040-ES. This form and its instructions were not available when we went to press, but you can get a copy by calling 1-800-TAX-FORM.

Regular or Annualized Method

Once you know the total amount of estimated tax payments you'll have to make during the year, there are two ways to compute the dollar amount you must pay for each quarter: the regular installment method and the annualized income installment method.

The regular installment method works by dividing your total amount of estimated payments for the year by four. On each payment due date, you pay one-fourth of the total tax due for the year. The IRS prefers this method, and it's by far the simplest to use.

If your business is of the type that doesn't receive income evenly throughout the year (for example, you sell surfboards year-round in the Northeast), you may want to use the second method. Under this method, your required estimated tax payment for one or more periods may be less than the amount figured using the regular installment method.

If you elect to use this method, you will have to file Form 2210, *Underpayment of Estimated Tax by Individuals, Estates, and Trusts,* with your regular individual income tax return for 2000. Using this method is more complicated than simply determining your net income for each quarter, and figuring the tax on it. For complete instructions, talk to your tax advisor or get a copy of the IRS's free Publication 505, *Tax Withholding and Estimated Tax.*

How to Make Estimated Tax Payments

You can make your estimated tax payments in two ways:

- by crediting all or part of any overpayment on your annual tax return towards your next year's estimated tax (rather than getting a refund)

- by sending in your estimated tax payments with payment vouchers using Form 1040-ES, *Estimated Tax For Individuals*

When to Make Estimated Tax Payments

For estimated tax payment purposes, a year is divided into four payment periods. Each period has a specific payment due date. If you don't pay enough tax by the due date of each of the payment periods, you may be charged a penalty for underpayment of tax until the underpayment is made up. This means that you may be charged a penalty for a particular quarter even if you're due a refund when you file your income tax return for the entire year! For calendar year taxpayers, your estimated tax payment due dates are:

For the Period	Due Date
January 1-March 31	April 15
April 1-May 31	June 15
June 1-August 31	September 15
September 1-December 31	January 15 (of the following year)

If at least two-thirds of your annual income comes from farming or fishing, you have only one payment due date for your estimated taxes — January 15. The first three payment periods don't apply.

Fiscal Year Filers

If you operate your business on a fiscal year, your estimated tax payment due dates are:

- the 15th day of the fourth month of your fiscal year

- the 15th day of the sixth month of your fiscal year

- the 15th day of the ninth month of your fiscal year

- the 15th day of the first month after the end of your fiscal year

Again, if at least two-thirds of your annual income comes from farming or fishing, and your operate on a fiscal tax year, you have only one payment due date for your estimated taxes — the 15th day of the first month after the end of your fiscal year. The first three payment periods don't apply.

If the due date for making an estimated tax payment falls on a Saturday, Sunday, or legal holiday, the payment must be made on the next day that is not a Saturday, Sunday, or legal holiday.

Filing Early in Lieu of Making Last Payment

There is a special rule in the tax law that excuses you from filing fourth quarter estimated taxes if you file your annual tax return (Form 1040, etc.), and pay any tax due by January 31 (for calendar year taxpayers). If you are a fiscal year taxpayer, you don't have to make the last quarterly estimated tax payment if you file your income tax return by the last day of the first month after the end of your fiscal year and pay all the tax you owe with your return.

Example

Stella, a self-employed individual with no tax withheld, does not make an estimated tax payment for the fourth quarter of 1999 but files a Form 1040 and pays the tax due as shown on the return on January 14, 2000. Although she did not make a fourth quarter payment of tax, she is excused from doing so because she filed her return on or before January 31, 2000, and paid the full amount due. In fact, she is deemed to have timely made a fourth quarter payment on January 14, 2000, for estimated tax payment penalty purposes.

Some of the advantages of filing your annual return by January 31 include:

- a 16-day (from January 15 to January 31) interest-free loan from the IRS

- one less payment that can be potentially lost in the mail — of course, it remains good practice to send estimated payments or final returns via certified or registered mail, to make sure the mail is received by the IRS

However, there are pitfalls to filing early:

- It's difficult to be accurate on your final tax return when you might not have received all the 1099s and other information you need to complete the forms.

- If you have computed your estimated tax payments based on a figure of less than 100 percent of the final tax amount shown on the return (i.e., the lesser of 90 percent of the final amount shown on the return or 100 percent of the tax shown on the preceding year's return) you will have to come up with the balance by January 31, rather than having the luxury of waiting until April 15.

Of course even if you think it's a good idea, filing early isn't always possible due to factors beyond your control. You may not have received documents that must be attached to your final tax return (Form W-2 for example). Or, if you are a partner or S corporation shareholder, you may not have received Schedule K-1s containing important tax information needed to complete your annual return. Finally, as a business owner, you simply may not have had sufficient time to compile the tax information needed to complete your Schedule C, *Profit or Loss From Business.*

INTEREST AND PENALTIES FOR UNDERPAYMENT OR LATE RETURNS

What happens if you don't file a tax return or pay taxes that you owe by their due date? Generally, in this situation the IRS will send you a notice hitting you with interest and penalties.

Interest

The IRS will charge you interest on taxes not paid by their due date, even if you've been granted an extension of time to file your return. Since July of 1994, the interest rates have fluctuated between 8 percent and 10 percent, and as we go to press, the most recently announced interest rate on underpayments of tax is 8 percent.

Interest is also charged on the penalties imposed for failure to file a return, as well as other penalties imposed for inaccuracy, fraud, etc. This interest is charged on the penalty from the due date of the return, including extensions.

Penalties

If you pay your taxes late, the penalty is usually 0.5 percent of the unpaid amount for each month or part of a month the tax is not paid. The penalty can't be more than 25 percent of the unpaid amount and applies to any unpaid tax on the return. Please note, this penalty is *in addition* to the interest charged for late payments.

The IRS will also hit you with a penalty if you file your return late. In that case, the penalty is usually 5 percent of the amount due for each month or part of a month your return is late, unless you have a reasonable explanation. If you think you have a reasonable explanation, write it down in a statement and attach it to your return, and you might be able to avoid the penalty. In any case, the penalty usually can't be more than 25 percent of the tax due. However, if your return is more than 60 days late, the minimum penalty will be $100 or the amount of any tax you owe, whichever is smaller.

Estimated Tax Penalty

What happens if you underpay your estimated tax? You may have to pay a penalty in the form of interest on the underpayment for the period when the underpayment occurred. The penalty is figured separately for each payment period, and you may owe a penalty for an earlier payment period even if you later paid enough to make up the underpayment.

As a matter of fact, if you didn't pay enough tax by the due date of each of the payment periods, you may owe a penalty even if you are due a refund from the IRS when you file your income tax return.

Example

Cherilyn is employed as a teacher and runs her own tutoring business as well. She didn't make any estimated tax payments during 1999 because she *thought she had enough tax withheld from her teaching wages. Early in January 2000, she estimated her total 1999 tax and realized that her withholding was $2,000 less than the amount needed to avoid a penalty for underpayment of estimated tax. So on January 11, Cherilyn made an estimated tax payment of $2,000, the difference between her withholding and her estimate of her total tax.*

When she files her final return, Cherilyn's total tax is $50 less than she originally figured, so she is due a refund from the IRS. However, Cherilyn will owe a penalty through January 11 for her underpayments for the earlier payment periods. (She won't owe a penalty for the January 15 estimated tax payment.)

You can request a waiver of the penalty if the underpayment was caused by a casualty, disaster, or some other unusual circumstance that would make its imposition unfair. The IRS may also waive the penalty for reasonable cause during the first two years after a taxpayer retires upon reaching age 62 or becomes disabled. Form 2210, *Underpayment of Estimated Tax by Individuals, Estates, and Trusts,* must be filed to request a waiver.

You can use Form 2210 to calculate your estimated tax penalty. But this form is very complicated, and generally, you aren't required to complete it. When you file your tax return, the IRS will usually figure the penalty for you and send you a bill. Depending on what you pay your tax pro, it may be more beneficial to you to let the IRS do the calculations.

What other situations might require you to file Form 2210? Other than when you request a waiver, you must file Form 2210 when:

- You use the annualized income installment method.

- You use your actual withholding for each payment period for estimated tax purposes.

- You base any of your required installments on the tax shown on the previous year's return and you filed or are filing a joint return for either that previous year or the present year, but not for both years.

Save Money

The IRS has been authorized by Congress to grant a 90-day grace period if you are unable to fulfill any of your tax obligations because of an actual Y2K computer failure. To get this relief, you must have made good-faith efforts to avoid Y2K problems. At the time we went to press, the IRS had not released details on how to claim Y2K relief. Consult your tax advisor or call the IRS at 1-800-TAX-1040 for more information.

HOW TO HANDLE AN AUDIT

There are two pieces of advice that you should keep in mind about audits:

- If you've done your homework, kept good records, and your return is truthful, you don't have anything to worry about.

- It's better not to be audited.

Minimize the Risk of Being Audited

First, let's talk about the second point.

The average taxpayer has a very small chance of being audited. But if you are self-employed, your return is definitely not typical of the millions of returns filed by employees. You may be waving some red flags at the IRS and increasing your chances of being audited.

Suggestions for Minimizing Audit Risk

The IRS does not provide details on its audit criteria — in fact, they are a closely guarded secret. However, we offer the following suggestions for minimizing your risk:

- Make sure that the information provided on any W-2 forms you receive from employers, and 1099s or 1098s you receive from banks, mutual funds, brokerages, retirement plans, or any other source, are accurately reflected on your return. If there is a mistake, get the issuer of the form to correct it. The IRS computer matches these figures with the figures on your return, and it will question any mismatch. If you have many of these forms, report each one separately somewhere on your tax return. The computer will not catch it if you lump the numbers together.

- If you are claiming an unusual deduction or there is something confusing on your return, attach a written explanation. Any statements should be as brief and to the point as possible — don't ramble or provide unessential details.

- If you are claiming home office expenses or significant travel or entertainment expenses, make sure you have the records. The IRS scrutinizes these expenses very carefully. The same is true of all business expenses if you haven't yet established a track record, and especially if your business is not profitable.

- Sign your return. Fill out all the information required. For example, it's common to omit the Social Security number of an ex-spouse from a return, but you are required to supply it if you are paying alimony. Make sure your return is complete.

- Make sure your math is correct. Arithmetic errors are the most common errors turned up by the IRS. If you are doing your own return with a calculator, after you've done all the computations, we suggest you start at the amount of your refund (or tax you owe) and work backwards to check your work (e.g., add back your payments, subtract your other taxes, and add back your credits to see whether you arrive at the same tax amount; continue in this vein for the rest of the return).

- Make sure that all Social Security numbers for your dependents are correct.

What to Expect if You Are Audited

The IRS has several different levels of audits. If questions arise about your math, items seem to be omitted from your return, or your figures don't match those on your W-2s, 1099s, or 1098s, the IRS may simply request a correction or explanation by mail.

Respond to the request as quickly as possible and, if you have doubts about the answer, consult your tax professional if you have one.

Work Smart

The IRS makes mistakes, too. Don't assume the IRS notice is correct. Check things out. Computer-generated forms, which include the forms most commonly sent out to deal with small errors, are notorious for automatically adding penalties that may not apply in your situation. If you are in doubt, call the IRS and ask them about anything you don't understand.

The first level of inquiry that can truly be considered an "audit" occurs when you get a letter requesting that you come into the IRS office to review one or more areas on your return. This is a true audit because the IRS is asking for proof of items on your return that goes beyond your word. If you have kept records, including bills, receipts, and canceled checks (see Chapter 2), you shouldn't worry. The IRS may end up interpreting your situation differently than you, but there is no crime in having differences of opinion. Nevertheless, professional help may be in order with an office audit, particularly if you yourself suspect that there are errors or omissions in your tax return.

Work Smart

You can attend an audit yourself, but you don't have to. You can authorize your accountant, lawyer, or other tax professional to handle it without you. Often this is the best way to prevent the audit from escalating beyond the original areas that piqued the IRS's interest. Experienced professional advisors are less likely to become emotional or to make statements that lead to more IRS questioning.

As rare as audits are, the dreaded knock on the door from the IRS agent is even rarer. Individuals are almost never audited in this way. On-site or "field audits" are used mainly for larger businesses, particularly when records are not portable. If you do get a notice of a field audit, professional help is definitely recommended.

Glossary of Tax Terms

Accelerated depreciation. A depreciation method that allows larger deductions in the early years of an asset's "life" and smaller deductions at the end of the period. (See "Straight-line depreciation.")

Accrual method (or accrual basis). One of two main accounting methods for determining when a transaction has tax significance. The accrual method says that a transaction is taxed when an obligation to pay or a right to receive payment is created (for example, at the time products are delivered, services rendered, billings sent, etc.). This method is used by all but the smallest businesses. (See "Cash method (or cash basis).")

Adjusted basis. The cost of property (or a substitute figure—see "Basis") with adjustments made to account for depreciation (in the case of business property), improvements (in the case of real estate), withdrawals or reinvestment (in the case of securities, funds, accounts, insurance or annuities), etc. Adjusted basis is part of the computation for determining gain or loss on a sale or exchange and for depreciation.

Adjusted gross income. The amount of income considered actually "available" to be taxed. Adjusted gross income is gross income reduced principally by business expenses incurred to earn the income and other specified reductions (such as alimony).

Alternative minimum tax. An alternative tax system that says your tax shall not go below this level. The alternative minimum tax works by negating (or minimizing) the effects of tax preferences or loopholes.

Amortization. The write-off of an amount spent for certain capital assets, similar to depreciation. This tax meaning is different from the common meaning of the term that describes, for example, payment schedules of loans.

Applicable Federal Rates (AFRs). Minimum interest rates that must be charged on various transactions that involve payments over a number of years. If the parties to a transaction do not adhere to these rates, the IRS will impute the interest. (See "Imputed interest.")

At-risk rules. Rules that limit an investor's deductible losses from an investment to the amount invested. Complications arise when investors finance their investment through loans that they are not personally on the hook for (nonrecourse financing). Without these rules, investors could raise their deduction limit considerably without being at-risk for the actual loss.

Basis. The starting point for computing gain or loss on a sale or exchange of property or for depreciation. (See "Adjusted basis.") For property that is purchased, basis is its cost. The basis of inherited property is its value at the date of death (or alternative valuation date). The basis of property received as a gift or a nontaxable transaction is based on the adjusted basis of the transferor (with some adjustments). Special rules govern property transferred between corporations and their shareholders, partners and their partnership, etc.

Cafeteria plan. A plan maintained by an employer that allows employees to select from a menu of taxable and nontaxable benefits.

Capital expenditures. Amounts spent to acquire or improve assets with useful lives of more than one year. These expenditures may not be deducted, but are added to the basis of the property (See "Adjusted basis.") and, for business property, may be converted into deductions through depreciation or amortization.

Capital gain or loss. Gain or loss from the sale or exchange of investment property, personal property (such as a home) or other "capital asset," which is often entitled to preferential tax treatment.

Carrybacks and carryforwards. Deductions that may be transferred to a year other than the current year because they exceeded certain limits. These deductions are typically carried back to earlier years first and, if they exceed the limits for those years, are then carried forward to later years until the deduction is used up. Charitable contributions and net operating losses are examples of deductions that may be carried back or forward.

Cash method (or cash basis). One of two main accounting methods for determining when a transaction has tax significance. The cash method says that a transaction is taxed when payment is made. This method is used by most individuals. (See "Accrual method (or accrual basis).")

Community property. A system governing spousal ownership of property and income that is the law in certain western and southern states and Wisconsin. The differences between community property and "common law" can change how federal tax law applies to spouses. For example: married taxpayers filing separately in a common law state do not have to report income earned by the other spouse. They do have to report income earned in a community property state.

Deferred compensation. An arrangement that allows an employee to receive part of a year's pay in a later year and not be taxed in the year the money was earned.

Depletion. A system similar to depreciation that allows the owner of natural resources (for example: a coal mine or an oil well) to deduct a portion of the cost of the asset during each year of its presumed productive life.

Depreciation. A system that allows a business or individual to deduct a portion of the cost of an asset ("recover its cost") during each year of its predetermined "life" (or "recovery period").

Earned income. Income earned by working for it. Interest, dividends and other kinds of profits are examples of *un*earned income.

Earned income credit. A tax credit available to individuals with low earned income. An individual is entitled to the full amount of this credit even if it exceeds the amount of tax otherwise due.

Employee stock ownership plan (ESOP). A type of profit-sharing plan in which benefits come in the form of stock in the employer.

Estimated tax. Quarterly down payments on a year's taxes that are required (on April 15, June 15, September 15, and January 15) if the total year's taxes will exceed $1,000 and the amount is not covered by withholding.

Federal Insurance Contributions Act (FICA). Social security taxes (for both old-age, survivors and disability insurance—OASDI—and Medicare).

Federal Unemployment Tax Act (FUTA). Unemployment taxes.

Filing status. One of four tax ranks determined by your marital status, your dependents and the way you file your tax return: (1) single, (2) married filing jointly, (3) married filing separately and (4) head of household. Filing status determines your tax rates and your eligibility for various tax benefits (for example: alimony deduction, IRA deduction, standard deduction, etc.).

First-in, first-out (FIFO). A rule that applies to the sale of part of a group of similar items (such as inventory, shares of the same stock, etc.) that assumes the first ones acquired were the first ones sold. This is important if the items in the group were acquired or manufactured at different times or for different costs. The rule may be overridden by identifying the specific item sold, if possible. (See "Last-in, first-out (LIFO).")

Generation-skipping transfer tax. An extra tax on gifts or on-death transfers of money or property that would otherwise escape the once-per-generation transfer taxes that apply to gifts and estates. For example: a gift from a grandfather to a granddaughter skips a generation and might be subject to this tax.

Golden parachutes. Bonuses payable to key executives in the event control of their corporation changes, as in the case of a takeover. "Excess" golden parachute payments are subject to tax penalties.

Gross income. All income that might be subject to tax. Most "realized" increases in wealth are considered income. The main exceptions for individuals are gifts, inheritances, increases in value of property *prior* to sale, loan repayments and some personal injury awards. For businesses, investments in their capital are not considered income.

Head of household. A filing status available to qualifying single parents (or others supporting certain dependents) that allows lower taxes than the normal rates for singles.

Imputed interest. A portion of a future payment that is treated as interest if parties to the transaction do not provide a stated amount of interest at a rate acceptable to the IRS. (See "Applicable Federal Rates (AFRs).") This prevents improper use of certain tax advantages (capital gains rates or tax deferral). For example: if a business sells an asset on the installment basis, part of all future payments is treated as interest whether the transaction states it or not.

Incentive stock option. A stock option that may be granted to an employee under tax-favored terms.

Itemized deductions. Personal deductions that may be taken if they total more than the standard deduction. (See "Standard deduction.") The following deductions are then itemized or listed on Schedule A of Form 1040: medical expenses, charitable contributions, state and local taxes, home mortgage interest, real estate taxes, casualty losses, unreimbursed employee expenses, investment expenses and others.

Investment credit. A credit against tax available for investment in a limited range of business property. The *general* investment credit was repealed in 1986, but this type of credit has been enacted and repealed repeatedly throughout history.

Involuntary conversion. The conversion of property into money under circumstances beyond the control of the owner. For example: (1) property that is destroyed and "converted" into an insurance settlement or (2) property that is seized by the government and "converted" into a condemnation award. Owners may avoid tax on any gain that may result (if the insurance settlement or condemnation award exceeds the adjusted basis of the property) by reinvesting in similar property within certain time limits.

Joint return. An optional filing status available to married taxpayers that offers generally (but not always) lower taxes than "married filing separately."

Keogh plan. A retirement plan available to self-employed individuals.

Last-in, first-out (LIFO). A rule that applies to the sale of part of a group of similar items in an inventory that assumes the last ones acquired were the first ones sold. This is important if the items in the group were acquired or manufactured at different times or for different costs. (See "First-in, first-out (FIFO).")

Like-kind exchanges. Tax-free swaps of investment property. Commonly used for real estate.

Limited liability company (LLC). A legal structure that allows a business to be taxed like a partnership but function generally like a corporation. An LLC offers members (among other things) protection against liability for claims against the business that is not available in a partnership.

Listed property. Property listed in the tax code or by the IRS that must comply with special rules before depreciation may be claimed. Cars and personal computers are examples of listed property. The special rules are designed to prevent deductions where the property is used for personal rather than business purposes.

Medical Spending Accounts (MSAs). An investment fund similar to an IRA that can be used to pay more routine medical expenses, when used in conjunction with "high-deductible" health insurance, which pays the big bills. Only 750,000 of these MSAs are available nationwide under a pilot program that runs through the year 2000. To qualify, you have to be self-employed or employed by a small employer that offers the program.

Modified Accelerated Cost Recovery System (MACRS). The system for computing depreciation for most business assets.

Net operating loss. The excess of business expenses over income. A business may apply a net operating loss to get a refund of past taxes (or a reduction of future taxes) by carrying it back to profitable years as an additional deduction (or by carrying it forward as a deduction to future years).

Original issue discount (OID). The purchase discount offered on some bonds (and similar obligations) in lieu of interest. For example: zero-coupon bonds. OID is generally treated as interest income to the holder rather than as a capital gain.

Passive activity loss (PAL). Loss on an investment that is deductible only up to the limit of gains from similar investments. The limit mainly affects tax shelters and does not apply to stocks, bonds or investments in businesses in which the investor materially participates. Special rules apply to investments in real estate.

Qualified plan. A retirement or profit-sharing plan that meets requirements about who must be covered, the amount of benefits that are paid, information that must be given to plan participants, etc. Qualified plans are entitled to tax benefits unavailable to nonqualified plans.

Real estate investment trust (REIT). A kind of "mutual fund" that invests in real estate rather than stocks and bonds.

Real estate mortgage investment conduit (REMIC). A kind of "mutual fund" that invests in real estate mortgages rather than stocks and bonds.

Recapture. The undoing of a tax benefit if certain requirements are not met in future years. For example: (1) The low-income housing credit may be recaptured or added back to tax if the credit property ceases to be used as low-income housing for a minimum number of years. (2) The alimony deduction may be retroactively lost or recaptured if payments do not continue at the requisite level for a minimum number of years.

Regulated investment company (RIC). A mutual fund.

Rollover. The tax-free termination of one investment and reinvestment of the proceeds. For example: An individual may roll over a lump-sum distribution from an employer's retirement plan into an IRA.

S corporation. A corporation with no more than 35 shareholders that is not taxed, but treated similarly to a partnership, if other requirements are met.

Savings Incentive Match Plan for Employees (SIMPLE plans). A simplified retirement arrangement for small businesses that comes in two varieties: one similar to a 401(k) plan and one that funds IRAs for employees.

Standard deduction. A deduction allowed individuals instead of listing or itemizing deductible personal expenses. (See "Itemized deductions.") The amount depends on the individual's filing status. Additional amounts are available for taxpayers who are blind or are age 65 or over. Individuals may deduct either their standard deduction or the total of their itemized deductions, whichever is greater.

Straight-line depreciation. A depreciation method that allows equal deductions in each year of an asset's "life" or recovery period. (See "Accelerated depreciation.")

Swaps, tax-free. (1) Exchanges of like-kind property that result in no capital gains tax (commonly used for real estate). (2) Sales and repurchases of stock (or other securities) designed to realize a tax loss without discontinuing the investment. Transactions must comply with the wash sale rules to be effective. (See "Wash sales.")

Taxable income. What is left after all deductions are taken. This is the amount upon which tax is computed.

Taxpayer identification number (TIN). In the case of an individual, the Social Security number. In the case of a business (even an individual in business), the employer identification number.

Top-heavy plan. An employee retirement or profit-sharing plan that disproportionately benefits top executives.

Uniform capitalization rules (Unicap). A set of uniform rules for computing the cost of goods produced by a business that prevents current deductions for costs that must be capitalized (See "Capital expenditures.") or added to inventory.

Wash sales. Simultaneous or near-simultaneous purchases and sales of the same property, usually stocks or bonds, made to generate deductible tax losses without discontinuing the investment. Losses on the transactions are ignored for tax purposes, however, unless a 30-day waiting period is observed between them.

Withholding allowances. Adjustments made to assure correct withholding on wages for individuals who may have unusually large deductions or who may be subject to other special circumstances.

1999 Tax Forms

The blank forms included in this section are ready for you to photocopy, or to use "as is."

As we go to press, the IRS has not yet released the final version of all of the forms you might need. If you need a form that is not included here, there are a number of other ways to obtain free copies.

Many forms are available at local libraries, post offices, and banks. You can also obtain a copy of any form by stopping by a local IRS office, or by calling the IRS at 1-800-TAX-FORM. If you call, allow at least a week for the form to arrive.

If you have a fax machine, you can call the IRS at 703-368-9694 to obtain a free copy of most forms by fax. However, you'll need to know the fax order numbers of the forms you need, which are listed on page 7 of the 1999 Form 1040 Instructions.

You can also obtain most forms by downloading them from the IRS's Internet site, at www.irs.gov. While not all forms and instructions are available, the IRS has made a concerted effort to increase the number of the forms that are posted.

Tax Forms Included

SS-4	Form 2106-EZ
Form 1040EZ	Form 2441
Form 1040A	Form 3903
Schedule 1	Form 4562
Schedule 2	Form 4684
Schedule 3	Form 4797
Form 1040	Form 4868
Schedules A&B	Form 4972
Schedule C	Form 5213
Schedule C-EZ	Form 6251
Schedule D	Form 6252
Schedule E	Form 8283
Schedule EIC	Form 8582
Schedule F	Form 8615
Schedule H	Form 8812
Schedule R	Form 8814
Schedule SE	Form 8822
Form 1040-V	Form 8829
Form 1040X	Form 8839
Form 1116	1999 Tax Table
Form 2106	1999 Tax Rate Schedules

Form **SS-4**

(Rev. February 1998)

Department of the Treasury
Internal Revenue Service

Application for Employer Identification Number

(For use by employers, corporations, partnerships, trusts, estates, churches,
government agencies, certain individuals, and others. See instructions.)

▶ Keep a copy for your records.

EIN

OMB No. 1545-0003

Please type or print clearly.

1 Name of applicant (legal name) (see instructions)	
2 Trade name of business (if different from name on line 1)	**3** Executor, trustee, "care of" name
4a Mailing address (street address) (room, apt., or suite no.)	**5a** Business address (if different from address on lines 4a and 4b)
4b City, state, and ZIP code	**5b** City, state, and ZIP code
6 County and state where principal business is located	
7 Name of principal officer, general partner, grantor, owner, or trustor—SSN or ITIN may be required (see instructions) ▶	

8a Type of entity (Check only one box.) (see instructions)

Caution: *If applicant is a limited liability company, see the instructions for line 8a.*

☐ Sole proprietor (SSN) _____
☐ Partnership   ☐ Personal service corp.
☐ REMIC   ☐ National Guard
☐ State/local government   ☐ Farmers' cooperative
☐ Church or church-controlled organization
☐ Other nonprofit organization (specify) ▶ _____
☐ Other (specify) ▶

☐ Estate (SSN of decedent) _____
☐ Plan administrator (SSN) _____
☐ Other corporation (specify) ▶ _____
☐ Trust
☐ Federal government/military
(enter GEN if applicable) _____

8b If a corporation, name the state or foreign country
(if applicable) where incorporated

State	Foreign country

9 Reason for applying (Check only one box.) (see instructions)
☐ Started new business (specify type) ▶ _____
☐ Hired employees (Check the box and see line 12.)
☐ Created a pension plan (specify type) ▶
☐ Banking purpose (specify purpose) ▶ _____
☐ Changed type of organization (specify new type) ▶ _____
☐ Purchased going business
☐ Created a trust (specify type) ▶ _____
☐ Other (specify) ▶

10 Date business started or acquired (month, day, year) (see instructions)

11 Closing month of accounting year (see instructions)

12 First date wages or annuities were paid or will be paid (month, day, year). **Note:** *If applicant is a withholding agent, enter date income will first be paid to nonresident alien. (month, day, year)* . . . . ▶

	Nonagricultural	Agricultural	Household
13 Highest number of employees expected in the next 12 months. **Note:** *If the applicant does not expect to have any employees during the period, enter -0-. (see instructions)* . . . . ▶			

14 Principal activity (see instructions) ▶

15 Is the principal business activity manufacturing? . . . . ☐ Yes ☐ No
If "Yes," principal product and raw material used ▶

16 To whom are most of the products or services sold? Please check one box. ☐ Business (wholesale)
☐ Public (retail)   ☐ Other (specify) ▶   ☐ N/A

17a Has the applicant ever applied for an employer identification number for this or any other business? . . . . ☐ Yes ☐ No
Note: *If "Yes," please complete lines 17b and 17c.*

17b If you checked "Yes" on line 17a, give applicant's legal name and trade name shown on prior application, if different from line 1 or 2 above.
Legal name ▶   Trade name ▶

17c Approximate date when and city and state where the application was filed. Enter previous employer identification number if known.

Approximate date when filed (mo., day, year)	City and state where filed	Previous EIN

Under penalties of perjury, I declare that I have examined this application, and to the best of my knowledge and belief, it is true, correct, and complete.

Business telephone number (include area code)

Fax telephone number (include area code)

Name and title (Please type or print clearly.) ▶

Signature ▶   Date ▶

Note: *Do not write below this line. For official use only.*

Please leave blank ▶	Geo.	Ind.	Class	Size	Reason for applying

For Paperwork Reduction Act Notice, see page 4.   Cat. No. 16055N   Form **SS-4** (Rev. 2-98)

Form **1040EZ**

Department of the Treasury—Internal Revenue Service

Income Tax Return for Single and Joint Filers With No Dependents

(99) **1999**   OMB No. 1545-0675

Use the IRS label here

Your first name and initial | Last name

If a joint return, spouse's first name and initial | Last name

Home address (number and street). If you have a P.O. box, see page 12. | Apt. no.

City, town or post office, state, and ZIP code. If you have a foreign address, see page 12.

Your social security number

Spouse's social security number

▲ **IMPORTANT!** ▲
You **must** enter your SSN(s) above.

Presidential Election Campaign
(See page 12.)

Note. *Checking "Yes" will not change your tax or reduce your refund.*

Do you want $3 to go to this fund? ▶ Yes ☐ No ☐

If a joint return, does your spouse want $3 to go to this fund? ▶ Yes ☐ No ☐

Income

Attach Copy B of Form(s) W-2 here. Enclose, but do not staple, any payment.

Dollars | Cents

1 Total wages, salaries, and tips. This should be shown in box 1 of your W-2 form(s). Attach your W-2 form(s).   1

2 Taxable interest. If the total is over $400, you cannot use Form 1040EZ.   2

3 Unemployment compensation, qualified state tuition program earnings, and Alaska Permanent Fund dividends (see page 14).   3

4 Add lines 1, 2, and 3. This is your **adjusted gross income.**   4

Note. You **must check** Yes or No.

5 Can your parents (or someone else) claim you on their return?

Yes. Enter amount from worksheet on back. ☐

No. If **single,** enter 7,050.00. If **married,** enter 12,700.00. See back for explanation. ☐   5

6 Subtract line 5 from line 4. If line 5 is larger than line 4, enter 0. This is your **taxable income.**   ▶ 6

Payments and tax

7 Enter your Federal income tax withheld from box 2 of your W-2 form(s).   7

8a Earned income credit (see page 15).
b Nontaxable earned income: enter type and amount below.

Type _____ | $ _____   8a

9 Add lines 7 and 8a. These are your **total payments.**   9

10 **Tax.** Use the amount on **line 6 above** to find your tax in the tax table on pages 24–28 of the booklet. Then, enter the tax from the table on this line.   10

Refund

Have it directly deposited! See page 20 and fill in 11b, 11c, and 11d.

11a If line 9 is larger than line 10, subtract line 10 from line 9. This is your **refund.**   11a

▶ **b** Routing number

▶ **c** Type: Checking ☐   Savings ☐   **d** Account number

Amount you owe

12 If line 10 is larger than line 9, subtract line 9 from line 10. This is the **amount you owe.** See page 21 for details on how to pay.   12

1 2 3 4 5

Sign here

I have read this return. Under penalties of perjury, I declare that to the best of my knowledge and belief, the return is true, correct, and accurately lists all amounts and sources of income I received during the tax year.

Your signature | Spouse's signature if joint return. See page 11.

Keep copy for your records.

Date | Your occupation | Date | Spouse's occupation

For Official Use Only

6 7 8 9 10

For Disclosure, Privacy Act, and Paperwork Reduction Act Notice, see page 23.   Cat. No. 11329W   **1999 Form 1040EZ**

Use this form if

- Your filing status is single or married filing jointly.
- You do not claim any dependents.
- You do not claim a student loan interest deduction (see page 8) or an education credit.
- You had **only** wages, salaries, tips, taxable scholarship or fellowship grants, unemployment compensation, qualified state tuition program earnings, or Alaska Permanent Fund dividends, and your taxable interest was not over $400. **But** if you earned tips, including allocated tips, that are not included in box 5 and box 7 of your W-2, you may not be able to use Form 1040EZ. See page 13. If you are planning to use Form 1040EZ for a child who received Alaska Permanent Fund dividends, see page 14.
- You did not receive any advance earned income credit payments.

- You (and your spouse if married) were under 65 on January 1, 2000, and not blind at the end of 1999.
- Your taxable income (line 6) is less than $50,000.

If you are not sure about your filing status, see page 11. If you have questions about dependents, use TeleTax topic 354 (see page 6). If you **cannot use this form,** use TeleTax topic 352 (see page 6).

Filling in your return

For tips on how to avoid common mistakes, see page 29.

Enter your (and your spouse's if married) social security number on the front. Because this form is read by a machine, please print your numbers inside the boxes like this:

9 8 7 6 5 4 3 2 1 0

Do not type your numbers. Do not use dollar signs.

If you received a scholarship or fellowship grant or tax-exempt interest income, such as on municipal bonds, see the booklet before filling in the form. Also, see the booklet if you received a Form 1099-INT showing Federal income tax withheld or if Federal income tax was withheld from your unemployment compensation or Alaska Permanent Fund dividends.

Remember, you must report all wages, salaries, and tips even if you do not get a W-2 form from your employer. You must also report all your taxable interest, including interest from banks, savings and loans, credit unions, etc., even if you do not get a Form 1099-INT.

Worksheet for dependents who checked "Yes" on line 5

(keep a copy for your records)

Use this worksheet to figure the amount to enter on line 5 if someone can claim you (or your spouse if married) as a dependent, even if that person chooses not to do so. To find out if someone can claim you as a dependent, use TeleTax topic 354 (see page 6).

A. Amount, if any, from line 1 on front _____

+ 250.00 Enter total ▶ A. _____

B. Minimum standard deduction . . . . B. _____ 700.00

C. Enter the LARGER of line A or line B here . . . . C. _____

D. Maximum standard deduction. If **single,** enter 4,300.00; if **married,** enter 7,200.00 . . . . D. _____

E. Enter the SMALLER of line C or line D here. This is your standard deduction . . . . E. _____

F. Exemption amount.
- If single, enter 0.
- If married and—
—both you and your spouse can be claimed as dependents, enter 0.
—only one of you can be claimed as a dependent, enter 2,750.00.

F. _____

G. Add lines E and F. Enter the total here and on line 5 on the front . . G. _____

If you checked "No" on line 5 because no one can claim you (or your spouse if married) as a dependent, enter on line 5 the amount shown below that applies to you.

- Single, enter 7,050.00. This is the total of your standard deduction (4,300.00) and your exemption (2,750.00).

- Married, enter 12,700.00. This is the total of your standard deduction (7,200.00), your exemption (2,750.00), and your spouse's exemption (2,750.00).

Mailing return

Mail your return by **April 17, 2000.** Use the envelope that came with your booklet. If you do not have that envelope, see page 32 for the address to use.

Paid preparer's use only

See page 21.

Under penalties of perjury, I declare that I have examined this return, and to the best of my knowledge and belief, it is true, correct, and accurately lists all amounts and sources of income received during the tax year. This declaration is based on all information of which I have any knowledge.

Preparer's signature ▶	Date	Check if self-employed ☐	Preparer's SSN or PTIN
Firm's name (or yours if self-employed) and address ▶		EIN	
		ZIP code	

Form **1040EZ** (1999)

Form **1040A**

Department of the Treasury—Internal Revenue Service

U.S. Individual Income Tax Return (99) **1999** IRS Use Only—Do not write or staple in this space.

OMB No. 1545-0085

Label
(See page 19.)

Use the IRS label.

Otherwise, please print or type.

L A B E L   H E R E

Your first name and initial | Last name | Your social security number

If a joint return, spouse's first name and initial | Last name | Spouse's social security number

Home address (number and street). If you have a P.O. box, see page 20. | Apt. no.

City, town or post office, state, and ZIP code. If you have a foreign address, see page 20.

▲ **IMPORTANT!** ▲

You **must** enter your SSN(s) above.

Presidential Election Campaign Fund (See page 20.)

| | Yes | No |
Do you want $3 to go to this fund? . . . . | | |
If a joint return, does your spouse want $3 to go to this fund? | | |

Note. Checking "Yes" will not change your tax or reduce your refund.

Filing status

Check only one box.

1 ☐ Single

2 ☐ Married filing joint return (even if only one had income)

3 ☐ Married filing separate return. Enter spouse's social security number above and full name here. ▶

4 ☐ Head of household (with qualifying person). (See page 21.) If the qualifying person is a child but not your dependent, enter this child's name here. ▶

5 ☐ Qualifying widow(er) with dependent child (year spouse died ▶ 19___). (See page 22.)

Exemptions

If more than seven dependents, see page 22.

6a ☐ **Yourself.** If your parent (or someone else) can claim you as a dependent on his or her tax return, **do not** check box 6a.

b ☐ **Spouse**

c **Dependents:**		**(2)** Dependent's social security number	**(3)** Dependent's relationship to you	**(4)** ✓ if qualifying child for child tax credit (see page 23)
(1) First name Last name				
				☐
				☐
				☐
				☐
				☐
				☐
				☐

No. of boxes checked on 6a and 6b ____

No. of your children on 6c who:
● lived with you ____
● did not live with you due to divorce or separation (see page 24) ____

Dependents on 6c not entered above ____

Add numbers entered on lines above ☐

d Total number of exemptions claimed.

Income

Attach Copy B of your Form(s) W-2 here. Also attach Form(s) 1099-R if tax was withheld.

If you did not get a W-2, see page 25.

Enclose, but do not staple, any payment.

7 Wages, salaries, tips, etc. Attach Form(s) W-2. | 7

8a **Taxable** interest. Attach Schedule 1 if required. | 8a

b **Tax-exempt** interest. DO NOT include on line 8a. | 8b

9 Ordinary dividends. Attach Schedule 1 if required. | 9

10a Total IRA distributions. | 10a | **10b** Taxable amount (see page 25). | 10b

11a Total pensions and annuities. | 11a | **11b** Taxable amount (see page 26). | 11b

12 Unemployment compensation, qualified state tuition program earnings, and Alaska Permanent Fund dividends. | 12

13a Social security benefits. | 13a | **13b** Taxable amount (see page 28). | 13b

14 Add lines 7 through 13b (far right column). This is your **total income.** ▶ | 14

Adjusted gross income

15 IRA deduction (see page 30). | 15

16 Student loan interest deduction (see page 30). | 16

17 Add lines 15 and 16. These are your **total adjustments.** | 17

18 Subtract line 17 from line 14. This is your **adjusted gross income.** ▶ | 18

For Disclosure, Privacy Act, and Paperwork Reduction Act Notice, see page 53. Cat. No. 11327A Form **1040A** (1999)

Taxable income	**19**	Enter the amount from line 18.	**19**

20a Check if: ☐ **You** were 65 or older ☐ Blind ⎱ **Enter number of**
☐ **Spouse** was 65 or older ☐ Blind ⎰ **boxes checked ▶** 20a ☐

b If you are married filing separately and your spouse itemizes deductions, see page 32 and check here . . . . . . ▶ 20b ☐

21 Enter the **standard deduction** for your filing status. **But** see page 33 if you checked any box on line 20a or 20b **OR** if someone can claim you as a dependent.
- Single—$4,300 • Married filing jointly or Qualifying widow(er)—$7,200
- Head of household—$6,350 • Married filing separately—$3,600   **21**

22 Subtract line 21 from line 19. If line 21 is more than line 19, enter -0-. **22**

23 Multiply $2,750 by the total number of exemptions claimed on line 6d. **23**

24 Subtract line 23 from line 22. If line 23 is more than line 22, enter -0-. This is your **taxable income.** ▶ **24**

Tax, credits, and payments	**25**	Find the tax on the amount on line 24 (see page 34). **25**

26 Credit for child and dependent care expenses. Attach Schedule 2. 26

27 Credit for the elderly or the disabled. Attach Schedule 3. 27

28 Child tax credit (see page 35). 28

29 Education credits. Attach Form 8863. 29

30 Adoption credit. Attach Form 8839. 30

31 Add lines 26 through 30. These are your **total credits.** **31**

32 Subtract line 31 from line 25. If line 31 is more than line 25, enter -0-. **32**

33 Advance earned income credit payments from Form(s) W-2. **33**

34 Add lines 32 and 33. This is your **total tax.** ▶ **34**

35 Total Federal income tax withheld from Forms W-2 and 1099. 35

36 1999 estimated tax payments and amount applied from 1998 return. 36

37a **Earned income credit.** Attach Schedule EIC if you have a qualifying child. 37a

b Nontaxable earned income:
amount ▶   and type ▶

38 Additional child tax credit. Attach Form 8812. 38

39 Add lines 35, 36, 37a, and 38. These are your **total payments.** ▶ **39**

Refund	**40**	If line 39 is more than line 34, subtract line 34 from line 39. This is the amount you **overpaid.** **40**

Have it directly deposited! See page 47 and fill in 41b, 41c, and 41d.

41a Amount of line 40 you want **refunded to you.** 41a

▶ b Routing number ☐☐☐☐☐☐☐☐☐ **▶ c** Type: ☐ Checking ☐ Savings

▶ d Account number ☐☐☐☐☐☐☐☐☐☐☐☐☐☐☐☐☐

42 Amount of line 40 you want **applied to your 2000 estimated tax.** 42

Amount you owe	**43**	If line 34 is more than line 39, subtract line 39 from line 34. This is the **amount you owe.** For details on how to pay, see page 48. **43**
	44	Estimated tax penalty (see page 48). 44

Sign here

Under penalties of perjury, I declare that I have examined this return and accompanying schedules and statements, and to the best of my knowledge and belief, they are true, correct, and accurately list all amounts and sources of income I received during the tax year. Declaration of preparer (other than the taxpayer) is based on all information of which the preparer has any knowledge.

Joint return? See page 20. Keep a copy for your records.

Your signature	Date	Your occupation	Daytime telephone number (optional) ( )
Spouse's signature. If joint return, BOTH must sign.	Date	Spouse's occupation	

Paid preparer's use only

Preparer's signature ▶	Date	Check if self-employed ☐	Preparer's SSN or PTIN
Firm's name (or yours if self-employed) and address ▶			EIN
			ZIP code

Form **1040A** (1999)

Schedule 1
(Form 1040A)

Department of the Treasury—Internal Revenue Service

**Interest and Ordinary Dividends
for Form 1040A Filers** (99)

1999

OMB No. 1545-0085

Name(s) shown on Form 1040A

Your social security number

Part I

Interest

(See page 60 and the instructions for Form 1040A, line 8a.)

Note. If you received a Form 1099-INT, Form 1099-OID, or substitute statement from a brokerage firm, enter the firm's name and the total interest shown on that form.

1 List name of payer. If any interest is from a seller-financed mortgage and the buyer used the property as a personal residence, see page 60 and list this interest first. Also, show that buyer's social security number and address.

Amount

| | 1 | |

2 Add the amounts on line 1. — **2**

3 Excludable interest on series EE and I U.S. savings bonds issued after 1989 from Form 8815, line 14. You **must** attach Form 8815. — **3**

4 Subtract line 3 from line 2. Enter the result here and on Form 1040A, line 8a. — **4**

Part II

Ordinary dividends

(See page 60 and the instructions for Form 1040A, line 9.)

Note. If you received a Form 1099-DIV or substitute statement from a brokerage firm, enter the firm's name and the ordinary dividends shown on that form.

5 List name of payer

Amount

| | 5 | |

6 Add the amounts on line 5. Enter the total here and on Form 1040A, line 9. — **6**

For Paperwork Reduction Act Notice, see Form 1040A instructions.   Cat. No. 12075R   Schedule 1 (Form 1040A) 1999

Schedule 2
(Form 1040A)

Department of the Treasury—Internal Revenue Service

Child and Dependent Care Expenses for Form 1040A Filers (99) 1999

OMB No. 1545-0085

Name(s) shown on Form 1040A

Your social security number

Before you begin, you need to understand the following terms. See **Definitions** on page 61.
● **Dependent Care Benefits** ● **Qualifying Person(s)** ● **Qualified Expenses** ● **Earned Income**

Part I

Persons or organizations who provided the care

You MUST complete this part.

1

(a) Care provider's name	(b) Address (number, street, apt. no., city, state, and ZIP code)	(c) Identifying number (SSN or EIN)	(d) Amount paid (see page 62)

(If you need more space, use the bottom of page 2.)

Did you receive **dependent care benefits?**	**No** ⟶ Complete only Part II below.
	Yes ⟶ Complete Part III on the back next.

Caution. If the care was provided in your home, you may owe employment taxes. If you do, you must use Form 1040. See **Schedule H** and its instructions for details.

Part II

Credit for child and dependent care expenses

2 Information about your **qualifying person(s).** If you have more than two qualifying persons, see page 62.

(a) Qualifying person's name		(b) Qualifying person's social security number	(c) Qualified expenses you incurred and paid in 1999 for the person listed in column (a)
First	Last		

3 Add the amounts in column (c) of line 2. DO NOT enter more than $2,400 for one qualifying person or $4,800 for two or more persons. If you completed Part III, enter the amount from line 24. | **3** | |

4 Enter YOUR **earned income.** | **4** | |

5 If married filing a joint return, enter YOUR SPOUSE'S earned income (if your spouse was a student or was disabled, see page 63); **all others,** enter the amount from line 4 | **5** | |

6 Enter the **smallest** of line 3, 4, or 5. | **6** | |

7 Enter the amount from Form 1040A, line 19. **7** | |

8 Enter on line 8 the decimal amount shown below that applies to the amount on line 7.

If line 7 is—		Decimal amount is	If line 7 is—		Decimal amount is
Over	But not over		Over	But not over	
$0	10,000	.30	$20,000	22,000	.24
10,000	12,000	.29	22,000	24,000	.23
12,000	14,000	.28	24,000	26,000	.22
14,000	16,000	.27	26,000	28,000	.21
16,000	18,000	.26	28,000	No limit	.20
18,000	20,000	.25			

8 ×.

9 Multiply **line 6** by the decimal amount on line 8. Enter the result here and on Form 1040A, line 26. But if this amount is more than the amount on Form 1040A, line 25, **or** you paid 1998 expenses in 1999, see page 63 for the amount to enter on line 26. | **9** | |

For Paperwork Reduction Act Notice, see Form 1040A instructions.   Cat. No. 10749I   Schedule 2 (Form 1040A) 1999

Part III

Dependent care benefits

10 Enter the total amount of **dependent care benefits** you received for 1999. This amount should be shown in box 10 of your W-2 form(s). DO NOT include amounts that were reported to you as wages in box 1 of Form(s) W-2.

10

11 Enter the amount forfeited, if any. See page 63.

11

12 Subtract line 11 from line 10.

12

13 Enter the total amount of **qualified expenses** incurred in 1999 for the care of the qualifying person(s).

13

14 Enter the **smaller** of line 12 or 13.

14

15 Enter YOUR **earned income.**

15

16 If married filing a joint return, enter YOUR SPOUSE'S earned income (if your spouse was a student or was disabled, see the instructions for line 5); if married filing a separate return, see the instructions for the amount to enter; **all others,** enter the amount from line 15.

16

17 Enter the **smallest** of line 14, 15, or 16.

17

18 **Excluded benefits.** Enter here the **smaller** of the following:
  • The amount from line 17, or
  • $5,000 ($2,500 if married filing a separate return **and** you were required to enter your spouse's earned income on line 16).

18

19 **Taxable benefits.** Subtract line 18 from line 12. Also, include this amount on Form 1040A, line 7. In the space to the left of line 7, enter "DCB."

19

To claim the child and dependent care credit, complete lines 20–24 below.

20 Enter $2,400 ($4,800 if two or more qualifying persons).

20

21 Enter the amount from line 18.

21

22 Subtract line 21 from line 20. If zero or less, **STOP.** You cannot take the credit. **Exception.** If you paid 1998 expenses in 1999, see the instructions for line 9.

22

23 Complete line 2 on the front of this schedule. DO NOT include in column (c) any benefits shown on line 18 above. Then, add the amounts in column (c) and enter the total here.

23

24 Enter the **smaller** of line 22 or 23 here. Also, enter this amount on line 3 on the front of this schedule and complete lines 4–9.

24

Schedule 3
(Form 1040A)

Department of the Treasury—Internal Revenue Service

**Credit for the Elderly or the Disabled
for Form 1040A Filers**

(99) **1999**

OMB No. 1545-0085

Name(s) shown on Form 1040A | Your social security number

You may be able to take this credit and reduce your tax if by the end of 1999:
- You were age 65 or older, **OR**
- You were under age 65, you retired on **permanent and total** disability, and you received taxable disability income.

But you must also meet other tests. See the separate instructions for Schedule 3.

TIP In most cases, the IRS can figure the credit for you. See the instructions.

Part I

Check the box for your filing status and age

If your filing status is:	And by the end of 1999:	Check only one box:

Single, Head of household, or Qualifying widow(er) with dependent child

1 You were 65 or older . . . . 1 ☐

2 You were under 65 and you retired on permanent and total disability . . . . 2 ☐

Married filing a joint return

3 Both spouses were 65 or older . . . . 3 ☐

4 Both spouses were under 65, but only one spouse retired on permanent and total disability . . . . 4 ☐

5 Both spouses were under 65, and both retired on permanent and total disability . . . . 5 ☐

6 One spouse was 65 or older, and the other spouse was under 65 and retired on permanent and total disability . . . . 6 ☐

7 One spouse was 65 or older, and the other spouse was under 65 and **NOT** retired on permanent and total disability . . . . 7 ☐

Married filing a separate return

8 You were 65 or older and you lived apart from your spouse for all of 1999 . . . . 8 ☐

9 You were under 65, you retired on permanent and total disability, and you lived apart from your spouse for all of 1999 . . . . 9 ☐

Did you check box 1, 3, 7, or 8? — Yes ➔ Skip Part II and complete Part III on the back.
— No ➔ Complete Parts II and III.

Part II

Statement of permanent and total disability

Complete this part **only** if you checked box 2, 4, 5, 6, or 9 above.

IF: **1** You filed a physician's statement for this disability for 1983 or an earlier year, or you filed or got a statement for tax years after 1983 and your physician signed line B on the statement, **AND**

2 Due to your continued disabled condition, you were unable to engage in any substantial gainful activity in 1999, check this box . . . . ▶ ☐
- If you checked this box, you do not have to get another statement for 1999.
- If you **did not** check this box, have your physician complete the statement on page 4 of the instructions. You **must** keep the statement for your records.

For Paperwork Reduction Act Notice, see Form 1040A instructions.   Cat. No. 12064K   **Schedule 3 (Form 1040A) 1999**

Part III

Figure your credit

10 If you checked (in Part I):   **Enter:**

Box 1, 2, 4, or 7 . . . . $5,000

Box 3, 5, or 6 . . . . $7,500

Box 8 or 9 . . . . $3,750   **10**

> **Did you check box 2, 4, 5, 6, or 9 in Part I?** —— **Yes** ——▶ You **must** complete line 11.
>
> —— **No** ——▶ Enter the amount from line 10 on line 12 and go to line 13.

11 • If you checked box 6 in Part I, add $5,000 to the taxable disability income of the spouse who was under age 65. Enter the total.

• If you checked box 2, 4, or 9 in Part I, enter your taxable disability income.

• If you checked box 5 in Part I, add your taxable disability income to your spouse's taxable disability income. Enter the total.

TIP For more details on what to include on line 11, see the instructions.   **11**

12 If you completed line 11, enter the **smaller** of line 10 or line 11; **all others,** enter the amount from line 10.   **12**

13 Enter the following pensions, annuities, or disability income that you (and your spouse if filing a joint return) received in 1999.

a Nontaxable part of social security benefits, and

Nontaxable part of railroad retirement benefits treated as social security. See instructions.   **13a**

b Nontaxable veterans' pensions and any other pension, annuity, or disability benefit that is excluded from income under any other provision of law. See instructions.   **13b**

c Add lines 13a and 13b. (Even though these income items are not taxable, they **must** be included here to figure your credit.) If you did not receive any of the types of nontaxable income listed on line 13a or 13b, enter -0- on line 13c.   **13c**

14 Enter the amount from Form 1040A, line 19.   **14**

15 **If you checked (in Part I):**   **Enter:**

Box 1 or 2 . . . . $7,500

Box 3, 4, 5, 6, or 7 . . . . . $10,000

Box 8 or 9 . . . . $5,000   **15**

16 Subtract line 15 from line 14. If zero or less, enter -0-.   **16**

17 Enter one-half of line 16.   **17**

18 Add lines 13c and 17.   **18**

19 Subtract line 18 from line 12. If zero or less, **stop;** you **cannot** take the credit. Otherwise, go to line 20.   **19**

20 Multiply line 19 by 15% (.15). Enter the result here and on Form 1040A, line 27. But if this amount is more than the amount on Form 1040A, line 25, **or** you are filing Schedule 2 (Form 1040A), see the instructions for the amount of credit you may take.   **20**

Form **1040**

Department of the Treasury—Internal Revenue Service

U.S. Individual Income Tax Return **1999**

IRS Use Only—Do not write or staple in this space.

For the year Jan. 1–Dec. 31, 1999, or other tax year beginning _____ , 1999, ending _____ , OMB No. 1545-0074

Label

(See instructions on page 18.)

Use the IRS label. Otherwise, please print or type.

L A B E L H E R E

Your first name and initial	Last name	Your social security number
If a joint return, spouse's first name and initial	Last name	Spouse's social security number

Home address (number and street). If you have a P.O. box, see page 18. | Apt. no.

City, town or post office, state, and ZIP code. If you have a foreign address, see page 18.

▲ **IMPORTANT!** ▲ You **must** enter your SSN(s) above.

Presidential Election Campaign
(See page 18.)

▶ Do you want $3 to go to this fund? . . . .
If a joint return, does your spouse want $3 to go to this fund? . . . .

| | Yes | No | Note. Checking "Yes" will not change your tax or reduce your refund. |

Filing Status

Check only one box.

1 ☐ Single
2 ☐ Married filing joint return (even if only one had income)
3 ☐ Married filing separate return. Enter spouse's social security no. above and full name here. ▶ _____
4 ☐ Head of household (with qualifying person). (See page 18.) If the qualifying person is a child but not your dependent, enter this child's name here. ▶ _____
5 ☐ Qualifying widow(er) with dependent child (year spouse died ▶ 19___). (See page 18.)

Exemptions

If more than six dependents, see page 19.

6a ☐ **Yourself.** If your parent (or someone else) can claim you as a dependent on his or her tax return, **do not** check box 6a. . . . .
b ☐ **Spouse** . . . .

c Dependents:

(1) First name Last name	(2) Dependent's social security number	(3) Dependent's relationship to you	(4)✓ if qualifying child for child tax credit (see page 19)
			☐
			☐
			☐
			☐
			☐
			☐

d Total number of exemptions claimed . . . .

No. of boxes checked on 6a and 6b _____

No. of your children on 6c who:
• lived with you _____
• did not live with you due to divorce or separation (see page 19) _____

Dependents on 6c not entered above _____

Add numbers entered on lines above ▶ ☐

Income

Attach Copy B of your Forms W-2 and W-2G here. Also attach Form(s) 1099-R if tax was withheld.

If you did not get a W-2, see page 20.

Enclose, but do not staple, any payment. Also, please use Form 1040-V.

7	Wages, salaries, tips, etc. Attach Form(s) W-2	**7**
8a	**Taxable** interest. Attach Schedule B if required	**8a**
b	**Tax-exempt** interest. DO NOT include on line 8a . . . **8b**	
9	Ordinary dividends. Attach Schedule B if required	**9**
10	Taxable refunds, credits, or offsets of state and local income taxes (see page 21) . .	**10**
11	Alimony received	**11**
12	Business income or (loss). Attach Schedule C or C-EZ . . .	**12**
13	Capital gain or (loss). Attach Schedule D if required. If not required, check here ▶ ☐	**13**
14	Other gains or (losses). Attach Form 4797	**14**
15a	Total IRA distributions . **15a**	b Taxable amount (see page 22)	**15b**
16a	Total pensions and annuities **16a**	b Taxable amount (see page 22)	**16b**
17	Rental real estate, royalties, partnerships, S corporations, trusts, etc. Attach Schedule E	**17**
18	Farm income or (loss). Attach Schedule F	**18**
19	Unemployment compensation	**19**
20a	Social security benefits . **20a**	b Taxable amount (see page 24)	**20b**
21	Other income. List type and amount (see page 24) ---------------	**21**
22	Add the amounts in the far right column for lines 7 through 21. This is your **total income** ▶	**22**

Adjusted Gross Income

23	IRA deduction (see page 26)	**23**	
24	Student loan interest deduction (see page 26)	**24**	
25	Medical savings account deduction. Attach Form 8853 .	**25**	
26	Moving expenses. Attach Form 3903	**26**	
27	One-half of self-employment tax. Attach Schedule SE .	**27**	
28	Self-employed health insurance deduction (see page 28)	**28**	
29	Keogh and self-employed SEP and SIMPLE plans . .	**29**	
30	Penalty on early withdrawal of savings	**30**	
31a	Alimony paid b Recipient's SSN ▶	**31a**	
32	Add lines 23 through 31a		**32**
33	Subtract line 32 from line 22. This is your **adjusted gross income** . . . . . . ▶		**33**

For Disclosure, Privacy Act, and Paperwork Reduction Act Notice, see page 54.   Cat. No. 11320B   Form **1040** (1999)

Tax and Credits	34	Amount from line 33 (adjusted gross income)	**34**	
	35a	Check if: ☐ **You** were 65 or older, ☐ Blind; ☐ **Spouse** was 65 or older, ☐ Blind. Add the number of boxes checked above and enter the total here . . . . ▶ **35a**		
	b	If you are married filing separately and your spouse itemizes deductions or you were a dual-status alien, see page 30 and check here . . . . . . ▶ **35b** ☐		

Standard Deduction for Most People

Single: $4,300

Head of household: $6,350

Married filing jointly or Qualifying widow(er): $7,200

Married filing separately: $3,600

36	Enter your **itemized deductions** from Schedule A, line 28, **OR standard deduction** shown on the left. **But** see page 30 to find your standard deduction if you checked any box on line 35a or 35b **or** if someone can claim you as a dependent	**36**	
37	Subtract line 36 from line 34	**37**	
38	If line 34 is $94,975 or less, multiply $2,750 by the total number of exemptions claimed on line 6d. If line 34 is over $94,975, see the worksheet on page 31 for the amount to enter .	**38**	
39	**Taxable income.** Subtract line 38 from line 37. If line 38 is more than line 37, enter -0-	**39**	
40	**Tax** (see page 31). Check if any tax is from **a** ☐ Form(s) 8814 **b** ☐ Form 4972 . . ▶	**40**	
41	Credit for child and dependent care expenses. Attach Form 2441	**41**	
42	Credit for the elderly or the disabled. Attach Schedule R . .	**42**	
43	Child tax credit (see page 33)	**43**	
44	Education credits. Attach Form 8863	**44**	
45	Adoption credit. Attach Form 8839	**45**	
46	Foreign tax credit. Attach Form 1116 if required . .	**46**	
47	Other. Check if from **a** ☐ Form 3800 **b** ☐ Form 8396 **c** ☐ Form 8801 **d** ☐ Form (specify) _____	**47**	
48	Add lines 41 through 47. These are your **total credits**	**48**	
49	Subtract line 48 from line 40. If line 48 is more than line 40, enter -0- . . . . . ▶	**49**	

Other Taxes	50	Self-employment tax. Attach Schedule SE	**50**	
	51	Alternative minimum tax. Attach Form 6251	**51**	
	52	Social security and Medicare tax on tip income not reported to employer. Attach Form 4137 .	**52**	
	53	Tax on IRAs, other retirement plans, and MSAs. Attach Form 5329 if required . .	**53**	
	54	Advance earned income credit payments from Form(s) W-2	**54**	
	55	Household employment taxes. Attach Schedule H	**55**	
	56	Add lines 49 through 55. This is your **total tax** . . . . ▶	**56**	

Payments	57	Federal income tax withheld from Forms W-2 and 1099 . .	**57**	
	58	1999 estimated tax payments and amount applied from 1998 return .	**58**	
	59a	**Earned income credit.** Attach Sch. EIC if you have a qualifying child		
	b	Nontaxable earned income: amount . . ▶ [____] and type ▶ -------------------------------	**59a**	
	60	Additional child tax credit. Attach Form 8812	**60**	
	61	Amount paid with request for extension to file (see page 48)	**61**	
	62	Excess social security and RRTA tax withheld (see page 48)	**62**	
	63	Other payments. Check if from **a** ☐ Form 2439 **b** ☐ Form 4136	**63**	
	64	Add lines 57, 58, 59a, and 60 through 63. These are your **total payments** . . . . ▶	**64**	

Refund	65	If line 64 is more than line 56, subtract line 56 from line 64. This is the amount you **OVERPAID**	**65**	
Have it directly deposited! See page 48 and fill in 66b, 66c, and 66d.	66a	Amount of line 65 you want **REFUNDED TO YOU** . . . . ▶	**66a**	
	▶ b	Routing number [_____] ▶ **c** Type: ☐ Checking ☐ Savings		
	▶ d	Account number [_____]		
	67	Amount of line 65 you want **APPLIED TO YOUR 2000 ESTIMATED TAX** ▶	**67**	

Amount You Owe	68	If line 56 is more than line 64, subtract line 64 from line 56. This is the **AMOUNT YOU OWE**. For details on how to pay, see page 49 . . . . ▶	**68**	
	69	Estimated tax penalty. Also include on line 68	**69**	

Sign Here Joint return? See page 18. Keep a copy for your records.	Under penalties of perjury, I declare that I have examined this return and accompanying schedules and statements, and to the best of my knowledge and belief, they are true, correct, and complete. Declaration of preparer (other than taxpayer) is based on all information of which preparer has any knowledge.

Your signature	Date	Your occupation	Daytime telephone number (optional) ( )
▶			
Spouse's signature. If a joint return, BOTH must sign.	Date	Spouse's occupation	
▶			

Paid Preparer's Use Only	Preparer's signature ▶	Date	Check if self-employed ☐	Preparer's SSN or PTIN
	Firm's name (or yours if self-employed) and address ▶			EIN
				ZIP code

Form **1040** (1999)

SCHEDULES A&B
(Form 1040)

Department of the Treasury
Internal Revenue Service (99)

OMB No. 1545-0074

1999

Attachment
Sequence No. 07

Schedule A—Itemized Deductions

(Schedule B is on back)

▶ Attach to Form 1040. ▶ See Instructions for Schedules A and B (Form 1040).

Name(s) shown on Form 1040

Your social security number

Medical and Dental Expenses

Caution. Do not include expenses reimbursed or paid by others.

1 Medical and dental expenses (see page A-1) . . . . | 1 |
2 Enter amount from Form 1040, line 34 . | 2 | |
3 Multiply line 2 above by 7.5% (.075) . . . . . . | 3 |
4 Subtract line 3 from line 1. If line 3 is more than line 1, enter -0- . . . . . . | 4 |

Taxes You Paid

(See page A-2.)

5 State and local income taxes . . . . | 5 |
6 Real estate taxes (see page A-2) . . . . . . | 6 |
7 Personal property taxes . . . . | 7 |
8 Other taxes. List type and amount ▶ ----------------- | 8 |
9 Add lines 5 through 8 . . . . | 9 |

Interest You Paid

(See page A-3.)

Note.
Personal interest is not deductible.

10 Home mortgage interest and points reported to you on Form 1098 | 10 |
11 Home mortgage interest not reported to you on Form 1098. If paid to the person from whom you bought the home, see page A-3 and show that person's name, identifying no., and address ▶ | 11 |
12 Points not reported to you on Form 1098. See page A-3 for special rules . . . . | 12 |
13 Investment interest. Attach Form 4952 if required. (See page A-3.) . . . . | 13 |
14 Add lines 10 through 13 . . . . | 14 |

Gifts to Charity

If you made a gift and got a benefit for it, see page A-4.

15 Gifts by cash or check. If you made any gift of $250 or more, see page A-4 . . . . . . | 15 |
16 Other than by cash or check. If any gift of $250 or more, see page A-4. You **MUST** attach Form 8283 if over $500 | 16 |
17 Carryover from prior year . . . . . . | 17 |
18 Add lines 15 through 17 . . . . . . | 18 |

Casualty and Theft Losses

19 Casualty or theft loss(es). Attach Form 4684. (See page A-5.) . . . . . . | 19 |

Job Expenses and Most Other Miscellaneous Deductions

(See page A-5 for expenses to deduct here.)

20 Unreimbursed employee expenses—job travel, union dues, job education, etc. You **MUST** attach Form 2106 or 2106-EZ if required. (See page A-5.) ▶ ----------------- | 20 |
21 Tax preparation fees . . . . | 21 |
22 Other expenses—investment, safe deposit box, etc. List type and amount ▶ ----------------- | 22 |
23 Add lines 20 through 22 . . . . . . | 23 |
24 Enter amount from Form 1040, line 34 . | 24 | |
25 Multiply line 24 above by 2% (.02) . . . . . | 25 |
26 Subtract line 25 from line 23. If line 25 is more than line 23, enter -0- . . . . | 26 |

Other Miscellaneous Deductions

27 Other—from list on page A-6. List type and amount ▶ ----------------- | 27 |

Total Itemized Deductions

28 Is Form 1040, line 34, over $126,600 (over $63,300 if married filing separately)?

☐ **No.** Your deduction is not limited. Add the amounts in the far right column for lines 4 through 27. Also, enter this amount on Form 1040, line 36. ▶ | 28 |

☐ **Yes.** Your deduction may be limited. See page A-6 for the amount to enter.

For Paperwork Reduction Act Notice, see Form 1040 instructions. Cat. No. 11330X Schedule A (Form 1040) 1999

Name(s) shown on Form 1040. Do not enter name and social security number if shown on other side.

Your social security number

Schedule B—Interest and Ordinary Dividends

Attachment
Sequence No. **08**

Note. If you had over $400 in taxable interest, you must also complete Part III.

			Amount
Part I **Interest** (See page B-1 and the instructions for Form 1040, line 8a.) **Note.** If you received a Form 1099-INT, Form 1099-OID, or substitute statement from a brokerage firm, list the firm's name as the payer and enter the total interest shown on that form.	**1**	List name of payer. If any interest is from a seller-financed mortgage and the buyer used the property as a personal residence, see page B-1 and list this interest first. Also, show that buyer's social security number and address ▶	**1**
	2	Add the amounts on line 1	**2**
	3	Excludable interest on series EE and I U.S. savings bonds issued after 1989 from Form 8815, line 14. You **MUST** attach Form 8815	**3**
	4	Subtract line 3 from line 2. Enter the result here and on Form 1040, line 8a ▶	**4**

Note. If you had over $400 in ordinary dividends, you must also complete Part III.

			Amount
Part II **Ordinary** **Dividends** (See page B-1 and the instructions for Form 1040, line 9.) **Note.** If you received a Form 1099-DIV or substitute statement from a brokerage firm, list the firm's name as the payer and enter the ordinary dividends shown on that form.	**5**	List name of payer. Include only ordinary dividends. If you received any capital gain distributions, see the instructions for Form 1040, line 13 ▶	**5**
	6	Add the amounts on line 5. Enter the total here and on Form 1040, line 9 . ▶	**6**

			Yes	No
Part III **Foreign** **Accounts** **and Trusts** (See page B-2.)	You must complete this part if you **(a)** had over $400 of interest or ordinary dividends; **(b)** had a foreign account; or **(c)** received a distribution from, or were a grantor of, or a transferor to, a foreign trust.			
	7a	At any time during 1999, did you have an interest in or a signature or other authority over a financial account in a foreign country, such as a bank account, securities account, or other financial account? See page B-2 for exceptions and filing requirements for Form TD F 90-22.1		
	b	If "Yes," enter the name of the foreign country ▶		
	8	During 1999, did you receive a distribution from, or were you the grantor of, or transferor to, a foreign trust? If "Yes," you may have to file Form 3520. See page B-2		

For Paperwork Reduction Act Notice, see Form 1040 instructions.

Schedule B (Form 1040) 1999

SCHEDULE C (Form 1040) Department of the Treasury Internal Revenue Service (99)	**Profit or Loss From Business** (Sole Proprietorship) ▶ Partnerships, joint ventures, etc., must file Form 1065 or Form 1065-B. ▶ **Attach to Form 1040 or Form 1041.** ▶ See Instructions for Schedule C (Form 1040).	OMB No. 1545-0074 **1999** Attachment Sequence No. **09**

Name of proprietor	Social security number (SSN)

A Principal business or profession, including product or service (see page C-1)

B Enter code from pages C-8 & 9 ▶

C Business name. If no separate business name, leave blank.

D Employer ID number (EIN), if any

E Business address (including suite or room no.) ▶ ....
City, town or post office, state, and ZIP code

F Accounting method: **(1)** ☐ Cash **(2)** ☐ Accrual **(3)** ☐ Other (specify) ▶ ....

G Did you "materially participate" in the operation of this business during 1999? If "No," see page C-2 for limit on losses . ☐ Yes ☐ No

H If you started or acquired this business during 1999, check here . . . . ▶ ☐

Part I Income

1	Gross receipts or sales. **Caution:** *If this income was reported to you on Form W-2 and the "Statutory employee" box on that form was checked, see page C-2 and check here* . . . . ▶ ☐	**1**	
2	Returns and allowances	**2**	
3	Subtract line 2 from line 1	**3**	
4	Cost of goods sold (from line 42 on page 2)	**4**	
5	**Gross profit.** Subtract line 4 from line 3	**5**	
6	Other income, including Federal and state gasoline or fuel tax credit or refund (see page C-3) . . .	**6**	
7	**Gross income.** Add lines 5 and 6 . . . . ▶	**7**	

Part II Expenses. Enter expenses for business use of your home **only** on line 30.

8	Advertising	**8**		19 Pension and profit-sharing plans	**19**	
9	Bad debts from sales or services (see page C-3) . .	**9**		20 Rent or lease (see page C-4):		
				a Vehicles, machinery, and equipment .	**20a**	
10	Car and truck expenses (see page C-3) . .	**10**		b Other business property . .	**20b**	
				21 Repairs and maintenance . .	**21**	
11	Commissions and fees . .	**11**		22 Supplies (not included in Part III) .	**22**	
12	Depletion	**12**		23 Taxes and licenses . . .	**23**	
13	Depreciation and section 179 expense deduction (not included in Part III) (see page C-3) . .	**13**		24 Travel, meals, and entertainment: a Travel	**24a**	
14	Employee benefit programs (other than on line 19) . . .	**14**		b Meals and entertainment .		
15	Insurance (other than health) .	**15**		c Enter nondeductible amount included on line 24b (see page C-5) .		
16	Interest:					
a	Mortgage (paid to banks, etc.) .	**16a**		d Subtract line 24c from line 24b .	**24d**	
b	Other	**16b**		25 Utilities	**25**	
17	Legal and professional services	**17**		26 Wages (less employment credits) .	**26**	
18	Office expense	**18**		27 Other expenses (from line 48 on page 2)	**27**	

28	**Total expenses** before expenses for business use of home. Add lines 8 through 27 in columns . ▶	**28**	
29	Tentative profit (loss). Subtract line 28 from line 7	**29**	
30	Expenses for business use of your home. Attach **Form 8829**	**30**	
31	**Net profit or (loss).** Subtract line 30 from line 29. ● If a profit, enter on **Form 1040, line 12,** and ALSO on **Schedule SE, line 2** (statutory employees, see page C-6). Estates and trusts, enter on Form 1041, line 3. ● If a loss, you MUST go on to line 32.	**31**	
32	If you have a loss, check the box that describes your investment in this activity (see page C-6). ● If you checked 32a, enter the loss on **Form 1040, line 12,** and ALSO on **Schedule SE, line 2** (statutory employees, see page C-6). Estates and trusts, enter on Form 1041, line 3. ● If you checked 32b, you MUST attach **Form 6198.**	**32a** ☐ All investment is at risk. **32b** ☐ Some investment is not at risk.	

For Paperwork Reduction Act Notice, see Form 1040 instructions. Cat. No. 11334P **Schedule C (Form 1040) 1999**

Part III   Cost of Goods Sold (see page C-6)

33   Method(s) used to value closing inventory: **a** ☐ Cost   **b** ☐ Lower of cost or market   **c** ☐ Other (attach explanation)

34   Was there any change in determining quantities, costs, or valuations between opening and closing inventory? If "Yes," attach explanation .   ☐ Yes   ☐ No

35 Inventory at beginning of year. If different from last year's closing inventory, attach explanation	**35**	
36 Purchases less cost of items withdrawn for personal use	**36**	
37 Cost of labor. Do not include any amounts paid to yourself	**37**	
38 Materials and supplies	**38**	
39 Other costs	**39**	
40 Add lines 35 through 39	**40**	
41 Inventory at end of year	**41**	
42 **Cost of goods sold.** Subtract line 41 from line 40. Enter the result here and on page 1, line 4	**42**	

Part IV   **Information on Your Vehicle.** Complete this part **ONLY** if you are claiming car or truck expenses on line 10 and are not required to file Form 4562 for this business. See the instructions for line 13 on page C-3 to find out if you must file.

43   When did you place your vehicle in service for business purposes? (month, day, year) ▶ .... / .... / ....

44   Of the total number of miles you drove your vehicle during 1999, enter the number of miles you used your vehicle for:

   a Business .... **b** Commuting .... **c** Other ....

45   Do you (or your spouse) have another vehicle available for personal use? .   ☐ Yes   ☐ No

46   Was your vehicle available for use during off-duty hours? .   ☐ Yes   ☐ No

47a   Do you have evidence to support your deduction? .   ☐ Yes   ☐ No

   b   If "Yes," is the evidence written? .   ☐ Yes   ☐ No

Part V   **Other Expenses.** List below business expenses not included on lines 8–26 or line 30.

....		
....		
....		
....		
....		
....		
....		
48 **Total other expenses.** Enter here and on page 1, line 27	**48**	

SCHEDULE C-EZ (Form 1040)

Department of the Treasury
Internal Revenue Service (99)

Net Profit From Business
(Sole Proprietorship)

▶ Partnerships, joint ventures, etc., must file Form 1065 or 1065-B.

▶ Attach to Form 1040 or Form 1041. ▶ See instructions on back.

OMB No. 1545-0074

1999

Attachment
Sequence No. **09A**

Name of proprietor

Social security number (SSN)

Part I — General Information

You May Use Schedule C-EZ Instead of Schedule C Only If You:

- Had business expenses of $2,500 or less.
- Use the cash method of accounting.
- Did not have an inventory at any time during the year.
- Did not have a net loss from your business.
- Had only one business as a sole proprietor.

And You:

- Had no employees during the year.
- Are not required to file **Form 4562**, Depreciation and Amortization, for this business. See the instructions for Schedule C, line 13, on page C-3 to find out if you must file.
- Do not deduct expenses for business use of your home.
- Do not have prior year unallowed passive activity losses from this business.

A Principal business or profession, including product or service

B Enter code from pages C-8 & 9
▶

C Business name. If no separate business name, leave blank.

D Employer ID number (EIN), if any

E Business address (including suite or room no.). Address not required if same as on Form 1040, page 1.

City, town or post office, state, and ZIP code

Part II — Figure Your Net Profit

1 **Gross receipts. Caution:** *If this income was reported to you on Form W-2 and the "Statutory employee" box on that form was checked, see* **Statutory Employees** *in the instructions for Schedule C, line 1, on page C-2 and check here* . . . . ▶ ☐ | **1** |

2 **Total expenses.** If more than $2,500, you **must** use Schedule C. See instructions . . . . . | **2** |

3 **Net profit.** Subtract line 2 from line 1. If less than zero, you **must** use Schedule C. Enter on **Form 1040, line 12,** and ALSO on **Schedule SE, line 2.** (Statutory employees **do not** report this amount on Schedule SE, line 2. Estates and trusts, enter on Form 1041, line 3.) . . . . . | **3** |

Part III — Information on Your Vehicle. Complete this part ONLY if you are claiming car or truck expenses on line 2.

4 When did you place your vehicle in service for business purposes? (month, day, year) ▶ ....../....../...... .

5 Of the total number of miles you drove your vehicle during 1999, enter the number of miles you used your vehicle for:

a Business .... **b** Commuting .... **c** Other ....

6 Do you (or your spouse) have another vehicle available for personal use? . . . . ☐ Yes ☐ No

7 Was your vehicle available for use during off-duty hours? . . . . ☐ Yes ☐ No

8a Do you have evidence to support your deduction? . . . . ☐ Yes ☐ No

b If "Yes," is the evidence written? . . . . ☐ Yes ☐ No

For Paperwork Reduction Act Notice, see Form 1040 instructions.   Cat. No. 14374D   Schedule C-EZ (Form 1040) 1999

Instructions

You may use Schedule C-EZ instead of Schedule C if you operated a business or practiced a profession as a sole proprietorship and you have met all the requirements listed in Part I of Schedule C-EZ.

Line A

Describe the business or professional activity that provided your principal source of income reported on line 1. Give the general field or activity and the type of product or service.

Line B

Enter the six-digit code that identifies your principal business or professional activity. See pages C-8 and C-9 for the list of codes.

Line D

You need an employer identification number (EIN) only if you had a Keogh plan or were required to file an employment, excise, estate, trust, or alcohol, tobacco, and firearms tax return. If you need an EIN, file **Form SS-4,** Application for Employer Identification Number. If you do not have an EIN, leave line D blank. **Do not** enter your SSN.

Line E

Enter your business address. Show a street address instead of a box number. Include the suite or room number, if any.

Line 1

Enter gross receipts from your trade or business. Include amounts you received in your trade or business that were properly shown on **Forms 1099-MISC.** If the total amounts that were reported in box 7 of Forms 1099-MISC are more than the total you are reporting on line 1, attach a statement explaining the difference. You must show all items of taxable income actually or constructively received during the year (in cash, property, or services). Income is constructively received when it is credited to your account or set aside for you to use. Do not offset this amount by any losses.

Line 2

Enter the total amount of all deductible business expenses you actually paid during the year. Examples of these expenses include advertising, car and truck expenses, commissions and fees, insurance, interest, legal and professional services, office expense, rent or lease expenses, repairs and maintenance, supplies, taxes, travel, the allowable percentage of business meals and entertainment, and utilities (including telephone). For details, see the instructions for Schedule C, Parts II and V, on pages C-3 through C-7. If you wish, you may use the optional worksheet below to record your expenses.

If you claim car or truck expenses, be sure to complete Part III of Schedule C-EZ.

Optional Worksheet for Line 2 (keep a copy for your records)

a Business meals and entertainment	**a**			
b Enter nondeductible amount included on line **a** (see the instructions for lines 24b and 24c on page C-5)	**b**			
c Deductible business meals and entertainment. Subtract line **b** from line **a**		**c**	
d		**d**	
e		**e**	
f		**f**	
g		**g**	
h		**h**	
i		**i**	
j Total. Add lines **c** through **i.** Enter here and on line 2		**j**	

SCHEDULE D
(Form 1040)

Department of the Treasury
Internal Revenue Service   (99)

Capital Gains and Losses

▶ Attach to Form 1040.   ▶ See Instructions for Schedule D (Form 1040).

▶ Use Schedule D-1 for more space to list transactions for lines 1 and 8.

OMB No. 1545-0074

1999

Attachment
Sequence No. 12

Name(s) shown on Form 1040

Your social security number

Part I — Short-Term Capital Gains and Losses—Assets Held One Year or Less

(a) Description of property (Example: 100 sh. XYZ Co.)	(b) Date acquired (Mo., day, yr.)	(c) Date sold (Mo., day, yr.)	(d) Sales price (see page D-5)	(e) Cost or other basis (see page D-5)	(f) GAIN or (LOSS) Subtract (e) from (d)	
1						

2 Enter your short-term totals, if any, from Schedule D-1, line 2 . . . . | **2** | | | | |

3 **Total short-term sales price amounts.** Add column (d) of lines 1 and 2 . . . . . | **3** | | | |

4 Short-term gain from Form 6252 and short-term gain or (loss) from Forms 4684, 6781, and 8824 . . . . | **4** | |

5 Net short-term gain or (loss) from partnerships, S corporations, estates, and trusts from Schedule(s) K-1 . . . . | **5** | |

6 Short-term capital loss carryover. Enter the amount, if any, from line 8 of your 1998 Capital Loss Carryover Worksheet . . . . | **6** | ( ) |

7 **Net short-term capital gain or (loss).** Combine lines 1 through 6 in column (f) ▶ | **7** | |

Part II — Long-Term Capital Gains and Losses—Assets Held More Than One Year

(a) Description of property (Example: 100 sh. XYZ Co.)	(b) Date acquired (Mo., day, yr.)	(c) Date sold (Mo., day, yr.)	(d) Sales price (see page D-5)	(e) Cost or other basis (see page D-5)	(f) GAIN or (LOSS) Subtract (e) from (d)	(g) 28% RATE GAIN or (LOSS) * (see instr. below)
8						

9 Enter your long-term totals, if any, from Schedule D-1, line 9 . . . . | **9** | | | | |

10 **Total long-term sales price amounts.** Add column (d) of lines 8 and 9 . . . . . | **10** | | | | |

11 Gain from Form 4797, Part I; long-term gain from Forms 2439 and 6252; and long-term gain or (loss) from Forms 4684, 6781, and 8824 . . . . | **11** | |

12 Net long-term gain or (loss) from partnerships, S corporations, estates, and trusts from Schedule(s) K-1 . . . . | **12** | |

13 Capital gain distributions. See page D-1 . . . . | **13** | |

14 Long-term capital loss carryover. Enter in both columns (f) and (g) the amount, if any, from line 13 of your 1998 Capital Loss Carryover Worksheet . . . . . . | **14** | ( ) | ( ) |

15 Combine lines 8 through 14 in column (g) . . . . | **15** | |

16 **Net long-term capital gain or (loss).** Combine lines 8 through 14 in column (f) ▶ | **16** | |
Next: Go to Part III on the back.

*28% Rate Gain or Loss includes all "collectibles gains and losses" (as defined on page D-5) and up to 50% of the eligible gain on qualified small business stock (see page D-4).

For Paperwork Reduction Act Notice, see Form 1040 instructions.   Cat. No. 11338H   Schedule D (Form 1040) 1999

Part III   Summary of Parts I and II

17 Combine lines 7 and 16. If a loss, go to line 18. If a gain, enter the gain on Form 1040, line 13 | **17** |

    Next: Complete Form 1040 through line 39. Then, go to **Part IV** to figure your tax if:
- Both lines 16 and 17 are gains, **and**
- Form 1040, line 39, is more than zero.

18 If line 17 is a loss, enter here and as a (loss) on Form 1040, line 13, the **smaller** of these losses:
- The loss on line 17, **or**
- ($3,000) or, if married filing separately, ($1,500) . . . . | **18** | (|) |

    Next: Skip **Part IV** below. Instead, complete Form 1040 through line 37. Then, complete the **Capital Loss Carryover Worksheet** on page D-6 if:
- The loss on line 17 exceeds the loss on line 18, **or**
- Form 1040, line 37, is a loss.

Part IV   Tax Computation Using Maximum Capital Gains Rates

19 Enter your taxable income from Form 1040, line 39 . . . . | **19** |

20 Enter the **smaller** of line 16 or line 17 of Schedule D . . . . . | **20** |

21 If you are filing Form 4952, enter the amount from Form 4952, line 4e | **21** |

22 Subtract line 21 from line 20. If zero or less, enter -0- . . . . . | **22** |

23 Combine lines 7 and 15. If zero or less, enter -0- . . . . . . | **23** |

24 Enter the **smaller** of line 15 or line 23, but not less than zero . . . | **24** |

25 Enter your unrecaptured section 1250 gain, if any, from line 16 of the worksheet on page D-7 . . . . | **25** |

26 Add lines 24 and 25. . . . . | **26** |

27 Subtract line 26 from line 22. If zero or less, enter -0- . . . . | **27** |

28 Subtract line 27 from line 19. If zero or less, enter -0- . . . . | **28** |

29 Enter the **smaller** of:
- The amount on line 19, **or**
- $25,750 if single; $43,050 if married filing jointly or qualifying widow(er); $21,525 if married filing separately; or $34,550 if head of household } . . . . . | **29** |

30 Enter the **smaller** of line 28 or line 29 . . . . . . | **30** |

31 Subtract line 22 from line 19. If zero or less, enter -0- . . . . . | **31** |

32 Enter the **larger** of line 30 or line 31 . . . . . . ▶ | **32** |

33 Figure the tax on the amount on line 32. Use the Tax Table or Tax Rate Schedules, whichever applies | **33** |

    Note. If line 29 is less than line 28, go to line 38.

34 Enter the amount from line 29 . . . . | **34** |

35 Enter the amount from line 28 . . . . | **35** |

36 Subtract line 35 from line 34. If zero or less, enter -0- . . . . ▶ | **36** |

37 Multiply line 36 by 10% (.10) . . . . | **37** |

    Note. If line 27 is more than zero **and** equal to line 36, go to line 52.

38 Enter the **smaller** of line 19 or line 27 . . . . | **38** |

39 Enter the amount from line 36 . . . . | **39** |

40 Subtract line 39 from line 38 . . . . ▶ | **40** |

41 Multiply line 40 by 20% (.20) . . . . | **41** |

    Note. If line 25 is zero or blank, skip lines 42 through 47 and read the note above line 48.

42 Enter the **smaller** of line 22 or line 25 . . . . | **42** |

43 Add lines 22 and 32. . . . . | **43** |

44 Enter the amount from line 19 . . . . | **44** |

45 Subtract line 44 from line 43. If zero or less, enter -0- . . . . . | **45** |

46 Subtract line 45 from line 42. If zero or less, enter -0- . . . . ▶ | **46** |

47 Multiply line 46 by 25% (.25) . . . . | **47** |

    Note. If line 24 is zero or blank, go to line 52.

48 Enter the amount from line 19 . . . . | **48** |

49 Add lines 32, 36, 40, and 46 . . . . | **49** |

50 Subtract line 49 from line 48 . . . . | **50** |

51 Multiply line 50 by 28% (.28) . . . . | **51** |

52 Add lines 33, 37, 41, 47, and 51. . . . . | **52** |

53 Figure the tax on the amount on line 19. Use the Tax Table or Tax Rate Schedules, whichever applies | **53** |

54 **Tax on all taxable income (including capital gains).** Enter the **smaller** of line 52 or line 53 here and on Form 1040, line 40. . . . . | **54** |

SCHEDULE E	Supplemental Income and Loss	OMB No. 1545-0074
(Form 1040)	(From rental real estate, royalties, partnerships, S corporations, estates, trusts, REMICs, etc.)	**1999**
Department of the Treasury Internal Revenue Service (99)	► Attach to Form 1040 or Form 1041. ► See Instructions for Schedule E (Form 1040).	Attachment Sequence No. **13**

Name(s) shown on return   Your social security number

Part I   **Income or Loss From Rental Real Estate and Royalties**   Note: *Report income and expenses from your business of renting personal property on* **Schedule C** *or* **C-EZ** *(see page E-1). Report farm rental income or loss from* **Form 4835** *on page 2, line 39.*

1 Show the kind and location of each **rental real estate property:**

A ....

B ....

C ....

2 For each rental real estate property listed on line 1, did you or your family use it during the tax year for personal purposes for more than the greater of:

- 14 days, **or**
- 10% of the total days rented at fair rental value?

(See page E-1.)

	Yes	No
A		
B		
C		

Income:		Properties A	B	C	Totals (Add columns A, B, and C.)
3 Rents received	3				3
4 Royalties received	4				4
Expenses:					
5 Advertising	5				
6 Auto and travel (see page E-2) .	6				
7 Cleaning and maintenance . . .	7				
8 Commissions	8				
9 Insurance	9				
10 Legal and other professional fees	10				
11 Management fees	11				
12 Mortgage interest paid to banks, etc. (see page E-2)	12				12
13 Other interest	13				
14 Repairs	14				
15 Supplies	15				
16 Taxes	16				
17 Utilities	17				
18 Other (list) ►	18				
19 Add lines 5 through 18	19				19
20 Depreciation expense or depletion (see page E-3)	20				20
21 Total expenses. Add lines 19 and 20	21				
22 Income or (loss) from rental real estate or royalty properties. Subtract line 21 from line 3 (rents) or line 4 (royalties). If the result is a (loss), see page E-3 to find out if you must file **Form 6198**. . .	22				
23 Deductible rental real estate loss. **Caution:** *Your rental real estate loss on line 22 may be limited. See page E-3 to find out if you must file* **Form 8582**. *Real estate professionals must complete line 42 on page 2*	23	( )	( )	( )	

24 Income. Add positive amounts shown on line 22. **Do not** include any losses . . . . | 24 |

25 Losses. Add royalty losses from line 22 and rental real estate losses from line 23. Enter total losses here | 25 | ( ) |

26 Total rental real estate and royalty income or (loss). Combine lines 24 and 25. Enter the result here. If Parts II, III, IV, and line 39 on page 2 do not apply to you, also enter this amount on Form 1040, line 17. Otherwise, include this amount in the total on line 40 on page 2 . . . . | 26 |

For Paperwork Reduction Act Notice, see Form 1040 instructions.   Cat. No. 11344L   Schedule E (Form 1040) 1999

Name(s) shown on return. Do not enter name and social security number if shown on other side.	Your social security number

Note: *If you report amounts from farming or fishing on Schedule E, you must enter your gross income from those activities on line 41 below. Real estate professionals must complete line 42 below.*

Part II	Income or Loss From Partnerships and S Corporations	Note: *If you report a loss from an at-risk activity, you MUST check either column (e) or (f) on line 27 to describe your investment in the activity. See page E-5. If you check column (f), you must attach Form 6198.*

27

	(a) Name	(b) Enter P for partnership; S for S corporation	(c) Check if foreign partnership	(d) Employer identification number	Investment At Risk? (e) All is at risk	(f) Some is not at risk
A						
B						
C						
D						
E						

	Passive Income and Loss		Nonpassive Income and Loss		
	(g) Passive loss allowed (attach Form 8582 if required)	(h) Passive income from Schedule K–1	(i) Nonpassive loss from Schedule K–1	(j) Section 179 expense deduction from Form 4562	(k) Nonpassive income from Schedule K–1
A					
B					
C					
D					
E					
28a Totals					
b Totals					

29	Add columns (h) and (k) of line 28a	29	
30	Add columns (g), (i), and (j) of line 28b	30 (	)
31	Total partnership and S corporation income or (loss). Combine lines 29 and 30. Enter the result here and include in the total on line 40 below	31	

Part III	Income or Loss From Estates and Trusts

32

	(a) Name	(b) Employer identification number
A		
B		

	Passive Income and Loss		Nonpassive Income and Loss	
	(c) Passive deduction or loss allowed (attach Form 8582 if required)	(d) Passive income from Schedule K–1	(e) Deduction or loss from Schedule K–1	(f) Other income from Schedule K–1
A				
B				
33a Totals				
b Totals				

34	Add columns (d) and (f) of line 33a	34	
35	Add columns (c) and (e) of line 33b	35 (	)
36	Total estate and trust income or (loss). Combine lines 34 and 35. Enter the result here and include in the total on line 40 below	36	

Part IV	Income or Loss From Real Estate Mortgage Investment Conduits (REMICs)—Residual Holder

37

	(a) Name	(b) Employer identification number	(c) Excess inclusion from Schedules Q, line 2c (see page E-6)	(d) Taxable income (net loss) from Schedules Q, line 1b	(e) Income from Schedules Q, line 3b

38	Combine columns (d) and (e) only. Enter the result here and include in the total on line 40 below	38	

Part V	Summary

39	Net farm rental income or (loss) from **Form 4835**. Also, complete line 41 below	39	
40	TOTAL income or (loss). Combine lines 26, 31, 36, 38, and 39. Enter the result here and on Form 1040, line 17 ▶	40	

41	**Reconciliation of Farming and Fishing Income.** Enter your **gross** farming and fishing income reported on Form 4835, line 7; Schedule K-1 (Form 1065), line 15b; Schedule K-1 (Form 1120S), line 23; and Schedule K-1 (Form 1041), line 14 (see page E-6)	41	
42	**Reconciliation for Real Estate Professionals.** If you were a real estate professional (see page E-4), enter the net income or (loss) you reported anywhere on Form 1040 from all rental real estate activities in which you materially participated under the passive activity loss rules . .	42	

Schedule E (Form 1040) 1999

Earned Income Credit
Qualifying Child Information

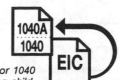

*Complete and attach to Form 1040A or 1040
only if you have a qualifying child.*

OMB No. 1545-0074

1999

Attachment
Sequence No. **43**

Name(s) shown on return | Your social security number

Before you begin: See the instructions for Form 1040A, lines 37a and 37b, or Form 1040, lines 59a and 59b, to make sure that (1) you can take the EIC and (2) you have a qualifying child.

- If you take the EIC even though you are not eligible, you may not be allowed to take the credit for up to 10 years. See back of schedule for details.
- It will take us longer to process your return and issue your refund if you do not fill in all lines that apply for each qualifying child.
- If you do not enter the child's correct social security number on line 4, at the time we process your return, we may reduce or disallow your EIC.

Qualifying Child Information	Child 1		Child 2	
1 Child's name If you have more than two qualifying children, you only have to list two to get the maximum credit.	First name	Last name	First name	Last name
2 Child's year of birth	Year ___ ___ ___ ___ *If born after 1980, skip lines 3a and 3b; go to line 4.*		Year ___ ___ ___ ___ *If born after 1980, skip lines 3a and 3b; go to line 4.*	
3 If the child was born before 1981— **a** Was the child under age 24 at the end of 1999 and a student?	☐ **Yes.** *Go to line 4.*	☐ **No.** *Continue*	☐ **Yes.** *Go to line 4.*	☐ **No.** *Continue*
b Was the child permanently and totally disabled during any part of 1999?	☐ **Yes.** *Continue*	☐ **No.** The child is not a qualifying child.	☐ **Yes.** *Continue*	☐ **No.** The child is not a qualifying child.
4 Child's social security number (SSN) The child must have an SSN as defined on page 42 of the Form 1040A instructions or page 41 of the Form 1040 instructions unless the child was born and died in 1999. If your child was born and died in 1999 and did not have an SSN, enter "Died" on this line and attach a copy of the child's birth certificate.				
5 Child's relationship to you (for example, son, daughter, grandchild, foster child, etc.)				
6 Number of months child lived with you in the United States during 1999 • If the child lived with you for more than half of 1999 but less than 7 months, enter "7". • If the child was born or died in 1999 and your home was the child's home for the entire time he or she was alive during 1999, enter "12".	___ months *Do not enter more than 12 months.*		___ months *Do not enter more than 12 months.*	

Do you want part of the EIC added to your take-home pay in 2000? To see if you qualify, get Form W-5 from your employer or by calling the IRS at 1-800-TAX-FORM (1-800-829-3676).

Purpose of Schedule

The purpose of this schedule is to give the IRS information about your qualifying child after you have figured your earned income credit.

To figure the amount of your credit, or to have the IRS figure it for you, see the instructions for Form 1040A, lines 37a and 37b, or Form 1040, lines 59a and 59b.

Taking the EIC When Not Eligible. If you take the EIC even though you are not eligible and it is determined that your error is due to reckless or intentional disregard of the EIC rules, you will not be allowed to take the credit for 2 years even if you are otherwise eligible to do so. If you fraudulently take the EIC, you will not be allowed to take the credit for 10 years. You may also have to pay penalties.

Qualifying Child

A qualifying child is a child who is your . . .

Son	Grandchild
Daughter	Stepchild
Adopted child	Foster child*

* A foster child is any child you cared for as your own child.

was at the end of 1999 . . .

Under age 19
OR
Under age 24 and a student
OR
Any age and permanently and totally disabled

who . . .

Lived with you in the United States for more than half of 1999 or, if a foster child, for all of 1999.
If the child did not live with you for the required time, see Exception to "Time Lived With You" Condition on page 42 of the Form 1040A instructions or page 41 of the Form 1040 instructions.

Note. If the child was married or meets the conditions to be a qualifying child of another person (other than your spouse if filing a joint return), special rules apply. For details, see page 42 of the Form 1040A instructions or page 41 of the Form 1040 instructions.

SCHEDULE F (Form 1040) Department of the Treasury Internal Revenue Service (99)	**Profit or Loss From Farming** ▶ Attach to Form 1040, Form 1041, Form 1065, or Form 1065-B. ▶ See Instructions for Schedule F (Form 1040).	OMB No. 1545-0074 **1999** Attachment Sequence No. **14**

Name of proprietor	Social security number (SSN)

A Principal product. Describe in one or two words your principal crop or activity for the current tax year.

B Enter code from Part IV ▶

D Employer ID number (EIN), if any

C Accounting method: (1) ☐ Cash (2) ☐ Accrual

E Did you "materially participate" in the operation of this business during 1999? If "No," see page F-2 for limit on passive losses. ☐ Yes ☐ No

Part I Farm Income—Cash Method. Complete Parts I and II (Accrual method taxpayers complete Parts II and III, and line 11 of Part I.)
Do not include sales of livestock held for draft, breeding, sport, or dairy purposes; report these sales on Form 4797.

1	Sales of livestock and other items you bought for resale	**1**	
2	Cost or other basis of livestock and other items reported on line 1	**2**	
3	Subtract line 2 from line 1		**3**
4	Sales of livestock, produce, grains, and other products you raised		**4**
5a	Total cooperative distributions (Form(s) 1099-PATR) **5a**	**5b** Taxable amount	**5b**
6a	Agricultural program payments (see page F-2) **6a**	**6b** Taxable amount	**6b**
7	Commodity Credit Corporation (CCC) loans (see page F-3):		
a	CCC loans reported under election		**7a**
b	CCC loans forfeited **7b**	**7c** Taxable amount	**7c**
8	Crop insurance proceeds and certain disaster payments (see page F-3):		
a	Amount received in 1999 **8a**	**8b** Taxable amount	**8b**
c	If election to defer to 2000 is attached, check here ▶ ☐	**8d** Amount deferred from 1998	**8d**
9	Custom hire (machine work) income		**9**
10	Other income, including Federal and state gasoline or fuel tax credit or refund (see page F-3)		**10**
11	**Gross income.** Add amounts in the right column for lines 3 through 10. If accrual method taxpayer, enter the amount from page 2, line 51 ▶		**11**

Part II Farm Expenses—Cash and Accrual Method. Do not include personal or living expenses such as taxes, insurance, repairs, etc., on your home.

12	Car and truck expenses (see page F-4—also attach **Form 4562**)	**12**		25	Pension and profit-sharing plans	**25**
13	Chemicals	**13**		26	Rent or lease (see page F-5):	
14	Conservation expenses (see page F-4)	**14**		a	Vehicles, machinery, and equipment	**26a**
15	Custom hire (machine work)	**15**		b	Other (land, animals, etc.)	**26b**
16	Depreciation and section 179 expense deduction not claimed elsewhere (see page F-4)	**16**		27	Repairs and maintenance	**27**
				28	Seeds and plants purchased	**28**
17	Employee benefit programs other than on line 25	**17**		29	Storage and warehousing	**29**
				30	Supplies purchased	**30**
18	Feed purchased	**18**		31	Taxes	**31**
19	Fertilizers and lime	**19**		32	Utilities	**32**
20	Freight and trucking	**20**		33	Veterinary, breeding, and medicine	**33**
21	Gasoline, fuel, and oil	**21**		34	Other expenses (specify):	
22	Insurance (other than health)	**22**		a	....	**34a**
23	Interest:			b	....	**34b**
a	Mortgage (paid to banks, etc.)	**23a**		c	....	**34c**
b	Other	**23b**		d	....	**34d**
24	Labor hired (less employment credits)	**24**		e	....	**34e**
				f	....	**34f**

35	**Total expenses.** Add lines 12 through 34f ▶	**35**
36	**Net farm profit or (loss).** Subtract line 35 from line 11. If a profit, enter on **Form 1040, line 18,** and ALSO on **Schedule SE, line 1.** If a loss, you MUST go on to line 37 (estates, trusts, and partnerships, see page F-6)	**36**
37	If you have a loss, you MUST check the box that describes your investment in this activity (see page F-6). • If you checked 37a, enter the loss on **Form 1040, line 18,** and ALSO on **Schedule SE, line 1.** • If you checked 37b, you MUST attach **Form 6198.**	**37a** ☐ All investment is at risk. **37b** ☐ Some investment is not at risk.

For Paperwork Reduction Act Notice, see Form 1040 instructions. Cat. No. 11346H Schedule F (Form 1040) 1999

Part III **Farm Income—Accrual Method** (see page F-6)

Do not include sales of livestock held for draft, breeding, sport, or dairy purposes; report these sales on Form 4797 and do not include this livestock on line 46 below.

38	Sales of livestock, produce, grains, and other products during the year.			**38**	
39a	Total cooperative distributions (Form(s) 1099-PATR)	39a	39b Taxable amount	**39b**	
40a	Agricultural program payments	40a	40b Taxable amount	**40b**	
41	Commodity Credit Corporation (CCC) loans:				
a	CCC loans reported under election			**41a**	
b	CCC loans forfeited	41b	41c Taxable amount	**41c**	
42	Crop insurance proceeds			**42**	
43	Custom hire (machine work) income			**43**	
44	Other income, including Federal and state gasoline or fuel tax credit or refund			**44**	
45	Add amounts in the right column for lines 38 through 44			**45**	
46	Inventory of livestock, produce, grains, and other products at beginning of the year.	46			
47	Cost of livestock, produce, grains, and other products purchased during the year.	47			
48	Add lines 46 and 47	48			
49	Inventory of livestock, produce, grains, and other products at end of year	49			
50	Cost of livestock, produce, grains, and other products sold. Subtract line 49 from line 48*			**50**	
51	**Gross income.** Subtract line 50 from line 45. Enter the result here and on page 1, line 11 ▶			**51**	

*If you use the unit-livestock-price method or the farm-price method of valuing inventory and the amount on line 49 is larger than the amount on line 48, subtract line 48 from line 49. Enter the result on line 50. Add lines 45 and 50. Enter the total on line 51.

Part IV **Principal Agricultural Activity Codes**

Caution. File **Schedule C** (Form 1040), Profit or Loss From Business, or **Schedule C-EZ** (Form 1040), Net Profit From Business, instead of Schedule F if:

• Your principal source of income is from providing agricultural services such as soil preparation, veterinary, farm labor, horticultural, or management for a fee or on a contract basis, or

• You are engaged in the business of breeding, raising, and caring for dogs, cats, or other pet animals.

These codes for the Principal Agricultural Activity classify farms by the type of activity they are engaged in to facilitate the administration of the Internal Revenue Code. These six-digit codes are based on the North American Industry Classification System (NAICS).

Select one of the following codes and enter the six-digit number on page 1, line B:

Crop Production

111100	Oilseed and grain farming
111210	Vegetable and melon farming
111300	Fruit and tree nut farming
111400	Greenhouse, nursery, and floriculture production
111900	Other crop farming

Animal Production

112111	Beef cattle ranching and farming
112112	Cattle feedlots
112120	Dairy cattle and milk production
112210	Hog and pig farming
112300	Poultry and egg production
112400	Sheep and goat farming
112510	Animal aquaculture
112900	Other animal production

Forestry and Logging

113000	Forestry and logging (including forest nurseries and timber tracts)

SCHEDULE H (Form 1040)	Household Employment Taxes	OMB No. 1545-0074

SCHEDULE H
(Form 1040)

Department of the Treasury
Internal Revenue Service (99)

Household Employment Taxes

(For Social Security, Medicare, Withheld Income, and Federal Unemployment (FUTA) Taxes)

▶ **Attach to Form 1040, 1040NR, 1040NR-EZ, 1040-SS, or 1041.**
▶ **See separate instructions.**

OMB No. 1545-0074

1999

Attachment
Sequence No. **44**

Name of employer

Social security number

Employer identification number

A Did you pay **any one** household employee cash wages of $1,100 or more in 1999? (If any household employee was your spouse, your child under age 21, your parent, or anyone under age 18, see the line A instructions on page 3 before you answer this question.)

☐ **Yes.** Skip lines B and C and go to line 1.
☐ **No.** Go to line B.

B Did you withhold Federal income tax during 1999 for any household employee?

☐ **Yes.** Skip line C and go to line 5.
☐ **No.** Go to line C.

C Did you pay **total** cash wages of $1,000 or more in **any** calendar **quarter** of 1998 or 1999 to household employees? (**Do not** count cash wages paid in 1998 or 1999 to your spouse, your child under age 21, or your parent.)

☐ **No.** **Stop.** Do not file this schedule.
☐ **Yes.** Skip lines 1–9 and go to line 10 on the back.

Part I Social Security, Medicare, and Income Taxes

1	Total cash wages subject to social security taxes (see page 3) . . . [1]	
2	Social security taxes. Multiply line 1 by 12.4% (.124)	2
3	Total cash wages subject to Medicare taxes (see page 3) . . . . [3]	
4	Medicare taxes. Multiply line 3 by 2.9% (.029)	4
5	Federal income tax withheld, if any	5
6	**Total social security, Medicare, and income taxes** (add lines 2, 4, and 5)	6
7	Advance earned income credit (EIC) payments, if any	7
8	**Net taxes** (subtract line 7 from line 6)	8

9 Did you pay **total** cash wages of $1,000 or more in **any** calendar **quarter** of 1998 or 1999 to household employees? (**Do not** count cash wages paid in 1998 or 1999 to your spouse, your child under age 21, or your parent.)

☐ **No.** **Stop.** Enter the amount from line 8 above on Form 1040, line 55. If you are not required to file Form 1040, see the line 9 instructions on page 4.

☐ **Yes.** Go to line 10 on the back.

For Paperwork Reduction Act Notice, see Form 1040 instructions.   Cat. No. 12187K   **Schedule H (Form 1040) 1999**

Part II   Federal Unemployment (FUTA) Tax

			Yes	No
10	Did you pay unemployment contributions to only one state?	10		
11	Did you pay all state unemployment contributions for 1999 by April 17, 2000? Fiscal year filers, see page 4	11		
12	Were all wages that are taxable for FUTA tax also taxable for your state's unemployment tax? . . .	12		

Next: If you checked the **"Yes"** box on **all** the lines above, complete Section A.

If you checked the **"No"** box on **any** of the lines above, skip Section A and complete Section B.

Section A

13	Name of the state where you paid unemployment contributions ▶		
14	State reporting number as shown on state unemployment tax return ▶		
15	Contributions paid to your state unemployment fund (see page 4) .	**15**	
16	Total cash wages subject to FUTA tax (see page 4)	**16**	
17	**FUTA tax.** Multiply line 16 by .008. Enter the result here, skip Section B, and go to line 26 . .	**17**	

Section B

18   Complete all columns below that apply (if you need more space, see page 4):

(a) Name of state	(b) State reporting number as shown on state unemployment tax return	(c) Taxable wages (as defined in state act)	(d) State experience rate period		(e) State experience rate	(f) Multiply col. (c) by .054	(g) Multiply col. (c) by col. (e)	(h) Subtract col. (g) from col. (f). If zero or less, enter -0-.	(i) Contributions paid to state unemployment fund
			From	To					

19	Totals	**19**		
20	Add columns (h) and (i) of line 19	**20**		
21	Total cash wages subject to FUTA tax (see the line 16 instructions on page 4)	**21**	
22	Multiply line 21 by 6.2% (.062)	**22**	
23	Multiply line 21 by 5.4% (.054)	**23**	
24	Enter the **smaller** of line 20 or line 23	**24**	
25	**FUTA tax.** Subtract line 24 from line 22. Enter the result here and go to line 26	**25**	

Part III   Total Household Employment Taxes

26	Enter the amount from line 8	**26**	
27	Add line 17 (or line 25) and line 26	**27**	

28   Are you required to file Form 1040?

☐ **Yes.**   **Stop.** Enter the amount from line 27 above on Form 1040, line 55. **Do not** complete Part IV below.

☐ **No.**   You may have to complete Part IV. See page 4 for details.

Part IV   Address and Signature—Complete this part **only** if required. See the line 28 instructions on page 4.

Address (number and street) or P.O. box if mail is not delivered to street address

Apt., room, or suite no.

City, town or post office, state, and ZIP code

Under penalties of perjury, I declare that I have examined this schedule, including accompanying statements, and to the best of my knowledge and belief, it is true, correct, and complete. No part of any payment made to a state unemployment fund claimed as a credit was, or is to be, deducted from the payments to employees.

▶ _____   ▶ _____
  Employer's signature   Date

Schedule R
(Form 1040)

Department of the Treasury
Internal Revenue Service   (99)

Credit for the Elderly or the Disabled

▶ Attach to Form 1040.   ▶ See separate instructions for Schedule R.

OMB No. 1545-0074

1999

Attachment
Sequence No. **16**

Name(s) shown on Form 1040

Your social security number

You may be able to take this credit and reduce your tax if by the end of 1999:

- You were age 65 or older, **OR** • You were under age 65, you retired on **permanent and total** disability, and you received taxable disability income.

But you must also meet other tests. See the separate instructions for Schedule R.

TIP In most cases, the IRS can figure the credit for you. See the instructions.

Part I   Check the Box for Your Filing Status and Age

If your filing status is:	And by the end of 1999:	Check only one box:
Single, Head of household, or Qualifying widow(er) with dependent child	**1** You were 65 or older **1**	☐
	2 You were under 65 and you retired on permanent and total disability **2**	☐
	3 Both spouses were 65 or older. **3**	☐
	4 Both spouses were under 65, but only one spouse retired on permanent and total disability **4**	☐
Married filing a joint return	**5** Both spouses were under 65, and both retired on permanent and total disability **5**	☐
	0 One spouse was 65 or older, and the other spouse was under 65 and retired on permanent and total disability **6**	☐
	7 One spouse was 65 or older, and the other spouse was under 65 and **NOT** retired on permanent and total disability **7**	☐
Married filing a separate return	**8** You were 65 or older and you lived apart from your spouse for all of 1999 . . . **8**	☐
	9 You were under 65, you retired on permanent and total disability, and you lived apart from your spouse for all of 1999 . . . . **9**	☐

Did you check box 1, 3, 7, or 8?	— Yes ——▶ Skip Part II and complete Part III on back.
	— No ——▶ Complete Parts II and III.

Part II   Statement of Permanent and Total Disability (Complete **only** if you checked box 2, 4, 5, 6, or 9 above.)

IF: 1 You filed a physician's statement for this disability for 1983 or an earlier year, or you filed or got a statement for tax years after 1983 and your physician signed line B on the statement, **AND**

2 Due to your continued disabled condition, you were unable to engage in any substantial gainful activity in 1999, check this box . . . . ▶ ☐

- If you checked this box, you do not have to get another statement for 1999.

- If you **did not** check this box, have your physician complete the statement on page 4 of the instructions. You **must** keep the statement for your records.

For Paperwork Reduction Act Notice, see Form 1040 instructions.   Cat. No. 11359K   Schedule R (Form 1040) 1999

Part III   **Figure Your Credit**

10   If you checked (in Part I):   Enter:

     Box 1, 2, 4, or 7 . . . . $5,000 ⎫

     Box 3, 5, or 6 . . . . $7,500 ⎬ **10**

     Box 8 or 9 . . . . $3,750 ⎭

     ┌──────────────┐

     │ **Did you check** │ ─── Yes ───▶ You **must** complete line 11.

     │ **box 2, 4, 5, 6,** │

     │ **or 9 in Part I?** │ ─── No ───▶ Enter the amount from line 10

     └──────────────┘   on line 12 and go to line 13.

11   If you checked:

- Box 6 in Part I, add $5,000 to the taxable disability income
 of the spouse who was under age 65. Enter the total. ⎫

- Box 2, 4, or 9 in Part I, enter your taxable disability income. ⎬ **11**

- Box 5 in Part I, add your taxable disability income to your
 spouse's taxable disability income. Enter the total. ⎭

(TIP) For more details on what to include on line 11, see the instructions.

12   If you completed line 11, enter the **smaller** of line 10 or line 11; **all others,** enter the amount from line 10 . . . . **12**

13   Enter the following pensions, annuities, or disability income that you (and your spouse if filing a joint return) received in 1999:

   a   Nontaxable part of social security benefits, and ⎫

     Nontaxable part of railroad retirement benefits ⎬ . . . **13a**

     treated as social security. See instructions. ⎭

   b   Nontaxable veterans' pensions, and ⎫

     Any other pension, annuity, or disability benefit that ⎬ . . . **13b**

     is excluded from income under any other provision

     of law. See instructions. ⎭

   c   Add lines 13a and 13b. (Even though these income items are not taxable, they **must** be included here to figure your credit.) If you did not receive any of the types of nontaxable income listed on line 13a or 13b, enter -0- on line 13c **13c**

14   Enter the amount from Form 1040, line 34 . . . . **14**

15   If you checked (in Part I):   Enter:

     Box 1 or 2 . . . . . . $7,500 ⎫

     Box 3, 4, 5, 6, or 7 . . . $10,000 ⎬ **15**

     Box 8 or 9 . . . . . . $5,000 ⎭

16   Subtract line 15 from line 14. If zero or less, enter -0- **16**

17   Enter one-half of line 16 . . . . **17**

18   Add lines 13c and 17 . . . . **18**

19   Subtract line 18 from line 12. If zero or less, **stop;** you **cannot** take the credit. Otherwise, go to line 20 . . . . **19**

20   Multiply line 19 by 15% (.15). Enter the result here and on Form 1040, line 42. But if this amount is more than the amount on Form 1040, line 40, **or** you are filing Form 2441, see the instructions for the amount of credit you may take **20**

SCHEDULE SE	Self-Employment Tax	OMB No. 1545-0074

SCHEDULE SE
(Form 1040)

Department of the Treasury
Internal Revenue Service   (99)

Self-Employment Tax

▶ See Instructions for Schedule SE (Form 1040).

▶ Attach to Form 1040.

OMB No. 1545-0074

1999

Attachment
Sequence No. **17**

Name of person with **self-employment** income (as shown on Form 1040)	Social security number of person with **self-employment** income ▶	

Who Must File Schedule SE

You must file Schedule SE if:

- You had net earnings from self-employment from **other than** church employee income (line 4 of Short Schedule SE or line 4c of Long Schedule SE) of $400 or more, **OR**
- You had church employee income of $108.28 or more. Income from services you performed as a minister or a member of a religious order **is not** church employee income. See page SE-1.

Note: *Even if you had a loss or a small amount of income from self-employment, it may be to your benefit to file Schedule SE and use either "optional method" in Part II of Long Schedule SE. See page SE-3.*

Exception. If your only self-employment income was from earnings as a minister, member of a religious order, or Christian Science practitioner **and** you filed Form 4361 and received IRS approval not to be taxed on those earnings, **do not** file Schedule SE. Instead, write "Exempt–Form 4361" on Form 1040, line 50.

May I Use Short Schedule SE or MUST I Use Long Schedule SE?

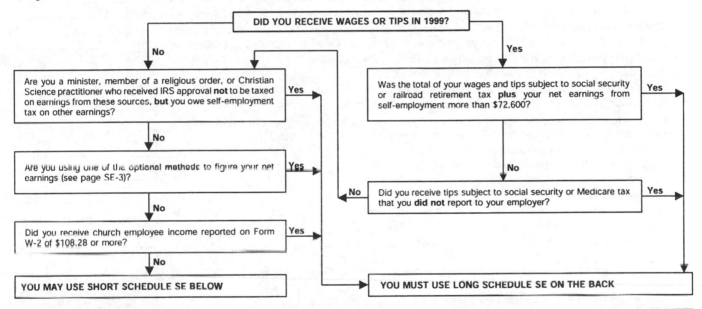

YOU MAY USE SHORT SCHEDULE SE BELOW

YOU MUST USE LONG SCHEDULE SE ON THE BACK

Section A—Short Schedule SE. Caution: *Read above to see if you can use Short Schedule SE.*

1	Net farm profit or (loss) from Schedule F, line 36, and farm partnerships, Schedule K-1 (Form 1065), line 15a	**1**	
2	Net profit or (loss) from Schedule C, line 31; Schedule C-EZ, line 3; Schedule K-1 (Form 1065), line 15a (other than farming); and Schedule K-1 (Form 1065-B), box 9. Ministers and members of religious orders, see page SE-1 for amounts to report on this line. See page SE-2 for other income to report	**2**	
3	Combine lines 1 and 2	**3**	
4	**Net earnings from self-employment.** Multiply line 3 by 92.35% (.9235). If less than $400, **do not** file this schedule; you do not owe self-employment tax . . . . ▶	**4**	
5	**Self-employment tax.** If the amount on line 4 is: • $72,600 or less, multiply line 4 by 15.3% (.153). Enter the result here and on **Form 1040, line 50.** • More than $72,600, multiply line 4 by 2.9% (.029). Then, add $9,002.40 to the result. Enter the total here and on **Form 1040, line 50.**	**5**	
6	**Deduction for one-half of self-employment tax.** Multiply line 5 by 50% (.5). Enter the result here and on **Form 1040, line 27**	**6**	

For Paperwork Reduction Act Notice, see Form 1040 instructions.   Cat. No. 11358Z   **Schedule SE (Form 1040) 1999**

Name of person with **self-employment** income (as shown on Form 1040)	Social security number of person with **self-employment** income ▶		

Section B—Long Schedule SE

Part I   Self-Employment Tax

Note: *If your only income subject to self-employment tax is* **church employee income,** *skip lines 1 through 4b. Enter -0- on line 4c and go to line 5a. Income from services you performed as a minister or a member of a religious order* **is not** *church employee income. See page SE-1.*

A   If you are a minister, member of a religious order, or Christian Science practitioner **and** you filed Form 4361, but you had $400 or more of **other** net earnings from self-employment, check here and continue with Part I . . . . . . ▶ ☐

1	Net farm profit or (loss) from Schedule F, line 36, and farm partnerships, Schedule K-1 (Form 1065), line 15a. **Note:** *Skip this line if you use the farm optional method. See page SE-3* . .	**1**		
2	Net profit or (loss) from Schedule C, line 31; Schedule C-EZ, line 3; Schedule K-1 (Form 1065), line 15a (other than farming); and Schedule K-1 (Form 1065-B), box 9. Ministers and members of religious orders, see page SE-1 for amounts to report on this line. See page SE-2 for other income to report. **Note:** *Skip this line if you use the nonfarm optional method. See page SE-3.*	**2**		
3	Combine lines 1 and 2	**3**		
4a	If line 3 is more than zero, multiply line 3 by 92.35% (.9235). Otherwise, enter amount from line 3	**4a**		
b	If you elected one or both of the optional methods, enter the total of lines 15 and 17 here . .	**4b**		
c	Combine lines 4a and 4b. If less than $400, **do not** file this schedule; you do not owe self-employment tax. **Exception.** If less than $400 and you had **church employee income,** enter -0- and continue ▶	**4c**		
5a	Enter your **church employee income** from Form W-2. **Caution:** *See page SE-1 for definition of church employee income* **5a**			
b	Multiply line 5a by 92.35% (.9235). If less than $100, enter -0-	**5b**		
6	**Net earnings from self-employment.** Add lines 4c and 5b	**6**		
7	Maximum amount of combined wages and self-employment earnings subject to social security tax or the 6.2% portion of the 7.65% railroad retirement (tier 1) tax for 1999	**7**	72,600	00
8a	Total social security wages and tips (total of boxes 3 and 7 on Form(s) W-2) and railroad retirement (tier 1) compensation **8a**			
b	Unreported tips subject to social security tax (from Form 4137, line 9) **8b**			
c	Add lines 8a and 8b	**8c**		
9	Subtract line 8c from line 7. If zero or less, enter -0- here and on line 10 and go to line 11 . ▶	**9**		
10	Multiply the **smaller** of line 6 or line 9 by 12.4% (.124)	**10**		
11	Multiply line 6 by 2.9% (.029)	**11**		
12	**Self-employment tax.** Add lines 10 and 11. Enter here and on **Form 1040, line 50**	**12**		
13	**Deduction for one-half of self-employment tax.** Multiply line 12 by 50% (.5). Enter the result here and on **Form 1040, line 27** **13**			

Part II   Optional Methods To Figure Net Earnings (See page SE-3.)

Farm Optional Method. You may use this method **only** if:

• Your gross farm income[1] was not more than $2,400, **or**

• Your net farm profits[2] were less than $1,733.

14	Maximum income for optional methods	**14**	1,600	00
15	Enter the **smaller** of: two-thirds (⅔) of gross farm income[1] (not less than zero) **or** $1,600. Also include this amount on line 4b above	**15**		

Nonfarm Optional Method. You may use this method **only** if:

• Your net nonfarm profits[3] were less than $1,733 and also less than 72.189% of your gross nonfarm income,[4] **and**

• You had net earnings from self-employment of at least $400 in 2 of the prior 3 years.

Caution: *You may use this method no more than five times.*

16	Subtract line 15 from line 14	**16**		
17	Enter the **smaller** of: two-thirds (⅔) of gross nonfarm income[4] (not less than zero) **or** the amount on line 16. Also include this amount on line 4b above	**17**		

[1] From Sch. F, line 11, and Sch. K-1 (Form 1065), line 15b.   [3] From Sch. C, line 31; Sch. C-EZ, line 3; Sch. K-1 (Form 1065), line 15a; and Sch. K-1 (Form 1065-B), box 9.
[2] From Sch. F, line 36, and Sch. K-1 (Form 1065), line 15a.   [4] From Sch. C, line 7; Sch. C-EZ, line 1; Sch. K-1 (Form 1065), line 15c; and Sch. K-1 (Form 1065-B), box 9.

1999 Form 1040-V

Department of the Treasury
Internal Revenue Service

What Is Form 1040-V and Do You Have To Use It?

It is a statement you send with your check or money order for any balance due on line 68 of your **1999 Form 1040.** Using Form 1040-V allows us to process your payment more accurately and efficiently. We strongly encourage you to use Form 1040-V, but there is no penalty if you do not do so.

How To Fill In Form 1040-V

Box 1. Enter the amount you are paying by check or money order.

Box 2. Enter the first four letters of your last name. See examples below.

Name	Enter	Name	Enter
John Brown	BROW	Nancy McCarthy	MCCA
Juan DeJesus	DEJE	Helen O'Neill	ONEI
Joan A. Lee	LEE	Pedro Torres-Lopez	TORR

Boxes 3 and 4. Enter your social security number (SSN) in box 3. If you are filing a joint return, enter in box 3 the SSN shown first on your return and in box 4 the SSN shown second.

Box 5. Enter your name(s) and address as shown on your return.

How To Prepare Your Payment

● Make your check or money order payable to the **"United States Treasury." Do not** send cash.

● Make sure your name and address appear on your check or money order.

● Enter "1999 Form 1040," your daytime telephone number, and your SSN on your check or money order. If you are filing a joint return, enter the SSN shown **first** on your return.

● To help us process your payment, enter the amount on the right side of your check like this: $ XXX.XX. **Do not** use dashes or lines (for example, do not enter "$ XXX—" or "$ XXX $\frac{XX}{100}$").

How To Send In Your Return, Payment, and Form 1040-V

● Detach Form 1040-V along the dotted line.

● **Do not** staple or otherwise attach your payment or Form 1040-V to your return or to each other. Instead, just put them loose in the envelope.

● If an envelope came with your tax package, please use it to mail your 1999 tax return, payment, and Form 1040-V.

● If you do not have that envelope or you moved or used a paid preparer, mail your tax return, payment, and Form 1040-V to the Internal Revenue Service at the address shown on the back that applies to you.

Note. If you filed electronically, send your check or money order and Form 1040-V to the applicable address shown on the back.

Paperwork Reduction Act Notice. We ask for the information on Form 1040-V to help us carry out the Internal Revenue laws of the United States. If you use Form 1040-V, you must provide the requested information. Your cooperation will help us ensure that we are collecting the right amount of tax.

You are not required to provide the information requested on a form that is subject to the Paperwork Reduction Act unless the form displays a valid OMB control number. Books or records relating to a form or its instructions must be retained as long as their contents may become material in the administration of any Internal Revenue law. Generally, tax returns and return information are confidential, as required by Internal Revenue Code section 6103.

The time needed to complete and mail Form 1040-V will vary depending on individual circumstances. The estimated average time is 10 minutes. If you have comments about the accuracy of this time estimate or suggestions for making Form 1040-V simpler, we would be happy to hear from you. See the Instructions for Form 1040.

Cat. No. 20975C   ▼ **DETACH HERE AND MAIL WITH YOUR PAYMENT** ▼   Form **1040-V** (1999)

Form **1040-V**

Department of the Treasury
Internal Revenue Service (99)

Payment Voucher

▶ **Do not staple or attach this voucher to your payment.**

OMB No. 1545-0074

1999

1 Enter the amount you are paying by check or money order	2 Enter the first four letters of your last name	3 Enter your social security number
▶ $.		

4 If a joint return, enter the SSN shown second on that return	5 Enter your name(s)
	Enter your address
	Enter your city, state, and ZIP code

Cat. No. 20975C

IF you live in . . .	THEN use this address if you:		
	Prepared your own return . . .	Used a paid preparer . . .	Filed electronically . . .
Florida, South Carolina	Atlanta, GA 39901-0002	P.O. Box 105093 Atlanta, GA 30348-5093	P.O. Box 6223 Chicago, IL 60680-6223
Georgia	Atlanta, GA 39901-0002	P.O. Box 105093 Atlanta, GA 30348-5093	P.O. Box 1214 Charlotte, NC 28201-1214
New Jersey, New York (New York City and counties of Nassau, Rockland, Suffolk, and Westchester)	Holtsville, NY 00501-0002	P.O. Box 1187 Newark, NJ 07101-1187	P.O. Box 371361 Pittsburgh, PA 15250-7361
New York (all other counties), Connecticut, Maine, Massachusetts, New Hampshire, Rhode Island, Vermont	Andover, MA 05501-0002	P.O. Box 371361 Pittsburgh, PA 15250-7361	P.O. Box 371361 Pittsburgh, PA 15250-7361
Illinois, Iowa, Minnesota, Missouri, Wisconsin	Kansas City, MO 64999-0002	P.O. Box 970011 St. Louis, MO 63197-0011	P.O. Box 970016 St. Louis, MO 63197-0016
Delaware, District of Columbia, Maryland, Pennsylvania, Virginia	Philadelphia, PA 19255-0002	P.O. Box 8530 Philadelphia, PA 19162-8530	P.O. Box 371361 Pittsburgh, PA 15250-7361
Indiana, Kentucky, Michigan, Ohio, West Virginia	Cincinnati, OH 45999-0002	P.O. Box 6223 Chicago, IL 60680-6223	P.O. Box 6223 Chicago, IL 60680-6223
Kansas, New Mexico, Oklahoma, Texas	Austin, TX 73301-0002	P.O. Box 970016 St. Louis, MO 63197-0016	P.O. Box 970016 St. Louis, MO 63197-0016
Alaska, Arizona, California (counties of Alpine, Amador, Butte, Calaveras, Colusa, Contra Costa, Del Norte, El Dorado, Glenn, Humboldt, Lake, Lassen, Marin, Mendocino, Modoc, Napa, Nevada, Placer, Plumas, Sacramento, San Joaquin, Shasta, Sierra, Siskiyou, Solano, Sonoma, Sutter, Tehama, Trinity, Yolo, and Yuba), Colorado, Idaho, Montana, Nebraska, Nevada, North Dakota, Oregon, South Dakota, Utah, Washington, Wyoming	Ogden, UT 84201-0002	P.O. Box 7704 San Francisco, CA 94120-7704	P.O. Box 7704 San Francisco, CA 94120-7704
California (all other counties), Hawaii	Fresno, CA 93888-0002	P.O. Box 60000 Los Angeles, CA 90060-6000	P.O. Box 7704 San Francisco, CA 94120-7704
Alabama, Arkansas, Louisiana, Mississippi, North Carolina, Tennessee	Memphis, TN 37501-0002	P.O. Box 1214 Charlotte, NC 28201-1214	P.O. Box 1214 Charlotte, NC 28201-1214
All APO and FPO addresses, American Samoa, nonpermanent residents of Guam or the Virgin Islands*, Puerto Rico (or if excluding income under section 933), a foreign country (or if a dual-status alien): U.S. citizens or those filing Form 2555, Form 2555-EZ, or Form 4563	Philadelphia, PA 19255-0215	P.O. Box 7328 Philadelphia, PA 19162-7328	P.O. Box 371361 Pittsburgh, PA 15250-7361

* Permanent residents of Guam or the Virgin Islands should not use Form 1040-V.

Form **1040X**
(Rev. November 1999)

Department of the Treasury—Internal Revenue Service

Amended U.S. Individual Income Tax Return

▶ See separate instructions.

OMB No. 1545-0091

This return is for calendar year ▶ _____ , OR fiscal year ended ▶ _____

Please print or type

Your first name and initial	Last name	Your social security number

If a joint return, spouse's first name and initial	Last name	Spouse's social security number

Home address (no. and street) or P.O. box if mail is not delivered to your home	Apt. no.	Telephone number (optional) ( )

City, town or post office, state, and ZIP code. If you have a foreign address, see page 2 of the instructions.	**For Paperwork Reduction Act Notice, see page 6.**

A If the name or address shown above is different from that shown on the original return, check here . . . . . ▶ ☐

B Has the original return been changed or audited by the IRS or have you been notified that it will be? . . ☐ Yes ☐ No

C Filing status. Be sure to complete this line. **Note.** You cannot change from joint to separate returns after the due date.

On original return ▶ ☐ Single ☐ Married filing joint return ☐ Married filing separate return ☐ Head of household ☐ Qualifying widow(er)

On this return ▶ ☐ Single ☐ Married filing joint return ☐ Married filing separate return ☐ Head of household* ☐ Qualifying widow(er)

* If the qualifying person is a child but not your dependent, see page 2.

USE PART II ON THE BACK TO EXPLAIN ANY CHANGES

Income and Deductions (see pages 2–5)		A. Original amount or as previously adjusted (see page 2)	B. Net change—amount of increase or (decrease)—explain in Part II	C. Correct amount
1 Adjusted gross income (see page 3)	**1**			
2 Itemized deductions or standard deduction (see page 3)	**2**			
3 Subtract line 2 from line 1	**3**			
4 Exemptions. If changing, fill in Parts I and II on the back	**4**			
5 Taxable income. Subtract line 4 from line 3	**5**			
6 Tax (see page 4). Method used in col. C _____	**6**			
7 Credits (see page 4)	**7**			
8 Subtract line 7 from line 6. Enter the result but not less than zero	**8**			
9 Other taxes (see page 4)	**9**			
10 Total tax. Add lines 8 and 9	**10**			

Tax Liability

Payments

11 Federal income tax withheld and excess social security and RRTA tax withheld. If changing, see page 4	**11**			
12 Estimated tax payments, including amount applied from prior year's return	**12**			
13 Earned income credit	**13**			
14 Additional child tax credit from Form 8812	**14**			
15 Credits from Form 4136 or Form 2439	**15**			
16 Amount paid with request for extension of time to file (see page 4)			**16**	
17 Amount of tax paid with original return plus additional tax paid after it was filed			**17**	
18 Total payments. Add lines 11 through 17 in column C			**18**	

Refund or Amount You Owe

19 Overpayment, if any, as shown on original return or as previously adjusted by the IRS	**19**	
20 Subtract line 19 from line 18 (see page 5)	**20**	
21 **AMOUNT YOU OWE.** If line 10, column C, is more than line 20, enter the difference and see page 5	**21**	
22 If line 10, column C, is less than line 20, enter the difference	**22**	
23 Amount of line 22 you want **REFUNDED TO YOU**	**23**	
24 Amount of line 22 you want **APPLIED TO YOUR** **ESTIMATED TAX**	**24**	

Sign Here
Joint return?
See page 2.
Keep a copy for your records.

Under penalties of perjury, I declare that I have filed an original return and that I have examined this amended return, including accompanying schedules and statements, and to the best of my knowledge and belief, this amended return is true, correct, and complete. Declaration of preparer (other than taxpayer) is based on all information of which the preparer has any knowledge.

Your signature	Date	Spouse's signature. If a joint return, BOTH must sign.	Date

Paid Preparer's Use Only

Preparer's signature	Date	Check if self-employed ☐	Preparer's SSN or PTIN
Firm's name (or yours if self-employed) and address			EIN
			ZIP code

Cat. No. 11360L

Form **1040X** (Rev. 11-99)

Part I **Exemptions.** See Form 1040 or 1040A instructions.

If you are **not changing your exemptions,** do not complete this part.
If claiming **more exemptions,** complete lines 25–31.
If claiming **fewer exemptions,** complete lines 25–30.

	A. Original number of exemptions reported or as previously adjusted	**B. Net change**	**C. Correct number** of exemptions
25 Yourself and spouse **25**			
Caution. If your parents (or someone else) can claim you as a dependent (even if they chose not to), you cannot claim an exemption for yourself.			
26 Your dependent children who lived with you **26**			
27 Your dependent children who did not live with you due to divorce or separation **27**			
28 Other dependents **28**			
29 Total number of exemptions. Add lines 25 through 28 . . . . . **29**			

30 Multiply the number of exemptions claimed on line 29 by the amount listed below for the tax year you are amending. Enter the result here and on line 4.

Tax year	Exemption amount	**But see the instructions for line 4 on page 3 if the amount on line 1 is over:**
1999	$2,750	$94,975
1998	2,700	93,400
1997	2,650	90,900
1996	2,550	88,475

30

31 Dependents (children and other) not claimed on original (or adjusted) return:

Note. For tax years after 1997, do not complete column (e) below. For tax years before 1998, do not complete column (d) below.

No. of your children on line 31 who:

(a) First name Last name	**(b)** Dependent's social security number. If born in the tax year you are amending, see page 5.	**(c)** Dependent's relationship to you	**(d)** ✓ if qualifying child for child tax credit (see page 5)	**(e)** No. of months lived in your home
			☐	
			☐	
			☐	
			☐	
			☐	
			☐	

- **lived with you** . . ▶ ☐
- **did not** live with you due to divorce or separation (see page 5) . . ▶ ☐

Dependents on line 31 not entered above ▶ ☐

Part II **Explanation of Changes to Income, Deductions, and Credits**

Enter the line number from the front of the form for each item you are changing and give the reason for each change. Attach only the supporting forms and schedules for the items changed. If you do not attach the required information, your Form 1040X may be returned. Be sure to include your name and social security number on any attachments.

If the change relates to a net operating loss carryback or a general business credit carryback, attach the schedule or form that shows the year in which the loss or credit occurred. See page 1 of the instructions. Also, check here . . . . . . ▶ ☐

_____

_____

_____

_____

_____

_____

Part III **Presidential Election Campaign Fund.** Checking below will not increase your tax or reduce your refund.

If you did not previously want $3 to go to the fund but now want to, check here . . . . ▶ ☐
If a joint return and your spouse did not previously want $3 to go to the fund but now wants to, check here . . . . ▶ ☐

Form **1040X** (Rev. 11-99)

Form **1116**

Department of the Treasury
Internal Revenue Service (99)

Foreign Tax Credit

(Individual, Estate, Trust, or Nonresident Alien Individual)
▶ Attach to Form 1040, 1040NR, 1041, or 990-T.
▶ See separate instructions.

OMB No. 1545-0121

1999

Attachment
Sequence No. **19**

Name	Identifying number as shown on page 1 of your tax return

Use a separate Form 1116 for each category of income listed below. See **Categories of Income** on page 3 of the instructions. Check only one box on each Form 1116. Report all amounts in U.S. dollars except where specified in Part II below.

a ☐ Passive income
b ☐ High withholding tax interest
c ☐ Financial services income

d ☐ Shipping income
e ☐ Dividends from a DISC or former DISC
f ☐ Certain distributions from a foreign sales corporation (FSC) or former FSC

g ☐ Lump-sum distributions
h ☐ Section 901(j) income
i ☐ Income re-sourced by treaty
j ☐ General limitation income

k Resident of (name of country) ▶

Note: If you paid taxes to only one foreign country or U.S. possession, use column A in Part I and line A in Part II. If you paid taxes to **more than one** foreign country or U.S. possession, use a separate column and line for each country or possession.

Part I   Taxable Income or Loss From Sources Outside the United States (for Category Checked Above)

		Foreign Country or U.S. Possession			Total
		A	**B**	**C**	(Add cols. A, B, and C.)
l	Enter the name of the foreign country or U.S. possession . . . . ▶				
1	Gross income from sources within country shown above and of the type checked above. See page 7 of the instructions:				**1**
	Deductions and losses (*Caution: See pages 7 through 9 of the instructions*):				
2	Expenses **definitely related** to the income on line 1 (attach statement)				
3	Pro rata share of other deductions **not definitely related**:				
a	Certain itemized deductions or standard deduction. See instructions				
b	Other deductions (attach statement)				
c	Add lines 3a and 3b				
d	Gross foreign source income. See instructions .				
e	Gross income from all sources. See instructions				
f	Divide line 3d by line 3e. See instructions . .				
g	Multiply line 3c by line 3f				
4	Pro rata share of interest expense. See instructions:				
a	Home mortgage interest (use worksheet on page 9 of the instructions)				
b	Other interest expense				
5	Losses from foreign sources				
6	Add lines 2, 3g, 4a, 4b, and 5				**6**
7	Subtract line 6 from line 1. Enter the result here and on line 14, page 2 . . . . ▶			**7**	

Part II   Foreign Taxes Paid or Accrued (See page 9 of the instructions.)

Country	Credit is claimed for taxes (you must check one) (m) ☐ Paid (n) ☐ Accrued	Foreign taxes paid or accrued								
		In foreign currency				In U.S. dollars				
		Taxes withheld at source on:			(s) Other foreign taxes paid or accrued	Taxes withheld at source on:			(w) Other foreign taxes paid or accrued	(x) Total foreign taxes paid or accrued (add cols. (t) through (w))
	(o) Date paid or accrued	(p) Dividends	(q) Rents and royalties	(r) Interest		(t) Dividends	(u) Rents and royalties	(v) Interest		
A										
B										
C										

8   Add lines A through C, column (x). Enter the total here and on line 9, page 2 . . . . ▶ | **8** |

For Paperwork Reduction Act Notice, see page 12 of the instructions.   Cat. No. 11440U   Form **1116** (1999)

Part III **Figuring the Credit**

9	Enter amount from line 8. These are your total foreign taxes paid or accrued for the category of income checked above Part I	**9**	
10	Carryback or carryover (attach detailed computation)	**10**	
11	Add lines 9 and 10	**11**	
12	Reduction in foreign taxes. See page 10 of the instructions . . .	**12**	
13	Subtract line 12 from line 11. This is the total amount of foreign taxes available for credit		**13**
14	Enter amount from line 7. This is your taxable income or (loss) from sources outside the United States (before adjustments) for the category of income checked above Part I. See page 10 of the instructions . .	**14**	
15	Adjustments to line 14. See page 10 of the instructions.	**15**	
16	Combine the amounts on lines 14 and 15. This is your net foreign source taxable income. (If the result is zero or less, you have no foreign tax credit for the category of income you checked above Part I. Skip lines 17 through 21.)	**16**	
17	**Individuals:** Enter amount from Form 1040, line 37. If you are a nonresident alien, enter amount from Form 1040NR, line 36. **Estates and trusts:** Enter your taxable income without the deduction for your exemption	**17**	
	Caution: *If you figured your tax using the special rates on capital gains, see page 12 of the instructions.*		
18	Divide line 16 by line 17. If line 16 is more than line 17, enter "1".		**18**
19	**Individuals:** Enter amount from Form 1040, line 40, **less** any amounts on Form 1040, lines 41 through 45, and any mortgage interest credit (from Form 8396) and District of Columbia first-time homebuyer credit (from Form 8859) on line 47. If you are a nonresident alien, enter amount from Form 1040NR, line 39, less any amount on Form 1040NR, lines 40, 41, 42, and any mortgage interest credit (from Form 8396) and District of Columbia first-time homebuyer credit (from Form 8859) on line 44. **Estates and trusts:** Enter amount from Form 1041, Schedule G, line 1c, or Form 990-T, lines 36 and 37 .	**19**	
20	Multiply line 19 by line 18 (maximum amount of credit)	**20**	
21	Enter the amount from line 13 or line 20, whichever is **smaller**. If this is the only Form 1116 you are completing, skip lines 22 through 29 and enter this amount on line 30. Otherwise, complete the appropriate line in Part IV. See page 12 of the instructions. . . . . ▶	**21**	

Part IV **Summary of Credits From Separate Parts III** (See page 12 of the instructions.)

22	Credit for taxes on passive income	**22**	
23	Credit for taxes on high withholding tax interest	**23**	
24	Credit for taxes on financial services income	**24**	
25	Credit for taxes on shipping income	**25**	
26	Credit for taxes on dividends from a DISC or former DISC and certain distributions from a FSC or former FSC	**26**	
27	Credit for taxes on lump-sum distributions	**27**	
28	Credit for taxes on income re-sourced by treaty	**28**	
29	Credit for taxes on general limitation income	**29**	
30	Add lines 22 through 29.		**30**
31	Reduction of credit for international boycott operations. See instructions for line 12 on page 10 . .		**31**
32	Subtract line 31 from line 30. This is your **foreign tax credit.** Enter here and on Form 1040, line 46; Form 1040NR, line 43; Form 1041, Schedule G, line 2a; or Form 990-T, line 39a. . . . . . ▶		**32**

Form **2106**

Department of the Treasury
Internal Revenue Service (99)

Employee Business Expenses

▶ See separate instructions.

▶ Attach to Form 1040.

OMB No. 1545-0139

1999

Attachment
Sequence No. **54**

Your name	Occupation in which you incurred expenses	Social security number

Part I — Employee Business Expenses and Reimbursements

STEP 1   Enter Your Expenses

		Column A Other Than Meals and Entertainment		Column B Meals and Entertainment	
1	Vehicle expense from line 22c or line 29. (Rural mail carriers: See instructions.)	1			
2	Parking fees, tolls, and transportation, including train, bus, etc., that **did not** involve overnight travel or commuting to and from work . .	2			
3	Travel expense while away from home overnight, including lodging, airplane, car rental, etc. **Do not** include meals and entertainment	3			
4	Business expenses not included on lines 1 through 3. **Do not** include meals and entertainment	4			
5	Meals and entertainment expenses (see instructions)	5			
6	**Total expenses.** In Column A, add lines 1 through 4 and enter the result. In Column B, enter the amount from line 5	6			

Note: *If you were not reimbursed for any expenses in Step 1, skip line 7 and enter the amount from line 6 on line 8.*

STEP 2   Enter Reimbursements Received From Your Employer for Expenses Listed in STEP 1

7	Enter reimbursements received from your employer that were **not** reported to you in box 1 of Form W-2. Include any reimbursements reported under code "L" in box 13 of your Form W-2 (see instructions)	7			

STEP 3   Figure Expenses To Deduct on Schedule A (Form 1040)

8	Subtract line 7 from line 6. If zero or less, enter -0-. However, if line 7 is greater than line 6 in Column A, report the excess as income on Form 1040, line 7	8			
	Note: *If both columns of line 8 are zero, you cannot deduct employee business expenses. Stop here and attach Form 2106 to your return.*				
9	In Column A, enter the amount from line 8. In Column B, multiply line 8 by 50% (.50). (Employees subject to Department of Transportation (DOT) hours of service limits: Multiply meal expenses by 55% (.55) instead of 50%. For more details, see instructions.)	9			
10	Add the amounts on line 9 of both columns and enter the total here. **Also, enter the total on Schedule A (Form 1040), line 20.** (Fee-basis state or local government officials, qualified performing artists, and individuals with disabilities: See the instructions for special rules on where to enter the total.) . . . . ▶	10			

Cat. No. 11700N

Form **2106** (1999)

Part II — Vehicle Expenses

Section A—General Information (You must complete this section if you are claiming vehicle expenses.)

		(a) Vehicle 1	(b) Vehicle 2
11	Enter the date the vehicle was placed in service.	/ /	/ /
12	Total miles the vehicle was driven during 1999	miles	miles
13	Business miles included on line 12	miles	miles
14	Percent of business use. Divide line 13 by line 12	%	%
15	Average daily roundtrip commuting distance	miles	miles
16	Commuting miles included on line 12	miles	miles
17	Other miles. Add lines 13 and 16 and subtract the total from line 12	miles	miles

18 Do you (or your spouse) have another vehicle available for personal use? ☐ Yes ☐ No

19 If your employer provided you with a vehicle, is personal use during off-duty hours permitted? ☐ Yes ☐ No ☐ Not applicable

20 Do you have evidence to support your deduction? ☐ Yes ☐ No

21 If "Yes," is the evidence written? ☐ Yes ☐ No

Section B—Standard Mileage Rate (See the instructions for Part II to find out whether to complete this section or Section C.)

22a	Multiply business miles driven **before** April 1, 1999, by 32½¢ (.325)	22a
b	Multiply business miles driven **after** March 31, 1999, by 31¢ (.31)	22b
c	Add lines 22a and 22b. Enter the result here and on line 1	22c

Section C—Actual Expenses

		(a) Vehicle 1		(b) Vehicle 2	
23	Gasoline, oil, repairs, vehicle insurance, etc.				
24a	Vehicle rentals				
b	Inclusion amount (see instructions)				
c	Subtract line 24b from line 24a				
25	Value of employer-provided vehicle (applies only if 100% of annual lease value was included on Form W-2—see instructions)				
26	Add lines 23, 24c, and 25				
27	Multiply line 26 by the percentage on line 14				
28	Depreciation. Enter amount from line 38 below				
29	Add lines 27 and 28. Enter total here and on line 1				

Section D—Depreciation of Vehicles (Use this section only if you owned the vehicle and are completing Section C for the vehicle.)

		(a) Vehicle 1		(b) Vehicle 2	
30	Enter cost or other basis (see instructions)				
31	Enter amount of section 179 deduction (see instructions)				
32	Multiply line 30 by line 14 (see instructions if you elected the section 179 deduction)				
33	Enter depreciation method and percentage (see instructions)				
34	Multiply line 32 by the percentage on line 33 (see instructions)				
35	Add lines 31 and 34				
36	Enter the limit from the table in the line 36 instructions				
37	Multiply line 36 by the percentage on line 14				
38	Enter the **smaller** of line 35 or line 37. Also enter this amount on line 28 above				

Form **2106-EZ**

Department of the Treasury
Internal Revenue Service (99)

Unreimbursed Employee Business Expenses

▶ **Attach to Form 1040.**

OMB No. 1545-1441

1999

Attachment
Sequence No. **54A**

Your name	Occupation in which you incurred expenses	Social security number

You May Use This Form ONLY if ALL of the Following Apply:

- You are an employee deducting expenses attributable to your job.
- You **do not** get reimbursed by your employer for any expenses (amounts your employer included in box 1 of your Form W-2 are not considered reimbursements).
- If you are claiming vehicle expense, you are using the standard mileage rate for 1999.

Caution: *You can use the standard mileage rate for 1999 only if: (a) you owned the vehicle and used the standard mileage rate for the first year you placed the vehicle in service, OR (b) you leased the vehicle and used the standard mileage rate for the portion of the lease period after 1997.*

Part I   **Figure Your Expenses**

1	Vehicle expense using the standard mileage rate. Complete Part II and then go to line 1a below.	
a	Multiply business miles driven **before** April 1, 1999, by 32½¢ (.325) **1a**	
b	Multiply business miles driven **after** March 31, 1999, by 31¢ (.31) **1b**	
c	Add lines 1a and 1b	**1c**
2	Parking fees, tolls, and transportation, including train, bus, etc., that **did not** involve overnight travel or commuting to and from work	**2**
3	Travel expense while away from home overnight, including lodging, airplane, car rental, etc. **Do not** include meals and entertainment	**3**
4	Business expenses not included on lines 1 through 3. **Do not** include meals and entertainment	**4**
5	Meals and entertainment expenses: $ _____ x 50% (.50) (Employees subject to Department of Transportation (DOT) hours of service limits: Multiply meal expenses by 55% (.55) instead of 50%. For more details, see instructions.)	**5**
6	**Total expenses.** Add lines 1c through 5. Enter here and **on line 20 of Schedule A (Form 1040).** (Fee-basis state or local government officials, qualified performing artists, and individuals with disabilities: See the instructions for special rules on where to enter this amount.) . . .	**6**

Part II   **Information on Your Vehicle.** Complete this part **ONLY** if you are claiming vehicle expense on line 1.

7   When did you place your vehicle in service for business use? (month, day, year) ▶ .... / .... / ....

8   Of the total number of miles you drove your vehicle during 1999, enter the number of miles you used your vehicle for:

a Business ....   b Commuting ....   c Other ....

9   Do you (or your spouse) have another vehicle available for personal use? . . . .   ☐ Yes   ☐ No

10   Was your vehicle available for use during off-duty hours? . . . .   ☐ Yes   ☐ No

11a   Do you have evidence to support your deduction? . . . .   ☐ Yes   ☐ No

b   If "Yes," is the evidence written? . . . .   ☐ Yes   ☐ No

General Instructions

Section references are to the Internal Revenue Code.

A Change To Note

The standard mileage rate has decreased to 31 cents for each mile of business use **after** March 31, 1999. See line 1 above.

Purpose of Form

You may use Form 2106-EZ instead of Form 2106 to claim your unreimbursed employee business expenses if you meet all the requirements listed above Part I.

Recordkeeping

You cannot deduct expenses for travel (including meals, unless you used the standard meal allowance), entertainment, gifts, or use of a car or other listed property, unless you keep records to prove the time, place, business purpose, business relationship (for entertainment and gifts), and amounts of these expenses. Generally, you must also have receipts for all lodging expenses (regardless of the amount) and any other expense of $75 or more.

Additional Information

If you need more information about employee business expenses, you will find the following publications helpful:

Pub. 463, Travel, Entertainment, Gift, and Car Expenses

Pub. 529, Miscellaneous Deductions

Pub. 587, Business Use of Your Home (Including Use by Day-Care Providers)

Pub. 946, How To Depreciate Property

For Paperwork Reduction Act Notice, see back of form.   Cat. No. 20604Q   Form **2106-EZ** (1999)

Specific Instructions

Part I—Figure Your Expenses

Line 2. See the line 8b instructions for the definition of commuting.

Line 3. Enter lodging and transportation expenses connected with overnight travel away from your tax home (defined below). You cannot deduct expenses for travel away from your tax home for any period of temporary employment of more than 1 year. **Do not** include expenses for meals and entertainment. For more details, including limits, see Pub. 463.

Generally, your **tax home** is your main place of business or post of duty regardless of where you maintain your family home. If you do not have a regular or main place of business because of the nature of your work, then your tax home is the place where you regularly live. If you do not fit in either of these categories, you are considered an itinerant and your tax home is wherever you work. As an itinerant, you are never away from home and cannot claim a travel expense deduction. For more details on your tax home, see Pub. 463.

Line 4. Enter other job-related expenses not listed on any other line of this form. Include expenses for business gifts, education (tuition and books), home office, trade publications, etc. For details, including limits, see Pub. 463 and Pub. 529. If you are deducting home office expenses, see Pub. 587 for special instructions on how to report these expenses. If you are deducting depreciation or claiming a section 179 deduction on a cellular telephone or other similar telecommunications equipment, a home computer, etc., see **Form 4562,** Depreciation and Amortization, to figure the depreciation and section 179 deduction to enter on line 4.

Do not include expenses for meals and entertainment, taxes, or interest on line 4. Deductible taxes are entered on lines 5 through 9 of Schedule A (Form 1040). Employees **cannot** deduct car loan interest.

Note: *If line 4 is your only entry, do not complete Form 2106-EZ unless you are claiming:*

- *Expenses for performing your job as a fee-basis state or local government official,*
- *Performing-arts-related business expenses as a qualified performing artist, or*
- *Impairment-related work expenses as an individual with a disability.*

See the line 6 instructions for definitions. If you are not required to file Form 2106-EZ, enter your expenses directly on Schedule A (Form 1040), line 20.

Line 5. Generally, you may deduct only 50% of your business meal and entertainment expenses, including meals incurred while away from home on business. If you were an employee subject to the Department of Transportation (DOT) hours of service limits, that percentage is increased to 55% for business meals consumed during, or incident to, any period of duty for which those limits are in effect.

Employees subject to the DOT hours of service limits include certain air transportation employees, such as pilots, crew, dispatchers, mechanics, and control tower operators; interstate truck operators and interstate bus drivers; certain railroad employees, such as engineers, conductors, train crews, dispatchers, and control operations personnel; and certain merchant mariners.

Instead of actual cost, you may be able to claim the **standard meal allowance** for your daily meals and incidental expenses while away from your tax home overnight. Under this method, you deduct a specified amount, depending on where you travel, instead of keeping records of your actual meal expenses. However, you must still keep records to prove the time, place, and business purpose of your travel. See Pub. 463 to figure your deduction using the standard meal allowance.

Line 6. If you were a **fee-basis state or local government official** (defined below), include the expenses you incurred for services performed in that job in the total on Form 1040, line 32. Write "FBO" and the amount in the space to the left of line 32. Your employee business expenses are deductible whether or not you itemize deductions. A fee-basis state or local government official is an official who is an employee of a state or political subdivision of a state and is compensated, in whole or in part, on a fee basis.

If you were a **qualified performing artist** (defined below), include your performing-arts-related expenses in the total on Form 1040, line 32. Write "QPA" and the amount in the space to the left of line 32. Your performing-arts-related business expenses are deductible whether or not you itemize deductions. The expenses are not subject to the 2% limit that applies to most other employee business expenses.

A qualified performing artist is an individual who:

1. Performed services in the performing arts as an employee for at least two employers during the tax year,

2. Received from at least two of those employers wages of $200 or more per employer,

3. Had allowable business expenses attributable to the performing arts of more than 10% of gross income from the performing arts, and

4. Had adjusted gross income of $16,000 or less before deducting expenses as a performing artist.

To be treated as a qualified performing artist, a married individual must also file a joint return, unless the individual and his or her spouse lived apart for all of 1999. On a joint return, requirements **1**, **2**, and **3** must be figured separately for each spouse. However, requirement **4** applies to the combined adjusted gross income of both spouses.

If you were an **individual with a disability** and are claiming impairment-related work expenses (defined below), enter the part of the line 6 amount attributable to those expenses on Schedule A (Form 1040), line 27, instead of on Schedule A (Form 1040), line 20. Your impairment-related work expenses are not subject to the 2% limit that applies to most other employee business expenses. Impairment-related work expenses are the allowable expenses of an individual with physical or mental disabilities for attendant care at his or her place of employment. They also include other expenses in connection with the place of employment that enable the employee to work. See Pub. 463 for more details.

Part II—Information on Your Vehicle

If you claim vehicle expense, you must provide certain information on the use of your vehicle by completing Part II. Include an attachment listing the information requested in Part II for any additional vehicles you used for business during the year.

Line 7. Date placed in service is generally the date you first start using your vehicle. However, if you first start using your vehicle for personal use and later convert it to business use, the vehicle is treated as placed in service on the date you started using it for business.

Line 8a. Do not include commuting miles on this line; commuting miles are not considered business miles. See below for the definition of commuting.

Line 8b. If you do not know the total actual miles you used your vehicle for commuting during the year, figure the amount to enter on line 8b by multiplying the number of days during the year that you used your vehicle for commuting by the average daily roundtrip commuting distance in miles.

Generally, **commuting** is travel between your home and a work location. However, travel that meets **any** of the following conditions is not commuting.

1. You have at least one regular work location away from your home and the travel is to a temporary work location in the same trade or business, regardless of the distance. A temporary work location is one where you perform services on an irregular or short-term basis (generally 1 year or less).

2. The travel is to a temporary work location outside the metropolitan area where you live and normally work.

3. Your home is your principal place of business under section 280A(c)(1)(A) (for purposes of deducting expenses for business use of your home) and the travel is to another work location in the same trade or business, regardless of whether that location is regular or temporary and regardless of distance.

Paperwork Reduction Act Notice. We ask for the information on this form to carry out the Internal Revenue laws of the United States. You are required to give us the information. We need it to ensure that you are complying with these laws and to allow us to figure and collect the right amount of tax.

You are not required to provide the information requested on a form that is subject to the Paperwork Reduction Act unless the form displays a valid OMB control number. Books or records relating to a form or its instructions must be retained as long as their contents may become material in the administration of any Internal Revenue law. Generally, tax returns and return information are confidential, as required by section 6103.

The time needed to complete and file this form will vary depending on individual circumstances. The estimated average time is:

Recordkeeping . . . . . . 40 min.

Learning about the law or the form 5 min.

Preparing the form . . . . . 28 min.

Copying, assembling, and sending the form to the IRS . . . . . 20 min.

If you have comments concerning the accuracy of these time estimates or suggestions for making this form simpler, we would be happy to hear from you. See the Instructions for Form 1040.

Form **2441**	**Child and Dependent Care Expenses**	OMB No. 1545-0068
Department of the Treasury Internal Revenue Service (99)	▶ Attach to Form 1040. ▶ See separate instructions.	**1999** Attachment Sequence No. **21**

Name(s) shown on Form 1040	Your social security number

Before you begin, you need to understand the following terms. See **Definitions** on page 1 of the instructions.

- **Dependent Care Benefits**
- **Qualifying Person(s)**
- **Qualified Expenses**
- **Earned Income**

Part I — **Persons or Organizations Who Provided the Care**—You **must** complete this part.
(If you need more space, use the bottom of page 2.)

1	(a) Care provider's name	(b) Address (number, street, apt. no., city, state, and ZIP code)	(c) Identifying number (SSN or EIN)	(d) Amount paid (see instructions)

Did you receive **dependent care benefits?**
- **No** ⟶ Complete only Part II below.
- **Yes** ⟶ Complete Part III on the back next.

Caution: *If the care was provided in your home, you may owe employment taxes. See the instructions for Form 1040, line 55.*

Part II — **Credit for Child and Dependent Care Expenses**

2 Information about your **qualifying person(s).** If you have more than two qualifying persons, see the instructions.

(a) Qualifying person's name — First / Last		(b) Qualifying person's social security number	(c) **Qualified expenses** you incurred and paid in 1999 for the person listed in column (a)
First	Last		

3	Add the amounts in column (c) of line 2. DO NOT enter more than $2,400 for one qualifying person or $4,800 for two or more persons. If you completed Part III, enter the amount from line 24	**3**	
4	Enter YOUR **earned income**	**4**	
5	If married filing a joint return, enter YOUR SPOUSE'S earned income (if your spouse was a student or was disabled, see the instructions); **all others,** enter the amount from line 4	**5**	
6	Enter the **smallest** of line 3, 4, or 5	**6**	
7	Enter the amount from Form 1040, line 34 . . . . . [**7**]		

8 Enter on line 8 the decimal amount shown below that applies to the amount on line 7

If line 7 is—		Decimal amount is	If line 7 is—		Decimal amount is
Over	But not over		Over	But not over	
$0	10,000	.30	$20,000	22,000	.24
10,000	12,000	.29	22,000	24,000	.23
12,000	14,000	.28	24,000	26,000	.22
14,000	16,000	.27	26,000	28,000	.21
16,000	18,000	.26	28,000	No limit	.20
18,000	20,000	.25			

8	X .

9	Multiply **line 6** by the decimal amount on line 8. Enter the result here and on Form 1040, line 41. But if this amount is more than the amount on Form 1040, line 40, **or** you paid 1998 expenses in 1999, see the instructions for the amount to enter on line 41 . . .	**9**	

For Paperwork Reduction Act Notice, see page 3 of the instructions.   Cat. No. 11862M   Form **2441** (1999)

Part III Dependent Care Benefits

10 Enter the total amount of **dependent care benefits** you received for 1999. This amount should be shown in box 10 of your W-2 form(s). DO NOT include amounts that were reported to you as wages in box 1 of Form(s) W-2 . . . . | **10** |

11 Enter the amount forfeited, if any. See the instructions . . . . | **11** |

12 Subtract line 11 from line 10 . . . . | **12** |

13 Enter the total amount of **qualified expenses** incurred in 1999 for the care of the **qualifying person(s)** . . . | **13** |

14 Enter the **smaller** of line 12 or 13 . . . . | **14** |

15 Enter YOUR **earned income** . . . . | **15** |

16 If married filing a joint return, enter YOUR SPOUSE'S earned income (if your spouse was a student or was disabled, see the instructions for line 5); if married filing a separate return, see the instructions for the amount to enter; **all others,** enter the amount from line 15 . . . | **16** |

17 Enter the **smallest** of line 14, 15, or 16 . . . . . . | **17** |

18 **Excluded benefits.** Enter here the **smaller** of the following:

   • The amount from line 17, or
   • $5,000 ($2,500 if married filing a separate return **and** you were required to enter your spouse's earned income on line 16). . . . . | **18** |

19 **Taxable benefits.** Subtract line 18 from line 12. Also, include this amount on Form 1040, line 7. On the dotted line next to line 7, enter "DCB" . . . . | **19** |

To claim the child and dependent care
credit, complete lines 20–24 below.

20 Enter $2,400 ($4,800 if two or more qualifying persons) . . . . | **20** |

21 Enter the amount from line 18 . . . . | **21** |

22 Subtract line 21 from line 20. If zero or less, **STOP.** You cannot take the credit. **Exception.** If you paid 1998 expenses in 1999, see the instructions for line 9 . . . . | **22** |

23 Complete line 2 on the front of this form. DO NOT include in column (c) any benefits shown on line 18 above. Then, add the amounts in column (c) and enter the total here . | **23** |

24 Enter the **smaller** of line 22 or 23. Also, enter this amount on line 3 on the front of this form and complete lines 4–9 . . . . | **24** |

Form **3903**

(Rev. October 1998)

Department of the Treasury
Internal Revenue Service

Moving Expenses

▶ **Attach to Form 1040.**

OMB No. 1545-0062

Attachment
Sequence No. **62**

Name(s) shown on Form 1040

Your social security number

Before you begin, see the **Distance Test** and **Time Test** in the instructions to make sure you can take this deduction. If you are a member of the armed forces, see the instructions to find out how to complete this form.

1 Enter the amount you paid for transportation and storage of household goods and personal effects (see instructions)	**1**	
2 Enter the amount you paid for travel and lodging expenses in moving from your old home to your new home. **Do not** include meals (see instructions)	**2**	
3 Add lines 1 and 2	**3**	
4 Enter the total amount your employer paid you for the expenses listed on lines 1 and 2 that is **not** included in the wages box (box 1) of your W-2 form. This amount should be identified with code **P** in box 13 of your W-2 form	**4**	

Is line 3 more than line 4?

Yes. Go to line 5.

No. You **cannot** deduct your moving expenses. If line 3 is less than line 4, subtract line 3 from line 4 and include the result on the "Wages, salaries, tips, etc." line of Form 1040.

5 Subtract line 4 from line 3. Enter the result here and on the "Moving expenses" line of Form 1040. This is your **moving expense deduction**	**5**	

General Instructions

A Change To Note

Beginning in 1998, include on lines 1 and 2 of Form 3903 **only** the amounts you actually paid for the expenses listed. Include on those lines the total amount you paid even if your employer reimbursed you for the expenses. Use line 4 to report amounts your employer paid directly to you for the expenses listed on lines 1 and 2 if they are **not** reported to you as wages on Form W-2.

Do not include on Form 3903 any amount your employer paid to a third party (such as a moving or storage company). Also, do not include the value of any services your employer provided in kind.

Purpose of Form

Use Form 3903 to figure your moving expense deduction if:

● You moved to a new principal place of work (workplace) within the United States or its possessions, OR

● You moved to a new workplace outside the United States or its possessions and you are a U.S. citizen or resident alien.

If you qualify to deduct expenses for more than one move, use a separate Form 3903 for each move.

For more details, see **Pub. 521,** Moving Expenses.

Who May Deduct Moving Expenses

If you moved to a different home because of a change in job location, you may be able to deduct your moving expenses. You may be able to take the deduction whether you are self-employed or an employee. But you must meet certain tests explained next.

Distance Test

Your new principal workplace must be at least 50 miles farther from your old home than your old workplace was. For example, if your old workplace was 3 miles from your old home, your new workplace must be at least 53 miles from that home. If you did not have an old workplace, your new workplace must be at least 50 miles from

your old home. The distance between the two points is the shortest of the more commonly traveled routes between them.

TIP: *If you are not sure if you meet the distance test, use the worksheet on this page.*

Time Test

If you are an employee, you must work full time in the general area of your new workplace for at least 39 weeks during the 12 months right after you move. If you are self-employed, you must work full time in the general area of your new workplace for at least 39 weeks during the first 12 months and a total of at least 78 weeks during the 24 months right after you move.

What If You Do Not Meet the Time Test Before Your Return Is Due? If you expect to meet the time test, you may deduct

---

Distance Test Worksheet (keep a copy for your records)

1. Enter the number of miles from your **old home** to your **new workplace**	**1.** _____	miles
2. Enter the number of miles from your **old home** to your **old workplace**	**2.** _____	miles
3. Subtract line 2 from line 1. If zero or less, enter -0-	**3.** _____	miles

Is line 3 at least 50 miles?

Yes. You meet this test.

No. You do not meet this test. You **cannot** deduct your moving expenses. **Do not** complete Form 3903.

For Paperwork Reduction Act Notice, see back of form.

Cat. No. 12490K

Form **3903** (Rev. 10-98)

your moving expenses in the year you move. But if you do not meet the time test, you must either:

1. Amend your tax return for the year you claimed the deduction (use **Form 1040X,** Amended U.S. Individual Income Tax Return, to do this), **or**

2. For the year you cannot meet the time test, report as income the amount of your moving expense deduction that reduced your income tax for the year you moved. For more details, see **Time Test** in Pub. 521.

If you do not deduct your moving expenses in the year you move and you later meet the time test, you may take the deduction by filing an amended return for the year you moved. To do this, use Form 1040X.

Example. You are an employee who moved to a new workplace in September 1998. Because you expect to meet the 39-week test by the end of 1999, you deduct your moving expenses on your 1998 return. If you do not meet the time test in 1999 and none of the exceptions to the time test (see below) apply, you must either amend your 1998 tax return to figure your tax without the moving expense deduction **or** report as income on your 1999 tax return the portion of your moving expense deduction that reduced your 1998 income tax.

Exceptions to the Time Test. The time test does not have to be met if any of the following apply:

● Your job ends because of disability.

● You are transferred for your employer's benefit.

● You are laid off or discharged for a reason other than willful misconduct.

● You meet the requirements (explained later) for retirees or survivors living outside the United States.

● You are filing this form for a decedent.

Members of the Armed Forces

If you are in the armed forces, you do not have to meet the **distance and time tests** if the move is due to a permanent change of station. A permanent change of station includes a move in connection with and within 1 year of retirement or other termination of active duty.

How To Complete the Form

Do not include on lines 1 and 2 any expenses for moving services that were provided by the government. If you and your spouse and dependents are moved to or from different locations, treat the moves as a single move.

On line 4, enter the total reimbursements and allowances you received from the government in connection with the expenses you claimed on lines 1 and 2. **Do not** include the value of moving services provided by the government. Complete line 5 if applicable.

Retirees or Survivors Living Outside the United States

If you are a retiree or survivor who moved to a home in the United States or its possessions and you meet the following requirements, you are treated as if you moved to a new workplace located in the United States. You are subject to the distance test.

Retirees

You may deduct moving expenses for a move to a new home in the United States when you actually retire if both your old principal workplace and your old home were outside the United States.

Survivors

You may deduct moving expenses for a move to a home in the United States if you are the spouse or dependent of a person whose principal workplace at the time of death was outside the United States. In addition, the expenses must be for a move **(1)** that begins within 6 months after the decedent's death, and **(2)** from a former home outside the United States that you lived in with the decedent at the time of death.

Reimbursements

You may choose to deduct moving expenses in the year you are reimbursed by your employer, even though you paid the expenses in a different year. However, special rules apply. See **How To Report** in Pub. 521.

Filers of Form 2555

If you file **Form 2555,** Foreign Earned Income, to exclude any of your income or housing costs, report the full amount of your deductible moving expenses on Form 3903 and on Form 1040. Report the part of your moving expenses that is not allowed because it is allocable to the excluded income on the appropriate line of Form 2555. For details on how to figure the part allocable to the excluded income, see **Pub. 54,** Tax Guide for U.S. Citizens and Resident Aliens Abroad.

Specific Instructions

You may deduct the following expenses you paid to move your family and dependent household members. Do not deduct expenses for employees such as a maid, nanny, or nurse.

Caution: See **A Change To Note** on page 1 before you complete lines 1 and 2.

Line 1

Moves Within or to the United States or its Possessions. Enter the amount you paid to pack, crate, and move your household goods and personal effects. You may also include the amount you paid to store and insure household goods and personal effects within any period of 30 days in a row after the items were moved from your old home and before they were delivered to your new home.

Moves Outside the United States or its Possessions. Enter the amount you paid to pack, crate, move, store, and insure your household goods and personal effects. Also, include the amount you paid to move your possessions to and from storage and to store them for all or part of the time the new workplace continues to be your principal workplace.

TIP: *You do not have to complete this form if you moved in an earlier year, you are claiming only storage fees during your absence from the United States, and any amount your employer paid for the storage fees is included in the wages box of your W-2 form. Instead, enter the storage fees on the "Moving expenses" line of Form 1040, and write "Storage" next to the amount.*

Line 2

Enter the amount you paid to travel from your old home to your new home. This includes transportation and lodging on the way. Include costs for the day you arrive. Although not all the members of your household have to travel together or at the same time, you may only include expenses for one trip per person.

If you use your own car(s), you may figure the expenses by using either:

● Actual out-of-pocket expenses for gas and oil, or

● Mileage at the rate of 10 cents a mile.

You may add parking fees and tolls to the amount claimed under either method. Keep records to verify your expenses.

Paperwork Reduction Act Notice. We ask for the information on this form to carry out the Internal Revenue laws of the United States. You are required to give us the information. We need it to ensure that you are complying with these laws and to allow us to figure and collect the right amount of tax.

You are not required to provide the information requested on a form that is subject to the Paperwork Reduction Act unless the form displays a valid OMB control number. Books or records relating to a form or its instructions must be retained as long as their contents may become material in the administration of any Internal Revenue law. Generally, tax returns and return information are confidential, as required by Internal Revenue Code section 6103.

The time needed to complete and file this form will vary depending on individual circumstances. The estimated average time is: **Recordkeeping,** 33 min.; **Learning about the law or the form,** 9 min.; **Preparing the form,** 13 min.; and **Copying, assembling, and sending the form to the IRS,** 14 min.

If you have comments concerning the accuracy of these time estimates or suggestions for making this form simpler, we would be happy to hear from you. See the Instructions for Form 1040.

Depreciation and Amortization
(Including Information on Listed Property)

▶ See separate instructions.   ▶ Attach this form to your return.

OMB No. 1545-0172

1999

Attachment
Sequence No. **67**

Name(s) shown on return	Business or activity to which this form relates	Identifying number

Part I   Election To Expense Certain Tangible Property (Section 179) (Note: *If you have any "listed property," complete Part V before you complete Part I.*)

1	Maximum dollar limitation. If an enterprise zone business, see page 2 of the instructions . .	**1**	$19,000
2	Total cost of section 179 property placed in service. See page 2 of the instructions	**2**	
3	Threshold cost of section 179 property before reduction in limitation	**3**	$200,000
4	Reduction in limitation. Subtract line 3 from line 2. If zero or less, enter -0-	**4**	
5	Dollar limitation for tax year. Subtract line 4 from line 1. If zero or less, enter -0-. If married filing separately, see page 2 of the instructions	**5**	

(a) Description of property	(b) Cost (business use only)	(c) Elected cost	
6			

7	Listed property. Enter amount from line 27.	**7**	
8	Total elected cost of section 179 property. Add amounts in column (c), lines 6 and 7 . . .	**8**	
9	Tentative deduction. Enter the smaller of line 5 or line 8	**9**	
10	Carryover of disallowed deduction from 1998. See page 2 of the instructions	**10**	
11	Business income limitation. Enter the smaller of business income (not less than zero) or line 5 (see instructions)	**11**	
12	Section 179 expense deduction. Add lines 9 and 10, but do not enter more than line 11 . .	**12**	
13	Carryover of disallowed deduction to 2000. Add lines 9 and 10, less line 12 ▶	**13**	

Note: *Do not use Part II or Part III below for listed property (automobiles, certain other vehicles, cellular telephones, certain computers, or property used for entertainment, recreation, or amusement). Instead, use Part V for listed property.*

Part II   MACRS Depreciation for Assets Placed in Service ONLY During Your 1999 Tax Year (Do Not Include Listed Property.)

Section A—General Asset Account Election

14   If you are making the election under section 168(i)(4) to group any assets placed in service during the tax year into one or more general asset accounts, check this box. See page 3 of the instructions . . . . ▶ ☐

Section B—General Depreciation System (GDS) (See page 3 of the instructions.)

(a) Classification of property	(b) Month and year placed in service	(c) Basis for depreciation (business/investment use only—see instructions)	(d) Recovery period	(e) Convention	(f) Method	(g) Depreciation deduction
15a 3-year property						
b 5-year property						
c 7-year property						
d 10-year property						
e 15-year property						
f 20-year property						
g 25-year property			25 yrs.		S/L	
h Residential rental property			27.5 yrs.	MM	S/L	
			27.5 yrs.	MM	S/L	
i Nonresidential real property			39 yrs.	MM	S/L	
				MM	S/L	

Section C—Alternative Depreciation System (ADS) (See page 5 of the instructions.)

16a Class life					S/L	
b 12-year			12 yrs.		S/L	
c 40-year			40 yrs.	MM	S/L	

Part III   Other Depreciation (Do Not Include Listed Property.) (See page 5 of the instructions.)

17	GDS and ADS deductions for assets placed in service in tax years beginning before 1999 .	**17**	
18	Property subject to section 168(f)(1) election	**18**	
19	ACRS and other depreciation	**19**	

Part IV   Summary (See page 6 of the instructions.)

20	Listed property. Enter amount from line 26.	**20**	
21	**Total.** Add deductions on line 12, lines 15 and 16 in column (g), and lines 17 through 20. Enter here and on the appropriate lines of your return. Partnerships and S corporations—see instructions . .	**21**	
22	For assets shown above and placed in service during the current year, enter the portion of the basis attributable to section 263A costs . .	**22**	

| **Part V** | Listed Property—Automobiles, Certain Other Vehicles, Cellular Telephones, Certain Computers, and Property Used for Entertainment, Recreation, or Amusement |

Note: *For any vehicle for which you are using the standard mileage rate or deducting lease expense, complete **only** 23a, 23b, columns (a) through (c) of Section A, all of Section B, and Section C if applicable.*

Section A—Depreciation and Other Information (Caution: *See page 7 of the instructions for limits for passenger automobiles.*)

23a Do you have evidence to support the business/investment use claimed? ☐ **Yes** ☐ **No**   **23b** If "Yes," is the evidence written? ☐ **Yes** ☐ **No**

(a) Type of property (list vehicles first)	(b) Date placed in service	(c) Business/ investment use percentage	(d) Cost or other basis	(e) Basis for depreciation (business/investment use only)	(f) Recovery period	(g) Method/ Convention	(h) Depreciation deduction	(i) Elected section 179 cost
24 Property used more than 50% in a qualified business use (See page 6 of the instructions.):								
		%						
		%						
		%						
25 Property used 50% or less in a qualified business use (See page 6 of the instructions.):								
		%				S/L –		
		%				S/L –		
		%				S/L –		

26 Add amounts in column (h). Enter the total here and on line 20, page 1 . . . . . . **26**

27 Add amounts in column (i). Enter the total here and on line 7, page 1 . . . . **27**

Section B—Information on Use of Vehicles

Complete this section for vehicles used by a sole proprietor, partner, or other "more than 5% owner," or related person.

If you provided vehicles to your employees, first answer the questions in Section C to see if you meet an exception to completing this section for those vehicles.

	(a) Vehicle 1		(b) Vehicle 2		(c) Vehicle 3		(d) Vehicle 4		(e) Vehicle 5		(f) Vehicle 6	
28 Total business/investment miles driven during the year (DO NOT include commuting miles—see page 1 of the instructions) . . .												
29 Total commuting miles driven during the year												
30 Total other personal (noncommuting) miles driven												
31 Total miles driven during the year. Add lines 28 through 30.												
	Yes	**No**	**Yes**	**No**	**Yes**	**No**	**Yes**	**No**	**Yes**	**No**	**Yes**	**No**
32 Was the vehicle available for personal use during off-duty hours?												
33 Was the vehicle used primarily by a more than 5% owner or related person?												
34 Is another vehicle available for personal use?												

Section C—Questions for Employers Who Provide Vehicles for Use by Their Employees

*Answer these questions to determine if you meet an exception to completing Section B for vehicles used by employees who **are not** more than 5% owners or related persons.*

	Yes	No
35 Do you maintain a written policy statement that prohibits all personal use of vehicles, including commuting, by your employees?		
36 Do you maintain a written policy statement that prohibits personal use of vehicles, except commuting, by your employees? See page 8 of the instructions for vehicles used by corporate officers, directors, or 1% or more owners		
37 Do you treat all use of vehicles by employees as personal use?		
38 Do you provide more than five vehicles to your employees, obtain information from your employees about the use of the vehicles, and retain the information received?		
39 Do you meet the requirements concerning qualified automobile demonstration use? See page 8 of the instructions . .		

Note: *If your answer to 35, 36, 37, 38, or 39 is "Yes," you need not complete Section B for the covered vehicles.*

| **Part VI** | **Amortization** |

(a) Description of costs	(b) Date amortization begins	(c) Amortizable amount	(d) Code section	(e) Amortization period or percentage	(f) Amortization for this year
40 Amortization of costs that begins during your 1999 tax year:					

41 Amortization of costs that began before 1999 . . . . **41**

42 **Total.** Enter here and on "Other Deductions" or "Other Expenses" line of your return . . . **42**

Form **4684**

Department of the Treasury
Internal Revenue Service

Casualties and Thefts

▶ See separate instructions.
▶ Attach to your tax return.
▶ Use a separate Form 4684 for each different casualty or theft.

OMB No. 1545-0177

1999

Attachment
Sequence No. **26**

Name(s) shown on tax return	Identifying number

SECTION A—Personal Use Property (Use this section to report casualties and thefts of property **not** used in a trade or business or for income-producing purposes.)

1 Description of properties (show type, location, and date acquired for each):

Property **A** ....

Property **B** ....

Property **C** ....

Property **D** ....

		Properties (Use a separate column for each property lost or damaged from one casualty or theft.)			
		A	**B**	**C**	**D**
2 Cost or other basis of each property	**2**				
3 Insurance or other reimbursement (whether or not you filed a claim). See instructions **Note:** If line 2 is **more than** line 3, skip line 4.	**3**				
4 Gain from casualty or theft. If line 3 is **more than** line 2, enter the difference here and skip lines 5 through 9 for that column. See instructions if line 3 includes insurance or other reimbursement you did not claim, or you received payment for your loss in a later tax year	**4**				
5 Fair market value **before** casualty or theft	**5**				
6 Fair market value **after** casualty or theft	**6**				
7 Subtract line 6 from line 5	**7**				
8 Enter the **smaller** of line 2 or line 7	**8**				
9 Subtract line 3 from line 8. If zero or less, enter -0-	**9**				

10 Casualty or theft loss. Add the amounts on line 9. Enter the total	**10**		
11 Enter the amount from line 10 or $100, whichever is **smaller**	**11**		
12 Subtract line 11 from line 10	**12**		
Caution: Use only one Form 4684 for lines 13 through 18.			
13 Add the amounts on line 12 of all Forms 4684	**13**		
14 Combine the amounts from line 4 of all Forms 4684	**14**		
15 ● If line 14 is **more than** line 13, enter the difference here and on Schedule D. Do not complete the rest of this section (see instructions). ● If line 14 is **less than** line 13, enter -0- here and continue with the form. ● If line 14 is **equal to** line 13, enter -0- here. Do not complete the rest of this section.	**15**		
16 If line 14 is **less than** line 13, enter the difference	**16**		
17 Enter 10% of your adjusted gross income (Form 1040, line 34). Estates and trusts, see instructions	**17**		
18 Subtract line 17 from line 16. If zero or less, enter -0-. Also enter result on Schedule A (Form 1040), line 19. Estates and trusts, enter on the "Other deductions" line of your tax return	**18**		

For Paperwork Reduction Act Notice, see page 4 of separate instructions.   Cat. No. 12997O   Form **4684** (1999)

Name(s) shown on tax return. Do not enter name and identifying number if shown on other side. | Identifying number

SECTION B—Business and Income-Producing Property

Part I Casualty or Theft Gain or Loss (Use a separate Part I for each casualty or theft.)

19 Description of properties (show type, location, and date acquired for each):

Property **A** ....

Property **B** ....

Property **C** ....

Property **D** ....

Properties (Use a separate column for each property lost or damaged from one casualty or theft.)

		A	B	C	D
20	Cost or adjusted basis of each property				
21	Insurance or other reimbursement (whether or not you filed a claim). See the instructions for line 3. **Note:** *If line 20 is **more than** line 21, skip line 22.*				
22	Gain from casualty or theft. If line 21 is **more than** line 20, enter the difference here and on line 29 or line 34, column (c), except as provided in the instructions for line 33. Also, skip lines 23 through 27 for that column. See the instructions for line 4 if line 21 includes insurance or other reimbursement you did not claim, or you received payment for your loss in a later tax year.				
23	Fair market value **before** casualty or theft				
24	Fair market value **after** casualty or theft				
25	Subtract line 24 from line 23				
26	Enter the **smaller** of line 20 or line 25. **Note:** *If the property was totally destroyed by casualty or lost from theft, enter on line 26 the amount from line 20.*				
27	Subtract line 21 from line 26. If zero or less, enter -0-				
28	Casualty or theft loss. Add the amounts on line 27. Enter the total here and on line 29 **or** line 34 (see instructions).		**28**		

Part II Summary of Gains and Losses (from separate Parts I)

(a) Identify casualty or theft	(b) Losses from casualties or thefts		(c) Gains from casualties or thefts includible in income
	(i) Trade, business, rental or royalty property	*(ii)* Income-producing and employee property	

Casualty or Theft of Property Held One Year or Less

		(b)(i)	(b)(ii)	(c)
29		( )	( )	
		( )	( )	
30	Totals. Add the amounts on line 29 **30**	( )	( )	
31	Combine line 30, columns (b)(i) and (c). Enter the net gain or (loss) here and on Form 4797, line 14. If Form 4797 is not otherwise required, see instructions		**31**	
32	Enter the amount from line 30, column (b)(ii) here. Individuals, enter the amount from income-producing property on Schedule A (Form 1040), line 27, and enter the amount from property used as an employee on Schedule A (Form 1040), line 22. Estates and trusts, partnerships, and S corporations, see instructions		**32**	

Casualty or Theft of Property Held More Than One Year

		(b)(i)	(b)(ii)	(c)
33	Casualty or theft gains from Form 4797, line 32	**33**		
34		( )	( )	
		( )	( )	
35	Total losses. Add amounts on line 34, columns (b)(i) and (b)(ii) **35**	( )	( )	
36	Total gains. Add lines 33 and 34, column (c)		**36**	
37	Add amounts on line 35, columns (b)(i) and (b)(ii)		**37**	

38 If the loss on line 37 is **more than** the gain on line 36:

  a Combine line 35, column (b)(i) and line 36, and enter the net gain or (loss) here. Partnerships (except electing large partnerships) and S corporations, see the note below. All others, enter this amount on Form 4797, line 14. If Form 4797 is not otherwise required, see instructions. **38a**

  b Enter the amount from line 35, column (b)(ii) here. Individuals, enter the amount from income-producing property on Schedule A (Form 1040), line 27, and enter the amount from property used as an employee on Schedule A (Form 1040), line 22. Estates and trusts, enter on the "Other deductions" line of your tax return. Partnerships (except electing large partnerships) and S corporations, see the note below. Electing large partnerships, enter on Form 1065-B, Part II, line 11. **38b**

39 If the loss on line 37 is **less than** or **equal to** the gain on line 36, combine lines 36 and 37 and enter here. Partnerships (except electing large partnerships), see the note below. All others, enter this amount on Form 4797, line 3, column (g) **39**

    Note: *Partnerships, enter the amount from line 38a, 38b, or line 39 on Form 1065, Schedule K, line 7. S corporations, enter the amount from line 38a or 38b on Form 1120S, Schedule K, line 6.*

Form **4797**	**Sales of Business Property**	OMB No. 1545-0184
Department of the Treasury Internal Revenue Service (99)	(Also Involuntary Conversions and Recapture Amounts Under Sections 179 and 280F(b)(2)) ▶ Attach to your tax return. ▶ See separate instructions.	**1999** Attachment Sequence No. **27**

Name(s) shown on return	Identifying number

1 Enter here the gross proceeds from the sale or exchange of real estate reported to you for 1999 on Form(s) 1099-S (or a substitute statement) that you will be including on line 2, 10, or 20 . . . . **1**

Part I Sales or Exchanges of Property Used in a Trade or Business and Involuntary Conversions From Other Than Casualty or Theft—Property Held More Than 1 Year

(a) Description of property	(b) Date acquired (mo., day, yr.)	(c) Date sold (mo., day, yr.)	(d) Gross sales price	(e) Depreciation allowed or allowable since acquisition	(f) Cost or other basis, plus improvements and expense of sale	(g) GAIN or (LOSS) Subtract (f) from the sum of (d) and (e)
2						

3 Gain, if any, from Form 4684, line 39 . . . . **3**

4 Section 1231 gain from installment sales from Form 6252, line 26 or 37 . . . . **4**

5 Section 1231 gain or (loss) from like-kind exchanges from Form 8824 . . . . **5**

6 Gain, if any, from line 32, from other than casualty or theft **6**

7 Combine lines 2 through 6. Enter the gain or (loss) here and on the appropriate line as follows: **7**

Partnerships (except electing large partnerships). Report the gain or (loss) following the instructions for Form 1065, Schedule K, line 6. Skip lines 8, 9, 11, and 12 below.

S corporations. Report the gain or (loss) following the instructions for Form 1120S, Schedule K, lines 5 and 6. Skip lines 8, 9, 11, and 12 below, unless line 7 is a gain and the S corporation is subject to the capital gains tax.

All others. If line 7 is zero or a loss, enter the amount from line 7 on line 11 below and skip lines 8 and 9. If line 7 is a gain and you did not have any prior year section 1231 losses, or they were recaptured in an earlier year, enter the gain from line 7 as a long-term capital gain on Schedule D and skip lines 8, 9, and 12 below.

8 Nonrecaptured net section 1231 losses from prior years (see instructions) **8**

9 Subtract line 8 from line 7. If zero or less, enter -0-. Also enter on the appropriate line as follows (see instructions): **9**

S corporations. Enter any gain from line 9 on Schedule D (Form 1120S), line 14, and skip lines 11 and 12 below.

All others. If line 9 is zero, enter the gain from line 7 on line 12 below. If line 9 is more than zero, enter the amount from line 8 on line 12 below, and enter the gain from line 9 as a long-term capital gain on Schedule D.

Part II Ordinary Gains and Losses

10 Ordinary gains and losses not included on lines 11 through 17 (include property held 1 year or less):

11 Loss, if any, from line 7 . . . . **11** ( )

12 Gain, if any, from line 7 or amount from line 8, if applicable **12**

13 Gain, if any, from line 31 . . . . **13**

14 Net gain or (loss) from Form 4684, lines 31 and 38a **14**

15 Ordinary gain from installment sales from Form 6252, line 25 or 36 . . . . **15**

16 Ordinary gain or (loss) from like-kind exchanges from Form 8824 . . . . **16**

17 Recapture of section 179 expense deduction for partners and S corporation shareholders from property dispositions by partnerships and S corporations (see instructions) **17**

18 Combine lines 10 through 17. Enter the gain or (loss) here, and on the appropriate line as follows: **18**

a For all except individual returns: Enter the gain or (loss) from line 18 on the return being filed.

b For individual returns:

(1) If the loss on line 11 includes a loss from Form 4684, line 35, column (b)(ii), enter that part of the loss here. Enter the part of the loss from income-producing property on Schedule A (Form 1040), line 27, and the part of the loss from property used as an employee on Schedule A (Form 1040), line 22. Identify as from "Form 4797, line 18b(1)." See instructions . . . . **18b(1)**

(2) Redetermine the gain or (loss) on line 18, excluding the loss, if any, on line 18b(1). Enter here and on Form 1040, line 14 . . . . **18b(2)**

For Paperwork Reduction Act Notice, see separate instructions.   Cat. No. 13086I   Form **4797** (1999)

Part III Gain From Disposition of Property Under Sections 1245, 1250, 1252, 1254, and 1255

19	(a) Description of section 1245, 1250, 1252, 1254, or 1255 property:	(b) Date acquired (mo., day, yr.)	(c) Date sold (mo., day, yr.)
A			
B			
C			
D			

	These columns relate to the properties on lines 19A through 19D. ▶		Property A	Property B	Property C	Property D
20	Gross sales price (**Note:** *See line 1 before completing.*)	20				
21	Cost or other basis plus expense of sale	21				
22	Depreciation (or depletion) allowed or allowable	22				
23	Adjusted basis. Subtract line 22 from line 21	23				
24	Total gain. Subtract line 23 from line 20	24				
25	**If section 1245 property:**					
a	Depreciation allowed or allowable from line 22	25a				
b	Enter the **smaller** of line 24 or 25a	25b				
26	**If section 1250 property:** If straight line depreciation was used, enter -0- on line 26g, except for a corporation subject to section 291.					
a	Additional depreciation after 1975 (see instructions)	26a				
b	Applicable percentage multiplied by the **smaller** of line 24 or line 26a (see instructions)	26b				
c	Subtract line 26a from line 24. If residential rental property or line 24 is not more than line 26a, skip lines 26d and 26e	26c				
d	Additional depreciation after 1969 and before 1976	26d				
e	Enter the **smaller** of line 26c or 26d	26e				
f	Section 291 amount (corporations only)	26f				
g	Add lines 26b, 26e, and 26f	26g				
27	**If section 1252 property:** Skip this section if you did not dispose of farmland or if this form is being completed for a partnership (other than an electing large partnership).					
a	Soil, water, and land clearing expenses	27a				
b	Line 27a multiplied by applicable percentage (see instructions)	27b				
c	Enter the **smaller** of line 24 or 27b	27c				
28	**If section 1254 property:**					
a	Intangible drilling and development costs, expenditures for development of mines and other natural deposits, and mining exploration costs (see instructions)	28a				
b	Enter the **smaller** of line 24 or 28a	28b				
29	**If section 1255 property:**					
a	Applicable percentage of payments excluded from income under section 126 (see instructions)	29a				
b	Enter the **smaller** of line 24 or 29a (see instructions)	29b				

Summary of Part III Gains. Complete property columns A through D through line 29b before going to line 30.

30	Total gains for all properties. Add property columns A through D, line 24	30	
31	Add property columns A through D, lines 25b, 26g, 27c, 28b, and 29b. Enter here and on line 13	31	
32	Subtract line 31 from line 30. Enter the portion from casualty or theft on Form 4684, line 33. Enter the portion from other than casualty or theft on Form 4797, line 6	32	

Part IV Recapture Amounts Under Sections 179 and 280F(b)(2) When Business Use Drops to 50% or Less (See instructions.)

			(a) Section 179	(b) Section 280F(b)(2)
33	Section 179 expense deduction or depreciation allowable in prior years	33		
34	Recomputed depreciation. See instructions	34		
35	Recapture amount. Subtract line 34 from line 33. See the instructions for where to report	35		

Form 4868

Department of the Treasury
Internal Revenue Service (99)

Application for Automatic Extension of Time To File U.S. Individual Income Tax Return

OMB No. 1545-0188

1999

General Instructions

A Change To Note

You may be able to use a credit card to get an extension of time to file without sending in Form 4868. See **Extension of Time To File Using a Credit Card** below for more details.

Purpose of Form

Use Form 4868 to apply for 4 more months to file **Form 1040EZ, Form 1040A, Form 1040, Form 1040NR-EZ,** or **Form 1040NR.**

To get the extra time you **MUST:**

- Properly estimate your 1999 tax liability using the information available to you,
- Enter your tax liability on line 9 of Form 4868, **AND**
- File Form 4868 by the regular due date of your return.

You are not required to make a payment of the tax you estimate as due. But remember, Form 4868 does not extend the time to pay taxes. If you do not pay the amount due by the regular due date, you will owe interest. You may also be charged penalties. For more details, see **Interest** and **Late Payment Penalty** on page 3. Any remittance you make with your application for extension will be treated as a payment of tax.

You do not have to explain why you are asking for the extension. We will contact you only if your request is denied.

Do not file Form 4868 if you want the IRS to figure your tax or you are under a court order to file your return by the regular due date.

If you need an additional extension, see **If You Need Additional Time** on page 3.

Note: Generally, an extension of time to file your 1999 **calendar year** income tax return also extends the time to file a gift or generation-skipping transfer (GST) tax return **(Form 709 or 709-A)** for 1999. Special rules apply if the donor dies during the year in which the gifts were made. See the Instructions for Form 709.

Extension of Time To File Using a Credit Card

You generally can get an extension by phone if you pay part or all of your estimate of income tax due by using a credit card (American Express® Card, MasterCard®, or Discover® Card). To pay by credit card, call **1-888-2PAY-TAX** (1-888-272- 9829) toll free by April 17, 2000, and follow the instructions. Your payment must be at least $1 to use this system. Before you call, fill in Form 4868 as a worksheet. You will be asked to enter certain items from the form during the call. A convenience fee will be charged by the credit card processor based on the amount you are paying. You will be told what the fee is when you call and you will have the option to either continue or cancel the call. You can also find out what the fee will be on the Internet at **www.8882paytax.com.**

You will be given a confirmation number at the end of the call. Keep the confirmation number with your records. Once you receive your confirmation number, you have completed the requirements for requesting an extension of time to file. **Do not** send in Form 4868.

Note: Although an extension of time to file your income tax return also extends the time to file Form 709 or 709-A, you cannot make payments of the gift or GST tax with a credit card. To make a payment of the gift or GST tax, send a check or money order to the service center where the donor's income tax return will be filed. Enter "1999 Form 709" and the donor's name and social security number on the payment. **Do not** send in Form 4868.

Out of the Country

If you already had 2 extra months to file because you were a U.S. citizen or resident and were out of the country, use this form to obtain an additional 2 months to file. Write "Taxpayer Abroad" across the top of Form 4868. "Out of the country" means either **(a)** you live outside the United States and Puerto Rico **and** your main place of work is outside the United States and Puerto Rico, **or (b)** you are in military or naval service outside the United States and Puerto Rico.

For Privacy Act and Paperwork Reduction Act Notice, see page 4.

Cat. No. 13141W

Form **4868** (1999)

▼ DETACH HERE ▼

Form 4868

Department of the Treasury
Internal Revenue Service (99)

Application for Automatic Extension of Time To File U.S. Individual Income Tax Return

For calendar year 1999, or other tax year beginning , 1999, ending , .

OMB No. 1545-0188

1999

Part I Identification	**Part III** Individual Income Tax
1 Your name(s) (see instructions)	4 Total tax liability on your income tax return for 1999 $ _____
	5 Total 1999 payments . . . . _____
Address (see instructions)	6 **Balance.** Subtract 5 from 4 . . . . _____

Part IV Gift/GST Tax—If you are **not filing** a gift or GST tax return, go to Part V now. See the instructions.

Part I (City)	**Part IV**
City, town or post office, state, and ZIP code	
2 Your social security number	3 Spouse's social security number	7 Your gift or GST tax payment. . . $ _____
		8 **Your spouse's** gift/GST tax payment .

Part II Complete ONLY If Filing Gift/GST Tax Return

Part V Total

This form also extends the time for filing a gift or generation-skipping transfer (GST) tax return if you file a calendar (not fiscal) year income tax return. Enter your gift or GST tax payment(s) in Part IV and:

Check this box ▶ ☐ if **you** are requesting a **GIFT or GST TAX** return extension.

Check this box ▶ ☐ if **your spouse** is requesting a **GIFT or GST TAX** return extension.

Checking box(es) may result in correspondence if Form 709 or 709-A is not filed.

9 **Total liability.** Add lines 6, 7, and 8 $ _____

10 Amount you are paying. . . . . ▶ _____

If line 10 is less than line 9, you may be liable for interest and penalties. See page 3.

Form **4868** (1999)

Where To File

If you live in:	And you are making a payment, send Form 4868 with your payment to IRS:	And you are NOT making a payment, send Form 4868 to Internal Revenue Service Center:
Florida, Georgia, South Carolina	P.O. Box 105073 Atlanta, GA 30348-5073	Atlanta, GA 39901
New Jersey, New York (*New York City and counties of Nassau, Rockland, Suffolk, and Westchester*)	P.O. Box 22423 Newark, NJ 07101-2423	Holtsville, NY 00501
New York (*all other counties*), Connecticut, Maine, Massachusetts, New Hampshire, Rhode Island, Vermont	P.O. Box 371410 Pittsburgh, PA 15250-7410	Andover, MA 05501
Illinois, Iowa, Minnesota, Missouri, Wisconsin	P.O. Box 970028 St. Louis, MO 63197-0028	Kansas City, MO 64999
Delaware, District of Columbia, Maryland, Pennsylvania, Virginia	P.O. Box 7990 Philadelphia, PA 19162-7990	Philadelphia, PA 19255
Indiana, Kentucky, Michigan, Ohio, West Virginia	P.O. Box 6252 Chicago, IL 60680-6252	Cincinnati, OH 45999
Kansas, New Mexico, Oklahoma, Texas	P.O. Box 970027 St. Louis, MO 63197-0027	Austin, TX 73301
Alaska, Arizona, California (*counties of Alpine, Amador, Butte, Calaveras, Colusa, Contra Costa, Del Norte, El Dorado, Glenn, Humboldt, Lake, Lassen, Marin, Mendocino, Modoc, Napa, Nevada, Placer, Plumas, Sacramento, San Joaquin, Shasta, Sierra, Siskiyou, Solano, Sonoma, Sutter, Tehama, Trinity, Yolo, and Yuba*), Colorado, Idaho, Montana, Nebraska, Nevada, North Dakota, Oregon, South Dakota, Utah, Washington, Wyoming	P.O. Box 7122 San Francisco, CA 94120-7122	Ogden, UT 84201
California (*all other counties*), Hawaii	P.O. Box 54916 Los Angeles, CA 90054-0916	Fresno, CA 93888
Alabama, Arkansas, Louisiana, Mississippi, North Carolina, Tennessee	P.O. Box 1236 Charlotte, NC 28201-1236	Memphis, TN 37501
American Samoa or Puerto Rico (*or exclude income under section 933);* are a nonpermanent resident of Guam or the Virgin Islands; have an APO, FPO, or foreign address; are a dual-status alien; or file Form 2555, 2555-EZ, or 4563	P.O. Box 7990 Philadelphia, PA 19162-7990	Philadelphia, PA 19255
Guam: 　Permanent residents	Send Form 4868 and payments to:	Department of Revenue and Taxation Government of Guam P.O. Box 23607 GMF, GU 96921
Virgin Islands: 　Permanent residents	Send Form 4868 and payments to:	V.I. Bureau of Internal Revenue 9601 Estate Thomas Charlotte Amalie St. Thomas, VI 00802

Form **4972**	**Tax on Lump-Sum Distributions** **From Qualified Retirement Plans** ▶ Attach to Form 1040 or Form 1041. ▶ See separate instructions.	OMB No. 1545-0193 **1999**
Department of the Treasury Internal Revenue Service (99)		Attachment Sequence No. **28**
Name of recipient of distribution		Identifying number

Part I Complete this part to see if you qualify to use Form 4972

			Yes	No
1	Was this a distribution of a plan participant's entire balance from all of an employer's qualified plans of one kind (pension, profit-sharing, or stock bonus)? If "No," do not use this form	**1**		
2	Did you roll over any part of the distribution? If "Yes," do not use this form	**2**		
3	Was this distribution paid to you as a beneficiary of a plan participant who died after reaching age 59½ (or who had been born before 1936)?	**3**		
4	Were you a plan participant who received this distribution after reaching age 59½ **and** having been in the plan for at least 5 years before the year of the distribution? . . . . If you answered "No" to both questions 3 **and** 4, do not use this form.	**4**		
5a	Did you use Form 4972 after 1986 for a previous distribution from your own plan? If "Yes," do not use this form for a 1999 distribution from your own plan	**5a**		
b	If you are receiving this distribution as a beneficiary of a plan participant who died, did you use Form 4972 for a previous distribution received for that plan participant after 1986? If "Yes," you may not use the form for this distribution	**5b**		

Part II Complete this part to choose the 20% capital gain election (See instructions.) Do not complete this part unless the participant was born **before** 1936.

6	Capital gain part from box 3 of Form 1099-R	**6**	
7	Multiply line 6 by 20% (.20) . . . . If you also choose to use Part III, go to line 8. Otherwise, include the amount from line 7 in the total on Form 1040, line 40, or Form 1041, Schedule G, line 1b, whichever applies.	**7**	

Part III Complete this part to choose the 5- or 10-year tax option (See instructions.)

8	Ordinary income from Form 1099-R, box 2a minus box 3. If you did not complete Part II, enter the taxable amount from box 2a of Form 1099-R		**8**		
9	Death benefit exclusion for a beneficiary of a plan participant who died before August 21, 1996		**9**		
10	Total taxable amount. Subtract line 9 from line 8		**10**		
11	Current actuarial value of annuity (from Form 1099 R, box 8)		**11**		
12	Adjusted total taxable amount. Add lines 10 and 11. If this amount is $70,000 or more, **skip** lines 13 through 16, and enter this amount on line 17		**12**		
13	Multiply line 12 by 50% (.50), but **do not** enter more than $10,000	**13**			
14	Subtract $20,000 from line 12. If the result is less than zero, enter -0-	**14**			
15	Multiply line 14 by 20% (.20)	**15**			
16	Minimum distribution allowance. Subtract line 15 from line 13		**16**		
17	Subtract line 16 from line 12		**17**		
18	Federal estate tax attributable to lump-sum distribution		**18**		
19	Subtract line 18 from line 17		**19**		
	If line 11 is blank, skip lines 20 through 22 and go to line 23.				
20	Divide line 11 by line 12 and enter the result as a decimal (rounded to at least four places) . .		**20**	.	
21	Multiply line 16 by the decimal on line 20		**21**		
22	Subtract line 21 from line 11		**22**		

For Paperwork Reduction Act Notice, see separate instructions.   Cat. No. 13187U   Form **4972** (1999)

Part III	5- or 10-year tax option—CONTINUED

5-year tax option	**23**	Multiply line 19 by 20% (.20)	**23**
	24	Tax on amount on line 23. Use the Tax Rate Schedule for the 5-Year Tax Option in the instructions	**24**
	25	Multiply line 24 by five (5). If line 11 is blank, skip lines 26 through 28, and enter this amount on line 29	**25**
	26	Multiply line 22 by 20% (.20) **26**	
	27	Tax on amount on line 26. Use the Tax Rate Schedule for the 5-Year Tax Option in the instructions **27**	
	28	Multiply line 27 by five (5)	**28**
	29	Subtract line 28 from line 25. (Multiple recipients, see page 2 of the instructions.) . . .	**29**

Note: *Complete lines 30 through 36 ONLY if the participant was born before 1936. Otherwise, enter the amount from line 29 on line 37.*

10-year tax option	**30**	Multiply line 19 by 10% (.10)	**30**
	31	Tax on amount on line 30. Use the Tax Rate Schedule for the 10-Year Tax Option in the instructions	**31**
	32	Multiply line 31 by ten (10). If line 11 is blank, skip lines 33 through 35, and enter this amount on line 36	**32**
	33	Multiply line 22 by 10% (.10) **33**	
	34	Tax on amount on line 33. Use the Tax Rate Schedule for the 10-Year Tax Option in the instructions **34**	
	35	Multiply line 34 by ten (10)	**35**
	36	Subtract line 35 from line 32. (Multiple recipients, see page 2 of the instructions.) . . .	**36**

37	Compare lines 29 and 36. Generally, you should enter the **smaller** amount here (see instructions) . . . . ▶	**37**
38	Tax on lump-sum distribution. Add lines 7 and 37. Also, include this amount in the total on Form 1040, line 40, or Form 1041, Schedule G, line 1b, whichever applies . . . . . ▶	**38**

Form **4972** (1999)

Form **5213**	**Election To Postpone Determination**	
(Rev. August 1997)	**as To Whether the Presumption Applies That an**	OMB No. 1545-0195
Department of the Treasury Internal Revenue Service	**Activity Is Engaged in for Profit** ▶ To be filed by individuals, estates, trusts, partnerships, and S corporations.	

Name(s) as shown on tax return	Identifying number as shown on tax return

Address (number and street, apt. no., rural route) (or P.O. box number if mail is not delivered to street address)

City, town or post office, state, and ZIP code

The taxpayer named above elects to postpone a determination as to whether the presumption applies that the activity described below is engaged in for profit. The determination is postponed until the close of:

- The 6th tax year, for an activity that consists mainly of breeding, training, showing, or racing horses; or
- The 4th tax year for any other activity,

after the tax year in which the taxpayer first engaged in the activity.

1 Type of taxpayer engaged in the activity (check the box that applies):

☐ Individual ☐ Partnership ☐ S corporation ☐ Estate or trust

2a Description of activity for which you elect to postpone a determination

2b First tax year you engaged in activity described in 2a

Under penalties of perjury, I declare that I have examined this election, including accompanying schedules, and to the best of my knowledge and belief, it is true, correct, and complete.

(Signature of taxpayer or fiduciary)	(Date)
(Signature of taxpayer's spouse, if joint return was filed)	(Date)
(Signature of general partner authorized to sign partnership return)	(Date)
(Signature and title of officer, if an S corporation)	(Date)

For Paperwork Reduction Act Notice, see Instructions on back. Cat. No. 42361U Form **5213** (Rev. 8-97)

General Instructions

Purpose of Form

This form is used to elect to postpone an IRS determination as to whether the presumption applies that an activity is engaged in for profit.

General Information

Generally, if you are an individual, estate, trust, partnership, or S corporation in an activity not engaged in for profit, some of your deductions may not be allowed. For information on the limits on deductions in not-for-profit activities, get **Pub. 535,** Business Expenses.

However, an activity is presumed to be engaged in for profit (and, therefore, deductions are not limited) if the gross income exceeds the deductions:

● From an activity that consists mainly of breeding, training, showing, or racing horses for each of 2 or more of the tax years in the period of 7 consecutive tax years ending with the tax year in question; or

● From any other activity for each of 3 or more of the tax years in the period of 5 consecutive tax years ending with the tax year in question.

Who Should File

Individuals, estates, trusts, partnerships (including limited liability companies or other entities that are treated as partnerships for Federal tax purposes), and S corporations should use this form if they want to postpone an IRS determination as to whether the presumption applies that they are engaged in an activity for profit. Partnerships and S corporations make the election, which is binding on all persons who were partners or shareholders at any time during the presumption period.

You may not use this form if you have been engaged in:

● Breeding, training, showing, or racing horses for more than 7 years; or

● Any other activity for more than 5 years.

If you elect a postponement and file this form on time, the IRS will generally postpone the determination until after the end of the 4th consecutive tax year (6th tax year for an activity that consists mainly of breeding, training, showing, or racing horses) after the tax year in which you first engaged in the activity. This period of 5 (or 7) tax years is called the "presumption period." The election to postpone covers the entire presumption period.

Joint Returns

If you and your spouse filed a joint return, both of you must elect to postpone the determination even if only one of you is engaged in the activity.

How Many Forms To File

Generally, if you want a postponement for more than one activity, you must file a separate Form 5213 for each activity.

However, you may file one form for more than one activity if all of the activities have the same presumption period. Be sure to describe each activity in detail and list the first tax year in which you were engaged in the activities.

Generally, in determining whether you are engaged in more than one activity, you must consider all of the following:

● The similarity of the activities;

● The business purpose that is (or might be) served by carrying on the activities separately or together in a trade or business or investment setting; and

● The organizational and economic interrelationship of the activities.

When To File

File this form within 3 years after the due date of your return (determined without extensions) for the first tax year in which you engaged in the activity.

However, if you received a written notice that the IRS proposes to disallow deductions attributable to an activity not engaged in for profit (under Internal Revenue Code section 183) and you want a postponement of the determination, you must file this form within 60 days of receiving the notice. This 60-day period does not extend the 3-year period referred to in the above paragraph.

Where To File

File this form with the Internal Revenue Service Center where you are required to file your return. Do not send it in with any other return because that will delay processing the election to postpone.

However, if the IRS notifies you about proposing to disallow deductions for an activity not engaged in for profit, file the form with the IRS office that sent you the notification.

Automatic Extension of Period of Limitations

Generally, filing this form automatically extends the period of limitations for assessing any income tax deficiency specifically attributable to the activity during any year in the presumption period. The extension also applies to partners or shareholders in the activity.

The period is extended until 2 years after the due date for filing the return (determined without extensions) for the last tax year in the presumption period. For example, for an activity subject to a 5-year presumption period that began in 1994 and ends in 1998, the period of limitations automatically extends to April 16, 2001, for all tax years in the presumption period that would otherwise expire before that date. Periods of limitations for tax years in the 5-year period expiring after April 16, 2001, would remain open until their normal expiration date. However, early termination of the presumption period does not terminate the automatic extension of the period of limitations.

The automatic extension applies only to those deductions attributable to the activity and to any deductions (such as medical expenses or charitable contribution deductions) that are affected by changes made to adjusted gross income.

The automatic extension does not affect general waivers of the statute of limitations that may be executed.

Specific Instructions

Name and Identifying Number as Shown on Tax Return

Enter your name(s) and identifying number as shown on your tax return for the first tax year in which you engaged in the activity.

If you are an individual, your identifying number is your social security number. If you are other than an individual, your identifying number is your employer identification number.

If you and your spouse filed a joint return, enter both your name and your spouse's name as they were shown on your tax return. Enter the social security number that was shown first on your return as your identifying number.

Signature and Date

Be sure to sign and date the form on the appropriate line or lines. Keep a copy for your records.

Paperwork Reduction Act Notice.—We ask for the information on this form to carry out the Internal Revenue laws of the United States. You are required to give us the information. We need it to ensure that you are complying with these laws and to allow us to figure and collect the right amount of tax.

You are not required to provide the information requested on a form that is subject to the Paperwork Reduction Act unless the form displays a valid OMB control number. Books or records relating to a form or its instructions must be retained as long as their contents may become material in the administration of any Internal Revenue law. Generally, tax returns and return information are confidential, as required by Internal Revenue Code section 6103.

The time needed to complete and file this form will vary depending on individual circumstances. The estimated average time is:

Recordkeeping	7 min.
Learning about the law or the form	7 min.
Preparing the form	10 min.
Copying, assembling, and sending the form to the IRS .	20 min.

If you have comments concerning the accuracy of these time estimates or suggestions for making this form simpler, we would be happy to hear from you. You can write to the Tax Forms Committee, Western Area Distribution Center, Rancho Cordova, CA 95743-0001. **DO NOT** send the form to this address. Instead, see **Where To File** on this page.

Form **6251**	**Alternative Minimum Tax—Individuals**	OMB No. 1545-0227
Department of the Treasury Internal Revenue Service (99)	▶ See separate instructions. ▶ Attach to Form 1040 or Form 1040NR.	**19**99 Attachment Sequence No. **32**

Name(s) shown on Form 1040	Your social security number

Part I — Adjustments and Preferences

1	If you itemized deductions on Schedule A (Form 1040), go to line 2. Otherwise, enter your standard deduction from Form 1040, line 36, here and go to line 6	**1**	
2	Medical and dental. Enter the smaller of Schedule A (Form 1040), line 4 **or** 2½% of Form 1040, line 34	**2**	
3	Taxes. Enter the amount from Schedule A (Form 1040), line 9	**3**	
4	Certain interest on a home mortgage **not** used to buy, build, or improve your home	**4**	
5	Miscellaneous itemized deductions. Enter the amount from Schedule A (Form 1040), line 26 . . .	**5**	
6	Refund of taxes. Enter any tax refund from Form 1040, line 10 or line 21	**6**	( )
7	Investment interest. Enter difference between regular tax and AMT deduction	**7**	
8	Post-1986 depreciation. Enter difference between regular tax and AMT depreciation	**8**	
9	Adjusted gain or loss. Enter difference between AMT and regular tax gain or loss	**9**	
10	Incentive stock options. Enter excess of AMT income over regular tax income	**10**	
11	Passive activities. Enter difference between AMT and regular tax income or loss	**11**	
12	Beneficiaries of estates and trusts. Enter the amount from Schedule K-1 (Form 1041), line 9 . . .	**12**	
13	Tax-exempt interest from private activity bonds issued after 8/7/86	**13**	

14 Other. Enter the amount, if any, for each item below and enter the total on line 14.

a Circulation expenditures .		**h** Loss limitations		
b Depletion		**i** Mining costs . . .		
c Depreciation (pre-1987) .		**j** Patron's adjustment . .		
d Installment sales . . .		**k** Pollution control facilities .		
e Intangible drilling costs .		**l** Research and experimental		
f Large partnerships . .		**m** Section 1202 exclusion . .		
g Long-term contracts . .		**n** Tax shelter farm activities .		
		o Related adjustments . .		**14**

15	**Total Adjustments and Preferences.** Combine lines 1 through 14 . . . . ▶	**15**	

Part II — Alternative Minimum Taxable Income

16	Enter the amount from **Form 1040, line 37.** If less than zero, enter as a (loss) . . . . . . ▶	**16**	
17	Net operating loss deduction, if any, from Form 1040, line 21. Enter as a positive amount	**17**	
18	If Form 1040, line 34, is over $126,600 (over $63,300 if married filing separately), and you itemized deductions, enter the amount, if any, from line 9 of the worksheet for Schedule A (Form 1040), line 28	**18**	( )
19	Combine lines 15 through 18 . . . . ▶	**19**	
20	Alternative tax net operating loss deduction. See page 6 of the instructions	**20**	
21	**Alternative Minimum Taxable Income.** Subtract line 20 from line 19. (If married filing separately and line 21 is more than $165,000, see page 7 of the instructions.) . . . . ▶	**21**	

Part III — Exemption Amount and Alternative Minimum Tax

22 **Exemption Amount.** (If this form is for a child under age 14, see page 7 of the instructions.)

IF your filing status is . . .	AND line 21 is not over . . .	THEN enter on line 22 . . .		
Single or head of household	$112,500	$33,750	}	
Married filing jointly or qualifying widow(er) .	150,000	45,000		**22**
Married filing separately.	75,000	22,500		

If line 21 is **over** the amount shown above for your filing status, see page 7 of the instructions.

23	Subtract line 22 from line 21. If zero or less, enter -0- here and on lines 26 and 28 . . . . . ▶	**23**	
24	If you reported capital gain distributions directly on Form 1040, line 13, **or** you completed Schedule D (Form 1040) and have an amount on line 25 or line 27 (or would have had an amount on either line if you had completed Part IV) (as refigured for the AMT, if necessary), go to Part IV of Form 6251 to figure line 24. **All others:** If line 23 is $175,000 or less ($87,500 or less if married filing separately), multiply line 23 by 26% (.26). Otherwise, multiply line 23 by 28% (.28) and subtract $3,500 ($1,750 if married filing separately) from the result . . . . ▶	**24**	
25	Alternative minimum tax foreign tax credit. See page 7 of the instructions	**25**	
26	Tentative minimum tax. Subtract line 25 from line 24 . . . . ▶	**26**	
27	Enter your tax from Form 1040, line 40 (minus any tax from Form 4972 and any foreign tax credit from Form 1040, line 46)	**27**	
28	**Alternative Minimum Tax.** Subtract line 27 from line 26. If zero or less, enter -0-. Enter here and on Form 1040, line 51 . . . . ▶	**28**	

For Paperwork Reduction Act Notice, see page 8 of the instructions.   Cat. No. 13600G   Form **6251** (1999)

Part IV Line 24 Computation Using Maximum Capital Gains Rates

Caution: *If you* **did not** *complete Part IV of Schedule D (Form 1040), see page 8 of the instructions before you complete this part.*

29 Enter the amount from Form 6251, line 23 . . . . **29**

30 Enter the amount from Schedule D (Form 1040), line 27 (as refigured for the AMT, if necessary). See page 8 of the instructions **30**

31 Enter the amount from Schedule D (Form 1040), line 25 (as refigured for the AMT, if necessary). See page 8 of the instructions **31**

32 Add lines 30 and 31 . . . . **32**

33 Enter the amount from Schedule D (Form 1040), line 22 (as refigured for the AMT, if necessary). See page 8 of the instructions **33**

34 Enter the **smaller** of line 32 or line 33 . . . . **34**

35 Subtract line 34 from line 29. If zero or less, enter -0- . . . . ▶ **35**

36 If line 35 is $175,000 or less ($87,500 or less if married filing separately), multiply line 35 by 26% (.26). Otherwise, multiply line 35 by 28% (.28) and subtract $3,500 ($1,750 if married filing separately) from the result **36**

37 Enter the amount from Schedule D (Form 1040), line 36 (as figured for the regular tax). See page 8 of the instructions **37**

38 Enter the **smallest** of line 29, line 30, or line 37 . . . . ▶ **38**

39 Multiply line 38 by 10% (.10) **39**

40 Enter the **smaller** of line 29 or line 30 . . . . **40**

41 Enter the amount from line 38 . . . . **41**

42 Subtract line 41 from line 40 . . . . ▶ **42**

43 Multiply line 42 by 20% (.20) **43**

Note: *If line 31 is zero or blank, go to line 48.*

44 Enter the amount from line 29 . . . . **44**

45 Add lines 35, 38, and 42 . . . . **45**

46 Subtract line 45 from line 44 . . . . **46**

47 Multiply line 46 by 25% (.25) **47**

48 Add lines 36, 39, 43, and 47 . . . . **48**

49 If line 29 is $175,000 or less ($87,500 or less if married filing separately), multiply line 29 by 26% (.26). Otherwise, multiply line 29 by 28% (.28) and subtract $3,500 ($1,750 if married filing separately) from the result **49**

50 Enter the **smaller** of line 48 or line 49 here and on line 24 . . . . **50**

Form **6251** (1999)

Form **6252**	**Installment Sale Income**	OMB No. 1545-0228
Department of the Treasury Internal Revenue Service	▶ See separate instructions. ▶ Attach to your tax return. ▶ Use a separate form for each sale or other disposition of property on the installment method.	**1999** Attachment Sequence No. **79**

Name(s) shown on return | Identifying number

1 Description of property ▶ ....

2a Date acquired (month, day, year) ▶ [___/___/___] **b** Date sold (month, day, year) ▶ [___/___/___]

3 Was the property sold to a related party after May 14, 1980? See instructions. If "No," skip line 4 . . . ☐ Yes ☐ No

4 Was the property you sold to a related party a marketable security? If "Yes," complete Part III. If "No,"
complete Part III for the year of sale and the 2 years after the year of sale . . . . ☐ Yes ☐ No

Part I **Gross Profit and Contract Price.** Complete this part for the year of sale only.

5	Selling price including mortgages and other debts. **Do not** include interest whether stated or unstated	**5**	
6	Mortgages and other debts the buyer assumed or took the property subject to, but not new mortgages the buyer got from a bank or other source .	**6**	
7	Subtract line 6 from line 5	**7**	
8	Cost or other basis of property sold	**8**	
9	Depreciation allowed or allowable	**9**	
10	Adjusted basis. Subtract line 9 from line 8	**10**	
11	Commissions and other expenses of sale.	**11**	
12	Income recapture from Form 4797, Part III. See instructions . .	**12**	
13	Add lines 10, 11, and 12	**13**	
14	Subtract line 13 from line 5. If zero or less, **stop here. Do not** complete the rest of this form .	**14**	
15	If the property described on line 1 above was your main home, enter the amount of your excluded gain. Otherwise, enter -0-. See instructions	**15**	
16	**Gross profit.** Subtract line 15 from line 14	**16**	
17	Subtract line 13 from line 6. If zero or less, enter -0-	**17**	
18	**Contract price.** Add line 7 and line 17	**18**	

Part II **Installment Sale Income.** Complete this part for the year of sale **and** any year you receive a payment or
have certain debts you must treat as a payment on installment obligations.

19	Gross profit percentage. Divide line 16 by line 18. For years after the year of sale, see instructions	**19**	
20	**For year of sale only:** Enter amount from line 17 above; otherwise, enter -0-	**20**	
21	Payments received during year. See instructions. **Do not** include interest whether stated or unstated	**21**	
22	Add lines 20 and 21	**22**	
23	Payments received in prior years. See instructions. **Do not** include interest whether stated or unstated **23**		
24	**Installment sale income.** Multiply line 22 by line 19	**24**	
25	Part of line 24 that is ordinary income under recapture rules. See instructions	**25**	
26	Subtract line 25 from line 24. Enter here and on Schedule D or Form 4797. See instructions .	**26**	

Part III **Related Party Installment Sale Income. Do not** complete if you received the final payment this tax year.

27 Name, address, and taxpayer identifying number of related party ....
....

28 Did the related party, during this tax year, resell or dispose of the property ("second disposition")? . . . ☐ Yes ☐ No

29 If the answer to question 28 is "Yes," complete lines 30 through 37 below unless one of the following conditions is
met. Check only the box that applies.

a ☐ The second disposition was more than 2 years after the first disposition (other than dispositions
of marketable securities). If this box is checked, enter the date of disposition (month, day, year) ▶ [___/___/___]

b ☐ The first disposition was a sale or exchange of stock to the issuing corporation.

c ☐ The second disposition was an involuntary conversion where the threat of conversion occurred after the first disposition.

d ☐ The second disposition occurred after the death of the original seller or buyer.

e ☐ It can be established to the satisfaction of the Internal Revenue Service that tax avoidance was not a principal purpose
for either of the dispositions. If this box is checked, attach an explanation. See instructions.

30	Selling price of property sold by related party	**30**	
31	Enter contract price from line 18 for year of first sale	**31**	
32	Enter the **smaller** of line 30 or line 31	**32**	
33	Total payments received by the end of your 1999 tax year. See instructions	**33**	
34	Subtract line 33 from line 32. If zero or less, enter -0-	**34**	
35	Multiply line 34 by the gross profit percentage on line 19 for year of first sale	**35**	
36	Part of line 35 that is ordinary income under recapture rules. See instructions	**36**	
37	Subtract line 36 from line 35. Enter here and on Schedule D or Form 4797. See instructions .	**37**	

For Paperwork Reduction Act Notice, see back of form. Cat. No. 13601R Form **6252** (1999)

Paperwork Reduction Act Notice. We ask for the information on this form to carry out the Internal Revenue laws of the United States. You are required to give us the information. We need it to ensure that you are complying with these laws and to allow us to figure and collect the right amount of tax.

You are not required to provide the information requested on a form that is subject to the Paperwork Reduction Act unless the form displays a valid OMB control number. Books or records relating to a form or its instructions must be retained as long as their contents may become material in the administration of any Internal Revenue law. Generally, tax returns and return information are confidential, as required by Internal Revenue Code section 6103.

The time needed to complete and file this form will vary depending on individual circumstances. The estimated average time is:

Recordkeeping . . 1 hr., 25 min.
**Learning about the law
or the form** . . . . . . 40 min.
Preparing the form . . . 56 min.
**Copy, assembling, and
sending the form
to the IRS** . . . . . . 20 min.

If you have comments concerning the accuracy of these time estimates or suggestions for making this form simpler, we would be happy to hear from you. See the instructions for the tax return with which this form is filed.

Form **8283** (Rev. October 1998) Department of the Treasury Internal Revenue Service	**Noncash Charitable Contributions** ▶ Attach to your tax return if you claimed a total deduction of over $500 for all contributed property. ▶ See separate instructions.	OMB No. 1545-0908 Attachment Sequence No. **55**
Name(s) shown on your income tax return		Identifying number

Note: *Figure the amount of your contribution deduction before completing this form. See your tax return instructions.*

Section A—List in this section **only** items (or groups of similar items) for which you claimed a deduction of $5,000 or less. Also, list certain publicly traded securities even if the deduction is over $5,000 (see instructions).

Part I	Information on Donated Property—If you need more space, attach a statement.

1	**(a)** Name and address of the donee organization	**(b)** Description of donated property
A		
B		
C		
D		
E		

Note: *If the amount you claimed as a deduction for an item is $500 or less, you do not have to complete columns (d), (e), and (f).*

	(c) Date of the contribution	**(d)** Date acquired by donor (mo., yr.)	**(e)** How acquired by donor	**(f)** Donor's cost or adjusted basis	**(g)** Fair market value	**(h)** Method used to determine the fair market value
A						
B						
C						
D						
E						

Part II	Other Information—Complete line 2 if you gave less than an entire interest in property listed in Part I. Complete line 3 if conditions were attached to a contribution listed in Part I.

2 If, during the year, you contributed less than the entire interest in the property, complete lines a–e.

a Enter the letter from Part I that identifies the property ▶ _____. If Part II applies to more than one property, attach a separate statement.

b Total amount claimed as a deduction for the property listed in Part I: **(1)** For this tax year ▶ _____ .
(2) For any prior tax years ▶ _____ .

c Name and address of each organization to which any such contribution was made in a prior year (complete only if different from the donee organization above):

Name of charitable organization (donee)

Address (number, street, and room or suite no.)

City or town, state, and ZIP code

d For tangible property, enter the place where the property is located or kept ▶ _____

e Name of any person, other than the donee organization, having actual possession of the property ▶ _____

3 If conditions were attached to any contribution listed in Part I, answer questions a – c and attach the required statement (see instructions).

		Yes	No
a	Is there a restriction, either temporary or permanent, on the donee's right to use or dispose of the donated property?		
b	Did you give to anyone (other than the donee organization or another organization participating with the donee organization in cooperative fundraising) the right to the income from the donated property or to the possession of the property, including the right to vote donated securities, to acquire the property by purchase or otherwise, or to designate the person having such income, possession, or right to acquire?		
c	Is there a restriction limiting the donated property for a particular use?		

For Paperwork Reduction Act Notice, see page 4 of separate instructions.   Cat. No. 62299J   Form **8283** (Rev. 10-98)

Name(s) shown on your income tax return	Identifying number

Section B—Appraisal Summary—List in this section only items (or groups of similar items) for which you claimed a deduction of more than $5,000 per item or group. **Exception.** Report contributions of certain publicly traded securities only in Section A.

If you donated art, you may have to attach the complete appraisal. See the **Note** in Part I below.

| **Part I** | **Information on Donated Property**—To be completed by the taxpayer and/or appraiser. |

4   Check type of property:

☐ Art* (contribution of $20,000 or more)   ☐ Real Estate   ☐ Gems/Jewelry   ☐ Stamp Collections

☐ Art* (contribution of less than $20,000)   ☐ Coin Collections   ☐ Books   ☐ Other

*Art includes paintings, sculptures, watercolors, prints, drawings, ceramics, antique furniture, decorative arts, textiles, carpets, silver, rare manuscripts, historical memorabilia, and other similar objects.

Note: *If your total art contribution deduction was $20,000 or more, you must attach a complete copy of the signed appraisal. See instructions.*

5	(a) Description of donated property (if you need more space, attach a separate statement)	(b) If tangible property was donated, give a brief summary of the overall physical condition at the time of the gift	(c) Appraised fair market value
A			
B			
C			
D			

	(d) Date acquired by donor (mo., yr.)	(e) How acquired by donor	(f) Donor's cost or adjusted basis	(g) For bargain sales, enter amount received	See instructions	
					(h) Amount claimed as a deduction	(i) Average trading price of securities
A						
B						
C						
D						

| **Part II** | **Taxpayer (Donor) Statement**—List each item included in Part I above that the appraisal identifies as having a value of $500 or less. See instructions. |

I declare that the following item(s) included in Part I above has to the best of my knowledge and belief an appraised value of not more than $500 (per item). Enter identifying letter from Part I and describe the specific item. See instructions. ▶ _____

Signature of taxpayer (donor) ▶ _____   Date ▶ _____

| **Part III** | **Declaration of Appraiser** |

I declare that I am not the donor, the donee, a party to the transaction in which the donor acquired the property, employed by, or related to any of the foregoing persons, or married to any person who is related to any of the foregoing persons. And, if regularly used by the donor, donee, or party to the transaction, I performed the majority of my appraisals during my tax year for other persons.

Also, I declare that I hold myself out to the public as an appraiser or perform appraisals on a regular basis; and that because of my qualifications as described in the appraisal, I am qualified to make appraisals of the type of property being valued. I certify that the appraisal fees were not based on a percentage of the appraised property value. Furthermore, I understand that a false or fraudulent overstatement of the property value as described in the qualified appraisal or this appraisal summary may subject me to the penalty under section 6701(a) (aiding and abetting the understatement of tax liability). I affirm that I have not been barred from presenting evidence or testimony by the Director of Practice.

Sign Here

Signature ▶	Title ▶	Date of appraisal ▶

Business address (including room or suite no.)	Identifying number
City or town, state, and ZIP code	

| **Part IV** | **Donee Acknowledgment**—To be completed by the charitable organization. |

This charitable organization acknowledges that it is a qualified organization under section 170(c) and that it received the donated property as described in Section B, Part I, above on ▶ _____

(Date)

Furthermore, this organization affirms that in the event it sells, exchanges, or otherwise disposes of the property described in Section B, Part I (or any portion thereof) within 2 years after the date of receipt, it will file **Form 8282,** Donee Information Return, with the IRS and give the donor a copy of that form. This acknowledgment does not represent agreement with the claimed fair market value.

Does the organization intend to use the property for an unrelated use? . . . . ▶ ☐ Yes   ☐ No

Name of charitable organization (donee)	Employer identification number
Address (number, street, and room or suite no.)	City or town, state, and ZIP code
Authorized signature	Title	Date

Form **8582**	**Passive Activity Loss Limitations**	OMB No. 1545-1008
Department of the Treasury Internal Revenue Service (99)	▶ See separate instructions. ▶ Attach to Form 1040 or Form 1041.	**19**99 Attachment Sequence No. **88**

Name(s) shown on return

Identifying number

Part I — 1999 Passive Activity Loss

Caution: *See the instructions for Worksheets 1 and 2 on page 7 before completing Part I.*

Rental Real Estate Activities With Active Participation (For the definition of active participation see **Active Participation in a Rental Real Estate Activity** on page 3.)

1a Activities with net income (enter the amount from Worksheet 1, column (a))	**1a**	
b Activities with net loss (enter the amount from Worksheet 1, column (b))	**1b** (	)
c Prior years unallowed losses (enter the amount from Worksheet 1, column (c))	**1c** (	)
d Combine lines 1a, 1b, and 1c	**1d**	

All Other Passive Activities

2a Activities with net income (enter the amount from Worksheet 2, column (a))	**2a**	
b Activities with net loss (enter the amount from Worksheet 2, column (b))	**2b** (	)
c Prior years unallowed losses (enter the amount from Worksheet 2, column (c))	**2c** (	)
d Combine lines 2a, 2b, and 2c	**2d**	

3 Combine lines 1d and 2d. If the result is net income or zero, all losses are allowed, including any prior year unallowed losses entered on line 1c or 2c. **Do not** complete Form 8582. Take the losses to the form or schedule you normally report them on.
If this line and line 1d are losses, go to Part II. Otherwise, enter -0- on line 9 and go to line 10 . | **3** |

Part II — Special Allowance for Rental Real Estate With Active Participation

Note: *Enter all numbers in Part II as positive amounts. See page 7 for examples.*

Note: *If your filing status is married filing separately and you lived with your spouse at any time during the year, do not complete Part II. Instead, enter -0- on line 9 and go to line 10.*

4 Enter the **smaller** of the loss on line 1d or the loss on line 3	**4**	
5 Enter $150,000. If married filing separately, see page 7	**5**	
6 Enter modified adjusted gross income, but not less than zero (see page 7)	**6**	

Note: *If line 6 is greater than or equal to line 5, skip lines 7 and 8, enter -0- on line 9, and go to line 10. Otherwise, go to line 7.*

7 Subtract line 6 from line 5	**7**	
8 Multiply line 7 by 50% (.5). **Do not** enter more than $25,000. If married filing separately, see page 8	**8**	
9 Enter the **smaller** of line 4 or line 8	**9**	

Part III — Total Losses Allowed

10 Add the income, if any, on lines 1a and 2a and enter the total	**10**	
11 **Total losses allowed from all passive activities for 1999.** Add lines 9 and 10. See page 9 to find out how to report the losses on your tax return	**11**	

For Paperwork Reduction Act Notice, see page 11.

Cat. No. 63704F

Form **8582** (1999)

Caution: *The worksheets are not required to be filed with your tax return and may be detached before filing Form 8582. Keep a copy of the worksheets for your records.*

Worksheet 1—For Form 8582, Lines 1a, 1b, and 1c (See page 7.)

Name of activity	Current year		Prior years	Overall gain or loss	
	(a) Net income (line 1a)	(b) Net loss (line 1b)	(c) Unallowed loss (line 1c)	(d) Gain	(e) Loss
Total. Enter on Form 8582, lines 1a, 1b, and 1c. . . . . ▶					

Worksheet 2—For Form 8582, Lines 2a, 2b, and 2c (See page 7.)

Name of activity	Current year		Prior years	Overall gain or loss	
	(a) Net income (line 2a)	(b) Net loss (line 2b)	(c) Unallowed loss (line 2c)	(d) Gain	(e) Loss
Total. Enter on Form 8582, lines 2a, 2b, and 2c. . . . . ▶					

Worksheet 3—Use this worksheet if an amount is shown on Form 8582, line 9 (See page 8.)

Name of activity	Form or schedule to be reported on	(a) Loss	(b) Ratio	(c) Special allowance	(d) Subtract column (c) from column (a)
Total . . . . ▶			1.00		

Worksheet 4—Allocation of Unallowed Losses (See page 8.)

Name of activity	Form or schedule to be reported on	(a) Loss	(b) Ratio	(c) Unallowed loss
Total . . . . ▶			1.00	

Worksheet 5—Allowed Losses (See page 8.)

Name of activity	Form or schedule to be reported on	(a) Loss	(b) Unallowed loss	(c) Allowed loss
Total . . . . ▶				

Form **8615**

Department of the Treasury
Internal Revenue Service (99)

**Tax for Children Under Age 14
Who Have Investment Income of More Than $1,400**

▶ Attach ONLY to the child's Form 1040, Form 1040A, or Form 1040NR.

OMB No. 1545-0998

1999

Attachment
Sequence No. **33**

Child's name shown on return | Child's social security number

A Parent's name (first, initial, and last). **Caution:** *See instructions on back before completing.*

B Parent's social security number

C Parent's filing status (check one):

☐ Single ☐ Married filing jointly ☐ Married filing separately ☐ Head of household ☐ Qualifying widow(er)

Part I	**Child's Net Investment Income**		
1	Enter the child's investment income, such as taxable interest and dividends. See instructions. If this amount is $1,400 or less, **stop;** do not file this form	1	
2	If the child **did not** itemize deductions on **Schedule A** (Form 1040 or Form 1040NR), enter $1,400. If the child **did** itemize deductions, see instructions	2	
3	Subtract line 2 from line 1. If the result is zero or less, **stop;** do not complete the rest of this form but **do** attach it to the child's return	3	
4	Enter the child's **taxable income** from Form 1040, line 39; Form 1040A, line 24; or Form 1040NR, line 38	4	
5	Enter the **smaller** of line 3 or line 4	5	

Part II	**Tentative Tax Based on the Tax Rate of the Parent Listed on Line A**		
6	Enter the parent's **taxable income** from Form 1040, line 39; Form 1040A, line 24; Form 1040EZ, line 6; TeleFile Tax Record, line K; Form 1040NR, line 38; or Form 1040NR-EZ, line 14. If less than zero, enter -0-	6	
7	Enter the total net investment income, if any, from Forms 8615, line 5, of **all other** children of the parent identified above. **Do not** include the amount from line 5 above	7	
8	Add lines 5, 6, and 7	8	
9	Enter the tax on line 8 based on the **parent's** filing status. See instructions. If the **Capital Gain Tax Worksheet** or **Schedule D** or **J** (Form 1040) is used to figure the tax, check here ▶ ☐	9	
10	Enter the parent's tax from Form 1040, line 40; Form 1040A, line 25; Form 1040EZ, line 10; TeleFile Tax Record, line K; Form 1040NR, line 39; or Form 1040NR-EZ, line 15. If any tax is from **Form 4972** or **8814,** see instructions. If the **Capital Gain Tax Worksheet** or **Schedule D** or **J** (Form 1040) was used to figure the tax, check here . . . . ▶ ☐	10	
11	Subtract line 10 from line 9 and enter the result. If line 7 is blank, also enter this amount on line 13 and go to **Part III**	11	
12a	Add lines 5 and 7	12a		
b	Divide line 5 by line 12a. Enter the result as a decimal (rounded to at least three places) . .	12b	× .
13	Multiply line 11 by line 12b	13	

Part III	**Child's Tax**—If lines 4 and 5 above are the same, enter -0- on line 15 and go to line 16.		
14	Subtract line 5 from line 4	14		
15	Enter the tax on line 14 based on the **child's** filing status. See instructions. If the **Capital Gain Tax Worksheet** or **Schedule D** or **J** (Form 1040) is used to figure the tax, check here ▶ ☐	15	
16	Add lines 13 and 15	16	
17	Enter the tax on line 4 based on the **child's** filing status. See instructions. If the **Capital Gain Tax Worksheet** or **Schedule D** or **J** (Form 1040) is used to figure the tax, check here ▶ ☐	17	
18	Enter the **larger** of line 16 or line 17 here and on Form 1040, line 40; Form 1040A, line 25; or Form 1040NR, line 39	18	

General Instructions

Purpose of Form

For children under age 14, investment income over $1,400 is taxed at the parent's rate if the parent's rate is higher than the child's rate. If the child's investment income is more than $1,400, use this form to figure the child's tax.

See **Pub. 929,** Tax Rules for Children and Dependents, if the child, the parent, or any of the parent's other children under age 14 received capital gain distributions or farm income. It has information on how

to figure the tax using the **Capital Gain Tax Worksheet** or **Schedule D** or **J,** which may result in less tax.

Investment Income

For this form, "investment income" includes all taxable income other than earned income as defined on page 2. It includes taxable interest, dividends, capital gains, rents, royalties, etc. It also includes taxable social security benefits, pension and annuity income, and income (other than earned income) received as the beneficiary of a trust.

Who Must File

Generally, Form 8615 must be filed for any child who was under age 14 on January 1, 2000, had more than $1,400 of investment income, and is required to file a tax return. But if neither parent was alive on December 31, 1999, do not use Form 8615. Instead, figure the child's tax in the normal manner.

Note: *The parent may be able to elect to report the child's interest and dividends (including capital gain distributions) on the parent's return. If the parent makes this election, the child will not have to file a return or Form 8615. However, the Federal*

For Paperwork Reduction Act Notice, see back of form.   Cat. No. 64113U   Form **8615** (1999) *income tax on the child's income, including captial gain distributions, may be **higher** if this election is made. For more details, see **Form 8814**, Parents' Election To Report Child's Interest and Dividends.*

Additional Information

For more details, see Pub. 929.

Incomplete Information for Parent or Other Children

If the parent's taxable income or filing status or the net investment income of the parent's other children is not known by the due date of the child's return, reasonable estimates may be used. Enter "Estimated" next to the appropriate line(s) of Form 8615. For more details, see Pub. 929.

Amended Return

If after the child's return is filed the parent's taxable income changes or the net investment income of any of the parent's other children changes, the child's tax must be refigured using the adjusted amounts. If the child's tax changes, file **Form 1040X**, Amended U.S. Individual Income Tax Return, to correct the child's tax.

Alternative Minimum Tax

A child whose tax is figured on Form 8615 may owe the alternative minimum tax. For details, see **Form 6251**, Alternative Minimum Tax—Individuals, and its instructions.

Line Instructions

Lines A and B

If the child's parents were married to each other and filed a joint return, enter the name and social security number (SSN) of the parent who is listed first on the joint return.

If the parents were married but filed separate returns, enter the name and SSN of the parent who had the **higher** taxable income. If you do not know which parent had the higher taxable income, see Pub. 929.

If the parents were unmarried, treated as unmarried for Federal income tax purposes, or separated either by a divorce or separate maintenance decree, enter the name and SSN of the parent who had custody of the child for most of the year (the custodial parent).

Exception. If the custodial parent remarried and filed a joint return with his or her new spouse, enter the name and SSN of the person listed first on the joint return, even if that person is not the child's parent. If the custodial parent and his or her new spouse filed separate returns, enter the name and SSN of the person with the **higher** taxable income, even if that person is not the child's parent.

Note: *If the parents were unmarried but lived together during the year with the child, enter the name and SSN of the parent who had the **higher** taxable income.*

Child's Investment Income Worksheet—Line 1 (keep a copy for your records)

1. Enter the amount from the child's Form 1040, line 22; Form 1040A, line 14; or Form 1040NR, line 23, whichever applies . . . . . **1.** _____

2. Enter the child's **earned income** (defined on this page) plus any deduction the child claims on Form 1040, line 30, or Form 1040NR, line 30, whichever applies . . . . **2.** _____

3. Subtract line 2 from line 1. Enter the result here and on Form 8615, line 1 . . . . **3.** _____

Line 1

If the child had no earned income (defined later), enter the child's adjusted gross income from Form 1040, line 34; Form 1040A, line 19; or Form 1040NR, line 34.

If the child had earned income, use the worksheet on this page to figure the amount to enter on line 1. But if the child files **Form 2555** or **2555-EZ** (relating to foreign earned income), has a net loss from self-employment, or claims a net operating loss deduction, you **must** use the worksheet in Pub. 929 instead.

Earned income includes wages, tips, and other payments received for personal services performed. Generally, it is the total of the amounts reported on Form 1040, lines 7, 12, and 18; Form 1040A, line 7; or Form 1040NR, lines 8, 13, and 19.

Line 2

If the child itemized deductions, enter the **greater** of:

● $1,400, **or**

● $700 plus the portion of the amount on **Schedule A** (Form 1040), line 28 (or line 17 of the Form 1040NR Schedule A), that is directly connected with the production of the investment income on Form 8615, line 1.

Line 6

If the parent filed a joint return, enter the taxable income shown on that return even if the parent's spouse is not the child's parent.

Line 9

Figure the tax using the Tax Table, Tax Rate Schedules, the **Capital Gain Tax Worksheet**, or **Schedule D** or **J,** whichever applies. If any net capital gain is included on line 5, 6, or 7, Schedule D must be used to figure the tax unless the Capital Gain Tax Worksheet may be used. See Pub. 929 for details on how to figure the net capital gain included on line 8. If any farm income is included on line 5, 6, or 7, the tax may be less if you use Schedule J.

Line 10

If the parent filed a joint return, enter the tax shown on that return even if the parent's spouse is not the child's parent. If the parent filed **Form 4972, do not** include any tax from that form on line 10. If the parent filed **Form 8814,** enter "Form 8814" and the total tax from line 9 of Form(s) 8814 on the dotted line next to line 10 of Form 8615.

Line 15

Figure the tax using the Tax Table, Tax Rate Schedule X, the Capital Gain Tax Worksheet, or Schedule D or J, whichever applies. If line 14 includes any net capital gain, use Schedule D to figure the tax unless the Capital Gain Tax Worksheet may be used. See Pub. 929 for details on how to figure the net capital gain included on line 14. If any farm income is included on line 14, the tax may be less if you use Schedule J.

Line 17

Figure the tax as if these rules did not apply. For example, if the child has a net capital gain, use Schedule D to figure the child's tax unless the Capital Gain Tax Worksheet may be used.

Paperwork Reduction Act Notice. We ask for the information on this form to carry out the Internal Revenue laws of the United States. You are required to give us the information. We need it to ensure that you are complying with these laws and to allow us to figure and collect the right amount of tax.

You are not required to provide the information requested on a form that is subject to the Paperwork Reduction Act unless the form displays a valid OMB control number. Books or records relating to a form or its instructions must be retained as long as their contents may become material in the administration of any Internal Revenue law. Generally, tax returns and return information are confidential, as required by Internal Revenue Code section 6103.

The time needed to complete and file this form will vary depending on individual circumstances. The estimated average time is: **Recordkeeping,** 13 min.; **Learning about the law or the form,** 13 min.; **Preparing the form,** 45 min.; and **Copying, assembling, and sending the form to the IRS,** 17 min.

If you have comments concerning the accuracy of these time estimates or suggestions for making this form simpler, we would be happy to hear from you. See the instructions for the tax return with which this form is filed.

Form **8812**

Department of the Treasury
Internal Revenue Service

Additional Child Tax Credit

1040
1040A
→
8812

Complete and attach to Form 1040 or 1040A.

OMB No. 1545-1620

1999

Attachment
Sequence No. **47**

Name(s) shown on return

Your social security number

Before you begin:
✓ Complete the Child Tax Credit Worksheet that applies to you. See the instructions for Form 1040, line 43, or Form 1040A, line 28.

✓ Have your W-2 form(s) available.

✓ If you, or your spouse if filing jointly, had more than one employer for 1999 and total wages of over $53,700, figure any excess social security and railroad retirement (RRTA) taxes withheld. See the instructions for Form 1040, line 62, or Form 1040A, line 39.

1	Enter the total of the social security and Medicare taxes from Form(s) W-2, boxes 4 and 6. • If married filing jointly, include your spouse's amounts with yours. • If you worked for a railroad, see the instructions on back.	**1**
2	**1040 filers:** Enter the total of the amounts from Form 1040, lines 27 and 52, plus any uncollected social security and Medicare or RRTA taxes included on line 56. **1040A filers:** Enter -0-.	**2**
3	Add lines 1 and 2.	**3**
4	**1040 filers:** Enter the total of the amounts from Form 1040, lines 59a and 62. **1040A filers:** Enter the total of the amount from Form 1040A, line 37a, plus any excess social security and RRTA taxes withheld that you entered to the left of line 39.	**4**

5 Is the amount on line 3 more than the amount on line 4?

☐ **No.** (STOP)
You cannot take this credit.
Complete the rest of your
Form 1040 or Form 1040A.

☐ **Yes** Subtract line 4 from line 3,

5

6 Enter the amount from line 1 of your Child Tax Credit Worksheet on page 34 of the Form 1040 instructions or page 36 of the Form 1040A instructions. If you used Pub. 972, enter the amount from line 8 of the worksheet on page 2 of the publication.

6

7 Enter the amount from Form 1040, line 43, or Form 1040A, line 28.

7

8 Is the amount on line 6 more than the amount on line 7?

☐ **No.** (STOP)
You cannot take this credit.
Complete the rest of your
Form 1040 or Form 1040A.

☐ **Yes.** Subtract line 7 from line 6.

8

9 Is the amount on line 5 more than the amount on line 8?

☐ **No.** Enter the amount from line 5.

☐ **Yes.** Enter the amount from line 8.

} **This is your additional child tax credit.**

9

1040
1040A
◄
Enter this amount on Form 1040, line 60, or Form 1040A, line 38.

Cat. No. 10644E Form **8812** (1999)

Instructions

Purpose of Form

Use Form 8812 to figure the additional child tax credit.

 The additional child tax credit may give you a refund even if you do not owe any tax.

Who Should Use Form 8812

First, complete the Child Tax Credit Worksheet that applies to you. See the instructions for Form 1040, line 43, or Form 1040A, line 28. Then, use the following chart to see if you should use Form 8812.

IF you completed the Child Tax Credit Worksheet in . . .	AND on the worksheet . . .	THEN . . .
The Instructions for Form 1040 or Form 1040A	• You answered "Yes" on line 4 or line 5, **and** • Line 1 is $1,500 or more	Use Form 8812 to see if you can take the additional child tax credit.
Pub. 972	• You answered "Yes" on line 13, **and** • Line 1 is $1,500 or more	

Railroad Employees

If you worked for a railroad, include the following taxes in the total on line 1 of Form 8812.

• Tier 1 tax withheld from your pay. This tax should be shown in box 14 of your W-2 form(s) and identified as "Tier 1 tax."

• If you were an employee representative, 50% of the total Tier 1 tax and Tier 1 Medicare tax you paid for 1999.

Paperwork Reduction Act Notice

We ask for the information on this form to carry out the Internal Revenue laws of the United States. You are required to give us the information. We need it to ensure that you are complying with these laws and to allow us to figure and collect the right amount of tax.

You are not required to provide the information requested on a form that is subject to the Paperwork Reduction Act unless the form displays a valid OMB control number. Books or records relating to a form or its instructions must be retained as long as their contents may become material in the administration of any Internal Revenue law. Generally, tax returns and return information are confidential, as required by Internal Revenue Code section 6103.

The time needed to complete and file this form will vary depending on individual circumstances. The estimated average time is:

Recordkeeping	7 min.
Learning about the law or the form	5 min.
Preparing the form	18 min.
Copying, assembling, and sending the form to the IRS	20 min.

If you have comments concerning the accuracy of these time estimates or suggestions for making this form simpler, we would be happy to hear from you. See the Instructions for Form 1040 or Form 1040A.

Form **8814**

Department of the Treasury
Internal Revenue Service (99)

**Parents' Election To Report
Child's Interest and Dividends**
▶ See instructions below and on back.
▶ Attach to parents' Form 1040 or Form 1040NR.

OMB No. 1545-1128

1999

Attachment
Sequence No. **40**

Name(s) shown on your return

Your social security number

Caution: *The Federal income tax on your child's income, including capital gain distributions, may be less if you file a separate tax return for the child instead of making this election. This is because you cannot take certain tax benefits that your child could take on his or her own return. For details, see* **Tax Benefits You May Not Take** *on the back.*

A	Child's name (first, initial, and last)	B Child's social security number

c If more than one Form 8814 is attached, check here . . . . ▶ ☐

Part I — Child's Interest and Dividends To Report on Your Return

1a	Enter your child's **taxable** interest. If this amount is different from the amounts shown on the child's Forms 1099-INT and 1099-OID, see the instructions	**1a**		
b	Enter your child's **tax-exempt** interest. **DO NOT** include this amount on line 1a	**1b**		
2	Enter your child's ordinary dividends, including any Alaska Permanent Fund dividends. If your child received any ordinary dividends as a nominee, see the instructions	**2**		
3	Enter your child's capital gain distributions. If your child received any capital gain distributions as a nominee, see the instructions	**3**		
4	Add lines 1a, 2, and 3. If the total is $1,400 or less, skip lines 5 and 6 and go to line 7. If the total is $7,000 or more, **do not** file this form. Your child **must** file his or her own return to report the income	**4**		
5	Base amount	**5**	1,400	00
6	Subtract line 5 from line 4. If you checked the box on line C above or if you entered an amount on line 3, see the instructions. Also, include this amount in the total on Form 1040, line 21, or Form 1040NR, line 21. In the space next to line 21, enter "Form 8814" and show the amount. Go to line 7 below . . . . ▶	**6**		

Part II — Tax on the First $1,400 of Child's Interest and Dividends

7	Amount not taxed	**7**	700	00
8	Subtract line 7 from line 4. If the result is zero or less, enter -0-	**8**		
9	**Tax.** Is the amount on line 8 less than $700? ☐ **No.** Enter $105 here and see the **Note** below. ☐ **Yes.** Multiply line 8 by 15% (.15). Enter the result here and see the **Note** below.	**9**		

Note: *If you checked the box on line C above, see the instructions. Otherwise, include the amount from line 9 in the tax you enter on Form 1040, line 40, or Form 1040NR, line 39. Be sure to check box* **a** *on Form 1040, line 40, or Form 1040NR, line 39.*

General Instructions

Purpose of Form. Use this form if you elect to report your child's income on your return. If you do, your child will not have to file a return. You can make this election if your child meets **all** of the following conditions.

● Was under age 14 on January 1, 2000.

● Is required to file a 1999 return.

● Had income only from interest and dividends, including Alaska Permanent Fund dividends.

● Had gross income for 1999 that was less than $7,000.

● Had no estimated tax payments for 1999 (including any overpayment of tax from his or her 1998 return applied to 1999 estimated tax).

● Had no Federal income tax withheld from his or her income.

You must also qualify. See **Parents Who Qualify To Make the Election** below.

How To Make the Election. To make the election, complete and attach Form(s) 8814 to your tax return and file your return by the due date (including extensions). A separate Form 8814 must be filed for **each** child whose income you choose to report.

Parents Who Qualify To Make the Election. You qualify to make this election if you file Form 1040 or Form 1040NR and **any** of the following apply.

● You are filing a joint return for 1999 with the child's other parent.

● You and the child's other parent were married to each other but file separate

returns for 1999 AND you had the **higher** taxable income. If you do not know if you had the higher taxable income, see **Pub. 929,** Tax Rules for Children and Dependents.

● You were unmarried, treated as unmarried for Federal income tax purposes, or separated from the child's other parent by a divorce or separate maintenance decree. You must have had custody of your child for most of the year (you were the custodial parent). If you were the custodial parent and you remarried, you may make the election on a joint return with your new spouse. But if you and your new spouse do not file a joint return, you qualify to make the election only if you had **higher** taxable income than your new spouse.

(continued)

For Paperwork Reduction Act Notice, see back of form.   Cat. No. 10750J   Form **8814** (1999)

Note: *If you and the child's other parent were not married but lived together during the year with the child, you qualify to make the election only if you are the parent with the **higher** taxable income.*

Tax Benefits You May Not Take. If you elect to report your child's income on your return, you may not take any of the following deductions that your child could take on his or her own return.

- Standard deduction of $1,750 for a blind child.
- Penalty on early withdrawal of child's savings.
- Itemized deductions such as child's investment expenses or charitable contributions.

If your child received **capital gain distributions,** you may pay up to $35 more tax on those distributions if you make this election instead of filing a separate tax return for the child. This is because the tax rate on the child's income between $700 and $1,400 is 15% if you make the election. However, if you file a separate return for the child, the tax rate on those distributions may be 10% because of the preferential capital gains tax rates.

If any of the above apply to your child, first figure the tax on your child's income as if he or she is filing a return. Next, figure the tax as if you are electing to report your child's income on **your** return. Then, compare the methods to determine which results in the lower tax.

Alternative Minimum Tax. If your child received tax-exempt interest (or exempt-interest dividends paid by a regulated investment company) from certain private activity bonds, you must take this into account in determining if you owe the alternative minimum tax. See **Form 6251,** Alternative Minimum Tax—Individuals, and its instructions for details.

Investment Interest Expense. Your child's income (other than Alaska Permanent Fund dividends and capital gain distributions) that you report on your return is considered to be **your** investment income for purposes of figuring your investment interest expense deduction. If your child received Alaska Permanent Fund dividends or capital gain distributions, see **Pub. 550,** Investment Income and Expenses, to figure the amount you may treat as your investment income.

Foreign Accounts and Trusts. Complete Part III of **Schedule B** (Form 1040) for your child if he or she **(1)** had a foreign financial account, or **(2)** received a distribution from, or was the grantor of, or transferor to, a foreign trust. If you answer "Yes" to either question, you must file this Schedule B with **your** return. Enter "Form 8814" next to line 7a or line 8, whichever applies. Also, complete line 7b if applicable.

Change of Address. If your child filed a return for a year before 1999 and the address shown on the last return filed is not your child's current address, be sure to notify the IRS, in writing, of the new address. To do this, you may:

- Use **Form 8822,** Change of Address, or
- Write to the Internal Revenue Service Center where your child's last return was filed, or
- Write to the Chief, Customer Service Division, in your local IRS district office.

Additional Information. See Pub. 929 for more details.

Line Instructions

Name and Social Security Number. If filing a joint return, include your spouse's name but enter the social security number of the person whose name is shown first on the return.

Line 1a. Enter **ALL** taxable interest income received by your child in 1999. If your child received a **Form 1099-INT** for tax-exempt interest, such as from municipal bonds, enter the amount and "Tax-exempt interest" on the dotted line next to line 1a. **Do not** include this interest in the total for line 1a but be sure to include it on line 1b.

If your child received, as a **nominee,** interest that actually belongs to another person, enter the amount and "ND" (for nominee distribution) on the dotted line next to line 1a. **Do not** include amounts received as a nominee in the total for line 1a.

If your child had accrued interest that was paid to the seller of a bond, amortizable bond premium (ABP) allowed as a reduction to interest income, or if any original issue discount (OID) included on line 1a is less than the amount shown on your child's **Form 1099-OID,** follow the instructions above for nominee interest to see how to report the nontaxable amounts. But on the dotted line next to line 1a, enter the nontaxable amount and "Accrued interest," "ABP adjustment," or "OID adjustment," whichever applies. **Do not** include any nontaxable amounts in the total for line 1a.

Line 1b. If your child received any tax-exempt interest income, such as from certain state and municipal bonds, report it on line 1b. Also, include any exempt-interest dividends your child received as a shareholder in a mutual fund or other regulated investment company.

Note: *If line 1b includes tax-exempt interest or exempt-interest dividends paid by a regulated investment company from private activity bonds, see **Alternative Minimum Tax** on this page.*

Line 2. Enter the ordinary dividends received by your child in 1999. Ordinary dividends should be shown in box 1 of **Form 1099-DIV.** Also, include ordinary dividends your child received through a partnership, an S corporation, or an estate or trust.

If your child received, as a **nominee,** ordinary dividends that actually belong to another person, enter the amount and "ND" on the dotted line next to line 2. **Do not** include amounts received as a nominee in the total for line 2.

Line 3. Enter the capital gain distributions received by your child in 1999. Capital gain distributions should be shown in box 2a of Form 1099-DIV. Also, see the instructions for line 6.

If your child received, as a **nominee,** capital gain distributions that actually belong to another person, enter the amount and "ND" on the dotted line next to line 3. **Do not** include amounts received as a nominee in the total for line 3.

Line 6. If you checked the box on line C, add the amounts from line 6 of **all** your Forms 8814. Include the total on line 21 of Form 1040 or Form 1040NR, whichever applies. Be sure to enter "Form 8814" and the total of the line 6 amounts in the space next to line 21.

If your child received capital gain distributions, part or all of those distributions must be reported on your **Schedule D** (Form 1040) or on Form 1040 or on Form 1040NR instead of on Form 8814, line 6. See Pub. 929 for details.

Line 9. If you checked the box on line C, add the amounts from line 9 of **all** your Forms 8814. Include the total on Form 1040, line 40, or Form 1040NR, line 39. Be sure to check box **a** on that line.

Paperwork Reduction Act Notice. We ask for the information on this form to carry out the Internal Revenue laws of the United States. You are required to give us the information. We need it to ensure that you are complying with these laws and to allow us to figure and collect the right amount of tax.

You are not required to provide the information requested on a form that is subject to the Paperwork Reduction Act unless the form displays a valid OMB control number. Books or records relating to a form or its instructions must be retained as long as their contents may become material in the administration of any Internal Revenue law. Generally, tax returns and return information are confidential, as required by Internal Revenue Code section 6103.

The time needed to complete and file this form will vary depending on individual circumstances. The estimated average time is: **Recordkeeping,** 26 min.; **Learning about the law or the form,** 10 min.; **Preparing the form,** 24 min.; and **Copying, assembling, and sending the form to the IRS,** 17 min.

If you have comments concerning the accuracy of these time estimates or suggestions for making this form simpler, we would be happy to hear from you. See the instructions for the tax return with which this form is filed.

Form **8822**
(Rev. Oct. 1997)
Department of the Treasury
Internal Revenue Service

Change of Address

▶ Please type or print.

▶ See instructions on back.　　▶ Do not attach this form to your return.

OMB No. 1545-1163

Part I	Complete This Part To Change Your Home Mailing Address

Check **ALL** boxes this change affects:

1 ☐ Individual income tax returns (Forms 1040, 1040A, 1040EZ, 1040NR, etc.)

　　▶ If your last return was a joint return and you are now establishing a residence separate
　　　from the spouse with whom you filed that return, check here . . . . ▶ ☐

2 ☐ Gift, estate, or generation-skipping transfer tax returns (Forms 706, 709, etc.)

　　▶ For Forms 706 and 706-NA, enter the decedent's name and social security number below.

　　▶ Decedent's name　　　　　　　　　　　　　▶ Social security number

3a Your name (first name, initial, and last name)	3b Your social security number
4a Spouse's name (first name, initial, and last name)	4b Spouse's social security number

5　Prior name(s). See instructions.

6a Old address (no., street, city or town, state, and ZIP code). If a P.O. box or foreign address, see instructions.	Apt. no.
6b Spouse's old address, if different from line 6a (no., street, city or town, state, and ZIP code). If a P.O. box or foreign address, see instructions.	Apt. no.
7 New address (no., street, city or town, state, and ZIP code). If a P.O. box or foreign address, see instructions.	Apt. no.

Part II	Complete This Part To Change Your Business Mailing Address or Business Location

Check **ALL** boxes this change affects:

8 ☐ Employment, excise, and other business returns (Forms 720, 940, 940-EZ, 941, 990, 1041, 1065, 1120, etc.)

9 ☐ Employee plan returns (Forms 5500, 5500-C/R, and 5500-EZ). See instructions.

10 ☐ Business location

11a Business name	11b Employer identification number
12 Old mailing address (no., street, city or town, state, and ZIP code). If a P.O. box or foreign address, see instructions.	Room or suite no.
13 New mailing address (no., street, city or town, state, and ZIP code). If a P.O. box or foreign address, see instructions.	Room or suite no.
14 New business location (no., street, city or town, state, and ZIP code). If a foreign address, see instructions.	Room or suite no.

Part III	Signature

Daytime telephone number of person to contact (optional) ▶ (　　)　　　

Please Sign Here

▶ _____ Your signature　　　Date

▶ _____ If Part II completed, signature of owner, officer, or representative　Date

▶ _____ If joint return, spouse's signature　Date

Title

For Privacy Act and Paperwork Reduction Act Notice, see back of form.　　Cat. No. 12081V　　Form **8822** (Rev. 10-97)

Purpose of Form

You may use Form 8822 to notify the Internal Revenue Service if you changed your home or business mailing address or your business location. Generally, complete only one Form 8822 to change your home and business addresses. If this change also affects the mailing address for your children who filed income tax returns, complete and file a separate Form 8822 for each child. If you are a representative signing for the taxpayer, attach to Form 8822 a copy of your power of attorney.

Note: *If you moved after you filed your return and you are expecting a refund, also notify the post office serving your old address. This will help forward your check to your new address.*

Prior Name(s)

If you or your spouse changed your name because of marriage, divorce, etc., complete line 5. Also, be sure to notify the **Social Security Administration** of your new name so that it has the same name in its records that you have on your tax return. This prevents delays in processing your return and issuing refunds. It also safeguards your future social security benefits.

Addresses

Be sure to include any apartment, room, or suite number in the space provided.

P.O. Box

If your post office does not deliver mail to your street address, show your P.O. box number instead of your street address.

Foreign Address

If your address is outside the United States or its possessions or territories, enter the information in the following order: city, province or state, and country. Follow the country's practice for entering the postal code. Please **do not** abbreviate the country name.

Employee Plan Returns

A change in the mailing address for employee plan returns must be shown on a separate Form 8822 unless the **Exception** below applies.

Exception. If the employee plan returns were filed with the same service center as your other returns (individual, business, employment, gift, estate, etc.), you do not have to use a separate Form 8822. See **Where To File** on this page.

Signature

If you are completing Part II, the owner, an officer, or a representative must sign. An officer is the president, vice president, treasurer, chief accounting officer, etc. A representative is a person who has a valid power of attorney to handle tax matters.

Where To File

Send this form to the **Internal Revenue Service Center** shown below for your old mailing address. But if you checked the box on line 9 (employee plan returns), send it to the address shown in the far right column.

IF your old mailing address was in . . .	THEN use this address. . .
Florida, Georgia, South Carolina	Atlanta, GA 39901
New Jersey, New York (New York City and counties of Nassau, Rockland, Suffolk, and Westchester)	Holtsville, NY 00501
New York (all other counties), Connecticut, Maine, Massachusetts, New Hampshire, Rhode Island, Vermont	Andover, MA 05501
Alaska, Arizona, California (counties of Alpine, Amador, Butte, Calaveras, Colusa, Contra Costa, Del Norte, El Dorado, Glenn, Humboldt, Lake, Lassen, Marin, Mendocino, Modoc, Napa, Nevada, Placer, Plumas, Sacramento, San Joaquin, Shasta, Sierra, Siskiyou, Solano, Sonoma, Sutter, Tehama, Trinity, Yolo, and Yuba), Colorado, Idaho, Montana, Nebraska, Nevada, North Dakota, Oregon, South Dakota, Utah, Washington, Wyoming	Ogden, UT 84201
California (all other counties), Hawaii	Fresno, CA 93888
Indiana, Kentucky, Michigan, Ohio, West Virginia	Cincinnati, OH 45999
Kansas, New Mexico, Oklahoma, Texas	Austin, TX 73301
Delaware, District of Columbia, Maryland, Pennsylvania, Virginia	Philadelphia, PA 19255
Alabama, Arkansas, Louisiana, Mississippi, North Carolina, Tennessee	Memphis, TN 37501
Illinois, Iowa, Minnesota, Missouri, Wisconsin	Kansas City, MO 64999
American Samoa	Philadelphia, PA 19255
Guam: Permanent residents	Department of Revenue and Taxation Government of Guam P.O. Box 23607 GMF, GU 96921
Guam: Nonpermanent residents Puerto Rico (or if excluding income under Internal Revenue Code section 933) Virgin Islands: Nonpermanent residents	Philadelphia, PA 19255
Virgin Islands: Permanent residents	V. I. Bureau of Internal Revenue 9601 Estate Thomas Charlotte Amalie St. Thomas, VI 00802
Foreign country: U.S. citizens and those filing Form 2555, Form 2555-EZ, or Form 4563 All APO and FPO addresses	Philadelphia, PA 19255

Employee Plan Returns ONLY (Form 5500 series)

IF the principal office of the plan sponsor or the plan administrator was in . . .	THEN use this address . . .
Connecticut, Delaware, District of Columbia, Maine, Maryland, Massachusetts, New Hampshire, New Jersey, New York, Pennsylvania, Puerto Rico, Rhode Island, Vermont, Virginia	Holtsville, NY 00501
Alabama, Alaska, Arkansas, California, Florida, Georgia, Hawaii, Idaho, Louisiana, Mississippi, Nevada, North Carolina, Oregon, South Carolina, Tennessee, Washington	Atlanta. GA 39901
Arizona, Colorado, Illinois, Indiana, Iowa, Kansas, Kentucky, Michigan, Minnesota, Missouri, Montana, Nebraska, New Mexico, North Dakota, Ohio, Oklahoma, South Dakota, Texas, Utah, West Virginia, Wisconsin, Wyoming	Memphis, TN 37501
Foreign country	Holtsville, NY 00501
All Form 5500-EZ filers	Memphis, TN 37501

Privacy Act and Paperwork Reduction Act Notice. We ask for the information on this form to carry out the Internal Revenue laws of the United States. We may give the information to the Department of Justice and to other Federal agencies, as provided by law. We may also give it to cities, states, the District of Columbia, and U.S. commonwealths or possessions to carry out their tax laws. And we may give it to foreign governments because of tax treaties they have with the United States.

You are not required to provide the information requested on a form that is subject to the Paperwork Reduction Act unless the form displays a valid OMB control number. Books or records relating to a form or its instructions must be retained as long as their contents may become material in the administration of any Internal Revenue law. Generally, tax returns and return information are confidential, as required by Internal Revenue Code section 6103.

If you fail to provide the Internal Revenue Service with your current mailing address, you may not receive a notice of deficiency or a notice and demand for tax. Despite the failure to receive such notices, penalties and interest will continue to accrue on the tax deficiencies.

The time needed to complete and file this form will vary depending on individual circumstances. The estimated average time is 16 minutes.

If you have comments concerning the accuracy of this time estimate or suggestions for making this form simpler, we would be happy to hear from you. You can write to the Tax Forms Committee, Western Area Distribution Center, Rancho Cordova, CA 95743-0001. **DO NOT** send the form to this address. Instead, see **Where To File** on this page.

Form **8829**	**Expenses for Business Use of Your Home**	OMB No. 1545-1266
Department of the Treasury Internal Revenue Service (99)	▶ File only with Schedule C (Form 1040). Use a separate Form 8829 for each home you used for business during the year. ▶ See separate instructions.	**1999** Attachment Sequence No. **66**

Name(s) of proprietor(s) | Your social security number

Part I — Part of Your Home Used for Business

1	Area used regularly and exclusively for business, regularly for day care, or for storage of inventory or product samples. See instructions	**1**	
2	Total area of home	**2**	
3	Divide line 1 by line 2. Enter the result as a percentage	**3**	%

- For day-care facilities not used exclusively for business, also complete lines 4–6.
- All others, skip lines 4–6 and enter the amount from line 3 on line 7.

4	Multiply days used for day care during year by hours used per day	**4**	hr.
5	Total hours available for use during the year (365 days × 24 hours). See instructions	**5**	8,760 hr.
6	Divide line 4 by line 5. Enter the result as a decimal amount	**6**	.
7	Business percentage. For day-care facilities not used exclusively for business, multiply line 6 by line 3 (enter the result as a percentage). All others, enter the amount from line 3 ▶	**7**	%

Part II — Figure Your Allowable Deduction

8	Enter the amount from Schedule C, line 29, **plus** any net gain or (loss) derived from the business use of your home and shown on Schedule D or Form 4797. If more than one place of business, see instructions		**8**	

See instructions for columns **(a)** and **(b)** before completing lines 9–20.

		(a) Direct expenses	(b) Indirect expenses		
9	Casualty losses. See instructions	**9**			
10	Deductible mortgage interest. See instructions	**10**			
11	Real estate taxes. See instructions	**11**			
12	Add lines 9, 10, and 11	**12**			
13	Multiply line 12, column (b) by line 7		**13**		
14	Add line 12, column (a) and line 13			**14**	
15	Subtract line 14 from line 8. If zero or less, enter -0-			**15**	
16	Excess mortgage interest. See instructions	**16**			
17	Insurance	**17**			
18	Repairs and maintenance	**18**			
19	Utilities	**19**			
20	Other expenses. See instructions	**20**			
21	Add lines 16 through 20	**21**			
22	Multiply line 21, column (b) by line 7		**22**		
23	Carryover of operating expenses from 1998 Form 8829, line 41		**23**		
24	Add line 21 in column (a), line 22, and line 23			**24**	
25	Allowable operating expenses. Enter the **smaller** of line 15 or line 24			**25**	
26	Limit on excess casualty losses and depreciation. Subtract line 25 from line 15			**26**	
27	Excess casualty losses. See instructions		**27**		
28	Depreciation of your home from Part III below		**28**		
29	Carryover of excess casualty losses and depreciation from 1998 Form 8829, line 42		**29**		
30	Add lines 27 through 29			**30**	
31	Allowable excess casualty losses and depreciation. Enter the **smaller** of line 26 or line 30			**31**	
32	Add lines 14, 25, and 31			**32**	
33	Casualty loss portion, if any, from lines 14 and 31. Carry amount to **Form 4684**, Section B			**33**	
34	Allowable expenses for business use of your home. Subtract line 33 from line 32. Enter here and on Schedule C, line 30. If your home was used for more than one business, see instructions ▶			**34**	

Part III — Depreciation of Your Home

35	Enter the **smaller** of your home's adjusted basis or its fair market value. See instructions	**35**	
36	Value of land included on line 35	**36**	
37	Basis of building. Subtract line 36 from line 35	**37**	
38	Business basis of building. Multiply line 37 by line 7	**38**	
39	Depreciation percentage. See instructions	**39**	%
40	Depreciation allowable. Multiply line 38 by line 39. Enter here and on line 28 above. See instructions	**40**	

Part IV — Carryover of Unallowed Expenses to 2000

41	Operating expenses. Subtract line 25 from line 24. If less than zero, enter -0-	**41**	
42	Excess casualty losses and depreciation. Subtract line 31 from line 30. If less than zero, enter -0-	**42**	

For Paperwork Reduction Act Notice, see page 4 of separate instructions.   Cat. No. 13232M   Form **8829** (1999)

Form **8839**

Department of the Treasury
Internal Revenue Service

Qualified Adoption Expenses

▶ Attach to Form 1040 or 1040A.

▶ See separate instructions.

OMB No. 1545-1552

1999

Attachment Sequence No. **38**

Name(s) shown on return

Your social security number

Before you begin, you need to understand the following terms. See **Definitions** on page 1 of the instructions.

- **Eligible Child**
- **Employer-Provided Adoption Benefits**
- **Qualified Adoption Expenses**

Part I   Information About Your Eligible Child or Children—You **must** complete this part. See the instructions for details, including what to do if you need more space.

1

	(a) Child's name		(b) Child's year of birth	(c) born **before 1981** and was disabled	(d) a child with special needs	(e) a foreign child	(f) Child's identifying number
	First	Last					
Child 1			19	☐	☐	☐	
Child 2			19	☐	☐	☐	

Caution: *If the child was a foreign child, see **Special Rules** in the instructions for line 1, column (e), before you complete Part II or Part III. If you received **employer-provided adoption benefits**, complete Part III on the back next.*

Part II   Adoption Credit

			Child 1		Child 2			
2	Enter $5,000 ($6,000 for a child with special needs)	2						
3	Did you file a 1997 or 1998 Form 8839? ☐ **No.** Enter -0-. ☐ **Yes.** See the instructions for the amount to enter.	3						
4	Subtract line 3 from line 2	4						
5	Enter the total **qualified adoption expenses** you paid in: • 1998 if the adoption was not final by the end of 1999 • 1998 and 1999 if the adoption was final in 1999. • 1999 if the adoption was final before 1999.	5						
6	Enter the **smaller** of line 4 or line 5 . . .	6						
7	Add the amounts on line 6. If zero, skip lines 8-11 and enter -0- on line 12					7		
8	Enter your modified adjusted gross income (see instructions) . .	8						
9	If line 8 is $75,000 or less, skip lines 9 and 10 and enter -0- on line 11. If line 8 is over $75,000, subtract $75,000 from the amount on line 8	9						
10	Divide line 9 by $40,000. Enter the result as a decimal (rounded to at least three places). Do not enter more than "1.000"					10	✕ .	
11	Multiply line 7 by line 10					11		
12	Subtract line 11 from line 7					12		
13	Enter any credit carryforward from 1997 (line 15 of your 1998 Form 8839)					13		
14	Enter any credit carryforward from 1998 (line 16 of your 1998 Form 8839)					14		
15	Add lines 12, 13, and 14. Then, see the instructions for the amount of credit to enter on Form 1040, line 45, or Form 1040A, line 30					15		
16	**1997 credit carryforward to 2000** (see instructions)	16						
17	**1998 credit carryforward to 2000** (see instructions)	17						
18	**1999 credit carryforward to 2000** (see instructions)	18						

For Paperwork Reduction Act Notice, see page 4 of instructions.

Cat. No. 22843L

Form **8839** (1999)

Part III Employer-Provided Adoption Benefits

		Child 1		Child 2				
19	Enter $5,000 ($6,000 for a child with special needs)	**19**						
20	Did you receive **employer-provided adoption benefits** for 1997 or 1998? ☐ **No.** Enter -0-. ☐ **Yes.** See the instructions for the amount to enter.	**20**						
21	Subtract line 20 from line 19. If zero or less, enter -0-	**21**						
22	Enter the total amount of your employer-provided adoption benefits received in 1999. This amount should be shown in box 13 of your 1999 W-2 form(s) with code **T**	**22**						
23	Add the amounts on line 22					**23**		
24	Enter the **smaller** of line 21 or line 22	**24**						
25	Add the amounts on line 24. If zero, skip lines 26-29, enter -0- on line 30, and go to line 31		**25**					
26	Enter your modified adjusted gross income (from the worksheet in the instructions)	**26**						
27	If line 26 is $75,000 or less, skip lines 27 and 28 and enter -0- on line 29. If line 26 is over $75,000, subtract $75,000 from the amount on line 26	**27**						
28	Divide line 27 by $40,000. Enter the result as a decimal (rounded to at least three places). Do not enter more than "1.000" . . .		**28**	✕ .				
29	Multiply line 25 by line 28		**29**					
30	**Excluded benefits.** Subtract line 29 from line 25					**30**		
31	**Taxable benefits.** Subtract line 30 from line 23. Also, include this amount on Form 1040, line 7, or Form 1040A, line 7. On the line next to line 7, enter "AB".					**31**		

If the total adoption expenses you paid in 1999 were not fully reimbursed by your employer **AND** the adoption was final in or before 1999, you may be able to claim the adoption credit in Part II on the front of this form.

1999 Tax Table

Use if your taxable income is less than $100,000.
If $100,000 or more, use the Tax Rate Schedules.

Example. Mr. and Mrs. Brown are filing a joint return. Their taxable income on line 39 of Form 1040 is $25,300. First, they find the $25,300–25,350 income line. Next, they find the column for married filing jointly and read down the column. The amount shown where the income line and filing status column meet is $3,799. This is the tax amount they should enter on line 40 of their Form 1040.

Sample Table

At least	But less than	Single	Married filing jointly *	Married filing sepa-rately	Head of a house-hold
			Your tax is—		
25,200	25,250	3,784	3,784	4,265	3,784
25,250	25,300	3,791	3,791	4,279	3,791
25,300	25,350	3,799	(3,799)	4,293	3,799
25,350	25,400	3,806	3,806	4,307	3,806

If line 39 (taxable income) is— At least	But less than	Single	Married filing jointly *	Married filing sepa-rately	Head of a house-hold
			Your tax is—		
0	5	0	0	0	0
5	15	2	2	2	2
15	25	3	3	3	3
25	50	6	6	6	6
50	75	9	9	9	9
75	100	13	13	13	13
100	125	17	17	17	17
125	150	21	21	21	21
150	175	24	24	24	24
175	200	28	28	28	28
200	225	32	32	32	32
225	250	36	36	36	36
250	275	39	39	39	39
275	300	43	43	43	43
300	325	47	47	47	47
325	350	51	51	51	51
350	375	54	54	54	54
375	400	58	58	58	58
400	425	62	62	62	62
425	450	66	66	66	66
450	475	69	69	69	69
475	500	73	73	73	73
500	525	77	77	77	77
525	550	81	81	81	81
550	575	84	84	84	84
575	600	88	88	88	88
600	625	92	92	92	92
625	650	96	96	96	96
650	675	99	99	99	99
675	700	103	103	103	103
700	725	107	107	107	107
725	750	111	111	111	111
750	775	114	114	114	114
775	800	118	118	118	118
800	825	122	122	122	122
825	850	126	126	126	126
850	875	129	129	129	129
875	900	133	133	133	133
900	925	137	137	137	137
925	950	141	141	141	141
950	975	144	144	144	144
975	1,000	148	148	148	148

1,000

At least	But less than	Single	Married filing jointly *	Married filing sepa-rately	Head of a house-hold
1,000	1,025	152	152	152	152
1,025	1,050	156	156	156	156
1,050	1,075	159	159	159	159
1,075	1,100	163	163	163	163
1,100	1,125	167	167	167	167
1,125	1,150	171	171	171	171
1,150	1,175	174	174	174	174
1,175	1,200	178	178	178	178
1,200	1,225	182	182	182	182
1,225	1,250	186	186	186	186
1,250	1,275	189	189	189	189
1,275	1,300	193	193	193	193

If line 39 (taxable income) is— At least	But less than	Single	Married filing jointly *	Married filing sepa-rately	Head of a house-hold
			Your tax is—		
1,300	1,325	197	197	197	197
1,325	1,350	201	201	201	201
1,350	1,375	204	204	204	204
1,375	1,400	208	208	208	208
1,400	1,425	212	212	212	212
1,425	1,450	216	216	216	216
1,450	1,475	219	219	219	219
1,475	1,500	223	223	223	223
1,500	1,525	227	227	227	227
1,525	1,550	231	231	231	231
1,550	1,575	234	234	234	234
1,575	1,600	238	238	238	238
1,600	1,625	242	242	242	242
1,625	1,650	246	246	246	246
1,650	1,675	249	249	249	249
1,675	1,700	253	253	253	253
1,700	1,725	257	257	257	257
1,725	1,750	261	261	261	261
1,750	1,775	264	264	264	264
1,775	1,800	268	268	268	268
1,800	1,825	272	272	272	272
1,825	1,850	276	276	276	276
1,850	1,875	279	279	279	279
1,875	1,900	283	283	283	283
1,900	1,925	287	287	287	287
1,925	1,950	291	291	291	291
1,950	1,975	294	294	294	294
1,975	2,000	298	298	298	298

2,000

At least	But less than	Single	Married filing jointly *	Married filing sepa-rately	Head of a house-hold
2,000	2,025	302	302	302	302
2,025	2,050	306	306	306	306
2,050	2,075	309	309	309	309
2,075	2,100	313	313	313	313
2,100	2,125	317	317	317	317
2,125	2,150	321	321	321	321
2,150	2,175	324	324	324	324
2,175	2,200	328	328	328	328
2,200	2,225	332	332	332	332
2,225	2,250	336	336	336	336
2,250	2,275	339	339	339	339
2,275	2,300	343	343	343	343
2,300	2,325	347	347	347	347
2,325	2,350	351	351	351	351
2,350	2,375	354	354	354	354
2,375	2,400	358	358	358	358
2,400	2,425	362	362	362	362
2,425	2,450	366	366	366	366
2,450	2,475	369	369	369	369
2,475	2,500	373	373	373	373
2,500	2,525	377	377	377	377
2,525	2,550	381	381	381	381
2,550	2,575	384	384	384	384
2,575	2,600	388	388	388	388
2,600	2,625	392	392	392	392
2,625	2,650	396	396	396	396
2,650	2,675	399	399	399	399
2,675	2,700	403	403	403	403

If line 39 (taxable income) is— At least	But less than	Single	Married filing jointly *	Married filing sepa-rately	Head of a house-hold
			Your tax is—		
2,700	2,725	407	407	407	407
2,725	2,750	411	411	411	411
2,750	2,775	414	414	414	414
2,775	2,800	418	418	418	418
2,800	2,825	422	422	422	422
2,825	2,850	426	426	426	426
2,850	2,875	429	429	429	429
2,875	2,900	433	433	433	433
2,900	2,925	437	437	437	437
2,925	2,950	441	441	441	441
2,950	2,975	444	444	444	444
2,975	3,000	448	448	448	448

3,000

At least	But less than	Single	Married filing jointly *	Married filing sepa-rately	Head of a house-hold
3,000	3,050	454	454	454	454
3,050	3,100	461	461	461	461
3,100	3,150	469	469	469	469
3,150	3,200	476	476	476	476
3,200	3,250	484	484	484	484
3,250	3,300	491	491	491	491
3,300	3,350	499	499	499	499
3,350	3,400	506	506	506	506
3,400	3,450	514	514	514	514
3,450	3,500	521	521	521	521
3,500	3,550	529	529	529	529
3,550	3,600	536	536	536	536
3,600	3,650	544	544	544	544
3,650	3,700	551	551	551	551
3,700	3,750	559	559	559	559
3,750	3,800	566	566	566	566
3,800	3,850	574	574	574	574
3,850	3,900	581	581	581	581
3,900	3,950	589	589	589	589
3,950	4,000	596	596	596	596

4,000

At least	But less than	Single	Married filing jointly *	Married filing sepa-rately	Head of a house-hold
4,000	4,050	604	604	604	604
4,050	4,100	611	611	611	611
4,100	4,150	619	619	619	619
4,150	4,200	626	626	626	626
4,200	4,250	634	634	634	634
4,250	4,300	641	641	641	641
4,300	4,350	649	649	649	649
4,350	4,400	656	656	656	656
4,400	4,450	664	664	664	664
4,450	4,500	671	671	671	671
4,500	4,550	679	679	679	679
4,550	4,600	686	686	686	686
4,600	4,650	694	694	694	694
4,650	4,700	701	701	701	701
4,700	4,750	709	709	709	709
4,750	4,800	716	716	716	716
4,800	4,850	724	724	724	724
4,850	4,900	731	731	731	731
4,900	4,950	739	739	739	739
4,950	5,000	746	746	746	746

Continued on next page

* This column must also be used by a qualifying widow(er).

5,000

At least	But less than	Single	Married filing jointly *	Married filing separately	Head of a household
5,000	5,050	754	754	754	754
5,050	5,100	761	761	761	761
5,100	5,150	769	769	769	769
5,150	5,200	776	776	776	776
5,200	5,250	784	784	784	784
5,250	5,300	791	791	791	791
5,300	5,350	799	799	799	799
5,350	5,400	806	806	806	806
5,400	5,450	814	814	814	814
5,450	5,500	821	821	821	821
5,500	5,550	829	829	829	829
5,550	5,600	836	836	836	836
5,600	5,650	844	844	844	844
5,650	5,700	851	851	851	851
5,700	5,750	859	859	859	859
5,750	5,800	866	866	866	866
5,800	5,850	874	874	874	874
5,850	5,900	881	881	881	881
5,900	5,950	889	889	889	889
5,950	6,000	896	896	896	896

6,000

At least	But less than	Single	Married filing jointly *	Married filing separately	Head of a household
6,000	6,050	904	904	904	904
6,050	6,100	911	911	911	911
6,100	6,150	919	919	919	919
6,150	6,200	926	926	926	926
6,200	6,250	934	934	934	934
6,250	6,300	941	941	941	941
6,300	6,350	949	949	949	949
6,350	6,400	956	956	956	956
6,400	6,450	964	964	964	964
6,450	6,500	971	971	971	971
6,500	6,550	979	979	979	979
6,550	6,600	986	986	986	986
6,600	6,650	994	994	994	994
6,650	6,700	1,001	1,001	1,001	1,001
6,700	6,750	1,009	1,009	1,009	1,009
6,750	6,800	1,016	1,016	1,016	1,016
6,800	6,850	1,024	1,024	1,024	1,024
6,850	6,900	1,031	1,031	1,031	1,031
6,900	6,950	1,039	1,039	1,039	1,039
6,950	7,000	1,046	1,046	1,046	1,046

7,000

At least	But less than	Single	Married filing jointly *	Married filing separately	Head of a household
7,000	7,050	1,054	1,054	1,054	1,054
7,050	7,100	1,061	1,061	1,061	1,061
7,100	7,150	1,069	1,069	1,069	1,069
7,150	7,200	1,076	1,076	1,076	1,076
7,200	7,250	1,084	1,084	1,084	1,084
7,250	7,300	1,091	1,091	1,091	1,091
7,300	7,350	1,099	1,099	1,099	1,099
7,350	7,400	1,106	1,106	1,106	1,106
7,400	7,450	1,114	1,114	1,114	1,114
7,450	7,500	1,121	1,121	1,121	1,121
7,500	7,550	1,129	1,129	1,129	1,129
7,550	7,600	1,136	1,136	1,136	1,136
7,600	7,650	1,144	1,144	1,144	1,144
7,650	7,700	1,151	1,151	1,151	1,151
7,700	7,750	1,159	1,159	1,159	1,159
7,750	7,800	1,166	1,166	1,166	1,166
7,800	7,850	1,174	1,174	1,174	1,174
7,850	7,900	1,181	1,181	1,181	1,181
7,900	7,950	1,189	1,189	1,189	1,189
7,950	8,000	1,196	1,196	1,196	1,196

8,000

At least	But less than	Single	Married filing jointly *	Married filing separately	Head of a household
8,000	8,050	1,204	1,204	1,204	1,204
8,050	8,100	1,211	1,211	1,211	1,211
8,100	8,150	1,219	1,219	1,219	1,219
8,150	8,200	1,226	1,226	1,226	1,226
8,200	8,250	1,234	1,234	1,234	1,234
8,250	8,300	1,241	1,241	1,241	1,241
8,300	8,350	1,249	1,249	1,249	1,249
8,350	8,400	1,256	1,256	1,256	1,256
8,400	8,450	1,264	1,264	1,264	1,264
8,450	8,500	1,271	1,271	1,271	1,271
8,500	8,550	1,279	1,279	1,279	1,279
8,550	8,600	1,286	1,286	1,286	1,286
8,600	8,650	1,294	1,294	1,294	1,294
8,650	8,700	1,301	1,301	1,301	1,301
8,700	8,750	1,309	1,309	1,309	1,309
8,750	8,800	1,316	1,316	1,316	1,316
8,800	8,850	1,324	1,324	1,324	1,324
8,850	8,900	1,331	1,331	1,331	1,331
8,900	8,950	1,339	1,339	1,339	1,339
8,950	9,000	1,346	1,346	1,346	1,346

9,000

At least	But less than	Single	Married filing jointly *	Married filing separately	Head of a household
9,000	9,050	1,354	1,354	1,354	1,354
9,050	9,100	1,361	1,361	1,361	1,361
9,100	9,150	1,369	1,369	1,369	1,369
9,150	9,200	1,376	1,376	1,376	1,376
9,200	9,250	1,384	1,384	1,384	1,384
9,250	9,300	1,391	1,391	1,391	1,391
9,300	9,350	1,399	1,399	1,399	1,399
9,350	9,400	1,406	1,406	1,406	1,406
9,400	9,450	1,414	1,414	1,414	1,414
9,450	9,500	1,421	1,421	1,421	1,421
9,500	9,550	1,429	1,429	1,429	1,429
9,550	9,600	1,436	1,436	1,436	1,436
9,600	9,650	1,444	1,444	1,444	1,444
9,650	9,700	1,451	1,451	1,451	1,451
9,700	9,750	1,459	1,459	1,459	1,459
9,750	9,800	1,466	1,466	1,466	1,466
9,800	9,850	1,474	1,474	1,474	1,474
9,850	9,900	1,481	1,481	1,481	1,481
9,900	9,950	1,489	1,489	1,489	1,489
9,950	10,000	1,496	1,496	1,496	1,496

10,000

At least	But less than	Single	Married filing jointly *	Married filing separately	Head of a household
10,000	10,050	1,504	1,504	1,504	1,504
10,050	10,100	1,511	1,511	1,511	1,511
10,100	10,150	1,519	1,519	1,519	1,519
10,150	10,200	1,526	1,526	1,526	1,526
10,200	10,250	1,534	1,534	1,534	1,534
10,250	10,300	1,541	1,541	1,541	1,541
10,300	10,350	1,549	1,549	1,549	1,549
10,350	10,400	1,556	1,556	1,556	1,556
10,400	10,450	1,564	1,564	1,564	1,564
10,450	10,500	1,571	1,571	1,571	1,571
10,500	10,550	1,579	1,579	1,579	1,579
10,550	10,600	1,586	1,586	1,586	1,586
10,600	10,650	1,594	1,594	1,594	1,594
10,650	10,700	1,601	1,601	1,601	1,601
10,700	10,750	1,609	1,609	1,609	1,609
10,750	10,800	1,616	1,616	1,616	1,616
10,800	10,850	1,624	1,624	1,624	1,624
10,850	10,900	1,631	1,631	1,631	1,631
10,900	10,950	1,639	1,639	1,639	1,639
10,950	11,000	1,646	1,646	1,646	1,646

11,000

At least	But less than	Single	Married filing jointly *	Married filing separately	Head of a household
11,000	11,050	1,654	1,654	1,654	1,654
11,050	11,100	1,661	1,661	1,661	1,661
11,100	11,150	1,669	1,669	1,669	1,669
11,150	11,200	1,676	1,676	1,676	1,676
11,200	11,250	1,684	1,684	1,684	1,684
11,250	11,300	1,691	1,691	1,691	1,691
11,300	11,350	1,699	1,699	1,699	1,699
11,350	11,400	1,706	1,706	1,706	1,706
11,400	11,450	1,714	1,714	1,714	1,714
11,450	11,500	1,721	1,721	1,721	1,721
11,500	11,550	1,729	1,729	1,729	1,729
11,550	11,600	1,736	1,736	1,736	1,736
11,600	11,650	1,744	1,744	1,744	1,744
11,650	11,700	1,751	1,751	1,751	1,751
11,700	11,750	1,759	1,759	1,759	1,759
11,750	11,800	1,766	1,766	1,766	1,766
11,800	11,850	1,774	1,774	1,774	1,774
11,850	11,900	1,781	1,781	1,781	1,781
11,900	11,950	1,789	1,789	1,789	1,789
11,950	12,000	1,796	1,796	1,796	1,796

12,000

At least	But less than	Single	Married filing jointly *	Married filing separately	Head of a household
12,000	12,050	1,804	1,804	1,804	1,804
12,050	12,100	1,811	1,811	1,811	1,811
12,100	12,150	1,819	1,819	1,819	1,819
12,150	12,200	1,826	1,826	1,826	1,826
12,200	12,250	1,834	1,834	1,834	1,834
12,250	12,300	1,841	1,841	1,841	1,841
12,300	12,350	1,849	1,849	1,849	1,849
12,350	12,400	1,856	1,856	1,856	1,856
12,400	12,450	1,864	1,864	1,864	1,864
12,450	12,500	1,871	1,871	1,871	1,871
12,500	12,550	1,879	1,879	1,879	1,879
12,550	12,600	1,886	1,886	1,886	1,886
12,600	12,650	1,894	1,894	1,894	1,894
12,650	12,700	1,901	1,901	1,901	1,901
12,700	12,750	1,909	1,909	1,909	1,909
12,750	12,800	1,916	1,916	1,916	1,916
12,800	12,850	1,924	1,924	1,924	1,924
12,850	12,900	1,931	1,931	1,931	1,931
12,900	12,950	1,939	1,939	1,939	1,939
12,950	13,000	1,946	1,946	1,946	1,946

13,000

At least	But less than	Single	Married filing jointly *	Married filing separately	Head of a household
13,000	13,050	1,954	1,954	1,954	1,954
13,050	13,100	1,961	1,961	1,961	1,961
13,100	13,150	1,969	1,969	1,969	1,969
13,150	13,200	1,976	1,976	1,976	1,976
13,200	13,250	1,984	1,984	1,984	1,984
13,250	13,300	1,991	1,991	1,991	1,991
13,300	13,350	1,999	1,999	1,999	1,999
13,350	13,400	2,006	2,006	2,006	2,006
13,400	13,450	2,014	2,014	2,014	2,014
13,450	13,500	2,021	2,021	2,021	2,021
13,500	13,550	2,029	2,029	2,029	2,029
13,550	13,600	2,036	2,036	2,036	2,036
13,600	13,650	2,044	2,044	2,044	2,044
13,650	13,700	2,051	2,051	2,051	2,051
13,700	13,750	2,059	2,059	2,059	2,059
13,750	13,800	2,066	2,066	2,066	2,066
13,800	13,850	2,074	2,074	2,074	2,074
13,850	13,900	2,081	2,081	2,081	2,081
13,900	13,950	2,089	2,089	2,089	2,089
13,950	14,000	2,096	2,096	2,096	2,096

* This column must also be used by a qualifying widow(er).

Continued on next page

14,000

At least	But less than	Single	Married filing jointly*	Married filing separately	Head of a household
14,000	14,050	2,104	2,104	2,104	2,104
14,050	14,100	2,111	2,111	2,111	2,111
14,100	14,150	2,119	2,119	2,119	2,119
14,150	14,200	2,126	2,126	2,126	2,126
14,200	14,250	2,134	2,134	2,134	2,134
14,250	14,300	2,141	2,141	2,141	2,141
14,300	14,350	2,149	2,149	2,149	2,149
14,350	14,400	2,156	2,156	2,156	2,156
14,400	14,450	2,164	2,164	2,164	2,164
14,450	14,500	2,171	2,171	2,171	2,171
14,500	14,550	2,179	2,179	2,179	2,179
14,550	14,600	2,186	2,186	2,186	2,186
14,600	14,650	2,194	2,194	2,194	2,194
14,650	14,700	2,201	2,201	2,201	2,201
14,700	14,750	2,209	2,209	2,209	2,209
14,750	14,800	2,216	2,216	2,216	2,216
14,800	14,850	2,224	2,224	2,224	2,224
14,850	14,900	2,231	2,231	2,231	2,231
14,900	14,950	2,239	2,239	2,239	2,239
14,950	15,000	2,246	2,246	2,246	2,246

15,000

At least	But less than	Single	Married filing jointly*	Married filing separately	Head of a household
15,000	15,050	2,254	2,254	2,254	2,254
15,050	15,100	2,261	2,261	2,261	2,261
15,100	15,150	2,269	2,269	2,269	2,269
15,150	15,200	2,276	2,276	2,276	2,276
15,200	15,250	2,284	2,284	2,284	2,284
15,250	15,300	2,291	2,291	2,291	2,291
15,300	15,350	2,299	2,299	2,299	2,299
15,350	15,400	2,306	2,306	2,306	2,306
15,400	15,450	2,314	2,314	2,314	2,314
15,450	15,500	2,321	2,321	2,321	2,321
15,500	15,550	2,329	2,329	2,329	2,329
15,550	15,600	2,336	2,336	2,336	2,336
15,600	15,650	2,344	2,344	2,344	2,344
15,650	15,700	2,351	2,351	2,351	2,351
15,700	15,750	2,359	2,359	2,359	2,359
15,750	15,800	2,366	2,366	2,366	2,366
15,800	15,850	2,374	2,374	2,374	2,374
15,850	15,900	2,381	2,381	2,381	2,381
15,900	15,950	2,389	2,389	2,389	2,389
15,950	16,000	2,396	2,396	2,396	2,396

16,000

At least	But less than	Single	Married filing jointly*	Married filing separately	Head of a household
16,000	16,050	2,404	2,404	2,404	2,404
16,050	16,100	2,411	2,411	2,411	2,411
16,100	16,150	2,419	2,419	2,419	2,419
16,150	16,200	2,426	2,426	2,426	2,426
16,200	16,250	2,434	2,434	2,434	2,434
16,250	16,300	2,441	2,441	2,441	2,441
16,300	16,350	2,449	2,449	2,449	2,449
16,350	16,400	2,456	2,456	2,456	2,456
16,400	16,450	2,464	2,464	2,464	2,464
16,450	16,500	2,471	2,471	2,471	2,471
16,500	16,550	2,479	2,479	2,479	2,479
16,550	16,600	2,486	2,486	2,486	2,486
16,600	16,650	2,494	2,494	2,494	2,494
16,650	16,700	2,501	2,501	2,501	2,501
16,700	16,750	2,509	2,509	2,509	2,509
16,750	16,800	2,516	2,516	2,516	2,516
16,800	16,850	2,524	2,524	2,524	2,524
16,850	16,900	2,531	2,531	2,531	2,531
16,900	16,950	2,539	2,539	2,539	2,539
16,950	17,000	2,546	2,546	2,546	2,546

17,000

At least	But less than	Single	Married filing jointly*	Married filing separately	Head of a household
17,000	17,050	2,554	2,554	2,554	2,554
17,050	17,100	2,561	2,561	2,561	2,561
17,100	17,150	2,569	2,569	2,569	2,569
17,150	17,200	2,576	2,576	2,576	2,576
17,200	17,250	2,584	2,584	2,584	2,584
17,250	17,300	2,591	2,591	2,591	2,591
17,300	17,350	2,599	2,599	2,599	2,599
17,350	17,400	2,606	2,606	2,606	2,606
17,400	17,450	2,614	2,614	2,614	2,614
17,450	17,500	2,621	2,621	2,621	2,621
17,500	17,550	2,629	2,629	2,629	2,629
17,550	17,600	2,636	2,636	2,636	2,636
17,600	17,650	2,644	2,644	2,644	2,644
17,650	17,700	2,651	2,651	2,651	2,651
17,700	17,750	2,659	2,659	2,659	2,659
17,750	17,800	2,666	2,666	2,666	2,666
17,800	17,850	2,674	2,674	2,674	2,674
17,850	17,900	2,681	2,681	2,681	2,681
17,900	17,950	2,689	2,689	2,689	2,689
17,950	18,000	2,696	2,696	2,696	2,696

18,000

At least	But less than	Single	Married filing jointly*	Married filing separately	Head of a household
18,000	18,050	2,704	2,704	2,704	2,704
18,050	18,100	2,711	2,711	2,711	2,711
18,100	18,150	2,719	2,719	2,719	2,719
18,150	18,200	2,726	2,726	2,726	2,726
18,200	18,250	2,734	2,734	2,734	2,734
18,250	18,300	2,741	2,741	2,741	2,741
18,300	18,350	2,749	2,749	2,749	2,749
18,350	18,400	2,756	2,756	2,756	2,756
18,400	18,450	2,764	2,764	2,764	2,764
18,450	18,500	2,771	2,771	2,771	2,771
18,500	18,550	2,779	2,779	2,779	2,779
18,550	18,600	2,786	2,786	2,786	2,786
18,600	18,650	2,794	2,794	2,794	2,794
18,650	18,700	2,801	2,801	2,801	2,801
18,700	18,750	2,809	2,809	2,809	2,809
18,750	18,800	2,816	2,816	2,816	2,816
18,800	18,850	2,824	2,824	2,824	2,824
18,850	18,900	2,831	2,831	2,831	2,831
18,900	18,950	2,839	2,839	2,839	2,839
18,950	19,000	2,846	2,846	2,846	2,846

19,000

At least	But less than	Single	Married filing jointly*	Married filing separately	Head of a household
19,000	19,050	2,854	2,854	2,854	2,854
19,050	19,100	2,861	2,861	2,861	2,861
19,100	19,150	2,869	2,869	2,869	2,869
19,150	19,200	2,876	2,876	2,876	2,876
19,200	19,250	2,884	2,884	2,884	2,884
19,250	19,300	2,891	2,891	2,891	2,891
19,300	19,350	2,899	2,899	2,899	2,899
19,350	19,400	2,906	2,906	2,906	2,906
19,400	19,450	2,914	2,914	2,914	2,914
19,450	19,500	2,921	2,921	2,921	2,921
19,500	19,550	2,929	2,929	2,929	2,929
19,550	19,600	2,936	2,936	2,936	2,936
19,600	19,650	2,944	2,944	2,944	2,944
19,650	19,700	2,951	2,951	2,951	2,951
19,700	19,750	2,959	2,959	2,959	2,959
19,750	19,800	2,966	2,966	2,966	2,966
19,800	19,850	2,974	2,974	2,974	2,974
19,850	19,900	2,981	2,981	2,981	2,981
19,900	19,950	2,989	2,989	2,989	2,989
19,950	20,000	2,996	2,996	2,996	2,996

20,000

At least	But less than	Single	Married filing jointly*	Married filing separately	Head of a household
20,000	20,050	3,004	3,004	3,004	3,004
20,050	20,100	3,011	3,011	3,011	3,011
20,100	20,150	3,019	3,019	3,019	3,019
20,150	20,200	3,026	3,026	3,026	3,026
20,200	20,250	3,034	3,034	3,034	3,034
20,250	20,300	3,041	3,041	3,041	3,041
20,300	20,350	3,049	3,049	3,049	3,049
20,350	20,400	3,056	3,056	3,056	3,056
20,400	20,450	3,064	3,064	3,064	3,064
20,450	20,500	3,071	3,071	3,071	3,071
20,500	20,550	3,079	3,079	3,079	3,079
20,550	20,600	3,086	3,086	3,086	3,086
20,600	20,650	3,094	3,094	3,094	3,094
20,650	20,700	3,101	3,101	3,101	3,101
20,700	20,750	3,109	3,109	3,109	3,109
20,750	20,800	3,116	3,116	3,116	3,116
20,800	20,850	3,124	3,124	3,124	3,124
20,850	20,900	3,131	3,131	3,131	3,131
20,900	20,950	3,139	3,139	3,139	3,139
20,950	21,000	3,146	3,146	3,146	3,146

21,000

At least	But less than	Single	Married filing jointly*	Married filing separately	Head of a household
21,000	21,050	3,154	3,154	3,154	3,154
21,050	21,100	3,161	3,161	3,161	3,161
21,100	21,150	3,169	3,169	3,169	3,169
21,150	21,200	3,176	3,176	3,176	3,176
21,200	21,250	3,184	3,184	3,184	3,184
21,250	21,300	3,191	3,191	3,191	3,191
21,300	21,350	3,199	3,199	3,199	3,199
21,350	21,400	3,206	3,206	3,206	3,206
21,400	21,450	3,214	3,214	3,214	3,214
21,450	21,500	3,221	3,221	3,221	3,221
21,500	21,550	3,229	3,229	3,229	3,229
21,550	21,600	3,236	3,236	3,243	3,236
21,600	21,650	3,244	3,244	3,257	3,244
21,650	21,700	3,251	3,251	3,271	3,251
21,700	21,750	3,259	3,259	3,285	3,259
21,750	21,800	3,266	3,266	3,299	3,266
21,800	21,850	3,274	3,274	3,313	3,274
21,850	21,900	3,281	3,281	3,327	3,281
21,900	21,950	3,289	3,289	3,341	3,289
21,950	22,000	3,296	3,296	3,355	3,296

22,000

At least	But less than	Single	Married filing jointly*	Married filing separately	Head of a household
22,000	22,050	3,304	3,304	3,369	3,304
22,050	22,100	3,311	3,311	3,383	3,311
22,100	22,150	3,319	3,319	3,397	3,319
22,150	22,200	3,326	3,326	3,411	3,326
22,200	22,250	3,334	3,334	3,425	3,334
22,250	22,300	3,341	3,341	3,439	3,341
22,300	22,350	3,349	3,349	3,453	3,349
22,350	22,400	3,356	3,356	3,467	3,356
22,400	22,450	3,364	3,364	3,481	3,364
22,450	22,500	3,371	3,371	3,495	3,371
22,500	22,550	3,379	3,379	3,509	3,379
22,550	22,600	3,386	3,386	3,523	3,386
22,600	22,650	3,394	3,394	3,537	3,394
22,650	22,700	3,401	3,401	3,551	3,401
22,700	22,750	3,409	3,409	3,565	3,409
22,750	22,800	3,416	3,416	3,579	3,416
22,800	22,850	3,424	3,424	3,593	3,424
22,850	22,900	3,431	3,431	3,607	3,431
22,900	22,950	3,439	3,439	3,621	3,439
22,950	23,000	3,446	3,446	3,635	3,446

* This column must also be used by a qualifying widow(er).

Continued on next page

Column header (applies to all three panels):

If line 39 (taxable income) is— At least	But less than	And you are— Single	Married filing jointly *	Married filing separately	Head of a household

Note: * This column must also be used by a qualifying widow(er). Your tax is—

23,000

At least	But less than	Single	Married filing jointly	Married filing separately	Head of a household
23,000	23,050	3,454	3,454	3,649	3,454
23,050	23,100	3,461	3,461	3,663	3,461
23,100	23,150	3,469	3,469	3,677	3,469
23,150	23,200	3,476	3,476	3,691	3,476
23,200	23,250	3,484	3,484	3,705	3,484
23,250	23,300	3,491	3,491	3,719	3,491
23,300	23,350	3,499	3,499	3,733	3,499
23,350	23,400	3,506	3,506	3,747	3,506
23,400	23,450	3,514	3,514	3,761	3,514
23,450	23,500	3,521	3,521	3,775	3,521
23,500	23,550	3,529	3,529	3,789	3,529
23,550	23,600	3,536	3,536	3,803	3,536
23,600	23,650	3,544	3,544	3,817	3,544
23,650	23,700	3,551	3,551	3,831	3,551
23,700	23,750	3,559	3,559	3,845	3,559
23,750	23,800	3,566	3,566	3,859	3,566
23,800	23,850	3,574	3,574	3,873	3,574
23,850	23,900	3,581	3,581	3,887	3,581
23,900	23,950	3,589	3,589	3,901	3,589
23,950	24,000	3,596	3,596	3,915	3,596

24,000

At least	But less than	Single	Married filing jointly	Married filing separately	Head of a household
24,000	24,050	3,604	3,604	3,929	3,604
24,050	24,100	3,611	3,611	3,943	3,611
24,100	24,150	3,619	3,619	3,957	3,619
24,150	24,200	3,626	3,626	3,971	3,626
24,200	24,250	3,634	3,634	3,985	3,634
24,250	24,300	3,641	3,641	3,999	3,641
24,300	24,350	3,649	3,649	4,013	3,649
24,350	24,400	3,656	3,656	4,027	3,656
24,400	24,450	3,664	3,664	4,041	3,664
24,450	24,500	3,671	3,671	4,055	3,671
24,500	24,550	3,679	3,679	4,069	3,679
24,550	24,600	3,686	3,686	4,083	3,686
24,600	24,650	3,694	3,694	4,097	3,694
24,650	24,700	3,701	3,701	4,111	3,701
24,700	24,750	3,709	3,709	4,125	3,709
24,750	24,800	3,716	3,716	4,139	3,716
24,800	24,850	3,724	3,724	4,153	3,724
24,850	24,900	3,731	3,731	4,167	3,731
24,900	24,950	3,739	3,739	4,181	3,739
24,950	25,000	3,746	3,746	4,195	3,746

25,000

At least	But less than	Single	Married filing jointly	Married filing separately	Head of a household
25,000	25,050	3,754	3,754	4,209	3,754
25,050	25,100	3,761	3,761	4,223	3,761
25,100	25,150	3,769	3,769	4,237	3,769
25,150	25,200	3,776	3,776	4,251	3,776
25,200	25,250	3,784	3,784	4,265	3,784
25,250	25,300	3,791	3,791	4,279	3,791
25,300	25,350	3,799	3,799	4,293	3,799
25,350	25,400	3,806	3,806	4,307	3,806
25,400	25,450	3,814	3,814	4,321	3,814
25,450	25,500	3,821	3,821	4,335	3,821
25,500	25,550	3,829	3,829	4,349	3,829
25,550	25,600	3,836	3,836	4,363	3,836
25,600	25,650	3,844	3,844	4,377	3,844
25,650	25,700	3,851	3,851	4,391	3,851
25,700	25,750	3,859	3,859	4,405	3,859
25,750	25,800	3,870	3,866	4,419	3,866
25,800	25,850	3,884	3,874	4,433	3,874
25,850	25,900	3,898	3,881	4,447	3,881
25,900	25,950	3,912	3,889	4,461	3,889
25,950	26,000	3,926	3,896	4,475	3,896

26,000

At least	But less than	Single	Married filing jointly	Married filing separately	Head of a household
26,000	26,050	3,940	3,904	4,489	3,904
26,050	26,100	3,954	3,911	4,503	3,911
26,100	26,150	3,968	3,919	4,517	3,919
26,150	26,200	3,982	3,926	4,531	3,926
26,200	26,250	3,996	3,934	4,545	3,934
26,250	26,300	4,010	3,941	4,559	3,941
26,300	26,350	4,024	3,949	4,573	3,949
26,350	26,400	4,038	3,956	4,587	3,956
26,400	26,450	4,052	3,964	4,601	3,964
26,450	26,500	4,066	3,971	4,615	3,971
26,500	26,550	4,080	3,979	4,629	3,979
26,550	26,600	4,094	3,986	4,643	3,986
26,600	26,650	4,108	3,994	4,657	3,994
26,650	26,700	4,122	4,001	4,671	4,001
26,700	26,750	4,136	4,009	4,685	4,009
26,750	26,800	4,150	4,016	4,699	4,016
26,800	26,850	4,164	4,024	4,713	4,024
26,850	26,900	4,178	4,031	4,727	4,031
26,900	26,950	4,192	4,039	4,741	4,039
26,950	27,000	4,206	4,046	4,755	4,046

27,000

At least	But less than	Single	Married filing jointly	Married filing separately	Head of a household
27,000	27,050	4,220	4,054	4,769	4,054
27,050	27,100	4,234	4,061	4,783	4,061
27,100	27,150	4,248	4,069	4,797	4,069
27,150	27,200	4,262	4,076	4,811	4,076
27,200	27,250	4,276	4,084	4,825	4,084
27,250	27,300	4,290	4,091	4,839	4,091
27,300	27,350	4,304	4,099	4,853	4,099
27,350	27,400	4,318	4,106	4,867	4,106
27,400	27,450	4,332	4,114	4,881	4,114
27,450	27,500	4,346	4,121	4,895	4,121
27,500	27,550	4,360	4,129	4,909	4,129
27,550	27,600	4,374	4,136	4,923	4,136
27,600	27,650	4,388	4,144	4,937	4,144
27,650	27,700	4,402	4,151	4,951	4,151
27,700	27,750	4,416	4,159	4,965	4,159
27,750	27,800	4,430	4,166	4,979	4,166
27,800	27,850	4,444	4,174	4,993	4,174
27,850	27,900	4,458	4,181	5,007	4,181
27,900	27,950	4,472	4,189	5,021	4,189
27,950	28,000	4,486	4,196	5,035	4,196

28,000

At least	But less than	Single	Married filing jointly	Married filing separately	Head of a household
28,000	28,050	4,500	4,204	5,049	4,204
28,050	28,100	4,514	4,211	5,063	4,211
28,100	28,150	4,528	4,219	5,077	4,219
28,150	28,200	4,542	4,226	5,091	4,226
28,200	28,250	4,556	4,234	5,105	4,234
28,250	28,300	4,570	4,241	5,119	4,241
28,300	28,350	4,584	4,249	5,133	4,249
28,350	28,400	4,598	4,256	5,147	4,256
28,400	28,450	4,612	4,264	5,161	4,264
28,450	28,500	4,626	4,271	5,175	4,271
28,500	28,550	4,640	4,279	5,189	4,279
28,550	28,600	4,654	4,286	5,203	4,286
28,600	28,650	4,668	4,294	5,217	4,294
28,650	28,700	4,682	4,301	5,231	4,301
28,700	28,750	4,696	4,309	5,245	4,309
28,750	28,800	4,710	4,316	5,259	4,316
28,800	28,850	4,724	4,324	5,273	4,324
28,850	28,900	4,738	4,331	5,287	4,331
28,900	28,950	4,752	4,339	5,301	4,339
28,950	29,000	4,766	4,346	5,315	4,346

29,000

At least	But less than	Single	Married filing jointly	Married filing separately	Head of a household
29,000	29,050	4,780	4,354	5,329	4,354
29,050	29,100	4,794	4,361	5,343	4,361
29,100	29,150	4,808	4,369	5,357	4,369
29,150	29,200	4,822	4,376	5,371	4,376
29,200	29,250	4,836	4,384	5,385	4,384
29,250	29,300	4,850	4,391	5,399	4,391
29,300	29,350	4,864	4,399	5,413	4,399
29,350	29,400	4,878	4,406	5,427	4,406
29,400	29,450	4,892	4,414	5,441	4,414
29,450	29,500	4,906	4,421	5,455	4,421
29,500	29,550	4,920	4,429	5,469	4,429
29,550	29,600	4,934	4,436	5,483	4,436
29,600	29,650	4,948	4,444	5,497	4,444
29,650	29,700	4,962	4,451	5,511	4,451
29,700	29,750	4,976	4,459	5,525	4,459
29,750	29,800	4,990	4,466	5,539	4,466
29,800	29,850	5,004	4,474	5,553	4,474
29,850	29,900	5,018	4,481	5,567	4,481
29,900	29,950	5,032	4,489	5,581	4,489
29,950	30,000	5,046	4,496	5,595	4,496

30,000

At least	But less than	Single	Married filing jointly	Married filing separately	Head of a household
30,000	30,050	5,060	4,504	5,609	4,504
30,050	30,100	5,074	4,511	5,623	4,511
30,100	30,150	5,088	4,519	5,637	4,519
30,150	30,200	5,102	4,526	5,651	4,526
30,200	30,250	5,116	4,534	5,665	4,534
30,250	30,300	5,130	4,541	5,679	4,541
30,300	30,350	5,144	4,549	5,693	4,549
30,350	30,400	5,158	4,556	5,707	4,556
30,400	30,450	5,172	4,564	5,721	4,564
30,450	30,500	5,186	4,571	5,735	4,571
30,500	30,550	5,200	4,579	5,749	4,579
30,550	30,600	5,214	4,586	5,763	4,586
30,600	30,650	5,228	4,594	5,777	4,594
30,650	30,700	5,242	4,601	5,791	4,601
30,700	30,750	5,256	4,609	5,805	4,609
30,750	30,800	5,270	4,616	5,819	4,616
30,800	30,850	5,284	4,624	5,833	4,624
30,850	30,900	5,298	4,631	5,847	4,631
30,900	30,950	5,312	4,639	5,861	4,639
30,950	31,000	5,326	4,646	5,875	4,646

31,000

At least	But less than	Single	Married filing jointly	Married filing separately	Head of a household
31,000	31,050	5,340	4,654	5,889	4,654
31,050	31,100	5,354	4,661	5,903	4,661
31,100	31,150	5,368	4,669	5,917	4,669
31,150	31,200	5,382	4,676	5,931	4,676
31,200	31,250	5,396	4,684	5,945	4,684
31,250	31,300	5,410	4,691	5,959	4,691
31,300	31,350	5,424	4,699	5,973	4,699
31,350	31,400	5,438	4,706	5,987	4,706
31,400	31,450	5,452	4,714	6,001	4,714
31,450	31,500	5,466	4,721	6,015	4,721
31,500	31,550	5,480	4,729	6,029	4,729
31,550	31,600	5,494	4,736	6,043	4,736
31,600	31,650	5,508	4,744	6,057	4,744
31,650	31,700	5,522	4,751	6,071	4,751
31,700	31,750	5,536	4,759	6,085	4,759
31,750	31,800	5,550	4,766	6,099	4,766
31,800	31,850	5,564	4,774	6,113	4,774
31,850	31,900	5,578	4,781	6,127	4,781
31,900	31,950	5,592	4,789	6,141	4,789
31,950	32,000	5,606	4,796	6,155	4,796

* This column must also be used by a qualifying widow(er).

Continued on next page

1999 Tax Table—*Continued*

If line 39 (taxable income) is—		And you are—			
At least	But less than	Single	Married filing jointly *	Married filing sepa-rately	Head of a house-hold
		Your tax is—			
32,000					
32,000	**32,050**	5,620	4,804	6,169	4,804
32,050	**32,100**	5,634	4,811	6,183	4,811
32,100	**32,150**	5,648	4,819	6,197	4,819
32,150	**32,200**	5,662	4,826	6,211	4,826
32,200	**32,250**	5,676	4,834	6,225	4,834
32,250	**32,300**	5,690	4,841	6,239	4,841
32,300	**32,350**	5,704	4,849	6,253	4,849
32,350	**32,400**	5,718	4,856	6,267	4,856
32,400	**32,450**	5,732	4,864	6,281	4,864
32,450	**32,500**	5,746	4,871	6,295	4,871
32,500	**32,550**	5,760	4,879	6,309	4,879
32,550	**32,600**	5,774	4,886	6,323	4,886
32,600	**32,650**	5,788	4,894	6,337	4,894
32,650	**32,700**	5,802	4,901	6,351	4,901
32,700	**32,750**	5,816	4,909	6,365	4,909
32,750	**32,800**	5,830	4,916	6,379	4,916
32,800	**32,850**	5,844	4,924	6,393	4,924
32,850	**32,900**	5,858	4,931	6,407	4,931
32,900	**32,950**	5,872	4,939	6,421	4,939
32,950	**33,000**	5,886	4,946	6,435	4,946
33,000					
33,000	**33,050**	5,900	4,954	6,449	4,954
33,050	**33,100**	5,914	4,961	6,463	4,961
33,100	**33,150**	5,928	4,969	6,477	4,969
33,150	**33,200**	5,942	4,976	6,491	4,976
33,200	**33,250**	5,956	4,984	6,505	4,984
33,250	**33,300**	5,970	4,991	6,519	4,991
33,300	**33,350**	5,984	4,999	6,533	4,999
33,350	**33,400**	5,998	5,006	6,547	5,006
33,400	**33,450**	6,012	5,014	6,561	5,014
33,450	**33,500**	6,026	5,021	6,575	5,021
33,500	**33,550**	6,040	5,029	6,589	5,029
33,550	**33,600**	6,054	5,036	6,603	5,036
33,600	**33,650**	6,068	5,044	6,617	5,044
33,650	**33,700**	6,082	5,051	6,631	5,051
33,700	**33,750**	6,096	5,059	6,645	5,059
33,750	**33,800**	6,110	5,066	6,659	5,066
33,800	**33,850**	6,124	5,074	6,673	5,074
33,850	**33,900**	6,138	5,081	6,687	5,081
33,900	**33,950**	6,152	5,089	6,701	5,089
33,950	**34,000**	6,166	5,096	6,715	5,096
34,000					
34,000	**34,050**	6,180	5,104	6,729	5,104
34,050	**34,100**	6,194	5,111	6,743	5,111
34,100	**34,150**	6,208	5,119	6,757	5,119
34,150	**34,200**	6,222	5,126	6,771	5,126
34,200	**34,250**	6,236	5,134	6,785	5,134
34,250	**34,300**	6,250	5,141	6,799	5,141
34,300	**34,350**	6,264	5,149	6,813	5,149
34,350	**34,400**	6,278	5,156	6,827	5,156
34,400	**34,450**	6,292	5,164	6,841	5,164
34,450	**34,500**	6,306	5,171	6,855	5,171
34,500	**34,550**	6,320	5,179	6,869	5,179
34,550	**34,600**	6,334	5,186	6,883	5,190
34,600	**34,650**	6,348	5,194	6,897	5,204
34,650	**34,700**	6,362	5,201	6,911	5,218
34,700	**34,750**	6,376	5,209	6,925	5,232
34,750	**34,800**	6,390	5,216	6,939	5,246
34,800	**34,850**	6,404	5,224	6,953	5,260
34,850	**34,900**	6,418	5,231	6,967	5,274
34,900	**34,950**	6,432	5,239	6,981	5,288
34,950	**35,000**	6,446	5,246	6,995	5,302

If line 39 (taxable income) is—		And you are—			
At least	But less than	Single	Married filing jointly *	Married filing sepa-rately	Head of a house-hold
		Your tax is—			
35,000					
35,000	**35,050**	6,460	5,254	7,009	5,316
35,050	**35,100**	6,474	5,261	7,023	5,330
35,100	**35,150**	6,488	5,269	7,037	5,344
35,150	**35,200**	6,502	5,276	7,051	5,358
35,200	**35,250**	6,516	5,284	7,065	5,372
35,250	**35,300**	6,530	5,291	7,079	5,386
35,300	**35,350**	6,544	5,299	7,093	5,400
35,350	**35,400**	6,558	5,306	7,107	5,414
35,400	**35,450**	6,572	5,314	7,121	5,428
35,450	**35,500**	6,586	5,321	7,135	5,442
35,500	**35,550**	6,600	5,329	7,149	5,456
35,550	**35,600**	6,614	5,336	7,163	5,470
35,600	**35,650**	6,628	5,344	7,177	5,484
35,650	**35,700**	6,642	5,351	7,191	5,498
35,700	**35,750**	6,656	5,359	7,205	5,512
35,750	**35,800**	6,670	5,366	7,219	5,526
35,800	**35,850**	6,684	5,374	7,233	5,540
35,850	**35,900**	6,698	5,381	7,247	5,554
35,900	**35,950**	6,712	5,389	7,261	5,568
35,950	**36,000**	6,726	5,396	7,275	5,582
36,000					
36,000	**36,050**	6,740	5,404	7,289	5,596
36,050	**36,100**	6,754	5,411	7,303	5,610
36,100	**36,150**	6,768	5,419	7,317	5,624
36,150	**36,200**	6,782	5,426	7,331	5,638
36,200	**36,250**	6,796	5,434	7,345	5,652
36,250	**36,300**	6,810	5,441	7,359	5,666
36,300	**36,350**	6,824	5,449	7,373	5,680
36,350	**36,400**	6,838	5,456	7,387	5,694
36,400	**36,450**	6,852	5,464	7,401	5,708
36,450	**36,500**	6,866	5,471	7,415	5,722
36,500	**36,550**	6,880	5,479	7,429	5,736
36,550	**36,600**	6,894	5,486	7,443	5,750
36,600	**36,650**	6,908	5,494	7,457	5,764
36,650	**36,700**	6,922	5,501	7,471	5,778
36,700	**36,750**	6,936	5,509	7,485	5,792
36,750	**36,800**	6,950	5,516	7,499	5,806
36,800	**36,850**	6,964	5,524	7,513	5,820
36,850	**36,900**	6,978	5,531	7,527	5,834
36,900	**36,950**	6,992	5,539	7,541	5,848
36,950	**37,000**	7,006	5,546	7,555	5,862
37,000					
37,000	**37,050**	7,020	5,554	7,569	5,876
37,050	**37,100**	7,034	5,561	7,583	5,890
37,100	**37,150**	7,048	5,569	7,597	5,904
37,150	**37,200**	7,062	5,576	7,611	5,918
37,200	**37,250**	7,076	5,584	7,625	5,932
37,250	**37,300**	7,090	5,591	7,639	5,946
37,300	**37,350**	7,104	5,599	7,653	5,960
37,350	**37,400**	7,118	5,606	7,667	5,974
37,400	**37,450**	7,132	5,614	7,681	5,988
37,450	**37,500**	7,146	5,621	7,695	6,002
37,500	**37,550**	7,160	5,629	7,709	6,016
37,550	**37,600**	7,174	5,636	7,723	6,030
37,600	**37,650**	7,188	5,644	7,737	6,044
37,650	**37,700**	7,202	5,651	7,751	6,058
37,700	**37,750**	7,216	5,659	7,765	6,072
37,750	**37,800**	7,230	5,666	7,779	6,086
37,800	**37,850**	7,244	5,674	7,793	6,100
37,850	**37,900**	7,258	5,681	7,807	6,114
37,900	**37,950**	7,272	5,689	7,821	6,128
37,950	**38,000**	7,286	5,696	7,835	6,142

If line 39 (taxable income) is—		And you are—			
At least	But less than	Single	Married filing jointly *	Married filing sepa-rately	Head of a house-hold
		Your tax is—			
38,000					
38,000	**38,050**	7,300	5,704	7,849	6,156
38,050	**38,100**	7,314	5,711	7,863	6,170
38,100	**38,150**	7,328	5,719	7,877	6,184
38,150	**38,200**	7,342	5,726	7,891	6,198
38,200	**38,250**	7,356	5,734	7,905	6,212
38,250	**38,300**	7,370	5,741	7,919	6,226
38,300	**38,350**	7,384	5,749	7,933	6,240
38,350	**38,400**	7,398	5,756	7,947	6,254
38,400	**38,450**	7,412	5,764	7,961	6,268
38,450	**38,500**	7,426	5,771	7,975	6,282
38,500	**38,550**	7,440	5,779	7,989	6,296
38,550	**38,600**	7,454	5,786	8,003	6,310
38,600	**38,650**	7,468	5,794	8,017	6,324
38,650	**38,700**	7,482	5,801	8,031	6,338
38,700	**38,750**	7,496	5,809	8,045	6,352
38,750	**38,800**	7,510	5,816	8,059	6,366
38,800	**38,850**	7,524	5,824	8,073	6,380
38,850	**38,900**	7,538	5,831	8,087	6,394
38,900	**38,950**	7,552	5,839	8,101	6,408
38,950	**39,000**	7,566	5,846	8,115	6,422
39,000					
39,000	**39,050**	7,580	5,854	8,129	6,436
39,050	**39,100**	7,594	5,861	8,143	6,450
39,100	**39,150**	7,608	5,869	8,157	6,464
39,150	**39,200**	7,622	5,876	8,171	6,478
39,200	**39,250**	7,636	5,884	8,185	6,492
39,250	**39,300**	7,650	5,891	8,199	6,506
39,300	**39,350**	7,664	5,899	8,213	6,520
39,350	**39,400**	7,678	5,906	8,227	6,534
39,400	**39,450**	7,692	5,914	8,241	6,548
39,450	**39,500**	7,706	5,921	8,255	6,562
39,500	**39,550**	7,720	5,929	8,269	6,576
39,550	**39,600**	7,734	5,936	8,283	6,590
39,600	**39,650**	7,748	5,944	8,297	6,604
39,650	**39,700**	7,762	5,951	8,311	6,618
39,700	**39,750**	7,776	5,959	8,325	6,632
39,750	**39,800**	7,790	5,966	8,339	6,646
39,800	**39,850**	7,804	5,974	8,353	6,660
39,850	**39,900**	7,818	5,981	8,367	6,674
39,900	**39,950**	7,832	5,989	8,381	6,688
39,950	**40,000**	7,846	5,996	8,395	6,702
40,000					
40,000	**40,050**	7,860	6,004	8,409	6,716
40,050	**40,100**	7,874	6,011	8,423	6,730
40,100	**40,150**	7,888	6,019	8,437	6,744
40,150	**40,200**	7,902	6,026	8,451	6,758
40,200	**40,250**	7,916	6,034	8,465	6,772
40,250	**40,300**	7,930	6,041	8,479	6,786
40,300	**40,350**	7,944	6,049	8,493	6,800
40,350	**40,400**	7,958	6,056	8,507	6,814
40,400	**40,450**	7,972	6,064	8,521	6,828
40,450	**40,500**	7,986	6,071	8,535	6,842
40,500	**40,550**	8,000	6,079	8,549	6,856
40,550	**40,600**	8,014	6,086	8,563	6,870
40,600	**40,650**	8,028	6,094	8,577	6,884
40,650	**40,700**	8,042	6,101	8,591	6,898
40,700	**40,750**	8,056	6,109	8,605	6,912
40,750	**40,800**	8,070	6,116	8,619	6,926
40,800	**40,850**	8,084	6,124	8,633	6,940
40,850	**40,900**	8,098	6,131	8,647	6,954
40,900	**40,950**	8,112	6,139	8,661	6,968
40,950	**41,000**	8,126	6,146	8,675	6,982

* This column must also be used by a qualifying widow(er).

Continued on next page

If line 39 (taxable income) is—		And you are—			
At least	But less than	Single	Married filing jointly *	Married filing separately	Head of a household
		Your tax is—			

41,000

At least	But less than	Single	Married filing jointly	Married filing separately	Head of a household
41,000	41,050	8,140	6,154	8,689	6,996
41,050	41,100	8,154	6,161	8,703	7,010
41,100	41,150	8,168	6,169	8,717	7,024
41,150	41,200	8,182	6,176	8,731	7,038
41,200	41,250	8,196	6,184	8,745	7,052
41,250	41,300	8,210	6,191	8,759	7,066
41,300	41,350	8,224	6,199	8,773	7,080
41,350	41,400	8,238	6,206	8,787	7,094
41,400	41,450	8,252	6,214	8,801	7,108
41,450	41,500	8,266	6,221	8,815	7,122
41,500	41,550	8,280	6,229	8,829	7,136
41,550	41,600	8,294	6,236	8,843	7,150
41,600	41,650	8,308	6,244	8,857	7,164
41,650	41,700	8,322	6,251	8,871	7,178
41,700	41,750	8,336	6,259	8,885	7,192
41,750	41,800	8,350	6,266	8,899	7,206
41,800	41,850	8,364	6,274	8,913	7,220
41,850	41,900	8,378	6,281	8,927	7,234
41,900	41,950	8,392	6,289	8,941	7,248
41,950	42,000	8,406	6,296	8,955	7,262

42,000

At least	But less than	Single	Married filing jointly	Married filing separately	Head of a household
42,000	42,050	8,420	6,304	8,969	7,276
42,050	42,100	8,434	6,311	8,983	7,290
42,100	42,150	8,448	6,319	8,997	7,304
42,150	42,200	8,462	6,326	9,011	7,318
42,200	42,250	8,476	6,334	9,025	7,332
42,250	42,300	8,490	6,341	9,039	7,346
42,300	42,350	8,504	6,349	9,053	7,360
42,350	42,400	8,518	6,356	9,067	7,374
42,400	42,450	8,532	6,364	9,081	7,388
42,450	42,500	8,546	6,371	9,095	7,402
42,500	42,550	8,560	6,379	9,109	7,416
42,550	42,600	8,574	6,386	9,123	7,430
42,600	42,650	8,588	6,394	9,137	7,444
42,650	42,700	8,602	6,401	9,151	7,458
42,700	42,750	8,616	6,409	9,165	7,472
42,750	42,800	8,630	6,416	9,179	7,486
42,800	42,850	8,644	6,424	9,193	7,500
42,850	42,900	8,658	6,431	9,207	7,514
42,900	42,950	8,672	6,439	9,221	7,528
42,950	43,000	8,686	6,446	9,235	7,542

43,000

At least	But less than	Single	Married filing jointly	Married filing separately	Head of a household
43,000	43,050	8,700	6,454	9,249	7,556
43,050	43,100	8,714	6,465	9,263	7,570
43,100	43,150	8,728	6,479	9,277	7,584
43,150	43,200	8,742	6,493	9,291	7,598
43,200	43,250	8,756	6,507	9,305	7,612
43,250	43,300	8,770	6,521	9,319	7,626
43,300	43,350	8,784	6,535	9,333	7,640
43,350	43,400	8,798	6,549	9,347	7,654
43,400	43,450	8,812	6,563	9,361	7,668
43,450	43,500	8,826	6,577	9,375	7,682
43,500	43,550	8,840	6,591	9,389	7,696
43,550	43,600	8,854	6,605	9,403	7,710
43,600	43,650	8,868	6,619	9,417	7,724
43,650	43,700	8,882	6,633	9,431	7,738
43,700	43,750	8,896	6,647	9,445	7,752
43,750	43,800	8,910	6,661	9,459	7,766
43,800	43,850	8,924	6,675	9,473	7,780
43,850	43,900	8,938	6,689	9,487	7,794
43,900	43,950	8,952	6,703	9,501	7,808
43,950	44,000	8,966	6,717	9,515	7,822

44,000

At least	But less than	Single	Married filing jointly	Married filing separately	Head of a household
44,000	44,050	8,980	6,731	9,529	7,836
44,050	44,100	8,994	6,745	9,543	7,850
44,100	44,150	9,008	6,759	9,557	7,864
44,150	44,200	9,022	6,773	9,571	7,878
44,200	44,250	9,036	6,787	9,585	7,892
44,250	44,300	9,050	6,801	9,599	7,906
44,300	44,350	9,064	6,815	9,613	7,920
44,350	44,400	9,078	6,829	9,627	7,934
44,400	44,450	9,092	6,843	9,641	7,948
44,450	44,500	9,106	6,857	9,655	7,962
44,500	44,550	9,120	6,871	9,669	7,976
44,550	44,600	9,134	6,885	9,683	7,990
44,600	44,650	9,148	6,899	9,697	8,004
44,650	44,700	9,162	6,913	9,711	8,018
44,700	44,750	9,176	6,927	9,725	8,032
44,750	44,800	9,190	6,941	9,739	8,046
44,800	44,850	9,204	6,955	9,753	8,060
44,850	44,900	9,218	6,969	9,767	8,074
44,900	44,950	9,232	6,983	9,781	8,088
44,950	45,000	9,246	6,997	9,795	8,102

45,000

At least	But less than	Single	Married filing jointly	Married filing separately	Head of a household
45,000	45,050	9,260	7,011	9,809	8,116
45,050	45,100	9,274	7,025	9,823	8,130
45,100	45,150	9,288	7,039	9,837	8,144
45,150	45,200	9,302	7,053	9,851	8,158
45,200	45,250	9,316	7,067	9,865	8,172
45,250	45,300	9,330	7,081	9,879	8,186
45,300	45,350	9,344	7,095	9,893	8,200
45,350	45,400	9,358	7,109	9,907	8,214
45,400	45,450	9,372	7,123	9,921	8,228
45,450	45,500	9,386	7,137	9,935	8,242
45,500	45,550	9,400	7,151	9,949	8,256
45,550	45,600	9,414	7,165	9,963	8,270
45,600	45,650	9,428	7,179	9,977	8,284
45,650	45,700	9,442	7,193	9,991	8,298
45,700	45,750	9,456	7,207	10,005	8,312
45,750	45,800	9,470	7,221	10,019	8,326
45,800	45,850	9,484	7,235	10,033	8,340
45,850	45,900	9,498	7,249	10,047	8,354
45,900	45,950	9,512	7,263	10,061	8,368
45,950	46,000	9,526	7,277	10,075	8,382

46,000

At least	But less than	Single	Married filing jointly	Married filing separately	Head of a household
46,000	46,050	9,540	7,291	10,089	8,396
46,050	46,100	9,554	7,305	10,103	8,410
46,100	46,150	9,568	7,319	10,117	8,424
46,150	46,200	9,582	7,333	10,131	8,438
46,200	46,250	9,596	7,347	10,145	8,452
46,250	46,300	9,610	7,361	10,159	8,466
46,300	46,350	9,624	7,375	10,173	8,480
46,350	46,400	9,638	7,389	10,187	8,494
46,400	46,450	9,652	7,403	10,201	8,508
46,450	46,500	9,666	7,417	10,215	8,522
46,500	46,550	9,680	7,431	10,229	8,536
46,550	46,600	9,694	7,445	10,243	8,550
46,600	46,650	9,708	7,459	10,257	8,564
46,650	46,700	9,722	7,473	10,271	8,578
46,700	46,750	9,736	7,487	10,285	8,592
46,750	46,800	9,750	7,501	10,299	8,606
46,800	46,850	9,764	7,515	10,313	8,620
46,850	46,900	9,778	7,529	10,327	8,634
46,900	46,950	9,792	7,543	10,341	8,648
46,950	47,000	9,806	7,557	10,355	8,662

47,000

At least	But less than	Single	Married filing jointly	Married filing separately	Head of a household
47,000	47,050	9,820	7,571	10,369	8,676
47,050	47,100	9,834	7,585	10,383	8,690
47,100	47,150	9,848	7,599	10,397	8,704
47,150	47,200	9,862	7,613	10,411	8,718
47,200	47,250	9,876	7,627	10,425	8,732
47,250	47,300	9,890	7,641	10,439	8,746
47,300	47,350	9,904	7,655	10,453	8,760
47,350	47,400	9,918	7,669	10,467	8,774
47,400	47,450	9,932	7,683	10,481	8,788
47,450	47,500	9,946	7,697	10,495	8,802
47,500	47,550	9,960	7,711	10,509	8,816
47,550	47,600	9,974	7,725	10,523	8,830
47,600	47,650	9,988	7,739	10,537	8,844
47,650	47,700	10,002	7,753	10,551	8,858
47,700	47,750	10,016	7,767	10,565	8,872
47,750	47,800	10,030	7,781	10,579	8,886
47,800	47,850	10,044	7,795	10,593	8,900
47,850	47,900	10,058	7,809	10,607	8,914
47,900	47,950	10,072	7,823	10,621	8,928
47,950	48,000	10,086	7,837	10,635	8,942

48,000

At least	But less than	Single	Married filing jointly	Married filing separately	Head of a household
48,000	48,050	10,100	7,851	10,649	8,956
48,050	48,100	10,114	7,865	10,663	8,970
48,100	48,150	10,128	7,879	10,677	8,984
48,150	48,200	10,142	7,893	10,691	8,998
48,200	48,250	10,156	7,907	10,705	9,012
48,250	48,300	10,170	7,921	10,719	9,026
48,300	48,350	10,184	7,935	10,733	9,040
48,350	48,400	10,198	7,949	10,747	9,054
48,400	48,450	10,212	7,963	10,761	9,068
48,450	48,500	10,226	7,977	10,775	9,082
48,500	48,550	10,240	7,991	10,789	9,096
48,550	48,600	10,254	8,005	10,803	9,110
48,600	48,650	10,268	8,019	10,817	9,124
48,650	48,700	10,282	8,033	10,831	9,138
48,700	48,750	10,296	8,047	10,845	9,152
48,750	48,800	10,310	8,061	10,859	9,166
48,800	48,850	10,324	8,075	10,873	9,180
48,850	48,900	10,338	8,089	10,887	9,194
48,900	48,950	10,352	8,103	10,901	9,208
48,950	49,000	10,366	8,117	10,915	9,222

49,000

At least	But less than	Single	Married filing jointly	Married filing separately	Head of a household
49,000	49,050	10,380	8,131	10,929	9,236
49,050	49,100	10,394	8,145	10,943	9,250
49,100	49,150	10,408	8,159	10,957	9,264
49,150	49,200	10,422	8,173	10,971	9,278
49,200	49,250	10,436	8,187	10,985	9,292
49,250	49,300	10,450	8,201	10,999	9,306
49,300	49,350	10,464	8,215	11,013	9,320
49,350	49,400	10,478	8,229	11,027	9,334
49,400	49,450	10,492	8,243	11,041	9,348
49,450	49,500	10,506	8,257	11,055	9,362
49,500	49,550	10,520	8,271	11,069	9,376
49,550	49,600	10,534	8,285	11,083	9,390
49,600	49,650	10,548	8,299	11,097	9,404
49,650	49,700	10,562	8,313	11,111	9,418
49,700	49,750	10,576	8,327	11,125	9,432
49,750	49,800	10,590	8,341	11,139	9,446
49,800	49,850	10,604	8,355	11,153	9,460
49,850	49,900	10,618	8,369	11,167	9,474
49,900	49,950	10,632	8,383	11,181	9,488
49,950	50,000	10,646	8,397	11,195	9,502

* This column must also be used by a qualifying widow(er).

Continued on next page

If line 39 (taxable income) is—		And you are—				If line 39 (taxable income) is—		And you are—				If line 39 (taxable income) is—		And you are—			
At least	But less than	Single	Married filing jointly *	Married filing separately	Head of a house-hold	At least	But less than	Single	Married filing jointly *	Married filing separately	Head of a house-hold	At least	But less than	Single	Married filing jointly *	Married filing separately	Head of a house-hold
		Your tax is—						Your tax is—						Your tax is—			
50,000						**53,000**						**56,000**					
50,000	50,050	10,660	8,411	11,209	9,516	53,000	53,050	11,500	9,251	12,079	10,356	56,000	56,050	12,340	10,091	13,009	11,196
50,050	50,100	10,674	8,425	11,223	9,530	53,050	53,100	11,514	9,265	12,094	10,370	56,050	56,100	12,354	10,105	13,024	11,210
50,100	50,150	10,688	8,439	11,237	9,544	53,100	53,150	11,528	9,279	12,110	10,384	56,100	56,150	12,368	10,119	13,040	11,224
50,150	50,200	10,702	8,453	11,251	9,558	53,150	53,200	11,542	9,293	12,125	10,398	56,150	56,200	12,382	10,133	13,055	11,238
50,200	50,250	10,716	8,467	11,265	9,572	53,200	53,250	11,556	9,307	12,141	10,412	56,200	56,250	12,396	10,147	13,071	11,252
50,250	50,300	10,730	8,481	11,279	9,586	53,250	53,300	11,570	9,321	12,156	10,426	56,250	56,300	12,410	10,161	13,086	11,266
50,300	50,350	10,744	8,495	11,293	9,600	53,300	53,350	11,584	9,335	12,172	10,440	56,300	56,350	12,424	10,175	13,102	11,280
50,350	50,400	10,758	8,509	11,307	9,614	53,350	53,400	11,598	9,349	12,187	10,454	56,350	56,400	12,438	10,189	13,117	11,294
50,400	50,450	10,772	8,523	11,321	9,628	53,400	53,450	11,612	9,363	12,203	10,468	56,400	56,450	12,452	10,203	13,133	11,308
50,450	50,500	10,786	8,537	11,335	9,642	53,450	53,500	11,626	9,377	12,218	10,482	56,450	56,500	12,466	10,217	13,148	11,322
50,500	50,550	10,800	8,551	11,349	9,656	53,500	53,550	11,640	9,391	12,234	10,496	56,500	56,550	12,480	10,231	13,164	11,336
50,550	50,600	10,814	8,565	11,363	9,670	53,550	53,600	11,654	9,405	12,249	10,510	56,550	56,600	12,494	10,245	13,179	11,350
50,600	50,650	10,828	8,579	11,377	9,684	53,600	53,650	11,668	9,419	12,265	10,524	56,600	56,650	12,508	10,259	13,195	11,364
50,650	50,700	10,842	8,593	11,391	9,698	53,650	53,700	11,682	9,433	12,280	10,538	56,650	56,700	12,522	10,273	13,210	11,378
50,700	50,750	10,856	8,607	11,405	9,712	53,700	53,750	11,696	9,447	12,296	10,552	56,700	56,750	12,536	10,287	13,226	11,392
50,750	50,800	10,870	8,621	11,419	9,726	53,750	53,800	11,710	9,461	12,311	10,566	56,750	56,800	12,550	10,301	13,241	11,406
50,800	50,850	10,884	8,635	11,433	9,740	53,800	53,850	11,724	9,475	12,327	10,580	56,800	56,850	12,564	10,315	13,257	11,420
50,850	50,900	10,898	8,649	11,447	9,754	53,850	53,900	11,738	9,489	12,342	10,594	56,850	56,900	12,578	10,329	13,272	11,434
50,900	50,950	10,912	8,663	11,461	9,768	53,900	53,950	11,752	9,503	12,358	10,608	56,900	56,950	12,592	10,343	13,288	11,448
50,950	51,000	10,926	8,677	11,475	9,782	53,950	54,000	11,766	9,517	12,373	10,622	56,950	57,000	12,606	10,357	13,303	11,462
51,000						**54,000**						**57,000**					
51,000	51,050	10,940	8,691	11,489	9,796	54,000	54,050	11,780	9,531	12,389	10,636	57,000	57,050	12,620	10,371	13,319	11,476
51,050	51,100	10,954	8,705	11,503	9,810	54,050	54,100	11,794	9,545	12,404	10,650	57,050	57,100	12,634	10,385	13,334	11,490
51,100	51,150	10,968	8,719	11,517	9,824	54,100	54,150	11,808	9,559	12,420	10,664	57,100	57,150	12,648	10,399	13,350	11,504
51,150	51,200	10,982	8,733	11,531	9,838	54,150	54,200	11,822	9,573	12,435	10,678	57,150	57,200	12,662	10,413	13,365	11,518
51,200	51,250	10,996	8,747	11,545	9,852	54,200	54,250	11,836	9,587	12,451	10,692	57,200	57,250	12,676	10,427	13,381	11,532
51,250	51,300	11,010	8,761	11,559	9,866	54,250	54,300	11,850	9,601	12,466	10,706	57,250	57,300	12,690	10,441	13,396	11,546
51,300	51,350	11,024	8,775	11,573	9,880	54,300	54,350	11,864	9,615	12,482	10,720	57,300	57,350	12,704	10,455	13,412	11,560
51,350	51,400	11,038	8,789	11,587	9,894	54,350	54,400	11,878	9,629	12,497	10,734	57,350	57,400	12,718	10,469	13,427	11,574
51,400	51,450	11,052	8,803	11,601	9,908	54,400	54,450	11,892	9,643	12,513	10,748	57,400	57,450	12,732	10,483	13,443	11,588
51,450	51,500	11,066	8,817	11,615	9,922	54,450	54,500	11,906	9,657	12,528	10,762	57,450	57,500	12,746	10,497	13,458	11,602
51,500	51,550	11,080	8,831	11,629	9,936	54,500	54,550	11,920	9,671	12,544	10,776	57,500	57,550	12,760	10,511	13,474	11,616
51,550	51,600	11,094	8,845	11,643	9,950	54,550	54,600	11,934	9,685	12,559	10,790	57,550	57,600	12,774	10,525	13,489	11,630
51,600	51,650	11,108	8,859	11,657	9,964	54,600	54,650	11,948	9,699	12,575	10,804	57,600	57,650	12,788	10,539	13,505	11,644
51,650	51,700	11,122	8,873	11,671	9,978	54,650	54,700	11,962	9,713	12,590	10,818	57,650	57,700	12,802	10,553	13,520	11,658
51,700	51,750	11,136	8,887	11,685	9,992	54,700	54,750	11,976	9,727	12,606	10,832	57,700	57,750	12,816	10,567	13,536	11,672
51,750	51,800	11,150	8,901	11,699	10,006	54,750	54,800	11,990	9,741	12,621	10,846	57,750	57,800	12,830	10,581	13,551	11,686
51,800	51,850	11,164	8,915	11,713	10,020	54,800	54,850	12,004	9,755	12,637	10,860	57,800	57,850	12,844	10,595	13,567	11,700
51,850	51,900	11,178	8,929	11,727	10,034	54,850	54,900	12,018	9,769	12,652	10,874	57,850	57,900	12,858	10,609	13,582	11,714
51,900	51,950	11,192	8,943	11,741	10,048	54,900	54,950	12,032	9,783	12,668	10,888	57,900	57,950	12,872	10,623	13,598	11,728
51,950	52,000	11,206	8,957	11,755	10,062	54,950	55,000	12,046	9,797	12,683	10,902	57,950	58,000	12,886	10,637	13,613	11,742
52,000						**55,000**						**58,000**					
52,000	52,050	11,220	8,971	11,769	10,076	55,000	55,050	12,060	9,811	12,699	10,916	58,000	58,050	12,900	10,651	13,629	11,756
52,050	52,100	11,234	8,985	11,784	10,090	55,050	55,100	12,074	9,825	12,714	10,930	58,050	58,100	12,914	10,665	13,644	11,770
52,100	52,150	11,248	8,999	11,800	10,104	55,100	55,150	12,088	9,839	12,730	10,944	58,100	58,150	12,928	10,679	13,660	11,784
52,150	52,200	11,262	9,013	11,815	10,118	55,150	55,200	12,102	9,853	12,745	10,958	58,150	58,200	12,942	10,693	13,675	11,798
52,200	52,250	11,276	9,027	11,831	10,132	55,200	55,250	12,116	9,867	12,761	10,972	58,200	58,250	12,956	10,707	13,691	11,812
52,250	52,300	11,290	9,041	11,846	10,146	55,250	55,300	12,130	9,881	12,776	10,986	58,250	58,300	12,970	10,721	13,706	11,826
52,300	52,350	11,304	9,055	11,862	10,160	55,300	55,350	12,144	9,895	12,792	11,000	58,300	58,350	12,984	10,735	13,722	11,840
52,350	52,400	11,318	9,069	11,877	10,174	55,350	55,400	12,158	9,909	12,807	11,014	58,350	58,400	12,998	10,749	13,737	11,854
52,400	52,450	11,332	9,083	11,893	10,188	55,400	55,450	12,172	9,923	12,823	11,028	58,400	58,450	13,012	10,763	13,753	11,868
52,450	52,500	11,346	9,097	11,908	10,202	55,450	55,500	12,186	9,937	12,838	11,042	58,450	58,500	13,026	10,777	13,768	11,882
52,500	52,550	11,360	9,111	11,924	10,216	55,500	55,550	12,200	9,951	12,854	11,056	58,500	58,550	13,040	10,791	13,784	11,896
52,550	52,600	11,374	9,125	11,939	10,230	55,550	55,600	12,214	9,965	12,869	11,070	58,550	58,600	13,054	10,805	13,799	11,910
52,600	52,650	11,388	9,139	11,955	10,244	55,600	55,650	12,228	9,979	12,885	11,084	58,600	58,650	13,068	10,819	13,815	11,924
52,650	52,700	11,402	9,153	11,970	10,258	55,650	55,700	12,242	9,993	12,900	11,098	58,650	58,700	13,082	10,833	13,830	11,938
52,700	52,750	11,416	9,167	11,986	10,272	55,700	55,750	12,256	10,007	12,916	11,112	58,700	58,750	13,096	10,847	13,846	11,952
52,750	52,800	11,430	9,181	12,001	10,286	55,750	55,800	12,270	10,021	12,931	11,126	58,750	58,800	13,110	10,861	13,861	11,966
52,800	52,850	11,444	9,195	12,017	10,300	55,800	55,850	12,284	10,035	12,947	11,140	58,800	58,850	13,124	10,875	13,877	11,980
52,850	52,900	11,458	9,209	12,032	10,314	55,850	55,900	12,298	10,049	12,962	11,154	58,850	58,900	13,138	10,889	13,892	11,994
52,900	52,950	11,472	9,223	12,048	10,328	55,900	55,950	12,312	10,063	12,978	11,168	58,900	58,950	13,152	10,903	13,908	12,008
52,950	53,000	11,486	9,237	12,063	10,342	55,950	56,000	12,326	10,077	12,993	11,182	58,950	59,000	13,166	10,917	13,923	12,022

* This column must also be used by a qualifying widow(er).

Continued on next page

59,000 – 61,000

If line 39 (taxable income) is— At least	But less than	Single	Married filing jointly*	Married filing separately	Head of a household
			Your tax is—		
59,000					
59,000	59,050	13,180	10,931	13,939	12,036
59,050	59,100	13,194	10,945	13,954	12,050
59,100	59,150	13,208	10,959	13,970	12,064
59,150	59,200	13,222	10,973	13,985	12,078
59,200	59,250	13,236	10,987	14,001	12,092
59,250	59,300	13,250	11,001	14,016	12,106
59,300	59,350	13,264	11,015	14,032	12,120
59,350	59,400	13,278	11,029	14,047	12,134
59,400	59,450	13,292	11,043	14,063	12,148
59,450	59,500	13,306	11,057	14,078	12,162
59,500	59,550	13,320	11,071	14,094	12,176
59,550	59,600	13,334	11,085	14,109	12,190
59,600	59,650	13,348	11,099	14,125	12,204
59,650	59,700	13,362	11,113	14,140	12,218
59,700	59,750	13,376	11,127	14,156	12,232
59,750	59,800	13,390	11,141	14,171	12,246
59,800	59,850	13,404	11,155	14,187	12,260
59,850	59,900	13,418	11,169	14,202	12,274
59,900	59,950	13,432	11,183	14,218	12,288
59,950	60,000	13,446	11,197	14,233	12,302
60,000					
60,000	60,050	13,460	11,211	14,249	12,316
60,050	60,100	13,474	11,225	14,264	12,330
60,100	60,150	13,488	11,239	14,280	12,344
60,150	60,200	13,502	11,253	14,295	12,358
60,200	60,250	13,516	11,267	14,311	12,372
60,250	60,300	13,530	11,281	14,326	12,386
60,300	60,350	13,544	11,295	14,342	12,400
60,350	60,400	13,558	11,309	14,357	12,414
60,400	60,450	13,572	11,323	14,373	12,428
60,450	60,500	13,586	11,337	14,388	12,442
60,500	60,550	13,600	11,351	14,404	12,456
60,550	60,600	13,614	11,365	14,419	12,470
60,600	60,650	13,628	11,379	14,435	12,484
60,650	60,700	13,642	11,393	14,450	12,498
60,700	60,750	13,656	11,407	14,466	12,512
60,750	60,800	13,670	11,421	14,481	12,526
60,800	60,850	13,684	11,435	14,497	12,540
60,850	60,900	13,698	11,449	14,512	12,554
60,900	60,950	13,712	11,463	14,528	12,568
60,950	61,000	13,726	11,477	14,543	12,582
61,000					
61,000	61,050	13,740	11,491	14,559	12,596
61,050	61,100	13,754	11,505	14,574	12,610
61,100	61,150	13,768	11,519	14,590	12,624
61,150	61,200	13,782	11,533	14,605	12,638
61,200	61,250	13,796	11,547	14,621	12,652
61,250	61,300	13,810	11,561	14,636	12,666
61,300	61,350	13,824	11,575	14,652	12,680
61,350	61,400	13,838	11,589	14,667	12,694
61,400	61,450	13,852	11,603	14,683	12,708
61,450	61,500	13,866	11,617	14,698	12,722
61,500	61,550	13,880	11,631	14,714	12,736
61,550	61,600	13,894	11,645	14,729	12,750
61,600	61,650	13,908	11,659	14,745	12,764
61,650	61,700	13,922	11,673	14,760	12,778
61,700	61,750	13,936	11,687	14,776	12,792
61,750	61,800	13,950	11,701	14,791	12,806
61,800	61,850	13,964	11,715	14,807	12,820
61,850	61,900	13,978	11,729	14,822	12,834
61,900	61,950	13,992	11,743	14,838	12,848
61,950	62,000	14,006	11,757	14,853	12,862

62,000 – 64,000

If line 39 (taxable income) is— At least	But less than	Single	Married filing jointly*	Married filing separately	Head of a household
			Your tax is—		
62,000					
62,000	62,050	14,020	11,771	14,869	12,876
62,050	62,100	14,034	11,785	14,884	12,890
62,100	62,150	14,048	11,799	14,900	12,904
62,150	62,200	14,062	11,813	14,915	12,918
62,200	62,250	14,076	11,827	14,931	12,932
62,250	62,300	14,090	11,841	14,946	12,946
62,300	62,350	14,104	11,855	14,962	12,960
62,350	62,400	14,118	11,869	14,977	12,974
62,400	62,450	14,132	11,883	14,993	12,988
62,450	62,500	14,146	11,897	15,008	13,002
62,500	62,550	14,162	11,911	15,024	13,016
62,550	62,600	14,177	11,925	15,039	13,030
62,600	62,650	14,193	11,939	15,055	13,044
62,650	62,700	14,208	11,953	15,070	13,058
62,700	62,750	14,224	11,967	15,086	13,072
62,750	62,800	14,239	11,981	15,101	13,086
62,800	62,850	14,255	11,995	15,117	13,100
62,850	62,900	14,270	12,009	15,132	13,114
62,900	62,950	14,286	12,023	15,148	13,128
62,950	63,000	14,301	12,037	15,163	13,142
63,000					
63,000	63,050	14,317	12,051	15,179	13,156
63,050	63,100	14,332	12,065	15,194	13,170
63,100	63,150	14,348	12,079	15,210	13,184
63,150	63,200	14,363	12,093	15,225	13,198
63,200	63,250	14,379	12,107	15,241	13,212
63,250	63,300	14,394	12,121	15,256	13,226
63,300	63,350	14,410	12,135	15,272	13,240
63,350	63,400	14,425	12,149	15,287	13,254
63,400	63,450	14,441	12,163	15,303	13,268
63,450	63,500	14,456	12,177	15,318	13,282
63,500	63,550	14,472	12,191	15,334	13,296
63,550	63,600	14,487	12,205	15,349	13,310
63,600	63,650	14,503	12,219	15,365	13,324
63,650	63,700	14,518	12,233	15,380	13,338
63,700	63,750	14,534	12,247	15,396	13,352
63,750	63,800	14,549	12,261	15,411	13,366
63,800	63,850	14,565	12,275	15,427	13,380
63,850	63,900	14,580	12,289	15,442	13,394
63,900	63,950	14,596	12,303	15,458	13,408
63,950	64,000	14,611	12,317	15,473	13,422
64,000					
64,000	64,050	14,627	12,331	15,489	13,436
64,050	64,100	14,642	12,345	15,504	13,450
64,100	64,150	14,658	12,359	15,520	13,464
64,150	64,200	14,673	12,373	15,535	13,478
64,200	64,250	14,689	12,387	15,551	13,492
64,250	64,300	14,704	12,401	15,566	13,506
64,300	64,350	14,720	12,415	15,582	13,520
64,350	64,400	14,735	12,429	15,597	13,534
64,400	64,450	14,751	12,443	15,613	13,548
64,450	64,500	14,766	12,457	15,628	13,562
64,500	64,550	14,782	12,471	15,644	13,576
64,550	64,600	14,797	12,485	15,659	13,590
64,600	64,650	14,813	12,499	15,675	13,604
64,650	64,700	14,828	12,513	15,690	13,618
64,700	64,750	14,844	12,527	15,706	13,632
64,750	64,800	14,859	12,541	15,721	13,646
64,800	64,850	14,875	12,555	15,737	13,660
64,850	64,900	14,890	12,569	15,752	13,674
64,900	64,950	14,906	12,583	15,768	13,688
64,950	65,000	14,921	12,597	15,783	13,702

65,000 – 67,000

If line 39 (taxable income) is— At least	But less than	Single	Married filing jointly*	Married filing separately	Head of a household
			Your tax is—		
65,000					
65,000	65,050	14,937	12,611	15,799	13,716
65,050	65,100	14,952	12,625	15,814	13,730
65,100	65,150	14,968	12,639	15,830	13,744
65,150	65,200	14,983	12,653	15,845	13,758
65,200	65,250	14,999	12,667	15,861	13,772
65,250	65,300	15,014	12,681	15,876	13,786
65,300	65,350	15,030	12,695	15,892	13,800
65,350	65,400	15,045	12,709	15,907	13,814
65,400	65,450	15,061	12,723	15,923	13,828
65,450	65,500	15,076	12,737	15,938	13,842
65,500	65,550	15,092	12,751	15,954	13,856
65,550	65,600	15,107	12,765	15,969	13,870
65,600	65,650	15,123	12,779	15,985	13,884
65,650	65,700	15,138	12,793	16,000	13,898
65,700	65,750	15,154	12,807	16,016	13,912
65,750	65,800	15,169	12,821	16,031	13,926
65,800	65,850	15,185	12,835	16,047	13,940
65,850	65,900	15,200	12,849	16,062	13,954
65,900	65,950	15,216	12,863	16,078	13,968
65,950	66,000	15,231	12,877	16,093	13,982
66,000					
66,000	66,050	15,247	12,891	16,109	13,996
66,050	66,100	15,262	12,905	16,124	14,010
66,100	66,150	15,278	12,919	16,140	14,024
66,150	66,200	15,293	12,933	16,155	14,038
66,200	66,250	15,309	12,947	16,171	14,052
66,250	66,300	15,324	12,961	16,186	14,066
66,300	66,350	15,340	12,975	16,202	14,080
66,350	66,400	15,355	12,989	16,217	14,094
66,400	66,450	15,371	13,003	16,233	14,108
66,450	66,500	15,386	13,017	16,248	14,122
66,500	66,550	15,402	13,031	16,264	14,136
66,550	66,600	15,417	13,045	16,279	14,150
66,600	66,650	15,433	13,059	16,295	14,164
66,650	66,700	15,448	13,073	16,310	14,178
66,700	66,750	15,464	13,087	16,326	14,192
66,750	66,800	15,479	13,101	16,341	14,206
66,800	66,850	15,495	13,115	16,357	14,220
66,850	66,900	15,510	13,129	16,372	14,234
66,900	66,950	15,526	13,143	16,388	14,248
66,950	67,000	15,541	13,157	16,403	14,262
67,000					
67,000	67,050	15,557	13,171	16,419	14,276
67,050	67,100	15,572	13,185	16,434	14,290
67,100	67,150	15,588	13,199	16,450	14,304
67,150	67,200	15,603	13,213	16,465	14,318
67,200	67,250	15,619	13,227	16,481	14,332
67,250	67,300	15,634	13,241	16,496	14,346
67,300	67,350	15,650	13,255	16,512	14,360
67,350	67,400	15,665	13,269	16,527	14,374
67,400	67,450	15,681	13,283	16,543	14,388
67,450	67,500	15,696	13,297	16,558	14,402
67,500	67,550	15,712	13,311	16,574	14,416
67,550	67,600	15,727	13,325	16,589	14,430
67,600	67,650	15,743	13,339	16,605	14,444
67,650	67,700	15,758	13,353	16,620	14,458
67,700	67,750	15,774	13,367	16,636	14,472
67,750	67,800	15,789	13,381	16,651	14,486
67,800	67,850	15,805	13,395	16,667	14,500
67,850	67,900	15,820	13,409	16,682	14,514
67,900	67,950	15,836	13,423	16,698	14,528
67,950	68,000	15,851	13,437	16,713	14,542

* This column must also be used by a qualifying widow(er).

Continued on next page

If line 39 (taxable income) is— / And you are—

* This column must also be used by a qualifying widow(er).

At least	But less than	Single	Married filing jointly*	Married filing separately	Head of a household
68,000					
68,000	68,050	15,867	13,451	16,729	14,556
68,050	68,100	15,882	13,465	16,744	14,570
68,100	68,150	15,898	13,479	16,760	14,584
68,150	68,200	15,913	13,493	16,775	14,598
68,200	68,250	15,929	13,507	16,791	14,612
68,250	68,300	15,944	13,521	16,806	14,626
68,300	68,350	15,960	13,535	16,822	14,640
68,350	68,400	15,975	13,549	16,837	14,654
68,400	68,450	15,991	13,563	16,853	14,668
68,450	68,500	16,006	13,577	16,868	14,682
68,500	68,550	16,022	13,591	16,884	14,696
68,550	68,600	16,037	13,605	16,899	14,710
68,600	68,650	16,053	13,619	16,915	14,724
68,650	68,700	16,068	13,633	16,930	14,738
68,700	68,750	16,084	13,647	16,946	14,752
68,750	68,800	16,099	13,661	16,961	14,766
68,800	68,850	16,115	13,675	16,977	14,780
68,850	68,900	16,130	13,689	16,992	14,794
68,900	68,950	16,146	13,703	17,008	14,808
68,950	69,000	16,161	13,717	17,023	14,822
69,000					
69,000	69,050	16,177	13,731	17,039	14,836
69,050	69,100	16,192	13,745	17,054	14,850
69,100	69,150	16,208	13,759	17,070	14,864
69,150	69,200	16,223	13,773	17,085	14,878
69,200	69,250	16,239	13,787	17,101	14,892
69,250	69,300	16,254	13,801	17,116	14,906
69,300	69,350	16,270	13,815	17,132	14,920
69,350	69,400	16,285	13,829	17,147	14,934
69,400	69,450	16,301	13,843	17,163	14,948
69,450	69,500	16,316	13,857	17,178	14,962
69,500	69,550	16,332	13,871	17,194	14,976
69,550	69,600	16,347	13,885	17,209	14,990
69,600	69,650	16,363	13,899	17,225	15,004
69,650	69,700	16,378	13,913	17,240	15,018
69,700	69,750	16,394	13,927	17,256	15,032
69,750	69,800	16,409	13,941	17,271	15,046
69,800	69,850	16,425	13,955	17,287	15,060
69,850	69,900	16,440	13,969	17,302	15,074
69,900	69,950	16,456	13,983	17,318	15,088
69,950	70,000	16,471	13,997	17,333	15,102
70,000					
70,000	70,050	16,487	14,011	17,349	15,116
70,050	70,100	16,502	14,025	17,364	15,130
70,100	70,150	16,518	14,039	17,380	15,144
70,150	70,200	16,533	14,053	17,395	15,158
70,200	70,250	16,549	14,067	17,411	15,172
70,250	70,300	16,564	14,081	17,426	15,186
70,300	70,350	16,580	14,095	17,442	15,200
70,350	70,400	16,595	14,109	17,457	15,214
70,400	70,450	16,611	14,123	17,473	15,228
70,450	70,500	16,626	14,137	17,488	15,242
70,500	70,550	16,642	14,151	17,504	15,256
70,550	70,600	16,657	14,165	17,519	15,270
70,600	70,650	16,673	14,179	17,535	15,284
70,650	70,700	16,688	14,193	17,550	15,298
70,700	70,750	16,704	14,207	17,566	15,312
70,750	70,800	16,719	14,221	17,581	15,326
70,800	70,850	16,735	14,235	17,597	15,340
70,850	70,900	16,750	14,249	17,612	15,354
70,900	70,950	16,766	14,263	17,628	15,368
70,950	71,000	16,781	14,277	17,643	15,382

At least	But less than	Single	Married filing jointly*	Married filing separately	Head of a household
71,000					
71,000	71,050	16,797	14,291	17,659	15,396
71,050	71,100	16,812	14,305	17,674	15,410
71,100	71,150	16,828	14,319	17,690	15,424
71,150	71,200	16,843	14,333	17,705	15,438
71,200	71,250	16,859	14,347	17,721	15,452
71,250	71,300	16,874	14,361	17,736	15,466
71,300	71,350	16,890	14,375	17,752	15,480
71,350	71,400	16,905	14,389	17,767	15,494
71,400	71,450	16,921	14,403	17,783	15,508
71,450	71,500	16,936	14,417	17,798	15,522
71,500	71,550	16,952	14,431	17,814	15,536
71,550	71,600	16,967	14,445	17,829	15,550
71,600	71,650	16,983	14,459	17,845	15,564
71,650	71,700	16,998	14,473	17,860	15,578
71,700	71,750	17,014	14,487	17,876	15,592
71,750	71,800	17,029	14,501	17,891	15,606
71,800	71,850	17,045	14,515	17,907	15,620
71,850	71,900	17,060	14,529	17,922	15,634
71,900	71,950	17,076	14,543	17,938	15,648
71,950	72,000	17,091	14,557	17,953	15,662
72,000					
72,000	72,050	17,107	14,571	17,969	15,676
72,050	72,100	17,122	14,585	17,984	15,690
72,100	72,150	17,138	14,599	18,000	15,704
72,150	72,200	17,153	14,613	18,015	15,718
72,200	72,250	17,169	14,627	18,031	15,732
72,250	72,300	17,184	14,641	18,046	15,746
72,300	72,350	17,200	14,655	18,062	15,760
72,350	72,400	17,215	14,669	18,077	15,774
72,400	72,450	17,231	14,683	18,093	15,788
72,450	72,500	17,246	14,697	18,108	15,802
72,500	72,550	17,262	14,711	18,124	15,816
72,550	72,600	17,277	14,725	18,139	15,830
72,600	72,650	17,293	14,739	18,155	15,844
72,650	72,700	17,308	14,753	18,170	15,858
72,700	72,750	17,324	14,767	18,186	15,872
72,750	72,800	17,339	14,781	18,201	15,886
72,800	72,850	17,355	14,795	18,217	15,900
72,850	72,900	17,370	14,809	18,232	15,914
72,900	72,950	17,386	14,823	18,248	15,928
72,950	73,000	17,401	14,837	18,263	15,942
73,000					
73,000	73,050	17,417	14,851	18,279	15,956
73,050	73,100	17,432	14,865	18,294	15,970
73,100	73,150	17,448	14,879	18,310	15,984
73,150	73,200	17,463	14,893	18,325	15,998
73,200	73,250	17,479	14,907	18,341	16,012
73,250	73,300	17,494	14,921	18,356	16,026
73,300	73,350	17,510	14,935	18,372	16,040
73,350	73,400	17,525	14,949	18,387	16,054
73,400	73,450	17,541	14,963	18,403	16,068
73,450	73,500	17,556	14,977	18,418	16,082
73,500	73,550	17,572	14,991	18,434	16,096
73,550	73,600	17,587	15,005	18,449	16,110
73,600	73,650	17,603	15,019	18,465	16,124
73,650	73,700	17,618	15,033	18,480	16,138
73,700	73,750	17,634	15,047	18,496	16,152
73,750	73,800	17,649	15,061	18,511	16,166
73,800	73,850	17,665	15,075	18,527	16,180
73,850	73,900	17,680	15,089	18,542	16,194
73,900	73,950	17,696	15,103	18,558	16,208
73,950	74,000	17,711	15,117	18,573	16,222

At least	But less than	Single	Married filing jointly*	Married filing separately	Head of a household
74,000					
74,000	74,050	17,727	15,131	18,589	16,236
74,050	74,100	17,742	15,145	18,604	16,250
74,100	74,150	17,758	15,159	18,620	16,264
74,150	74,200	17,773	15,173	18,635	16,278
74,200	74,250	17,789	15,187	18,651	16,292
74,250	74,300	17,804	15,201	18,666	16,306
74,300	74,350	17,820	15,215	18,682	16,320
74,350	74,400	17,835	15,229	18,697	16,334
74,400	74,450	17,851	15,243	18,713	16,348
74,450	74,500	17,866	15,257	18,728	16,362
74,500	74,550	17,882	15,271	18,744	16,376
74,550	74,600	17,897	15,285	18,759	16,390
74,600	74,650	17,913	15,299	18,775	16,404
74,650	74,700	17,928	15,313	18,790	16,418
74,700	74,750	17,944	15,327	18,806	16,432
74,750	74,800	17,959	15,341	18,821	16,446
74,800	74,850	17,975	15,355	18,837	16,460
74,850	74,900	17,990	15,369	18,852	16,474
74,900	74,950	18,006	15,383	18,868	16,488
74,950	75,000	18,021	15,397	18,883	16,502
75,000					
75,000	75,050	18,037	15,411	18,899	16,516
75,050	75,100	18,052	15,425	18,914	16,530
75,100	75,150	18,068	15,439	18,930	16,544
75,150	75,200	18,083	15,453	18,945	16,558
75,200	75,250	18,099	15,467	18,961	16,572
75,250	75,300	18,114	15,481	18,976	16,586
75,300	75,350	18,130	15,495	18,992	16,600
75,350	75,400	18,145	15,509	19,007	16,614
75,400	75,450	18,161	15,523	19,023	16,628
75,450	75,500	18,176	15,537	19,038	16,642
75,500	75,550	18,192	15,551	19,054	16,656
75,550	75,600	18,207	15,565	19,069	16,670
75,600	75,650	18,223	15,579	19,085	16,684
75,650	75,700	18,238	15,593	19,100	16,698
75,700	75,750	18,254	15,607	19,116	16,712
75,750	75,800	18,269	15,621	19,131	16,726
75,800	75,850	18,285	15,635	19,147	16,740
75,850	75,900	18,300	15,649	19,162	16,754
75,900	75,950	18,316	15,663	19,178	16,768
75,950	76,000	18,331	15,677	19,193	16,782
76,000					
76,000	76,050	18,347	15,691	19,209	16,796
76,050	76,100	18,362	15,705	19,224	16,810
76,100	76,150	18,378	15,719	19,240	16,824
76,150	76,200	18,393	15,733	19,255	16,838
76,200	76,250	18,409	15,747	19,271	16,852
76,250	76,300	18,424	15,761	19,286	16,866
76,300	76,350	18,440	15,775	19,302	16,880
76,350	76,400	18,455	15,789	19,317	16,894
76,400	76,450	18,471	15,803	19,333	16,908
76,450	76,500	18,486	15,817	19,348	16,922
76,500	76,550	18,502	15,831	19,364	16,936
76,550	76,600	18,517	15,845	19,379	16,950
76,600	76,650	18,533	15,859	19,395	16,964
76,650	76,700	18,548	15,873	19,410	16,978
76,700	76,750	18,564	15,887	19,426	16,992
76,750	76,800	18,579	15,901	19,441	17,006
76,800	76,850	18,595	15,915	19,457	17,020
76,850	76,900	18,610	15,929	19,472	17,034
76,900	76,950	18,626	15,943	19,488	17,048
76,950	77,000	18,641	15,957	19,503	17,062

Continued on next page

77,000 – 79,000

At least	But less than	Single	Married filing jointly *	Married filing separately	Head of a household
77,000					
77,000	77,050	18,657	15,971	19,519	17,076
77,050	77,100	18,672	15,985	19,534	17,090
77,100	77,150	18,688	15,999	19,550	17,104
77,150	77,200	18,703	16,013	19,565	17,118
77,200	77,250	18,719	16,027	19,581	17,132
77,250	77,300	18,734	16,041	19,596	17,146
77,300	77,350	18,750	16,055	19,612	17,160
77,350	77,400	18,765	16,069	19,627	17,174
77,400	77,450	18,781	16,083	19,643	17,188
77,450	77,500	18,796	16,097	19,658	17,202
77,500	77,550	18,812	16,111	19,674	17,216
77,550	77,600	18,827	16,125	19,689	17,230
77,600	77,650	18,843	16,139	19,705	17,244
77,650	77,700	18,858	16,153	19,720	17,258
77,700	77,750	18,874	16,167	19,736	17,272
77,750	77,800	18,889	16,181	19,751	17,286
77,800	77,850	18,905	16,195	19,767	17,300
77,850	77,900	18,920	16,209	19,782	17,314
77,900	77,950	18,936	16,223	19,798	17,328
77,950	78,000	18,951	16,237	19,813	17,342
78,000					
78,000	78,050	18,967	16,251	19,829	17,356
78,050	78,100	18,982	16,265	19,844	17,370
78,100	78,150	18,998	16,279	19,860	17,384
78,150	78,200	19,013	16,293	19,875	17,398
78,200	78,250	19,029	16,307	19,891	17,412
78,250	78,300	19,044	16,321	19,906	17,426
78,300	78,350	19,060	16,335	19,922	17,440
78,350	78,400	19,075	16,349	19,937	17,454
78,400	78,450	19,091	16,363	19,953	17,468
78,450	78,500	19,106	16,377	19,968	17,482
78,500	78,550	19,122	16,391	19,984	17,496
78,550	78,600	19,137	16,405	19,999	17,510
78,600	78,650	19,153	16,419	20,015	17,524
78,650	78,700	19,168	16,433	20,030	17,538
78,700	78,750	19,184	16,447	20,046	17,552
78,750	78,800	19,199	16,461	20,061	17,566
78,800	78,850	19,215	16,475	20,077	17,580
78,850	78,900	19,230	16,489	20,092	17,594
78,900	78,950	19,246	16,503	20,108	17,608
78,950	79,000	19,261	16,517	20,123	17,622
79,000					
79,000	79,050	19,277	16,531	20,139	17,636
79,050	79,100	19,292	16,545	20,154	17,650
79,100	79,150	19,308	16,559	20,170	17,664
79,150	79,200	19,323	16,573	20,185	17,678
79,200	79,250	19,339	16,587	20,201	17,692
79,250	79,300	19,354	16,601	20,216	17,706
79,300	79,350	19,370	16,615	20,234	17,720
79,350	79,400	19,385	16,629	20,252	17,734
79,400	79,450	19,401	16,643	20,270	17,748
79,450	79,500	19,416	16,657	20,288	17,762
79,500	79,550	19,432	16,671	20,306	17,776
79,550	79,600	19,447	16,685	20,324	17,790
79,600	79,650	19,463	16,699	20,342	17,804
79,650	79,700	19,478	16,713	20,360	17,818
79,700	79,750	19,494	16,727	20,378	17,832
79,750	79,800	19,509	16,741	20,396	17,846
79,800	79,850	19,525	16,755	20,414	17,860
79,850	79,900	19,540	16,769	20,432	17,874
79,900	79,950	19,556	16,783	20,450	17,888
79,950	80,000	19,571	16,797	20,468	17,902

80,000 – 82,000

At least	But less than	Single	Married filing jointly *	Married filing separately	Head of a household
80,000					
80,000	80,050	19,587	16,811	20,486	17,916
80,050	80,100	19,602	16,825	20,504	17,930
80,100	80,150	19,618	16,839	20,522	17,944
80,150	80,200	19,633	16,853	20,540	17,958
80,200	80,250	19,649	16,867	20,558	17,972
80,250	80,300	19,664	16,881	20,576	17,986
80,300	80,350	19,680	16,895	20,594	18,000
80,350	80,400	19,695	16,909	20,612	18,014
80,400	80,450	19,711	16,923	20,630	18,028
80,450	80,500	19,726	16,937	20,648	18,042
80,500	80,550	19,742	16,951	20,666	18,056
80,550	80,600	19,757	16,965	20,684	18,070
80,600	80,650	19,773	16,979	20,702	18,084
80,650	80,700	19,788	16,993	20,720	18,098
80,700	80,750	19,804	17,007	20,738	18,112
80,750	80,800	19,819	17,021	20,756	18,126
80,800	80,850	19,835	17,035	20,774	18,140
80,850	80,900	19,850	17,049	20,792	18,154
80,900	80,950	19,866	17,063	20,810	18,168
80,950	81,000	19,881	17,077	20,828	18,182
81,000					
81,000	81,050	19,897	17,091	20,846	18,196
81,050	81,100	19,912	17,105	20,864	18,210
81,100	81,150	19,928	17,119	20,882	18,224
81,150	81,200	19,943	17,133	20,900	18,238
81,200	81,250	19,959	17,147	20,918	18,252
81,250	81,300	19,974	17,161	20,936	18,266
81,300	81,350	19,990	17,175	20,954	18,280
81,350	81,400	20,005	17,189	20,972	18,294
81,400	81,450	20,021	17,203	20,990	18,308
81,450	81,500	20,036	17,217	21,008	18,322
81,500	81,550	20,052	17,231	21,026	18,336
81,550	81,600	20,067	17,245	21,044	18,350
81,600	81,650	20,083	17,259	21,062	18,364
81,650	81,700	20,098	17,273	21,080	18,378
81,700	81,750	20,114	17,287	21,098	18,392
81,750	81,800	20,129	17,301	21,116	18,406
81,800	81,850	20,145	17,315	21,134	18,420
81,850	81,900	20,160	17,329	21,152	18,434
81,900	81,950	20,176	17,343	21,170	18,448
81,950	82,000	20,191	17,357	21,188	18,462
82,000					
82,000	82,050	20,207	17,371	21,206	18,476
82,050	82,100	20,222	17,385	21,224	18,490
82,100	82,150	20,238	17,399	21,242	18,504
82,150	82,200	20,253	17,413	21,260	18,518
82,200	82,250	20,269	17,427	21,278	18,532
82,250	82,300	20,284	17,441	21,296	18,546
82,300	82,350	20,300	17,455	21,314	18,560
82,350	82,400	20,315	17,469	21,332	18,574
82,400	82,450	20,331	17,483	21,350	18,588
82,450	82,500	20,346	17,497	21,368	18,602
82,500	82,550	20,362	17,511	21,386	18,616
82,550	82,600	20,377	17,525	21,404	18,630
82,600	82,650	20,393	17,539	21,422	18,644
82,650	82,700	20,408	17,553	21,440	18,658
82,700	82,750	20,424	17,567	21,458	18,672
82,750	82,800	20,439	17,581	21,476	18,686
82,800	82,850	20,455	17,595	21,494	18,700
82,850	82,900	20,470	17,609	21,512	18,714
82,900	82,950	20,486	17,623	21,530	18,728
82,950	83,000	20,501	17,637	21,548	18,742

83,000 – 85,000

At least	But less than	Single	Married filing jointly *	Married filing separately	Head of a household
83,000					
83,000	83,050	20,517	17,651	21,566	18,756
83,050	83,100	20,532	17,665	21,584	18,770
83,100	83,150	20,548	17,679	21,602	18,784
83,150	83,200	20,563	17,693	21,620	18,798
83,200	83,250	20,579	17,707	21,638	18,812
83,250	83,300	20,594	17,721	21,656	18,826
83,300	83,350	20,610	17,735	21,674	18,840
83,350	83,400	20,625	17,749	21,692	18,854
83,400	83,450	20,641	17,763	21,710	18,868
83,450	83,500	20,656	17,777	21,728	18,882
83,500	83,550	20,672	17,791	21,746	18,896
83,550	83,600	20,687	17,805	21,764	18,910
83,600	83,650	20,703	17,819	21,782	18,924
83,650	83,700	20,718	17,833	21,800	18,938
83,700	83,750	20,734	17,847	21,818	18,952
83,750	83,800	20,749	17,861	21,836	18,966
83,800	83,850	20,765	17,875	21,854	18,980
83,850	83,900	20,780	17,889	21,872	18,994
83,900	83,950	20,796	17,903	21,890	19,008
83,950	84,000	20,811	17,917	21,908	19,022
84,000					
84,000	84,050	20,827	17,931	21,926	19,036
84,050	84,100	20,842	17,945	21,944	19,050
84,100	84,150	20,858	17,959	21,962	19,064
84,150	84,200	20,873	17,973	21,980	19,078
84,200	84,250	20,889	17,987	21,998	19,092
84,250	84,300	20,904	18,001	22,016	19,106
84,300	84,350	20,920	18,015	22,034	19,120
84,350	84,400	20,935	18,029	22,052	19,134
84,400	84,450	20,951	18,043	22,070	19,148
84,450	84,500	20,966	18,057	22,088	19,162
84,500	84,550	20,982	18,071	22,106	19,176
84,550	84,600	20,997	18,085	22,124	19,190
84,600	84,650	21,013	18,099	22,142	19,204
84,650	84,700	21,028	18,113	22,160	19,218
84,700	84,750	21,044	18,127	22,178	19,232
84,750	84,800	21,059	18,141	22,196	19,246
84,800	84,850	21,075	18,155	22,214	19,260
84,850	84,900	21,090	18,169	22,232	19,274
84,900	84,950	21,106	18,183	22,250	19,288
84,950	85,000	21,121	18,197	22,268	19,302
85,000					
85,000	85,050	21,137	18,211	22,286	19,316
85,050	85,100	21,152	18,225	22,304	19,330
85,100	85,150	21,168	18,239	22,322	19,344
85,150	85,200	21,183	18,253	22,340	19,358
85,200	85,250	21,199	18,267	22,358	19,372
85,250	85,300	21,214	18,281	22,376	19,386
85,300	85,350	21,230	18,295	22,394	19,400
85,350	85,400	21,245	18,309	22,412	19,414
85,400	85,450	21,261	18,323	22,430	19,428
85,450	85,500	21,276	18,337	22,448	19,442
85,500	85,550	21,292	18,351	22,466	19,456
85,550	85,600	21,307	18,365	22,484	19,470
85,600	85,650	21,323	18,379	22,502	19,484
85,650	85,700	21,338	18,393	22,520	19,498
85,700	85,750	21,354	18,407	22,538	19,512
85,750	85,800	21,369	18,421	22,556	19,526
85,800	85,850	21,385	18,435	22,574	19,540
85,850	85,900	21,400	18,449	22,592	19,554
85,900	85,950	21,416	18,463	22,610	19,568
85,950	86,000	21,431	18,477	22,628	19,582

* This column must also be used by a qualifying widow(er).

Continued on next page

86,000

If line 39 (taxable income) is— At least	But less than	Single	Married filing jointly *	Married filing separately	Head of a household
86,000	86,050	21,447	18,491	22,646	19,596
86,050	86,100	21,462	18,505	22,664	19,610
86,100	86,150	21,478	18,519	22,682	19,624
86,150	86,200	21,493	18,533	22,700	19,638
86,200	86,250	21,509	18,547	22,718	19,652
86,250	86,300	21,524	18,561	22,736	19,666
86,300	86,350	21,540	18,575	22,754	19,680
86,350	86,400	21,555	18,589	22,772	19,694
86,400	86,450	21,571	18,603	22,790	19,708
86,450	86,500	21,586	18,617	22,808	19,722
86,500	86,550	21,602	18,631	22,826	19,736
86,550	86,600	21,617	18,645	22,844	19,750
86,600	86,650	21,633	18,659	22,862	19,764
86,650	86,700	21,648	18,673	22,880	19,778
86,700	86,750	21,664	18,687	22,898	19,792
86,750	86,800	21,679	18,701	22,916	19,806
86,800	86,850	21,695	18,715	22,934	19,820
86,850	86,900	21,710	18,729	22,952	19,834
86,900	86,950	21,726	18,743	22,970	19,848
86,950	87,000	21,741	18,757	22,988	19,862

87,000

At least	But less than	Single	Married filing jointly *	Married filing separately	Head of a household
87,000	87,050	21,757	18,771	23,006	19,876
87,050	87,100	21,772	18,785	23,024	19,890
87,100	87,150	21,788	18,799	23,042	19,904
87,150	87,200	21,803	18,813	23,060	19,918
87,200	87,250	21,819	18,827	23,078	19,932
87,250	87,300	21,834	18,841	23,096	19,946
87,300	87,350	21,860	18,855	23,114	19,960
87,350	87,400	21,865	18,869	23,132	19,974
87,400	87,450	21,881	18,883	23,150	19,988
87,450	87,500	21,896	18,897	23,168	20,002
87,500	87,550	21,912	18,911	23,186	20,016
87,550	87,600	21,927	18,925	23,204	20,030
87,600	87,650	21,943	18,939	23,222	20,044
87,650	87,700	21,958	18,953	23,240	20,058
87,700	87,750	21,974	18,967	23,258	20,072
87,750	87,800	21,989	18,981	23,276	20,086
87,800	87,850	22,005	18,995	23,294	20,100
87,850	87,900	22,020	19,009	23,312	20,114
87,900	87,950	22,036	19,023	23,330	20,128
87,950	88,000	22,051	19,037	23,348	20,142

88,000

At least	But less than	Single	Married filing jointly *	Married filing separately	Head of a household
88,000	88,050	22,067	19,051	23,366	20,156
88,050	88,100	22,082	19,065	23,384	20,170
88,100	88,150	22,098	19,079	23,402	20,184
88,150	88,200	22,113	19,093	23,420	20,198
88,200	88,250	22,129	19,107	23,438	20,212
88,250	88,300	22,144	19,121	23,456	20,226
88,300	88,350	22,160	19,135	23,474	20,240
88,350	88,400	22,175	19,149	23,492	20,254
88,400	88,450	22,191	19,163	23,510	20,268
88,450	88,500	22,206	19,177	23,528	20,282
88,500	88,550	22,222	19,191	23,546	20,296
88,550	88,600	22,237	19,205	23,564	20,310
88,600	88,650	22,253	19,219	23,582	20,324
88,650	88,700	22,268	19,233	23,600	20,338
88,700	88,750	22,284	19,247	23,618	20,352
88,750	88,800	22,299	19,261	23,636	20,366
88,800	88,850	22,315	19,275	23,654	20,380
88,850	88,900	22,330	19,289	23,672	20,394
88,900	88,950	22,346	19,303	23,690	20,408
88,950	89,000	22,361	19,317	23,708	20,422

89,000

At least	But less than	Single	Married filing jointly *	Married filing separately	Head of a household
89,000	89,050	22,377	19,331	23,726	20,436
89,050	89,100	22,392	19,345	23,744	20,450
89,100	89,150	22,408	19,359	23,762	20,464
89,150	89,200	22,423	19,373	23,780	20,478
89,200	89,250	22,439	19,387	23,798	20,494
89,250	89,300	22,454	19,401	23,816	20,509
89,300	89,350	22,470	19,415	23,834	20,525
89,350	89,400	22,485	19,429	23,852	20,540
89,400	89,450	22,501	19,443	23,870	20,556
89,450	89,500	22,516	19,457	23,888	20,571
89,500	89,550	22,532	19,471	23,906	20,587
89,550	89,600	22,547	19,485	23,924	20,602
89,600	89,650	22,563	19,499	23,942	20,618
89,650	89,700	22,578	19,513	23,960	20,633
89,700	89,750	22,594	19,527	23,978	20,649
89,750	89,800	22,609	19,541	23,996	20,664
89,800	89,850	22,625	19,555	24,014	20,680
89,850	89,900	22,640	19,569	24,032	20,695
89,900	89,950	22,656	19,583	24,050	20,711
89,950	90,000	22,671	19,597	24,068	20,726

90,000

At least	But less than	Single	Married filing jointly *	Married filing separately	Head of a household
90,000	90,050	22,687	19,611	24,086	20,742
90,050	90,100	22,702	19,625	24,104	20,757
90,100	90,150	22,718	19,639	24,122	20,773
90,150	90,200	22,733	19,653	24,140	20,788
90,200	90,250	22,749	19,667	24,158	20,804
90,250	90,300	22,764	19,681	24,176	20,819
90,300	90,350	22,780	19,695	24,194	20,835
90,350	90,400	22,795	19,709	24,212	20,850
90,400	90,450	22,811	19,723	24,230	20,866
90,450	90,500	22,826	19,737	24,248	20,881
90,500	90,550	22,842	19,751	24,266	20,897
90,550	90,600	22,857	19,765	24,284	20,912
90,600	90,650	22,873	19,779	24,302	20,928
90,650	90,700	22,888	19,793	24,320	20,943
90,700	90,750	22,904	19,807	24,338	20,959
90,750	90,800	22,919	19,821	24,356	20,974
90,800	90,850	22,935	19,835	24,374	20,990
90,850	90,900	22,950	19,849	24,392	21,005
90,900	90,950	22,966	19,863	24,410	21,021
90,950	91,000	22,981	19,877	24,428	21,036

91,000

At least	But less than	Single	Married filing jointly *	Married filing separately	Head of a household
91,000	91,050	22,997	19,891	24,446	21,052
91,050	91,100	23,012	19,905	24,464	21,067
91,100	91,150	23,028	19,919	24,482	21,083
91,150	91,200	23,043	19,933	24,500	21,098
91,200	91,250	23,059	19,947	24,518	21,114
91,250	91,300	23,074	19,961	24,536	21,129
91,300	91,350	23,090	19,975	24,554	21,145
91,350	91,400	23,105	19,989	24,572	21,160
91,400	91,450	23,121	20,003	24,590	21,176
91,450	91,500	23,136	20,017	24,608	21,191
91,500	91,550	23,152	20,031	24,626	21,207
91,550	91,600	23,167	20,045	24,644	21,222
91,600	91,650	23,183	20,059	24,662	21,238
91,650	91,700	23,198	20,073	24,680	21,253
91,700	91,750	23,214	20,087	24,698	21,269
91,750	91,800	23,229	20,101	24,716	21,284
91,800	91,850	23,245	20,115	24,734	21,300
91,850	91,900	23,260	20,129	24,752	21,315
91,900	91,950	23,276	20,143	24,770	21,331
91,950	92,000	23,291	20,157	24,788	21,346

92,000

At least	But less than	Single	Married filing jointly *	Married filing separately	Head of a household
92,000	92,050	23,307	20,171	24,806	21,362
92,050	92,100	23,322	20,185	24,824	21,377
92,100	92,150	23,338	20,199	24,842	21,393
92,150	92,200	23,353	20,213	24,860	21,408
92,200	92,250	23,369	20,227	24,878	21,424
92,250	92,300	23,384	20,241	24,896	21,439
92,300	92,350	23,400	20,255	24,914	21,455
92,350	92,400	23,415	20,269	24,932	21,470
92,400	92,450	23,431	20,283	24,950	21,486
92,450	92,500	23,446	20,297	24,968	21,501
92,500	92,550	23,462	20,311	24,986	21,517
92,550	92,600	23,477	20,325	25,004	21,532
92,600	92,650	23,493	20,339	25,022	21,548
92,650	92,700	23,508	20,353	25,040	21,563
92,700	92,750	23,524	20,367	25,058	21,579
92,750	92,800	23,539	20,381	25,076	21,594
92,800	92,850	23,555	20,395	25,094	21,610
92,850	92,900	23,570	20,409	25,112	21,625
92,900	92,950	23,586	20,423	25,130	21,641
92,950	93,000	23,601	20,437	25,148	21,656

93,000

At least	But less than	Single	Married filing jointly *	Married filing separately	Head of a household
93,000	93,050	23,617	20,451	25,166	21,672
93,050	93,100	23,632	20,465	25,184	21,687
93,100	93,150	23,648	20,479	25,202	21,703
93,150	93,200	23,663	20,493	25,220	21,718
93,200	93,250	23,679	20,507	25,238	21,734
93,250	93,300	23,694	20,521	25,256	21,749
93,300	93,350	23,710	20,535	25,274	21,765
93,350	93,400	23,725	20,549	25,292	21,780
93,400	93,450	23,741	20,563	25,310	21,796
93,450	93,500	23,756	20,577	25,328	21,811
93,500	93,550	23,772	20,591	25,346	21,827
93,550	93,600	23,787	20,605	25,364	21,842
93,600	93,650	23,803	20,619	25,382	21,858
93,650	93,700	23,818	20,633	25,400	21,873
93,700	93,750	23,834	20,647	25,418	21,889
93,750	93,800	23,849	20,661	25,436	21,904
93,800	93,850	23,865	20,675	25,454	21,920
93,850	93,900	23,880	20,689	25,472	21,935
93,900	93,950	23,896	20,703	25,490	21,951
93,950	94,000	23,911	20,717	25,508	21,966

94,000

At least	But less than	Single	Married filing jointly *	Married filing separately	Head of a household
94,000	94,050	23,927	20,731	25,526	21,982
94,050	94,100	23,942	20,745	25,544	21,997
94,100	94,150	23,958	20,759	25,562	22,013
94,150	94,200	23,973	20,773	25,580	22,028
94,200	94,250	23,989	20,787	25,598	22,044
94,250	94,300	24,004	20,801	25,616	22,059
94,300	94,350	24,020	20,815	25,634	22,075
94,350	94,400	24,035	20,829	25,652	22,090
94,400	94,450	24,051	20,843	25,670	22,106
94,450	94,500	24,066	20,857	25,688	22,121
94,500	94,550	24,082	20,871	25,706	22,137
94,550	94,600	24,097	20,885	25,724	22,152
94,600	94,650	24,113	20,899	25,742	22,168
94,650	94,700	24,128	20,913	25,760	22,183
94,700	94,750	24,144	20,927	25,778	22,199
94,750	94,800	24,159	20,941	25,796	22,214
94,800	94,850	24,175	20,955	25,814	22,230
94,850	94,900	24,190	20,969	25,832	22,245
94,900	94,950	24,206	20,983	25,850	22,261
94,950	95,000	24,221	20,997	25,868	22,276

* This column must also be used by a qualifying widow(er).

Continued on next page

If line 39 (taxable income) is—		And you are—				If line 39 (taxable income) is—		And you are—			
At least	But less than	Single	Married filing jointly *	Married filing separately	Head of a household	At least	But less than	Single	Married filing jointly *	Married filing separately	Head of a household
		Your tax is—						Your tax is—			

95,000

95,000	95,050	24,237	21,011	25,886	22,292	98,000	98,050	25,167	21,851	26,966	23,222
95,050	95,100	24,252	21,025	25,904	22,307	98,050	98,100	25,182	21,865	26,984	23,237
95,100	95,150	24,268	21,039	25,922	22,323	98,100	98,150	25,198	21,879	27,002	23,253
95,150	95,200	24,283	21,053	25,940	22,338	98,150	98,200	25,213	21,893	27,020	23,268
95,200	95,250	24,299	21,067	25,958	22,354	98,200	98,250	25,229	21,907	27,038	23,284
95,250	95,300	24,314	21,081	25,976	22,369	98,250	98,300	25,244	21,921	27,056	23,299
95,300	95,350	24,330	21,095	25,994	22,385	98,300	98,350	25,260	21,935	27,074	23,315
95,350	95,400	24,345	21,109	26,012	22,400	98,350	98,400	25,275	21,949	27,092	23,330
95,400	95,450	24,361	21,123	26,030	22,416	98,400	98,450	25,291	21,963	27,110	23,346
95,450	95,500	24,376	21,137	26,048	22,431	98,450	98,500	25,306	21,977	27,128	23,361
95,500	95,550	24,392	21,151	26,066	22,447	98,500	98,550	25,322	21,991	27,146	23,377
95,550	95,600	24,407	21,165	26,084	22,462	98,550	98,600	25,337	22,005	27,164	23,392
95,600	95,650	24,423	21,179	26,102	22,478	98,600	98,650	25,353	22,019	27,182	23,408
95,650	95,700	24,438	21,193	26,120	22,493	98,650	98,700	25,368	22,033	27,200	23,423
95,700	95,750	24,454	21,207	26,138	22,509	98,700	98,750	25,384	22,047	27,218	23,439
95,750	95,800	24,469	21,221	26,156	22,524	98,750	98,800	25,399	22,061	27,236	23,454
95,800	95,850	24,485	21,235	26,174	22,540	98,800	98,850	25,415	22,075	27,254	23,470
95,850	95,900	24,500	21,249	26,192	22,555	98,850	98,900	25,430	22,089	27,272	23,485
95,900	95,950	24,516	21,263	26,210	22,571	98,900	98,950	25,446	22,103	27,290	23,501
95,950	96,000	24,531	21,277	26,228	22,586	98,950	99,000	25,461	22,117	27,308	23,516

96,000 | ## 99,000

96,000	96,050	24,547	21,291	26,246	22,602	99,000	99,050	25,477	22,131	27,326	23,532
96,050	96,100	24,562	21,305	26,264	22,617	99,050	99,100	25,492	22,145	27,344	23,547
96,100	96,150	24,578	21,319	26,282	22,633	99,100	99,150	25,508	22,159	27,362	23,563
96,150	96,200	24,593	21,333	26,300	22,648	99,150	99,200	25,523	22,173	27,380	23,578
96,200	96,250	24,609	21,347	26,318	22,664	99,200	99,250	25,539	22,187	27,398	23,594
96,250	96,300	24,624	21,361	26,336	22,679	99,250	99,300	25,554	22,201	27,416	23,609
96,300	96,350	24,640	21,375	26,354	22,695	99,300	99,350	25,570	22,215	27,434	23,625
96,350	96,400	24,655	21,389	26,372	22,710	99,350	99,400	25,585	22,229	27,452	23,640
96,400	96,450	24,671	21,403	26,390	22,726	99,400	99,450	25,601	22,243	27,470	23,656
96,450	96,500	24,686	21,417	26,408	22,741	99,450	99,500	25,616	22,257	27,488	23,671
96,500	96,550	24,702	21,431	26,426	22,757	99,500	99,550	25,632	22,271	27,506	23,687
96,550	96,600	24,717	21,445	26,444	22,772	99,550	99,600	25,647	22,285	27,524	23,702
96,600	96,650	24,733	21,459	26,462	22,788	99,600	99,650	25,663	22,299	27,542	23,718
96,650	96,700	24,748	21,473	26,480	22,803	99,650	99,700	25,678	22,313	27,560	23,733
96,700	96,750	24,764	21,487	26,498	22,819	99,700	99,750	25,694	22,327	27,578	23,749
96,750	96,800	24,779	21,501	26,516	22,834	99,750	99,800	25,709	22,341	27,596	23,764
96,800	96,850	24,795	21,515	26,534	22,850	99,800	99,850	25,725	22,355	27,614	23,780
96,850	96,900	24,810	21,529	26,552	22,865	99,850	99,900	25,740	22,369	27,632	23,795
96,900	96,950	24,826	21,543	26,570	22,881	99,900	99,950	25,756	22,383	27,650	23,811
96,950	97,000	24,841	21,557	26,588	22,896	99,950	100,000	25,771	22,397	27,668	23,826

97,000

97,000	97,050	24,857	21,571	26,606	22,912		
97,050	97,100	24,872	21,585	26,624	22,927		
97,100	97,150	24,888	21,599	26,642	22,943		
97,150	97,200	24,903	21,613	26,660	22,958		
97,200	97,250	24,919	21,627	26,678	22,974		
97,250	97,300	24,934	21,641	26,696	22,989		
97,300	97,350	24,950	21,655	26,714	23,005		
97,350	97,400	24,965	21,669	26,732	23,020		
97,400	97,450	24,981	21,683	26,750	23,036		
97,450	97,500	24,996	21,697	26,768	23,051		
97,500	97,550	25,012	21,711	26,786	23,067		
97,550	97,600	25,027	21,725	26,804	23,082		
97,600	97,650	25,043	21,739	26,822	23,098		
97,650	97,700	25,058	21,753	26,840	23,113		
97,700	97,750	25,074	21,767	26,858	23,129		
97,750	97,800	25,089	21,781	26,876	23,144		
97,800	97,850	25,105	21,795	26,894	23,160		
97,850	97,900	25,120	21,809	26,912	23,175		
97,900	97,950	25,136	21,823	26,930	23,191		
97,950	98,000	25,151	21,837	26,948	23,206		

$100,000 or over — use the Tax Rate Schedules on page 69

* This column must also be used by a qualifying widow(er).

1999
Tax Rate
Schedules

 CAUTION

Use **only** if your taxable income (Form 1040, line 39) is $100,000 or more. If less, use the **Tax Table.** Even though you cannot use the Tax Rate Schedules below if your taxable income is less than $100,000, all levels of taxable income are shown so taxpayers can see the tax rate that applies to each level.

Schedule X—Use if your filing status is **Single**

If the amount on Form 1040, line 39, is: Over—	But not over—	Enter on Form 1040, line 40	of the amount over—
$0	$25,750	.... 15%	$0
25,750	62,450	$3,862.50 + 28%	25,750
62,450	130,250	14,138.50 + 31%	62,450
130,250	283,150	35,156.50 + 36%	130,250
283,150	....	90,200.50 + 39.6%	283,150

Schedule Y-1—Use if your filing status is **Married filing jointly** or **Qualifying widow(er)**

If the amount on Form 1040, line 39, is: Over—	But not over—	Enter on Form 1040, line 40	of the amount over—
$0	$43,050	.... 15%	$0
43,050	104,050	$6,457.50 + 28%	43,050
104,050	158,550	23,537.50 + 31%	104,050
158,550	283,150	40,432.50 + 36%	158,550
283,150	....	85,288.50 + 39.6%	283,150

Schedule Y-2—Use if your filing status is **Married filing separately**

If the amount on Form 1040, line 39, is: Over—	But not over—	Enter on Form 1040, line 40	of the amount over—
$0	$21,525	.... 15%	$0
21,525	52,025	$3,228.75 + 28%	21,525
52,025	79,275	11,768.75 + 31%	52,025
79,275	141,575	20,216.25 + 36%	79,275
141,575	....	42,644.25 + 39.6%	141,575

Schedule Z—Use if your filing status is **Head of household**

If the amount on Form 1040, line 39, is: Over—	But not over—	Enter on Form 1040, line 40	of the amount over—
$0	$34,550	.... 15%	$0
34,550	89,150	$5,182.50 + 28%	34,550
89,150	144,400	20,470.50 + 31%	89,150
144,400	283,150	37,598.00 + 36%	144,400
283,150	....	87,548.00 + 39.6%	283,150

Index

T

. . . *Generating Sales from New and Repeat Customers?*

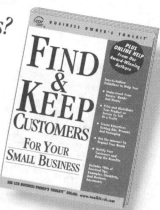

Find & Keep Customers addresses the top priority for small business owners—creating loyal customers. This clear-language, no nonsense guide shows readers how to find a profitable niche; research and develop a realistic marketing plan; sell, price, communicate and compete in today's rapidly changing marketplace; and understand the advantagees and requirements of electronic commerce.

Simply put, the key to finding and keeping customers is solving customers' problems and getting them to see the benefits of your solutions. By using this book, you will learn how to target your time, money and energy toward those prospects who will offer you the highest chances for long-term success.

224 pages / Book No. 0-5180-100 **$16.**⁹⁵***

. . . *Dealing with Complicated Employment Issues?*

Hire Manage & Retain Employees for Your Small Business is a complete, easy-to-use resource for small business employees. The tax and legal implications of employing people are complex and full of pitfalls for the average entrepreneur. In addition to providing detailed information, state-by-state tables, and business forms to guide the reader, this book coaches business owners through the human side of managing people.

"Clear language, no-nonsense advice, meaningful worksheets and an excellent layout make this one of the best books on the subject of hiring, managing and retaining employees I have seen to date . . . It belongs on your 'most important' bookshelf." — *Paul Tulenko, syndicated small business columnist*

$19.⁹⁵*** *320 pages / Book No. 0-5377-100*

. . . *Formulating and Writing an Effective Business Plan?*

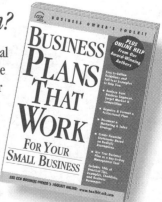

Business Plans That Work for Your Small Business clearly translates complicated marketing and financial concepts into down-to-earth practical advice, explains all the essential elements and formulas, and offers concrete examples throughout. Five sample plans from real small businesses provide readers with the blueprints for their own plans, as well as a wealth of detailed information about how a successful small business should operate

This book will appeal not only to budding entrepreneurs who are planning a new venture on paper to see whether it will fly, but also to new or existing business owners who need a business plan document as part of a business loan application, and to established owners who want to create a plan for internal use.

304 pages / Book No. 0-5346-100 **$19.**⁹⁵***

*Plus shipping, handling and applicable sales tax

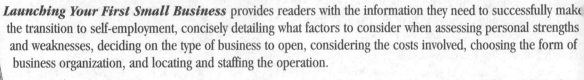